Economic Efficiency
and Social Welfare

To Milton Friedman
with affection and respect

Economic Efficiency and Social Welfare

Selected Essays on Fundamental Aspects of the Economic Theory of Social Welfare

E. J. MISHAN

London
GEORGE ALLEN & UNWIN
Boston   Sydney

British Library Cataloguing in Publication Data

Mishan, E. J.
    Economic efficiency and social welfare.
    1. Welfare economics
    I. Title
    330.15'5   HB99.3

ISBN 0-04-330314-5
ISBN 0-04-330315-3 Pbk

Set in 9 on 11 point Times by Fotographics, Bedford
and printed in Great Britain
by Mackays of Chatham.

Contents

Preface

The essays reproduced in this volume cover a period of about two decades. The first, which appeared in *Economica* in 1957, was written soon after my appointment as assistant lecturer at the London School of Economics in November 1956. The last was written just before I resigned my chair there in September 1977.

The essays have been selected by me either because they contain elements of theoretical novelty that have not as yet been wholly absorbed into current economic thinking, or because they are less accessible to students, or because they open perspectives within the five areas I have chosen – which areas, between them, cover a large part of the literature on welfare and resource allocation. The papers in each of the five sections are arranged so as to impart a sense of the development of ideas which, as it happens, does not always coincide with the chronology.

For any one of the three reasons above I have omitted quite a number of my published journal articles. My 'Survey of welfare economics' (*Economic Journal*, 1960) has been reprinted many times and is easily accessible to students. So too has my minor survey paper 'How to make a burden of the public debt' (*Journal of Political Economy*, 1963). Again, the ideas in my 'Welfare criteria for external effects' (*American Economic Review*, 1961) were more ingeniously exploited in my 'Optimality and the law' paper of 1967 (reproduced in this volume) and those in my 'Reflections on recent development in the concept of external effects' (*Canadian Journal of Economics*, 1965) as well as those in 'The relationship between joint products, collective goods and external effects' (*Journal of Political Economy*, 1969) were, to a large extent, assimilated into the later survey paper 'The postwar literature on externalities: an interpretative essay', 1971 (reproduced in this volume). Omitted also are critiques of the books or papers of others, or papers that are too specialised to be of general interest.

Some of the essays in this volume will, I hope, be found useful, perhaps provocative, by professional economists and teachers. But they have been selected chiefly with an eye to offering the economics student a broad sample of the treatment of theoretical issues in allocative economics. The student I have in mind is not necessarily one who is specialising in allocation or political economy. He may well be primarily interested in positive or quantitative economics. Yet he is more likely than not to find some of these essays relevant to his work, if not disturbing to his equanimity. The simple technique of maximising some welfare function subject to familiar constraints so as to shake out the first-order (and, possibly, second-order) conditions is – as is made clear in a number of these essays – more often a way of evading a problem than of solving it.

Apart from a few sceptical asides, all the essays in Parts One to Four are developed within the framework of traditional economic assumptions. The essays in Part Five, on the other hand, are inspired by more philosophical considerations bearing on the question of social welfare. In consequence, the familiar economic premises are themselves subject to criticism.

The last essay in this volume, 'Whatever happened to progress?', is easily the most sceptical in its examination of the economic approach to welfare, and the most pessimistic in its assessment of the consequences of continued economic growth. Those students in whom it strikes a chord, either of sympathy or of antipathy, may find time to peruse a more thorough-going critique of economic growth, my *Economic Growth Debate: An Assessment* (1977).

E. J. MISHAN
London

PART ONE

Economic Criteria

Comparative Statics

1

A Reappraisal of the Principles of Resource Allocation

I

A rejection of the theories of welfare economics carries with it the judgment that there is at present no rule or method by which we may judge of the relative efficiency of alternative forms of economic organisation; indeed, that any conceivable set of production plans or any conceivable set of prices, no matter how arbitrary, are – in our present state of knowledge – to be considered as good as any others.

Few economists, even among those who are wont to treat welfare economics with extreme scepticism, will go as far as this to avoid courting the subject while economists of the liberal school who talk of a presumption in favour of the market mechanisms must, if they are to rationalise this presumption, invoke some theory of welfare. Put at its bluntest then it is in pursuit of an answer to the question, by what lights are we to distinguish between a good allocation and a chaotic one, that we are led willy-nilly into the domain of welfare economics.

Notwithstanding the logic of this conclusion a great deal continues to be written concerning economic efficiency which deliberately eschews the language of welfare economics, relying instead on apparently more acceptable criteria – for instance, the 'common sense' rule that total receipts should be able to cover total costs supplemented, perhaps, by rules about marginal equalities. For the abiding impression seems to be that by confining oneself to the traditional rules governing the allocation of resources one somehow circumvents the tenuous concepts and fine paradoxes of welfare economics. After all, there are critiques and counter-

I am indebted to Mr Ralph Turvey on whose advice I have removed a great deal of controversial and difficult material from a previous draft thereby increasing the readability and relevance of the present paper, to Professor James Meade for several important suggestions and to Mr Richard Lipsey for valuable and detailed criticism.

critiques of welfare economics and in the process a great deal of smoke and subtlety is generated. But the principles of resource allocation are of more solid stuff. They are ever with us and in continual application.

This view, however, does not bear close examination. A byproduct of this paper will be the demonstration that certain familiar welfare criteria and the so-called optimum conditions of resource allocation are raised on the same foundation: they stand or fall together. In fact the relationship is so close it is almost inevitable that allocative criteria be examined by the techniques which have proved so popular in welfare economics.[1]

II

It is hard to exaggerate how fundamental is the idea of resource allocation in the theory and application of economics. If competition and unimpeded international trade and mobility of capital and labour are good things this is so, we are given to understand, because they are conducive to allocative efficiency. For opposite reasons monopoly, tariffs, price controls and most kinds of taxes are bad things. And if these judgments have been attacked the attack has not been levelled at the allocative principles on their own ground so to speak. Rather it is the relevance of these principles to the real world, the world of uncertainty, flux, and growth, that has been brought into question. Adjustments which may be demanded by allocative criteria alone, it is argued, may interfere with the more important factors making for growth.[2] Furthermore, to speak of resources being organised to meet the wants of the community is somewhat fanciful in view of the opinion that in advanced economies, at least, consumers may be persuaded to want almost anything if enough resources are devoted to the task of persuasion.

Weighty as these criticisms are I wish to make it plain from the start that my concern is with the narrower but less controversial aspect: with the validity of allocative criteria within their own limited framework. Let us be certain what this framework encompasses. First, an unchanging population of 'rational' and 'responsible' beings. Rational in two senses, (a) that the choices made by each individual in any situation are consistent with all his other choices and (b) that the well-being of the individual depends only on his own real income and not at all on those of others. Responsible in that each individual is taken to be the best judge of his own wants. Clearly both senses of rational are simplifications which may or may not be generally true, while individual responsibility is an ethical judgment without which nothing may be said about allocation. Furthermore – in order to ease the exposition but not necessary for its conclusions – the factor endowment of the economy is fixed[3] as also is the number of finished goods in the economy.[4] Arbitrary assumptions are usually made in order to deal with the government as a supplier of goods and services.[5] But since our conclusions do not depend in any way upon such assumptions we will confine our attention to the market sector of the economy. Uncertainty, which gives rise to theoretical difficulties at many points, is conceded to be the preserve of dynamics, and is therefore excluded from an analysis which is basically static.

As to ethical presuppositions, other than individual responsibility already mentioned, we shall follow tradition in stating that the community as a whole is better off if at least one person is made better off and no person is made worse off.

We now proceed to inquire whether, within the confines of our assumptions and simplifications, a movement toward an optimum allocation of resources, defined with reference to the familiar marginal equalities,[6] is an actual improvement for the community in this sense.[7] If it is not an actual improvement is it, we ask, a *potential* improvement in accordance with the definition advanced in the New Welfare Economics: that a situation *II* is to be preferred to a situation *I* if the community as a whole *could* be made better off by a movement to *II*. And in order to answer this question satisfactorily we shall, further, seek to be free from commitment in the matter of distribution – as indeed we ought to be if we are to accommodate the many economists who persistently invoke allocative criteria while shunning the question of better or worse distributions of welfare – by regarding *II* as superior to *I* only if it is a potential improvement over *I* for all conceivable distributions of welfare.

The conclusion of this paper briefly stated is this: that in principle an optimum allocation of resources is neither actually nor potentially superior on welfare grounds to a non-optimum allocation of resources. Nevertheless, though an optimum allocation *per se* cannot be vindicated as a norm to be pursued some virtue may be detected in the 'lower level' optima of exchange and production. If, therefore, one disregards allocative criteria to the extent of trespassing upon these lower level optimum conditions the welfare of the community is liable to be damaged.

In an endeavour to hold the interest of those readers who are not on familiar terms with some of the basic technique of welfare economics the following two sections will be taken up in elaborating the properties of community indifference curves essential to the analysis and in examining briefly the various criteria put forward in the development of the New Welfare Economics. Readers already aware of the power, and limitations, of these constructs may pass on immediately to section V.

III

The need for a welfare criterion of the type now common enough in the literature arises from a consideration of the following sort of dilemma. The definition of an improvement in the collective welfare which commands general assent requires that at least one individual be made better off without any individual being made worse off. However, it is usually recognised that any change in the economic situation all too frequently affects the distribution of welfare in some degree. Consequently an actual improvement in welfare which conforms with the above definition is apt to be a rare event. To accept, therefore, only an actual improvement in this sense would be an extremely frustrating axiom for the welfare economist to adopt.

The formulation of a new welfare criterion by Kaldor and Hicks[8] was the outcome of an endeavour to circumvent this source of frustration by defining an improvement in the collective welfare in such a way as to be independent of the actual distribution of welfare among the individuals. The criterion alighted upon was one which involved a *potential* improvement in welfare: if everyone in the community *could* be better off by moving from an existing situation *I* to a new situation *II* – in other words, if the gainers from the movement to *II* could more than compensate the losers – then the criterion was fulfilled. Accordingly, the movement from *I* to *II* was to be treated as an improvement in welfare regardless of whether or not compensation was paid.

Soon after the formulation of this criterion Scitovsky proved that it was capable of self-contradiction.[9] Though the gainers might indeed be able to compensate the losers from a movement to *II* and yet remain better off than they were at *I*, this fact did not rule out the possibility that the losers in question might, after the movement to *II*, be in a position to bribe the gainers to agree to return to the *I* situation.

Subtle though this certainty was, it could be cast into a more obvious form and one through which the elusive nature of the apparent contradiction might be uncovered. The Kaldor-Hicks criterion made use of a comparison between two product aggregates *I* and *II* which was based on the distribution of welfare attaching to the *I* aggregate. To apply the Scitovsky reversal test, however, we must compare the two aggregates on the basis of the welfare distribution attaching to the *II* aggregate. The Scitovsky criterion was fulfilled if the result of this reversal test did not contradict that reached by the original Kaldor–Hicks criterion.

If the comparison based on the *II* distribution of welfare did in fact give a result contrary to that reached when the comparison was based on the *I* distribution of welfare then indeed nothing could be said of the potential welfare superiority of either *I* or *II*.[10] Nor should we stop here. For if we are to remain truly independent of all welfare distributions there is no case for confining a comparison of *I* and *II* to criteria based on the particular welfare distribution attaching to each. A truly comprehensive criterion, and the one we shall adopt from now on, involves a comparison of *I* and *II* with reference to *all conceivable distributions of welfare*. This comprehensive criterion is fulfilled if *II* is shown to be superior to *I* for every conceivable distribution of welfare. Unless this criterion is fulfilled the possibility of contradiction is not fully eliminated.[11]

IV

The reason why this apparent contradiction can arise in a comparison between two situations may be made clear with the aid of Figure 1. The point *P* in the co-ordinate system with origin *O* fixes the quantities of *X* and *Y* available to the community. *P* may also be regarded as the other corner of the conventional box diagram for these quantities of *X* and *Y* which are to be shared between two individuals, *J* and *K*. The mutual tangency, and the individual ordering, of the two sets of indifference curves, representing respectively the welfare functions of the individuals *J* and *K*, are indicated at several points along the contract curve *ORSP*.

Irrespective of the manner of division of the total

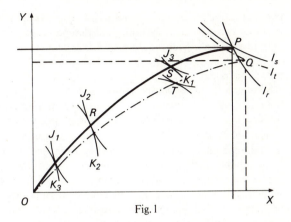

Fig. 1

product *P* between the two individuals the community indifference curve must, of course, pass through point *P*. But the *angle* at which it passes through *P* depends directly on the division between them of this aggregate product. Since at each point on a properly constructed community indifference curve[12] – and therefore also at the particular point *P* – the rate of substitution of *Y* for *X* must be the same for each individual, the locus of efficient divisions of the total product between the individuals is given by the contract curve *ORSP*.[13]

However, for any two points along the contract curve, representing two different divisions of the product *P*, the rate of substitution of *Y* for *X* is, in general, different for both individuals. For example, if we divide the product *P* between the two individuals in the manner indicated by *R* on the contract curve, the community indifference curve *I_r* passing through *P* (and representing along its length the sum of the individual welfares determined by this division) is parallel to the slope of mutual tangency at *R*. If, on the other hand, we begin with a division between the two individuals which is indicated by *S* on the contract curve, the community indifference curve *I_s* passes through *P* at an angle parallel to that of the mutual tangency at *S*.

In general we may say that the rate of substitution at *P*, and therefore the slope of the community indifference curve at *P*, is uniquely determined by the division of the product between the individuals as represented by a point on the contract curve.[14]

If we now introduce another combination of goods, *Q*, with similar possibilities of division between these two individuals, we can again construct a whole pencil of community indifference curves passing through *Q*. In order to make a welfare comparison between *P* and *Q* we must select two community indifference curves, one passing through *P* and one passing through *Q*, that are *comparable* with each other; which is to say that the two curves selected may be regarded as parts of a properly constructed community indifference map – a map in which a higher indifference curve denotes that no individual is worse off and that at least one individual is better off.

This condition of comparability is less restrictive than it may first appear. For any one community indifference curve derived from some particular division of P, such as I_r, there will be many community indifference curves passing through Q each deriving from a slightly different distribution along Q's contract curve, which are directly comparable with I_r.[15] Consequently all these comparable curves will at all points be above I_r. All of them will reveal the same thing, that Q is above P for the community as a whole.[16]

As we cannot legitimately talk of the same or similar welfare distributions existing at different levels of collective welfare[17] we shall, for terminological convenience, speak of any two distributions of welfare from which two comparable community indifference curves are generated as being *comparable welfare distributions.* For the same reason a comparison of, say, P and Q using I_r on the one hand and, on the other, any one of the comparable community indifference curves passing through Q, may be spoken of as a welfare comparison *based on* the I_r indifference curve or, alternatively, a comparison of P and Q *based on* the R distribution of welfare.

Suppose now that the aggregate of goods represented by Q differed from that represented by P in its having one less of Y and one more of X and that we chose to make a welfare comparison of P and Q based on I_r, I_r being the community indifference curve generated from the existing division at R of the product P. If the community's rate of substitution at R, and therefore also at I_r as it passes through P, were $2Y:1X$ then I_r is practically sure to pass below Q. On a comparison based on the R distribution then, Q is a better welfare position for the community than P.

If instead we chose to compare P and Q on the basis of the T division of the product Q, I_t is the community indifference curve generated for Q, a comparable one for P being I_s. If with the division T the community's rate of substitution were $2X:1Y$ the community indifference curve I_t will almost certainly pass below P. A comparison based on the T distribution of welfare would then reveal P to be a better welfare position for the community than Q.

If P is taken to be the initial situation, and Q the new alternative situation, the Kaldor–Hicks criterion is fulfilled by a movement to Q. For, beginning with the existing distribution, R, everyone *could* be made better off by a movement to Q. Having moved to Q, but com-

pensation not having been paid, the welfare distribution is now that indicated by T. The relative valuations of the two goods are, as a concomitant of the new distribution at T, so changed that once again it is apparent that everyone can be made better off by a movement back to P – I_s being a higher community indifference curve comparable with I_t.

This is the essence of the Scitovsky paradox. And it has been shown that it stems from the interdependence of relative prices and welfare distributions.[18]

V

The apparent contradiction which can arise with the use of these welfare criteria has, however, been demonstrated only for a comparison of given product aggregates without reference to the conditions under which they are brought into being. If we wish to bring these criteria into relation with the traditional principles governing the proper allocation of resources – which ensure that each class of factor is distributed over the economy so that in all lines of production the value of its marginal product is the same – we must bring the production conditions into the picture.

In taking account of these conditions, however, we may for the present allow that production is efficiently organised; that the rates of substitution between any two factors is the same in the production of all goods in the economy.[19] On the other hand, we have already seen that the use of community indifference curves implies that the rate of substitution between any two goods is the same for all individuals. Therefore, in an economy where all firms maximise profits without recourse to discrimination between individuals and without regard to the supply curves of the factors, the two 'lower level' optima – the production optimum and the exchange optimum – will be simultaneously realised. Granted this much, we can focus our attention on the significance of divergences in the ratios of prices to marginal costs.

What is now to be examined is what we may call an economic *plan.* The plan is identified by a particular aggregate of goods from the many producible with the resources at the disposal of the economy *plus* the differential in the ratio of the product prices to the ratio of their respective marginal costs. For brevity this differential may be referred to as the *price–cost ratio.* In diagrammatic terms, whereas the community's aggregate of goods is represented by a point on the co-ordinate system, a plan is represented by the intersection, or tangency, of a community indifference curve with the production possibility curve – the angle between them, if any, measuring the price–cost ratio.

Now in the absence of all forms of external economies, the 'ideal' allocation is said to be found in a situation in which marginal cost everywhere is equal to price or, on our simplification of fixed factor supplies, in which the ratio of price to marginal cost is the same for all products. Any situation, or plan, having this 'ideal' allocation is commonly spoken of as a complete optimum and is represented diagrammatically by the tangency of the community indifference curve with the production possibility curve.

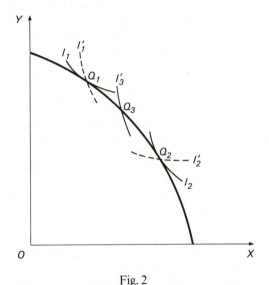

Fig. 2

Can we now compare two optimum plans, such as Q_1, with the community indifference curve I_1 in Figure 2, and Q_2 with community indifference curve I_2? The answer is no, and the reason easy to illustrate. For if we hypothetically redivide the aggregate product Q_2 in order to derive therefrom a community indifference curve, say I_2', which is comparable with I_1 in the sense defined, then in effect what is now being compared with the optimum situation at Q_1 is no longer an optimum at Q_2 which has a welfare distribution comparable with that attaching to Q_1, but instead a non-optimum plan at Q_2, since I_2' *cuts* the production possibility curve at Q_2. The same thing happens of course if we try to base the comparison on the I_2 community indifference curve by redividing the product Q_1 between the individuals so as to generate I_1', a community indifference curve comparable with I_2.

We conclude that welfare comparisons between optimum plans is logically impossible: the attempt to make use of such comparisons entails a destruction of

the essential characteristic of at least one of the optimum plans – the equality of the ratio of prices and marginal costs.

Moreover, and this is more to the purpose, we can demonstrate by analogous reasoning that, in principle, an optimum plan cannot be made comparable with a non-optimum plan and therefore cannot be said to be superior to it. Consider, for example (Figure 2), the optimum plan Q_1 with the community indifference curve I_1, and the non-optimum plan Q_3 with the community indifference curve I_3'. To attempt a comparison of the two plans through the medium of a community indifference map based on the I_3' curve requires a comparable community indifference curve through Q_1, say I_1'. But this manifestly destroys the optimum characteristic of the plan at Q_1, and therefore vitiates the desired comparison. In a like manner an attempted comparison based instead on the community indifference curve I_1 requires the construction of a community indifference curve passing through Q_3 at an angle differing from the original, in this way contravening the particular price–cost characteristic of the non-optimum plan at Q_3. Hence it is not possible, in principle, to compare by means of hypothetical compensation optimum with non-optimum plans or, for that matter, optimum plans with one another.

The words *in principle* should be stressed, for there may be cases where the community indifference curves initially attaching to the plans to be compared already form part of a consistent community indifference map. Here a direct comparison is possible without invoking the technique of hypothetical compensation (which, as we have just seen, destroys the price–cost ratio characteristic of at least one of the plans). Since the two plans are directly comparable – for instance, plan Q_1 with I_1 and plan Q_2 with I_2' – one is actually and unambiguously superior to the other. When, however, two plans are not directly comparable in this way, a comparison of potential welfare is, in the nature of things, impossible.

It is surely at this juncture that we sense acutely the need to answer the question: what virtue resides in an optimum plan that is absent in a non-optimum plan? And the answer will, I think, emerge most clearly if we compare an optimum and a non-optimum plan with a particular aggregate of goods common to both – let us say the optimum plan Q_1 with I_1 and the non-optimum plan Q_1 with I_1' in Figure 3.

Of the optimum plan at Q_1 it may be asserted that, with the particular division of the aggregate Q_1 as summarised in the community indifference curve I_1 at that point, no improvement is possible for both the individuals within the bounds of the given production possibilities, themselves determined by the resources and technology available to the economy. This statement, however, does not hold for the non-optimum position at Q_1 – that is, for the division of the aggregate product Q_1 which is summarised in the community indifference curve I_1' at that point, for we can clearly construct a community indifference curve comparable with I_1' which is an improvement for both individuals and yet is below the production possibility curve along some of its length. One such comparable community indifference curve, I_2, will just touch the production possibility curve at a point Q_2 thereby forming an optimum plan at that point. With this resulting division of the aggregate product Q_2 no further improvement for both individuals is possible.[20]

It is manifest therefore that for each point on the production possibility curve, representing as it does a combination of goods, there corresponds a *unique* distribution of those goods which invests it with the properties of an optimum and therefore a *unique* community indifference curve which determines the pattern of individual welfares.[21]

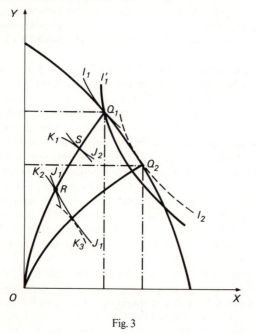

Fig. 3

We conclude therefore that so long as we have no rule for the ranking of welfare distributions (a) comparisons between optimum plans are not possible and (b) comparisons between optimum and non-optimum plans are, in general, not possible. They are not possible because whenever the distribution of one of the plans

has to be altered for the purposes of comparison – welfare distribution being inseparable from relative prices – the identity of one of the plans is destroyed. (c) If the optimum and non-optimum plans to be compared already form part of the existing community indifference map then the method of hypothetical compensation is superfluous, the optimum being actually and unambiguously superior to the non-optimum.

Conclusion (c) is, however, not so much of an exception as it may first appear, not merely because as the number of individuals in the community increases the likelihood of this eventuality rapidly diminishes but because of our aim to be neutral as between different welfare distributions. If, from an existing non-optimum plan we move directly to a comparable optimum plan, everyone being better off, this improvement in welfare is unambiguous for the existing distributions of welfare. For other distributions of welfare the previously optimal plan is a non-optimum plan and, as such, it will be actually inferior to some other plans, optimum and non-optimum; which is to say, once more, that only by abandoning the endeavour to be neutral in the matter of welfare distributions – or, more positively, by selecting one reachable distribution of product quantities above all others available from the given resources – can we define an unambiguous optimum position.

The full force of these conclusions must now be apparent. Far from an optimum allocation of resources representing some kind of an ideal output separable from and independent of interpersonal comparisons of welfare, a particular output retains its optimum characteristics only in so far as we commit ourselves to the particular welfare distribution uniquely associated with it. *If, therefore, we insist on eschewing interpersonal comparisons of welfare the logic of choice impels us to be indifferent as between 'good' and 'bad' allocations of resources.*

To those who, like myself, do not at first take kindly to these conclusions some additional persuasion may be necessary. Let us then turn aside from the price–cost constraints imposed by allocative criteria and briefly reconsider the matter in the light of more familiar welfare comparisons. Toward the end of section III we stated that in order for our results to be truly independent of welfare distributions we were required to employ the comprehensive criterion which would define *II* as an unambiguous potential improvement over *I* if, for all conceivable distributions of welfare, *II* proved to be superior to *I*.

Now in a comparison of the two particular product aggregates in section IV we illustrated the possibility of alternative welfare distributions giving contrary results. If we now introduce the constraint that the product aggregates to be compared are points on a production possibility curve contrary results are certain. Therefore the comprehensive criterion can never be fulfilled. For there will be always, at least, two sets of comparable community indifference curves which give contrary results. One set will be based on a welfare distribution yielded by the community indifference curve which passes through one of the two points at a tangent to the production possibility curve – say I_2 in Figure 3. The other set will be based on the welfare distribution which is derived from the community indifference curve tangent to the production possibility curve which passes through the other point – say I_1 in Figure 3. These two sets of community indifference curves will always intersect, one set based on I_2 revealing Q_2 to be superior to Q_1, the other set based on I_1 revealing Q_1 to be superior to Q_2.

It follows – provided we do not opt for any particular pattern of welfare – that no one of these possible combinations of goods represented by the production possibility curve is unambiguously potentially superior to any other. But each one is superior to all others for some distribution.

Only by preferring above all others, on account of the welfare distribution it entails, the community indifference curve passing tangentially through a particular point on the production possibility curve can we avoid contradiction, since we thereby commit ourselves to *the* optimum; that is to say, only an indifference map built around our chosen community indifference curve has a right to be considered, all other indifference maps built around other tangential community indifference curves being irrelevant. Hence, to repeat our conclusion, there can be no proper allocation of resources independent of a judgment as to the best distribution of welfare.

VI

The conclusions reached in the previous section may indeed give us pause, for the principles governing the proper allocation of resources, and therefore the notion of an optimum, have long enjoyed an unshakable eminence in the theory and application of economic policy. As was suggested at the beginning of this chapter, if they were challenged at all the challenge was directed toward their restrictive assumptions. Granted these assumptions, however, and due allowances being made for divergences between private and social costs, equalising the marginal conditions was the accepted and apparently inescapable formula.

What is left of this formula? If there is now nothing to choose between an optimum and a non-optimum situation are we to go on to say that any arbitrary system of quantities and prices is as good as any other? Fortunately this is not the case. Though the top of the edifice, the complete optimum, has been shown to be illusory the lower levels of optima are fairly substantial. In particular, the exchange optimum which we required for the construction of the community indifference curves and the production optimum which was necessary for the construction of the production possibility curve may be vindicated, the former completely, the latter partially.

In regard to the exchange optimum, if individuals place different relative valuations on the same range of goods, some at least can profit by exchange until the rate of substitution between pairs of goods is the same for each individual in the community. Irrespective of the distribution of welfare, a movement to or toward an exchange optimum is an unambiguous *actual* improvement in the welfare of the community. In other words, some people will always be better off – and none will be worse off – if exchange between individuals of their initial product endowments is permitted.

As for the production optimum, this in general is less certain. Within limits it fulfills the comprehensive criterion. For if it is not fulfilled – if the ratio of the marginal physical products is not the same in all lines of production – then we are at a point inside the production possibility curve, say at q in Figure 4. Any combination of X and Y on the segment of the production frontier between Q_1 and Q_2 – the segment contained in the quadrant northeast of q – represents a net addition to output without additional sacrifice by the community. Hence for *any* conceivable welfare distribution existing at q and a comparable distribution of any product combination along the segment Q_1Q_2 the latter combination yields a higher welfare for the community. This is clear common sense since, starting from *any* distribution, some additional products can be distributed to make all or some of the individuals better off without making anyone worse off.[22]

Provided, then, that a movement to, or toward, a production optimum is one which entails the production of more of one good without reducing the production of another the new output will be unambiguously *potentially* superior to the old output. It need hardly be added that the further removed is the economy from the production optimum the greater is the scope for unambiguous potential welfare improvements.

To sum up, we began our inquiry by affirming that all questions concerned with allocation economics lay

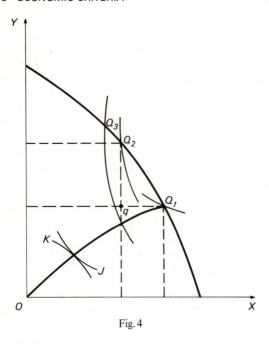

Fig. 4

within the domain of welfare economics and therefore could be treated with and tested by the techniques evolved in welfare economics. Starting, therefore, from a widely acceptable definition of an improvement in the collective welfare – that the community is better off if no one is worse off and at least one person is better off – we proceeded to inquire whether a movement toward an optimum allocation of resources results in an unambiguous improvement either in the *actual* or in the *potential* welfare of the community. We concluded (1) that an exchange optimum is perfectly reliable. From any non-optimum position at this level individuals who avail themselves of exchange opportunities will better themselves without harming any one else. A movement to, or toward, an exchange optimum is therefore an unambiguous actual improvement in the welfare of the community. (2) A production optimum is less reliable. A movement to or toward an optimum production point is an un-ambiguous potential improvement with certainty only if the movement toward the optimum entails an increased production of at least one good without reducing the production of another good. (3) Granted that the exchange and production optima are achieved, the 'top layer' optimum, reached by equalising the ratio of prices to marginal costs, is in general no improvement actual or potential as com-pared with a non-optimum position. Failing interpersonal comparisons, no optimum at this level is

superior to a non-optimum. Put otherwise, in a non-interpersonal welfare economics there is no case for equalising the ratios of prices and marginal costs.

VII

Many propositions in economics require modification in the light of these conclusions. For instance, monopoly may continue to be condemned for various reasons but no longer for the reason that in an otherwise competitive economy it causes a malallocation of resources. More generally, it can no longer be main-tained that an aggregate output in which the ratio of prices to marginal costs is the same for all products is in any way ideal, or to be preferred on welfare grounds to an aggregate output in which this ratio differs from one product to another.

As another instance, the long controversy between the welfare effects of direct and indirect taxation now takes a new turn, and it may be of general interest to describe this briefly before ending.

Since we are to be concerned with the *excess* burden of taxation we may follow custom and suppose that any tax the individual pays is directly refunded to him. If then after the tax the community as a whole, on any chosen criterion, is worse off the method of taxation imposes an excess burden.

On the basis of partial analysis it was for some time widely believed that indirect taxation imposed burdens on the economy from which direct taxation was free. About a decade ago the question was reopened by several economists, along them Henderson,[23] who demonstrated that direct taxes imposed a welfare burden on the individual inasmuch as he would be better off if, instead, the same amount were collected by a poll tax. Neverthless, argued Henderson, indirect taxation was worse still, for it was equivalent to an income tax with its concomitant loss of welfare *plus* an additional loss of welfare arising from the tax-distortion of product prices.

Three years later, Little[24] attempted to prove that, in general, there was nothing to choose as between direct and indirect taxation. Illustrating his thesis with three goods, two products and leisure, he pointed out that an income tax, inasmuch as it raised the price of income relative to that of leisure, in effect raised the prices of the two products relative to that of leisure. There was no essential welfare difference between this effect and that of an indirect tax on either or both of the two products.

However, an investigation of the welfare effects of taxation on the individual may yield results different from those which arise when we re-examine the matter at the community level, for it is at this level that relative prices and welfare distributions are interdependent.

If we remove the assumption of fixed factor supplies and assume that no institutional rigidities prevent the individual from equating his rate of substitution between leisure and X and Y to the resultant market rates of exchange between these three goods, the production possibility curve for products X and Y which emerges may be viewed as the cross-section, at a certain level of leisure for the community, of a three-dimensional production possibility surface, any point on which indicates a combination of total X, Y, and leisure available for distribution among the community. This total amount, or level, of leisure is, of course, determined along with the total amounts of X and Y by the point at which the community indifference surface touches the production possibility surface.

An indirect tax on X alone, or on X and on Y, alters for each individual the preferred pattern between leisure and the quantity of X and of Y consumed. A direct tax on income, being an equiproportional tax on X and Y does the same thing. Either tax moves the economy to a new aggregate combination of X, Y, and leisure. In this new position, however, the community indifference surface *cuts* the production possibility surface in a manner which reflects the divergences between marginal costs and the new market prices. Either tax position has the characteristics of a non-optimum position.

Formally, then, the argument moves on lines parallel to those of Little. The conclusion we reach does not contradict that of Little, though it is more radical. The interpretation of this formal similarity is, however, quite different. Since Little was dealing with a single individual he constructed a unique indifference map and derived a unique optimum. Both direct and indirect taxation took the individual to essentially similar suboptimal points and were therefore equally indictable on welfare grounds. A poll tax, or a tax on earnable capacity, did not move the individual from his optimum and was therefore clearly preferable.

If we turn to consider the community as a whole, any direct or indirect tax not only causes a divergence between marginal costs and prices of some or all of the products, but concomitantly alters the distribution of welfare among the individuals. In general the new community indifference surface which cuts the production possibility surface is not comparable with the initial community indifference surface. Once again, therefore, we are constrained to employ the method of hypothetical compensation in order to compare the two positions. We have already demonstrated, however, the impossibility of comparing, in general, non-optimum and optimum positions at the highest level or, put more strictly, the impossibility of having any optimum unambiguously potentially superior to any non-optimum position.

In the absence of interpersonal comparisons and provided, as we have assumed, that all taxes leave us somewhere on the production possibility surface, we cannot on welfare grounds justify any choice as between a poll tax, a direct tax, an indirect tax or no tax at all.

Notes: Chapter 1

1 To those who have followed the development of the New Welfare Economics it can hardly be surprising that resource allocation should be linked with, and capable of being tested by, welfare criteria. If allocative criteria have managed to survive unscathed despite difficulties in formulating unambiguous welfare criteria the explanation is surely that the connection between the two, though apprehended, has not yet been made explicit.
2 For some very forcible arguments in this connection see chapter 12 of Schumpeter's *Socialism, Capitalism and Democracy* (London, 1943). For a recent attack on allocation economics see P. Wiles, 'Growth versus choice', *Economic Journal* (June 1956); also a comment on this article by K. Klappholz in the same journal for June 1957.
3 Investment and saving can be, and often are, brought into the scheme of things since allocation has a time as well as a space dimension. We do not introduce it here simply because we are interested in testing the validity of the basic principles of resource allocation and not in their extended application.
4 The introduction of a new good, however, may be treated in its effects on welfare as a reduction in the price of an existing good.
5 For some interesting controversy over the treatment of government activity see J. R. Hicks, 'The valuation of the social income', *Economica* (1940), in particular his section 6 on 'Public finance'; and Simon Kuznets, 'On the valuation of social income – reflections on Professor Hicks' article', *Economica* (1948), pt I, section 3; also J. R. Hicks, 'The valuation of the social income – a comment on Professor Kuznets' reflections', *Economica* (1948).
6 For a compact treatment of the relevant marginal equalities consult Melvin W. Reder, *Studies in the Theory of Welfare Economics* (New York, 1947), in particular his chapter 2.
7 The answer, needless to say, is always affirmative if the community consists of only one individual. It is as soon as we have a community of two or more individuals that the problem arises.
    In this connection the frequent assumption in the treatment of welfare or allocative problems, that the utility functions of the population are all homogeneous and identical, enable one to reach conclusions which are

no more applicable to society than the conclusions arising from the analysis of a Crusoe economy.

This stricture is no less pertinent to 'second-best' solutions which build on this restrictive simplification. In this connection one might consult a recent and very fertile approach by R. Lipsey and K. Lancaster, 'The general theory of second best', *Review of Economic Studies,* vol. 24, no. 1 (1957), where because of the explicit initial assumption of homogeneous and identical utility functions the welfare conclusions reached apply in effect only to an individual but not to society.

Unless, that is, we can find some way of justifying the criteria of an optimum allocation of resources for society all the interesting propositions about monopoly, controls, taxation and trade barriers remain without any acceptable foundations. On the principle of first things first, then, we should seek to establish the apparently elusive rationale of the 'first best' before pursuing the logic of the second best.

8 The criterion was suggested by N. Kaldor in 'Welfare propositions and interpersonal comparisons of utility', *Economic Journal* (September 1938), and adopted by J. R. Hicks in his 'Foundations of welfare economics', *Economic Journal* (December 1939).

9 T. de Scitovsky, 'A note on welfare propositions in economics', *Review of Economic Studies,* vol. 9 (1941).

10 In a later paper, 'A reconsideration of the theory of tariffs', *Review of Economic Studies* (1942), Scitovsky says (pp. 94–5), 'If [the community indifference curves through two given situations] intersect . . . according to our convention we must regard the two situations as equally good'. This conclusion is hardly acceptable. Unfortunately Arrow, in his *Social Choice and Individual Values,* elected to treat this unwarrantable conclusion as a proposition of the New Welfare Economics (p. 44 ff.) and – manipulating a self-contradictory relationship as if it were instead a transitive one – discovered, not surprisingly, that it led to a self-contradictory conclusion.

11 That the fulfilment of the Scitovsky criterion – that is, the Kaldor–Hicks criterion and the Scitovsky reversal test both yield the same result – is by itself insufficient to guard against contradiction has been amply demonstrated by W. M. Gorman, 'The intransitivity of certain criteria used in welfare economics', *Oxford Economic Papers* (February 1955). Given that the relevant community indifference curves intersect, Gorman shows that, with more than two situations to compare, the Scitovsky criterion may be intransitive and, if consistently applied and acted upon, the community may be led into a clear reduction of its welfare. Only the comprehensive criterion is necessarily transitive and free from all possible contradiction.

12 For a simple geometric construction of a community indifference map derived directly from individual indifference maps, see my paper, 'The principle of compensation reconsidered', *Journal of Political Economy* (August 1952).

13 A division of the product given by a point off the contract curve is inefficient since by exchange both individuals can improve themselves. For the present we shall consider only those divisions of the product traced out by the contract curve. The exchange optimum is therefore fulfilled as indeed it will be in any economy in which each product has only one price and people are free to buy all they want.

14 Paul Samuelson, in his paper 'Social indifference curves', *Quarterly Journal of Economics* (February 1956), rejects community indifference curves simply because, as distinct from individual indifference curves, they do not enable welfare to be determined uniquely from the given amount of the products. They are then, according to Samuelson, not capable of generating group demand or of being of much service in the technique of revealed preference.

Now one can always 'fix' a community indifference map, making the welfare of the community depend only on the quantities of the goods involved, by using some method such as lump sum transfers in order to maintain constant the initial distribution of welfare. This is in essence what Samuelson's 'social indifference curves' amount to. Such a construction, however, is rather a vehicle for bypassing the crucial problem posed by the interdependence of prices and distribution than a device for its investigation.

That is to say, if the community indifference curves have to be constructed with due regard to this interdependence constraint it is not a defect in them but a virtue. Properly understood it makes explicit a relationship which we overlook to our cost, a relationship which plays a key role in this paper.

15 These curves are not, of course, comparable with one another (since as we pass from one to the other one individual has a little more, the other a little less) but any *one* of them is comparable with I_r. Whichever one we choose to work with, to the exclusion of the others, it will, in a comparison of the two positions, give us the same answer.

16 Since we shall continue from now on to deal with comparable community indifference curves it may be worth while emphasising that in moving from a particular community indifference curve to one above that is comparable with it, the only condition to be fulfilled is that at least one member of the community be better off, none being worse off. Thus, a higher comparable curve may entail an improvement for all the individuals in the community, for some of the individuals, or only for one individual, no one being worse off. Having somewhat different distributions of welfare such curves will be slightly different from one another but, as stated, any *one* of them will be comparable with the curve below.

Having chosen one comparable community indifference curve with reference to the one already given, they both form part of a consistent indifference map – indeed, they could, on this principle of construction, form part of many such maps each differing in some degree in the arrangement of the curves above and below this pair. The curves of such a map cannot, of course, intersect.

17 We cannot, for example, say that in a situation *II* everyone in the community is 20 per cent better off than he was in a situation *I*, and that therefore the distribution of welfare remains unchanged, without admitting cardinal utility into welfare.

18 It may be noted in passing that if, as in the above example, the *I* situation appears superior to *II* when a comparison is made with the *II* distribution (or, in Figure 1, if *P* appears superior to *Q* when the comparison is made using the distribution pertaining to the latter) it may *not* be interpreted as if 'potential losers could bribe potential gainers to oppose the change to *II*' as in fact it very frequently is. For this expression turns the apparent contradiction into a real one. It says (i) that individual *J* can bribe individual *K* to make the change to *II* while, *at the same time,* (ii) individual *K* can successfully bribe *J* to oppose the change. Or, in other words, everybody could be made better off (i)

by moving to *II* and (ii) by staying at *I*. These are logically contradictory propositions. Both cannot simultaneously be correct.

Stated correctly, the apparent contradiction should read: (i) individual *J* could bribe individual *K* to make the change from *I* to *II*, but (ii) *having made the change to II,* and no compensation having been paid, individual *K* could bribe individual *J* to return to *I*.

19 It is not necessary, of course, to hold factor supplies fixed to describe a production possibility curve. We need only assume consistent preferences of factor-owners as between the alternative types of activity open to them, including leisure. A production possibility curve could therefore be constructed in such a way that at every point along it the additional condition is met that the rate of substitution for any class of factor as between one activity and another is the same for each factor-owner at the margin.

20 In more detail, I_1 at the point Q_1 in Figure 3 is parallel with the point of mutual tangency *S* on the contract curve $ORSQ_1$, the respective welfares of the individuals *J* and *K* being denoted by the individual indifference curves J_2 and K_1. I_1 therefore represents the proper summation of K_1 and J_2.

Since I_1 is above the production frontier at all points save Q_1 it is not possible for either individual to become better off without the other becoming worse off.

On the other hand, I_1' at the point Q_1 is parallel to the point of mutual tangency at *R* and represents the proper summation of the individual indifference curves J_1 and K_2. But as I_1' is below the production frontier along part of its length it is obvious that both individuals can be made better off. This is achieved, for example, with the community indifference curve I_2 which is tangent to the production frontier thereby forming an optimum plan at Q_2.

For simplicity of construction, however, I_2 is drawn to represent the special case in which all the improvement in welfare accrues to the individual *K*, individual *J* remaining as well off but no better off than before. Thus, I_2 becomes the proper summation of J_1 (whose extension across the contract curve pertaining to the product Q_2 is possible inasmuch as the origin of *J*'s indifference map at *O* remains unchanged) and K_3 (measured from individual *K*'s new origin at Q_2), where K_3 is of course above K_2.

21 It may well be emphasised that an optimum has a sensible and precise meaning but one *inseparable from the distribution of welfare*. Any point on the production frontier may qualify for an optimum position, each of such optima being tied to a particular distribution of the quantities of goods represented by that point.

This inseparability has been recognised by Professor Meade in his *Theory of International Economic Policy,* Vol. 2. On page 76, for instance, he writes, 'Efficiency demands that the production programme should match the distribution of income which is judged proper on grounds of equity. The two sets of considerations cannot be separated.'

Certainly there is no inconsistency in Meade's concern with allocative efficiency for he explicitly admits interpersonal comparisons. Thus there is in his system of welfare an 'optimum' distribution of welfare.

In strict logic, of course, we cannot select an 'optimum' distribution of welfare as an *a priori* concept without invoking cardinal utility, for the choice of distribution is constrained by the possibilities provided by the range of optimum allocations. In other words, we can only compare the actual quantities distributed among the individuals for each point on the production frontier when each point is treated as an optimum. Having chosen among the various distributions of goods among the individuals that which we judge to be most desirable, we have effectively isolated the optimum position for society compared with which all other possibilities are unambiguously inferior.

Nevertheless, any change in tastes or in resources nullifies this ideal position and once again we have to choose among the new range of optimum positions for the most desired distribution of the product quantities.

22 To put the matter diagrammatically, consider the production-optimum output Q_1 (Figure 4) as divisible between individuals *J* and *K*, and examine the extreme case in which the whole of the output Q_1 accrues to the first individual. His preference for *X* over *Y* being stronger than that of individual *K*, the community indifference curve passing through Q_1 – in effect the indifference curve of individual *J* – is as flat as it can be at Q_1, any subsequent distribution in favour of *K* entailing an anticlockwise movement about Q_1 of the community indifference curve. Even if it were perfectly horizontal about Q_1 it must pass above *q* and, therefore, above the comparable community indifference curve passing through *q*. An analogous argument holds for the community indifference curve passing through Q_2 at the northern tip of the segment. Even if all the product accrues to *K*, the community indifference curve – in effect the indifference curve of *K* – passes above *q* and, therefore, above the comparable community indifference curve passing through *q*. Consequently, any other community indifference curve which may be generated through points Q_1 or Q_2, or through any points on the segment Q_1Q_2, will *a fortiori* pass above the comparable community indifference curve passing through *q*.

If, however, we move outside the Q_1Q_2 segment we can no longer ensure this result. If, for example, in equalising the ratio of the marginal physical products of the relevant factors we move from *q* to Q_3, a point on the production frontier at which a lot more of *Y* but a little less of *X* is available than at *q*, it is possible to conceive of an extreme distribution – say all, or almost all, of the product accruing to individual *K* – such that the community indifference curve generated will pass below *q*, as in Figure 4, and therefore below any comparable community indifference curve passing through *q*.

23 A. M. Henderson, 'The case for indirect taxation', *Economic Journal* (1948).

24 I. M. D. Little, 'Direct versus indirect taxes', *Economic Journal* (1951).

2

Second Thoughts on Second Best

While formal demonstration of the general theorem of second best[1] is, in substance, unassailable since, like other impossibility theorems,[2] its negative corollaries rest securely on the posited absence of empirical limitations, it must be admitted that its forceful presentation several years ago disturbed us somewhat and carried just so much further the process of disillusion with conventional welfare economics. Not that we had any right to be disturbed, for it is clear enough now that in talking of optimum conditions we were, in any case, saying precious little; no more, in fact, than (assuming the appropriate degree of differentiability in our functions) that a constrained maximum entails necessary conditions. This much being conceded, the second-best theorem does no more than point out that, if additional constraints are imposed, the necessary conditions for a maximum are in general more complex.[3] The obvious corollary follows that, in order to identify a maximum position in these conditions, it is necessary to forsake the optimum conditions that are strictly relevant only to the simple case of a single and familiar constraint.

It might seem proper then to say no more on the matter until a great deal more of information has been unearthed about the economic world we live in. But with welfare economics in the dumps now in consequence of several attacks in the last decade, those who have not yet abandoned hope will be prompted to scrutinize these theorems more closely if only with a view to setting limits to the gradual erosion of confidence in the subject. In regard to the second-best theory, for instance, we may admit that *in general* one can say nothing in the absence of universal optimization; further, that the vast and intricate knowledge required in order to derive quantitatively exact second-best solutions will be denied us in the foreseeable future. Yet we may still be able to indicate certain easily conceived conditions that permit us to say something useful; in particular we may be able to discover circumstances which enable us to derive guidance from the familiar optimum rules even though these rules are not universally met.

I

In order to face second-best theory on its chosen ground, we must ignore throughout complications arising from the possible dependence of a person's utility on the utility enjoyed by others, and from divergences between private and social benefit.[4] In short, we shall adopt all the assumptions necessary to warrant the proposition that a situation of perfectly competitive equilibrium entails an ideal allocation of resources. In addition to such assumptions, the employment by Lipsey and Lancaster of a unique utility function to illustrate and demonstrate their theorem is, of course, a permissible procedure. It can hardly be supposed that the introduction, instead, of a community of persons, each having a distinct utility function, would in any way detract from the formal conclusions they reach. Nevertheless, in the search for mathematical convenience some finer points have been overlooked which, if recognized, would have led to greater caution in their interpretations.

Thus, to take up a minor point first, the general case in which the utility function differs as between individuals presents no easy adding-up problem. Such a utility function depends upon the distribution of incomes, which incomes themselves depend upon factor and product prices. In the very process of approaching some optimum the distribution is being altered, with the result that the initial optimum aimed at may cease to be relevant. But if one has to be careful in moving from nonoptimal positions, one cannot feel very easy about optimal positions either. A Pareto optimum, as everyone knows, has the property that movement away from it in any direction cannot make some people better off without making others worse off, a property whose implications have been made explicit in the controversies over compensation tests. It has since been recognized that inasmuch as the set of product prices is itself a function of the distribution of the social product, the value of that product when it displays optimal characteristics is a maximum only for the distribution associated with that price set: it is a best position for society only in the sense that there is no movement from such a position that could make everyone better off.[5] Translated into the language of compensation tests, a movement from any non-optimal position to an optimal position meets only what Little has called 'the Scitovsky criterion'.[6] It does not necessarily meet the Kaldor–Hicks criterion: in other words, a movement to an optimum does not ensure that everyone in the optimum position could be made better off than he was in the nonoptimal position. Thus movements as between optimal and nonoptimal positions are prone to the same paradoxes as are movements as between nonoptimal positions themselves. In both cases, it is possible that each of the alternative positions appears superior in the light of its corresponding distribution, and a choice between the associated distributions becomes necessary if only for the purpose of reaching a determinate solution.

The implication of these preliminary remarks for second-best theory is that its occasional positive contributions carry no more weight than 'first-best' contributions. For instance, the Corlett and Hague[7] theorem that, in the absence of a poll tax, some system of excise taxes weighted in favor of goods complementary with leisure is superior to an income tax[8] was derived with the aid of a unique utility function. Once we bring into account that a change in the tax structure in general alters the distribution of income, and therefore the community utility function, it can no longer be asserted that the community as a whole is better off with the proposed tax system. For we can no longer be sure of meeting the Kaldor–Hicks test – of reaching a position in which everyone could be made better off with the new system than he was in the old income-tax system. Indeed, the Kaldor–Hicks test can contradict the result of the 'Scitovsky test,' and we can but conclude that movements to a second-best position, no less than movements to an optimal position, must be subjected to more searching criteria, such as those proposed by Little, before they can be comfortably accepted.

Having said all this, however, and recalling that 'the Scitovsky criterion' plus a 'better' distribution of income in the new position was one of the criteria suggested by Little, we may carry on with the argument on the supposition that a movement to an optimal position is a good thing.

II

A further, and also a relatively minor, point arises from the method of proof of the general theorem used by Lipsey and Lancaster. Translated in terms of sectors of the economy, the constraint takes the form of a ratio of two prices being unequal to the ratio of their marginal costs. Maximizing with respect to this constraint in addition to that of the transformation surface is enough to yield a quite complicated set of necessary conditions.[9] But in economics this constraint is really equivalent to two constraints – for example, price 10 per cent above marginal cost in X and 50 per cent above marginal cost in Y. Indeed, if there were only one constraint, say price in Y being 50 per cent above marginal cost, the second-best solution is well known and quite straightforward: set the prices in the remaining $(n-1)$ sectors 50 per cent above their corresponding marginal costs.[10] This solution, as it will transpire, is no less of an optimal solution that one wherein every price is set exactly equal to its marginal cost,[11] though, of course, it carries with it a different distribution of income. Consequently, if there is a price–marginal cost ratio common to all the constrained sectors in the economy, the rule is simple: adjust output in all the remaining 'free' sectors until the same ratio prevails there also.

Another issue, less obvious than the above, is obscure both by the form of the general proof and the two illustrations preceding it. In the former, the additional constraint consists of negating one of the necessary conditions for an initially restrained extremum where, as we have seen, these conditions are cast into ratio form. In the latter – the illustrations – it takes the particular form of setting price equal to marginal cost in one of the constrained sectors, greater than marginal cost in another constrained sector, and finding a second-best solution for the free sector. As a result of this method of attack, attention is focused on top-level optima, also on a particular kind of additional constraint, and, therefore, on a particular kind of second-best solution.

In order to remove these limitations, consider a popular three-tier optimum scheme: (1) an exchange optimum, in which rates of substitution between all pairs of goods (including, where necessary, *negative* goods – meaning factors supplied by individuals) are the same; (2) a production optimum, in which rates of substitution between pairs of factors are the same for each good produced in the economy; and (3) top-level optimum, in which the subjective rate of substitution between each pair of goods is equal to their technological rate of substitution.

However, before investigating the implications of this division for second-best theory, the reader should be reminded that in so far as the *individual* is concerned, utility maximization is an *assumption,* an assumption from which we may deduce necessary conditions. Again, for the firm, cost minimization is an assumption (a corollary of profit maximization) from which, again, we may deduce necessary conditions. It follows that the introduction of additional constraints of the form $f_i/f_j \neq p_i/p_j$ (the ps being prices) is not admissible for the individual or for the firm. If the fs are the marginal utilities of pairs of goods, this inequality is precluded by implication of maximizing behavior of the individual. If the fs are the marginal physical products of pairs of factors in the output of any good, then the inequality is again precluded by implication of the cost-minimizing axiom applied to firms.

On the community level, however, where it is no longer legitimate to suppose a unique utility function and to ignore distribution of the product, there can be no *assumption* of maximization; indeed, there would hardly be a problem if there were. One seeks instead the fulfillment of necessary conditions. If they are all fulfilled, we are enabled to *deduce* a maximum in some sense – in fact, in the sense indicated by a Pareto optimum. One or more of these conditions may well be unfulfilled in one sector or in several sectors. If there is no possibility of intervening in such sectors we are faced with the problem of prescribing a second-best solution.

These reminders, as it happens, do enable us at once to say something useful when considering constraints operating on levels (1) and (2), though we shall also have quite a bit to say, in section IV, about top-level constraints.

Thus, insofar as the individual is correctly apprised of all constraints, budget and otherwise, he must be deemed to attain a correct maximum solution – whether first or second-best – in virtue of the maximizing assumption. Even though it exceeds our mathematical ability to derive the specific conditions necessary for this maximum, they are implicitly realized: for whatever the individual's choice is, it has to be accepted as the best solution in the circumstances facing him. Once satisfied with his choice, we can but infer the condition that the marginal utility per penny expenditure is the same in all lines that are freely available at given prices and, therefore, that the ratio of marginal utilities must be equal to the ratio of these prices.

One can therefore immediately modify one serious impression left by the general second-best theorem to the effect that, if there are one or more constraints, the familiar optimal rules can no longer serve us. For we have just seen that whenever the individual's initially free choice is openly interfered with in the market there is no need for the economist to intervene. The individual finds his own way to maximize his utility. To illustrate, we can use the labor market where, in the nature of modern industrial organization, it is not feasible to permit the individual to choose the number of hours to work at each job. The optimum condition that requires the worker's subjective rate of substitution between each factor and product be made equal to the relevant real wage rate[12] cannot be met. Nor, therefore, can this subjective rate of substitution between factor and product, through its equation with the real wage rate, be equated to the technological rate of substitution between factor and product.[13] Each worker, constrained to accept, say, a 40-hour week in a particular firm, must then infringe the factor-product condition and make a decision on an all-or-nothing basis from the range of occupations and firms. He will accept some employment if his rent is positive – defining rent as the maximum sum he would pay to enter the employment in question when compared with other alternatives – and, by assumption, seeks that employment that maximizes his rent.

But the rent-maximizing choice on the all-or-nothing basis, and the consequent infringement of the factor-product condition, does not thereby nullify the applicability of the remaining optimal conditions. In meeting some of them we can ignore the interpretation of the calculus that would have us deal in small units, say hours of labor, and instead apply the optimal rule in terms of the amounts in which factors are customarily hired. Thus, in the production of each good the value of the 'marginal' product of each type of labor must be the same when the 'marginal' product is now measured as the minimum amount of labor that can be hired. Translated from factor to product terms, the price of each product must again be equated to its corresponding social marginal cost, the units of product being measured as the amounts produced by the successive weeks of hired labor. The top-level optimum condition continues then to be held in the same form, amended only by the unit of measurement. The production optimum, requiring the same factor rate of substitution in all goods, which when met, describes the boundary of the production transformation surface, is amended in exactly the same way. The exchange optimum condition, however, remains unamended. Finally, if in addition to a general factor-product constraint another constraint is introduced in the form of a monopolized good, the familiar second-best solution – that all other goods' prices be raised above social marginal cost in the same proportion – continues to apply.

III

We now turn to additional constraints which face individuals *qua* consumers. Two types will be considered – a constraint on the quantities purchasable and discriminatory pricing. In order to avoid constant qualification, we shall start in both cases from a position of overall optimum.

Introduce first a rationing system for a particular good, X. Clearly, if the ration is to make any difference to the consumer, it must be smaller than the maximum amount of X he would choose to buy at the current price. We shall assume this to be the case and, further, so as not to evade problems, we shall allow that, in general, the marginal valuation of the rationed quantity of X differs from one person to another.

Before examining how matters stand on level (1), the exchange level, let us turn for a moment to see how things fit in on other two levels. If the shortage of X were the result, say, of a harvest failure, levels (2) and (3) would have no relevance. We could then, with a clear conscience, pursue the familiar optimum conditions notwithstanding the rationing constraint.

Alternatively, the rationing of X may arise from the social policy imposed by the government, it having been decided that, all liberal arguments notwithstanding, people should buy less of X than they would buy if it were produced by unrestricted private enterprise. There must then necessarily be an output constraint on the production of X. But whatever the output that is deemed socially proper, it should still be produced efficiently. The economy, that is, must still produce on its production frontier and, therefore, the rule for factor combination must still hold – the production optimum (2) must be fulfilled. As for top-level optimum, inasmuch as the ratio is assumed effective, the marginal valuation–marginal cost ratio in X exceeds that in all other goods – though, of course, it will vary as between individuals. If, for the moment, however, we assume that for all individuals this ratio is the same, it might be thought that a second-best solution would involve merely raising all other prices above their corresponding marginal costs in the same proportion. But since this solution would entail an expansion of purchases of X, its adoption would necessarily defeat the government's social policy. If, therefore, we accept the social policy of the government, we are not at the same time at liberty to seek a second-best solution of this sort.

We return therefore to the exchange level, recognizing once more that individuals have different marginal valuations of X. Obviously, if consumers are permitted to sell their ration, X will acquire a market price at which anyone can buy or sell X. Apparently no one will be made worse off and some will increase their welfare. The method of securing a correct second-best solution on this exchange level would appear to be that of simply allowing a free market for X. Yet, once more,

if in pursuit of this social policy the exchange of X as between persons were prohibited by the government, a second-best solution of this kind must be ruled out of order. In that case each individual has to accept the rationing constraint, and maximizes therefore with that constraint in mind. The substance of these remarks is, of course, unaltered if more than one good is rationed by the government.

What of the case in which relative product prices differ as between consumers,[14] so violating the exchange optimum? Once again it should be manifest that the damage cannot be repaired by any new directives on the production level, since any departure from the rule for efficient production necessarily entails that, whatever the resulting output combination, it is smaller than is potentially producible. As for top-level rules, nothing useful can be accomplished by juggling with price–marginal cost ratios as between the various products, since the fault arises not from differences in such ratios but rather from different prices of the same product – some firms, or some industries, having two or more prices for exactly the same product. Indeed, if for any reasons this constraint is accepted, there is nothing one can do to improve matters by altering the other conditions. If, however, there is no warrant for this discriminatory pricing, it ought not to be accepted as a constraint. The government can act to remove it either by making such discrimination a legal offense or by disseminating relevant information among the buying public.

Both these forms of constraint may also operate at the production level. If the quantity of some input (raw material or factor) were arbitrarily rationed among a number of firms, each being forbidden to buy additional supplies from the other, cost of production would differ among them.[15] Firms that were least rationed (in terms of their output of the good in question) would produce at a lower cost than the others. By assumption each firm minimizes its cost by attributing a virtual price to this rationed input, but since these virtual prices differ as among the affected firms, the production optimum is not met, and the resultant output combination is to be found on an inferior range of production possibilities. If we now suppose that, for reasons of social policy, one cannot escape the constraint, the inferior locus of production possibilities has to be accepted, and one makes the best of this inferior locus by invoking the rule for a top-level tangency solution – in effect, an equiproportional, price–marginal cost ratio for all goods. In sum, notwithstanding the constraint which infringes the production optimum, we achieve a correct second-best solution by realizing top-level (and exchange) optimal conditions.

These remarks are equally relevant for a production constraint in which the costs of some given input are made different to different firms.[16]

IV

The impression from the preceding section is that, in virtue of the assumptions about the behavior of the individual and the firm, constraints imposed at the two lower-level optima do not cause much difficulty. Rather it is at the top level that the significance of second-best theory finds scope. There it does correct the view that if one or more sectors of the economy are 'out of line', and for any reason cannot be brought into line, the best thing to do is to go ahead and maximize within the remaining sectors – in the belief that if, after all, the constraints are genuine, there is nothing one can do about them, and one may as well concentrate therefore on reshuffling factors in the remaining sectors in order to maximize the value of their social product. However, equalizing the value of the marginal products in the controllable, or free, sectors does have repercussions on the value of the outputs in the constrained sectors. This follows from the simple proposition that, given an interdependent system, in response to a movement along any market demand curve, prices and quantities purchased in all other sectors cannot both be held constant. Thus if there were a *quantity* constraint in the production of X, any reallocation in the free sectors would in principle alter the price of X and, therefore, the value of the marginal product of factors used in X. If, alternatively, there were a *price–marginal cost* constraint in X, a reallocation of factors in the free sectors would in principle entail a change in the output of X. In either case then the value of output in X is altered. There is no warrant, therefore, for concluding that the set of all relative product prices thrown up from the process of optimizing in the free sectors only will be that at which the value of the social product of the entire economy (including, that is, the value of the product in the constrained sector X) is greater than it could be for any conceivable nonoptimal arrangement in the free sector.[17] This is the common sense of the second-best theorem when applied to top-level situations.[18]

But although nothing in general may be said at this level, and we cannot hope for quantitative estimates of a multitude of relevant interconnections in order to make decisions in specific cases, we need not shrug our shoulders and say nothing at all. For one thing, it would seem very reasonable to believe that (i) the smaller are the constrained sectors relative to the remaining ones,

and (ii) the larger are the initial discrepancies in the price–marginal cost ratios of the free sectors as compared with the constrained sectors, the surer we are to improve matters by optimizing in the free sectors alone than by standing by and sadly sucking our thumbs under the sign of second best.[19] We shall not improve matters quite as much as we might have done if we could have alighted on the complex of exact second-best rules and could have applied them at no greater cost. But by adopting the simple and familiar rules for the free sectors we may not be very far from this hypothetically ideal position. It is reasonable to believe this because the larger the initial discrepancies as between the free sectors of the economy, and the greater the part of the total economy accounted for by these sectors, the further away is the economy from an optimum. If, then, we applied a single price–marginal cost rule to all the free sectors, at the end of the process the economy could not be far from a complete optimum. For if the constrained sectors that remain out of line were small, then a relatively small reshuffling of factors as between the free and the constrained sectors could – if the constraints were removable – take us to a complete optimum.

In fact we may go a little further. The larger are the differences in price–marginal cost ratios as between industries in the free sectors relative to these differences in the constrained sectors, the more certain we are to improve matters – to come closer to an ideal allocation – by adopting as a rule for all the free sectors any one of the price–marginal cost ratios in the constrained sectors.

These remarks bring us to another proposition; namely, that if we had to choose a price-marginal cost ratio common to all the free sectors such a ratio should lie somewhere within the range set by the highest and the lowest ratios of the constrained sectors. To illustrate, if X and Y were the two constrained sectors at the extremes of the range of constrained sectors, X having a 50 per cent markup over marginal cost and Y having a 10 per cent markup, then the markup to be set for the free sectors should be between 10 per cent and 50 per cent. This is intuitively plausible, for if, instead, the markup set for the free sector is above 50 per cent or below 10 per cent, we widen price–marginal differentials and, inasmuch as we thereby increase the movement of factors that would be necessary for a complete optimum to be achieved, we move farther away from an optimum.

Nor need we stop here. We could surmise that the price-marginal cost ratio to be adopted by the free sectors would not be far removed from a correct second-best solution if it were calculated as an average of the ratios of the constrained sectors, each such ratio being weighted by the value added of that sector. Thus, if the value produced in the constrained sector X were large relative to that in the constrained sector Y, the rule to be adopted would be nearer to a 50 per cent markup than to a 10 per cent markup. Again, this has intuitive appeal. If we suppose Y's output dwindling toward zero, the markup to be adopted gradually approaches 50 per cent: it reaches 50 per cent in the case already mentioned, that in which all the constrained sectors have the same 50 per cent price–marginal cost ratio. This rough result does, however, assume that the goods produced in the constrained sectors are about equal substitutes with the goods produced in the free sectors of the economy. But the closer the substitutes the greater the change in outputs for a given differential in price–marginal cost ratios. As between complements, however, even large differentials in price–marginal cost ratios entail small changes in the patterns of outputs. In consequence, the more substitutable is a good produced by the constrained sectors with those in the free sectors of the economy, the more weight it should carry in striking an average; the more complementary it is with goods in the free sectors, the less weight it should carry. To illustrate briefly, suppose there are three highly substitutable goods in the free sectors of the economy, wine, beer, and cider, the constrained good being glass bottles. Since glass bottles accompany the purchases of each type of refreshment, a rise in the price of bottles reduces somewhat the demand for wine, beer, and cider. In the extreme case in which they are bought in fixed proportions, the rise in the bottled drink could be attributed as much to the contents of the bottle as to the bottle itself. If the fixed proportions are the same, in value terms, for each of the three drinks, it is a matter of indifference to the consumer if the price of the bottle alone rises, or the price of the drink alone rises, or whether the rise in price is spread partly on the bottle and partly on the drink. Thus in the case of extreme complementarity as between the good in the constrained sector and those of the free sectors, we could ignore completely the price–marginal cost ratio of any good in the constrained sector and proceed to an optimum simply by imposing a common ratio on all goods in the free sectors. If, now, wine entered the constrained sectors, since it is a strong substitute for cider and beer, the larger the discrepancy between its price–marginal cost ratio and that adopted for cider and beer, the larger the change in outputs demanded as compared with a situation in which all three had the same price–marginal cost ratio. In this case we should ignore the price–marginal cost ratio of bottles completely but

we should bring those of beer and cider into equality with that of wine in order to reach a correct second-best solution – one which, in this particular case, happens to be no different from that of a Pareto optimum.

Finally, there may be circumstances in which one may justify optimizing in some broad sector of the economy while explicitly neglecting what takes place in the remainder of the economy, circumstances which are frequently invoked in partial analysis. If the changes in outputs and relative prices in this broad sector happen to have negligible repercussions in the rest of the economy, we can proceed along these lines. For maximizing the product of this broad sector by equalizing the value of the marginal products of each factor class does not, by assumption, affect the value of the output in the rest of the economy. Thus, without doing any worse in the rest of the economy we can do better by reshuffling factors so as to maximize the social product in this broad sector. The same argument would, of course, apply to some geographical area which had tenuous economic links with the rest of the economy.

V

This is about as far as we should be prepared to go in offering practical suggestions which, although admittedly rough and ready – a sort of 'third best' – are much superior to the rather paralyzing conclusion that unless all optimal rules are everywhere met nothing at all may be said, a conclusion that is too often eagerly embraced as an anodyne against further thought. If second-best theory has a positive contribution to make it is that of serving notice that, in the presence of constraints, slapdash optimizing, wherever one can, may not improve matters: one has, in that case, to proceed cautiously – which is rather different from not proceeding at all.

Indeed, to descend for a moment to the exigencies of the real world, since time is taken to adjust the sizes of industries in response to continual changes in the overall pattern of demand, it is unlikely that at any instant of time we shall, even in the absence of all such constraints, attain a Pareto optimum, much less that we should for long maintain it. We can only hope to be moving in that direction most of the time and not to be too far away from an optimum for any prolonged period. It should not bother us too much then if we cannot pick out exact second-best solutions provided that we are able to adjust frequently toward positions which are fairly close to optimal.

Treated in this way and regarded in the light of the

last paragraph, second-best theory has had a good deal of its sting drawn. And this seems to point to a moral. Much of the recent disillusion with welfare economics has arisen from the rather depressing spectacle of familiar universal propositions being tripped up by facile possibility theorems of this sort. But though it is fashionable to wallow in skepticism about welfare propositions we can and must do better. We can turn our ingenuity to more constructive purpose by attempting to determine the range of conditions under which welfare propositions hold, or hold approximately, and to discover methods that enable us to come within satisfactory distance of an ideal position whose attainment is not practicable.

Notes: Chapter 2

1 See R. G. Lipsey and Kelvin Lancaster, 'The general theory of second best', *Review of Economic Studies,* vol. 24 (1957).
2 For instance, that of K. J. Arrow, 'A difficulty in the concept of social welfare', *Journal of Political Economy,* vol. 58 (1950).
3 ibid., p. 26.
4 The argument would remain unaltered if we corrected outputs in order that the value of the *social* marginal product of each class of factor were the same in all uses.
5 Where we could assume the existence of second-order derivatives at all points on the community's indifference map, we could go further and say that any movement from a Pareto optimum would take us to a position in which everyone could be made worse off than he was at the Pareto optimum.
6 See T. Scitovsky, 'A note on welfare propositions in economics', *Review of Economic Studies,* vol. 9 (1941), where a 'reversal' of the Kaldor-Hicks test is proposed. By 'Scitovsky criterion fulfilled', Little meant that from the new position gainers could not be bribed by losers to return to the old position.
7 'Complementarity and the excess burden of taxation', *Review of Economic Studies,* vol. 9.
8 On the rather far-fetched assumption that such goods, when identified, turn out to be complementary with leisure in much the same degree for all taxed individuals.
9 Their general proof proceeds as follows: in order to maximize some function $F(x_1, \ldots, x_n)$ subject to a constraint $\phi(x_1, \ldots, x_n)$, use the Lagrange method and maximize $W \equiv F - \lambda\phi$. Necessary conditions are $F_i = \lambda\phi_i$ $(i = 1, \ldots, n)$.

Now impose an additional constraint $F_1/F_n = k\phi_1/\phi_n$ $(k \neq 1)$, and maximize

$$W - \mu \left(\frac{F_1}{F_n} - \frac{k\phi}{\phi_n} \right)$$

The necessary conditions become

$$F_i - \lambda'\phi_i - \mu \left(\frac{F_n F_{1i} - F_1 F_{ni}}{F_{n^2}} - \frac{k \phi_n \phi_{1i} - \phi_1 \phi_{ni}}{\phi_{n^2}} \right)$$
$$= 0 \, (i = 1, \ldots . n)$$

10 See R. F. Kahn, 'Some notes on ideal output', *Economic Journal* (1935).
11 It is occasionally asserted that price-equals-marginal cost meets a further optimum condition that is not met in equi-proportional monopoly, namely the leisure-income condition. This mistaken view is corrected in section III, where it is pointed out that perfect competition, no less than imperfect competition, is consistent with the worker's being *unable* to equate income and leisure at the margin. He cannot adjust the hours of his work given the rate for the job but must also accept as a constraint the hours per week that go with the job.
12 This is the rule for adjusting the position as between income and leisure and for determining the number of hours to be worked in each occupation.
13 One could assume, as is common, a zero elasticity of supply of the factor (compounded of a zero substitution and a zero welfare effect), but it would be too much to assume that the fixed supply of the factors, independently decided upon by each worker, coincided exactly with the amounts required by the industries in question.
14 If relative prices were the same to each person but money prices differed as between them, exchange optimum would remain unaffected.
15 A rationing system applied at the production level is quite consistent with market equilibrium. Although there will be only one price for each commodity on the market, the firms that are least rationed (relatively to their outputs), and therefore make larger profits, will be unable to expand and replace other firms so long as the rationing system is in force. In the case of price discrimination, however, if there are no limits on the amounts that can be bought, firms that are enabled to buy inputs at a lower price will eventually displace less favored firms and competitive long-run equilibrium would be restored.
16 If, however, rationing were instead on an *industry* basis, the less-favored industries would suffer a steeper rise in prices relative to marginal costs (where the marginal cost of the good in question included the marginal cost of the rationed inputs, *not* their market value to industry). Moreover, since the marginal value of the rationed inputs, regarded as internal prices, differed as between industries, the conditions for the production optimum would be infringed. The combination of outputs produced will, therefore, be somewhere inside the locus of production possibilities.

One if rejects these constraints as undesirable, then obviously one take steps to abolish them. If, on the other hand, they are accepted as part of a desirable social policy, the fact that their implementation takes us away from an optimal position – or, rather, an optimal position built on market valuations – must also be accepted.

Similar remarks apply to price discrimination on an industry basis. If it is regarded as undesirable, it can be overcome by legislation and by other means. If, however, it is part of the government's social policy, there is no getting closer to an optimum without in some degree undoing the objectives of that policy.
17 Put otherwise, the implication of the tangency solution of the top-level optimum is that, at the ratio of product prices associated with it, the output combination has a value higher than any other output combination producible with the community's resources (measured in terms of any of the n goods regarded as numeraire). But maximizing in this way the value of $(n - x)$ goods with only part of the total

resources of the economy is to ignore the prices and the outputs of the remaining x goods. When account is taken of them, plus the constraints attaching to them, the pattern of outputs in the whole economy at the resulting $(n - 1)$ relative prices might not be that which yields a greater value than any other output combination of the $(n - x)$ goods that is consistent with the constraints on the remaining x goods.

18 One has, of course, to admit the same sort of deficiency in the 'piecemeal' approach in suboptimal situations. Thus, to assert that a movement of some factors out of X, where the value of the marginal product of factors is low, into Y, where it is high, will increase the value of the social product, and will therefore constitute a movement toward an optimum, is to ignore these secondary repercussions on all other market valuations. Each such transfer of factors from one product to another in principle alters all demand prices and, indeed, all factor prices also. Only in circumstances in which we can safely neglect these repercussions on all other prices can we proceed along this route with hope of approaching closer to an optimum – to a position in which there is no further scope for such factor transfers.

19 To be more cautious, we should require as a sufficient condition that all the goods (whose outputs will be affected by the process under discussion) be roughly equal substitutes. If the market substitutability of the goods were exactly equal, for each 1 per cent that price is in excess of its marginal cost the output of any such good would be x per cent smaller than the price-equals-marginal cost output. Under these conditions, the smaller are the constrained sectors relative to the free sectors, the smaller is the amount of unavoidable misallocation. Again, for any given size of the free sectors, the larger the initial price-marginal cost discrepancies, the larger the amount of 'potential improvement'.

3
The Recent Debate on Welfare Criteria

Three areas of development may be distinguished in theoretical welfare economics, (1) that which, aiming at complete generality, seeks to develop the formal apparatus necessary for attaining a unique social optimum. The set of conditions determining the boundary of production possibilities, or of the utility possibilities, is the more acceptable product of this approach, no rules for the selection therefrom of a unique social optimum, other than purely tautological ones, being provided. However, although recent contributions within this area have elaborated optimal conditions to cope with indivisibilities, nonconvexity, and other such awkward possibilities, more prominence has been given to discussions about the theoretical possibility of constructing, under certain circumstances, an apparatus of social choice to enable the unique social optimum to be reached. Though it lends itself to some fascinating philosophical speculation one must be inordinately optimistic to expect welfare propositions to emerge in the foreseeable future from these investigations.

(2) The more traditional interest in resource allocation closely associated with the development of the theory of value had elements of both a general and a partial approach to welfare problems. On the one hand, there was a stress on the allocative rules – in particular, the equality of marginal products in all lines of production – often coupled with the belief that every additional sector in which the rule was met placed the economy closer to optimum. On the other, there was the development of such partial concepts as consumer's surplus and rents and, to some extent, social cost often in connection with a comparison of the merits of various types of taxes and bounties. In this field can also be placed the propositions of second-best theories and many recent contributions intent on refining the concepts of consumer's surplus, social cost, and external effects.

(3) Beginning with the so-called New Welfare Economics, an interest over the last twenty-five years has sprung up in the possibility of formulating simple welfare criteria. The attempt to order all possible social states is consciously repudiated in the search only for sufficient criteria, based on widely acceptable value judgments that enable the community to choose between specified alternative forms of economic organization.

What hope there is for evolving a practical welfare economics seems to me to lie in this last field of endeavor. Justification for commending it to the attention of readers can count on more than this belief, however. The familiar rules of resource allocation, and their growing application through the spread of mathematical programming techniques, can be vindicated by recourse to those judgments of fact and value made explicit only in the search for satisfactory welfare criteria. Until such criteria are established, all recommendations deriving from allocative rules must be acknowledged as tentative and provisional.

The welfare criteria to be considered here are those initially proposed by Little[1] and since then subjected to much criticism. Though, as mentioned above, they can produce only an incomplete ordering, certain attributes are desirable, even essential: (a) the ethical judgments made should command a consensus,[2] and (b) the criteria should be logically tenable; in particular, they should be conceptually clear and unambiguous and, also, consistent in themselves if mutually contradictory recommendations are to be avoided.

Misgivings about whether Little's criteria did in fact possess these attributes have been the source of all the recent controversies. The questions raised in this connection may be grouped under three broad headings which we shall consider in the order that follows:

(1) the meaning of the alternatives under comparison, Q_1 and Q_2, and intermediate points such as H and J in Little's analysis;

(2) distributional problems in the application of Little's criteria; and

(3) transitivity of the two parts of the criteria, and the question of consistency of the criteria as a whole.

I

Prior to the analysis of the chief issues in the recent debate the reader should remind himself that it took place within the confines of Little's assumption A: that direct income transfers were not possible. Thus, only those distributions directly associated with the situation under comparison could be reached. Under that assumption the criteria proposed had two parts, a Pareto part involving a test of hypothetical compensation, and a distributional part. A position Q_2 was to be regarded as socially preferred to Q_1 either (1) if the change from Q_1 to Q_2 met the Kaldor–Hicks test – everyone[3] could be better off in the Q_2 position than he was in Q_1 – and the distribution in Q_2 was better[4] than in Q_1, or (2) if the same change met the 'Scitovsky' test[5] –that in changing from Q_2 to Q_1 everyone could not be made better off than he was at Q_2[6] – and, again, that the Q_2 distribution was better. Obviously if both criteria were met, Q_2 would be socially preferred to Q_1.

that the 'Scitovsky' test (the negation, in fact, of the latter reversal test) establishing the superiority of Q_2 could also be contradicted by a reversal test,[7] it is fitting that any demonstration of the force of Little's argument should be tested by assuming the appropriate reversal test to give a contradictory result in each case. At any rate this has been the practice, the standard method of representing the two criteria being shown in Figures 1 and 2. In a two-person community B's utility is measured on the vertical axis, A's utility on the horizontal axis.[8] In both diagrams the initial position is taken to be Q_1 on the U_1 utility possibility curve, the alternative position being Q_2 on the U_2 curve. In Figure 1, the Kaldor–Hicks test is met in a movement from Q_1 to Q_2, since by moving from Q_2 along U_2 a position J can be reached at which both individuals are better off than they were with Q_1. In Figure 2 the 'Scitovsky' test is met since by moving along the U_1 curve from Q_1 to H, both individuals are worse off than they were with Q_2. We need only add that, in some sense, Q_2 has a better distribution than Q_1, to meet, in each case, the requirements of one of Little's criteria establishing the superiority of Q_2 over Q_1.

No more than this conventional apparatus is needed in analyzing the issues raised in the controversy.

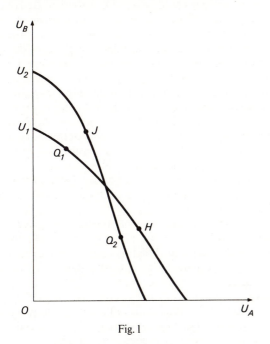

Fig. 1

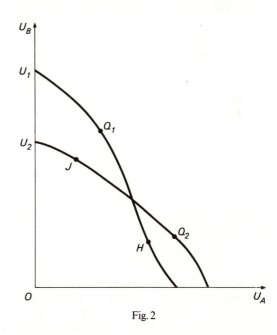

Fig. 2

Since Scitovsky had shown in 1941 [21] that the fulfillment of the Kaldor–Hicks test ranking Q_2 above Q_1 could be simultaneously contradicted by a reversal test that ranked Q_1 above Q_2, and it was later recognized

II The Meaning of Points Q_1, Q_2, and H, J

Although little has been heard in the recent discussion about the meaning of alternative organizations represented by Q_1 and Q_2 to which the criteria are to be applied, the tacit understanding being that they are to be regarded as alternative collections of goods distributed in a certain way among the community, Little had actually suggested other interpretations [10, p. 102] which I take up first as a ground-clearing operation. Indeed, Little was under the impression that he had illustrated the nature of the paradox of hypothetical compensation tests by initially interpreting Q_1 and Q_2 as positions chosen by a quantity-adjuster B in response to prices P_1 and P_2 set by a monopolist A in an economy composed of a given collection of goods.[9]

Presumably each individual already has some amounts of x and y and there remains to be shared between them the amounts of x and y indicated by the lengths of the two axes of the box diagram in Figure 3. The indifference curves of the price-setter A rise as we move in the northeastern direction, those of B rising as we move in the southwestern direction. The initial position is Q_1 chosen by B when faced with price P_1. If A now sets price at P_2 so that Q_2 is chosen, both individuals can be made better off than they were in position Q_1.

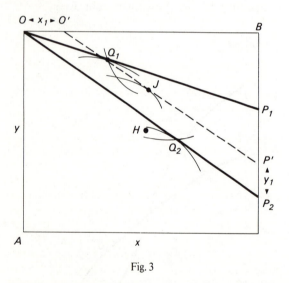

Fig. 3

Construct $P'O'$ parallel to OP_2 to pass through Q_1, and transfer an amount of y_1 or x_1 (or any appropriate combination of both at the P_2 price) from B to A. B is now faced, in effect, with a price line $O'P'$ and, therefore, chooses J. But at J both the individuals are on higher indifference curves than they were at Q_1, QED. The reverse is then proved by constructing, instead, a line parallel to OP_1 and passing through Q_2, the amount of y represented by the vertical distance between OP_1

and this line being transferred from A to B after A's raising the price from OP_2 to OP_1. The position H chosen by B represents a higher indifference curve for both parties as compared with Q_2.

However, this demonstration is unconvincing and when pressed against Little's analytical framework it tends to disintegrate. If, as Little allows, the monopolist is free to set prices, then, even if he began by setting price P_1 so inviting position Q_1, by continuing to set prices further exchange could move them to J (or any other mutually beneficial division) without recourse to this unnecessary and devious route which Little associates with the Kaldor–Hicks test. Indeed, since direct transfers of goods between them are also allowed, nothing is to prevent an exchange which takes them in one bound from Q_1 to J, or some point of mutual tangency. The paradox generated therefore arises only from the inability of A (the monopolist, price-setter, and transfer-arranger) to think straight, not from some inescapable economic relationships. If A had any sense and arranged matters so as to move to a position J on the contract curve to start with, such a 'paradox' could no longer be demonstrated.[10]

The other interpretation of Q_1 and Q_2 suggested by Little, that they could be factor endowments described by a frontier of production possibilities, must also be rejected, since one could establish the hypothetical superiority of the outer frontier, arising from the Q_2 endowment, only if it were possible to move freely along these frontiers choosing any collections of goods and, therefore, any of the distributions directly associated with them. But if the full range of distributions are realizable the second part of Little's dual criteria, which asks whether *the* distribution associated with Q_2 is more desirable than that associated with Q_1, is no longer applicable.

The upshot is that we must perforce continue to view Q_1 and Q_2 as alternative collections of goods in the customary way.[11]

Let us now return to the intermediate points H and J which have elicited much more controversy. Kennedy in 1953 [5] had argued that there was no need for such intermediate points; that a person should be able to compare Q_1 and Q_2 directly. Replying to this charge in his second edition of the *Critique* [10, p. 106] Little emphasized two things: the difficulty of specifying the new position Q_2, and the absence of well-ordered preferences by someone doing the ranking. It failed, however, to impress others. Robertson called it 'lame' [19, p. 228]. Robertson's understanding of the matter was that in moving (in thought) from Q_1 to H the total supply of such factors (work, saving, risk-taking)[12] should remain unchanged, a view, however, rejected by

Little [11, p. 230] who laid it down that a point such as H, northeast or southwest of Q_2, is that collection of goods reached by a lump sum transfer from Q_1.[13] Such an intermediate point, he argued, is a 'potential reality', and though incentives should not be affected inasmuch as lump sum transfers are involved, there can be wealth effects which, in general, alter the total supplies of the factors. On reflection it would seem that Robertson was correct though he might well have gone further and included as unchanged the collection of goods at H as well as the supplies of factors. In the first place, the 'potential reality' that Little wishes to make of H is a rather fuzzy concept.[14] One may be uncertain of economic consequences and one may have to do some guesswork in applying criteria to alternatives in the real world, but the criteria themselves rest on pure concepts, and if they are to be vindicated at all they must be crystal clear on the conceptual level in the first place. If it cannot be known whether the factors increase or decrease, or whether the goods increase or decrease in the imaginary journey from Q_1 to H, it has yet to be made plain by reference to Little's value judgments why it is a matter of indifference. Secondly, if H is a different collection of goods than Q_1, as well as being distributed differently – so as to be comparable, in some sense, with the Q_2 distribution – then, *in general,* it cannot be any easier to compare Q_1 with H than Q_1 with Q_2. In fact H simply ceases to have any essential characteristics of an intermediate point.[15] Thirdly, and most important of all, it is just not true, as Little asserts, that wealth effects involved in redistributing the collection must alter the factor supplies. For by continuously varying the price set as redistribution takes place one may ensure optimal exchange conditions so that, moving along the contract curve in effect, the total collection of goods and factors does not alter.[16] If this contract curve is defined, like the utility possibility curve, as the maximum satisfaction available to one person for given levels of satisfaction enjoyed by the other persons, the property that at any point along it the goods rate of substitution for each person be the same[17] is exhibited only in the absence of external economies or diseconomies of consumption. Nonetheless, even in the presence of such external effects there exists a clearly defined contract curve and so, also, a clearly defined utility possibility curve. Since none of the arguments put forward in the recent controversy invoked these external effects, and since in any case no essential part of the analysis is altered by their consideration, no further reference to them appears in the rest of this paper.

III The Question of Distribution

By substituting some single criterion such as maximizing social utility[18] or by invoking the concept of a social-welfare function we can, of course, continue to evade this issue. Apparently one measures total social utility by adding the individual utilities, presumed to be cardinal and comparable. In the absence of an agreed interpersonal cardinal measure we might accept as judgments of fact that tastes and capacities for enjoyment are pretty much the same, at least given time for human adaptation. We might further agree that the marginal utility of money income persistently diminishes after subsistence income. Ignoring the effects on the total product of a more equal distribution, we should then infer that an equal distribution of income issues in the maximum of total utility. It does not seem likely, however, that if the evidence revealed prodigious differences in the capacity to enjoy money and/or significant ranges of increasing marginal utility of income, many of the Cambridge economists would have accepted the distributional implications. Rather, I imagine, they would jettison the maximizing objective and come down in favor of a more equal distribution of income for its own sake. In the last resort, if distribution does matter then it should be separately acknowledged as a judgment to be taken into account explicitly in any welfare criterion; certainly not left as a byproduct of some single-minded pursuit in the hope that certain features in the real world would act to ensure that the resulting distribution would not be at variance with our ideas of fairness.

As for leaving it to the social-welfare function to specify the distribution, although many symbols have been expended in the endeavor to prove that under 'reasonable' conditions it is not possible to generate a social ordering from individual ones, it would not matter much if the contrary were established. Not only is any hope of obtaining such orderings from individuals chimerical; if such information were to be had it would certainly reveal orderings with wide and irreconcilable differences. The social-welfare function solution to this problem has no affinity with the ideal distribution which informs the distributional requirement of welfare criteria, like those of Little, that begin *ab initio* from value judgments designed for general acceptance and which, in any case, serve only an incomplete ordering. For such welfare criteria, a better or best distribution, is envisaged as a *structure,* one that holds irrespective of any of the conceivable permutations of individuals in the community.[19] On the fairness of a structure of distribution wide agreement may well be possible, while it is not in the least likely that much agreement would emerge if each individual were asked, instead, to write down *inter alia* the share of goods, or income, or wealth, to be received by himself, by Jones, by Smith, and by Robinson, and so on. We should think a person unwordly if he did not give his family and friends high priority, and unusually detached if he did not occasionally regard himself as rather worse off when, though his command over goods remained unimpaired, those around him managed to improve their lot. Such personal rankings, the stuff out of which social-welfare functions are supposed to be formed, along with the existence of 'interdependent utilities' would, therefore, seem to have no part to play in the distributional judgment which enters into such welfare criteria.

Several minor points can be dealt with quickly. I had suggested [**17,** p. 238] that 'more equal' distribution could be substituted for the noncommittal term 'better' distribution, since more specific statements, or statements about the pattern of some contemplated improvements in distribution, always made it clear that, for the West at least, more equal was synonymous with better. Some additional constraints might well be desirable[20] but otherwise the judgment that a more equal distribution of a given product was not likely to meet with opposition. It is of no analytic consequence, however, and were I shown to have misinterpreted the consensus in this respect I should gladly withdraw. In addition, I proposed that we cut the Gordian knot rather than forever be entangled in bitty arguments about real and money income or wealth [**18,** pp. 345–6]; indeed, that in a predominantly market economy our distributional value judgments could be expressed directly in terms of money – a value judgment that a more equal distribution of money incomes in allocating a given collection of goods was a social improvement might command widespread assent. Again, however, this proposal is no more than an attempt to fit some clothing on the bare part of Little's criteria and does not constitute any criticism or even any formal amendment of them. It should be noticed, however, that in a world in which there happened to be great variations in the capacity for enjoyment, the achievement of equality implies that aggregate utility could be raised by transferring income from those with smaller to those with larger worldly appetites. The forfeiture of this potential access of utility, even if we knew exactly how to realize it, is an implication I find easy enough to accept though I am aware of its power to upset others.[21]

IV Consistency and Transitivity

In his review [**13**] Meade pointed out that it was possible both for *H* to be distributionally preferred to

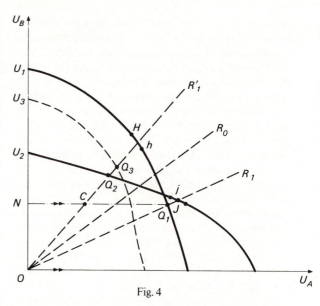

Fig. 4

Q_1 and for *J* to be distributionally preferred to Q_2 which, if accepted, would carry the interpretation that Q_2 was distributionally preferred to Q_1, and at the same time Q_1 was distributionally preferred to Q_2, so that in Figure 2, for example, we should be able to show, on Little's criterion, that Q_2 is socially preferred to Q_1 and vice versa. One could, of course, guard against this possibility by requiring in the 'Scitovsky' application of Little's criterion (illustrated in Figure 2) that, whenever any point *H* was distributionally preferred or indifferent to Q_1, all possible points *J* be distributionally worse than Q_2. Similarly in the Kaldor–Hicks version of the criterion (illustrated in Figure 1) we should require that for any Q_2 distributionally preferred or indifferent to *J*, Q_1 is distributionally worse than all possible points *H*.

This constraint is a bit clumsy, however, and would add to the difficulties of applying the criteria. We might discover a simpler way to avoid this possible contradiction if we could first ascertain how it arises. It soon transpires that the possibility of contradiction in the criteria is latent in the value judgments on which they are based: (i) that a change which makes everyone better off is a social improvement, and (ii) that a better distribution of the given product is a social improvement.[22] For if we effect a social improvement by realizing an ideal distribution of the product, and then effect a further social improvement by a Pareto improvement that gives the whole of the increase to one individual, the resulting distribution will be less than ideal; thus, a movement that ranks as a social improvement by reason of the (i) judgment may simultaneously appear as a socially inferior position in virtue of the (ii) judgment. The seed of the contradiction is sown.[23]

The way it insinuates itself into the criteria can be demonstrated quite simply if we suppose interpersonal cardinal utility, by reference to Figure 4, with the ray R_0 representing an ideal distribution of income, rays on either side being a worse distribution the further they are from R_0. Rays R_1 and R_1' are distributions that are ranked as equally desirable.[24] It will, further, be an advantage to adopt the following notation:

d to indicate distributionally preferred (since strong distributional ordering is generally adopted, $Q_2 dJ$ implies $J\tilde{d}Q_2$);
p to indicate Pareto preferred (in Figure 4 JpQ_1, and therefore $Q_1\tilde{p}J$);
$>$ to indicate socially preferred on either of Little's criterion ($Q_2 > Q_1$ implies $Q_1 \not> Q_2$).

Confining our attention to the U_1 and U_2 utility possibility curves, the Kaldor–Hicks–Little criterion takes the following form:

$$Q_2 dJQ_1, \quad \text{therefore} \quad Q_2 > Q_1 \qquad \text{(a)}$$

However, it is no less true that

$$Q_1 dHpQ_2, \quad \text{and therefore} \quad Q_1 > Q_2 \qquad \text{(b)}$$

The explanation of this paradox is not difficult. The ordering JpQ_1 admits a latent contradiction inasmuch as it is simultaneously true $Q_1 dJ$. If the same relationship exists between H and Q_2 as exists between J and Q_1, and Q_1 and Q_2 are distributionally indifferent, we have the result that $Q_2 dJ$ and $Q_1 dH$ at the same time as JpQ_1 and HpQ_2, the rankings from which (a) and (b) are derived. Indeed, we can go further. Since there is a whole range of possible intermediate points like J and H, in the northeastern quadrant of Q_1 and Q_2 respectively, by altering the position of such points – though without in any way altering the properties of Q_1 and Q_2, the collections under comparison – we could reach a consistent result that $Q_2 > Q_1$, or a consistent result that $Q_1 > Q_2$, or else (taking H and J to be the intermediate points) the result that both $Q_2 \not> Q_1$ and $Q_1 \not> Q_2$.

The need for some further restraint in the choice of such intermediate points is fairly obvious not only to eliminate contradictability and also the arbitrariness of an apparently consistent result, but also because value judgments that can be made to pull in opposite directions do not provide a steady enough foundation on which to raise welfare criteria. What was suggested therefore [**17**, p. 242] was that judgment (i) be amended

to (i') that society is better off if everyone is better off *without the distribution being made worse*. And to ensure that this judgment is met in applying such criteria, intermediate points such as H and J are required not merely to be Pareto comparable with Q_2 and Q_1 respectively, but 'equicomparable' also – which term serves to indicate the requirement that everyone at H or J be better off (or worse off) in the same proportion as compared with Q_2 and Q_1 respectively. The difficulty of discovering what would constitute a proportional increase in the welfare of all the individuals concerned is to be resolved simply by couching the distributional value judgment in terms of money.

Following these proposals, two further implications of such welfare criteria were pointed out by Kennedy [**6**]. First, that the unambiguous fulfillment of Little's Kaldor–Hicks welfare criterion is consistent with a movement to a smaller collection of goods. Thus, if we suppose for the moment that the ray R_1' in Figure 4 represented a better distribution than the ray R_1, we should legitimately infer from the (Kaldor–Hicks) Little criterion that Q_2 is socially preferred to Q_1. However, Q_3 being northeast of Q_2 and along the same ray R_1' is – by either judgment (i) or (i') – socially preferred to Q_2. Consistent application of the criterion would take us from Q_1 to Q_3 on the utility possibility curve U_3 which is generated from a collection having less of every good than the collection U_1 on which Q_1 is to be found.[25] Secondly, that judgments such as (i') and (ii) can be boiled down to judgment (iii) that there is a social improvement if the distribution of welfare is better, provided that not everyone is made worse off.[26] The limiting case which such a judgment could be made to cover is that in which, although the distribution has improved, everyone in the community is worse off except one person whose welfare remains unchanged. In a two-person community such a case is illustrated in Figure 4 by a movement from Q_1 to a point C on the ray R_1' which is in some degree a better distributional arrangement than the ray R_1. Such a limiting case could also involve a limiting shape for the U_2 utility possibility curve. J would coincide with Q_1 and the portion of the curve from J to N would run parallel with the horizontal axis. If, however, we are reluctant to accept a movement along the contract curve, from an initial position in which B has all the goods, which makes B no worse off while making A continuously better off, at least for some range, then the limiting point C must be in some degree higher than Q_1. (iii) would have to be revised to read (iii') that there is a social improvement if the distribution of welfare is better, provided at least one person is better off.[27]

It is important to notice in passing that these two implications depend in no way upon the proposed value judgment (i′) and the consequent constraints imposed on the intermediate points H and J. They are implications of Little's criteria applied to alternative collections of goods however the intermediate points are interpreted.[28]

V Further Reflections on Intransitivity

Since the two parts that make up each of Little's criteria rest on judgments that are different in kind they cannot, according to Kennedy, be treated as transitive, as they are by Little. Moreover, as we have indicated above, a movement that fulfills the unamended Pareto value judgment (i), may tacitly negate the distributional value judgment (ii), and, if this happens, mutually contradictory rankings may be derived. One way of overcoming this deficiency has been discussed at some lengths in the preceding section. Before going on, however, it is pertinent to inquire whether there exists any other consideration which might prevent the emergence of contradictory rankings. It could be alleged, for instance, that the original Little criteria are consistent with the ordering of what Graaff [3] has called a Pareto-type welfare function – one in which society is better off if no person is worse off and at least one is better off – or, possibly, that a Pareto improvement is never to be regarded as a worse distribution of welfare. Now, apart from the ethics of the matter, neither proposition can in fact save the original criteria. If they are supposed to be consistent with a Pareto-type ordering the constraints necessary to ensure this attribute should be clearly indicated, whereas no hint of their nature is to be found. As for the proposition that a Pareto improvement can never be judged a worse distribution, even if it were acceptable the effect would be merely to ignore the possibility of latent contradiction in the criteria. If, for example, in Figure 4, we assert that a latent movement from Q_1 to J is not only a Pareto improvement but a distributional improvement also, similarly for a movement from Q_2 to H, it would not prevent the outcome that Q_2 is socially preferred to Q_1 and Q_1 socially preferred to Q_2. We conclude that contradictory results can be insured against only by adopting value judgment (i′) instead of (i) and, therefore, in applying the criteria making use of equicomparable intermediate points or – since the latter can be effectively employed by recourse to money distributions – by comparing the money distributions of Q_1 and Q_2 directly. Alternatively the judgments (i′) and (ii), as also these amended criteria,

can be boiled down to a single judgment (iii), or (iii′) in which, again, money distributions are compared. True, when the criteria are transformed into judgments such as (iii′), that society is better off if distribution is improved and at least one person is better off, their luster is somewhat diminished. Nevertheless, experience of their application may give more satisfaction if in most cases the Q_2 adopted yielded something of a premium above this acceptable minimum. We might hope to find that in many cases quite a lot of people were made better off in addition to the distributional improvement.

Finally, even though the adoption of (i′) effectively bars the way to contradiction, we may not feel altogether comfortable. Considerations of symmetry at least would suggest that we also amend judgment (ii) to some sort of (ii′). And there is something to this. For we may rank Q_2 above Q_1, for instance, on the ground that Q_2 is distributionally preferred to J which is distributionally as good as, and also Pareto preferred to, Q_1 (see Figure 4). We can now choose a Q_3 that is distributionally as good as Q_2 and Pareto preferred to Q_2, in which case we rank Q_3 above Q_2 and, *a fortiori*, above Q_1. Yet we have already shown that Q_3 can have smaller amounts of every good than the collection Q_1. If we wanted to avoid such an outcome we should have to require, in comparing Q_2 and Q_1, that Q_2 is not only distributionally preferred to J but also Pareto preferred to it – or, at least, not Pareto inferior. This desideratum would be ensured if the distributional proviso (ii) were amended to (ii′), that there is a social improvement if the distribution of welfare is better provided no one is made worse off.[29]

This amended judgment (ii′) may seem pretty stringent, and it is obvious that, like (i′), it cannot be met by confining the change to a given collection of goods. Yet (i′) and (ii′) are not very different: (i′) is 'strong' on the Pareto requirement and 'weak' on distribution, the reverse being true for (ii′). An improvement that meets (i′) *alone* can be expected to meet (ii′) alone, and vice versa, since an improvement in which distribution is no worse and everyone better off may be expected to be one in which distribution is also better. The stringency really arises from requiring Pareto *and* distributional improvements in *both* movements, from Q_1 to the intermediate point, say J, and then from J to Q_2 also. Having to meet them successively in this way amounts to a judgment (iv) that there is a social improvement when everyone is better off and the distribution also is better off. Such a judgment is likely to command a wider consensus than, say, (iii′) though it is unlikely to be met as often as (iii′) and, in a large community, one would be surprised if it were ever completely met.

VI Summary and Conclusions Relevant for Resource Allocation

It is well known that a movement from a nonoptimal position Q_1 to a fully optimal position Q_2 meets the 'Scitovsky' compensation test, though it may fail the Kaldor–Hicks test: in other words, a redistribution of the Q_1 collection that made it comparable with the existing distribution of the optimal collection Q_2 would always reveal Q_2 as Pareto superior to Q_1, although it is simultaneously possible that a redistribution of the optimal collection Q_2 that rendered it comparable with the existing distribution of the Q_1 collection would reveal Q_2 to be Pareto inferior to Q_1.[30] Since the outcome of a hypothetical compensation test between optimal and nonoptimal positions depends, as it does also in such tests as between two nonoptimal positions, upon the distribution on which the test is based, it would appear that one could be sure of an unambiguous answer only after deciding which was the relevant distribution. If one agrees that the relevant distribution is the better distribution one is in fact led into contemplating dual welfare criteria – that is, criteria with distributional as well as Pareto requirements – as much to avoid ambiguity as for the ethical concern with distribution itself.

What has emerged from the recent controversy, however, is that unless these dual criteria are more carefully formulated than they were by Little the ambiguity remains after the distributional judgments are included in them. We have indicated that a point H distributionally preferred to Q_1 is not inconsistent with a point J distributionally preferred to Q_2 – or, in long hand, that a distribution of Q_1 comparable with the distribution of the optimal collection Q_2, which is judged better than the actual distribution of the Q_1 collection (on which grounds we assert Q_2 to be better distributed than Q_1), does not rule out the possibility that a distribution of the optimal Q_2 collection made comparable with the Q_1 distribution is better than the actual distribution of the Q_2 collection (which we interpret to mean that Q_1 has a better distribution than Q_2). Thus even an optimal position with a better distribution (in the Little sense) does not necessarily establish itself as being unambiguously superior to a particular nonoptimal position.

In the endeavor to eradicate this further source of ambiguity it was found necessary to amend Little's judgment (i) to (i') and, in consequence, it was found expedient to define uniquely the intermediate points H and J. In order to implement the more precise criteria, however, two further steps could scarcely be avoided. Though H and J were made conceptually precise, there was still the problem of how, in the real world, we should determine such points. If the transition to the real world is ever to be made I cannot see how we can avoid accepting the distribution of money incomes, or wealth, as an index of the distribution of welfare. Nor does this step seem to me at all questionable. If there was broad acceptance of the distributional judgment (ii) when framed in terms of money we could legitimately circumvent much of the fastidiousness on this question. Granted this much, however, the points H and J become otiose since their structures of distribution in terms of money are now no different from the distributional structures of Q_2 and Q_1 respectively. In applying these dual criteria, then, we should be able to compare the distributions of two alternative collections Q_1 and Q_2 directly without recourse to intermediate positions.[31]

Having gone so far, however, it would seem that we need not go to the trouble of employing these criteria based on hypothetical compensation. For once we seek to justify the two parts of the criteria by reference to judgments (i') and (ii) we become aware that, taken in succession, they yield (iii'), with distribution measured in money terms, which can be applied directly to Q_1 and Q_2. The dual welfare criteria become unnecessary. And since by definition of a Pareto optimum it is not possible to have an optimum position in which all individuals are worse off (or even in which all individuals are no better off) than any nonoptimal position, any optimal position Q_2 that has a better (money) structure of distribution than the nonoptimal position in question enables (iii') to be met.[32]

Notes: Chapter 3

1 See I. M. D. Little [9 and 10, esp. ch. vi].

2 One could sidestep methodological discussion by making these criteria conditional upon a consensus, or by pointing out to the individual that by accepting certain factual and value judgments he is logically impelled to accept the outcomes of applying the criteria – always under the assumption, of course, that they produce noncontradictory results.

3 We can assume perfect divisibility of goods and factors, also that each person's welfare is increased if he has more of any goods or supplies less of any factor. Though these assumptions are not necessary for the argument they would warrant the abbreviation 'everyone better off' for the more usual definition of a Pareto improvement: 'At least one person better off and nobody else worse off'.

4 Actually, Little only requires that the distribution in Q_2 be *no worse* than in Q_1. However, the logical status of his criteria can hardly be weakened by substituting the stronger requirement, that Q_2 have a *better* distribution than Q_1.

5 I follow my custom of writing 'Scitovsky' in quotes since Little inadvertently misrepresents Scitovsky's criterion [**10,** p. 101]. Scitovsky proposed that Q_2 be regarded as superior to Q_1 only if both the Kaldor–Hicks test was met and the reversal of the Kaldor–Hicks test negated. This latter test, the negation of the reversal test, is what Little refers to in table 1 [**10,** p. 101] when he speaks of the Scitovsky criterion.

6 'Strong' ordering has always been assumed in the discussion of these criteria: if, for example, in moving from Q_2 to Q_1 everyone could *not* be made better off, it is accepted that everyone in Q_1 could be made worse off than he was in Q_2.

7 Initially, in connection with the problem of index numbers as indicators of changes in welfare, see Kuznets [**8**], also Hicks's reply [**4**]. The reader who feels a bit rusty on these concepts will find a simplified treatment of their rationale in my survey paper [**16,** pp. 218–28].

8 There is no need to assume cardinal utility nor interpersonal comparisons. Apart from moving downward from left to right the shapes of the curves are arbitrary.

9 No other interpretation of Q_1 and Q_2 was explicitly introduced in the first edition of the *Critique*. In the second edition, the same box diagram was retained to illustrate the Kaldor–Hicks and 'Scitovsky' criteria before alternative interpretations of Q_1 and Q_2 were discussed.

10 How Little is able to represent such a case by a pair of utility possibility curves on his diagrams in figure VII [**10,** p. 104] is something of a mystery. According to Little [**10,** p. 102], each utility possibility curve gives the maximum utility attainable by one person given the utility of the other, this maximum depending upon what is fixed. If the set of goods *and* prices is fixed, he goes on to say, the curve traces out the utility levels of each person as direct transfers are made from one to the other. Allowing complete freedom of such direct transfers, however, would surely discover the contract curve itself as being the utility possibility curve. But there is only one contract curve and, therefore, only one utility possibility curve.

11 A fourth alternative, that a movement along the utility possibility curve represents 'what would actually happen as money was shifted between the individuals, the points being determined by the actual price and output policies' [**10,** p. 102], is not taken up at this point. Such an interpretation involves intermediate points H and J that have quantities of goods different from Q_1 and Q_2, an interpretation which I discuss in the latter part of this section and reveal to be untenable.

12 How risk-taking should be conceptually measured in this context is not at all clear.

13 In the same note [**11,** p. 230] Little, in reply to a criticism of Professor Meade, made it clear that Q_2 being distributionally preferred to Q_1 is to be taken to mean that some point H to the southwest or northeast of Q_2 which could actually be reached by lump sum transfers from Q_1 is better than Q_1. We consider this further in section III below.

14 Dobb's criticism of this interpretation of H is more explicit. If it were accepted, he says, it would be better to banish:

... the terminology and apparatus of the older

compensation debate and to say simply: 'there is no pretence that H is the equivalent of Q_1 in all respects save distribution: it is simply a point which it would be feasible to reach in given circumstances from Q_1; and when I say Q_2 is better than Q_1 I merely mean that such a point exists to the south-west of Q_2 which is preferable to Q_2'. [**2,** pp. 769–70].

15 A. K. Sen [**20,** pp. 774–6] interprets Little's position more intelligibly (1) by appointing H to a position outside Q_1's utility possibility curve and (2) by some other collection H which is worse than Q_2 though better than Q_1 then one can rank Q_2 above Q_1. But to accept this interpretation of the procedure would be a virtual abandonment of the attempt to formulate objective (or, rather intersubjective) welfare criteria. For what Sen is describing is a purely personal ranking with H no longer uniquely defined but merely a position any particular economist might chance to think on. Economists could, under this procedure, consistently take up opposite positions.

16 Individual indifference curves encompassing factor supplies can be constructed [**15**] and the maps of various individuals compounded into community indifference maps in the usual way [**16,** pp. 221–4]. For any given collection of goods and factors there will be a 'contract curve' giving a range of factor and product prices associated with the efficient distribution of these factors and products.

This concept incidentally lays to rest the shade of an old and favorite dilemma, brought to light by Meade in this connection [**13**], the conflict between equality and incentives. For the community is now seen to be ordering alternative collections in one of which there may be fewer factors and goods but which may not, however, preclude its meeting the tests of hypothetical compensation. See also [**17,** p. 236].

17 See my survey [**16,** pp. 228-9] and also Little's statement at the top of p. 102 [**11**].

18 See Kennedy [**5** and **6**].

19 It is for this reason that one of Arrow's strictures [**1**] of Little's *Critique* [**9**] is, perhaps, not so relevant as it appeared. The view that distributional comparisons of different collections imply both interpersonal and cardinal utility (which belief, if valid, would in any case apply no less to distributional comparisons of a single collection) is not true if one is concerned with comparing distributional *structures,* something which is feasible enough if we are content to work with the structure of money, income, or wealth.

20 A reduction in some measure of dispersion about the mean income is obviously consistent with a group of the very poor suffering a reduction in their average income. If compensation for such a group were not feasible, the relevant constraint would operate to prevent fulfillment of the criteria, notwithstanding that distribution was more equal in the Q_2 position.

21 Sen's criticism of the equality thesis [**20,** p. 777] amounts to concern with the possibility of this implication, though he chooses to illustrate his point with a two-person world in which A is a cheese-lover having all the cheese and B a beer-lover having all the beer, in an economy rich in cheese though poor in beer. In the process of

reaching welfare equality A has to sacrifice large quantities of cheese which, however, add very little to B's satisfaction. Without invoking so restrictive an example it should be clear that what is at issue is the large loss of utility by A with no commensurable gain by B in the pursuit of equality of total utility, an issue which is quite adequately illustrated, as above, by the more traditional concern with differences in capacity for enjoyment.

22 See Little's *Critique* [**9**, pp. 111 and 116]. Since Little's intermediate point H is open to the interpretation of being a collection of goods different from Q_1, he does not talk of a better distribution *of the given product* but merely of a better distribution of welfare. Though reasons have been given to reject this interpretation, the argument in the text is, nonetheless, still applicable even if H did represent a different collection from Q_1.

23 Kennedy [**6** and **7**] pointed out correctly that the two parts of the criteria are different in kind and therefore not transitive. See also Dobb [**2**, pp. 767–8]. I agree with this point, although I conclude that non-transitivity, in this instance at least, does not *necessarily* lead to contradiction. For we can take precautions to guard against this eventuality [**18**, p. 343].

24 The argument in the text is facilitated by this construction which helps us to keep our distributional bearings, but it holds as well for the usual construction of utility possibility curves.

25 Granted the proposed amendments, however, intransitivity is not involved. Since Q_3 has a *better* distribution than Q_1 it cannot be shown inferior to Q_1 – which is one good reason for substituting a *better* distribution for Little's *no worse* distribution.

26 To which one ought to add for completeness the judgment (i′) itself, that there is a social improvement even if the distribution remains unchanged provided everyone is made better off [**18**, p. 349]. Since it adds little to (iii), and its inclusion does not affect the rest of the analysis, we shall omit further reference to it.

27 It might be argued that external economies of consumption could result in a left-to-right upward-sloping portion of the utility possibility curve, leading to the conclusion that a Q_2 may be found in which *both* individuals are worse off along R_t' and yet, by these criteria, Q_2 is socially preferred to Q_1. However, if the contract curve is defined, as it ought to be, as a locus of positions in which both individuals cannot be made better off, such upward-sloping ranges, if they could be observed in the real world, would not form part of the effective utility possibility curve.

28 This should be emphasized because of the impression conveyed that they arise only in consequence of the proposed revision of Little's criteria [**18**, p. 347].

29 The implications of the intransitivity of a dual criterion and the need to impose further constraints to avoid contradiction can be illustrated by a homely example in which a person ranks various shades and qualities of some blue woollen material, preferring brightness of color and softness of texture. For BbA, read cloth B is preferred to A on grounds of brightness. For CsB read cloth C is preferred to B on grounds of softness. Applying, now, the logic of a dual criterion we would reason: (1) $CsBbA \rightarrow C > A$. However, it is not impossible that brightness and hardness are inversely related, so that comparing the same pairs in the reverse order for opposite qualities, we should reason: (2) $AsBbC \rightarrow A > C$.

To avoid contradictions of this sort, one could now lay down that $BbA \rightarrow B > A$ only if $A\tilde{s}B$. Assuming that statement (i) is allowed only after ensuring $A\tilde{s}B$, this effectively prevents us from asserting (ii). This requirement is analogous to that part of the proposed amended judgment (i′) that reads 'provided the distribution is not made worse'. But the requirement $A\tilde{s}B$, though sufficient to prevent contradiction, is not wholly satisfactory. We should further want to lay down that $CsB \rightarrow C > B$ only if $B\tilde{b}C$, otherwise CsBb, sA $\rightarrow C > A$ has C superior to B superior to A, notwithstanding the possibility that C is preferred to B on grounds of softness only and therefore when B, and indeed A also, may be brighter than C. It is for analogous reasons I suggest above an additional amendment to (ii). In an incomplete ordering guided by a sufficient criterion based on two nontransitive qualities, it seems to be the only satisfactory way of proceeding, though obviously it must reduce its successful application to such criteria.

30 See [**14**, esp. pp. 332–7]. This is one of the reasons why the supposed demonstrations that for any country free trade (or restricted trade) is better than no trade at all are unsatisfactory.

31 If, for any reason, we continue to use dual welfare criteria based on distributional judgments in terms of money and hypothetical compensation tests between Q_1 and Q_2, though we may not in practice have any need for intermediate points such as H and J, we might still want to retain them merely in order to illustrate how meeting those dual criteria issue in the fulfillment of judgments (i′) and (ii).

32 Meeting judgments (i) and (ii) in succession, which amounts to meeting (iv), is a good deal more ambitious. A movement from a nonoptimal to an optimal position that has both a better distribution and more of all goods than the nonoptimal one may still leave some individuals worse off and, therefore, fail to meet (iv).

References

1 Arrow, K., 'Little's critique of welfare economics', *American Economic Review* (1951).

2 Dobb, M., 'A further comment on the discussion of welfare criteria', *Economic Journal* (December 1963).

3 de V. Graaff, J., *Theoretical Welfare Economics* (Cambridge: Cambridge University Press, 1957).

4 Hicks, J. R., 'The valuation of the social income: a comment on Professor Kuznets' reflections', *Economica* (August 1948).

5 Kennedy, C. M., 'The economic welfare function and Dr Little's Criterion', *Review of Economic Studies,* vol. 20 (1952–3).

6 Kennedy, C. M., 'Welfare criteria – a further note', *Economic Journal* (June 1963).

7 Kennedy, C. M., 'Two comments (II)', *Economic Journal* (December 1963).

8 Kuznets, Simon, 'On the valuation of social income – reflections on Professor Hicks' article, part I', *Economica* (February 1948).

9 Little, I. M. D., *A Critique of Welfare Economics,* 1st edn (London: Oxford University Press, 1950).

10 Little, I. M. D., *A Critique of Welfare Economics,* 2nd edn (London: Oxford University Press, 1957).

11 Little, I. M. D., 'Welfare criteria: an exchange of notes. II: A comment', *Economic Journal* (March 1962).

12 Little, I. M. D., 'Welfare criteria: an exchange of notes. IV: A rejoinder', *Economic Journal* (March 1962).

13 Meade, J. E., Review of *A Critique of Welfare Economics,* 2nd edn, *Economic Journal* (March 1959).

14 Mishan, E. J., 'A re-appraisal of the principles of resource allocation', *Economica* (November 1957).

15 Mishan, E. J., 'Rent as a measure of welfare change', *American Economic Review* (June 1959).

16 Mishan, E. J., 'A survey of welfare economics, 1939–1959', *Economic Journal* (June 1960).

17 Mishan, E. J., 'Welfare criteria: an exchange of notes. V: A comment', *Economic Journal* (March 1962).

18 Mishan, E. J., 'Welfare criteria: are compensation tests necessary?', *Economic Journal* (June 1963).

19 Robertson, D. H., 'Welfare criteria: an exchange of notes. I: A note', *Economic Journal* (March 1962).

20 Sen, A. K., 'Distribution, transitivity and Little's welfare criteria', *Economic Journal* (December 1963).

21 Scitovsky, T., 'A note on welfare propositions in economics', *Review of Economic Studies,* vol. 9 (1941).

4

Welfare Criteria: Resolution of a Paradox

I Introduction

The ideas developed in this paper represent a continuation – a person less restrained than the writer might say, hopefully, a culmination – of the debate on welfare criteria that began in the late 1930s, was rekindled by Little in 1950, and flared up again in the early 1960s.[1] Today, bogged down by now familiar paradoxes, these welfare criteria continue to receive attention from time to time, but the excitement they once generated among the profession is a thing of the past. The excuse I offer for wilfully disturbing the somnolence that has gathered over the subject in the last few years is the belief that the apparent paradoxes can easily be resolved and, in being resolved, throw a more searching light on allocative propositions.

It is important to distinguish the 'piecemeal' approach to the ranking of alternative economic organisations from the theoretically more general approach associated with the notion of a social welfare function first introduced by Bergson (1938) and later developed by Arrow (1951) and others. Those captivated by the more cosmic concept of a social welfare function appear to have little patience with the problems and paradoxes generated by the more modest welfare criteria that are part of the piecemeal approach. Clearly, if one succeeds in constructing an acceptable social welfare function then, seen from the dizzy heights of the *optimum optimorum*, the ranking of alternative economic positions is indeed a slight and inconsequential achievement. On the other hand, those who regard the notion of a social welfare function as interesting but sterile believe that the economist can make a contribution to society's continual search for economic advantage only by persisting with the piecemeal approach.

The social welfare function, even when it is more narrowly defined as a ranking of all conceivable combinations of individual welfare, remains but a pleasing and nebulous abstraction.[2] It cannot be translated into practical guidance for economic policy. Even if there were no fundamental obstacles to its construction, or even if one could think up reasonable conditions under which a social welfare function could exist, there would remain the virtually impossible task of arranging for society to rank unambiguously all conceivable combinations of the individual welfares and moreover – in order to utilise this massive apparatus – to discover (without much cost) the effect on the welfare of each person in society (in terms of utilities, goods, or money) of the introduction of alternative economic organisations. For only if we have such data can we rank all existing and future economic possibilities and pronounce some to be socially superior to others. Although one can always claim that 'useful insights' have emerged from the attempts to construct theoretical social welfare functions, the belief that they can ever be translated into useful economic advice is chimerical.

In contrast, the more pedestrian welfare criteria, although analysed in abstract terms, can be translated into practical propositions. Modern societies do seek to rank projects or policies by some criterion of economic efficiency and to take account also of distributional consequences. Indeed, the debate has its origin in the concern with real policy issues – with Harrod (1938) arguing that unless economists were prepared to make interpersonal comparisons of utility they would have very little to contribute to economic policy. Though in some part anticipated by Hotelling (1938),[3] the clearest and most explicit expression of what came to be known as the New Welfare Economics came from Kaldor (1939) and, a little later, from Hicks (1939), both of whom laid it down that, without in any way invoking interpersonal comparisons of utility, a movement from a position *I* to a position *II* would qualify as an economic improvement if the gainers from the movement would be able to compensate all the losers and yet themselves be better off than before. In this sense, according to Kaldor, the repeal of the corn laws in 1846 could be vindicated on economic grounds, and without any weighting of the distributional effects.

II Summary of the Debate on Dual Welfare Criteria

The apparent paradox uncovered by Scitovsky (1941) in the initial formulation of the Kaldor–Hicks compensation test, and that later revealed by Kuznets (1948) in the index-number test proposed by Hicks (1940) and by ,Samuelson (1939), are by now a familiar part of the recent history of welfare economics. Although the logic of the apparent contradictions has been made clear (Mishan, 1957), the problems they give rise to have not as yet been satisfactorily resolved. One can, of course, take reasonable precautions to avoid inconsistencies – which is what the Scitovsky criterion was designed to do by requiring that the ranking of the two economic positions should be the same irrespective of which of the two was used as a base for comparison. Alternatively one could take the seemingly excessive precaution entailed by the Samuelson criterion (1950) which required that the ranking of the two positions be the same for every conceivable distribution of income.

Although distributional requirements had not been overlooked by these and other writers on the subject, it remained for Little (1950, 1957) to propose explicitly a dual criterion wherever *actual* compensation was not feasible; a hypothetical compensation test and a distribution test. Accordingly, a situation Q_2 was to be socially preferred to Q_1 if *either* the Kaldor–Hicks test was met (gainers in moving from Q_1 to Q_2 can more than compensate losers) *or* the 'reversal' test was met (gainers in moving from Q_2 to Q_1 cannot compensate the losers[4]), provided also that the distribution of income in Q_2 was no worse than it was in Q_1.

These dual criteria were believed to have their rationale embedded in two value judgments: (i) that there is a social improvement if someone is made better off and nobody is made worse off (abbreviated to 'everyone' is made better off) by the change in question, and (ii) that there is a social improvement if there is simply an improvement in the distribution of income.

The idea of basing recommendations on a dual criterion was soon adopted by economists interested in these aspects of the subject, [5] a scheme of things which continued even when it transpired that, as formulated, these dual criteria were capable also of yielding contradictory rankings. To illustrate, if in a comparison of two positions, Q_1 and Q_2, the movement from Q_1 to Q_2 were to meet both the required tests – say it met the Kaldor–Hicks test and also a distributional test – this result might be quite consistent with a construction in which a subsequent movement from Q_2 to Q_1 also met the Kaldor–Hicks test and in which the Q_1 distribution appeared better than that of Q_2.

This dual criterion paradox could not, however, be attributed wholly to the employment of two independent and unrelated tests since the paradox, as we have indicated, arises also in applying the single Kaldor–Hicks criterion. Though it is true that the consecutive use of two non-transitive tests embodied in a welfare criterion can indeed lead to apparent contradiction, it is not necessary that it should do so.[6] Indeed, in the dual criterion proposed by Little, a paradox arising from the application of the Kaldor–Hicks test alone could be circumvented by accepting an initial demonstration that a collection of goods Q_2 was by that test preferred to Q_1, notwithstanding that after moving to Q_2 it could then be demonstrated that Q_1 was preferred. Thus the possible paradox of the dual criterion had to be sought in its distributional proviso. Indeed, it emerged from the symposium of 1962 in the *Economic Journal* (Robertson, Meade, Little, Mishan) that, given the allocative part of the dual criterion as represented by tests of hypothetical compensation, the possible paradox arose from the devices adopted for enabling distributional comparisons to be made as between different collections of goods. For while distributional rankings of a single collection of goods were regarded as being unexceptionable, in comparing the distributions of two collections of goods recourse was had to any one of a wide range of hypothetical distributions of one of the collections – represented in utility space by any point along a segment of the collection's utility-possibility curve – that would render it distributionally comparable with the alternative collection. With so much latitude for discretion in this respect, it is hardly surprising that application of these dual welfare criteria could produce contradictory rankings.

In order to guard against the possibility of contradictory ranking, I suggested (1963) that the hypothetical distribution of the Q_1 collection of goods be chosen in all cases as to be 'distributionally indifferent' to the *actual* distribution of the Q_2 collection, the hypothetical distribution of the latter being treated likewise with respect to the actual distribution of Q_1. This requirement in the choice of hypothetical distributions would be ensured by amending the original Pareto value judgment (i) to a proposed (i'), that there is a social improvement if 'everyone' is made better off *without the distribution of welfare being made worse.*

Following this suggestion Kennedy (1963) alleged (and at the time I went along with him) that (i') and (ii) together could be boiled down to a single value judgment (iii), that there is a social improvement if the distribution of welfare is improved and at least one person is better off. He also showed that these judgments (i′) and (ii), or the criteria raised on them, could rank as socially preferred a collection Q_2 that has less of every good than a collection Q_1. Kennedy could have gone further than this, however, because although the Pareto value judgment had been revised to (i′), which in effect places a distributional restriction on its application, the distributional judgment (ii) had not been treated symmetrically. Indeed, symmetrical treatment would have entailed the inclusion in such judgment of a Pareto restriction, one ensuring that the distributional improvement could not make 'everyone' worse off. Thus, as was later shown by Ng (1971), repeated application of judgments (i′) and (ii), or criteria raised on them, could be made to recommend a movement to a new situation in which every person is worse off than before – although the distribution, at least, would be better[7]

This possibility is less surprising once we recognise that, following an allocative improvement that meets the (distributionally-restricted) Pareto value judgment (i′), a subsequent change that meets the unrestricted distributional value judgment (ii) can move us to a point in utility space that effectively undoes the Pareto improvement. In improving distribution it makes every person worse off.[8]

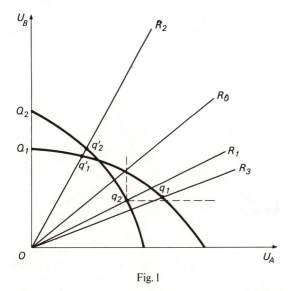

Fig. 1

The construction necessary to depict this result appears as Figure 1, which exhibits the utility-possibility curves as between two persons, A and B, corresponding to the Q_1 and Q_2 collections of goods.[9] Though not strictly necessary to the analysis, there are expositional advantages both in measuring cardinal utility for persons A and B along the two axes and in

assuming that the distributional rankings are determined only by the ratio of each person's total utility.[10]

Rather than deploy the hypothetical compensation tests and their distributional provisos in comparing the Q_1 and Q_2 collections of goods, we can operate directly with the value judgments (i′) and (ii) from which they stem. Thus we let p stand for Pareto-preferred, as an indicator that (i′) is met, and we let d stand for distributionally-preferred, as an indicator that value judgment (ii) is met. The positions that are to be ranked in accordance with these value judgments are q_1 and q_2 in Figure 1, these points indicating the actual distributions respectively of the Q_1 and Q_2 collections of goods whose utility-possibility curves are depicted in the figure.

The R_0 ray shows the best of all possible distributions, for any utility-possibility curve, as between persons A and B, say perfect equality. R_1 is the distributional ray passing through the actual distribution q_2 of Q_2, while R_3 is the distributional ray passing through the actual distribution q_1 of the Q_1 collection. R_1 is distributionally preferred to R_3. The construction of the utility-possibility curves for Q_1 and Q_2 is such that we can choose a distribution indicated by the ray R_2, to the left of R_0, one that is intermediate between R_1 and R_3; that is, R_1 d R_2 d R_3. The hypothetical distributions of Q_1 and Q_2 that accord with the R_2 distribution are q_1' and q_2' respectively.

The following ordering is then affirmed by reference to the figure: q_2 d q_2' p q_1' d q_1. Hence, q_2, in which both A and B are worse off than they are in q_1, is ranked by these value judgments as socially preferred to q_1.[11]

In my 1969 monograph I proposed, in passing, a way out of our troubles by observing that whenever potentially contradictory rankings arise, as they do when the actual distributions of the two collections of goods are to be found on either side of their intersecting utility-possibility curves, there is really no need to invoke dual welfare criteria. For if we continue to suppose that society can rank alternative distributions of a single collection of goods, say distributions q_2 and q_2' of the Q_2 collection in Figure 2, there is no apparent reason why it cannot continue to do so if we erase the Q_2 utility-possibility curve and concentrate directly on the two points in utility space. But if we can do this, we can also compare directly any other two points in utility space, say q_1 and q_2, even though they are attached to different utility-possibility curves.[12]

Put otherwise, if we continue to allow that society can rank distributions along a particular utility-possibility curve, there is apparently nothing to

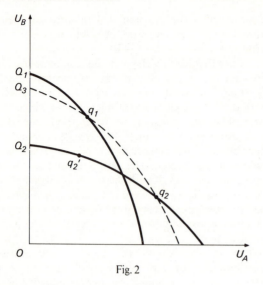

Fig. 2

III   Construction of the Required Hypothetical Collection, Q_3

A collection of two goods, x and y, to be shared between two persons A and B, is indicated in Figure 3 by a point Q_1 in the x–y co-ordinate system. Person A's indifference curves are ordered from the origin O, a_9 being one such curve. Person B's indifference curves are ordered from the origin at Q_1, b_4 being one such curve, and one that is – by the definition of exchange efficiency – tangent to person A's indifference curve a_9 at the point q_1 along the Q_1 contract curve. Since q_1 is chosen to be the actual distribution of the Q_1 collection, the mutual tangency at q_1 has the same slope as that of the community indifference curve I_1 as it passes through Q_1.[13] Another point Q_1' on this same community curve I_1 is the result of moving B's 'mobile' co-ordinate system, initially having Q_1 as origin, downward and rightward, so as to maintain mutual tangency between the individual indifference curves, b_4 and a_9 – indifference curve a_9 being set in the 'fixed' co-ordinate system having origin O.

prevent our construction of a *hypothetical* utility-possibility curve, arising from a hypothetical collection of goods Q_3, whose locus in utility space – indicated by the broken line in Figure 2 – passes through q_1 and q_2, these being the actual distributions of the collections Q_1 and Q_2 respectively. We should then be able to compare q_1 and q_2 directly on distributional grounds.

Now this construction of a hypothetical utility-possibility curve, passing through q_1 and q_2, is deemed to derive from the hypothetical collection of goods Q_3, as indicated above. But are we sure that such a collection of goods can always be found for such cases? If we hesitate a little, it is simply because these constructs in utility space are highly abstract. Certainly they are useful as a summary of logical possibilities yet they are also so facile to manipulate as to rob one of conviction about the validity of the results that can be contrived.

For this reason it is advisable to move back a stage in abstraction – from utility space to commodity space wherein the quantities of goods and their relative prices are clearly depicted. What has to be demonstrated then is that, wherever the use of hypothetical compensation tests discloses an apparent contradiction in the ranking of the two collections being compared, Q_1 and Q_2, there can indeed be at least one hypothetical collection of goods, say Q_3, which contains along its contract curve the actual welfare combinations of the original collection of goods Q_1 and Q_2. Following this demonstration, its interpretation will be discussed and further implications of the construction will be explored.

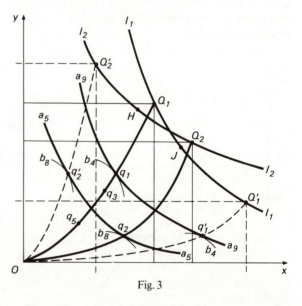

Fig. 3

Along the contract curve for Q_1', point q_1' also indicates the point of mutual tangency of individual indifference curves b_4 and a_9. Thus a path passing through q_1 q_1' describes all the points of mutual tangency of b_4 and a_9 along the contract curves of the continuum of collections of goods traced out by the community indifference curve I_1 (along which the combination of individual welfares b_4 and a_9 remains constant): and it is important to observe that this q_1 q_1' locus is identical with the a_9 indifference curve.

Now just as we generated a community indifference curve I_1 from the q_1 distribution of Q_1 between persons A and B, so may we generate for every distributional point along Q_1's contract curve a particular community indifference curve passing through Q_1. Each of these community indifference curves is identified as having the specific welfare combination corresponding to one particular point of mutual tangency on the contract curve of Q_1. And unless the indifference maps of the individuals are homogeneous and identical, this contract curve will not be a straight line, and the slopes of the mutual tangencies along it will vary. In general then, there will be a pencil of exchange-efficient community indifference curves passing through point Q_1, none of which are Pareto comparable[14] inasmuch as each such curve corresponds to a distinct distribution of Q_1 as between persons A and B. We shall, however, continue to suppose that society can *distributionally* rank these community indifference curves. Thus, moving along the Q_1 contract curve it may be said, for example, that q_3 is distributionally preferred to q_5 which is distributionally preferred to q_5 – where q_1 is, as indicated above, the distribution from which community indifference curve I_1 is generated.

We now introduce another collection of goods Q_2 having more of good x and less of good y as compared with the Q_1 collection. From the locus of all exchange-efficient distributions given by the Q_2 contract curve we choose the point q_2, which represents individual welfares a_5 and b_8, from which to generate a community indifference curve I_2. The slope of this community indifference curve at Q_2 is, of course, the same as that of the mutual tangency of the two individual indifference curves a_5 and b_8 at point q_2. Again, another point Q_2' on this same community indifference curve I_2 is the result of moving person B's 'mobile' co-ordinate system, initially having Q_2 as origin, upward and to the left so as to maintain the mutual tangency between the individual indifference curves a_5 and b_8 – indifference curve a_5 being set in the 'fixed' co-ordinate system with origin O. The locus of $q_2\,q_2'$ corresponding to I_2 is identical with the a_5 indifference curve.

Before taking the next step, we can assure ourselves that the construction of Figure 3 is such as to reveal an apparent contradiction in the application of the Kaldor–Hicks test. A movement from Q_1 to Q_2 clearly meets this test since both persons are indifferent as between Q_1 and some other point J on the same I_1 community indifference curve, while a further movement from J to Q_2 can make both persons better off. After moving to Q_2, however, the actual distribution will be that shown at q_2 – involving, as it does,

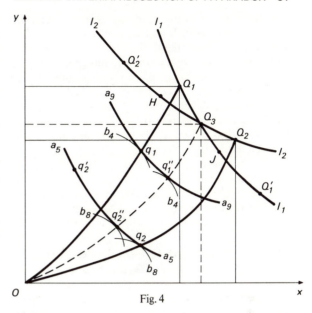

Fig. 4

individual welfares a_5 and b_8 – from which the community indifference curve I_2 is generated. The movement from Q_2 on I_2 to Q_1 on I_1 is now one that will also meet the Kaldor–Hicks test, for both persons are indifferent as between goods-combination Q_2 and some other point H on the same indifference curve, while a further movement from H to Q_1 can make both of them better off. In sum, if the comparison of Q_1 and Q_2 is made on the basis of the actual distribution of Q_1 then Q_2 appears superior to Q_1, whereas if the comparison is based on the actual distribution of Q_2 then Q_1 appears superior to Q_2.[15]

Now the hypothetical collection of goods, Q_3, that we seek is in fact given by the point of intersection of the community indifference curves I_1 and I_2 as depicted in Figure 4 (which reproduces the main outlines of Figure 3), the amounts of x and y contained in this new collection being indicated by the broken line co-ordinates from Q_3 to the x and y axes. Since for all goods-combinations described by the I_1 community indifference curve (representing individual welfares b_4 and a_9) the corresponding $q_1\,q_1'$ locus is identical with the a_9 indifference curve, the point q_1'' along it, and on the contract curve of Q_3, also represents the mutual tangency of b_4 and a_9. Similarly, for all goods-combinations described by the I_2 community indifference curve: the $q_2\,q_2'$ locus (representing welfares b_8 and a_5) is identical with the a_5 indifference curve. Hence the point q_2'' along it, and on the Q_3 contract curve, also represents the mutual tangency of b_8 and a_5.

If, therefore, as assumed, society is able to rank the distributions of a single collection of goods, then it is able also to rank those for the hypothetical Q_3 collection. In particular, it is able to rank points q_1'' and q_2'', these being exchange-efficient points along the Q_3 contract curve. If, for example, q_2'' is ranked by society as distributionally superior to q_1'', it must follow that q_2, the actual distribution of Q_2, is ranked above q_1, the actual distribution of Q_1. Indeed, the comparison between the original collections Q_1 and Q_2 is reducible to a comparison between q_1'' and q_2'' of Q_3; for whether we compare the original Q_1 and Q_2, or q_1'' and q_2'', we compare in either case the welfare combination (a_9, b_4) with the welfare combination (a_5, b_8) respectively.

IV   Construction of Hypothetical Collections Q_1 and Q_2 from a Q_3 Collection

In the preceding section we have shown that we can plot the welfare combinations attaching to two different collections of goods along the contract curve of a single collection of goods. Some additional light is cast on the relation between allocation and distribution by showing the reverse; showing that from two distributions of a *single* collection of goods we can generate two hypothetical collections of goods. In particular, we shall first generate two such collections that yield contradictory rankings when subjected to tests of hypothetical compensation.

As stated earlier, for any collection of goods such as Q_3 a pencil of exchange-efficient community indifference curves can be generated, passing through the point Q_3, as indicated in Figure 5. Each of such curves, as we know, corresponds to a distinct efficient distribution of the Q_3 collection of goods as between persons A and B. From these Pareto non-comparable community indifference curves we may select I_1 corresponding to the q_1 distribution along the Q_3 contract curve and I_2 corresponding to the q_2 distribution – for which distribution person B is better off and A is worse off as compared with q_1. On the I_1 community curve choose a point Q_1 that is above Q_3. On the I_2 community indifference curve choose a point Q_2 that is below Q_3. The points Q_1 and Q_2 then represent two possible collections of goods which, by construction, have identical welfare combinations to the q_1 and q_2 distributions respectively of the original Q_3 collection. Hypothetical compensation tests involving Q_1 and Q_2 will produce contradictory rankings.

Thus, by this construction, we can derive any number of hypothetical collections, and any number of pairs of such collections, that will yield contradictory

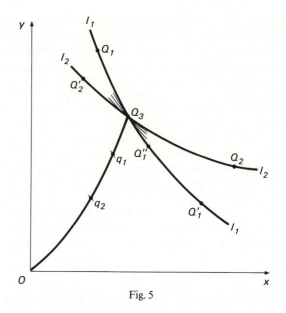

Fig. 5

rankings. All that is necessary in this construction to ensure a contradictory pair of collections is to locate a single point along each of two commodity indifference curves and on either side of Q_3. This contrived contradiction arises unavoidably from the plausible assumption that the individual consumption functions are not identical and homogeneous, since this is the assumption that produces a pencil of community indifference curves at Q_3 from which we are then able to select 'contradictory' pairs of collections.

From this section and the preceding one we generalise as follows: wherever there is an intersection of the community indifference curves that attach to the collections of goods being compared, the only tenable ranking is a distributional one. This proposition applies even where the comparison is between top-level optimal collections Q^*_1 and Q^*_2, where each top-level position is identified in Figure 6 by the tangency of its community indifference curve with the boundary of production possibilities. For, again, the welfare combination of each top-level optimal position is reducible to efficient distributions q^*_1 and q^*_2 along the contract curve of some hypothetical collection Q_3, which distributions can be ranked directly by society. Neither is it possible to rank by hypothetical compensation tests an optimal collection Q^*_1 on I_1 with a nonoptimal collection Q_2 on I'_2 that intersects with I_1. Yet by reference again to a hypothetical collection Q'_3 they can be distributionally compared inasmuch as the welfare combinations of these collections are identical with the distributions (q^*_1) and q_2 of the Q', hypothetical collection. Consequently Q_2, the non-optimal collection, could be ranked above the optimal collection Q^*_1 along the only valid scale, that of distribution.

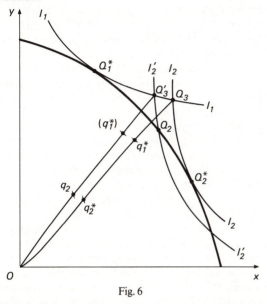

Fig. 6

The significant conclusion which emerges is that in all cases for which a hypothetical collection can be distributed so as to yield the welfare combinations attaching to the alternative and actual collections being compared – and such a hypothetical collection is always possible for a pair of 'contradictory' collections – Pareto tests are of no use. However, if society is deemed able to rank different distributions of a single collection of goods then these alternative collections can be ranked directly on their distributional merits. If, on the other hand, society is deemed unable to rank the distributions of a single collection of goods, nothing at all can be said about the ranking of the alternative collections. In either case Pareto criteria are ruled out, for we already know that there can be no Pareto comparisons between different efficient distributions of a single collection of goods.[16]

Finally, it is useful to note that the familiar 'contradictory' case – that in which the Kaldor–Hicks and the 'reversal' tests yield opposite rankings – can be detected in practice. A sufficient test, though not a necessary one, of the existence of such a case is provided by the 'contradictory' index number inequations. If, in comparing two situations (in which tastes have not changed) we discover that $\Sigma P_2 Q_2 > \Sigma P_2 Q_1$ and also that $\Sigma P_1 Q_1 > \Sigma P_1 Q_2$, we can be sure that compensation tests based respectively on the actual distributions of those Q_1 and Q_2 collections will also yield contradictory results. In consequence, one may legitimately make a direct comparison between the alternative collections.

V Interpretation of the Analysis

If transfers of income in this context were costless (or, at least, not so costly as to be thought impractical), and if identifying other collections of goods on the same community indifference curve were also costless, we should have no need of welfare criteria that invoke hypothetical compensation. For with costless transfers and with costless identification, we should be able to transform all *potential* Pareto comparisons – those which reveal that 'everyone' *could* be made better off – into direct Pareto comparisons in which 'everyone' is indeed made better off in one of the situations as compared with the other.

To illustrate with Figure 5, if we were required to compare Q_1 on I_1 with Q_2 on I_2 we should first have to identify, costlessly, another collection Q'_1 on I_1; one, therefore, that contains the identical welfare combination q_1 as does Q_1. Notwithstanding that Q_2 has more of each good than Q'_1, a movement from Q' to Q_2 in the *absence of any transfer payments* entails no more than a movement from the welfare combination indicated by q_1 to that indicated by q_2. Only if the additional goods in Q_2 are *in fact* distributed without cost among all members of the community so as to make 'everyone' in Q_2 better off than he was in Q'_1 or in Q_1, can it be said unambiguously that Q_2 is a Pareto improvement.[17] In this costless wonderland, that is, all comparisons of this sort resolve themselves into direct Pareto comparisons in which 'everyone' is actually to be made better off in the one situation as compared with the other.

It is only because costless transfers in this context were thought to be wholly unrealistic and that, therefore, any ranking of collections Q_1 and Q_2 had to be made on the assumption that their actual distributions could not be changed, that economists had perforce to compare them by reference to the concept of a *potential* Pareto improvement – a concept which, beginning with Kaldor–Hicks, took the form of welfare criteria based on hypothetical compensation. As we noticed earlier, whether such welfare criteria are single or dual (whether they do not, or whether they do, make provision also for a distributional test) they can always give rise to apparently contradictory results.

The question is how far does the analysis of the preceding two sections enable us to resolve this long-standing paradox.

From section IV we realise that, although they are not actually Pareto comparable, any two welfare combinations on the contract curve of some existing collection Q_3 can be made to appear *potentially* Pareto comparable. In particular, two such welfare combinations can be associated with two collections Q_1 and Q_2 that are located on either side of Q_3, so constituting a potentially contradictable pair of goods-collections. However, we already know that, in principle, q_1 and q_2 welfare combinations of an existing Q_3 collection can be ranked along a distributional scale. The process by which we transform q_1 and q_2 into the 'contradictable' collections Q_1 and Q_2, though interesting, does not of itself enable us to say any more that is useful about the ranking of q_1 and q_2.

The direction of the analysis in section III is more revealing. For while no unambiguous potential Pareto ranking can emerge from the existing 'contradictable' collections, we discover that the particular welfare combinations associated with them are in fact reducible to distributional points on the contract curve of a single collection of goods. Therefore, insofar as we continue to regard alternative distributions of a single collection of goods as not capable of being ranked on an allocative scale, but only on a distributional scale, we must conclude that 'contradictable' collections also can be ranked only on a distributional scale.

If the analysis and its interpretation are accepted, it would appear that the resolution of 'contradictory' rankings, arising from systematic application of conventional welfare criteria, is, in principle, wonderfully simple. If society is assumed able to rank distributions of a single collection of goods (which has been the traditional assumption) then 'contradictory' collections can be ranked unambiguously, albeit only on a distributional scale – irrespective of whether either, neither, or both collections are associated with top-level optima. If society is assumed unable to rank the distributions of a single collection of goods, then 'contradictory' collections cannot be ranked at all.

These findings do not, incidentally, depend upon actual identification of the required hypothetical collection of goods – Q_3 in Figures 4 and 5 – which is to contain the particular welfare combinations associated with the 'contradictable' collections Q_1 and Q_2. Indeed, nothing of significance results from knowing the composition of this hypothetical collection. For the analysis reveals that wherever there are 'contradictable' collections there will also be, necessarily, the appropriate hypothetical collection. And the purpose of confirming its existence is only to establish the fact that a comparison of 'contradictable' collections can always be reduced to a distributional ranking.

It should be clear, moreover, that the usefulness of the findings does not depend upon the ability of society

actually to rank the distributions associated with the 'contradictable' collections, Q_1 and Q_2. We conclude only that 'contradictable' collections can always be reduced to a distributional ordering, and only to a distributional ordering. If it happens that society is unable to place a distributional ordering on the 'contradictable' collections in question, then nothing at all can be said in that particular case.

Regard to the fact that in modern industrialised economies many thousands of goods are produced and distributed among millions of people makes distributional comparisons between alternative output combinations virtually impossible without recourse to the measuring rod of money. Even so, it may be the case that, for most of the choices that correspond in the real world to the 'contradictable' alternatives, the differences in distribution are barely perceptible. If so, little is lost in choosing arbitrarily one alternative rather than the other. But if, on occasion, the distribution of one of these alternatives is markedly regressive as compared with the other, we need have no hesitation in rejecting it in favour of the latter.

To sum up, the content of our conclusion is negative, but useful for all that. It bids us waste no more time and energy in seeking ways to rank 'contradictable' alternative positions on an allocative scale, and to resign ourselves to the fact that they can be ordered only on a distributional scale.

VI   Extension of the Analysis

So far we have restricted ourselves to the conclusion that wherever the collections of goods to be compared are 'contradictable' they can be ranked only on a distributional scale. But if these once-awkward cases are now easily resolved, it transpires that the more straightforward cases – those about which economists had no hesitation in ranking on an allocative scale – now become problematic. Thus where the two community indifference curves that pass respectively through two collections, such as Q''_1 and Q_2 in Figure 5, do not intersect between Q''_1 and Q_2 the 'contradiction' cannot arise. In that case the original Scitovsky criterion is met, which is to say that the hypothetical compensation test gives the same result whether the comparison is based on the Q''_1 distribution or on the Q_2 distribution. To some economists, Q_2 might then be regarded as allocatively superior to Q''_1. Certainly if the distribution of Q_2 was better than, or at least no worse than, that of the Q''_1 collection, the Little criteria would rank Q_2 as socially preferred to Q''_1.

A yet more comprehensive criterion would require that, using these tests of hypothetical compensation, the Q_2 collection should be superior to an alternative Q'_1 collection not only for the Q_2 and Q'_1 distributions, but for every conceivable distribution. A sufficient (though not necessary) condition for meeting this more searching criterion is that the collection Q_2 has more of each good than the Q'_1 collection. In two-good space, that is, Q_2 has to be located northeast of Q'_1, as it is in Figure 5.

Yet Q'_1 is one of the points on the community indifference curve I, that passes through Q_3 and Q_1. And collection Q_1, having by construction the identical welfare combination as Q'_1, clearly has a 'contradictable' relation with Q_2. Hence, notwithstanding that the Q_2 collection has more of each good than the Q'_1 collection, their respective welfare combinations can be plotted as alternative distributions q_2 and q_1 of the hypothetical Q_3 collection.[18]

Hypothetical compensation turns out to be an untrustworthy concept. Even where one collection has more of every good than another collection, so that a comprehensive criterion based on hypothetical compensation reveals the former to be superior for every conceivable distribution, it is yet possible by further research to discover another pair of collections having the identical welfare combinations as the first pair but yielding the reverse result. Thus, in these apparently best-of-all cases where one collection has more of every good than the other, as has Q_2 in Figure 5 compared with Q'_1, there is no simple way of discovering if these community indifference curves intersect at some other point, as they do at Q_3 in the figure, beyond which these curves reverse their position so yielding the reverse ranking. For in Figure 5, the collection Q_1, which has a welfare combination identical with the former unambiguously 'inferior' collection Q'_1, now appears as having more of every good than Q'_2 which new collection has a welfare combination identical with Q_2, the formerly unambiguously 'superior' collection. Unless the economist can be sure that no intersection of the relevant community indifference curves is possible, he has no warrant for adopting the ranking produced by the Samuelson comprehensive criterion. Where such an intersection is detected, however, the only valid ranking of the collections is a distributional one.

VII   Summary and Conclusion

In the light of the above analysis, a conclusion that criteria based on potential Pareto comparability should be used with greater circumspection is hardly necessary. The transparently 'contradictable' case, which is resolved in this paper, has always been a source of dissatisfaction. What is more disconcerting is the disclosure that the apparently 'non-contradictable' case – in which one collection has manifestly more of every good than the alternative collection – may turn out, on further investigation in goods space, to produce essentially the same sort of contradiction. Such cases are then also resolved only by reducing them to a distributional ranking of the collections in question.

As for *dual* welfare criteria – those based on hypothetical compensation tests *plus* a distributional proviso – they are now seen to be at least as misleading as single welfare criteria. For the justification of the former sort of criterion rested on the belief that – granted that distributional comparisons between different collections of goods were somehow possible – if it was met, a subsequent implementation of the change recommended would be tantamount to realising two things: (i) 'everyone' would be made better off, after which (ii) income would be redistributed but in such a way as to be at least no worse than the former distribution.[19]

This dual criterion is therefore met in the apparently unambiguous case in which a collection Q_M is northeast of Q_N, and Q_M has at least as good a distribution as Q_N. We would then have reasoned that the movement from actual Q_N to actual Q_M is equivalent to two successive changes: a movement from Q_N to a Q_M that has been redistributed so as to make 'everyone' better off than he was in Q_N, which is a direct Pareto improvement. Following this, the original Q_M distribution is restored, this distribution being no worse than that of the actual Q_N. But we now know that further exploration may uncover an intersection of the community indifference curves passing through such collections, and this is a sufficient condition for generating a 'contradictory' case. No unambiguous allocative statement is then possible. Only a distributional ranking is possible, and society may well be indifferent as between the distributions of Q_M and Q_N.[20]

The importance of these conclusions cannot be gauged without making some judgment about the facts. For the changes that the economist has to consider, the conclusions assume importance (a) the greater the distributional changes involved and (b) the stronger the relationship between distributional changes and changes in relative prices. In cost–benefit analysis, for example, the presumption is that the latter relationship is not strong, a presumption that is necessary inasmuch as cost–benefit analysis is largely an exercise in partial analysis in which all prices, other than those under scrutiny, are held constant. But for larger issues, for instance the free-trade-versus-tariff issue, the presumption would not be so acceptable.

The ranking of alternative or successive economic situations on the scale of better or worse by reference, in part at least, to a criterion based on potential Pareto comparability has never escaped suspicion, and not only for analytic reasons. The appeal of such a criterion has turned to some extent on the belief, or hope, that an improvement that is potential would somehow, sooner or later, realise its potential and make everybody (or nearly everybody) in society better off, at least in a material sense. And if some particular potential improvements would dislodge them and bring them to earth. But to a greater extent, I think, the appeal has improvements would dislodge thrm and bring them to earth. But to a greater extent, I think, the appeal has been to expediency rather than to ethics, for considered alone the ethics of such a criterion are not convincing. Economists, that is, recognised that if they rejected such a criterion in favour of an alternative based on an actual Pareto improvement, they would have to mute their voice considerably. All their expertise would avail them little when it came to ranking real situations, and they would virtually never be able to say on economic grounds that state A is better, or 'more efficient', than state B. For the set of alternative states likely to occur in the real world for which in fact 'everyone' in the one state will be better off than he is in an alternative or existing state cannot be very large.

Yet the belief that our attachment to potential Pareto criteria springs chiefly from mundane professional considerations is going to be difficult to swallow. There is always hope that a little more thought may enable us to discover some redeeming features of such criteria. In that hope I forbear from proposing that we abandon them.

Notes: Chapter 4

1 See in particular Robertson, Meade, Little, Mishan (all 1962), and Kennedy, Dobb, Sen, Mishan (all 1963). For a summary of the debate, see Mishan (1965).
2 The so-called Pareto-type welfare function, frequently assumed by economists, is in any case likely to be ethically unacceptable since it reveals as a social improvement some further impoverishment of the poor compensated by some further enrichment of the already rich.
3 It was even anticipated in passing by Pigou himself (1932, pp. 50–5) who, nonetheless, chose to raise his welfare economics on foundations of interpersonal comparisons of utility.
4 'Strong' ordering is assumed. Thus if gainers in moving to Q_1 are unable to compensate losers, then losers are assumed able to compensate them to return to Q_2.

5 An exception was Charles Kennedy who argued (1953, 1963) that two disparate tests could not be counted on to produce a consistent criterion.
6 Further remarks on the implications of using two consecutive non-transitive criteria can be found in Mishan (1965), especially section V.
7 In 1965, I proposed that money income distributions in the modern economy be accepted as a proxy for real income distributions. Ng (1971) has argued that if money distributions can indeed be taken accurately to reflect real distributions (and if a more equal distribution can be assumed to be a better distribution) then in the two-person case *all* utility-possibility curves are symmetric about the perfect-equality ray R_0 in Figure 1 – which implies that intersection of such utility-possibility curves takes place at two points, one on either side of R_0. Such a construction would prevent potential contradictions occurring.
8 If (ii) were revised in a symmetric way as to become (ii'), which would state that a social improvement takes place if the distribution of income is made better *provided nobody is made worse off,* then each of such value judgments, (i') and (ii'), could be met without 'undoing' the social improvement realised by the other. But they are obviously restrictive value judgements since all social improvements from an initial position have now to fall within the north-eastern quadrant in utility space.
9 Ng (1971) demonstrated this result earlier, though using a figure with four utility-possibility curves corresponding to four collections of goods.
10 If the reader demurs, he is at liberty to conceive the two axes as measuring ordinal utility. In that case, the distances on either axis can be multiplied by a scalar without, however, altering the negative slope of the utility-possibility curves. Though the distributional 'rays' would no longer be straight lines as in the figure, they would pass through the same points, and the same conclusions would be reached.

As for the assumption that distributional rankings are independent of the levels of total utility, this indeed is a possibility over the range of movement in question. Yet this assumption can also be relaxed without altering the conclusion.
11 Using a dual criterion it would have been argued that q_2 is strongly preferred to q_1. For a movement from q_2 to q'_1 meets the Kaldor-Hicks test, and q_2 is also a better distribution than q'_1. But q'_1 is already a better distribution of Q_1 than is q_1.
12 Which is perhaps what Charles Kennedy was getting at in 1953 (though without offering formal demonstrations).
13 Geometrically, this community indifference curve I_1 is constructed by holding individual A's indifference curve, a_9, fixed and then moving B's indifference curve, b_4 in tangency contact with it and in such a manner that B's origin, originally at Q_1, describes the I_1 community indifference curve. More detailed instructions are given in Mishan (1960).
14 More formally, if for each of n persons $w_i^2 \, r \, w_i^1$ $(i = 1, \ldots, n)$ where w_i^1 is any level of welfare for any ith person, w_i^2 is another level of welfare, and r stands for 'preferred or indifferent to', and if for at least one person, the jth, $w_j^2 \, p \, w_j^1$, where p stands for 'preferred to' then $I_2 \, p \, I_1$. This expression is interpreted as community indifference curve I_2 is Pareto-preferred to community indifference curve I_1, where $I_1 \equiv \overset{n}{\Sigma} \, w_i^1$ and $I_2 \equiv \overset{n}{\Sigma} \, w_i^2$, and there is no possibility, in

either of I_1 or I_2, of raising any individual's welfare level without lowering that of another.

Where either $I_2 p I_1$ or $I_1 p I_2$, we say that the community indifference curves I_1 and I_2 are *Pareto comparable*.

15 The reverse contradiction is, of course, also possible; that in which the q_1-based comparison shows Q_1 to be superior to Q_2, and the q_2-based comparison shows Q_2 to be superior to Q_1. This result would be shown by Figure 3 if H and Q_1 were to change places and J and Q_2 were to change places.

We need not treat this latter case, however, as it is perfectly symmetric with the one treated in the text.

16 The analysis can be extended to n persons and m goods without altering the conclusions. A community indifference curve for any number of persons can be built up in the same way as it is for two persons. Thus, after constructing a community indifference curve for two persons, one for three persons can be constructed by 'somersaulting' the axes of the third person's indifference map, and having its origin describe a three-person community indifference curve as this third person's chosen indifference curve is slid tangentially along that of the existing two-person community indifference curve. A four-person indifference curve is then constructed by adding the chosen indifference curve of a fourth person to the three-person community indifference curve, and so on for any number of persons. The quantity of goods Q_3, represented by any point on an n-person community indifference curve I_1, is associated with a unique slope, or goods-rate of substitution, which – since, by the tangency condition for exchange optimum, it is common to each of the n persons – uniquely specifies the amounts to be received by each person so as to maintain his initial welfare constant.

By construction, every point along the I_1 community indifference curve maintains constant the welfare level of each of the n persons. Now by choosing another efficient distribution of the Q_3 collection of goods among these n persons we can generate another community indifference curve I_2 which also passes through Q_3, but at a different slope to that of I_1. So constructed, the community indifference curves I_1 and I_2 are, of course, not Pareto comparable and intersect at Q_3.

As in Figure 5, another collection of goods Q_2, below and to the right of Q_3, can be chosen along the I_2 curve, and another collection Q_1, to the left of and above Q_3, can be chosen along the I_1 curve. Systematic application of hypothetical compensation tests will then reveal mutually contradictory rankings of Q_1 and Q_2. But we already know from our construction that the welfare combinations associated with I_1 and I_2, and therefore also with Q_1 and Q_2, can be reproduced as different distributions of the single collection Q_3, and, being Pareto noncomparable, can be ranked only on a distributional scale.

For additional goods additional axes are required, and the community indifference curves become surfaces. In general, the intersection of community indifference surfaces will consist of a set or continuum of points as distinct from a single point in the two-good case. For the three-good case, for example, there will be a curved line intersection of the two community indifference surfaces so extending the number of requisite hypothetical collections. But the conclusions remain unaltered.

17 If society, instead, happened to be at Q_2 then it would indeed be possible by costless redistribution to make 'everyone' actually better off by moving to Q_1.

It may seem strange that whether (a) we begin with Q_1 – having equivalent welfares to q_1 on the Q_3 contract curve – we are able to make 'everyone' actually better off than he was with Q_1 by moving to Q_2 (plus costless redistribution) or whether, instead, (b) we begin with Q_2 – with equivalent welfares to q_2 on the Q_3 contract curve – we are able to make 'everyone' better off than he was with Q_2 by moving to Q_1 (with costless redistribution). But it is not so strange if we bear in mind that the movement to Q_2, in (a), does *not* have the welfare equivalence of q_2 on the Q_3 contract curve. In order that 'everyone' actually be better off than he was in Q_1, the Q_2 collection does have to be (costlessly) redistributed. And this resulting welfare combination is different from that associated with Q_2 (and therefore with q_2) and is not to be found on the contract curve of Q_3. (In utility space, the *redistributed* Q_2 will be a point outside the Q_2 utility-possibility curve.) The same analysis applies to the *redistributed* Q_1 collection: it yields a welfare combination that is not to be found on the contract curve of Q_3.

18 For completeness we should also choose a collection Q'_2 on the I_2 curve having the same welfare combination as Q_2. However, it is the movement from Q'_2 to Q_1 that now offers more of each good and therefore also meets the comprehensive compensation criterion. Once again, however, the welfare combinations associated with Q'_2 and Q_1 are reducible to the distributions q_2 and q_1, respectively, of the Q_3 collection.

19 See Mishan (1960, pp. 226–7).

20 It is plausible to believe, however, that the further northeast of Q_N is Q_M situated, the smaller is the likelihood that their corresponding community indifference curves will intersect. Consequently the smaller is the likelihood of being able to reduce the welfare combinations associated respectively with collections Q_N and Q_M to alternative distributions of a hypothetical collection of goods.

References

Arrow, K., *Social Choice and Individual Values* (New York, 1951; 2nd edn, 1963).

Bergson, A., 'A reformulation of certain aspects of welfare economics', *Quarterly Journal of Economics* (1938).

Dobb, M., 'A further comment on the discussion of welfare criteria', *Economic Journal* (December 1963).

Harrod, R. F., 'Scope and methods of economics', *Economic Journal* (1938).

Hicks, J. R., 'The valuation of social income', *Economica* (1940), pp. 105–24.

Hicks, J. R., 'Foundations of welfare economics', *Economic Journal* (1939), pp. 694–712.

Hotelling, H., 'The general welfare in relation to the problems of taxation and of railway and utility rates', *Econometrica* (1938).

Kaldor, N., 'Welfare propositions in economics and interpersonal comparisons of utility', *Economic Journal* (September 1939), pp. 549–52.

Kennedy, C., 'The economic welfare function and Dr Little's criterion', *Review of Economic Studies* (1953), pp. 137–42.

Kennedy, C., 'Two comments (II)', *Economic Journal* (December 1963), pp. 780–1.

Kennedy, C., 'Welfare criteria – a further note', *Economic Journal* (June 1963), pp. 338–41.

Kuznets, S., 'On the valuation of social income – reflections on Professor Hicks' article, part I', *Economica* (February 1948).

Little, I. M. D., *A Critique of Welfare Economics* (London: Oxford University Press, 1950; 2nd edn, 1957).

Little, I. M. D., 'Welfare criteria: an exchange of notes. II: A comment', *Economic Journal* (March 1962).

Little, I. M. D., 'Welfare criteria: an exchange of notes. IV: A rejoinder', *Economic Journal* (March 1962).

Meade, J. E., 'Welfare criteria: an exchange of notes. III', *Economic Journal* (March 1962).

Mishan, E. J., 'A re-appraisal of the principles of resource allocation', *Economica* (November 1957), pp. 324–42.

Mishan, E. J., 'A survey of welfare economics, 1939–1959', *Economic Journal* (June 1960), pp. 197–256.

Mishan, E. J., 'Welfare criteria: an exchange of notes. V', *Economic Journal* (March 1962), pp. 234–44.

Mishan. E. J., 'Welfare criteria: are compensation tests necessary?', *Economic Journal* (June 1963), pp. 342–50.

Mishan, E. J., 'The recent debate on welfare criteria', *Oxford Economic Papers* (July 1965), pp. 219–36.

Mishan, E. J., *Welfare Economics: An Assessment* (Amsterdam: North-Holland, 1969).

Ng, Y-K., 'Little's welfare criterion under the equality assumptions', *Economic Record* (December 1971), pp. 579–83.

Pigou, A. C., *The Economics of Welfare,* 4th edn (London: Macmillan, 1932).

Robertson, D., 'Welfare criteria: an exchange of notes. I: A note', *Economic Journal* (March 1962), pp. 226–9.

Samuelson, P. A., 'The gains from international trade', *Canadian Journal of Economics* (May 1939), pp. 195–205.

Samuelson, P. A., 'Evaluation of real national income', *Oxford Economic Papers* (January 1950), pp. 1–40.

Scitovsky, T., 'A note on welfare propositions in economics', *Review of Economic Studies* (November 1941), pp. 77–88.

Sen, A. K., 'Distribution, transitivity, and Little's welfare criterion', *Economic Journal* (December 1963).

Dynamics

5

Economic Criteria for Intergenerational Comparisons

Abstract

It is argued in this paper that the generational time paths produced by economic models offer opportunities for the display of technical virtuosity, but shed no more light on the problem than did earlier neoclassical models on the problem of distribution within the community. In both these instances, economists unerringly select assumptions for their models that produce conclusions which, when they are not merely taxonomic, accord with the broadly accepted values of society. Although these new models are not quite so obvious as the earlier static neoclassical ones, cursory attention to their procedure reveals that the economist has really nothing of substance to contribute to the debate on the 'ideal' intergenerational time path. In effect, the models are 'cooked up' so as to give the imprimatur of science to what is, after all, no more than a popular ethical judgment.

I What is an Economic Criterion?

A sociological criterion is one that turns on the stability, progress or cohesion of society; a psychological criterion is one that turns on the development or fulfilment, in some sense, of the individual; whereas a political criterion is one that turns on the interests of the state or polity, however determined or expressed. But what is an economic criterion?

The classical definition of the scope of economics, proposed by Robbins in 1931, is that relating the allocation of scarce resources to the satisfaction of given ends. To the extent that the economist turns from the description and interpretation of economic data to the

I am indebted to Tony Fisher of the University of Maryland for drawing my attention to errors and ambiguities in a first draft.

formulation of rules and policies for the allocation of resources, under certain conditions at least, he is obviously employing a criterion of some sort. But what sort?

If we accept the traditional literature on these aspects of the subject, and the practical advice that is tendered by the economist to governments, the components of an economic criterion appear to be unambiguous.

The 'objective' and fundamental data for the economist engaged in normative or prescriptive analysis are in fact the subjective valuations of the individual as stated by him, or revealed by his market behaviour, at the relevant moment of time, or during some period of time, over which his tastes remain, or are assumed to remain, unchanged. We might leave this component of an economic criterion at that, except for the disturbing propensity of the economist to justify this recourse by reference to the liberalist dictum that each man must be supposed to know his own interest best. Certainly, if the supposition were true, it would impart some welfare significance to the economist's prescriptive propositions and policies.

Now, in so far as the individual is choosing between carrots at 60 cents a pound and peas at 50 cents, the dictum is reasonable. But it is suspect for larger and more complex choices, such as the allocation of the individual's time over the week or year, or the allocation of his income between broad categories of goods entailed by his adopted style of life. Indeed, in these regards, whereas for the economist the choices revealed by the individual are assumed to be the expression of his wants, for the psychotherapist they are assumed to be the expression of his problem. For the former, welfare is raised accordingly as the individual satisfies his expressed wants. For the latter, it is more often the case that the individual's welfare can be raised only according as such expressed wants can be altered in the interests of the individual's psychic harmony.

Be that as it may, this supposition is the singular

characteristic of the economist's method, one that informs all his allocative proposals and propositions. Vulnerable though it is, such an assumption, as indicated, need not impugn the relevance of an analysis restricted to relatively minor choices. But once this sort of analysis is extended to major choices, and also to more complex social issues bearing on foreign trade, industrial disputes, economic growth, and monetary and fiscal controls, the welfare validity of the economist's propositions and policies becomes questionable.

Such seemingly provocative remarks, I hasten to add, are not merely incidental to my purpose. Nor are they inspired chiefly by a desire to damp the enthusiasm of the young and eager. They are altogether pertinent in any assessment of economic criteria – intergenerational, intragenerational or other.

We reach now for the other component of prescriptive economics, one that takes us from the individual to the group: namely, the judgment that the welfare of the group is no more than the aggregate of the welfare of the individual members. Stated baldly in this way, it looks at least no less vulnerable than the preceding assumption. Yet, its adoption by economists is almost universal. Indeed, it is unthinkingly used in all that passes for orthodox economic advice and is the staple of all familiar quantitative techniques, such as mathematical programming, operations research and cost–benefit analysis.

However, this aggregation can take either of two forms. The more popular one today is an aggregation of individual values, in terms of money or numeraire, associated with Pareto. The other is an aggregation of the util-equivalent of these individual values, a procedure associated with the neoclassical school, in particular with the writings of Marshal and Pigou, and still fashionable in the more theoretical welfare constructions.

I am, of course, aware that, with the progress of economics toward increasing formalisation, we can regard both the Pareto and the neoclassical criteria as rather crude and perhaps limiting cases of the *social welfare function*, that grandiose but ineffectual excrescence on the body of welfare economics. Seen in retrospect, however, this billowing concept seems to have issued out of a growing sense of frustration. And though it has the merit of providing opportunities within the profession both for employment and for the display of technical virtuosity, no practising economist would regard it for an instant as one of the cutting tools of the trade. If I refer to it later on, it is only in the endeavour to gain perspective in reviewing developments in the field of normative economics.

II Models of Intergenerational Distribution

Let us now turn briefly to a number of economic models that produce generational time paths. Although there are quite a few of them, the best known, perhaps, being the early attempt by Ramsey (1928), the conclusions I wish to draw can be illustrated by inspecting a small but (hopefully) not too biased a sample. In addition to Ramsey's model, I have selected those of Strotz (1955), Dasgupta and Heal (1974), Solow (1974) and Page (1976). Some or all of these five models are likely to be familiar to most economists interested in theories of welfare or growth. Nonetheless, it seems sensible, first, to attempt to present recognisable caricatures of each of them, if only to make the paper more accessible to other economists with better things to do. Nothing is lost in looking at them in chronological order.

(1) *Ramsey*'s model, when purged of its technical finesse, appears as a simple extension of the neoclassical approach to the allocation problem, the traditional procedure being that of prescribing an allocation of goods and factors, at a point of time, among a given population so as to maximise aggregate utility. Starting from the same behaviour and resource base – that is, given tastes, given factors and given techniques – the intergenerational analogue is that of choosing a consumption path over time that again maximises aggregate utility.[1] The mathematical problem of this analogue is simplified by reducing the diversity of consumer goods, of capital goods and of labour services to homogeneous aggregates of consumption, capital and labour respectively. Thus, starting with some initial capital stock, taking the labour force to be constant over time, and making the common assumptions that both the returns to capital and the utility of consumption increase at a diminishing rate, there is only one decision to be made – the shape of the savings (investment) path over time. For, given the simplifications of the model, any time path of savings entails a corresponding time path of the capital stock, which in turn entails a corresponding time path of consumption and, therefore, one also of utility.

If we go along with Ramsey and reject the notion of discounting the utility of future generations as unimaginative and unethical, the path of the capital stock that maximises utility is described by the simple condition that the percentage rate of decline of marginal utility be equal always to the percentage rate of return on capital.[2]

In order to prevent the path of aggregate utility from growing indefinitely large, a ceiling is effectively imposed by postulating that the returns to capital eventually become zero and/or that the marginal utility of consumption eventually becomes zero. It transpires that the optimal consumption path is one that grows for a time at a diminishing rate until it settles down to a highest possible level. Once this point of bliss is attained, it is maintained for ever more.[3]

(2) *Strotz* is formally concerned with the consumption path of a single individual, say Robinson Crusoe. In order to focus more closely on the problem of consistent planning, he ignores production and starts off with a stock of consumption goods that never deteriorates. Crusoe's problem is how to distribute this stock over time so as to be satisfied at any subsequent point of time with all preceding plans. Although the utility of any given amount of consumption good is to be the same whenever Crusoe chooses to consume it, he can regard himself as a different person at different points of time, in so far as he attaches a different weight to the utility enjoyed at each point of time according to where he happens to be in time. Posed in this way, the problem can be reinterpreted as that of choosing an intergenerational consumption path, given that the typical individual of each generation has the same utility function as that of any other generation yet uses a pattern of generation weights different from those adopted by the typical individuals of other generations in choosing that distribution over time that maximises his own utility.

Identifying each point of time with a distinct generation-person then, there will be for each generation-person an indefinite number of feasible consumption paths to the terminal date, T, which are to be ranked according to some criterion.[4] The conventional ranking device, for, say, person *one* situated at time zero would be a ranking of all alternative consumption paths using person *one's* set of utility weights, bearing in mind, however, that utility of consumption increases at the same diminishing rate wherever it takes place. Any person τ uses the same procedure, except that he adopts his own τ set of utility weights.[5] Thus, the choice of consumption path for each individual will be that yielding him the maximum utility.

If we reject dictatorial solutions, the question arises: is it possible to produce a single consumption path that would be regarded as optimal by each person? The answer is that a sufficient condition for such a coincidence is the adoption by all persons of a particular exponential weighting device, one applying a common rate of time discount, r, to the utility of all future persons. If such a weighting device were universally adopted, the amount consumed by each person over time would be determined at the point for which the percentage decline in the marginal utility of consumption was equal to this rate r.[6]

For a positive r, this resulting time path of consumption, which coincides with the desires of each person, declines asymptotically.[7] In the limiting case of a zero r, the time path of consumption is constant and the marginal utility of consumption is everywhere constant.

In the absence of this sort of coincidence, however, the path of consumption in this model is one that is likely to decline in any case. For each generation can have no influence on past decisions, and can decide only what amount it will leave to the future from the amount it inherits from the preceding generation. True, if all generations happen to discount the future in exactly the same way, the future consumption path to T that each envisages will turn out to be the consumption time path that is in fact followed. Yet, there is nothing ethically commendable about consistency of this sort. And there is certainly no necessary relation between this consistent consumption path and one that would have been agreed upon by some hypothetical meeting of all generations prior to the events.

(3) *Dasgupta and Heal*'s model can be recognised as both a more elaborate and a more flexible version of the Ramsey model. Their production function contains, besides a stock of capital and inputs of labour, inputs from a depletable stock of natural resources. The consumption time path that emerges is made to depend upon a number of key parameters, behavioural and technological – in particular on the rate of discount, on the elasticity of marginal utility with respect to consumption, and on the elasticity of factor substitution in a CES production function. Without pretending to be realistic, we might instead adopt the simpler Cobb–Douglas production function, in which this elasticity is unity. In that case the time path will depend on the magnitude of the influence, with respect to output, of capital inputs relative to natural resource inputs, say a_1 relative to a_2.[8]

Holding labour (and population) constant throughout, and beginning with a stock of homogeneous capital and of homogeneous natural resources, we can generate any number of consumption time paths by accumulating capital and/or depleting the natural resource base at different rates. By making the assumption that a_1 exceeds a_2, the influence of the accumulation of capital on output is able to offset that of the depletion of the natural resource base to the extent, at any rate, of preventing output from ever falling to zero.

Clearly, the thing to be maximised is the utility of consumption over time when it is discounted at r, the discount rate, assuming as usual that utility increases with consumption but at a diminishing rate. The use of a specific form of the utility function,

$$U = -(C_t^{-v})$$

has the convenient property that the elasticity of marginal utility of consumption is a constant $(1 + v)$.

It transpires that, for any given positive rate of discount r, the optimal consumption path is one that (eventually) declines at a decreasing rate, although asymptotically. For high enough rates of discount, the optimal path declines continuously; for other positive discount rates the corresponding optimal time-paths grow at first to a peak before declining. As for the magnitude of v, the higher it is, the longer the time taken to reach the point of highest *per capita* consumption before declining.

In the limiting case of a zero discount rate – one dollar of consumption any time in the future being worth no less (in util terms) than a dollar of consumption today – the optimal consumption path is one that grows continuously along with a continuous growth in the stock of capital (bearing in mind that the requirement of a positive rate of return on investment is assured by the adoption of a Cobb–Douglas production function).

For this zero discount rate, however, the higher is the value of v (a reflection of the elasticity of the marginal utility of consumption), the higher is the initial level of consumption and the lower is its subsequent rate of ascent. In the limiting case in which v approaches infinity, the optimal consumption path approaches a constant level over time.[9]

(4) In its final version *Solow*'s model employs a production function similar to that used by the preceding writers and, in addition, assumes an exogenous rate of technological progress. Beginning, therefore, with a fixed stock of homogeneous capital, a given amount of labour and a fixed stock of depletable homogeneous resources, any number of consumption paths, or *per capita* consumption paths, can be generated from time zero to infinity. However, instead of using a typical neoclassical welfare function that aggregates the utility of consumption over time, appropriately discounted, Solow rejects any discounting procedure and, extending Rawls's principle of justice to an intergenerational context, proposes a maximin criterion for choosing among the alternative consumption paths that are feasible.

If we chopped time into discrete generation periods, we could write $U_0, U_1, \ldots, U_T$ for the amounts of utility experienced by the average persons in each of the successive generations $0, 1, \ldots, T$. The implication of the maximin criterion is that, if the τth period's consumption, and therefore, utility, is the lowest in a particular consumption path, the welfare index W of that consumption path can be raised only by raising U_τ, provided that the utility of no other period falls below U_τ. In effect, any additional utility of other generations above that of the generation having the lowest average utility does not count in this welfare index. It is therefore always possible to raise W if there is at least one lowest average utility generation, simply by transferring some consumption from other generations to this one – provided always that the transfers leave all generations above the previous lowest average. It should be apparent on reflection that, unless the average consumptions of all generations are equal, there is always scope (assuming sufficient divisibility) for improving W by spreading the consumption more equally, thereby raising the average utility of the lowest. The highest W corresponds therefore to the highest path of equal consumption over time – irrespective of the shape of the individual utility function, which is, however, deemed to be the same for each person of each generation.

We may note in passing that, if there were no exogenous technological progress in the model, no capital would ever be accumulated on this criterion, since, as compared with the highest path of equal consumption over time, any capital accumulated by a generation would reduce its consumption and so lower W. However, in so far as exogenous technical progress is built into the model, one can raise the first generation's consumption above the total returns to the existing stock of capital and labour simply by *decumulating* capital, maintaining consumption in subsequent periods through the effects of technical progress. Once we introduce a stock of depletable natural resources, we can also raise consumption by depleting the resource base as well as by depleting the capital stock.

(5) *Page*'s model. If one drops the fiction of a single person in the Strotz model and, as suggested, interprets it as an intergenerational model, each generation being represented by some average person, then the amounts to be consumed by each of these future average persons may be supposed to enter the utility function of the τth person. They can be regarded by him as a form of external economy, a *ceteris paribus* increase in the amount consumed by any future person, in effect, raising the utility of the τth person.

If there are exactly 100 generations of equal populations numbered zero to 99, the utility of the average person of the first generation can take the additive form

$$U^0(C) = U(C_0) + \alpha^1 U(C_1) + \ldots + \alpha^{99} U(C_{99})$$

where the utility experienced by any person is taken to

be the same for the given quantity consumed, irrespective of the period in generational time, and where the weights or discount factors, α^τ, attached to the utility of the amounts consumed by each future person are all positive and less than unity.

The problem of this first generation is obviously that of distributing a given stock of consumption goods among the generations so as to maximise $U^0(C)$. And the question of consistency arises at once, since each of the successive generations, say the τth generation, will also have to choose a distribution of its inherited stock of consumption goods over the remaining future generations so as to maximise its own utility, $U^\tau(C)$.[10] The consistency condition

$$\alpha^\tau = \left(\frac{1}{1+r}\right)^\tau$$

derived from the Strotz model is, of course, applicable to the problem as posed above. As indicated, it produces, in general, a declining consumption path over time.

Now, following Page, let us suppose that, in each average person's utility function, some weight is given not only to the consumption of successive generations but also to the consumption of preceding generations. We may then be more inclined to regard as a fair distribution over time that pattern of consumption which would emerge from maximising an aggregate-weighted utility of the consumption of all the generations – the aggregate of weights used for the consumption of any one generation being the sum of the different weights attached to it by each of the 100 generations.

If each person uses the same discount factor α and treats past and future symmetrically,[11] the resultant aggregated weights to be attached to the utility of each of the generations turn out to be roughly equal. With equal weights, and diminishing marginal utility, equal consumption over time maximises utility.[12]

III   Intragenerational Distribution Criteria

Bearing in mind that the economic criterion proper of each of the five intergenerational models considered has reference only to the particular form of the maximand adopted, and not to those components of the model which place limits on the feasible time paths, it may be illuminating first to review some of the earlier and better-known attempts by economists to deal with the distribution of the social product among an existing population.

The neoclassical approach, exemplified by Marshall and Pigou, leads to the income equalisation result as a corollary of maximising aggregate utility. Thus, according to the neoclassical analysis, at its most explicit in Pigou's *Economics of Welfare*, it is not enough to allocate resources so that (at the prevailing set of prices) simply the dollar value of the 'social dividend' is a maximum. It is necessary also that the aggregate *utility* from society's resources be a maximum. And a necessary condition for the fulfilment of the latter criterion is the realisation of that distribution of the aggregate output for which the marginal utility of a dollar is the same for everybody.

Now, in the absence of any constraint on the shape of the individual utility functions, this resulting distribution that, along with an ideal allocation of resources, maximises aggregate utility can take any form, including, of course, a highly regressive one. The egalitarian distribution can be assured, however, by imposing two sufficient conditions on the individual utility functions. The first is that the individual utility functions are all alike (at least with respect to real income), which implies that the innate capacity to enjoy a given real income is the same for every member of society – allowing perhaps for age, and also for the time needed to adapt to changes in real income. The second is that the marginal utility of real income is diminishing. Needless to remark, the neoclassical economists had no difficulty in believing that these two conditions reflected the facts of life. The belief in equal natural endowments was common to nearly all nineteenth-century reformers, for whom observed differences in capacity were to be ascribed to differences in nurture rather than in nature. As for the belief in diminishing marginal utility, it seemed to explain a lot, and in the last resort it could draw upon strong intuitive appeal.

Both these beliefs may still be thought true, or roughly true. We need not debate them here. The question that should interest us, however, is the position that would have been taken by, say, Pigou had he become convinced by the evidence that differences in capacity to enjoy goods are innate and irremediable. For then his adopted criterion, a maximum of the aggregate of individual utilities, might entail a highly unequal distribution of the product. Indeed, if the existing distribution of real income already happened to be roughly equal, aggregate utility might be raised simply by transferring income from persons with lower capacities to enjoy goods to persons with higher capacities. In effect, a natural and unalterable state of distributional injustice with respect to the inherited capacity to enjoy goods would then be compounded by man in pursuit of the utility-maximising goal.

This simple reflection should not be dismissed with impatience, for it takes us to the heart of the matter: the quandary the economist seeks to escape by his selection of particular assumptions about human behaviour. It is a quandary because there is no doubt that the economist, moved by the spirit of the times, believes that income ought to be more equally distributed. He may even go as far as to believe that distributional justice can be realised only by an equal distribution of income.

Thus, if the revealed and incontrovertible facts of human nature were such as to face the economist with a dilemma, either (1) to uphold the goal of maximising utility, or some related economic criterion, and therefore to recommend the political implementation of a resulting increase in income inequality, or else (2) to reject his criterion and support a more equal distribution of incomes, there could be little doubt about his resolution. He would almost certainly reject the economic criterion, no matter how engaging, and plump for a policy of increasing income equality.

In the circumstances, the best that can be said for the employment of economic criteria for resolving distributional questions is that it speaks for the good intentions of the economist who seeks to seal his moral convictions with the imprimatur of 'economic science'. But it reveals also a degree of wilful obtuseness, inasmuch as, if (or when) it comes to a critical choice, his moral judgment will prevail and his criterion will be scrapped. If I am right, the economist so occupied cannot be absolved of the charge of dilettantism: he is choosing to engage in unnecessary labour, using his ingenuity to produce results that either have to accord with his own or existing norms of justice or else have to be left in limbo.

Let us now consider the important shift of perspective introduced by Bergson's seminal paper in 1938. It then became clear that the neoclassical economists' utility criterion, along with their particular assumptions about the utility function, could be prised away from those efficiency propositions (bearing on the allocation of factors) which were held to be valid irrespective of the particular welfare criterion employed and, therefore, irrespective of distributional implications.

From Bergson's contribution sprang the notion of a 'social welfare function' by reference to which a person, or group, is supposed able to rank every conceivable economic situation open to society. Beginning with any prevailing technology and factor endowment, the highest-ranking economic situation derivable therefrom, the 'optimum optimorum', could be determined in the light of some specified social-welfare function. The difficulties of forming a socially acceptable social welfare function from the social welfare functions of each of the members of a society were disclosed in Arrow's famous monograph of 1951, which gave rise to a burgeoning literature aptly described by Samuelson as 'welfare politics'. But the idea of invoking an unspecified social-welfare function (to be chosen by society itself), so enabling the economist to dissociate himself from any ethical or political view, particularly in respect of distribution, proved to be a popular one.

Returning to Bergson's efficiency conditions, or optimality conditions, it is unsurprising that they were also an essential part of what came to be known as the New Welfare Economics associated with Hotelling (1938), Kaldor (1939), Hicks (1939) and Scitovsky (1941). The other and more interesting part of this New Welfare Economics, associated with the Kaldor–Hicks–Scitovsky criteria, can now be recognised as no more than a rehabilitation of the Pareto criterion – in its simplest expression, a ranking of alternative aggregations of individual valuations (at some given price set) without, that is, first transforming dollar values into utils, as is done in effect by the neoclassical criterion. Although some attention was given by the above-mentioned writers to the distributional implications arising from the use of this Pareto criterion, they are clearly disregarded by the criterion proper – a fact that provoked opposition to its acceptance, quite apart from the question of possible ambiguities.

This hostility toward its adoption might have been less if it had been explicitly realised at the time that such a criterion by itself need not be regarded as decisive in any social choice, perhaps not even the dominant consideration. Indeed, in 1950 Little did the profession a service by taking a first step toward this recognition by proposing a *dual* criterion: a Pareto test (the economic criterion) plus a distribution test (the 'non-economic' criterion). Accordingly, unless both parts of the dual criterion were met in a move to a new situation, the economist should not recommend the movement.[13]

It does not matter much, in the immediate context, whether Little's distributional proviso – worded cautiously in terms of a 'better' or a 'not worse' distribution – was to be determined by a political decision or by an ethical one. What is significant is the implied recognition that the distributional aspects of a socially acceptable criterion cannot be legitimately derived as a byproduct of a purely economic criterion.

However, one has to be unduly sanguine to expect that, in the economics profession, the most patent demonstration of this or any other impossibility will act to deter further attempts, in effect, to pour a quart out of a pint pot. It is therefore fitting we should end this section with a brief mention of two recent attempts to distil distributional propositions from economic criteria by ingenious use of that most accommodating of economic concepts, the external effect.

Hochman and Rodgers (1969) based their distributional conclusions on actual Pareto improvements resulting from interperson money transfers wherever the donor of a dollar gained more from giving it to someone else than from spending it himself. Such transfers can properly be called Pareto efficient, and the resulting redistribution from carrying this process to its limit may be identified as Pareto optimal. Not unexpectedly, the authors strove to persuade themselves that it was the richer members of society who sought to gratify themselves by giving away sums to the poorer members, and also that the existing tax structure could properly be regarded, *inter alia,* as an instrument designed by society to give expression to this latent benevolence.

With the tautological part of their analysis there can be no quarrel. All voluntary transfers are indeed classifiable as Pareto improvements. Any redistribution arising therefrom is Pareto efficient in the usual sense. However, two limitations of this process of voluntary transfers – allowing that it is taken to the limit – should not be overlooked. First, it can be agreed (1) that a Pareto-efficient redistribution may take us only part of the way toward some 'ideal' distribution, and also perhaps (2) that the amount of redistribution and its pattern will depend upon the initial distribution. It is therefore possible that, starting from two different initial distributions, the respective resulting Pareto-optimal distributions are wholly different. How, then, do we choose between them?

Secondly, and more important, is the fact that any substantive conclusion reached runs straight into the dilemma mentioned earlier. If the psychological assumptions adopted in order to reach an ethically or politically acceptable distributional conclusion happen to be empirically valid, the model is superfluous. If, on the other hand, these psychological assumptions are unwarranted – the psychological facts being such that Pareto improvements entail unacceptable distributional conclusions – the conclusions will be ignored.

This latter limitation applies also to Lester Thurow's imaginative proposal (1971) for selecting as the optimal distributional structure of incomes that structure which yields for society the largest aggregate algebraic sum of the individual compensating variations – each person in society, that is, putting a sum, positive or negative, on each of the possible distributional structures ordered along a complete spectrum.[14]

IV   Assessment of Intergenerational Models in the Light of these Observations

Ramsey's analysis is in harmony with those of the neoclassical writers. He too invests every one, or every generation, with the same diminishing marginal utility function. Faced with intergenerational comparisons, he follows the spirit of these writers in rejecting the use of a generational discount rate. Thus, given the production and behavioural features of the model, the optimal consumption path over the future is that which eventually remains constant over time at the highest possible utility level *per capita,* a conclusion that is wholly satisfactory.

Strotz, on the other hand, appears to be preoccupied, in the main, with consistency of planning, which requires that the future consumption paths chosen by the individual at each point in time coincide with the initially chosen consumption path. A constant consumption path is only a special case of his consistency requirement. But it is worth mentioning, since, once we extend the analysis to intergenerational time paths, results that have the virtue of consistency only may fail to meet ethical standards.

Dasgupta and Heal have managed to put together a neat little machine capable of churning out optimal consumption paths corresponding to any chosen values of their crucial parameters. Whether or not a_1 exceeds a_2 – whether, that is, we are doomed or not – the optimal consumption path is determined by the values adopted for the discount rate and for the elasticity of marginal utility with respect to consumption.

Their highly aggregated production and utility functions could, of course, be disaggregated in a number of different ways. But once having accepted the maximum utility criterion, the resulting analytic refinements would leave the essential procedure unchanged – and, of course, also the essential conclusion that the optimal path depends upon the magnitudes of the key parameters that describe the features of the now more elaborate model.

Page's model introduces the idea of symmetric weighting of the utility of future and past generations. The satisfaction each generation is assumed to receive from the utility or consumption of generations on either side may be seen as a form of that distributional externality which plays a direct part in the Hochman–Rodgers and Thurow analyses. But whereas in the latter analyses these externalities were enough to produce important distributional implications in a purely Pareto context, they are necessary but not sufficient in the Page model. This is because his externalities (in contrast to those of Hochman and Rodgers) are invariant to differences in *per capita* consumption. In a Pareto context, Page's equal weights (to be attached to the utility or consumption of each generation) would yield no distributional implication whatever. For the dollar value of the stock of consumption good would remain the same however it was distributed.

However, once equal capacities for enjoyment and diminishing marginal utility are brought into the model, as they are, we are home again in neoclassical territory, able again to derive the egalitarian distribution we seek. Thus, it transpires that the symmetric externality employed by Page serves the commendable purpose of rationalising on economic grounds a zero discount rate in evaluating the consumption of future generations – which zero discount rate Ramsey rationalises, however, on ethical grounds.

Turning, finally, to the maximin criterion adopted by Solow, it turns out to be the counterpart of a primitive L-shaped social welfare function, as shown in Figure 1. In this construction axes 1 and 2 measure respectively the cardinal utilities of persons one and two. If, from a position of exact equality, a, additional utility is enjoyed by person one, the welfare of society remains unchanged at W_2. In an intergenerational context, axes 1 and 2 measure respectively the *per capita* utility, and consumption, of generations one and two. According to the criterion, an addition of ab consumption for generation one counts for nothing. Thus, in a static setting, the equal division solution requires a conventionally drawn utility-possibility locus R_1R_1.[15] In the dynamic model, on the other hand, the ranking of a continuous range of feasible time paths of consumption implies the existence also of constant consumption-*per-capita* time paths, from which, of course, the maximin procedure picks out the highest.

It is evident, moreover, that the other components of the Solow model do not affect the ethical criterion, which is imported, so to speak, from outside economics. His successive introductions of increasing population, depletable natural resources and unlimited technical progress act only to alter the magnitude of the constant consumption path and to modify the necessary conditions for its attainment.

Solow himself is willing to make an ethical assessment of the constant consumption time path that results from the application of the maximin criterion. In fact, he suggests two 'difficulties': (1) such a time path requires a large initial capital stock, as otherwise it could perpetuate poverty; and (2) such an optimal time path is 'very conservative' – at least for a fixed population and unlimited technical progress – inasmuch as it dismisses the alternative of an exponentially

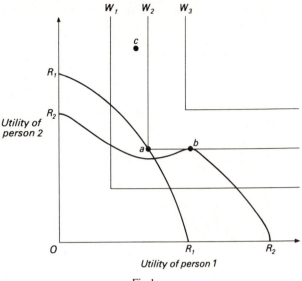

Fig. 1

rising consumption path in exchange for some initial sacrifice. These alleged difficulties, I imagine, will be conceded readily by economists who tend to dote on the notion of trade-off or who are irresistibly attracted by the idea of exponential growth. They are the same as the kind of 'difficulty' such economists would have in ranking a utility combination a in Figure 1 above that of c.

Before concluding this section, let me suggest another possible interpretation of economic egalitarianism. Solow's maximin procedure as depicted in Figure 1 expresses a 'weak' form of egalitarianism. A stronger form would require that, beginning with an equal distribution of income, any additional consumption for individual one alone actually reduces social welfare. Utility combination b would therefore be ranked below that of a. On the strictest egalitarian principle the two 'arms' of the welfare contour W_iW_i fold together to coincide along the 45° degree ray OD_0. Society has then to be deemed worse off if there is any deviation from an initial position of equality, no matter how much more utility everyone enjoys. If, for example, from a position of perfect equality everyone but person A receives twice his income, while A receives a little less than twice his income, social welfare declines.

This more uncompromising conception of equality generates a lexicographic ordering, as depicted in Figure 2: a point along the distributional ray OD_0 preferred to any point along the rays OD_1, and so on. Thus, in this construction the point a is preferred to b which is preferred to c.

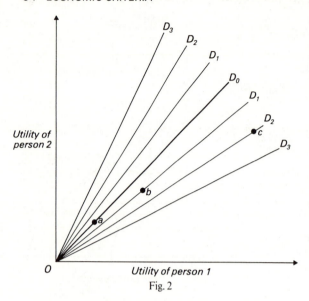

Fig. 2

Now, Rawls's (1971) concept of a 'just rate of saving' entails a departure from equal *per capita* consumption between generations. But this is not, in my view, because a just distribution of resources over time is not one producing equal *per capita* consumption.[16] The departure from the constant distribution over time that is the just distribution arises from what Rawls perceives to be a paramount objective: an accumulation of capital necessary to build the edifice of justice on secure foundations. To this extent, Rawls agrees with Solow's first difficulty in accepting a constant consumption time path. Given the prevailing material conditions, this edifice cannot be built without some sacrifices from the earlier generations, which sacrifices, however, are to be agreed upon behind the veil of ignorance. Once this edifice is complete, consumption *per capita* should remain constant from one generation to another for ever after. Indeed, the level to be attained is also a matter of grave decision if, as Rawls believes, consumption beyond some point can only hinder the administration and the enjoyment of justice.

V   Intergenerational and Intragenerational Equality Compared

I have so far associated an equal distribution of the product with a just distribution not simply for expositional convenience but also because it seems to reflect the prevailing (although not the universal) sense

of right in this respect, one that has become more popular and vociferous in the postwar era. Nevertheless, it is as well to state explicitly at this point that my general thesis – that the distributional implications of economic models are gratuitous and expendable – does not depend upon the particular distributional structure that is currently accepted as ethical by society as a whole.

The appeal of an equal division among all members of a community of the fruits of their collective efforts rests ultimately on a philosophical view, or rather an interpretation of the world or, in the last resort, a factual judgment: namely, that the material success of a person depends predominantly or entirely on factors outside his control – these being, primarily, his endowments of ability and character, the family that rears him, the social environment in which he grows, the people whom he happens to meet and the events that overtake him. A contrary interpretation of the world, one that regards such factors as minor influences, and believes that personal deficiencies are personally remediable, would explain differences in income between persons (within a unified economic area at least) as arising, in the main, from differences in personal decisions about the efforts and sacrifices to be made over the span of their lives.[17] Those who believe that differences in income arise chiefly from such causes are not likely to accept an equal sharing of the society's product as a just distribution. They would tend rather to support the dictum 'to each according to his work'.

The observations in the preceding paragraph, however, are germane to the distribution of the product within an existing society at some point of time, or over some short period of time. The case is different when we are to consider distributions over generational time, comparing the average real income or consumption in one generation with that in another. For whatever be our view of the fundamental factors explaining differences in existing incomes, we are likely to agree that an equal *per capita* real consumption for all generations is an eminently fair arrangement. Even if we take what seems today to be the less popular view, that one's income is primarily the fruit of one's effort, it is the *average* income of each generation, not the distribution within it, that is at issue. For, making the minor assumption (which can always be modified) that the average effort of each generation is about the same, the reasonable supposition that the distribution of relevant characteristics is much the same for one generation as for another impels us to the view that no generation deserves as of right to enjoy a higher standard than any other.

Irrespective, therefore, of the way in which each generation chooses to distribute its own outputs among its members, and irrespective also of the way in which we think any generation ought to distribute its outputs among them, we can agree on each generation's right to a natural resource and capital endowment that, with the same average effort, will produce for it the same *per capita* real consumption as that of any other generation. In sum, the ethical appeal of equality of *per capita* consumption over generational time is independent of a belief in the justice of an equal division of the product in any existing society, and is far more compelling.

VI Concluding Remarks

I began this paper by casting doubt on the dictum, fundamental to normative economics, that each man knows his own interest best, or, put more formally, that his revealed choices identify the combination of goods that, subject to institutional and budgetary constraints, maximises his utility. I do not say that it is imprudent to subscribe to this fiction. Indeed, in a society prone to excesses of democratic sentiment, any proposed amendment of it would be politically hazardous. Yet, were economists in earnest about social welfare, so basic an assumption about human behaviour would have to be subjected to psychological investigation.[18]

This observation is by the way, however. For suppose the dictum to be wholly true; suppose, that is, we discover a breed of men possessed of such worldly sagacity as to be able at all times to squeeze the most satisfaction from their expenditures, the moral worth of their accomplishment is not apparent. And if the individual's goal of maximising his utility has little ethical appeal, the goal of maximising the aggregated sum of the utilities of the members of society has even less. For, as suggested, the facts may be such that the goal can be attained only by a highly regressive distribution of income.

We might wish to put the matter otherwise by claiming to be concerned wholly with welfare. But we would soon come to an impasse. For although maximising utility may, in some circumstances, be a suitable criterion for the individual, its extension to society as a whole would be suitable only if men were perfectly indifferent about the distribution of the aggregate utility, which is manifestly untrue. The economist concerned with social welfare cannot, then, avoid this problem of distribution, a problem that is essentially ethical.

In the preceding sections we have indicated how economists, reluctant apparently to admit the limitations of their methods, have habitually addressed themselves to distributional aspects whether at a point of time or through generational time. Wielding a purely economic criterion, a maximand of some sort, their various attempts may be grouped as follows: (1) those that would, in effect, 'cook up' the utility function (and possibly other properties of the model) in order to ensure the emergence of an acceptable distribution or redistribution; (2) those that remain aloof from the distributional implications by constructing a framework in which the values of key parameters (assuming they can eventually be estimated) determine the distribution that maximises the utility function postulated; and (3) those which, attending to the allocative aspects of the problem only, go no further than the construction of a frontier of utility combinations, leaving it to a social welfare function selected by society to choose the combination yielding the highest social welfare.

Enough has already been said of the (1) and (2) procedures, not enough about the (3) procedure. The import of a socially determined social welfare function, in particular, still bothers me. When the economist invokes this *deus ex machina* to resolve the distributional problem, are we to suppose that he is proposing a political solution or an ethical one?

In the world we live in, political decisions dominate. Yet, the ethical sanction for political prescriptions are, in principle, no stronger than they are for economic prescriptions. In so far as political institutions are democratic, the collective choices that pass into legislation do, of course, have the formal assent of a majority. But once allowance is made for imperfect information, intellectual inertia, and the natural deficiencies of imagination and understanding, and once account is taken of campaigns overt and covert to influence public opinion by small groups having much to gain or lose by the decision in question, a good deal of the resulting legislation may yet tend to favour minority interests. Nonetheless, even in a hypothetical world in which political man could be assumed also to know his own long-term interests best, the resulting coincidence between majority vote and majority interest would have no relish of ethics in it. Good democrats are, in the last resort, bound to express faith in their institutions' ability to serve the common good, even when they also acknowledge that democracy, Western democracy at least, is primarily an institution for conflict resolution – which conflicts, incidentally, become more acute in time of rapid technological progress.

The democratic constitution, written or unwritten, is in effect a compact to abide by procedural rules in taking decisions – which rules, however, can themselves be changed over time. It may be defended persuasively in comparison with alternative political dispensations, but there can be no dependable safeguards in any democracy against grave misjudgment or consummate folly. And although the system may occasionally be inspired by ideals of social justice, wherever the implementation of such ideals entails material sacrifices by majorities, any enabling legislation is sure to run into political difficulties.

In particular, the difficulty of implementing distributional justice in a Western-type democracy arises not so much because men do not know 'in their hearts' what a just distribution of income would look like.[19] The real difficulty may properly be called political, meaning, in this context, that in the actual circumstances they find themselves in the world they inhabit, men are prone to have all too lively a regard for their own material interests.

In so far, therefore, as the determination of a just distribution is at issue, a political criterion turning on the result emerging from the sum of all votes, each individual vote being influenced by – or being a function of – a select number of variables, is of no more ethical consequence than an economic criterion turning on the aggregate of individual utilities. Both the political and the economic criterion address themselves to worldly man, man on this earth and in his unredeemed state – which is to say, the man of 'given tastes', as the economist would have it, but essentially man in his existing material circumstances and prone to all the illusions, vices and obsessions that plague ordinary men.

Thus, the convenient insertion of a D^* (distributional structure of real income) into economic man's utility function – or, as in Thurow's model, requiring the man to put a value on D^* – may enable the economist, under some conditions, to pull out of his model a collectively determined distributional ordering and possibly an optimal distributional pattern. If this is the sort of process implied in the construction of a social welfare function, and I think it is, it is clear that it carries with it no ethical sanction whatever.

As suggested by Rawls and others, ethical judgments are reached by men only when they meet in a hypothetical deliberative assembly wholly removed from all worldly interests, hopes and anticipations. According, then, as men have the courage and character to deliberate as though indeed they are part of this hypothetical assembly, so do their judgments approach the ethical. Yet, having said this much of ethical judgments in general, it must not be imagined that great difficulties invariably inhere in resolving broad ethical issues. We certainly do not have to await the official appointment of a conclave of bishops to resolve for us the pattern of a just distribution. As affirmed earlier, we know 'in our hearts' that an equal distribution of utility between men, or at least an equal *per capita* utility between generations, is a just distribution. And we may accept also that an equal distribution of goods, or of money income, would be as close a proxy for an equal distribution of utility in ordinary circumstances as any other distribution of money income.

In sum then, no economic criterion can produce acceptable answers to the distribution problem – whether at a point of time or over time – since the problem is basically an ethical one. I confess that this conclusion looks pretty obvious, and I would not be at all surprised if every economist assured me that he would gladly have conceded this from the start. While in the confessing vein, however, I may add also that I do not expect that anything I have said will have the slightest effect on diminishing the current popularity of intergenerational path pastimes among economists. No halt to any research is ever called by the researchers themselves merely because it does not look very promising.

Epilogue

Suppose, finally, economists are agreed that the ideal distribution is one of constant *per capita* real income over time, the problems of prescribing for it are formidable, especially at a time when the exhilarating vision of unlimited growth has begun to give way to the more sober vision of emerging limitations. The problem now becomes that of arranging our use of resources in order to generate this equitable time path over the future, bearing in mind the finiteness of natural resources, the finiteness of the biosphere's absorptive capacity, the finiteness of space, and the limitations on factor and product substitutability.[20]

Clearly, in a world coming to terms with emerging limitations the economist has a vital role to play. But it is a difficult role to discharge conscientiously, because in this new world measuring real income runs into a number of new problems. As a result of material abundance, man is being pushed up against limits he cannot reasonably be expected to overcome – limits on his time, limits on his absorptive capacity, limits on his hedonic capacity and limits to his adaptability. It is a brave economist, in these circumstances, who continues to suppose that there still exists a positive relation between an index of man-made goods and a psychological index of well-being.

Notes: Chapter 5

1 Ramsey's utility function is in fact the excess of the utility of consumption over the disutility of labour inputs. But nothing essential is lost in the conception of the model by holding constant through time the disutility of a fixed supply of labour.

2 This should be intuitively evident, for we should gain, on balance, by forgoing an extra dollar's consumption only if the percentage loss of utility is more than offset by a greater percentage gain from investing the dollar – an opportunity for gain that is maximised when (recalling that marginal utility and marginal returns are diminishing) we have reduced consumption to the point at which the condition mentioned in the text has been met.

3 The maximisation problem is, incidentally, converted by Ramsey into a minimisation one; that of minimising, starting from time zero, the *difference* between the bliss path and a feasible utility path.

4 Since for mathematical convenience Strotz and others adopt a continuous time to T, the device for ranking alternative time paths takes the form of a functional.

5 Thus for τth person, the functional is

$$\Phi_\tau \equiv \int_\tau^T \lambda^\tau(t) U(C_t, t) dt$$

where t runs from 0 to T, and λ^τ can take the form $e^{-r(t-\tau)}$

6 The proposition that each person, considered alone, will maximise his utility by distributing consumption of a given stock over future periods (persons) until his discounted marginal utility of consumption is the same for each period (person) is familiar enough. Added to this, we now require that the rate of discount used, r, be the same for each person.

7 This declining consumption path corresponds with a rising marginal utility of consumption over time, the rate of increase being

$$\frac{dU'}{dt} \cdot \frac{1}{U'} = r$$

8 In its Cobb–Douglas form their production function is

$$AK^{a_1} R^{a_2} L^{1-a_1-a_2}$$

where L may be taken as constant over time.

9 This is easily understood, starting with a position of equal amounts of consumption in two successive periods. For if one increment of consumption is transferred from the first period to the second, the utility loss to the first is extremely high, whereas the gain in utility from that increment to the second period is extremely low – both being the results of an extremely large decrease in the *increment* of utility associated with an increment of consumption.

10 Following the suggestion of Phelps and Pollack (1968), one way of representing possible inconsistencies under those assumptions (identical utility functions and diminishing marginal utility) emerges from splitting the term α^τ into two components, $\delta\beta^\tau$, where β^τ is a pure discount factor and δ is the constant weight attached by each generation to every future generation, such that

$$\beta^\tau = \left(\frac{1}{1+r}\right)^\tau \qquad 0 < \delta \leqslant 1$$

Assuming δ to be less than unity, it can be shown, as Krutilla and Fisher (1975) have done, that, say, generation two will want to consume more relative to generation three than generation one plans that it should.

This result is intuitively evident if we take a limiting case in which $r=0$, with δ less than unity, say $\delta=\frac{1}{2}$. Each generation then values the *n*th dollar of consumption of every future generation equally, and at one-half of the value of its own consumption of the *n*th dollar. Generation two will therefore want to allocate more consumption to itself than to generation three, whereas generation one (which will also want to allocate more to itself than to any future generation) will want to allocate equal amounts to generations two and three.

In the limiting case of δ equal to unity, α^τ is equal to β^τ, with r a constant discount factor, as in the text.

11 Thus, the τth person's utility function takes the form

$$U^\tau(C) = \sum_{t=0}^{T} U(C_t)\alpha^{|t-\tau|}$$

12 If instead of utils we evaluated benefits in terms of real dollars of consumption, each person would set his own dollar value on the dollar consumption of other generations. A Pareto criterion would then select that pattern of generation distribution having the largest (excess) dollar value. If the weights proposed in the text were used, the aggregated value attached to the dollar of consumption of each generation would be about the same, and therefore *any* distribution of consumption over time would have about the same value as any other.

The Pareto criterion would foster a more *equal* distribution of consumption over time only if the weights varied, not inversely with generational distance (as in the Page model), but inversely with generational *per capita* consumption. An equal distribution over time would produce the largest aggregate value only if any generation having more than average consumption perceived a net benefit from transferring a dollar of its consumption to any generation having less than average consumption – this being the limiting case of the Hochman and Rodgers assumption when applied to generations instead of to persons.

13 The apparent ambiguities that marred this otherwise commendable proposal were made explicit in my 1965 paper, and were resolved in my 1973 paper.

14 Daly and Giertz (1972) also make use of this handy concept of externality in contriving a case for transfers in kind rather than in money. I have suggested (1975) that their argument raises moral problems in addition to the distributional one mentioned above.

15 If, however the utility possibilities are those indicated by the locus R_2R_2, the highest social welfare is attained by the choice of the utility combination indicated by b, person one enjoying more consumption than person two.

16 Departures from equality can arise in cases of emergency also. If the harvest in an isolated community were so meagre that equal distribution among the inhabitants

would ensure their death by starvation, they might jointly agree to draw lots, allowing the winners to survive by sharing the whole of the harvest between them. This dire expedient in response to desperate hardship, however, suspends the *application* of distributional justice in the interests of collective survival, although without in any way weakening the ethical appeal of the former.

17 These include the investment of time and money in obtaining relevant information and in education, training, migration, and so on.

18 Although common experience impels us to reject the dictum regarded as a psychological truth, the full extent of the social damage perpetuated by economists in their routine advocacy of allocative rules, formalised techniques and economic policies, all of which build on it, should be a matter of profound concern and speculation. It is therefore encouraging to discover that so distinguished an economist as Scitovsky has, in his recent book (1976), made a frontal attack on this basic postulate.

19 Nor because political man shares the economic theorist's apprehension that, whatever the just distribution of money income adopted by society, changes in relative prices can alter the real distribution of welfare.

20 Talbot Page (1976) has made a modest but promising contribution to the understanding of this problem.

References

Arrow, K. J., *Social Choice and Individual Values* (New York, 1951; 2nd edn, 1963).

Bergson (Burk), A., 'A reformulation of certain aspects of welfare economics', *Quarterly Journal of Economics*, vol. 52 (1938), pp. 310–34.

Daly, G. and Giertz, F., 'Welfare economics and welfare reform', *American Economic Review*, vol. 62 (1972), pp. 131–8.

Dasgupta, P. and Heal, G., 'The optimal depletion of exhaustible resources', *Review of Economic Studies*, vol. 41 (1974), pp. 3–28.

Hicks, J. R., 'The foundations of welfare economics', *Economic Journal*, vol. 49 (1939), pp. 696–712.

Hochman, H. M. and Rodgers, J. R., 'Pareto optimal redistribution', *American Economic Review*, vol. 59 (1969), pp. 542–57.

Hotelling, H., 'The economics of exhaustible resources', *Journal of Political Economy*, vol. 39 (1931), pp. 137–75.

Hotelling, H., 'The general welfare in relation to the problems of taxation and of railway and utility rates', *Econometrica*, vol. 6 (1938), pp. 242–69.

Kaldor, N., 'Welfare propositions in economics and interpersonal comparisons of utility', *Economic Journal*, vol. 49 (1939), pp. 549–52.

Krutilla, J. and Fisher, A., *The Economics of Natural Environments* (Baltimore, 1975).

Little, I. M. D., *A Critique of Welfare Economics* (London: Oxford University Press, 1950; 2nd edn, 1957).

Mishan, E. J., 'The recent debate on welfare criteria', *Oxford Economic Papers*, vol. 17 (1965), pp. 219–36.

Mishan, E. J., 'Welfare criteria: resolution of a paradox', *Economic Journal*, vol. 83 (1973), pp. 747–67.

Mishan, E. J., 'The folklore of the market: an inquiry into the economic doctrines of the Chicago school', *Journal of Economic Issues*, vol. 10 (1975).

Page, T., *Conservation and Efficiency* (Baltimore, 1976).

Phelps, E. and Pollack, R., 'On second-best, national saving, and game-equilibrium growth', *Review of Economic Studies*, vol. 35 (1968), pp. 185–99.

Pigou, A. C., *The Economics of Welfare*, 4th edn (London: Macmillan, 1932).

Ramsey, F. P., 'A mathematical theory of saving', *Economic Journal*, vol. 38 (1928), pp. 543–59.

Rawls, J., *A Theory of Justice* (Cambridge, Mass., 1971).

Robbins, L., *The Nature and Significance of Economic Science* (London, 1931).

Samuelson, P. A., 'Evaluation of real national income', *Oxford Economic Papers*, vol. 2 (1950), pp. 1–29.

Scitovsky, T., 'A note on welfare propositions in economics', *Review of Economic Studies*, vol. 9 (1941), pp. 77–88.

Scitovsky, T., *The Joyless Economy* (Oxford, 1976).

Solow, R., 'Intergenerational equity and exhaustible resources', *Review of Economic Studies*, vol. 41 (1974), pp. 29–45.

Strotz, R., 'Myopia and inconsistency in dynamic utility maximisation', *Review of Economic Studies*, vol. 23 (1955–6), pp. 165–80.

Thurow, L., 'Income distribution as a pure public good', *Quarterly Journal of Economics*, vol. 85 (1971), pp. 327–36.

PART TWO

Economic Rent or Surplus

6

The Plain Truth About Consumer Surplus

In view of the rapid growth in the number of economic journals since the war, and the consequent shortage of conscientious and competent referees, in view also of the political biases and personal predilections to which the economic analysis of others can be subjected, the ambitious student can no longer count on being able to follow the evolution of some specialised aspect of the subject through a reading of the main journals. A few of the pertinent articles will generally turn out to be largely in error, and of those which advance the subject in some respects some will have created confusion in others.

So it has been with the recent literature on consumer surplus. True, if a subject is inherently complex, no expositional talent can render it simple. But in fact the analysis of consumer surplus is basically a straightforward matter, one which skill, patience, and misunderstanding, have combined to make difficult and misleading. The greater part of the unnecessary difficulty in this literature appears to have arisen from an imperfect appreciation, even among competent economists, of the full implications of the ordinalist revolution which, following the earlier writings of Pareto and Slutsky, was formally initiated by Hicks and Allen in 1934. The writings of Hicks between 1939 and 1944 produced definitions of consumer's surplus that are simple, unambiguous, and allocatively operative within a Pareto context. The concepts and the relevant analysis were further simplified in Hicks's *Revision of Demand Theory* (1956) from where they found their way into popular texts and surveys. And yet the journal articles on the subject appearing in the last few years[1] have managed to produce complications and paradoxes which unnerve the general reader and confuse the specialist. No graduate student today who is directed to this new literature emerges free from the impression that it is a tangled and slippery business at best. If he is left with any affirmative notions, they are likely to include some or all of the following:

(a) that the marginal utility of money is the crucial concept in any analysis designed to validate the use of consumer's surplus;

(b) that the difference, if any, between Hicks's compensating variation (CV) of consumer's surplus and his equivalent variation (EV) is attributable to a difference in the marginal utility of money income;

(c) in particular, that if there are zero income effects for the goods in question, so that CV is equal to EV, the marginal utility of money income will be constant over the relevant price changes;

(d) that in measuring the consumer's surplus for a simultaneous change in a number of prices, 'path independence' cannot be assumed, for, in general, the money measure of the consumer's surplus will vary with the order in which the price changes are taken; and

(e) that while neither the CV nor the EV is a reliable measure of the required change in the individual's welfare, the CV measure is the less useful of the two.

The aim of the present paper is, *inter alia,* to convince the reader that none of the above propositions can be vindicated.

In the treatment that follows, I shall resist the temptation to begin at the beginning with Marshall, cardinal utility, and all that. Chronological considerations will be sacrificed to pedagogical ones. Thus, in section I that follows, the Hicksian definitions will be restated, and their nature and application discussed. Those interested only in the authentication of the concept and its proper use in allocative economics need not read beyond the following section. For the connoisseur, for those who have written on the subject, and for those who have read and suffered, there are two further sections (supplemented by brief Notes); one on what we may call a Marshallian consumer's surplus, and a final and shorter section comparing the two alternative approaches in salient respects.

I The Hicksian Consumer's Surplus

It is a matter of methodological propriety to choose properties of the model that yield features which are generally acceptable for the purpose in hand; indeed, that are necessary in this instance for the interpretation of the proposed measure. Among these features are constancy of tastes and consistency of choices. Both can be assured by adopting an unchanged integrable utility function –visually, one for which any selection of indifference curves, as described in the model, will lie one above the other.

Such a utility function may, of course, appear somewhat restrictive in the light of mathematical possibilities. But for the economist who is primarily interested in economics, such restrictions can be justified on methodological grounds. In this particular case, since Hicks seeks a unique magnitude for each of his two measures – and, as we shall see presently, only a unique magnitude for either accords with economic sense – this integrable utility function has to be adopted. The relevant consequence of doing so is that the cross-partials, $\partial x_i/\partial p_j$ and $\partial p_j/\partial x_i$, are equal, this being a necessary and sufficient condition for what is known as path-independence. In the present context, this means simply that whether we take the order of price changes as Δp_i, Δp_j, ... or Δp_j, Δp_i, ... or whatever, the adopted measure of consumer surplus for the combination of these price changes is uniquely determined.

It is as well to remind ourselves also that Hicks's consumer surplus analysis, along with his theory of consumer's demand, is derived wholly from an ordinal utility hypothesis: we are to suppose, that is, that the individual can rank different levels of his utility only on the scale of more or less. He cannot attach real numbers to them. He cannot even rank *differences* in utility levels –which means that he cannot know whether the marginal utility of anything, including his money income, is increasing, decreasing, or constant.

Thus, without reference to the utility (marginal or average) of money income, the appropriate Hicksian definitions for the individual's surplus, CV and EV, are also as follows. The CV, in its most general form, is defined as that sum of money received by or from the individual which, following a welfare change, leaves him at his original level of welfare. In its most general form, the EV is defined as that sum received by or from the individual which (if he is denied the change in question) leaves him as well off as if he had the welfare change.[2]

Confining ourselves to the right-hand quadrant of Figure 1, a fall in the price of good x from p_0 to p_1, with income constant at y_0, yields a CV equal to $y_1 y_0$ (the most he would pay for the lower price p_1) and an EV equal to $y_2 y_0$ (the least he would accept to forgo the lower price p_1). According as the vertical distances between indifferent curves I_0 and I_1 increase (as in the figure), remain constant, or decrease, as we move leftward, $\partial X/\partial Y$ (the income effect on good x) is positive, zero, or negative respectively, and, correspondingly, the EV measure exceeds, is equal to, or is less than the CV measure.[3]

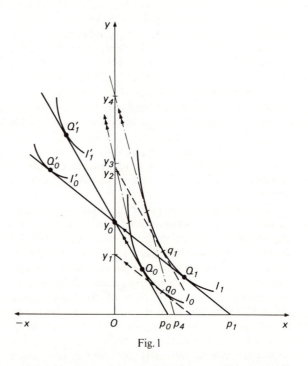

Fig. 1

For a rise, instead, of the price from p_1 to p_0, the correspondence is reversed. The CV required to maintain the individual at his I_1 welfare level is the receipt of a sum $y_2 y_0$. The EV required to move him to the I_0 welfare level when he is spared the higher price p_1 is his payment of $y_1 y_0$.

The price lines in the figure are extended to the right of the y axis so as to reveal the opportunities for the selling of x. Thus, if the indifference curves were drawn as $I_0' I_1'$, a rise in the price of x from p_1 to p_0 would move the individual from Q_0' on I_0' to Q_1' on the higher indifference curve I_1'. The CV and EV measures of this welfare gain can properly be regarded as rent whenever the distance from O along the $-x$ axis measures the sale of a factor x. These two measures are derived geometrically in the same way as they were for the change in product price; that is, by cutting the y axis with a price line parallel to p_0 and tangent to I_0' for the CV, and with a price line parallel to p_1 and tangent to I_1' for the EV (these parallel price lines, and the resulting CV and EV measures along the y axis, $y_1' y_0$ and $y_0 y_2'$ respectively, being omitted so as not to clutter up the figure). For a rise in the price of x that raises the welfare of the seller of x, the CV measure of the gain exceeds the EV measure for a positive income effect (or 'welfare effect') on x.[4]

More generally, for a change alone in any original *set* of prices p_0 (of both goods and factors) to a new set of prices p_1 which changes the individual's level of welfare from I_0 to I_1, the CV is defined as the sum of money Δy for which

$$I_0(p_0) = I_0(p_1, \Delta y)$$

while the EV is defined as the sum of money $\Delta' y$ for which

$$I_1(p_1) = I_1(p_0, \Delta' y)$$

The above exposition sums up the essentials of an ordinalist conception, and of the corresponding definitions, of consumer's surplus, as they were developed about a generation ago. Nothing that has been written since adds much to them. In view of the recent controversial literature, however, at least two propositions can bear emphasis.

(1) First, irrespective of the sign of the income effect and, therefore, irrespective of whether CV is less than, equal to or greater than EV, CV and the EV measures are not approximations to some real surplus; in particular, they are not to be viewed as two limiting estimates of ΔU (the increment of utility), being the results of dividing this ΔU by two different values of λ (the marginal utility of money income), one calculated before and the other after the change in price. They are both exact measures of the welfare change in question. They are in principle measurable, and – in an allocative context – they define the required valuation.

For any given welfare change, each poses a different question. But what is crucial about this difference can be inferred from the formal definitions above: each definition has reference to a different level of welfare. The CV has reference to the original level of welfare, the EV to the subsequent level. Thus, only if all relevant income effects are zero can we expect the CV and the EV measures to be identical.

However, granted that the difference between the CV and EV measures arises directly from the sign of the relevant income effects, is it possible also to explain this

difference on the view rejected above, as relating to a difference in the values of λ? If so, an EV greater than CV for a fall in the price of good x would follow not only from a positive income effect ($\partial x/\partial Y > 0$), but also from a fall in λ resulting from the fall in the price of x; that is, from $\partial \lambda/\partial p_x > 0$.[5] Now it may not be intuitively apparent, but it is easy to show formally (Mathematical Note B (a)) that from positive $\partial \lambda/\partial p_x$, derived from a specific utility function, the required positive $\partial x/\partial Y$ cannot be inferred. More important, in an ordinal system, the sign of $\partial \lambda/\partial p_x$ cannot in fact be uniquely determined (Mathematical Note B (b)).

In sum, the differences, if any, between the EV and the CV measures in the ordinal system can be explained entirely in terms of but one of its two chief operational categories, the income effect (the other being the substitution effect). For this explanatory purpose, reference to different values of λ is not only unnecessary, it is erroneous.

(2) Whatever definition of consumer's surplus we adopt, including CV and EV, wherever more than one price is altered, it is commonly alleged that the measure of the surplus, regarded as the value of a line integral, differs in general according to the order in which the price changes are taken.

A mathematical condition for 'path independence', required to ensure a unique measure regardless of the order in which the price changes are taken, is given by the so-called integrability condition,

$$\frac{\partial x_i}{\partial p_j} = \frac{\partial x_j}{\partial p_i}$$

As it happens, this condition is already a property of the Hicksian system for a given level of utility (Mathematical Note, equation (2)). But whether the CV or the EV definition is used, the logic of the situation clearly admits only of a unique sum whatever the order of price changes. After all, calculating say, the CV as a succession of price changes is simply one possible mathematical device for the calculation of the CV of a simultaneous change in a number of prices.[6]

The exercise is essentially one of comparative statics. For example, the individual is required to give an answer to the question: what is the most you would pay for a 60 per cent reduction in the price of x and a 30 per cent reduction in the price of y? For the consistent individual there can be only one answer to this question.

Even if one price happens to be reduced before the other, it can make no difference within this comparative static context, for the problem is *not* one involving a time path. The problem is simply that of comparing two alternative situations – an original situation *I* with a subsequent or alternative situation *II* in which p_x and p_y alone have fallen.[7] (If, for example, the individual is willing to offer for the *II* price-set a maximum of $100, the confidential information imparted to him that p_x has in fact been lowered before p_y, or vice versa, can make not a jot of difference to him in this comparative static context.)

The only problem that remains in this connection is that of a practical method for calculating the consumer's surplus where several prices are simultaneously changed. Its resolution requires two things; an operational procedure which, could it be implemented, would yield an unambiguous figure for the required *CV* (or *EV*), and, secondly, a close proxy for this procedure, one that in fact can be estimated.

The operational procedure involves adding in sequence the relevant areas under the compensated demand curves (at the I_0 welfare level for the *CV* measure) for each of the several goods whose prices have changed, paying special attention to the *ceteris paribus* clauses, as shown by Hicks (1956). To illustrate for a fall in the prices of two substitute goods, *x* and *y*, the *CV* for the joint price fall is the sum of the shaded areas *A* and *B* in Figure 2. Beginning with a fall from p_x to p_x', with p_y held constant, the *CV* for this price fall alone is given by the shaded area *A* under the compensated demand curve $D_x(p_y)$. With the new price p_x', the compensated demand curve for substitute good *y* shifts leftward from $D_y(p_x)$ to $D_y(p_x')$. Attending now to the fall from p_y to p_y' the additional *CV* gain is given by the shaded area *B*. Regard to consistency ensures that the sum of *CV*s is the same if we begin, instead, with a fall in p_y.

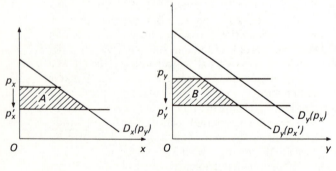

Fig. 2

As for a proxy for the compensated demand curve, it is obviously the ordinary uncompensated demand curve in which money income is held constant. The simple geometric relation between the ordinary demand curve and the two compensated demand

curves pertinent to the *CV* and *EV* measures is by now too familiar to warrant illustration here.[8] Very generally, the smaller is a person's expenditure on a good as a proportion of his total expenditure the smaller is the income effect and the closer, therefore, will the compensated demand curve lie in relation to the ordinary demand curve. And the closer the curves are, the more likely is the error in estimating the ordinary demand curve to swamp the divergence between the true ordinary demand curve and the two compensated demand curves.

There are, finally, two allegations about the Hicksian measures which, just because they appear to have been accepted by recent writers, invite comment. The first, made by Winch (1965) concerns a paradox in the measurement of the *CV* or *EV*, as a result of which he found in favour of the Marshallian measure of consumer's surplus. The second, made by Foster and Neuberger (1974) and by Hause (1975), is that the *EV* is a more reliable indicator of welfare change than the *CV*. Although neither allegation is of central importance they ought not to be evaded in a paper seeking also to vindicate the ordinalist concepts. Appraisal of their validity and relevance has been relegated to Note I at the end of the paper.

II   A Marshallian Consumer's Surplus

There is no need, in this article, to enter into the debate initiated by Friedman (1950) about the nature and purpose of Marshall's demand curve. It is fair to say, however, that the demand curve of the modern textbook conceived in terms of substitution and income effects does not correspond with Marshall's vision of the downward sloping demand curve as a reflection primarily of diminishing marginal utility of the good in question.

However that may be, Marshall's approach was neoclassic in two critical respects; (1) the utility function was 'cardinal' – to the extent, at least, of assuming diminishing marginal utility of goods and of real income, and (2) the capacity for enjoyment was held to be uniformly diffused in society, implying identical utility functions (given time for adjustment of all persons) and permitting 'interpersonal comparisons' of utility. To a neoclassic, what matters is 'real' income or utility, for which money income or wealth is just a proxy. And this primary concern with the actual changes in aggregate social utility which, under certain condition, could be captured by changes in money income is most evident in Marshall's argument supporting the use of the area under the *market* demand curve as yielding a good approximation of the increment in aggregate social utility following a price change.

From the two neoclassic assumptions above, it follows that the marginal utility of money income is lower for the rich than for the middle-class than for the poor. Nonetheless, according to Marshall, the area under the demand curve would serve as an index of the change in aggregate utility if the goods were used in unchanged proportions by each of the several income groups (otherwise alternative consumers' surpluses of equal dollar value might correspond to quite different amounts of aggregate utility).

This concern with utility or real income was of course, evident also in his treatment of the subject at the individual level. Since, ideally, a one-to-one correspondence was required between money changes (which could be observed) and utility changes (which could not), Marshall's intellectual conscience was troubled about the concomitant change in λ, the marginal utility of money income, whenever one or more prices changed. His observation, that the smaller the change in price the more likely was the ideal condition to be realised, brought out the weakness of the analysis. And Marshall, aware of this, became increasingly disillusioned with consumer's surplus.

Seen in historic perspective, it is this besetting concern to compare ultimately in real terms, rather than in terms of money or numeraire, that characterises, and sometimes oppresses, the welfare economics of Marshall and Pigou. It is far from certain that modern writers on this topic are afflicted by the same doctrinal compulsion, yet by following the neoclassic route they inevitably run into the same problems. Because they persevere with the mathematics, they push into them further But, in the end, they have little more to show for their efforts.

Such an approach to consumer's surplus, increasingly popular over the last few years, begins in the ordinary way by envisaging ΔU, a change in total utility that is the result, usually, of a change in one or more prices. The exercise then consists of determining the conditions, in terms of λ, under which a sum of money can be said to correspond exactly with this ΔU.

As Samuelson has shown (1942), it is not possible for λ to remain constant with respect *both* to prices *and* to income. It is therefore necessary to interpret Marshall's constancy of λ with respect *either* to one *or* the other. Attention to the issue leaves no room for doubt that, (bearing in mind the conventional price demand curve with unchanged money income) for Marshall's measure of consumer's surplus, the required constancy of λ is with respect to price movements only.

But, granted this interpretation, two problems arise; the first concerns the necessity of the constancy of λ with respect to prices over the relevant range. Related to it is the second problem of path-dependence mentioned earlier. If the constancy of λ is, indeed, necessary, then the money surplus corresponding to the $\Sigma \Delta p_i$ is uniquely determined only when this condition is met. And when it is met, there can be no path-dependent problem.[9] However, since writers on this subject cannot reasonably suppose the prevalence of this constancy of λ, it becomes virtually impossible for them to refrain from using up space in working out other less restrictive conditions for translating from money to utils or in discussing the approximation afforded by ordinary demand curves.

Thus, in an endeavour to face up to the first problem, and to free the dollar–util conversion from its alleged dependence upon a constant λ, Harberger (1971) observed, in effect, that the util measure of the dollar area of consumer's surplus might be accurately determined even in the absence of a constant λ. Allowing that λ does change with the price changes in question, Harberger proposed the adoption of an *average* change in λ in converting from an increment of money to an increment of utility.

While this device is formally valid (at least if we could suppose that all persons affected by the price changes happen to have identical utility functions), it does not really meet the difficulty as perceived by Marshall and others.[10] First, it assumes away the path-dependency problem, taking it for granted that the consumer's surplus so calculated from the price changes is invariant to the order in which they occur. Secondly, since the purpose of the consumer surplus measures is to enable the economist to compare alternative dollar consumer surpluses in the assurance that they reflect util consumer surpluses, the required one-to-one correspondence between the measured ΔYs and the ΔUs entails the requirement that the average change of λ involved in each of the alternative (sets of) price changes being compared be exactly the same. But this requirement also imposes a restriction on variations in λ hardly less than that of constancy. Of course, if we could actually measure this average change of λ in each of the alternatives being compared, we should then be able – in the absence of the aforementioned one-to-one correspondence – actually to calculate the ratio of any set of ΔUs for any set of measured ΔYs. But no one has yet claimed that such calculation is possible.

Turning now to this second problem, to this *bête noir* of 'path dependence' about which so much fuss is made by modern writers,[11] there is little that may usefully be said within a Marshallian context. It is not hard to derive an expression for the necessary and sufficient conditions for path independence in terms of λ. The form taken is

$$x_i \frac{\partial \lambda}{\partial p_j} = x_j \frac{\partial \lambda}{\partial p_i}$$

(see Mathematical Note, equation 7), a condition that is intuitively suggestive in requiring that λ change at the same rate for each of the price changes (when corrected by relative expenditures on the goods).

However, only a homothetic utility function meets this condition; a function that *inter alia* implies an income elasticity of unity for each of the goods.[12] This requirement is, of course, also met by the constancy of λ with respect to price changes, which constancy is clearly a special and more restrictive instance of the more general path-independence condition given above.

To conclude, so long as the economist plods doggedly along the route pioneered by Marshall, seeking all the time to convert dollar measures of consumer surplus into util measures, and vice versa, by reference to λ, he is eventually impelled either to throw in the sponge or – what effectively comes to the same thing – to invoke the constancy of λ as a plausible assumption for negligible price changes that do not, in any case, matter, and as a vain hope for large price changes that do matter.

III Summary and Conclusions

In the two preceding sections an attempt has been made to clarify distinctions between 'cardinal' and ordinal systems that have become blurred over time, to convince the more specialised reader that the relationships between the two systems are not those commonly supposed, and to persuade the ordinary reader that the adoption of the CV and EV measures of individual rent or surplus, proper to an ordinal system, is the only sensible course of action for those interested in allocative techniques and analysis.[13] For these two measures are unambiguously defined. They are simpler in concept than their Marshallian analogue and, in contrast to it, operationally valid within a Pareto context and for Pareto criteria – those criteria seeking to compare or to rank alternative situations in terms of money (or numeraire) rather than in terms of aggregate utility. Although the path-dependence problem is sure to suggest itself to the mathematical mind for the case in which a number of price changes occur, in view of the logic of the situation, as indicated in section I, the problem does not properly arise with the CV and EV measures.

Where, as in the neoclassic context, criteria turn on aggregate utility and, therefore, alternative situations have to be assessed ultimately in terms of aggregate utility, nothing less than constancy of λ will serve in comparing alternative surpluses, a condition that cannot be readily assumed wherever the price changes are important. Thus, although both Hicks and Marshall turn to the area under the demand curve as a proxy for the actual measurement of consumer surplus, the approximation for the CV and EV measures is in principle measurable and meaningful within the Pareto context. In contrast, the approximation of Marshall's real consumer surplus to the area under the demand curve is not measurable without relevant information above λ which, in practice, is impossible. And even if such information were readily available, or λ could be assumed constant, it is of no consequence whatever in the usual Pareto context.

Apart from a common recourse to the demand curves for approximate measures of their respective consumer surpluses there are no simple connections between Hicks's CV and EV and Marshall's consumer's surplus. This is apparent once we perceive that in a Hicksian ordinal system it is not possible even to identify a movement of λ with respect to price or money-income changes. To elaborate, if we choose a specific utility function such that over the relevant price changes λ remains constant (or increases, or decreases) there is always some monotone transform of this utility function for which the resulting marginal utility of money income does *not* remain constant (or does *not* increase, or decrease). It follows that there can be no unequivocal relation between the sign of $\partial x_i / \partial Y$ and the sign of $\partial \lambda / \partial p_i$ (Mathematical Note B (b)).

In particular, a zero income effect cannot be uniquely associated with constancy of λ with respect to price changes; therefore the price–quantity path of the compensated demand curve is *not,* in general, the price–quantity path of the 'ideal' Marshallian demand curve; that having a constant λ. Nor for that matter, then, can a positive income effect from x_i (EV exceeding CV for a fall in p_i) be uniquely associated with a positive sign of $\partial \lambda / \partial p_i$, and vice versa.

There is, not surprisingly, more scope for exploring connections between income effects and λ effects by turning instead to nonordinal or specific forms of the utility function. And since economics tends increasingly to be defined as that which economists write about, I will not trouble to dissuade any economist from undertaking such explorations. Among the contributions listed in the References, those of Samuelson are particularly recommended for their originality and virtuosity – though not, perhaps, for their assessment of the importance of the consumer-surplus concept in economics.

Note I

A. *The so-called nibble paradox.* In order to contrive this 'paradox', Winch (1965) makes use of an example in which person B's gain from a fall in the price of good x, accompanied as it is by person A's loss from a rise in the price of another good y, does not meet the Kaldor-Hicks test. If, however, the fall in the price of x from p_1 to p_2 is split into two stages at least – from p_1 to p_1' and then from p_1' to p_2 – and the rise in the price of y is treated similarly, the Kaldor–Hicks test can then be met. This discovery Winch called the nibble paradox.

This result arises because B's apparent gain, as measured by his CV, appears to be larger for a price fall when it is split into two stages. Assuming the same positive income effect for good y, the reverse is true for person A's loss as measured by his CV. But concentration on B alone will enable us to resolve this paradox, by showing that the splitting of the price change into two stages is not of itself enough to generate it. What is crucial to the paradox is the tacit supposition that accompanies this process, and effectively alters the question being asked of B.

Figure 3 shows B's ordinary demand curve for x, DD, cut by three compensated demand curves (or 'marginal indifference curves'); I' corresponding to B's welfare level when he can buy x at p_1, I'' corresponding to his welfare level when he can buy x at p_1' and I''' corresponding to his welfare level when he can buy x at p_2.

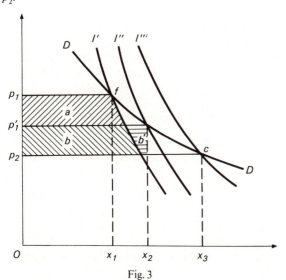

Fig. 3

For a straight fall from p_1 to p_2, B's gain as measured by his CV is equal to the area a plus the area b. Since his income effect is positive, however, the welfare gain from the fall in the price to p_2 shifts his compensated demand curve to the right, to I''', as a result of which he purchases Ox_3 of x. If, now, the price falls from p_1 but only as far as p_1', B's CV is equal to the area a alone. As a result of the welfare gain, his compensated demand curve shifts to I'', and he buys Ox_2 of x. If the price is now lowered the rest of the way to p_2, the resulting CV as measured by reference to I'' is equal to the area b plus area b'.

Apparently, then, his CV is larger when the price fall is taken in two stages rather than one. Indeed, the CV can be made to look larger still if the price fall is split up into more stages – in the limiting case being equal to the area under the demand curve, $p_1 p_2 cf$.

How does this 'paradox' arise? Once the price falls from p_1 to p_1', and the CV is equal to area a, we are ready for the next stage. But if the most that person B will pay for the remainder of the price fall, p_1' to p_2, is to be reckoned as equal to the areas b and b', we are effectively acknowledging that the question B is to answer in contemplating the full change from p_1 to p_2 is no longer (1): what is the most B can afford to pay for the whole of the price fall to p_2 if he is to maintain his welfare level at I' when p_1 alone is available to him? Instead, two successive questions are put to B which together amount to a different question to (1); namely, (1a) what is the most B can afford to pay for a fall in price only to p_1' if he is to maintain his welfare level at I' when only p_1 is available? followed by (1b), what is the most B can now afford to pay for the fall in price from p_1' to p_2 *if he is to maintain the welfare level I'' enjoyed with the p_1' price?* The italicised clause is crucial, since it clearly does not feature in the (1) question.

However, the second question (1b) pertinent to the two-stage price fall may be revised to (1b') so that (1a) and (1b') together do give effect to question (1) and, therefore, together yield the same CV as question (1) does.

In order to discover this (1b') question, consider the following procedure. Let the price fall from p_1 to p_1'. B's CV from answering question (1a) is, again, equal to the area a. Now let person B be taxed the amount a. As a result B's welfare becomes exactly the same as it was originally, I' when he enjoyed price p_1 only. Back on his I' compensated demand curve, his CV for the fall from p_1' to p_2 is then exactly equal to area b.

The required (1b') question is therefore: what is the most B can afford to pay for the fall from p_1' to p_2 *if he is to maintain the original I' level of welfare associated with the original price p_1?*

Comparing the italicised clauses of (1b) and (1b'), it is manifest that it is the inadvertent recourse to question (1b) in determining the CV of the $p_1'p_2$ price fall, instead of question (1b'), that results in a larger CV for the two-stage price fall. For the sum of the CVs in answer to questions (1a) and (1b') is exactly equal to the CV in answer to question (1).

In short, for consistency of the CV measure irrespective of the number of stages into which a given price change is divided, the individual is required at each stage to pay (or receive) the sum of money necessary to restore his original level of welfare, in this way continuing to derive the CV measure by reference to the original I' compensated demand curve.

B. *The alleged superiority of the EV measure.* According to Hause, 'the main theoretical blemish of the CV is that it may fail to order correctly ... the relative desirability of three or more bundles' (1975, p. 1150). The statement is easily illustrated.

From the formal definition of the EV in section I we may infer that, diagrammatically, the vertical EV distances along the y axis arise from its intersection by price lines that are parallel to y_0p_0 and tangent to the reference indifference curve. The higher the indifference curve I_i the higher the price line parallel to p_0 and the higher the EV measure y_iy_0. In Figure 1, for example, the I_1 curve is reached either by the budget line y_0p_1 or by a budget line y_4p_4 (a higher income than y_0 but a higher price than p_0 also). Nonetheless, the EV measure for each is exactly equal to y_2y_0, as it should be.

In contrast, the CV measure is taken by reference to whatever the new budget line happens to be. Thus in Figure 1, the CV measures of these alternative budget lines y_0p_1 and y_4p_4, both of which yield the same increment of welfare (I_1-I_0), are markedly different, being y_0y_1 and y_4y_3 respectively.

Perhaps the following simplified example will put the logic of the matter in bolder relief. A person having \$100 of income is faced with two choices, (a) all prices halved with constant money income, or (b) money income doubled with prices constant. Under familiar assumptions he should be indifferent between them. But for (a) the CV measure is 50 (the most he would pay for the halving of prices), whereas for (b) the CV measure is 100 (the most he would pay for the doubling of his money income).

This difference in the two CVs arises clearly because in (b) money is worth less (in fact exactly half) in terms of goods than it is in (a). In (b), that is, we have a relative 'inflation effect' – money prices higher in (b) than in (a) – which, therefore 'inflates' the CV. This 'inflation effect' is removed by the definition of EV which implies

that the person does not receive either (a) the price fall or (b) the income rise. He receives only a sum which, along with his original income and prices, leaves him with the equivalent gain in welfare. Thus for (a) the EV measure is 100 (the sum he must receive to induce him to go without the price fall), and for (b) the EV measure is also 100 (the sum he must receive to induce him to go without the income rise).

In a cost-benefit calculation, however, the alternatives being ranked are commonly that of a fall in the price of a good, or of its introduction by the project in question, and that of not introducing the project. Thus, possible perversities in individual CV rankings will not show up. For the actual measurements of the welfare changes are not derived from indifference maps, individual or communal. In practice, market demand curves are used for deriving consumer surplus measurements of price changes (in the estimation of which errors of measurement are, as indicated, likely to swamp differences between the true EV and CV measurements). And possible increases or decreases in money incomes directly associated with the project will, in practice, also be measured separately – again, *not* as part of a CV or an EV measure derived from sets of individual indifference surfaces.

Mathematical Note

Symbols

$u_i \quad = \dfrac{\partial x_i}{\partial u}$ where $u(x_i, \ldots, x_n)$ is the individual's utility function.

x_i, x_j = quantities of goods i and j purchased by the individual.

p_i, p_j = prices of goods i and j that face the individual.

$Y \quad$ = money income of the individual.

$\lambda \quad$ = Lagrange multiplier (equals $\dfrac{\partial u}{\partial Y}$, the marginal utility of money income).

$$U = \begin{vmatrix} u_{11} & u_{12} & \ldots & u_{1n} & p_1 \\ u_{21} & & \ldots & & p_2 \\ & & & & \cdot \\ & & & & \cdot \\ & & & & \cdot \\ u_{n1} & & \ldots & & p_n \\ p_1 & p_2 & \ldots & p_n & 0 \end{vmatrix}$$

U_{ij} is the cofactor of the element in the ith row and jth column. Since $u_{ij} = u_{ji}$, $U_{ij} = U_{ji}$.

A Path Independence

When a number of price-changes take place, a necessary and sufficient condition for the sum of the resulting consumer surpluses, measured with respect to the individual's demand curves, to remain the same irrespective of the order in which the surpluses are added, is $\frac{\partial x_i}{\partial p_j} = \frac{\partial x_j}{\partial p_i}$. (Whether, along the demand curves the level of utility or that of money income is held constant.)

(a) If the fundamental Slutsky–Hicks equation is written

$$\left(\frac{\partial x_i}{\partial p_j}\right)_{Y\,=\,\text{constant}} = \left(\frac{\partial x_i}{\partial p_j}\right)_{U\,=\,\text{constant}} - x_j\frac{\partial x_i}{\partial Y} \qquad (1)$$

then, since the Hicksian definitions of CV and EV always have reference to compensated demand curves (i.e. to those for which the level of utility is held constant), the relevant necessary and sufficient condition for path independence is

$$\left(\frac{\partial x_i}{\partial p_j}\right)_{U\,=\,\text{constant}} = \left(\frac{\partial x_j}{\partial p_i}\right)_{U\,=\,\text{constant}} \qquad (2)$$

But equation (2) itself is a property of the Hicksian system (see his appendix, p. 310), and therefore the condition is automatically met for his CV and EV definitions.

(b) The Marshallian measure of consumer's surplus is generally interpreted to have reference to a demand curve for which the level of money income is held constant. The relevant necessary and sufficient condition for path independence is therefore that

$$\left(\frac{\partial x_i}{\partial p_j}\right)_{Y\,=\,\text{constant}} = \left(\frac{\partial x_j}{\partial p_i}\right)_{Y\,=\,\text{constant}} \qquad (3)$$

(i) From equations (1) and (2), this condition (3) requires

$$x_j\frac{\partial x_i}{\partial Y} = x_i\frac{\partial x_j}{\partial Y}$$

or

$$\frac{\partial x_i}{\partial Y}\cdot\frac{Y}{x_i} = \frac{\partial x_j}{\partial Y}\cdot\frac{Y}{x_j} \qquad (4)$$

which requires that income elasticities of demand be the same for all goods whose prices have changed.

If there is to be path independence for any set of price changes, then the income elasticities for all goods must be the same, and therefore each income elasticity must be equal to unity. A utility function having this property must be homothetic – each indifference curve being, therefore, a radial extension of any indifference curve.

(ii) An alternative implication of the equation (3) requirement, in terms now of $\frac{\partial\lambda}{\partial p}$ (for Y constant), is obtained from the equation

$$\frac{\partial(\lambda x_i)}{\partial p_j} = \frac{\partial(\lambda x_j)}{\partial p_i} \qquad (5)[14]$$

$$\therefore \lambda\frac{\partial x_i}{\partial p_j} + x_i\frac{\partial\lambda}{\partial p_j} = \lambda\frac{\partial x_j}{\partial p_i} + x_j\frac{\partial\lambda}{\partial p_i} \qquad (6)$$

The requirement

$$\left(\frac{\partial x_i}{\partial p_j}\right)_{Y=\text{constant}} = \left(\frac{\partial x_j}{\partial p_i}\right)_{Y=\text{constant}}$$

implies therefore that

$$x_i\frac{\partial\lambda}{\partial p_j} = x_j\frac{\partial\lambda}{\partial p_i} \qquad (7)$$

is a necessary and sufficient condition for path independence, and equation (7) implies and is implied by equation (4).

Therefore $\frac{\partial\lambda}{\partial p_j} = \frac{\partial\lambda}{\partial p_i} = 0$ is a special case of equation (7) and a sufficient (though not necessary) condition for path independence.

B The Relation Between Marginal Utility of Money and the Income Effect

(a) In a 'cardinal' system $U = u(x_1, \ldots, x_n)$.

Following the procedure of Hicks's appendix we derive the equation

$$\frac{\partial\lambda}{\partial p_i} = -\lambda^2\frac{U_i}{U} + \lambda^2 x_i\frac{U_0}{U}$$

But since

$$\frac{U_i}{\lambda U} = \frac{\partial x_i}{\partial Y}, \text{ and } \frac{U_0}{\lambda^2 U} = \frac{\partial\lambda}{\partial Y}$$

we can write this as

$$\frac{\partial\lambda}{\partial p_i} + x_i\frac{\partial\lambda}{\partial Y} = -\lambda\frac{\partial x_i}{\partial Y}. \qquad (8)$$

(i) Clearly, if $\frac{\partial\lambda}{\partial p_i} = -\frac{\partial\lambda}{\partial Y}$, then $\frac{\partial x_i}{\partial Y} = 0$.

(ii) In particular, if $\dfrac{\partial \lambda}{\partial p_i} = \dfrac{\partial \lambda}{\partial Y} = 0$, then $\dfrac{\partial x_i}{\partial Y} = 0$.

(iii) However, if $\dfrac{\partial \lambda}{\partial p_i} = 0$, and $\dfrac{\partial \lambda}{\partial Y} \neq 0$, then $\dfrac{\partial x_i}{\partial Y} \neq 0$.

Since Marshall's exact measure of consumer surplus requires only that $\dfrac{\partial \lambda}{\partial p_i} = 0$, this requirement, if met, does not of itself imply a zero income effect for good x_i.

In general, for a *fall* in p_i $EV \gtreqless CV$ according as $\dfrac{\partial x_i}{\partial Y} \gtreqless 0$ (but *not* according as $\dfrac{\partial \lambda}{\partial p_i} \lesseqgtr 0$, since as stated above, there is no necessary relation between $\dfrac{\partial x_i}{\partial Y}$ and $\dfrac{\partial \lambda}{\partial p_i}$.

(b) We show now that if $\dfrac{\partial \lambda}{\partial Y}, \dfrac{\partial \lambda}{\partial p_i} \gtreqless 0$ in the preceding cardinal system, then $\dfrac{\partial \lambda'}{\partial Y}, \dfrac{\partial \lambda'}{\partial p_i}$ not necessarily $\gtreqless 0$, where λ' is the Lagrange multiplier (or marginal utility of money corresponding to any monotonic transform of the cardinal utility function).

(i) If we maximise $u(x_1, \ldots, x_m)$ subject to $\Sigma\, px = Y$, necessary conditions include

$$u_i = \lambda p_i \quad \left(\text{where } \lambda = \frac{\partial u}{\partial Y}\right) \tag{9}$$

Taking the differential of equation (1), $du_i = d(\lambda p_i)$, and expanding gives equation

$$\sum_i u_{ii} \frac{\partial x_j}{\partial Y} = p_i \frac{\partial \lambda}{\partial Y} \tag{10}$$

since $p_i > 0$ $\dfrac{\partial \lambda}{\partial Y} \gtreqless 0$ entails $\sum_i u_{ij} \dfrac{\partial x_j}{\partial Y} \gtreqless 0$.

(ii) Now maximise $w[u(x_i, \ldots, x_n)]$ subject to $\Sigma p_x = Y$. Necessary conditions include

$$w_i = \lambda' p_i \tag{11}$$

where $w_i \equiv w'\, u_i$ and $\lambda' = w'\lambda$.

Again, taking differentials and expanding as above, we have

$$\sum_i w_{ij} \frac{\partial x_j}{\partial Y} = p_i \frac{\partial \lambda'}{\partial Y} \tag{12}$$

Since $w_i = w'u_i$, $w_{ij} = w'u_{ij} + w''u_i u_j$.
Therefore, equation (12) can be written

$$w'\sum_i u_{ij} \frac{\partial x_j}{\partial Y} + w''u_i \sum_i u_j \frac{\partial x_j}{\partial Y} = p_i \frac{\partial \lambda'}{\partial Y} \tag{13}$$

(1) First, let $\dfrac{\partial \lambda}{\partial Y} = 0$, so that from equation (10) above, $\Sigma_i\, u_{ij} \dfrac{\partial x_j}{\partial Y} = 0$ and equation (13) becomes

$$w''u_i \sum_i u_j \frac{\partial x_j}{\partial Y} = p_i \tag{14}$$

Only if the left hand side of equation (14) is zero will $\dfrac{\partial \lambda'}{\partial Y}$ also be zero.

However, u_i, $u_j \neq 0$, and $\Sigma\, \dfrac{\partial x_j}{\partial Y} \neq 0$, and w'' is zero *only* if the monotone transform $w(u)$ is also a linear transform, $w = \alpha + \beta u$ which restriction cannot be assured,

therefore $\dfrac{\partial \lambda}{\partial Y} = 0$ does not entail $\dfrac{\partial \lambda'}{\partial Y} = 0$.

By similar methods we can also show that $\dfrac{\partial \lambda}{\partial p_i} = 0$ does not entail $\dfrac{\partial \lambda'}{\partial p_i} = 0$.

(2) Secondly, let $\dfrac{\partial \lambda}{\partial Y} > 0$, so that from equation (10) above, $\Sigma_i\, u_{ij} \dfrac{\partial x_j}{\partial Y} > 0$. Thus the first component of equation (13) is positive. But since a w can be chosen to produce a w'' that is negative and as large (absolutely) as desired, the left hand side of equation (13) can be made negative and, therefore, $\dfrac{\partial \lambda'}{\partial Y}$ also.

Mutatis mutandi, with $\dfrac{\partial \lambda}{\partial Y} < 0$, a w can be chosen so that $\dfrac{\partial \lambda'}{\partial Y} > 0$.

By similar methods we can also show that $\dfrac{\partial \lambda}{\partial p_i} > 0$ does not necessarily entail $\dfrac{\partial \lambda'}{\partial p_i} > 0$, and $\dfrac{\partial \lambda}{\partial p_i} < 0$ does not necessarily entail $\dfrac{\partial \lambda'}{\partial p_i} < 0$.

Notes: Chapter 6

1 Those in the better known journals include Burns (1973), Currie *et al.* (1971), Foster and Neuberger (1974), Glaister (1974), Harberger (1971), Hause (1975), Mohring (1971), Silberberg (1972) and Winch (1965).

2 It is possible, formally, for the *CV* or the *EV* measure to be

expressed either as a flow or as a stock, and either in terms of money or in terms of any commodity or group of commodities at fixed prices (or in fixed proportions).

3 In general, an indefinite number of consumer's surplus measurements can be produced from the Hicksian categories simply by imposing quantity constraints on the individual. Hicks (1944) suggested two, a CV with a quantity constraint equal to the amount bought after the price change, and an EV with a quantity constraint equal to amount bought before the price change. There may, of course, be circumstances in which these quantity-constrained CV and EV measures are appropriate, but they are not important enough to warrant diagrammatic exposition. The interested reader can consult my 1960 survey.

4 A detailed treatment of rent as a CV or EV measure of welfare change can be found in my 1959 paper.

5 This being the impression conveyed also by Burns's recent paper (1973, p. 341).

6 Indeed, Hicks (1942, pp. 131–2) develops a CV and EV formula for a simultaneous change in n prices (assuming straight line demand curves over the relevant range) without mention of path-dependence.

7 A simple treatment of this analysis, extended also to non-constant supply curves, can be found in Mishan (1976a).

8 The reader who is uncertain about the analysis should consult my 1960 survey.

9 This is easily seen if we write

$$\Delta Y = \int_{U_0^*}^{U_1^*} \frac{1}{\lambda} \ (U^*) \, dU^*,$$

where U_0^* and U_1^* are two different optimal levels of utility corresponding to two different sets of prices with constant money income. If $1/\lambda$ (say, dollars per util) is independent of U^* $(p_1, \ldots, p_n)$, the term $1/\lambda$ being a constant can be placed outside the integral, whence ΔY is directly related to $(U_1^* - U_0^*)$. The constancy of $1/\lambda$, however, is sufficient but not necessary for path independence (see Mathematical Note, equation (7)).

10 Since I am concerned here solely with consumer surplus, I ignore Harberger's treatment of 'producer surplus' which does not face up to the difficulties I pointed out in 1968.

11 'It would be nice', concludes Silberberg wistfully (1972, p. 951), 'if there were always a unique one-to-one correspondence between utility changes and money changes … However it is simply not so.'

For the guidance of the more specialised reader, I should add that Silberberg reaches this conclusion from concentrating, for the most part, on the Marshallian concept of consumer surplus. Morever, his terminology may confuse the student. For his so-called 'equivalent variations' have no affinity with the Hicksian EVs as correctly described in the test of this paper. According to Silberberg, they 'can be thought of as a generalisation of the area under the demand curve' (p. 943). And he sets out to show that such 'equivalent variations' will in fact 'depend upon a particular path of price … change' (p. 943). In short, Silberberg's 'equivalent variations' are no more than equivalent money sums of a Marshallian (constant money income) consumer surplus area, all of which, we agree, can differ – unless path independence is ensured by a homothetic utility function.

12 Since equation (4) in the Mathematical Note implies and is implied by equation (7).

13 As is well known by practitioners in this field of allocation economics, a choice as between the CV and the EV measure can be important if relative prices change sufficiently. There is, however, also a danger of detecting 'paradoxes' where none exists and of overstating difficulties which, though conceivable, may never occur. *Caveats* against these temptations are sounded in my 1976b paper.

14 The proof is given in Silberberg (1972, p. 947), but for completeness we can restate it as follows. From Hicks's appendix we know that

$$\left(\frac{\partial x_j}{\partial p_i}\right)_{Y=\text{constant}} = \frac{-\lambda U_{ij} - x_i \, U_{n+1, j}}{U} \ (i, j = 1, \ldots, n) \quad \text{(a)}$$

and

$$\left(\frac{\partial \lambda}{\partial p_i}\right)_{Y=\text{constant}} = \frac{-\lambda U_{i, \, n+1} - x_i \, U_{n+1, \, n+1}}{U} \quad \text{(b)}$$

Now

$$\frac{(\partial \lambda x_j)}{\partial p_i} = \lambda \frac{\partial x_j}{\partial p_i} + x_j \frac{\partial \lambda}{\partial p_i} \quad \text{(c)}$$

Substituting from equations (a) and (b), we rewrite equation (c) as

$$\frac{\partial (\lambda x_j)}{\partial p_i} = \lambda \left(\frac{-\lambda U_{ij} - x_i \, U_{n+1, j}}{U}\right) + x_j \left(\frac{-\lambda U_{i, \, n+1} - x_i \, U_{n+1, \, n+1}}{U}\right) \quad \text{(d)}$$

or

$$\frac{\partial (\lambda \, x_j)}{\partial p_i} = -\lambda \, U_{ij} - \lambda \, x_i \, U_{n+1, \, j} - \lambda \, x_j U_{i, \, n+1} - x_j \, x_i \, U_{n+1, \, n+1} \quad \text{(e)}$$

Similarly, we can show that

$$\frac{\partial (\lambda \, x_i)}{\partial p_j} = \lambda \, U_{ji} - \lambda \, x_j U_{n+1, \, i} - \lambda \, x_i \, U_{j, \, n+1} - x_i x_j \, U_{n+1, n+1} \quad \text{(f)}$$

Bearing in mind that $U_{ij} = U_{ji}$, it can be seen that the right hand sides of equations (e) and (f) are equal. Thus equation (5) in the test is shown to be true.

References

Burns, M. E., 'A note on the concept and measure of consumer's surplus', *American Economic Review*, vol. 63 (1973), pp. 335–44.

Currie, J. M., Murphy, J. A. and Schmitz, A., 'The concept of economic surplus, and its use in economic analysis', *Economic Journal*, vol. 81 (1971), pp. 741–99.

Foster, C. D. and Neuberger, H. L., 'The ambiguity of the consumer's surplus measure of welfare change', *Oxford Economic Papers*, vol. 26 (1974), pp. 66–77.

Friedman, M., 'The Marshallian demand curve', *Journal of Political Economy*, vol. 57 (1950), pp. 463-95.

Glaister, S., 'Generalised consumer surplus and public transport pricing', *Economic Journal*, vol. 83 (1974), pp. 849–67.

Harberger, A. C., 'Three basic postulates for applied welfare economics: an interpretive essay', *Journal of Economic Literature,* vol. 9 (1971), pp. 785–97.

Hause, J. C., 'The theory of welfare measurement', *Journal of Political Economy,* vol. 83 (1975), pp. 1145–82.

Hicks, J. R., 'Consumers' surplus and index numbers', *Review of Economic Studies,* vol. 9 (1942), pp. 126–37.

Hicks, J. R., 'The four consumers' surpluses', *Review of Economic Studies,* vol. 11 (1944), pp. 31–41.

Hicks, J. R., *Value and Capital,* 2nd edn (Oxford: Clarendon, 1948; first published 1939).

Hicks, J. R., *A Revision of Demand Theory* (Oxford: Clarendon, 1956).

Hicks, J. R. and Allen, R. G. D., 'A reconsideration of the theory of value', *Economica* (1934).

Marshall, A., *Principles of Economics*, 8th edn (London: Macmillan, 1920).

Mishan, E. J., 'Rent as a measure of welfare change', *American Economic Review,* vol. 49 (1959), pp. 386-95.

Mishan, E. J., 'A survey of welfare economics', *Economic Journal,* vol. 70 (1960), pp. 197–265.

Mishan, E. J., 'What is producer's surplus?', *American Economic Review,* vol. 58 (1968), pp. 1269–82.

Mishan, E. J. (1976a), *Cost-Benefit Analysis* (New York, 1976).

Mishan, E. J. (1976b), 'The use of compensating and equivalent variations in cost–benefit analysis', *Economica,* vol. 43 (1976), pp. 185–97.

Mohring, H., 'Alternative welfare gain and loss measures', *Western Economic Journal,* vol. 9 (1971), pp. 349–68.

Samuelson, P. A., *Foundations of Economic Analysis* (Cambridge, Mass., 1955), chs 7 and 8.
Economics and Econometrics (Chicago, 1942).

Samuelson, P. A., *Foundations of Economic Analysis* Cambridge, Mass., 1955). chs 7 and 8.

Silberberg, E., 'Duality and the many consumer's surpluses', *American Economic Review,* vol. 62 (1972), pp. 942–52.

Winch, D. M., 'Consumer's surplus and the compensation principle', *American Economic Review,* vol. 55 (1965), pp. 395–423.

7

Rent as a Measure of Welfare Change

The definitions of economic rent in current use fall easily into two categories: (1) a payment in excess of that necessary to maintain a resource in its current occupation. Thus, Frederick Benham[1] tells us that rents are 'the sums paid to the factors which need not be paid in order to retain the factors *in the industry*'. While to Kenneth Boulding[2] it is the payment to a factor 'in excess of the minimum amount necessary to keep that factor in its present occupation'. The second category (2) is the difference between the current earnings of a resource and its transfer earnings[3] – the latter term signifying its earnings in the next best alternative use.[4] For instance, Paul Samuelson[5] says, 'we should term the excess of his income above the alternative wage he could earn elsewhere as *a pure rent*'. Similarly, for George Stigler[6] the rent of a factor is 'the excess of its return in the best use over its possible return in other uses'.[7]

While the first type of definition is, as we shall see, unavoidably ambiguous, the second type is yet more inadequate. Among other things it would require that, in the choice of occupation, men were motivated solely by pecuniary considerations.

I   A Measure of Rent as an Economic Surplus

For the purpose of revealing ambiguities in the existing definitions of economic rent and of demonstrating the logic of the proposed definition, we shall find it no less convenient and a good deal more suggestive to take our bearings from a more generalized version of the traditional theory of consumer's choice.

Rather than maximizing the utility function $W[u(x_1, \ldots, x_n)]$, over the range in which $\partial W/\partial x_r > 0$ for all x_r, subject to the usual constraint $\Sigma p_r x_r = Y$, where Y is the individual's income,[8] we require our individual, in possession of given resources, or assets, to maximize such a function subject to $\Sigma p_r x_r = 0$. At least one of the xs is negative in order to indicate a quantity supplied per

period by the individual of a good or service and, of course, at least one of the xs is positive to indicate a quantity demanded per period of a good or service. The suggested constraint expresses nothing more than the proposition that, in all circumstances, the individual's current earnings are equal to the current value of his expenditure.[9] It is a significant amendment, however, because it brings to the fore the notion of simultaneous determination of the individual's allocation of his productive services and of his earnings in response to a given pattern of prices: an obvious point perhaps, but one frequently ignored in the analysis of the individual's demand and supply curves.

Maximizing the utility function subject to our new constraint, we derive the well-known equilibrium condition $\partial W/\partial x_r = \lambda p_r$ (λ being identified as the marginal utility of income) for all goods and services whether their magnitudes are positive or negative – whether, that is, they are demanded or supplied by the individual.[10] Or, dispensing with utility, we can write $\partial x_i/\partial x_j = p_j/p_i$ for any i and j.

It should be apparent that, although the substitution effect may be defined in the customary way, there can be no income effect, $\partial x_r/\partial Y$, since there is no necessary correspondence, using our new constraint, between changes in the individual's welfare and changes in his income, real or money. For with the new constraint, money income, Y, is no longer held constant; it is determined along with all the other variables. It may increase, remain unchanged, or diminish, with an improvement in the individual's welfare. In its place, therefore, we derive a *welfare* effect, $\partial x_r/\partial W$. In consequence, the effect on the quantity bought or sold of any chosen good or service of a given change in the set of prices is divided into a substitution effect and a welfare effect.

The implications of this less-restricted formulation, though straightforward enough, are worth recording. A change in the price of any good or service – whether it is supplied or demanded by the individual – changes, in general, the quantities of all goods and services which the individual buys and sells. Consequently it changes the value of his earnings and expenditure. A search for a useful definition of an 'incentive good' might begin with the implication that a fall in the price of any consumed good will, *inter alia,* increase or reduce the amount of work done by the individual as a result of the operation of the welfare effect. But this will not be pursued here.

Having extended the customary confines of the theory of consumer's choice we may now develop the argument largely in terms of two or three goods or services, but deriving from our hypothesis a more symmetrical construction of the individual indifference map. Since $\Sigma p_r x_r = 0$, the price hyperplane passes through the origin of an *n*-dimensional indifference map and is negative in slope with respect to all the axes. This means that in order to acquire (or surrender) more of one good or service, other goods or services must be surrendered (or acquired).

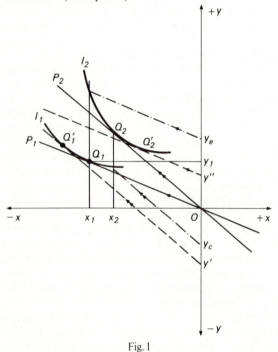

Fig. 1

A two-dimensional cross-section of this indifference map is represented in Figure 1. Any distance Ox to the right of the origin measures amount per unit period of x acquired by the individual. Any distance Ox to the left of the origin measures the amount of x per period given up by the individual. Similarly, Oy above the origin measures the quantity of y taken, and Oy below the origin, the quantity of y given up. Inasmuch as rent partakes of the nature of a surplus, and is to be measured in

exactly the same way as consumers' surplus is measured, it is advantageous to consider in some detail the simple problem of the individual supplying x, say a single type of productive service, 'labor', to the market in return for which y is demanded. Thus, we operate in the northwestern quadrant of the figure. And though we may not do so in an *n*-dimensional treatment of the problem, confined as we are to two dimensions, we may find it convenient to regard y as all other goods at fixed prices, the only price which alters being the price of x, labor.[11] We now seek a precise measure of the difference in welfare resulting from alternative supply prices of labor.

If we construct a price-line P_1 passing through the origin and tangent to Q_1 on the indifference curve I_1, the individual is represented as in equilibrium, giving up Ox_1 of labor and acquiring in exchange Oy_1 of income y. We now perform the familiar Hicksian experiment in order to have the supply effects on all fours with those of demand. The price of x is now increased from p_1 to p_2, the individual's new equilibrium being at Q_2 on the indifference curve I_2. The change in equilibrium positions consequent upon the change in the price of labor may be divided into the substitution effect, Q_1 to Q_1', and the welfare effect, Q_1' to Q_2 (or alternatively the welfare effect Q_1 to Q_2' and the substitution effect Q_2' to Q_2). Although the welfare effect can, of course, go either way, it should be noticed that a positive welfare effect on x, implying an increase in the *demand* for x, constitutes a reduction in its supply, which is to say that a positive or 'normal' welfare effect of a rise in the supply price of labor, or in the supply price of any good or service, is that of a reduction in the quantity supplied by the individual. The 'backward-bending' supply curve of labor is, then, the outcome of a strong positive, or normal, welfare effect, and not a negative, or perverse, welfare effect.

Suppose we are now to measure the increase in welfare following a rise in the price of x to p_2, we may follow Hicks's practice[12] and distinguish between two preliminary measures: the compensating variation (CV), and the equivalent variation (EV). The CV is the amount of y which, following a change in the price of x, has to be given to or taken from the individual in order that his initial welfare – indicated by the indifference curve I_1 in Figure 1 – remain unchanged. In this instance, the individual's welfare being improved as a result of the price change, Oy' measures the CV. For if Oy' were taken from his income he could still maintain his initial welfare position on I_1, given that the higher supply price P_2 is available to him. The EV, on the other hand, is the amount of y which has to be given to, or taken from, the individual to ensure that he reaches the new level of welfare when the change in price does not apply to him. Since in this instance the increment in welfare is positive he is to receive a money equivalent. If he receives Oy'' he can just reach I_2, the new level of welfare, with the old price P_1.

The concept of rent as an economic surplus, it is suggested here, should be measured as a CV or an EV in a manner symmetrical in all respects with the concept of consumer's surplus. In the example above, it arises as the difference in welfare experienced by the individual from the rise in the supply price to P_2, P_1 being regarded as the most preferred alternative open to him.[13] The rent obviously becomes larger the lower the initial supply price P_1. In the limiting case, P_1 will be a no-transactions price tangent to an indifference curve at the point where it crosses the vertical axis.

Since the current definitions treat rent as a surplus which may be appropriated without any effects on the supply of the individual's productive services in his current occupation, it is important to observe that in all cases in which the individual is made to pay or to receive compensation equal to the measures of rent suggested, the amount of the productive service he will then offer will differ from that which he originally supplied at the current price. For example, if, having reached Q_2 in Figure 1, he is made to pay the full CV, equal to Oy', he will no longer continue to supply Ox_2 of labor. Instead he will supply the amount indicated by the equilibrium point Q_1' – a larger amount than before if x is normal.

Finally it may be instructive to remove the restriction of a single occupation in our analysis and to consider briefly the case of the supply of productive services to two alternative occupations, A and B, in which, although the individual might choose to work part-time in each if that were feasible, he is obliged, owing to institutional arrangements, to work entirely in the one occupation or the other.

In Figure 2, a three-dimensional indifference map with a vertical y-axis and two horizontal axes, a and b, crossing at right angles, we cut a vertical slice along the negative ay plane and along the negative by plane as far as the y-axis and remove the segment. Hence, if we imagine our figure divided vertically into four quarters, we shall be looking into the space left after the removal of the vertical quarter in which a and b are both negative. The upper part of what meets the eye is represented in Figure 2. By removing the vertical quarter referred to, we have removed the possibility of combining employment A and B.

Despite the fact that both the rate of pay and the resultant earnings are higher in A than in B, the individual chooses to supply his services to B, his

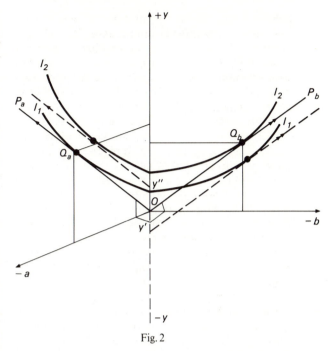

Fig. 2

equilibrium there being at Q_b on the indifference surface I_2 compared with the alternative equilibrium position Q_a on I_1. Nonetheless, he enjoys a positive economic rent in the lower-paid occupation B which can be measured by the CV, Oy' – the maximum he is prepared to pay to remain in B when A, at the existing wage-rate, is the only alternative open to him. It can also be measured by the EV, Oy'' – the minimum the individual must be paid in order to induce him to transfer his services from B to A.[14]

II Comparison with the Marshallian Concept

Let us now compare our results with Marshall's concept of rent. Though the *Principles* do not contain a formal definition of rent, the sense of most of Marshall's dicta on the subject points to a definition of rent as a surplus above that necessary to elicit the productive services of a resource.[15] This Marshallian definition, essentially that of category (1), suffers from the same imprecision as his definition of consumer's surplus.[16] For one thing, the surplus was treated as if it could be taxed away without affecting the supply of the productive service, which is manifestly false on our analysis. Once this is granted the difficulties are easily perceived. In order to persist with the Marshallian definition we have to interpret it to have reference to some unchanged amount of the productive service;

either (a) the amount supplied in the equilibrium position resulting from the price change (Ox_2 in Figure 1), or (b) that supplied in the original equilibrium position (Ox_1 in Figure 1). In either case we are saddled with an improbable and cumbersome measure inasmuch as we have to compel the individual to supply an amount of the productive service other than that which he would freely choose. For instance, if we adopt (a) we derive what may be called, for convenience, the Marshallian CV, equal to Oy_c. It represents the maximum amount of money the individual would surrender in order to retain P_2 if at the same time he were constrained to provide no more than Ox_2 of productive service – Ox_2 being the amount supplied at P_2 when he is free to choose. As we should expect, the restriction on his choice of quantity reduces the maximum he is prepared to pay for the privilege of the P_2 price. In a like manner, if we adopt (b), the Marshallian EV, we are left with a measure Oy_e. It is larger than the EV proper, Oy'', since the minimum payment to him must be greater if he is now compelled to provide the original quantity of productive services Ox_1 at the original price P_1 when his welfare is increased from I_1 to I_2. There is obviously nothing strictly illogical about such definitions, but on the grounds of plausibility and convenience they are to be rejected in favor of the CV and EV proper.

If, on the other hand, a Marshallian *measure* of economic rent is taken to be the area above the supply curve of the services of the individual's resource[17] – a measure which seems to correspond with the category (2) definition if the individual's supply curve represents maximum earnings of successive increments of productive services in alternative uses – for this measure to be of any use requires (i) an upward-sloping supply curve and (ii) exclusion of nonpecuniary considerations. Clearly this Marshallian measure, which is popular in textbooks, is inadequate since it represents no more than a first derivative of the locus of price-quantity equilibria of an indifference map. Nor is this derivative necessarily upward-sloping; it may be backward-bending in contrast to the *marginal* indifference curves which will always be upward-sloping. It appears yet more unsatisfactory if the restriction to pecuniary considerations is removed. We may then discover that differences between the earnings of the resource in its current occupation and those of the relevant alternative occupation are negative, a tribute to the individual's preference for his present occupation.

Hicks has done some admirable work in tracing the relationships between Marshall's definition of consumer's surplus, Marshall's way of measuring con-

sumer's surplus (the area under the individual's demand curve), and the two precise measures CV and EV which were initially suggested by his indifference curve analysis. Important as these contributions were in clarifying our ideas on this tangled subject, it can be held that the tracing of these precise relationships assumes a far greater importance on the neglected supply side. For it is surely just there that we cannot reasonably suppose that change in price has negligible effects on the welfare of the individual inasmuch as the supply of any one of his productive services enters significantly into his budget. To the extent it does so, the area above the individual's supply curve, especially in the case of only one productive service, is a much less reliable index of the surplus welfare than the area under his demand curve for any one good.

In the special case in which the welfare elasticity of the supply of x is zero there is a coincidence of the CV, EV, Marshallian CV, Marshallian EV, and the Marshallian measure, the area above the supply curve. (This same coincidence obtains when the rent is reckoned as between the current and alternative occupations in the case in which the choice between occupations rests on a purely pecuniary basis.) While in general, a zero elasticity of supply with respect to price does not entail a zero welfare elasticity, in the particular case in which the former derives from a zero substitutability *plus a zero welfare elasticity,* these four definitions and the Marshallian measure all come to the same thing. The zero substitutability implies no alternative uses and therefore a set of vertical *marginal* indifference curves. The zero welfare elasticity implies that all the marginal indifference curves will coincide. Ricardian land is a favorite example of a zero elasticity of supply of this sort. Its characteristic is that it has only one use, say wheat production. As a consequence of this characteristic (i) it cannot move elsewhere in response to changes in relative prices (zero substitution effect), and therefore (ii) *all* of a given acreage of land of uniform quality is brought into wheat production in response to any positive price per acre (zero welfare effect).[18]

III   Conclusion

Little further reflection is required to recognize that consumer's surplus and economic rent are both measures of the change in the individual's welfare when the set of prices facing him are changed or the constraints imposed upon him are altered. Any distinction between them is one of convenience only: consumer's surpluses have reference to demand prices, economic rent to supply prices. Furthermore, no consideration of logic precludes our measuring the individual's gain – in terms either of the *CV* or the *EV* – from, say, a simultaneous fall in the price of a good bought and a rise in the price of a service provided.

Indeed, in general, if any one, several, or even all prices change for the individual, some demand prices and some supply prices rising, others falling, the resulting change in the individual's welfare can, in principle, be measured by either of our definitions. The *CV* is an exact measure of the transfer, to or from the individual, following a change in the set of all prices, in order to maintain his initial level of welfare. In this case the amount transferred is measured in terms of any one good, in combinations of various goods, or in a combination of all goods dealt in, always using the *new* set of prices. This is quite possible since, given a set of prices, the amount of any one good is equivalent in value to various combinations of some particular goods or of all goods. More usefully, an amount of money calculated at the given set of prices will suffice to measure the *CV*.

On the other hand, the *EV* is an exact measure of the transfer necessary to bring the individual's level of welfare into equality with what it would have been if he were not, as he is, debarred from the new set of prices. The amount of the transfer is now calculated at the *old* prices, and may be expressed in money or in any combination of goods at these prices.

Notes: Chapter 7

1 F. Benham, *Economics* (London: Pitman, 1945), p. 227.
2 K. Boulding, *Economic Analysis* (New York: Harper & Row, 1948), p. 230.
3 To impart precision to this measure of economic rent the period of adjustment should be specified, as should, also, the area of comparison – within the industry, region, country, or within the world as a whole. But since the inadequacy of this definition of rent prevails irrespective of these distinctions, I shall make no further mention of them in this chapter.
4 Benham, op. cit., p. 328.
5 P. A. Samuelson, *Economics* (New York: McGraw-Hill, 1951), p. 593.
6 G. J. Stigler, *The Theory of Price* (New York: Macmillan, 1952), p. 99.
7 In all these cases the writers appear to be using 'factor' in the sense in which I shall use the term 'resource'. And though, generally, I prefer to reserve the term 'factor' for the productive service of the resource, it will avoid possible confusion if instead I adhere to the term 'productive service'.
8 J. R. Hicks, *Value and Capital* (Oxford: Clarendon, 1948), p. 305.
9 Strictly speaking his spending is equal to current earnings less current saving plus current dissaving. This could easily be allowed for without any modification of our conclusions. Over time, if his assets grow, his demand for goods and his disposal of productive services will, of course, alter. This problem is, however, common to all such static analysis.
10 Since we restrict ourselves to the range in which the marginal utilities of all goods and services are positive, the acquisition of goods and services from the individual's assets or resources subtracts from his total utility. Corresponding to the equilibrium conditions for goods purchased, the marginal utilities of the productive services supplied to the market are proportional to their corresponding supply prices.
11 This construction, and its later elaboration, are, I believe, to be preferred to the more common leisure–income diagram apart from the fact that the present diagram is derived directly from the more general condition in which the individual chooses to supply a combination of various goods and productive services to the market in amounts which depend upon the current set of prices: (1) Giving up leisure, a homogeneous good, does not have the same connotation as providing various kinds of services each of which requires a different skill and entails a different degree of hardship for the individual. (2) We need not evoke the artifice of a fixed amount of the good, leisure, say 24 hours a day, with the rather awkward result that an improvement in welfare may be represented along one axis as equivalent to more than 24 hours of leisure a day. In the construction used here, the shape of the indifference curves acts to limit the supply of any productive service furnished to the market, and our measure of welfare changes is in terms only of the good, *y*. Finally (3) the indifference map used here is the correct prior construction to that useful textbook diagram in which a downward-sloping line crosses the price-axis, to the right of which is represented the demand schedule and to the left, the supply schedule.
12 J. R. Hicks, *A Revision of Demand Theory* (Oxford: Clarendon, 1956), pp. 69–82.
13 Though we are working with a single productive service, labor, the notion and the definition of economic rent may, just as in the analysis of consumer's surplus, be extended to several services with obvious modifications. If, for example, the individual is providing two services, x_1 and x_2, then a rise in the supply price of both services yields a *CV* rent which is the maximum he is willing to pay – prices of all goods and services other than those of x_1 and x_2 remaining unchanged – rather than forgo these higher prices. This measure remains the same, as we might expect, if we measure each in turn and add them: the rent when the price of x_1 rises, all other prices, including that of x_2, being constant, plus the additional rent when now the price of x_2 rises, all other prices remaining constant with x_1 unchanged at its new price.

This argument is symmetrical with that of Hicks on consumer's surplus (op. cit., note 12, pp. 178–9), but the generalization on the conclusion of this paper goes further than Hicks's.
14 In all cases in which institutional arrangements preclude a combination of occupations – the individual having the choice only of putting the services of his resources entirely in *A* or in *B* – the coincidence of the four definitions and the Marshallian measure of rent no longer follow from a zero welfare elasticity, for the *EV* and the *CV* now arise from different cross-sections of the individual indifference map.

15 In particular see A. Marshall, *Principles of Economics,* 8th edn (London: Macmillan, 1920), pp. 155–62, 427–30. Elsewhere in the *Principles* Marshall talks of the additional earnings resulting from superior abilities as a surplus or rent (pp. 577–9), 623–7). What part of the additional earnings might be regarded as rent on the definition attributed to Marshall cannot be known without determining first what part of the additional earnings is necessary to attract the resource into that occupation. From the point of view of the firm, however, the additional payments for superior abilities must appear as efficiency payments.

16 ibid., p. 124. Marshall was, of course, aware of the slippery nature of his consumer's surplus (though not, apparently, of his economic rent) and tried to cover himself by specifying a change in the demand price for a particular good whose real-income effect was so small in relation to the individual's budget that the marginal utility of money income could be taken, for all practical purposes, as constant. The trouble with this is that it is double-edged: ambiguity is reduced by reducing the significance of what is being measured. Ambiguity disappears entirely only when the price change under consideration becomes zero and there is nothing left to measure.

17 ibid., p. 811. Here Marshall graphically illustrates consumer's surplus and producer's surplus for an *industry*. But even if we interpret the industry's supply curve as a marginal curve, the producer's surplus could be identified with the rent of resources in that industry only under restricted conditions. On the other hand, it would hardly be inconsistent with Marshall's view of things to interpret the measurement of the individual's rent in a manner symmetrical with his suggested measurement of the individual's consumer's surplus (pp. 125–7) as the area under the individual's demand curve.

18 The indifference curves in this special case would all be horizontal (signifying zero elasticity of substitution) up to a distance representing the maximum supply of productive service from the given resource. At this distance they would all become vertical and, hence, coincide. Rent however measured would, on this vertical limit, be equal to the vertical distance between the two price-lines in question.

8

What Is Producer's Surplus?

The term producer's surplus first appears in A. Marshall's *Principles of Economics* [**11,** p. 811, f. 2], taking shape as the area between the competitive equilibrium price and the supply curve, a curve that slopes upward as a result of placing the firms in order of diminishing efficiency. Thus the supply curve may be taken as a curve of marginal cost[1] for the industry with the producer's surplus derived therefrom being in the nature of a rent attributable ultimately to the specialized factors that initially confer differential advantages on the firms employing them. Discussing the term in connection with consumer's surplus in appendix K [**11,** pp. 830–1], Marshall appears to extend the term so as to comprehend all the surpluses a man derives as producer, including a 'worker's surplus' arising from the sale of his personal services and a 'saver's surplus' arising from the services of his capital.[2]

It is, of course, possible to introduce some refinement into these various forms of producer's surplus by reference to their spatial and temporal dimensions. A producer's surplus arising from the differential earnings of a special factor as between firms in a single industry is, in general, smaller than the differential earnings of the factor if instead the comparison is made between this industry and others, and this in turn is smaller than the relevant differential as between regions. As for temporal comparisons, the longer the period considered the smaller the rent – a particular instance being quasi-rent accruing to a firm's fixed capital in the Marshallian short period. But references to such refinements are incidental to the issue broached here; that turning on the validity of the concept of producer's surplus which remains in use in economics. It has been and continues to be regarded as a surplus accruing to the firm or industry, a concept commonly believed to be symmetric with, and commonly used in conjunction with, consumer's surplus. What is to be investigated then is the analytic status of producer's

surplus as a tool of partial welfare analysis especially in its application to competitive industry.

Let us prepare the way by revealing an ambiguity in the conception of producer's surplus arising out of an ambiguity in the construction of the supply curve.

I

In his *Principles of Public Finance*, Hugh Dalton derives an old-fashioned formula [**3**, p. 48], the ratio of the elasticity of demand to that of supply, for the burden of an excise tax on a competitive good as between buyers and sellers. This ratio is reckoned to be approximately equal to the ratio of the loss of consumer's surplus to the loss of producer's surplus. But whether this upward-sloping supply curve is relevant to the long period or short period is not stated. If, as is likely, the long-period perfectly competitive supply curve was intended, a difficulty arises. For in comparative statics a zero (Knightian) profit accrues to all equally efficient firms *ex hypothesi* both in the pretax and post-tax long-run equilibria.[3]

Similarly Mrs U. Hicks, in her volume on *Public Finance* [**7**], after offering a formula for the loss of consumer's surplus resulting from an excise tax, goes on to say, 'In practice, however, the situation will often be complicated by the fact that marginal costs are not constant; and we have therefore also to take account of the elasticity of the supply curve, and of the loss of producers' surplus' [**7**, p. 170]. However, she, also, fails to say whether the upward-sloping supply curve in her figure 3 is short or long-period. We may suppose, however, that it is the supply curve of a competitive industry as there is, following this analysis, a treatment of the case of monopoly.

A related but different difficulty arises in K. E. Boulding's treatment of the same problem in his *Economic Analysis* [**1**, pp. 772–3]. After discussing the symmetry between buyers' surplus and sellers' surplus, he applies the analysis to the well-known theorem that the revenue from an excise tax is less than the total loss

I wish to record my indebtedness to D. M. Winch for many valuable comments on a first draft of this paper.

of the combined surpluses. But the proposition in question has reference to production of goods, the supply curve being derived from the cost curves of competitive firms that combine factors in efficient proportions. Boulding's curve, in contrast, is no more than an offer curve derived from a given stock of goods.

In his classic *Econometrica* paper of 1938 H. Hotelling's explanation of the 'rising supply curve SB' in his figure 1 [8] is not altogether satisfactory. It is, he says, 'sometimes regarded as coinciding with the marginal-cost curve. Such a coincidence would arise if there were free competition among producers. However, 'This condition is approximate, for example, in most agriculture.' If agriculture were characterized by the Ricardian notion of applying increasing doses of labor and capital (in fixed proportions) to a given supply of land, then indeed the producer's surplus derived is equal to the Ricardian rent imputed to land. But competitive industry in manufactures is also possible in which case the supply curve is not a marginal cost curve, and the meaning of producer's surplus is again unclear.[4]

II

I shall argue first that, whatever the interpretation put on it, the producer's surplus that is measured as an area above the industry supply curve is not symmetric with consumer's surplus. Secondly, that in the long period at least, the area above the supply curve is not an unambiguous index of gain to any person or group in the economy.

Consider carefully the nature and application of consumer's surplus. For all practical purposes it is best regarded as a partial concept. It is true that the combined effect, positive or negative, on a person's welfare of a large number of price changes could, in principle, be exactly offset either by a change in his money income, by a change in the amount of any one good, or by a change in the amounts of several different goods.[5] But the fewer the number of price changes the easier it is to think in terms of a compensating money effect. In the limiting, but most practical, case of a change in the price of a single good, the value of money in which the change of consumer's surplus is measured is determined by the constancy of all prices save that under survey. In that case, the relevant area under the consumer's demand curve provides, under familiar conditions, a good measure of consumer's surplus.

In comparing producer's surplus with consumer's surplus in this limiting but practical case (in which the price of a single good or factor changes, all other prices

remaining constant), the first thing to bear in mind is that, provided the so-called income effect is not zero, J. R. Hicks's 'compensating variation' and 'equivalent variation' [6] are but different money measures of exactly the same alteration in a person's welfare resulting from a change in the price of some good. So long as firms are explicit profit-maximizers, they are uninfluenced by welfare effects and no such distinction need therefore be maintained for producer's surplus.[6] The only other concept which can be measured either as a compensating variation or as an equivalent variation is that of a person's economic rent which is perfectly symmetric with, indeed is no more than an extension of, his consumer's surplus. As has been indicated elsewhere [12] economic rent can be defined to provide a money measure of the welfare change arising from a movement of factor prices (product prices constant) in exactly the same way that consumer's surplus provides a money measure of the welfare change arising from a movement in product prices (factor prices constant). Both economic rent so defined and consumer's surplus are derived by operating on the given preference map of the individual.

Having defined economic rent this way (which covers Marshall's 'worker's surplus', just as consumer's surplus or producer's surplus can be made to cover his 'saver's surplus',[7] and having recognized it to be, like consumer's surplus, a measure of the gain or loss arising from a change in the terms of exchange facing a person, we must look elsewhere for an independent construct of producer's surplus.

III

Since cost curves and supply curves derive from production functions, it seems apparent that producer's surplus is to be traced by operating on the isoquant, or production indifference map. The K and L axes of the isoquant in Figure 1 measure respectively real units of capital and labor. If we relate this isoquant to the firm, its long-period cost curve (with unchanged factor prices) can be derived from the output path along OR which, for homogeneous production functions, is a ray through the origin. In order for the familiar U-shaped envelope curve to be generated it is necessary that along OR we first pass through an area of increasing returns to scale until we reach the isoproduct curve x_0 after which we pass through an area of decreasing returns to scale. Once a plant size, say K_0, is chosen by the firm, its short-period average inclusive cost, with minimum point at R_0, can be derived from the output path $K_0K'_0$. The actual short-period expansion path, with labor the only variable factor, follows that part of its marginal cost curve emerging from the lowest point of the average variable cost curve. Since all firms in the competitive industry are assumed equally efficient, and since factor prices are held constant, the short-period supply curve for the industry is no more than the horizontal sum of the short-run expansion paths of the firms.

If, on the other hand, we take the isoquant in Figure 1 to be that facing the industry as a whole, the expansion path is no longer a ray OR. In the long-period equilibrium there is for the industry a relation between its output and factor prices. If x is a capital-intensive good and capital is less than perfectly elastic in supply, an equilibrium expansion of the output of x results in a rise in the price of capital relative to labor and, therefore, a shift toward using an increased proportion of labor. The long-period expansion path of the industry would then be a line bending to the right as OR'. Conversely, if x is labor-intensive, such a line bends to the left.

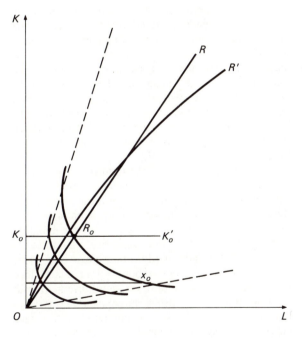

Fig. 1

This restatement of the familiar is necessary before examining the pertinence of the area above the supply curve as a measure of producer's surplus. Thus, the area above the industry's supply curve has a clear meaning only for the short period; for situations in which one factor, capital, is fixed in quantity and the

other factor, labor, fixed in price, is varied over the range of diminishing average returns to labor. Two familiar instances are formally identical, (a) Marshall's short-period quasi-rent and (b) Ricardian rent to a fixed supply of land in the economy.

(a) Marshallian quasi-rent in the industry is the sum of the surpluses made by each firm, where each firm's surplus is the sum of the surpluses it makes on each product sold. The surplus on each product is the excess of the price over the marginal cost of labor incurred in its production. Since the firm's surpluses are positive, they make a positive contribution to the firm's overheads, or capital costs, which contribution is attributable, ultimately, to the owners of capital. Within the short period, during which capital retains its specific form, the area above the supply curve as a measure of quasi-rent is clearly relevant: a decision to employ this capital equipment in one use rather than another is determined by a comparison of the resulting quasi-rents in the alternative uses.

(b) Ricardian rent, on the other hand, has reference to a long period over which labor and capital, both of them at fixed prices, (and therefore applied in fixed proportions[8]) can be varied without any alteration in the supply of land. Again, the surplus itself is identified as the sum of the surpluses on each unit of output, with each unit of surplus being defined as the excess of the price over the marginal cost of labor-and-capital incurred in its output. Over the long period the area above the supply curve[9] as a measure of rent is, again, clearly relevant: the decision to employ a certain piece of land, for example, in one use rather than another is determined by a comparison of the resulting rents.

Such instances as these, however, are properly regarded as examples of economic rent as previously defined [12], notwithstanding that they are apparently derived with reference to the production function and seemingly without reference to people's preference functions. The compensating variation definition of rent is the maximum sum a factor-owner would pay to have the full benefit of a rise in the price of his factor. The equivalent variation definition is the minimum sum he will accept to forgo the benefit of the price rise. If the income effect – or, more accurately, the welfare effect – is zero, either definition produces exactly the same measure. And if the factor-owner is concerned only with pecuniary advantage, this measure will be identical with the area above the supply curve reckoned as a sum of money. All of the Marshallian quasi-rent is to be imputed to the owners of specific capital equipment (at least in riskless situations). Ricardian rent is obviously to be imputed entirely to the owners of non-marginal land.

IV

The area above the long-period supply curve of an industry appears to offer, for policy purposes, the more significant measure of producer's surplus. Certainly it would seem that the criterion suggested by Hicks in 1940 [5], that (assuming universal perfect competition) consumer's surplus plus producer's surplus positive[10] would justify the introduction of a new commodity, implies a long period supply curve. If, in a limiting case, we took consumer's surplus to be zero, the criterion that producer's surplus be positive could be compared with the familiar investment criterion that $PV_i(A)$ be positive – where $PV_i(A)$ represents the present value of the A stream of net returns discounted at i. The positive producer's surplus would then be measured as the area above the long-period supply curve, an average curve that includes all capital charges.[11]

We turn therefore to the long-period supply curve for a competitive industry x[12] in which, following standard textbook procedure, we assume all firms are of equal size and efficiency. With unchanged techniques, some inelasticity in the supply of each factor, and an absence of external economies, the minimum long-period average inclusive cost curve for each firm rises as supply is expanded in response to increasing demand. This rise in the industry's supply curve reflects the growing scarcity of the factor that is intensive to the product x in question. With only two factors, capital and labor, the production of an increased supply of x entails a rise in the price of capital relative to labor and, owing to the greater weight of capital in x, a rise in its per unit cost relative to labor-intensive goods. With unchanged demand for an unchanged stock of money this translates into a rise in the average money cost of x.

Irrespective of the change in factor proportions as we move along the long-period supply curve of the industry, the size of each firm in terms of output (as determined by the minimum average inclusive cost) is given by technology. Consequently any long-period expansion of the total supply of x entails a larger number of firms.

What is significant, however, is that (always allowing for sufficient divisibility) each point on the long period industry supply curve SS' in Figure 2 represents the lowest average inclusive cost for that particular output to the industry and also to each firm in the industry. Thus, at industry outputs x_1, x_2, x_3, the minimum long-period average cost for each firm is, respectively, $x_1 m_1$, $x_2 m_2$, $x_3 m_3$, these being the lowest points on each of the typical envelope curves $s_1 s_1, s_2 s_2, s_3 s_3$, that correspond to these industry outputs x_1, x_2, x_3. These firms'

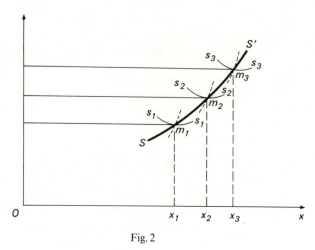

Fig. 2

minimum average costs for each of these industry outputs is also equal to their long-period marginal costs.

It should be clear that as we move along the industry's long-period supply curve SS' the rent of one factor will, in general, rise relative to the rent of the other factor – which, unless there are increasing returns to scale, will decline in real terms. And while it is manifest that the inelasticity of substitution, and therefore, the extent of the change in relative rents, is connected with the steepness of the industry supply curve, neither the slope of that curve nor the area above it can be associated with a net gain by both factors taken together, or a net gain by producers each of which in the long period makes zero profit.

For the purpose in hand, the industry supply curve SS' must be regarded as an average curve: at any equilibrium output, say Ox_2, $x_2 m_2$ is the average cost to each firm and to the industry. True, $x_2 m_2$ is also the marginal cost to each firm, but it is *not* the marginal cost to the industry. Put otherwise, the industry supply curve is, admittedly, an average cost curve *including* rents – the rents of both factors in fact, since these alter as the industry's equilibrium output expands. But it is *not* also a marginal curve *excluding* rent (as is the Ricardian average cost curve). An average curve including rent, equal to a marginal curve excluding rent, can be derived only in those cases in which rent accrues to a single fixed factor, all other factors being infinitely elastic. In the more general case, however, where the changes in rents of all factors are fully taken account of in the average curve, including of course the rental of capital (but no Knightian profit), the area above the rising industry supply curve carries no economic significance.[13]

V

To conclude, the area above the supply curve referred to as 'producer's surplus' may be used along with consumer's surplus only for a particular type of supply used in partial equilibrium analysis; namely, that constructed for a period during which the output of the good in question can be increased only by adding to fixed-factors amounts of other factors that are imperfect substitutes for it but are perfectly elastic in supply with respect to their money prices. In such cases the rent of the fixed factor is exactly equal to the area above the supply curve under the conditions mentioned – zero welfare effect and complete indifference to nonpecuniary advantages. The further we move from these conditions, especially the latter condition, the greater the divergence between the true rent (either compensating or equivalent variation) and the area in question. Provided price everywhere else is equal to social marginal cost the familiar qualitative tax-subsidy propositions, based on the geometry of consumer's and 'producer's surplus', hold true even though the areas involved are generally only an approximation to the combined losses or gains.

In contrast, we cannot derive a 'producer's surplus' from a supply curve along which all factors are variable. Thus we cannot derive a 'producer's surplus' from an industry's long-period supply curve. Such a curve is not marginal to an average curve that is made up of the cost of the other (variable) factors at fixed prices. In this more general case in which all factors are variable in supply, the industry's supply curve necessarily includes all factor prices and, therefore, all rents. Thus, the price of each factor, and the proportions in which each is combined with the others, must be known before the unit inclusive cost – equal to price in long-period competitive equilibrium – can be determined. Put differently, at each point on the long-period industry supply curve 'Euler's theorem' is met: the product is exhausted by paying to each of the contributing factors its full marginal product. Nothing is left as a surplus to any agent of production, and Knightian profit is zero.

In cases such as these the notion of 'producer's surplus' is inapplicable, and all welfare propositions deriving from areas above such long-period supply curves are invalid.

Finally, the term 'producer's surplus' has been placed in quotation marks in this final section as a reminder that the term is misleading and otiose. It is misleading inasmuch as the term producer is misleading: it may refer to the owners of the agents of production or it may refer to the entrepreneur.

Consequently, it may suggest rents, or it may suggest profits of some sort. It is otiose inasmuch as, in those special cases where the area above the supply curve may be taken as an accurate or approximate measure of the surplus, the money sum it represents is properly defined as economic rent to one of the factors of production, the concept of rent being therefore on all fours with the concept of consumer's surplus.

An additional advantage of excluding all reference to 'producer's surplus' and restricting our terminology to economic rent is that it obliges us to identify the particular factor that is, over some period of time, inelastic in supply and therefore also the factor-owners to whom the rents are to be imputed. We are then not likely to be deluded into measuring nonexisting surpluses. For these reasons I recommend that the term 'producer's surplus' be struck from the economist's vocabulary.

Appended Note

In this note we shall briefly examine the attempt to derive a producer's (and consumer's) surplus from a 'real' supply curve for a two-good economy – the marginal cost of one of the goods being expressed in terms of the other. From the convex transformation curve TT' and from the community indifference curve I_0I_0, in Figure (a), we construct respectively a curve of marginal opportunity cost ss' and a compensated demand curve dd' in Figure (b), both for units of x in terms of y.

The exposition will be more revealing if we adapt the Johnson analysis of the gains from removing a tariff [10, pp. 329–32] to the more extreme case of the gains arising from the complete removal of a previously prohibitive tariff. Once the tariff is completely abolished we move from Q_0, the autarkic collection of goods produced and consumed, to the completely free trade situation at the world terms of trade VV' at which C_1 indicates the batch consumed, P_1 the batch produced, with Q_1P_1 of y therefore being exchanged for Q_1C_1 of x. Adapting Johnson's argument to this special case, SR is to be identified with the *consumption cost* of the tariff and RV with the *production cost* of the tariff, both in terms of x at the world terms of trade. Their sum, SV, is the total gain from free trade.

In Figure (b) the substitution of the autarkic terms of trade UU' in Figure (a) for the world terms of trade VV' is translated into a reduction from the domestic price of x (in terms of y), p_0, to the international price of x, p_1. The distances SR, RV, and their total SV, along the x-axis of Figure (a), can be represented in Figure (b) as

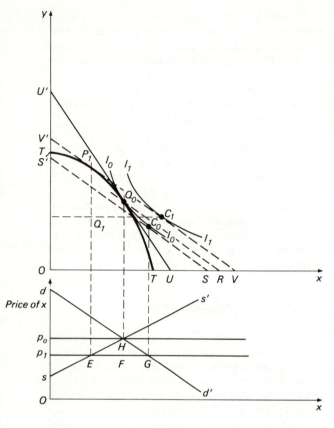

Figs. (a) and (b)

case zero for all (long period) equilibrium positions, whether in autarky or free trade, for a perfectly competitive economy.[17]

It appears then that the attempt to separate a consumer's surplus from a producer's surplus in the construction of Figure (a), or from its derived construction Figure (b), is arbitrary and erroneous. It must be recognized that we have constructed two Pareto-comparable community indifference curves, I_0I_0 and I_1I_1 in Figure (a), passing through the consumption batches in the autarkic and free trade situations respectively. And the welfare gain is no more than the difference between them measured here as a single compensating variation at the new international price ratio – as SV along the x-axis or as $S'V'$ along the y-axis.[18] Either can be interpreted as an exact measure of the gains for the community as a whole, or for a single person, in moving from the *consumption* possibilities presented by TT' to the new *consumption* possibilities presented by VV'.

Notes: Chapter 8

1 With commendable analytic finesse Marshall separates the rising supply curve resulting from differential advantages as between firms, 'the particular expenses curve', from the possible external economies which may predominate and act, therefore, to lower the unit cost as the total output of industry is increased. The contribution of external economies are taken as fixed at the equilibrium output, OH, of his figure 39 [**11**, p. 811]. This procedure is correct inasmuch as the area measures what the total number of firms take to be their rents or producer's surpluses. Nonetheless, since competitive firms ignore their contributions in reducing cost for all other firms, the equilibrium output OH will be below the 'ideal' output as would be indicated by the point of equality between the demand curve and a marginal curve taken from the downward-sloping supply curve (resulting from the dominance of external economies).

2 Marshall warns us that 'These two sets of surpluses (i.e., consumer's surplus and producer's surplus) are not independent . . . For when we have reduced the producer's surplus at the value of the general purchasing power which he derives from his labour or savings we have reckoned implicitly his consumer's surplus too' [**11**, p. 831]. Regarding consumer's surplus or producer's surplus as an absolute measure of the total surplus arising from his conjuncture, the statement is correct. If, in contrast, we are concerned with a money measure of the *change* in his welfare brought about by a change in the set of prices confronting him, it becomes possible to separate the contributions to his welfare effected by changes in both factor and product prices. In this connection see Mishan [**12**, p. 394].

3 The net long-period change in pure profit is therefore zero also. 'Normal' profit cannot be other than the return on capital in the long period in which each factor, including

triangles *FHG, FHE,* and *EHF,* respectively. What cannot be done, however, is to identify the gain in consumer's surplus as p_1p_0HG,[14] the loss of producer's surplus as p_1p_0HE, with triangle *EHG* measuring the net gain of consumer's surplus over the loss of producer's surplus. For if we constructed a Figure (b') (not shown here), with y measured along the horizontal axis and the price of y in terms of x on the vertical axis, exactly the same net gain would have to be interpreted instead as an excess of the gain of producer's surplus over the loss of consumer's surplus.[15] In the limiting case, if the country, either in trade or autarky, produces nothing but x the resulting producer's surplus in Figure (b) would appear as a maximum, whereas if it were depicted in Figure (b') (not shown) the producer's surplus would appear as zero. The division of the welfare gain from free trade into gains (or losses) of consumer's surpluses offset by losses (or gains) of producer's surpluses is, therefore, quite arbitrary. Indeed, if producer's surplus is defined as to be coterminous with pure profit[16] then it is in any capital, receives its normal supply price. In this long-period equilibrium there is no surplus left over for the firm, or the industry, in either situation. All added value is distributed among the factors employed.

4 There are more recent examples of failure to be specific about the upward-sloping supply curve. In their recent paper on Indian fertilizer projects, Tintner and Patel [13] do not specify whether the supply curve is long- or short-period. They are, however, concerned in the main with shifts of the supply curve induced by altering the proportion of fertilizer to labor and land. And with constant wages any changes in producer's surplus would, indeed, reflect changes in the gross rent of land. In Harry Johnson's analysis of customs unions [9] nothing is said about the upward-sloping supply curves used from which the conclusions are derived. But the context of the analysis leads one to suppose that Johnson intended them to be long-run supply curves of competitive industries. As will be indicated in the following section neither construct can be used for deriving a surplus. As a final example, W. M. Corden in his 1957 paper [2] constructs a supply curve HH' in his figure 1 from which he derives a measure of producer's surplus, but it is a supply curve for which money incomes and all prices *including* factor prices are to be held constant. Strictly speaking, this is not possible. The rise in supply price cannot take place if all factor prices remain unchanged. Even if variable factors, say labor and capital, did not change in price, the price of the fixed factor, say land, must rise.

5 The choice of numeraire in which to measure the welfare change arising, say, from the changes in product prices is an arbitrary matter to be decided by considerations of convenience. If, for example, there is a simultaneous change in the prices of two products, x and y, the consumer's surplus can be measured (a) in terms of a third good or in terms of a combination of several other goods at given prices, (b) in terms of x alone, (c) in terms of y alone, or (d) in terms of any combination of x and y. Again, using the numeraire suggested by any of the last three, the consumer's surplus can be measured either (i) as the maximum payment in terms of x and/or y (compensating variation for a price fall, equivalent variation for a price rise) required to restore the initial level of welfare, or (ii) as the minimum receipt of x and/or y (equivalent variation for a price fall, compensating variation for a price rise) necessary to achieve the new level of welfare without the change in price of x and/or y.

Alternatively, and more conveniently, the welfare change could be measured in terms of money income alone. In that case the worth of money is determined by reference to all goods, other than x and y, at their unchanged prices and by reference to x and y at their new prices if the compensating variation measure is used, or at their old prices if the equivalent variation is used. This holds irrespective of a rise or fall in the prices of x and y.

6 The explicit profit-maximization assumption is not essential to this critique of producer's surplus. If all but several of a large number of firms in a perfectly competitive industry maximized money profits and these profits were zero in long-period equilibrium, these several firms would make less than zero profits and could not cover their full costs. On the other hand, one can imagine an industry in which there was a general agreement among managers to produce outputs that were smaller than the profit-

maximizing outputs, deliberately sacrificing profit, or personal earnings, for greater leisure. All then may be better off than they would be maximizing profits. But the degree to which each is better off can be measured as a rent only by reference to his indifference map as between income and leisure, which information cannot be extracted from the firm's cost curve or the industry's supply curve.

7 If a man exchanges a stock of money for a security he can be thought of as buying a yielding asset in which case the welfare effects of a change in its price (with constant yield) can be measured as a consumer's surplus. Alternatively, he can be thought of as lending the services of his money for an annual fee in which case the welfare effects of a change in the rate of interest – payment for his factor services – can be measured as an economic rent.

8 With a homogeneous production function having negative second derivatives at all points along the isoproduct curves, efficient production implies that factor proportions are uniquely determined by relative factor prices.

9 It is, of course, a familiar proposition that in order to identify any quasi-rent, or rent, as the area above the supply curve, this curve must be conceived as a marginal curve exclusive of rent. Once the rent or quasi-rent is derived in this way, and is added at each point of output to the average cost of the *variable* factors, then the same supply curve can be taken to represent the average cost at each output including rent or quasi-rent to the fixed factors. In this connection see Ellis and Fellner [4, pp. 497–502].

10 In this paper [5] Hicks equated a constant marginal utility of money with zero income effect. Needless to say, zero income effect is consistent also with increasing or diminishing marginal utility of money.

11 Hicks calls his SS' curve in Figure 1 [5 p. 113] a marginal curve for the industry. Unless he is thinking of the Ricardian land case he must be following Marshall's assumptions: constant prices for all variable factors with the upward-sloping supply curve the result simply of ranking firms in order of efficiency. This construction is less general than the upward-sloping long period supply curve of the industry which results when firms of equal efficiency respond to an expanding market demand.

12 I have restricted myself in this paper to a critique of producer's surplus as popularly used in partial equilibrium analysis where it is thought to be the obvious counterpart to the consumer's surplus concept. The erroneous construct of producer's surplus drawn from a general equilibrium analysis requires different arguments, and is dealt with briefly in the Appended Note.

13 Although the measurement of producer's surplus is generally linked to the upward-sloping supply curve of a competitive industry, it may be observed in passing that the cost curve of a monopolist does not measure a producer's surplus either. Monopoly profit, or 'monopoly rent', arises strictly speaking from the 'exploitation' of the consumer's-demand curve. It is measured not by the area above the long-period cost curve (which curve may be horizontal), but by the area between the long-period cost curve and the price, *times* output: alternatively, by the net positive area enclosed between the marginal cost and marginal revenue curves. If the latter measure is used, one cannot associate a producer's surplus with the net positive area above the marginal cost curve alone, for the area below the marginal revenue curve is also a part of the

monopoly profit (and not, as required in the usual welfare treatment associated with this sort of geometry, a measure of consumer's surplus).

14 In deriving Figure (b) from Figure (a), the reader will observe that the point G in Figure (b) is taken to be directly below C_0. With as much justification G could be placed directly below C_1. Only if x has a zero 'income' effect (or, rather, welfare effect) could C_0 and C_1 be on the same vertical line and, therefore, the compensated demand curve uniquely determined. If it were uniquely determined, however, we could not *also* construct a unique compensated demand curve for y in terms of x.

15 It should be obvious that we would be counting the net gain from trade twice if we treated the net surpluses on both goods, x and y, as separate and addable – adding, that is, the excess consumer's surplus on x to the excess producer's surplus on y.

16 If, on the other hand, producer's surplus is to be defined as factor rents, it should be manifest that they cannot be determined from the data in Figure (a); only from a knowledge of people's preferences as between income and leisure. In general all we can say is that all factor prices change when we move from autarky to free trade. If, for example, x is labor-intensive, and the supply of labor is not perfectly elastic, the movement to free trade raises its price relative to that of capital. This entails a rise of rent to labor relative to rental of capital, but no overall net rise in rents.

17 If, on the other hand, the economy is imperfectly competitive, we cannot say whether a shift of production from y to x increases or reduces profits without knowing the markups on the two goods, information not yielded by Figure (a).

18 Alternatively, the welfare gains could be measured, again either in x or y, at the terms of trade UU' in the autarkic position. Needless to remark, though one will always show a gain by using the world terms of trade as an index, it is *possible* simultaneously to show a welfare loss in moving to the free trade situation using the autarkic terms of trade as an index.

References

1 K. E. Boulding, *Economic Analysis* (New York, 1948).
2 W. M. Corden, 'The calculation of the cost of protection', *Economic Record*, vol. 33 (April 1957), pp. 29–51.
3 H. Dalton, *Principles of Public Finance*, 4th edn (London, 1954).
4 H. S. Ellis and W. Fellner, 'External economies and diseconomies', *American Economic Reivew*, vol. 33 (1943), pp. 493–511.
5 J. R. Hicks, 'The rehabilitation of consumers' surpluses', *Review of Economic Studies*, vol. 8 (1940–1), pp. 108–16.
6 J. R. Hicks, 'The four consumers' surpluses', *Review of Economic Studies*, vol. 11 (1944), pp. 31–41.
7 U. K. Hicks, *Public Finance* (London and Cambridge, 1947).
8 H. Hotelling, 'The general welfare in relation to problems of taxation and of railway and utility rates', *Econometrica*, vol. 6 (July 1938), pp. 242–69.
9 H. G. Johnson, 'A Marshallian analysis of customs unions', *Indian Journal of Economics*, vol. 38 (July 1957), pp. 39–47; reprinted in *Money, Trade and Economic Growth* (London, 1962).
10 H. G. Johnson, 'The cost of protection and the scientific tariff', *Journal of Political Economy*, vol. 68 (August 1960), pp. 327–45.
11 A. Marshall, *Principles of Economics*, 8th edn (London, 1925).
12 E. J. Mishan, 'Rent as a measure of welfare change', *American Economic Review*, vol. 49 (June 1959), pp. 386–95.
13 G. Tintner and M. Patel, 'Evaluation of Indian fertilizer projects – an application of consumer's and producer's surplus', *Journal of Farm Economics*, vol. 48 (August 1966), pp. 704–10.

PART THREE

Externalities

9

Evaluation of Life and Limb: A Theoretical Approach

Abstract

None of the existing methods of evaluating loss or saving life, or assessing an increase or reduction in accidents resulting from investment projects, is satisfactory for a number of reasons. This is so chiefly because they are all inconsistent with the Pareto base of existing allocation theory and benefit–cost analysis. Strict application of the Pareto principle to changes in accidents and fatalities involves a calculation of the compensating variation associated with the changes in risk-bearing regarded as external effects. Several of these external effects are discussed at length.

As cost-benefit studies grow in popularity, it is increasingly important to make proper allowance for losses or gains arising from changes in the incidence of death, disablement, or disease caused by the operation of new projects or developments. What is at issue is not the reliability of the current estimates of economic gains or losses arising from the saving or losing of life or health but the appropriateness of the ideal or conceptual measures about which, so far, there is no consensus among economists. I propose, therefore, first to argue that the more familiar concepts employed in evaluating the loss or saving of life are all unsatisfactory and, secondly, by referring to the basic rationale of economic calculation, to determine how such losses and gains should, in principle, be evaluated.

Since the analysis of saving life is symmetrical with that of losing it, it will simplify the exposition if, initially, we confine ourselves to the analysis of loss of life and limb – or, more briefly, to loss of life alone – indicating the necessary extensions in the latter part of the paper.

I

(1) Despite repeated expressions of dissatisfaction with the method, the most common way of calculating the economic worth of a person's life and, therefore, the loss to the economy consequent upon his decease is that of discounting to the present the person's expected future earnings. A precise expression for the loss to the economy calculated on this method would be L_1, where

$$L_1 = \sum_{t=\tau}^{\infty} Y_t P_\tau^t (1+r)^{-(t-\tau)}$$

The Y_t is the expected gross earnings of (or, alternatively, value added by) the person during the tth year, exclusive of any yields from his ownership of nonhuman capital.[1] The P_τ^t is the probability in the current, or τth, year of the person being alive during the tth year, and r is the social rate of discount expected to rule during the tth year. This kind of calculation is occasionally supplemented by a suggestion that auxiliary calculations be made in order to take account of the suffering of the victim, the loss of his utility due to his demise, and/or of the bereavement of his family.[2] More recently, and as an example of the economist's finesse, it has been proposed that such calculations be supplemented by the cost of 'premature burial'[3] – the idea being that the present discounted value of the funeral expenses is higher if they are incurred sooner owing to an untimely death.

(2) A second method, which might be thought of as more refined than the first, is that of calculating the present discounted value of the losses over time accruing to *others only* as a result of the death of the person at age τ. A precise expression for the loss to the economy based on this method would be L_2, where

$$L_2 = \sum_{t=\tau}^{\infty} P_\tau^t (Y_t - C_t)(1+r)^{-(t-\tau)}$$

where C_t is the personal expenditure of the individual during the tth period that is expected at time τ. This kind of measure (sometimes referred to as being based on the 'net output' approach in order to distinguish it from the 'gross output' approach associated with the L_1 measure), although occasionally mentioned in the literature – for instance, by Devons (1961, p. 107) and Ridker (1967, p. 36) – has not been employed apparently because of the assumed policy implications.

(3) A third possible method would repudiate any direct calculation of the loss of potential earnings or spending. Instead, it would approach the problem from a 'social' point of view. Since society, through its political processes, does in fact take decisions on investment expenditures that occasionally increase or reduce the number of deaths, an implicit value of human life can be calculated. This approach receives occasional mention – for instance, by Fromm (1965, p. 193) and by Schelling (1968, p. 147) – and, indeed, the appeal to the political, or democratic, process is sometimes invoked to provide guidance on broader issues.[4]

(4) The insurance principle is a departure from any of the aforementioned methods. Predicated on the premium a man is willing to pay, and the probability of his being killed as a result of engaging in some specific activity, it is thought possible to calculate the value a man sets on his life. An example is given by Fromm (1965, p. 194).

II

Each of these four possible methods of measuring the loss of life is now briefly appraised.

Method (1), turning on the loss of potential future earnings, can be rationalized only if the criterion adopted in any economic reorganization turns on the value of its contribution to gross national product (GNP), or, more accurately, to net national product. But although financial journalists manage to convey the contrary impression, maximizing GNP is not an acceptable goal of economic policy. Notwithstanding its usage, most writers have mental reservations about its validity and tend to regard it as only part of the total measurement. For instance, Schelling (1968) makes a distinction between the value of likelihood, which is the L_1 measure, and the value of life, which poses a perplexing and possibly unsolvable problem.

The so-called net output method (2) might seem, at first glance, more acceptable than the gross output method. For, taking a cold-blooded attitude, what matters to the rest of society is simply the resulting loss, or gain, to society following the death of one or more of its members. This *ex post* approach, however, appears to strike some writers as either absurd or dangerous.[5] If accepted, it certainly follows that the death of any person whose L_2 measure is negative confers a net benefit on society. And this category of persons would certainly include all retired people irrespective of their ownership of property. Yet, from this undeniable inference, no dread policy implications follow. If the method were satisfactory on economic grounds, the inference would not, of itself, provide any reason for rejecting it. But the method is not satisfactory for the simple reason that it has no regard for the feelings of the potential decedents. It restricts itself to the interest only of the surviving members of society: it ignores society *ex ante* and concentrates wholly on society *ex post*.

As for the method (3) which would build on implicit values placed on human life by the political process, the justification appears somewhat circular even when we ignore the political realities of Western democracies. Assuming that democratic voting alone determines whether or not a particular investment project or part of a project is to be adopted, the idea of deriving quantitative values from the political process is clearly contrary to the idea of deriving them from an independent economic criterion. Where the outcome of the political debate calls upon the economist to provide a quantitative evaluation of the project under consideration, the economist fails to meet his brief insofar as he abandons the attempt to calculate any aspect of the project by reference to an economic criterion and, instead, attempts to extricate figures from previous political decisions.[6] By recourse to a method that refers a question, or part of a question, received from the political process back again to the political process, the economist appears to be concealing some deficiency in the relevant data or some weakness in the logic of his criteria.

Finally, there is method (4) based on the insurance principle. This has about it a superficial plausibility, enough, at any rate, to attract some attention. An early attempt, for instance, was made by Fromm (1965, pp. 193–6) to attribute a value for loss of life raised on the implied assumption of a straight-line relationship between the probability of a person being killed and the sum that he would pay to cover the risk. If, therefore, the premium y corresponding to the additional risk p is known, the value he places on his life is to be reckoned as y/p. Thus, if a man would pay $100 to reduce his chance of being killed by 1 per cent – say, from an existing chance of one-twentieth to two-fiftieths the value he places on his life is to be estimated as $10,000. (Or, to use Fromm's own calculation, if the probability of being killed in air travel were to be reduced from the existing figure of 0·0000017 per trip of 500 miles to zero, a person who values his life at $400,000 should be willing to pay 68 cents to reduce the existing risk to zero.)

The implied assumption of linearity, which has it that a man who accepts $100,000 for an assignment offering him a four-to-one chance of survival will agree to go to certain death for $500,000, is implausible, to say the least. And, indeed, this linearity assumption was later criticized by Fromm himself (1968, p. 174) when it was incidentally posited by Schelling (1968). But even if it were both plausible and proved, the insurance principle does not yield us the required valuation. For the insurance policy makes provision, in the event of a man's death, only for compensation to *others*. Thus, the amount of insurance a man takes out may be interpreted as a reflection, *inter alia*, of his concern for his family and dependents but hardly as an index of the value he sets on his own life.[7] A bachelor with no dependents could have no reason to take out flight insurance, notwithstanding the fact that he could be as reluctant as the next man to depart this fugacious life at short notice.

III

The crucial objection to each of these four methods, however, is that not one of them is consistent with the basic rationale of the economic calculus used in cost–benefit analysis. If we are concerned, as we are in all allocative problems, with increasing society's satisfaction in some sense, and if, in addition, we eschew interpersonal comparisons of satisfactions, we can always be guided in the ranking of alternative economic arrangements by the notion of a Pareto improvement – an improvement such that at least one person is made better off and nobody is made worse off. A *potential* Pareto improvement,[8] one in which the net gains *can* so be distributed that at least one person is made better off, with none being made worse off, provides an alternative criterion, or definition, of social gain. This alternative, as it happens, provides the rationale of all familiar allocative propositions in economics and, therefore, the rationale of all cost–benefit calculations.[9]

When the full range of its economic effects is brought into the calculus, the introduction of a specific investment project will make some of the community of n members better off on balance, some worse off on balance, the remainder being indifferent to it. If the jth person is made better off, a compensating variation

(CV) measures the full extent of his improvement, this CV being a maximum sum V_j he will pay rather than forgo the project, the sum being prefixed by a positive sign. *Per contra*, if the jth person is made worse off by the introduction of the project, his CV measures the full decline of his welfare as a minimal sum V_j he will accept to put up with the project, this sum being prefixed by a negative sign.[10] If, then, in response to the introduction of this specific project, the aggregate sum

$$\sum_{j}^{n} V_j > 0$$

(where j runs from 1 to n) – if, that is, the algebraic sum of all n individual CVs is positive – there is a potential Pareto improvement, its positive value being interpreted as the excess of benefits over costs arising from the introduction of the project.[11]

Consistency with the criterion of a potential Pareto improvement and, therefore, consistency with the principle of evaluation in cost–benefit analyses would require that the loss of a person's life be valued by reference to his CV; by reference, that is, to the minimum sum he is prepared to accept in exchange for its surrender. For unless a project that is held to be responsible for, say, an additional 1,000 deaths annually can show an excess of benefits over costs *after* meeting the compensatory sums necessary to restore the welfare of these 1,000 victims, it is not possible to make all members of the community better off by a redistribution of the net gains. A potential Pareto improvement cannot, then, be achieved, and the project in question ought not to be admitted.

If the argument is accepted, however, the requirements of consistency might seem to be highly restrictive. Since an increase in the annual number of deaths can be confidently predicted in connection with a number of particular developments – those, for example, which contribute to an increase in ground and air traffic – such developments would no longer appear as economically feasible. For it would not surprise us to discover that, in ordinary circumstances,[12] no sum of money is large enough to compensate a man for the loss of his life.

In conditions of certainty, the logic of the above proposition is unassailable. If, in ordinary circumstances, we face a person with the choice of continuing his life in the usual way or of ending it at noon the next day, a sum large enough to persuade him to choose the latter course of action may not exist. And, indeed, if the development in question unavoidably entailed the death of this specific person or, more generally, a number of specific persons, it is highly unlikely that any conceivable excess benefit over cost, *calculated in the absence of these fatalities*, would warrant its undertaking on the potential Pareto criterion.

It is never the case, however, that a specific person, or a number of specific persons, can be designated in advance as being those who are certain to be killed if a particular project is undertaken.[13] All that can be predicted, although with a high degree of confidence, is that out of a total of n members in the community an additional x members per annum will be killed (and, say, an additional $10x$ members will be seriously injured). In the absence, therefore, of any breakdown of the circumstances surrounding the additional number of accidents to be expected, the increment of risk of being killed imposed each year on any one member of the community can be taken as x/n (and $10x/n$ for the risk of being seriously injured). And it is this fact of complete ignorance of the identity of each of the potential victims that transforms the calculation. Assuming universal risk aversion,[14] the relevant sums to be subtracted from the benefit side are no longer those which compensate a specific number of persons for their certain death but are those sums which compensate each person in the community for *the additional risk* to which he is to be exposed.[15]

In general, of course, every activity will have attached to it some discernible degree of risk (even staying at home in bed bears some risk of mishap – the bed might collapse, the wind might blow the roof in, a marauder might enter). Any change, from one environment to another, from one style of living to another, can be said to alter the balance of risk, sometimes imperceptibly, sometimes substantially. Only the dead opt out of all risk. Yet the actual statistical risk attaching to some activity may be so small that only the hypersensitive would take account of it. In common with all other changes in economic arrangements, there is some *minimum sensible* beyond which an increment, or decrement, of risk will go unnoticed. More important, however, what is strictly relevant to the analysis is not the change in the statistical risk *per se* but the person's response, if any, to such a change. For the change in risk may go unperceived, and, if perceived, it may be improperly evaluated. Indeed, people do have difficulty in grasping the objective significance of large numbers and, where chance or risk is at issue, they are prone to underestimate it. One chance in 50,000 of winning a lottery, or of having one's house burned down, seems a better chance, or a greater risk, than it is in fact. If so, the existence of gambling and insurance by the same person is explicable without recourse to the ingenious Friedman–Savage hypothesis (1948).

The analysis which follows does not, however, depend upon the veracity of such conjectures. All the reader has to accept is the proposition that people's subjective preferences of the worth of a thing must be counted. In the market place, the price of a good or a 'bad' (such as labor input or other disutility) is fixed by the producer, and the buyer or seller determines the amount by reference to his subjective preferences. Where, however, the amount of a (collective) good, or 'bad' is fixed for each person – as may be the case with a change in risk – a person's subjective preference can only determine the price he will accept or offer for it; in short, his CV. People's imperfect knowledge of economic opportunities, their imprudence and unworldliness, have never prevented economists from accepting as basic data the amounts people freely choose at given prices. Such imperfections cannot, therefore, consistently be invoked to qualify people's choices when, instead, their preferences are exercised in placing a price on some increment of a good or 'bad'. True, attempts to observe the change of magnitude when people adjust the price to the change in quantity – rather than the more common assumption that they adjust the quantity to the change in price – does pose problems of measurement. But the problems of measurement must not be allowed to obscure the validity of the concept.

Placed within the broadest possible context then, any additional risk of death, associated with the provision of some new facility, takes its place as one of a number of economic consequences (including employment gains and losses, new purchase and sale opportunities, and the withdrawal of existing ones), all of which affect the welfare of each of the n members of the community.

IV

We shall now consider four types of risk, two of them direct, or physical, risks, the remaining two being indirect, or derivative, risks.

First, there are the direct, or physical, risks that people *voluntarily* assume whenever they choose to buy a product or avail themselves of a service or facility. Inasmuch as such risks are evaluated by each jth person as a CV, equal say to r^1_{jj}, his benefit from the service or facility is estimated net of such risk; that is, after r^1_{jj} has been subtracted from it. If smoking tobacco causes 20,000 deaths a year, no subtracting from the benefits, on account of this risk, need be entered in a cost–benefit analysis of the tobacco industry inasmuch as smokers are already aware that the tobacco habit is unhealthy. And if, notwithstanding their awareness, they continue to smoke, the economist has no choice but to assume that they consider themselves better off despite the risks. Indeed, the benefits to smokers, net of risk, that is, after subtracting the aggregate,

$$\sum_{j}^{n} r_{ij}^{1}$$

are reflected in the demand schedule for tobacco. Once the area under the demand curve has been estimated and used as an approximation of the benefit smokers derive from the use of tobacco, any further subtraction for such risks would entail double counting.

Another example will help clarify the principle and will extend the argument. In an initially riskless situation, the jth person's anticipated consumer's surplus on buying a new car can be expressed by

$$C_j = \int_0^M [v(m) - g'(m)]\, dm + g_0 - P$$

where $v(m)$ is the present discounted value of the maximum amounts he will pay (net of all operating costs) for each successive mile for which the car is to be used; $g'(m)$ is the derivative of $g(m)$, the present discounted value of the sum the car will fetch if sold after it has been driven m miles; g_0 is the discounted present value of the car if he holds it over time without driving it at all; P is the original price of the car (including tax); and M is the total number of miles he expects to drive the car. If we observe that he buys the car, we infer that C_j is positive; that, in his own estimation, he is better off with the car than without it.

The introduction, now, of some personal risk associated with driving the car does not alter this inference.[16] Once he is aware of the additional element of risk in driving the car, the consequent reduction in the jth person's welfare is valued at the risk compensation r_{jj}^1. If, in spite of the additional risk, the jth person still offers to buy the car, we are compelled to infer that $(C_j - r_{jj}^1) > 0$; that is, his original consumer's surplus exceeds the risk compensation or, put otherwise, his consumer's surplus *net of risk* is positive. The evaluation of a new automobile plant will, therefore, disregard this type of risk, since the benefits are roughly equal to the aggregate of consumer's surplus net of risk. Similarly, a cost–benefit study of a highway project which is expected to increase the number of casualties need make no allowance for the expected loss of life provided, again, that this is the only type of risk. For in this case, also, the benefits to be measured are, ultimately, the maximum sums motorists are willing to pay for the new highway system in full cognizance of the additional risks they choose to assume.

Occasionally, as in the automobile example, the risk assumed by each person will depend upon the numbers availing themselves of the service or facility. Since the additional degree of risk generated by all the others are imposed on each one, in addition to the risk he would assume in the absence of all others, the analysis must extend itself to include 'external diseconomies internal to the industry'.[17] If we let r_{ij}^1 stand for the risk-compensation sum required by the jth person for the risk imposed on him by the ith individual, the compensatory sums for the extra risks contributed by all other individuals is given by

$$\sum_{i}^{n} r_{ij}^{1} \quad (i \neq j)$$

Now, although these additional risks are imposed on the jth person, they can always be avoided by his refusal to avail himself of the new service or facility. If, however, he decides to avail himself of it, the economist cannot but assume that he believes he is better off with it than without it. Again, therefore, we must assume that

$$C_j - \sum_{i}^{n} r_{ij}^{1} > 0$$

where i now includes j so as to make provision also for the risk that person j would run if he alone enjoyed the new service or facility.[18] Aggregating over all n members, the net consumer's surplus is

$$\sum_{j}^{n} (C_j - \sum_{i}^{n} r_{ij}^{1})$$

which can be abbreviated to $(C - R^1)$.

Insofar, then, as additional risks associated with the service or facility are all *voluntarily* assumed, there is no call for intervention in the allocative solution to which the market tends. As for project evaluations, insofar as benefits are calculated by reference to estimates of consumers' surplus, no allowance need be made for additional risk of loss of life. For the sum each person is willing to pay for the services provided by the project is net of all the risks associated with them. However, once we turn from risks that can be voluntarily assumed to *involuntary* risks that cannot be avoided – or, rather, cannot be avoided without incurring expenses – special provision for them has to be made in any cost–benefit analysis.

V

The additional involuntary risks that are imposed on the community as a whole as a byproduct of some specific economic activity, and are, therefore, to be regarded as external diseconomies external to the industry, can be separated into three types. Although all three can be inflicted on the same person who could propose a single sum in compensation, it is useful to separate them, there being circumstances where only one or two types of risk are of any importance.

The *direct* involuntary risk of death that is inflicted on the jth person by some specific project can be compensated by the sum r_{jj}^2. For example, the establishment of a nuclear power station and the resulting disposal of radioactive waste materials are held to be responsible for an increase in the annual number of deaths. Again, if supersonic flights over inhabited areas are introduced as a regular service, we can anticipate an increase in the annual number of deaths, at least among the frail, the elderly, and among those suffering from heart ailments.

In addition to this primary risk, there is a secondary risk to which the jth person is exposed, which will arise in other instances. For example, in the absence of legal prohibition, an industry pours 'sewage' into the air and increases the incidence of death from a number of lung and heart diseases. Apart from those who are the direct victims of this activity, there will be a number of fatalities arising from infection through others. And this possibility of infection obviously increases the risk since, within a given area, every person becomes a source of risk to every other. In addition, therefore, to the sum r_{jj}^2 to compensate the jth person for the risk imposed on him even if he were the sole inhabitant, he requires also a sum

$$\sum_{i}^{n} r_{ij}^2 \qquad (i \neq j)$$

to compensate for the risk that each of the other $(n-1)$ persons imposes on him.

There does not seem to be any advantage, however, in upholding this distinction between primary and secondary physical risk. Where the risk of infection through others is acknowledged, it is difficult, if not impossible, to separate primary from secondary risk. In such cases the risk compensation required by each person covers both. We shall, therefore, employ the general term

$$\sum_{i}^{n} r_{ij}^2$$

for the jth person (which includes the term r_{jj}^2 for the risk he runs in the absence of others). Aggregating over the n members of the community this total risk compensation is to be valued at

$$\sum_{j}^{n} \sum_{i}^{n} r_{ij}^2$$

which can be denoted by R^2.

There are, finally, the *indirect*, or derivative, risks arising from the general concern of each of the n persons with the physical risks, voluntary and involuntary, to which any of the others is exposed. This additional concern to which, in general, each member is prone (as a result of the additional physical risks run by others) has both a financial and a psychic aspect.

(a) *The financial aspect.* If, on balance, the death of the ith person improves the financial position of the jth person, the additional chance of i's death is a benefit to j, and the risk-compensatory sum r_{ij}^3 is therefore positive. This means that the jth person is willing to pay up to a given sum for the improved chance of his losing some dependent or inheriting some asset – or of inheriting it sooner.[19] If, on the other hand, the death of the ith person would reduce j's real income, the sum r_{ij}^3 is negative; that is, the jth person would have to receive a sum of money to compensate him for the increased risk of suffering a reduction in his real income. Although the jth person's financial condition is likely to be affected by the death of only a few members of the community, his risk compensation, on this account, can be written in general as

$$\sum_{i}^{n} r_{ij}^3 \qquad (i \neq j)$$

Bearing in mind that most of the terms in the sum will be zero, the total expression will be positive or negative as the increased risk of death run by others makes the jth person on balance better off or worse off.

For this financial risk to which the community as a whole is exposed, the total risk compensation is obtained by aggregating the above expression over the n members to give

$$\sum_{j}^{n} \sum_{i}^{n} r_{ij}^3 \qquad (i \neq j)$$

which can be represented by R^3. This sum can, as suggested, be positive or negative according to the way the community as a whole expects to be made financially better off or worse of by the death of others.[20]

(b) *The psychic aspect.* It is convenient, as well as charitable, to suppose that this concern for the additional risks to which others are exposed entails a reduction in a person's welfare. Thus, the compensatory sum

$$\sum_{i}^{n} r_{ij}^4 \qquad (i \neq j)$$

for the jth person's increased risk of bereavement carries a negative sign, being the sum of money necessary to reconcile him to bearing the additional risk of death to which his friends and the members of his family are exposed.

The increased risk of bereavement to which the community as a whole is exposed is to be valued at a sum equal to the aggregate

$$\sum_{j}^{n}\sum_{i}^{n} r_{ij}^{4} \qquad (i \neq j)$$

which sum is abbreviated to R^4.

VI

Simplicity of exposition has restricted the analysis to an increase only in the risk of death. The qualifications necessary for the treatment of an increase also in the risk of injury and disease are too obvious to justify elaboration. Application of the above analysis to a *reduced* risk of death, and to a reduced risk of injury and disease, is perhaps slightly less obvious and it may reassure the reader if its symmetrical nature is briefly illustrated by an example. Just as an increase in the number of accidents and fatalities can be a byproduct of some growth in economic activity, so also can a reduction in the number of accidents and fatalities. More familiar, however, is public investment designed primarily to reduce the incidence of disease, suffering, and death. And, although such activity is to be regarded as a collective good, the relationship between collective goods and external effects (which can be thought of as incidental, 'nonoptional', collective goods and 'bads'), is close enough to permit us to make use of our conceptual apparatus without significant modification.

Suppose, then, that the government has a scheme for purifying the air over a vast region, one which is expected to save 20,000 lives annually.[21] The costs of enforcing a clean-air Act and of installing preventive devices needed has to be set against the above social benefits. In accordance with our scheme, they are to be evaluated as follows:

(1) Since, in this example, the reduced risk of death is a collective good, and not an external economy that is internal to some specific economic activity (as there could be, say, in a development that promoted horticulture, regarded as a healthy occupation), there is no R^1 term. There is here no question of how much a person will pay for some market good after making allowance for the *incidental* reduction of risk. The only good in question here is the collective reduction of risk itself.

(2) If the population of the area is 100 million, and the chance of dying from causes connected with air pollution is independent of age, location, occupa-

tion, physical condition, or other factors, the risk of death to each person in the region is reduced by 2/10,000. More generally, there is for the jth person a reduction of the risk of death from factors connected with air pollution (including infection by others suffering from air-pollution diseases) for which he is prepared to pay up to

$$\sum_{i}^{n} r_{ij}^{2}$$

which, on our assumption of universal risk aversion, is positive. Aggregating over the n members, the total sum R^2 is, therefore, also positive.[22]

(3) A reduction in the risk of death for everyone implies, for the jth person, a reduction in the chance of his being financially worse off or better off in the future. The risk compensation

$$\sum_{i}^{n} r_{ij}^{3} \qquad (i \neq j)$$

can therefore be positive or negative. The greater the proportion of aggregate income arising from nonhuman capital, the more likely is the total sum R^3 to be negative for the reduced risk.

(4) Finally, there is the reduced risk of the jth person's suffering bereavement over the future, the corresponding risk compensation

$$\sum_{i}^{n} r_{ij}^{4} \qquad (i \neq j)$$

being positive. The total sum R^4 will, therefore, also be positive.

Evaluation of the benefits of the government scheme is, then, to be based ultimately on the aggregate of maximal sums that all persons in the region affected are willing to pay for the estimated reduction of the risks of death, an aggregate which can be split usefully into three components, R^2, R^3, and R^4.

VII

A word on the deficiencies in the information available to each person concerning the degree of risk involved. These deficiencies of information necessarily contribute to the discrepancies experienced by people between anticipated and realized satisfactions. For all that, in determining whether a potential Pareto improvement has been met, economists are generally agreed – either as a canon of faith, as a political tenet, or as an act of expediency – to accept the dictum that each person knows best his own interest. If, therefore, the economist is told that a person, A, is indifferent regarding not assuming a particular risk or assuming it along with a sum of money, V, then, on the Pareto principle, the sum V has to be accepted as the relevant cost of his being exposed to that risk. It may be the case that, owing either to deficient information or congenital optimism, person A consistently overestimates his chances of survival. But once the dictum is accepted, as indeed it is in economists' appraisals of allocative efficiency, cost–benefit analysis has to accept V as the only relevant magnitude – this being the sum chosen by A in awareness of his relative ignorance.[23] Certainly all the rest of the economic data used in a cost–benefit analysis or any other allocative study, whether derived from market prices and quantities or by other methods of inquiry, is based on this principle of accepting as final only the individual's estimate of what an article is worth to him at the time the decision is to be made. The article in question may, of course, also have a direct worth, positive or negative, for persons other than its buyer or seller, a possibility which requires a consideration of external effects. Yet, again, on the above dictum, it is the values placed on this article by these other persons which will count. Thus, while it is scarcely necessary to urge that more economical ways of refining and disseminating information be explored, the economist engaged in allocative studies traditionally follows the practice of evaluating all social gains and losses solely on the basis of individuals' own evaluations of the relevant effects on their welfare, given the information they have at the time the decision is taken.

VIII

In sum, any expected loss of life or saving of life, any expected increase or reduction in suffering in consequence of economic activity, is to be evaluated for the economy by reference to the Pareto principle; in particular, by reference to what each member of the community is willing to pay or to receive for the estimated change of risk. The resulting aggregate of CVs for the community can be usefully regarded as comprised of four components, and, of these, R^1 – which encompasses all the voluntary risks (where they exist) – can be ignored on the grounds that the benefit to each individual of the direct activity in question (often estimated as equal to the area under the demand curve) is already net of this risk.

The other involuntary components of risk – R^2, R^3, R^4 –cannot, in general, be ignored, though one can surmise that with the growth in material prosperity their magnitude will tend to grow. On the other hand, with the growth in the welfare state, and in particular with an increasingly egalitarian structure of real disposable incomes, the financial risk compensation, R^3, will tend to decline. The gradual loosening of family ties and the decline of emotional interdependence should cause the magnitude of the bereavement risk compensation, R^4, to decline also. In a wholly impersonal society in which, for any jth person, the loss of any member of the community is easily replaceable in j's estimation by many others, R^4 will tend to vanish; R^2, however, is wholly selfish in the sense that it depends on people's preference for staying alive. Until such time as a genetic revolution turns men into pure altruists, or pure automatons, ready, like some species of ants, to sacrifice themselves at a moment's notice for the greater convenience of the whole, it can be expected that R^2 will grow over time.

Before concluding, however, it should be emphasized that the basic concept introduced in this paper is not simply an alternative to, or an auxiliary to, any existing methods[24] that have been proposed for measuring the loss or saving of life. It is the only economically justifiable concept. And this assertion does not rest on any novel ethical premise. It follows as a matter of consistency in the application of the Pareto principle in cost–benefit calculations.

Insofar as an immediate application of the concepts to the measurement of loss or saving of life is in issue, one's claims must be more muted. In the attempts to measure social benefits and losses, price–quantity statistics lend themselves better to the more familiar examples in which people choose quantities at given market prices than they do to examples in which people have to choose prices for the given quantities. For one can observe the quantities they choose, at least collectively, whereas one cannot generally observe their subjective valuations. In the circumstances, economists seriously concerned with coming to grips with the magnitudes may have to brave the disdain of their colleagues and consider the possibility that data yielded by surveys based on the questionnaire method are better than none, or better than data obtained by persisting with some of the current measures such as L_1 or L_2. In the last resort, one could invoke 'contingency calculations' (Mishan, 1969, p. 70) in order to determine, for example, whether the apparent excess benefit of a scheme (calculated in the absence of any allowance for the expected increase in fatalities and injuries) is likely or not to exceed any plausible estimate of the evaluation of the increased risk to which people are exposed.

In view of the existing quantomania, one may be forgiven for asserting that there is more to be said for rough estimates of the precise concept than precise estimates of economically irrelevant concepts. The caveat is more to be heeded in this case, bearing in mind that currently used and currently mooted measures of saving life or the loss of life – such as L_1, L_2, L_3, and L_4 – have no conceptual affinity with the Pareto basis of cost–benefit analysis.

Notes: Chapter 9

1 For the returns on his (nonhuman) assets continue after his death, or during his disablement.

2 For example, see Kneese (1966, p. 77) and Ridker (1967, p. 34). The suggestions, needless to remark, have not been taken up. Presumably they are made in response to an uneasy conscience about the methods actually being employed.

3 The expression occurs in Ridker's book (1967) on the costs of pollution. For those prone to morbid curiosity, the formula used is on page 39, and takes the form

$$C_a = C_O \left(1 - \sum_{n=a}^{\infty} \frac{P_a^n}{(1+r)^{n-a}} \right)$$

where C_a is the present value of the net expected gain from delaying burial at age a; C_o is the cost of burial; P_a^n is the probability that an individual age a will die at age n, and r is the discount rate. It is not impossible that these calculations were made with tongue in cheek, and, if so, it is perhaps an oversight on his part that he omitted a countervailing consideration; namely, that if the unfortunate person died at a very early age, some useful savings might be effected from the lower cost of a smaller coffin.

4 Indeed, Rothenberg (1961, pp. 309–36) ends his examination of social welfare criteria by proposing that the democratic process itself be regarded as such a criterion. More recently, Nath (1969, pp. 216–17) proposes that the task of the economist be limited to that of revealing the locus of 'efficient' economic production possibilities available to society, leaving it to democracy to select the collection of goods it wishes. If one favors a majority decision rule or some other democratic decision rule for top level choices, the question must arise: on what grounds is this decision rule withheld (in favor of the potential Pareto criterion) at lower levels of *optima* – for instance, in generating a locus of 'efficient' collection of goods? A movement from a non-efficient point *inside* the boundary to an efficient point *on* the boundary of production possibilities can claim no more than can a movement from a top-level nonoptimal boundary point to a top-level optimal boundary point. Both of such movements have distributional implications, both meet the 'Scitovsky' criterion, and both may be negated by the Kaldor-Hicks criterion.

5 For example, Devons (1961, p. 108) concludes ironically: 'Indeed if we could only kill off enough old people we could show a net gain on accidents as a whole!' As for Ridker (1967, p. 36), the net output method 'suggests that society should not interfere with the death of a person whose net value is negative'.

6 Which is not to deny that the economist's criterion or criteria – although independent of the outcome of any particular political process that is sanctioned by the constitution – must be vindicated ultimately by reference to value judgments widely held within the community. The reader interested in this aspect is referred to Mishan (1969, pp. 13–23).

7 An ingenious paper by Eisner and Strotz (1961), after some theorizing on the basis of the Neumann–Morgenstern axioms about the optimal amount of insurance a person should buy, addresses itself to the question of why people continue to buy air-accident insurance when ordinary life insurance is cheaper. They suggest, among other things, that flight insurance could be a gamble (related formally to the increasing marginal-utility segment of the income–utility curve), and they point also to the existence of imperfect knowledge, imperfect markets, and inertia. However, the paper does not, and is presumably not intended to, throw any light on this question of the valuation of human life. The observation that a man does not insure his life against some specific contingency cannot be taken as evidence that he is indifferent as between being alive and being dead.

8 A 'potential Pareto improvement' is an alternative and simpler nomenclature than 'hypothetical compensation test'. The problems associated with the concept are important, but need not concern us here if we accept the fact that cost–benefit analyses take place within a partial context, one in which changes in the prices of all the non-project goods can be ignored. If this much is granted, the relevant individuals' compensating variations, which is what we are after, will be uniquely determined.

9 For the arguments that tend to this conclusion, see Mishan (1969, pp. 66–73).

10 These sums may be calculated as annual transfers or as capital sums according to the method being used in the cost–benefit study. Since the flow of costs and benefits is to be valued at a point of time, consistency would require that the CVs also be reckoned as a capital sum at that point of time. If there are no external effects of saving for future generations, as posited by Marglin (1963), the existence of imperfect capital markets will result in different rates of time preference among the persons concerned. In that case, capitalizing their CVs reckoned as annual sums at some single rate of discount will result in corresponding capitalized CVs which would differ from those chosen directly by these same persons, which latter sums should, of course, prevail.

11 Within the same broad context, and allowing for sufficient divisibility in the construction of such projects, the corresponding rule necessary to determine the optimal output of such projects – or, in short periods, the optimal output of the goods of the existing project – takes the simple form that

$$\sum_{j}^{n} v_j = 0$$

where v_j is the CV of the jth person in response to a marginal increment in the size of the industry or (in the short period) the size of its output.

12 If a man and his family were so destitute and their prospects so hopeless that one or more members were likely to die of starvation, or at least to suffer from acute

deprivation, then the man might well be persuaded to sacrifice himself for the sake of his family. But without dependents or close and needy friends, the inducement to sacrifice himself for others is not strong.

13 Cf. Schelling's remarks (1968, pp. 142–6).

14 Risk aversion is assumed throughout (unless otherwise stated) solely in the interests of brevity. If some people enjoy the additional risk, their CVs will be positive. In general, if the aggregate of the CVs for the additional risk is negative, which is the case for universal risk aversion, there is a subtraction from the benefit side. If, on the other hand, it was positive, there would be an addition to the benefit side.

15 In a most engaging and highly perceptive paper, Schelling (1968) divides the problem into three parts: (a) society's interest, (b) an economic interest (in which category a man's contribution to GNP is placed), and (c) a 'consumer's interest'. Discussing this third interest in connection with a life-saving program, Schelling correctly poses the relevant question: what will people pay for a government program that reduces risk? (p. 142). But being uneasy about the actual measurement of such a sum, and absorbed with other fascinating, though in the context irrelevant, considerations, he does not develop the analysis systematically. Indeed, he goes on later to discuss the value of certain and inescapable loss of life and comes up with the suggestion that college professors would be prepared to pay an amount equal to something between ten and a hundred times their annual income in order to save the life of one of their family. If one is interested solely in the conceptual measure, as I am here, one can make use of the notion of external effects to develop the analysis. Fromm's hypercritical comments (1968), on the other hand, make use of external effects, along with the difficulties of measuring, largely to cast doubt upon this valid part of Schelling's paper.

16 The nice distinction made by Schelling (1968, pp. 132–5) between loss of life and loss of livelihood is, possibly, meaningful, but difficult to capture. Given the 'conjuncture' of circumstances in which a man finds himself, there is, in principle, some amount of money that will just induce him to assume a particular risk of being killed. But it is hardly likely that he will be able to apportion that sum as between 'life' and 'livelihood' – and it is not necessary, in this analysis, that he should be able to do so.

17 The distinction between external effects *internal* to the industry and those *external* to the industry is proposed in Mishan (1965).

18 The external diseconomies of traffic risk are, therefore, treated exactly as the external diseconomies of traffic congestion. But, as distinct from the problem of estimating the excess benefit of a project of given size, the determination of an *optimal* traffic flow does require intervention by the economist in consequence of these mutual external diseconomies. For the question raised in determining an optimal traffic flow is no longer one of showing that, for a given volume of traffic, total benefits (*net* of risk and congestion) exceed total costs. The question, now, is to *choose* a volume of traffic so as to *maximize* excess benefit over cost, this being realized by equating marginal social benefit to marginal cost. The standard argument is then invoked, namely, that although the effects on all others of risk and congestion grow with each additional car, the jth, or marginal

vehicle-owner, in deciding whether to use the highway, considers only the term

$$\sum_i^n r_{ij}^!$$

(ignoring the similar congestion term), as indeed does each of the other members, that is, he takes account only of the costs to him of each of the n vehicles on the road, including his own. What he does *not* take into account is the effect he himself produces on each of the others by his decision to add his vehicle to theirs; which is to say, he ignores the cost

$$\sum_i^n r_{ij}^! \qquad (i \neq j)$$

the costs imposed on each of the intramarginal vehicles by introducing his own jth vehicle. This latter term, therefore, represents the cost of those external diseconomies generated by the marginal vehicle, diseconomies that are internal to and absorbed by all intramarginal vehicles, and which are properly attributable to the marginal vehicle in determining the optimal flow of traffic.

19 It might, at first, appear that an asset which is transferred from the deceased to his beneficiaries cancels out, as it does in the L_1 or L_2 measure. But, if transfers are generally omitted from such calculations, it is simply because they take place between living persons: a transfer of $10,000 from person A to person B implies that the sum of their CVs is zero. On our criterion there is neither gain nor loss. However, where the issue is no longer a voluntary transfer of wealth but the risk of an involuntary transfer through death, the case is different. If there is an increased risk of person B losing his life, the CV for that risk is negative; that is, there is some minimum amount of money which will restore his welfare. To person A, however, who cares nothing for B's person but expects to inherit B's vast estate, the increased risk to which B is now exposed is a benefit for which he is willing to pay up to some maximum sum.

20 Only in an economy in which income was wholly from human capital would the R^3 component be comparable with the L_2 measure. A figure for the latter could be got by subtracting the net *losses* to the surviving members, arising from the death of breadwinners, from the net *gains* to the surviving members, arising from the death of dependents. As for R^3, the better the information, and the more constant the relation between income and utility along the relevant range, the closer the figure would be to the aggregate of the actuarial values of the net expected gain or loss to each person. It is the existence of non-human assets, and the possibility of their transfer from deceased to survivors, that adds to the positive value of R^3 and raises it above the L_2 measure.

21 Again, for simplicity of exposition we omit reference, in this example, to the reduction of suffering or the enjoyment of better health.

22 It is frequently alleged that at low levels risk can have a positive utility. (In the absence of 'income effects' one can, for example, hypothesize a curve relating the person's CV to increasing risk of death. Measuring risk on a horizontal axis, the CV curve is above it for low risk, and below it for all risk exceeding a critical level. As the probability of death rises toward unity, we should expect the curve to increase its rate of decline and become

asymptotic to a vertical axis passing through the unity point.) But whether this is so, and the extent to which it is so, would seem to depend upon the activity associated with the risk. Driving at 100 miles per hour increases the risk of a fatal accident. And if some people choose gratuitously to drive at this speed, it is not simply in response to the additional risk *per se*. It is partly because a test of skill, physical courage, or manhood is involved. Even where skill is absent, as in playing Russian roulette, there is a certain bravado in openly flirting with death. On the other hand, it is hard to imagine a man deriving positive utility from the information that henceforth he is to be exposed – though anonymously, along with millions of others – to an increased risk of death, one over which he has no semblance of choice or control. The risk of increased infection by some new disease or by increased radioactive fallout would be examples. Nevertheless, the question of whether risk, at some levels, has a positive or a negative utility, in any particular case, is an empirical one and does not affect the formal analysis.

23 Person *A*, for example, may find himself disabled for life and rue his decision to take the risk. But this example is only a more painful one of the fact that people come to regret a great many of the choices they make, notwithstanding which they would resent any interference with their future choices.

24 It is far from impossible that society may choose to refer decisions in matters involving life and death to a representative body or committee and that a decision may be reached that differs from the one which would arise from the consistent application of cost–benefit techniques. Nevertheless, the economist is free to criticize the decision, to point out inconsistencies, and to discover what features, if any, warrant a departure from the Pareto criterion. Consistency, in this instance, requires that the expected change in risk associated with any contemplated scheme be evaluated by reference to the same principle as all other relevant economic gains and losses. To evaluate the welfare effect of risk on some other principle, say, by a voting procedure, entails the adding together of incommensurables. Thus, an implicit figure for the effect of risk on welfare attributable to a decision taken by a smaller group (or even by the whole group), by the method of counting heads, is added to a figure for the other economic effects which, using the Pareto principle, aggregates the valuation of each member determined on a *CV* basis.

References

Devons, E., *Essays in Economics* (London: Allen & Unwin, 1961).

Eisner, R. and Strotz, R. H., 'Flight insurance and the theory of choice', *Journal of Political Economy,* vol. 69, no. 4 (August 1961), pp. 355–68.

Friedman, M. and Savage L. J., 'Utility analysis of choices involving risks', *Journal of Political Economy*, vol. 56, no. 4 (August 1948), pp. 279–304.

Fromm, G., 'Civil aviation expenditures', in *Measuring Benefits of Government Investment*, edited by R. Dorfman (Washington DC: Brookings Institution, 1965).

Fromm, G., 'Comment on T. C. Schelling's paper, "The life you save may be your own" ', in *Problems in Public Expenditure*, edited by S. B. Chase Jr (Washington DC: Brookings Institution, 1968).

Kneese, A. V., 'Research goals and progress toward them', in *Environmental Quality in a Growing Economy*, edited by H. Jarrett (Washington DC: Johns Hopkins, 1966).

Marglin, S., 'The social rate of discount and the optimal rate of investment', *Quarterly Journal of Economics*, vol. 77, no. 1 (February 1963), pp. 95–111.

Mishan, E. J., 'Rent as a measure of welfare change', *American Economic Review*, vol. 49, no. 3 (May 1959), pp. 386–94.

Mishan, E. J., 'Reflections on recent development in the concept of external effects', *Canadian Journal of Economics*, vol. 31, no. 1 (February 1965), pp. 3–34.

Mishan, E. J., *Welfare Economics: An Assessment* (Amsterdam: North-Holland, 1969).

Nath, S. K., *A Reappraisal of Welfare Economics* (London: Routledge & Kegan Paul, 1969).

Ridker, R. G., *The Economic Costs of Air Pollution* (New York: Praeger, 1967).

Rothenberg, J., *The Measurement of Social Welfare* (Englewood Cliffs, NJ: Prentice-Hall, 1961).

Schelling, T. C., 'The life you save may be your own', in *Problems in Public Expenditure*, edited by S. B. Chase Jr (Washington DC: Brookings Institution, 1968).

10

Interpretation of the Benefits of Private Transport

I

In this article I construct a hypothetical situation to reveal some of the circumstances under which consumers' surplus, when used as an index of the benefits to be derived from private automobile travel, may give perverse results – a rise in the index being accompanied by a reduction in the benefit experienced by motorists. Less surprisingly, it will also be shown that the use of consumers' surplus in determining optimal traffic flows, in benefit–cost studies, and in estimating rates of return in road investment results in solutions leading to overinvestment in road construction unless the alternatives to private automobile travel are properly priced.

Although not essential, it will simplify the analysis to assume (1) that in all sections of a fully employed economy, except those under examination, price is already equal to social marginal cost, and (2) provisionally at least, that there are no neighbourhood effects external to the transport industry that affect the amenity of the public. We estimate the consumer's surplus for each individual in terms of present discounted value of expected surpluses over the future, using as discount rate whatever rate is deemed appropriate. A measure of this consumer's surplus, represented by the compensating variation[1] on the purchase of a new automobile, requires the individual to anticipate at the time of purchase the total number of miles for which the car will be used, valuing each mile at its maximum present worth to him (net of all variable costs, including fuel and maintenance) and arranging these sums in descending order to the point of zero maximum worth. This arrangement produces a function $V(m)$ of total expected mileage. After completing M miles the automobile is to be sold for a sum having a present value of $£T$. If the car when bought costs $£B$, including tax,[2] the present discounted value of

the compensating-variation measure of consumer's surplus, CS, is equal to

$$\int_0^M V(m)dm - (B - T)$$

this sum being the maximum the individual would be prepared to pay in order to secure a permit to buy the car at the price $£B$, given his expectation of reselling for the sum mentioned after motoring M miles.

Phase I of the situation is one in which there is no private traffic. An efficient system of public transport, say a bus service, links all parts of the city. Individual A, typical of others, uses the bus daily to take him to the centre of the city in about 10 minutes. Public transport is also used for his occasional outings.

Phase II is the transitional one in which A buys a new car which in the circumstances prevailing (which he, shortsightedly, projects into the future) is expected to take him to the centre in 5 minutes. On his anticipations of the future he makes a CS of, say, £800. Provided that only A buys a car, and nothing else changes, A is to that extent better off in phase II than in phase I.

Phase III occurs after a large enough number of others follow A's example. Within two or three years, we may suppose, the increase in the number of private cars is such that it takes A 15 minutes to drive to work. He realises now that he was better off in phase I, but that opportunity is now closed to him. For, owing to the build-up of private traffic, the congestion is such that it would now take him 25 minutes to reach his office by bus. Moreover, since bus-drivers have had to be compensated for the increased difficulties and risk of driving, the bus fare has risen.

Phase III' is the situation after public transport has been withdrawn altogether, as may happen if commercial considerations alone prevail. Analytically, it differs from III only in being a more extreme case of it.

II

By assumption A is now worse off in phase III than he was in I. He would, of course, prefer II to either III or I. But II is a transitional phase only: it is no longer open to him, and could be reserved for him only if he were granted special privileges.

Since A is typical of other individuals who have changed from being passengers to being motorists, we can assume that I is *socially* preferred to III: dealers in motor cars and accessories may, themselves, be on balance better off, but we suppose that they could not compensate the rest of the community and remain as well off as they were in I.

There are two points to notice. First, under existing institutions there are no self-generating forces that can restore to the community the socially preferred phase I. Only a collective decision could return the community from the existing III or III' phase to the original I situation. Secondly, A's CS on his automobile in phase III will exceed that in phase II notwithstanding that he gets less benefit from it in phase III. It was, in fact, just because public transport was so cheap and efficient in phase I that the maximum amount he was prepared to pay for successive miles of private driving was lower then than it is now in phase III, in which the public transport alternative is less attractive. If now, for example, we move to phase III', in which the public transport alternative is completely withdrawn, a loss of welfare will certainly be experienced by the remaining passengers. Some of these ex-passengers will have little choice but to purchase automobiles. Nevertheless, compared with their new alternatives – those of walking to work and of not working in the city – the CS on their purchase will be positive, and may even be large. Since we may assume that the cars used by the displaced passengers in phase III' take up more road space than did the displaced buses, the motorists in phase III', of whom A was a typical example, will also be worse off than they were in III.

If the benefit conferred by the private automobile on its owner is measured by his CS, or any proxy measure, the chronological change through II, III and III' will appear to register a continuously increasing benefit, notwithstanding the continuous deterioration in his welfare in this respect.

A similar development could, of course, arise in other situations, for instance in a suburb linked by rail to the city. At the given rail fare n commuters are required for the railway to 'break even'. If, therefore, owing to an initial change from rail to road, only m commuters remain ($m < n$), the railway service must close down. The closure clearly makes the m com-

muters worse off. But it also makes worse off those who before the closure were travelling by private automobiles, because: (a) m commuters now have to travel by road and increase the congestion there, and (b) even though automobile travellers made no use of the railway, or used it infrequently, it did provide a form of insurance in case the car was out of service – or for any occasions when, for one reason or another, the motorist did not feel up to driving.

Again, however, despite the fact that everyone going into the city is adversely affected by the railway closure, the community's demand for road travel will be seen to have expanded and the individual and, therefore, the collective consumers' surplus of automobile-owners will reveal a gain. Each ex-train-commuter who has now perforce to purchase an automobile must reveal a positive CS. As for the remainder, once the railway service has been removed the only alternative, we may suppose, is walking to the city. The maximum amount any individual would be willing to pay for the ith journey by car is consequently greater.

These simple illustrations may serve to remind us that there are difficulties other than those of statistical measurement. Not only can the index of consumers' benefit rise over time without any actual experience of benefit – simply because 'real' income is increasing, and therefore people are prepared to pay more for the ith unit of any good, or service, whose actual utility to them in fact remains unchanged – but such an index can rise concurrently with an actual reduction of benefit. The more significant parts of the other factors which may affect any consumer's surplus (and rent) analysis relate to the constancy of the prices, and/or availabilities, of the close substitutes, and complements, for the good or service in question. The more effective is the good y as, say, a substitute for x, the smaller will be the consumer's surplus on purchase of x at the given prices. Raise the price of y, and ultimately withdraw it from the market, and this simultaneously *reduces* the welfare of the consumer and *increases* his measure of consumer's surplus on purchases of x.

III

We may now use the same two illustrations to show that any road-engineering recommendations flowing from such estimates of the demand curve for automobile travel are invalid in the absence of optimal outputs in all the alternative services. In the first illustration, as the community moves into phase III the transport engineer will continue to revise upward his estimate of the 'optimal traffic flow',[3] which appears to expand, therefore, along with the fall in motorists' welfare.[4]

The transport engineer may also use the data in *III* and *III'* to justify investment in road-widening, flyovers, freeways and bridges, in the attempt to accommodate the expanding number of private automobiles.

Now, if there were effective methods for imputing congestion costs in the first place, other recommendations would follow which, under our assumption that in all other sectors price was equal to social marginal cost, could be justified. Beginning with a satisfactory public transport in phase *I*, such a mechanism would require that full compensation for any inconvenience caused to every passenger and bus driver by the marginal private car be imputed to the marginal private car. Such a scheme would ensure that no additional car be allowed on the route(s) in question unless it were able to effect a Pareto improvement: the owner of the car being better off after compensating everyone else using the roads – bus passengers, bus-drivers, and intramarginal automobiles – than he would be without the use of his car. Such a requirement, which would ensure growing benefits from traffic, might well entail an optimal flow with very few private automobiles.

Be that as it may, it is only *after* this optimal flow is established that one may proceed to estimate correctly the returns to investment in road-widening, freeways and other traffic-accommodating projects. A traffic flow that has not been corrected implies that marginal congestion costs already exceed marginal benefit for some part of the existing traffic flow. Total congestion costs incurred being, then, greater than the optimally determined congestion costs, the saving by traffic investment will appear correspondingly greater. It is possible, therefore, that an initial optimal traffic flow might reveal no economic case for traffic investment, whereas failure to establish this optimal flow would allow traffic to pile up congestion costs and would consequently enable investment to appear profitable, in effect, by reducing excess traffic costs that were not warranted in the first place.

Similar remarks apply to our second illustration. If, as a consequence of rail closure, congestion occurs on the roads connecting the suburb to the centre of the city, the establishment of an optimal flow of motorised traffic must precede any estimate of the benefits of road investment. More important, the rationale of the proposed rail closure itself should be scrutinised before this requirement. A fall in the number of fare-paying passengers below some critical number *n* is generally irrelevant in this connection. The line should be kept running for the time being if, at any number of passengers for which price is equal to marginal operating costs, total benefit exceeds total operating costs.[5] Benefits may be reckoned as the sum of three items: (a) the fares that could be collected from all those willing to pay the marginal cost price (as determined by the existing demand schedule) *plus* the consumer's surplus of every such individual, (b) the insurance value of the railway service to those who do not anticipate any particular railway journeys, and (c) the sum total of any (additional) congestion costs that would be inflicted on all motorists having to use the suburb-to-city road after the railway closure.[6] It would not be surprising if many of the railway services closed or due for closure could prove economic viability by meeting these conditions.[7] At all events, closing a railway service which on this criterion ought not to be closed brings about a misallocation of scarce resources, including those released by closing the railway. After resources have been misallocated by closing the railway service, investment in roads that would otherwise (if the railway services were available) be clearly seen as wasteful might well appear profitable.

Before concluding, it is worth emphasising that the application of the consumer's surplus concept in transport economics goes far beyond its direct application in the analysis of optimal flows. Its use is implicit in cost-benefit analysis and in other transport investment criteria. Inasmuch as the estimated benefits of a bridge or new road will include savings in running costs and savings in motorists' time *as compared with existing alternatives*, the value of these benefits entails an upward revision of the individual's schedule of marginal valuation, roughly equal to his demand curve, with respect to motoring mileage. This being so, the withdrawal of any existing substitutes for private motoring raises all such marginal valuation schedules and shifts to the right the aggregate demand curve for motoring – the number of motoring journeys increasing as a result both of the induced rise in the motoring population and the induced rise in the average number of journeys per motorist. Thus, as public transport is withdrawn or rendered less efficient, *benefit–cost ratio* calculation is increased, since estimated 'benefits' of constructing a road or bridge begin to appear which would not have appeared under an optimally controlled traffic flow. Moreover, inasmuch as the expected returns from any capital investment in roads or bridges are derived from just such benefits, the resulting *internal rate of return* calculation also becomes inflated whenever the existing traffic flow exceeds the optimal flow. And though it is possible that, in some cases, this spurious rise in the estimated benefit–cost ratio or internal rate of return is not large, it may be enough to raise the estimates beyond the crucial figure at which the investment decision becomes operative.

IV

We have confined ourselves in this note to external diseconomies that are internal to private motoring, that is, to the mutual congestion costs of motorised traffic, following the popular custom of relegating to a parenthetical remark the unmeasurable, though probably much more important, effects on the physical environment. The private car carries along with it, however, another much neglected disamenity potential as the chief agent of urban sprawl and ribbon building. As 'developers' set up estates farther and yet farther from city centres, in the assurance that wherever they site their buildings families with private cars will be prepared to make the longer journey in order to live in country areas, the advantages of those families already settled in these areas are diminished.[8]

Even if we restrict the analysis to a given area (say the city and its dormitory areas), the continual visual disturbance, the pollution of the air by exhaust fumes, and the incessant engine noise and vibration generated by any n travellers using private transport are very many times greater than would be generated by the same number using public transport, especially if public transport were electrically powered. Hence, although an optimal flow of traffic calculated with respect only to mutual traffic frustration already favours public transport at the expense of private transport (comparing this optimal flow with the usual free-for-all that makes road investment appear so profitable), an optimal flow that also takes into consideration these other environment-damaging consequences – no less relevant or significant for being statistically elusive – would further reduce the warrantable flow of private traffic. If the number of private car journeys consistent with this more comprehensive measure of the optimal flow were believed to be few, the costs involved in their regulation might well suggest prohibition of all private traffic within a given area as the most economic solution – allowing, perhaps, for a given number of private taxis within the area for emergency purposes.

It may, of course, happen that, contrary to our initial assumption, an existing public transport system is already inefficient in coverage, speed and frequency. However, an analysis yielding a Pareto optimal solution requiring the provision of an efficient public transport service does not depend for its validity upon the chronological sequence posited.[9]

Notes: Chapter 10

1 In this context, the compensating variation is the maximum sum an individual will offer for the privilege of buying a good at a given price. See J. R. Hicks, 'The four consumers' surpluses', *Review of Economic Studies,* vol. 11, no. 2 (1944).

2 This tax may be an underestimate or overestimate of the costs of road maintenance and administration incurred by the community (exclusive of the costs of mutual congestion) in keeping the traffic moving on the existing system of roads. The analysis assumes that the tax is exactly equal to the costs incurred.

3 By calculating the marginal congestion cost of traffic

$$\frac{dC}{dN} = \frac{dC}{dT} \cdot \frac{dT}{dS} \cdot \frac{dS}{dN}$$

where C is total congestion cost, N the number of vehicles, T the total time taken by the traffic over the given route ($= tN$, where t is the average time taken per automobile) and S is the average speed of traffic over that route. The optimal traffic flow is that which equates marginal congestion costs dC/dN to the demand price $P(N)$ for that route.

4 Of course, in the event of phase III' being reached, there remaining no alternative but to walk to work, the elasticity of demand may be so low as to make little difference, if any, between the actual traffic flow and the optimal traffic flow.

5 Largely the earnings of *necessary* personnel, fuel and maintenance charges.

6 To be more exact, (c) should be included in so far as this contingent addition to congestion has not been anticipated. If it were wholly anticipated it would have raised the consumer's surpluses of existing, and potential, railway-users, and would also have raised the value of the railway to motorists who make no regular use of the railway.

7 Professor George Clayton, in private correspondence with me, points out that there is no common pattern of decision about rail closures, and that many lines have been closed or are threatened with closure even though they carried, or currently carry, heavy local traffic. In particular he cites the proposed closures of (1) the Liverpool–Southport electric line, carrying over 100,000 passengers a week, mainly during rush hours – but this proposal has been dropped pending further study; and (2) the Cardiff–Coryton line, which offers only a peak hour service – permission to close the line has been refused, owing to heavy commuter traffic, but eventual closure is still possible.

8 Again, however, if some institutional mechanism could be established whereby each additional home-buyer (who adds to the existing number in or near the area and so contributes to its transformation into a suburb) were obliged to compensate existing householders for the loss of amenity endured by his settling there, the criterion for a Pareto improvement could be met. Such external diseconomies would then be automatically corrected and urban sprawl be subject to a built-in check.

9 In general, if all vehicles differed in size and other relevant characteristics, and if the value attached

by their occupants to travelling the distance in question differed for any *i*th journey, we should determine the optimal traffic flow and its composition by maximising the social surplus. This is got by ranking the individual journeys by the excess of *CV* over the marginal congestion cost until the excess is zero. In the absence of welfare effects on the *CV* measure (these would be brought into operation by compensatory payments), the optimal flow and composition of the traffic are uniquely determined. For any flow having a social surplus smaller than this maximum indicates a potential Pareto improvement. Thus some journey(s) currently excluded by the composition of the existing traffic could replace some journey(s) currently included, and thereby increase the social surplus. The additional gain from such exchange operations could, of course, be distributed among the participants so as to make each of them better off.

11

Pareto Optimality and the Law

Over the past few years it has been generally recognized that the nature of any optimal solution depends, for two quite different reasons, on the existing distribution of income [10]. Inasmuch as the distribution of income is itself influenced by legislation – through taxes and subsidies, through price regulation and controls, and through a vast and growing public expenditure on goods and services – the optimal solutions attainable must depend also upon the laws of a country. In a modern economy in which external effects are rapidly spreading, the influence of the law both on the determination and the attainment of optimal solutions, makes itself felt in yet other ways. In cases of conflicting interest, according as the law, deliberately or by default, places the burden of reaching optimal arrangement on one party or group rather than on the other, both the characteristics of the optimal outcome and the costs of its attainment are altered. And the more important, as a component of welfare, are the external effects in question the greater, in these respects, is the impact of the law.

I

This paper then is concerned primarily with demonstrating (1) that the characteristics of an optimal solution are not uniquely specified but depend, in general, on the existing law, (2) that the costs incurred in realizing an optimal outcome, and the question therefore of its 'feasibility', also depend upon the existing law, and finally (3) that an optimal solution emerging from conflicts of interest is optimal only with respect to an implicit constraint requiring the area in question to be used in common by the groups or persons having conflicting interests. Once separate areas, or separate facilities, are introduced solutions appear that are Pareto superior to the familiar constrained optimal outcomes. The first two propositions are particularly relevant in connection with external diseconomies which, when uncorrected, engender conflicts of interest. The expositional scheme used

here, however, can just as well be extended to cover external economies.

Since the analysis has more heuristic than operational value, the problems of measurement are not touched upon. Nor do we introduce algorithms for determining solutions in the n-unit case. Again, though the treatment of external effects must be regarded as an exercise in partial statics, we circumvent familiar second-best obstacles by keeping to the path of *ceteris paribus* which, in this connection, requires that consequent changes in all prices, other than those directly under examination, be negligible: an 'improvement' within the sector under survey is, therefore, on the Pareto principle, an improvement for the economy as a whole, irrespective of the condition of the economy prior to this improvement.

We introduce, in addition, a number of simplifications into the analysis which facilitate the exposition without restricting unduly the range of its applicability: (1) The activity, exemptions from which involve compensatory payments, is measured over a given period without reference to the pattern of its distribution within that period. (2) The income, or welfare, effects, with respect to the activity in question, are taken to be 'normal'. (3) The compensatory payments used throughout the paper are defined as compensating variations. (4) The money equivalent of the net benefits arising from any Pareto improvement within the area in question is in all cases passed on to the government for distribution outside that area. A few words about each of these:

(1) Formally one can choose a period small enough as to make the question of the pattern of distribution within it appear trivial. But a limit is placed on the shortness of the period by the requirement, in any solution, that successive periods carry the same distributional pattern; for the characteristics of the solution must, within the framework of static analysis, be repeated in all periods. This neglect of the pattern of distribution within a period of minimum duration is convenient and frequently realistic, but not always. An

example will be given in note 29 to suggest how improvements may be brought about by changing the pattern of the distribution of the activity within the period.

(2) A 'normal' welfare effect, implying that an improvement in the individual's welfare raises his demand for the good, also implies that the maximum sum he will pay for a given amount of it (or, alternatively, the minimum sum he will accept to forgo a given amount of it) will arise with an increase in his welfare.[1] It has the further implication that the maximum he will pay for a thing[2] is less than the minimum sum he will accept to forgo it. Although the 'normal' welfare effect is plausible for the sort of activities exemplified in this paper, the results do not in the least depend upon it.

(3) In a general treatment of external effects – one that is not restricted to spillover effects that can be costed through the market – the distinction should be made between a compensating variation, CV, defined more generally as a measure of the money transfer necessary, following some economic change, to maintain the individual's welfare at his original level, and an equivalent variation, EV, defined more generally as a measure of the money transfer which, in the absence of the change in question, affords the individual an equivalent change in his welfare [10, p. 610]. Exactly the same distinction between CV and EV arises if we consider a reversal of some specific law from being, say, permissive with respect to an activity to being prohibitive.

To illustrate, if from a state of permissiveness with respect to smoking, a no-smoking order were introduced, the CV of a nonsmoker who gains from the change of law would be measured as a maximum sum per period, say $20, this being the amount he is willing to pay to have the permissive law reversed. The EV measure would be a transfer to him of some minimum amount, say $22, in lieu of the contemplated no-smoking order. If, later, the no-smoking order were revoked the CV would be a payment to him of this minimum sum, $22, while the EV would be a maximum sum of $20. The smoker's welfare is affected in the opposite way, but the pattern is equally symmetric.

Thus, if we are interested in the effects wrought by a reversal of the law, it would appear that for each person affected by the state of the law four measures of exact compensatory transfer are required; a CV and an EV corresponding to each of the two states of the law. However, it is evident from the above illustration that there is only a single difference notwithstanding the four measures, the individual's CV and EV for the

introduction of the no-smoking order being equal, respectively, to the EV and CV for a reversal of that order. Hence, for two alternative states of the law, one the reverse of the other, we need consider only the CV or only the EV. And our choice, here, will be influenced by the definition of a Pareto improvement as one that makes everyone affected better off (or some better off and others no worse off), beginning from the *status quo*. By adopting the CV measure, rather than the EV, we enjoy the convenience of identifying a Pareto improvement with a positive sum arising from the algebraic total of the CVs of all the individuals affected by the change in question. For those who are affected by a change can be divided into gainers and losers. The CV of each gainer is the maximum sum he would now pay (a sum which, if paid, would leave him no better off than he was before the change). The CV for each of the losers, on the other hand, is the minimum sum he can be made to accept as a *quid pro quo* (a sum which, if paid to him, would leave him no worse off than he was before the change). If, with respect to some change, the maximum sum the gainers would be willing to pay exceeds the minimum sum the losers would accept, that is, if the algebraic sum of the CVs is positive, that change offers a Pareto improvement.[3]

Reversing the law, we shall still want to ask whether a Pareto improvement can be effected by a change from it. We must again ask, that is, whether the algebraic sum of the CVs is positive.

(4) In comparing the distribution of welfare in the initial situation under the existing law with that which would emerge if the laws were reversed, we begin in each case from a position in which the external effects are uncorrected. Those made better off in reversing the existing law will subsequently be made worse off if, later, the law reverts to its previous state. The important implication, to be demonstrated, is that the outcome of each decision rule which may realize a Pareto improvement starting from the initial situation (with external effects uncorrected) is not uniquely determined. In general such outcomes will depend upon the law under which potential Pareto improvements are envisaged. Granted this much, it becomes a matter of great convenience that when comparing, under the existing law, the magnitude of the gain from one arrangement B with that of a previous arrangement A, the individual CVs continue to remain the same as those determined in the initial (uncorrected) situation notwithstanding any consequent redistribution of welfare resulting from the first, A, arrangement. Put otherwise, if the net benefit, NB, of an arrangement B, is the algebraic sum of the CVs compared with the initial situation under the existing law, and the NB of an

arrangement *A* is similarly defined, then it would be convenient to reckon the *excess* net benefit of *B* as compared with the net benefit of *A* as [*NB(B)* − *NB (A)*], where *NB(B)* and *NB(A)* are, respectively, the net benefits of *B* and of *A*, both measured with respect to the initial, uncorrected, situation. This desideratum may be accomplished by requiring that, after full compensation is paid within the group, the amount left over, the positive sum associated with an *NB* from any adopted arrangement, be paid in the government which may distribute it among people in the rest of the economy, for instance among the poor there. No individual within the group affected, therefore, is left better off or worse off than he was in the initial situation under the existing law in virtue of a positive *NB* arising from an *A, B, C,* or *D* arrangement. Nonetheless any positive *NB* constitutes a Pareto improvement for the economy as a whole, on this scheme, inasmuch as no one in the group is worse off and some others in the rest of the economy are made better off.

II

Prior to a more general formulation we shall consider the fairly common case of a population of individuals, firms, or families, the members of which are located within a given area. Each member enjoys the product of his own activity while, in varying degrees, resenting the products of the same activity of others. An example which may help to fix our ideas is that of a beach daily occupied by individuals, or families, each of which enjoys the sound of his own radio while disliking the sounds generated by each of the others. No distortion of the central features of the analysis arises from supposing that, notwithstanding differences in location of neighboring radios, differences in volume or program, each individual dislikes equally the noise created by any *r* numbers of radios, which noise, however, is more objectionable to him, by a determinate amount, than the noise produced by any (*r*–1) radios.

The existing state of the law, which we assume is permissive, is denoted by *L*, the reverse state of the law, *L̄*, being prohibitive. Whichever state of the law prevails, however, agreements reached by mutual consent to exempt one or more individuals from the existing law are always sanctioned. Under the permissive law *L*, then, each individual would have to be paid some minimum compensatory sum before agreeing to exempt himself from the existing freedom to play his own radio. On the other hand, in order to exempt some other individual from the existing law, *L*, he is prepared to pay some maximum sum by way of compensation.[4]

We construct below a simple numerical example, in which the relevant data under the *L* law for four individuals, *W, X, Y,* and *Z*, are shown in Table I.

	Table I				
W	−14	6	5	4	1
X	−33	9	7	3	−14
Y	−35	16	15	10	6
Z	−25	10	9	8	2

The first positive figure, 6 in the *W* row, indicates the maximum sum individual *W* would pay to have the first other radio turned off, whether it be that of *X, Y,* or *Z*. The following figure, 5, is the maximum sum he is prepared to contribute as compensation for any second radio that is turned off. The next figure, 4, is the maximum sum he will pay for the last remaining radio (excluding his own) to be turned off. This diminishing magnitude of the positive row figures for each person implies the 'normal' assumption of diminishing marginal utility (or, more precisely, marginal valuation) of a good – quiet, in this instance. The corresponding 'normal' case implied under the *L* law is increasing marginal disutility of the 'bad' – radio noise in this instance. Thus, under the *L̄* law, the *W* row would read 14, −4, −5, −6. Since the broad conclusions to be reached in this section about the ranking of the outcomes *A, B, C,* and *D*, are not affected if, instead, we assumed increasing marginal utility of a good and diminishing marginal disutility of a bad, we confine ourselves throughout the paper to the 'normal' case. Some particular features of the 'perverse' case are, however, indicated in Appendix 1.

Lastly, the −14 in the *W* row indicates that 14 is the minimum sum required by individual *W* as compensation for surrendering his right under the *L* law to play his radio; that is, to exempt him from the *L* law. We may assume that this sum is invariant to the number of other radios that are playing.[5] All other rows are interpreted in the same way.

On the right-hand side of the table is a column of figures, 1, −14, 6, 2, which are in fact the row totals. The figure 6 corresponding to the *Y* row, for example, being the total of compensatory sums proposed by *Y* to exempt every radio on the beach (including his own), is to be interpreted as the net value to *Y* of a reversal of the existing *L* law to *L̄*. In other words, *Y* is prepared to pay a maximum of 6 to have the beach change from an area in which all radios are permitted to play into one in which all are prohibited from playing their radios. The total for the *X* row, −14, reveals the minimum sum, 14, which *X* would regard as adequate compensation for replacing the *L* law by the *L̄* law.

With this information, and provisionally ignoring all costs incurred in moving from the *status quo* to any other arrangement, let us appraise four alternative rules or methods for reaching a decision on whether, and how, to depart from the initial situation under the *L* law, in which everyone is playing his radio: *A*, single-outcome voting, *B*, single-outcome bargaining, *C*, Pareto mixed outcome, and *D*, a separate facilities outcome.

A. This rule requires each individual to vote whether or not to reverse the existing *L* law into the *L̄* law, a majority to carry the decision. Bargaining between them being prohibited, each individual only weighs the advantage of listening to his own radio against the disadvantage of being exposed to the sounds of all the others. If his row total is positive he votes for the *L̄* law, otherwise he votes for a continuation of the *L* law.

In our numerical example, individuals *W*, *Y*, and *Z* all vote for the *L̄* law, *X* alone voting for a continuation of the *L* law. By the *A* decision rule, then, common agreement is secured to transform the permissive area into a prohibited area.

B. This decision rule differs from the one above in that each individual's vote no longer counts as one but, instead, is weighted according to the value of net advantage, or disadvantage, he attaches to a change from the *L* law. *W*, *Y*, and *Z*, between them offer a maximum of 9 for the change to *L̄*. Individual *X*, however, requires at least 14 as compensation.[6] In consequence the existing *L* law continues.

Under the provisional assumption of costless implementation of new arrangements, the *B* outcome can be regarded as Pareto superior to the *A* outcome, in that, wherever the *B* outcome differs from the *A* outcome, as it does in our example, it is possible to make everyone better off by substituting the *B* outcome for the *A* outcome. The *A* outcome in the above example entails a negative *NB* of 5 for the group as a whole as compared with the initial situation, since a change to *L̄* makes *W*, *Y*, and *Z* better off by 9, a sum which, if paid to *X*, would fall short by 5 of adequately compensating him. Compared with the *B* arrangements, then, the *A* outcome leaves *X* worse off by 5 with *W*, *Y*, and *Z* no better off and is, consequently, Pareto inferior to *B*.

C. The Pareto mixed outcome differs from *B* in the device of exempting one or more individuals from the existing *L* law, the others remaining subject to that law.

If one individual alone were persuaded not to play his radio, his loss is given by the negative number in his row, and the gain of each of the others by the first positive number in their rows. If the algebraic sum of these numbers were positive, the exempted individual could be fully compensated with some payment left

over as *NB* going to the government. For a second individual a positive *NB* is also possible if his negative number is more than offset by the sum of the second positive numbers in the rows of the other three, and so on. There are 4!, or 24 different ways of ranking the four individuals in successive order of exemption, an optimal ordering being one which produces the largest positive *NB* (if any) from the first *r* individuals – *r*, in our example, being any number from 1 to 3.[7]

Let us suppose that this has been done, and the result set out in Matrix I(*L*). The matrix arrangement differs from that in the table in the reordering of the rows necessary for an optimal outcome and in the placing of the negative numbers along the principal diagonal. The numbers carry the same interpretation as that in the table, and the row totals remain unaltered. The figures along the bottom of the matrix are the column totals, and these are significant for implementing the *C*-decision rule.

	W	*Z*	*X*	*Y*	
W	−14	6	5	4	1
Z	10	−25	9	8	2
X	9	7	−33	3	−14
Y	16	15	10	−35	6
	21	3	−9	−20	−5

Matrix I(*L*)

→

Reading down the *W* column, the first element, −14, is *W*'s compensatory payment for exempting himself, *W*, from the *L* law – a minimum payment of 14, that is, is required by *W*. The 10 below is *Z*'s compensatory payment for exempting *W*, a maximum of 10. The 9 and the 16 are, respectively, the maximum payments from *X* and from *Y* to exempt *W* from permission to play his radio. The amount by which the sum of these payments to prohibit *W* exceeds the compensation required by *W* is given by the algebraic total of the *W* column, 21 in this instance, and is the positive *NB* of exempting *W* alone from the *L* law as compared with the initial situation. The algebraic total of the next column being 3, we infer that the exemption of individual *Z*, in addition to individual *W*, adds another 3 to the *NB*, a total *NB* of 24 as compared with the initial situation. Further exemptions would not be admitted. For the exemption of *X* and/or *Y* would serve only to reduce the total positive *NB* of 24, since each of their algebraic totals are negative – the compensatory payments offered falling short of the minimum sums required.[8]

Compared with the initial situation (and, in this instance, also with the *B* outcome) the *C* outcome confers a positive *NB* of 24.

D. This rule requires that we substitute for the given areas to which the *C* outcome was constrained two separate areas, one to be placed under the *L* law and one to be placed under the *L̄* law, the law in each area being binding on all members placed therein. One can seek an algorithm for selecting individuals for the two areas as to maximize *NB*. Alternatively, one can reveal an increase in *NB* over that resulting from the *C* outcome[9] if, as in this example, some but not all of the column totals are positive, by placing in the separate *L̄* area those exempted under the *C* procedure (those having positive column totals), and placing the remainder in the separate *L* area. In this paper we restrict ourselves to demonstrating this latter proposition. Accordingly, we place *W* and *Z* in the separate *L̄* area and *Y* and *X* in the separate *L* area.

The increase in *NB* over the *C* outcome is easily shown by partitioning Matrix I(*L*) with reference to the *C* outcome; that is, by drawing a broken line separating the columns *W* and *Z* from the other columns, and a broken line separating the *W* and *Z* rows from the other rows, as indeed is shown in the matrix. Let us identify the northwestern, northeastern, southwestern and southeastern sub-matrices respectively as V^{11}, V^{12}, V^{21}, and V^{22}.

(a) Now, in the *C* outcome, in order that *W* and *Z* together be fully compensated for their exemption from the *L* law, their joint net minimum compensation requirement of 23 (equal to the negative of the algebraic sum of the elements in V^{11}, –14, 10, 6, –25), has to be met by joint payments to them from the group *X* and *Y*.[10] Once *W* and *Z* are placed in a separate *L̄* area, however, their required compensatory payment of 23 has no longer to be met. As a result *X* and *Y* between them dispose of an additional 23 as compared with the *C* outcome.

(b) However, *W* and *Z* have been moved from an *L* area into an *L̄* area.[11] From their row totals, 1 and 2, we know they are willing to pay a joint sum of 3 to change to an *L̄* area. Under the *D* arrangement they are placed in such an area without payment. They are therefore better off by this amount 3 as compared with the *C* outcome.[12].

The excess *NB* as compared with the *C* outcome is therefore 23 plus 3, or 26.[13] In summary, [*NB*(*D*) – *NB*(*C*)] has two components (a) – V^{11}I for *X* and *Y*, and (b) V^{11}+V^{12} (equal to row totals for *W* and *Z*). Hence,

$$NB(D) - NB(C) = (a) + (b) = V^{12}I$$

In this example $V^{12}I = 26$.[14] In the absence of all costs

associated with the change from one arrangement to another, these decision rules *A, B, C, D,* are ranked in ascending order of positive *NB*.

III

We now compare these results with those which would obtain if, instead of the *L* law, we started with the *L̄* law. In our example, the initial situation is now one in which radio-playing is totally prohibited and, as in the preceding section, we go on to consider the possible improvements of permitting exemptions by common consent according to each of the decision rules. Each individual would now pay some maximum sum for permission to play his own radio but would require some minimum compensation to suffer any of the others to play his. Perfectly symmetrical results are assured by assuming that each individual has a zero welfare effect with respect to radio sound, whether his own radio sound or someone else's. Under this assumption the matrix remains unchanged in every respect save that all the signs are reversed. The result is Matrix I(*L̄*).

Matrix I(*L̄*)

	W	*Z*	*X*	*Y*	
W	14	–6	–5	–4	–1
Z	–10	25	–9	–8	–2
X	–9	–7	33	–3	14
Y	–16	–15	–10	35	–6
	–21	–3	9	20	5 ↑

A. Individuals *W*, *Z*, and *Y* vote for remaining with the *L̄* law, and therefore have a majority over *X*'s solitary vote for the change to *L*. Under this rule the area is voted, as before, to be an *L̄* area, all radio-playing prohibited.

B. Individual *X*, however, can bribe the other three to change to the *L* law, and yet show an *NB* of 5. Again, therefore, the *L* law is the outcome.

C. The arrows serve to indicate the order of exemptions under the *C* rule (the reverse of the order under the *L* law), *Y* and *X* being successfully exempted from the *L̄* law. The *NB* is given by their column totals as 29, an excess of 24 over the *NB* yielded by the *B* outcome.[15] The result, again, is no different from that of the *C* outcome under the *L* law: in both cases, *X* and *Y* will continue to play their radios and *W* and *Z* will be prohibited from playing theirs.

D. Placing the *X* and *Y* individuals in a separate permissive (*L*) area and *W* and *Z* in a separate prohibited (*L̄*) area again increases the *NB* compared with the *C* outcome. In claiming their exemption from the $\bar{L}$ law under the *C* rule, *X* and *Y* were required to meet the compensatory demands of *W* and *Z*; that is, *X* and *Y* were required to pay 26 – equal, with sign reversed, to the algebraic sum of the elements in submatrix V^{12}. With the *W* and *Z* removed to a separate area this payment is no longer necessary, and the excess *NB* from the reduced *X* and *Y* columns is 26. In fact this 26 equal to – V^{12}I, is, once again, equal to the excess *NB* of the *D* outcome over the *C* outcome,[16] since *W* and *Z* are no better off and no worse off in the *D* outcome, in which they are placed in a separate prohibited area, than they would be remaining in a joint prohibited area under the *C* outcome and being compensated for the radio noise created by the exempted group *Y* and *X*.[17]

Greater interest, however, attaches to a comparison of the results under *L* and $\bar{L}$ when we remove the restrictive assumption of zero welfare effects for each individual. If, now, an individual is, on balance, better off in the initial (uncorrected) situation under the $\bar{L}$ law as compared with the *L* law, all his compensatory payments, positive and negative, will be revised upward (absolutely): if he is worse off under the $\bar{L}$ law all such payments will be revised downward. Individuals *W*, *Z*, and *Y* are each better off under the $\bar{L}$ law, since each, when under the *L* law, would have paid, on balance, some positive sum to have the *L* law reversed. The reverse is true only for *X*, who, when under the *L* law would have had to be bribed to agree to reverse the *L* law. Matrix I'($\bar{L}$) is constructed with these revisions in mind.[18] The negative row totals for *W*, *Z*, and *Y* are each larger (absolutely) in this new matrix than they were in Matrix I($\bar{L}$). The positive row total for individual *X*, on the other hand, is now smaller than it was in that matrix. As a result of these alterations, only the new *A* outcome is the same as that in the symmetric Matrix I($\bar{L}$). The outcomes of applying the decision rules *B*, *C*, and *D*, however, are all different.

Matrix I'($\bar{L}$)

	W	*Z*	*X*	*Y*	
W	15	–6	–6	–5	–2
Z	–12	29	–11	–9	–3
X	–8	–6	30	–4	12
Y	–18	–16	–11	37	–8 ↑
	–23	1	2	19	–1

In the *B* outcome with the *symmetric* Matrix I($\bar{L}$), individual *X* by 14 to 9 prevailed over the other three to change to the *L* law; in the new matrix *X* is prevailed upon by the other three, by 13 to 12, to remain with the $\bar{L}$ law. As for the *C* outcome, whereas only *X* and *Y* were

exempted from the $\bar{L}$ law under the symmetric matrix with an *NB* of 29, in the new matrix *X*, *Y*, and *Z* are exempted with an *NB* of 22. Turning finally to the *D* outcome, if we continued to place *X* and *Y* in a separate *L* area, and *W* and *Z* in a separate $\bar{L}$ area, the excess *NB* is, as before, measured by the sum of the elements in what would then be the V^{12} submatrix. For this measures the excess over the *NB* of the *C* outcome from *X* and *Y* no longer having to compensate *Z* and *W*, these latter themselves being no worse off in a separate prohibited area than they were in a joint prohibited area. This new excess *NB* is therefore 31 as compared with 26 under the symmetric matrix. If, on the other hand, we follow our rule and place in the separate *L* area all individuals whose column totals are positive, in this case *X*, *Y*, and *Z*, all of whom secure exemption from the $\bar{L}$ law under the *C* procedure, we partition the matrix as shown. V^{12} now contains –6, –6, –5, a total of –17, indicating that, under the *C* procedure, 17 was the minimum compensation required by *W* to exempt *X*, *Y*, and *Z* from the $\bar{L}$ law while he, *W*, remained in this area. When *W* is placed in a separate $\bar{L}$ area these payments are not needed, and the excess *NB* compared with the *C* outcome is 17.

A formal treatment of the *n*-person case is provided in Appendix 2.

IV

We now remove the provisional assumption of no costs of change and consider total costs incurred in implementing any of these four decision rules, additional to whatever costs are incurred in maintaining unchanged the existing situation under the *L* law. The total of these costs in implementing the *A* rule is denoted by *G*(*A*), that in implementing the *B* rule, by *G*(*B*), and so on. We must, therefore, revise our requirement for the *B* outcome to be regarded as a Pareto improvement, compared with the initial situation, from *NB*(*B*) > 0 to

$$NB(B) - G(B) > 0$$

Similarly, for the *D* outcome to be regarded as an improvement over the *C* outcome, it is required that

$$NB(D) - G(D) > NB(C) - G(C)$$

We may divide these total costs, *G*, associated with implementing any one of the four decision rules into three main groups: G_1 are the costs of reaching agreement to move from the existing situation under *L* to the outcome associated with the decision rule in question.

They include the costs of negotiation among members of a group having the same interest, and those arising from negotiations between groups having conflicting interests. G_2 are the costs of administration and supervision connected with maintaining the agreement reached. G_3 are the capital costs, if any, required to implement the outcome of the decision rule in question.

The G_3 costs may be important in the creation of separate facilities, though in the instances that come easily to mind – separate smoking and nonsmoking facilities in trains, cinemas, and restaurants, beaches where games, or radios, are prohibited, quiet study room in universities, pedestrian precincts – usually require little more than a revision of the law as it applies to existing facilities. However, there may be cases where the costs of partitioning areas, or of shifting equipment from one area to the other, may be substantial.[19]

The G_2 costs may be significant is supervising separate facilities, or in enforcing optimal arrangements under the C procedure. The weaker the sense of civic responsibility the greater are these costs likely to be. It is possible, however, that any increase of effort entailed in administration and supervision of the new arrangements, as compared with the arrangements under the *status quo*, is only an addition to the existing duties of personnel drawing fixed salaries. Though in real terms this counts, no additional demands appear to register on the resources of the economy.

The G_1 costs are easily the most significant of the three groups. Writing

$$G_1 = G_1(n, d, f)$$

it is suggested that G_1 varies directly with n, the number of individuals, or families, affected adversely or otherwise under the L law, who might benefit under any of the alternative solutions. G_1 also varies directly with d, regarded as some index of geographical dispersion of the n people within the area. Other factors that are less tangible, but which may also increase these costs considerably – ignorance of the identity of the members of an adversely affected group, ignorance of the law, lack of worldly experience or organizing ability within such a group – are summarized in the symbol f.

Although no reliable studies have been made in this connection, it seems likely that the costs both of collecting information and reaching agreement among a group adversely affected by some activity under the L law – agreement both in respect of compensation to offer to the party creating the damage, and in respect of contribution to be made by each member (in the case of

the C decision rule) – will rise exponentially with the magnitude of n. Whatever the values to be placed on the other factors, d and f, their effect on G will also be greater the larger the size of n. For the larger the number in any group that is adversely affected, the higher will be the costs incurred in overcoming geographical and other obstacles.

It is, of course, possible that the total of such G costs, so far as they can be estimated, are not so high as the potential gains from adopting the outcome of, say, the C or D decision rule, notwithstanding which such an arrangement is not undertaken. The obvious explanation is in terms of inertia, or lack of initiative. But it is tautological, as well as complacent, to infer from the observed fact that mutual arrangements, apparently profitable, are not undertaken, that costs – including 'costs of initiative' – are too high, and that potential Pareto improvements do not really exist.[20]

What makes such an inference tautological is, of course, the implicit valuation of the 'costs of initiative' as being, in all pertinent instances, a sum which is more than enough to bridge the gap by which estimated costs G fall short of the potential net benefit associated with some decision rule, usually C. Such a tautology is unnecessary. For it is quite feasible for the government, say, to set up an agency for the specific purpose of organizing the interests of such adversely affected groups in cases where the group was large and dispersed and inexperienced, thus setting a cost for the required initiative. If it did so under the existing law, voluntary arrangements hitherto neglected would now appear and would yield net benefits above all G costs (when these are revised to include the costs of initiative) so effecting Pareto improvements.[21]

What makes such a proposal complacent in addition is the unquestioned acceptance of the existing costs of altering the *status quo* as a datum. Thus, unless we choose to regard the existing L law, permissive in respect of a range of spillover effects on the community at large, as a constraint, we must admit the possibility of a wide range of voluntary agreements, tending to increase the community's net benefit, remaining unrealized.

The alterations in the outcomes that might follow a change from the L law to the $\bar{L}$ law are made explicit in the following section where we re-examine briefly the conventional conclusions of a variety of instances in the light of the above analysis.

V   Application of the Analysis to Particular Instances of Social Cost

(1) We may begin with the simplest case of one individual inflicting damage on another.[22] For each state of the law we have a 2×1 matrix. We can suppose that individual Y wishes to site a house in the country, though in a location that obscures the view from X's house. The decision rule obviously results in a tie. Therefore we consider the B decision rule, which in this simple two-person case, is the same as the C decision rule.

If the permissive L law prevailed then X is to be made worse off and Y better off by Y's decision, therefore unless X approaches Y with an offer Y is certain to build on his chosen site. Above the cost of the house to Y the value he places on the site is such that he will not accept less than $28,000 to abandon the site. If X is willing to pay a sum larger than this, say, $30,000, to induce Y to move elsewhere, the optimal outcome results in Y's choosing some other site. A change to $\bar{L}$ law, which prohibits any new building without consent of those affected will confirm this outcome. For the assumption of normal welfare effects implies that Y would offer to pay less than $28,000 for the site while X would require more than $30,000, as a result of which, again, Y must seek a site elsewhere.[23]

It is quite possible, however, to meet with cases in which the optimal outcome varies with the law. The figures in Matrix (i) are such that agreement cannot be reached under either law. If the L law prevails, the $25,000 maximum that X is willing to pay is below the $28,000 minimum that would induce Y to change his mind. Under the L law, therefore, Y sites his house and obscures X's view. On the other hand, if the $\bar{L}$ law prevailed instead, the maximum sum that Y could offer X for permission to site his new house would be $23,000 which sum, however, falls short of the $30,000 minimum that would be acceptable to X. Under the $\bar{L}$ law, therefore, Y cannot build his house to obscure X's view. It follows that under the L law the optimal outcome requires that Y build his house. Under the $\bar{L}$ law, the optimal outcome requires that Y does *not* build his house.

	Matrix (i)	
	L	$\bar{L}$
X	25,000	–30,000
Y	–28,000	23,000

Finally, if some factor affecting the interest of both parties could be varied the magnitude of the variation would, in general, depend upon the prevailing law.

Suppose that additions to the height of Y's new house would add to his satisfaction, though at a diminishing rate, while they would increase X's dissatisfaction, at an increasing rate. It is now supposed that under the L law X would pay a maximum of $15,000 to dissuade Y from building the lowest-height house contemplated. Y, however, could not be persuaded from building this squat house for less than $30,000. These figures are marked on the vertical axis of Figure 1. By assuming continuity between height of house and compensation we construct the solid lines X_L and Y_L. The highest point on the Y_L curve indicates the height, H_Y, that would be chosen by Y under the L law and in the absence of any agreement with X. At this height, however, the maximum compensation to be offered by X for a height-reduction of, say, 1 foot, exceeds the minimum sum acceptable to Y. While this condition is met agreement on successive height reductions can be reached until the optimal height H_L – that at which the marginal benefit to Y is equal to the marginal cost to X – is attained. The optimal height corresponds to the largest vertical distance between the Y_L and X_L curves and provides, therefore, the greatest surplus of benefit to Y above the loss to X. If now we change to $\bar{L}$ law, Y is prepared to pay a maximum of $25,000 for permission to build the lowest height structure while X will accept no less than $20,000. The curves $Y_{\bar{L}}$ and $X_{\bar{L}}$ trace the relation between height and compensation under the $\bar{L}$ law. In the absence of any approach by Y, no building will take place on the site in question. Yet Y is able to bribe X to permit a building of increasing height until $H_{\bar{L}}$ is reached, where $H_{\bar{L}}$ is the optimal height under the $\bar{L}$ law and is below H_L, the optimal height under the L law.[24]

(2) The topical example of aircraft noise differs from the above in two respects; first, in the obvious respect of the large numbers which, under the L law, suffer disturbance to their quiet, and secondly, in that the compensatory payments of the airline company are determined uniquely by reference to the market.[25] The maximum sum it will offer to continue operating planes from its airfield and the minimum it will accept to move elsewhere are exactly equal. Once again, there are no reciprocal effects, and for the n residents or families affected an $(n+1)×1$ matrix summarizes the position under either law if the airline company counts as one. Irrespective of the law, under the A decision rule, the voting would go against the company. The B and C decision rules are equivalent in this case because of the absence of reciprocal effects. Indeed if we group the compensatory payments of the n residents together, the problem can be collapsed to the two-party case having the possibilities already treated in the previous

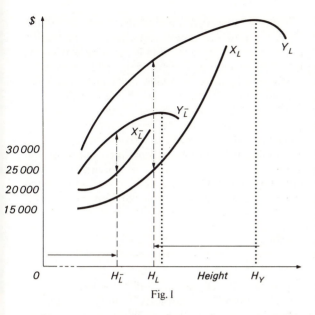

$ ↑

30 000
25 000
20 000
15 000

X_L Y_L
$Y_{\bar{L}}$
$X_{\bar{L}}$

0     $H_{\bar{L}}$ H_L Height H_Y

Fig. 1

problem. As for the variable factor, in this instance it could be represented by variation in the number of planes operating from the airfield.[26]

Matrix (ii) can be taken to summarize the position. Under the permissive law *L*, the *n* residents represented as *X* are able to afford a maximum payment of $30 million, which sum exceeds by $10 million the minimum compensation of $20 million demanded by the airline company. The figures for the $\bar{L}$ law are $50 million required by *X* and, again, $20 million for the company.[27]

Matrix (ii)

	L	$\bar{L}$
X	30m.	–50m.
Y	–20m.	20m.

Under the existing *L* law, the company could not be induced to move to another airfield if the total *G* costs exceeded $10 million. If such costs are accepted as unavoidable, the existing situation has to be accepted as the optimal outcome. But the unavoidability of such costs does not arise from the economic facts of life but from the legal facts. For if the *L* law were changed to $\bar{L}$, and made prohibitive of aircraft noise, the company would be obliged to make the approach. The G_1 costs now associated with the airline's reaching agreement on maximum compensation, would be slight compared with G_1 costs incurred by the *n* residents.

In this example, as it happens, the sum the company can afford to offer to bribe the residents into accepting the airfield in their midst would not suffice, and the

company, therefore, would be obliged to move elsewhere.

Once again, the outcome varies with the law, but not, as in the previous example. because of the welfare effects on compensatory payments. Indeed we could have supposed zero welfare effects for the residents, and substituted –30 instead of –50 in Matrix (ii), without altering the results. The excessive costs, especially the G_1 costs, associated with a large number of residents, implies [$NB(C)$–$G(C)$] is negative: since everyone cannot be made better off under the *L* law by a voluntary approach by residents to bribe the company, the existing outcome is accepted as optimal. Under the $\bar{L}$ law, on the other hand, the prohibition of aircraft from the residential area would be the optimal outcome: for the company could not operate the planes while making everyone better off.

(3) We may now turn to a mixed case in which some individuals of the population regard themselves as victims of the activities of others while the remainder regard themselves as beneficiaries of these activities, or less extreme but more realistic, one in which some people mind very little and others mind a great deal. We could think, in this connection, of a spacious residential area in which some *X*-type inhabitants were sensitive to automobile noise of others and/or attached little value to their own use of this form of transport. The *Y*-type inhabitants, on the other hand, are not unduly disturbed by such noises and/or attach great store by their automobiles. Under the permissive *L* law, the matrix would be like the *V* matrix, with all the $v_{ii} \leq 0$ and all the $v_{ij} \geq 0$ ($j \neq i$).[28] For the *X*-type, the v_{ii} will be (absolutely) smaller compared with their v_{ij}, the reverse being true for the *Y*-type. The row totals for the *X*-type are therefore positive: for the *Y*-type they may be negative, zero, or positive. The *A* outcome is determined by the number of *X*-types compared with *Y*-types, and the *B* outcome by the algebraic sum of the matrix elements. What makes this case interesting are two things: (a) as in the preceding case, the influence of the law on the *G* costs, and (b) the superiority of the separate facilities solution is particularly marked.

We illustrate with specific Matrices (iii)*L* and (iii)$\bar{L}$ in which there are two persons of each type. Since in a reversal of law from *L* to $\bar{L}$ *X*-types gain heavily, and *Y*-types lose heavily, the absolute values of the elements must be revised upward for the *X* rows in Matrix (iii)$\bar{L}$ and downward for the *Y* rows. The *A* and *B* decision rules give the same outcome under either law – a tie, and prohibition of motoring, respectively. Applying the *C* rule Y_1 and Y_2 will be left driving under the *L* law, while no one secures consent to drive under the $\bar{L}$ law.

Matrix (iii)L				
	X_1	X_2	Y_1	Y_2
X_1	-10	18	30	35	73
X_2	25	-12	20	30	63
Y_1	4	6	-62	10	-42
Y_2	4	6	10	-80	-60
	23	18	-2	-5	34

$\rightarrow$

Matrix (iii)$\overline{L}$				
	X_1	X_2	Y_1	Y_2
X_1	12	-20	-35	-40	-83
X_2	-30	15	-25	-30	-70
Y_1	-2	-4	55	-8	41
Y_2	-3	-5	-8	60	44
	-23	-14	-13	-18	-68

Once we recognize the magnitude of the G costs, in particular the G_1 costs, which are likely to rise rapidly with the numbers involved, incurred in a movement to the C outcome, the advantage lies predominantly with the group, or type, enjoying the *status quo*. In the absence of initiative by a government agency seeking to promote optimal outcomes under the existing law, the initial situation under the L law is likely to perpetuate itself notwithstanding the large potential NB of a C solution.

Finally, if we place individuals in separate areas according to their *row* totals in either matrix, the D outcome under either law captures a much greater NB than does the C outcome. Under the L law for instance, X_1 and X_2 would have paid row totals 73 and 63 respectively, a total of 136, to have the whole area converted into a nonmotoring zone, as between which and dwelling in a nonmotoring separate area they are deemed indifferent. Y_1 and Y_2 also gain. They would require under the L law minimum payments of 102 to consent to having the area made into a nonmotoring zone. Now they can be lodged in a separate permissive area which is superior to the existing permissive area inasmuch as they are not disturbed there by X_1 and X_2. Once in the separate area the minimum acceptable sum for each will rise by 10, a total of 20 (equal to the sum of the elements in the submatrix V^{21}). Compared with the initial situation, then, the D outcome provides an NB of 156 compared with 41 from the C outcome.

In general, the greater the population, and the larger are the absolute v_{ij} of the X-type of individual relative to the Y-type, the larger become the elements in V^{12} compared with those in V^{21}, and the greater the superiority of the D outcome compared with the C. The excess $NB(D)$ over $NB(C)$ is, however, equal to the sum of the elements in V^{12}.

Moreover, granted the initiative was there, the capital costs of providing separate facilities may not be heavy. The existing area, if large, may be partitioned into two separate and viable areas, and the costs of movement for either type may not be great relative to the expected advantage over a long period. There would be no, or practically no, additional costs of supervision and administration, as compared with a C outcome. Nor need there be heavy costs incurred in estimating the actual compensatory sums of the individuals. A simple question asked of each individual or family would suffice: if a separate area were created would you, if necessary, be prepared to move into it (with, or without, financial aid)?[29]

VI

The general belief, attacked in this paper, is that an optimal solution in a partial setting is uniquely determined [3, pp. 61-2; 4, p. 3; 15, p. 55], or that it may reasonably be treated as uniquely determined [2, p. 385], a belief that may appear justified if the treatment is confined to spillover effect as between firms or industries (as, for instance, in [8] and [5]) or if the estimate of damages inflicted on the public may be costed by reference to market prices. Even in such cases, however, the belief is unwarranted. Resorting once more to Pigou's smoky chimney example, the supposition that a given amount of soap is alone sufficient to undo the damage caused will still not determine an optimal output irrespective of the law. For the soap used by the victims of smoke damage may well be produced by an industry that disposes of its waste products by contaminating the air or polluting a river, so reducing the welfare of other sections of the public which, under the existing law, are unable – because of exorbitant G costs – to bribe the soap industry either to reduce its output or to install effective safeguards. Inasmuch as a change of law that puts the burden of compensation on the soap industry would raise its long-run costs (whether compensatory payments cause it to reduce its output, or whether, in operating anti-pollution devices, it increases its running costs and/or overheads) reference to the market price of soap under this new law entails higher costs and, consequently, a smaller optimal output in the smoky chimney industry. Nor need we stop here. Insofar as any of the inputs of the original smoky chimney industry, or any of the inputs of the soap industry, or any of the inputs of these inputs, would be produced at higher costs under a law that places the onus of compensation on those generating the external diseconomies the level of costs and outputs of the final and contributory industries are all affected. Thus, if we begin with what appears to be a set of optimal outputs and prices in the economy, a change of law in the respect indicated changes in general the whole set of optimal prices and outputs. The implication may be put otherwise: no output or set of outputs in the economy can be justified by the Pareto criterion without implicit support of the existing law bearing on the question of compensation.

There are, moreover, several reasons for expecting that the difference to the patterns of costs and outputs following such a change of law would be substantial. Significant external diseconomies involving the effects on the amenity of the public at large both of the operation of modern industry and the use of new commercial products are on the increase. Moreover, inasmuch as the external effects wrought on the environment enter heavily into a man's welfare they entail a significant differential between the maximum amount which (under the L law) he is willing to pay to rid himself of the unpleasantness in question and the minimum sum which (under an $\bar{L}$ law) he is willing to accept to bear it. Finally, according as the ratio of the number of people affected by noxious byproducts to the number of enterprises generating them increases so do the G_1 costs under the L law as compared with the G_1 costs under an $\bar{L}$ law.

Granted the general conclusion that the pattern of costs and outputs varies with the state of the law, is there a case for the economist supporting one kind of law as against the other? If we regard the existing law as being predominantly L law, that is, predominantly permissive with respect to incidental disamenities generated, then a case for a switchover to $\bar{L}$ law can be made on grounds (1) of efficiency, and (2) of equity.

(1) There are three reasons why a change to the $\bar{L}$ law may be expected to promote allocative efficiency:

(i) We have shown that, by provisionally ignoring all $\bar{G}$ costs, the pattern of 'optimal' outputs under an $\bar{L}$ law is, in general, different from that under the L law. What is relevant, with respect to allocative efficiency alone, however, is our proposition that the G costs (in particular, the G_1 costs) to be incurred in arranging to bring into effect an optimal output are small under $\bar{L}$ law compared with those incurred under L law. If, therefore, we begin, under either law, with a number of sectors in which outputs are uncorrected for net external diseconomies, there will be some of these sectors that yield a positive NB under an $\bar{L}$ law – the potential gain in moving to optimal outputs exceeding their corresponding G costs – but not

under the L law. Thus, under an $\bar{L}$ law it becomes cheaper for the economy to approach its pattern of potential optimum outputs than to do so under the L law.

(ii) Once the burden of full compensation for disamenities generated either in the production or use of the commodity or service is borne by the manufacturer, on a legal par with the costs incurred in compensating people for the use of their factors, he has an immediate and often powerful incentive to direct resources into discovering low cost devices – low enough on balance, that is, to reduce total costs *including* compensation under an $\bar{L}$ law – that enable him to increase his profits and extend his outputs. Under the L law, in contrast, there is no such incentive to switch part of his resources from current research into raising quality or reducing costs of existing goods to reducing, instead, the costs of eliminating the negative goods he inadvertently produces. For either he totally ignores these negative goods or, if it is forthcoming, accepts full compensation for curtailing his output or for installing known methods of combating them.

(iii) Finally, in those cases where it remains costly, in the state of current technology, to remove or appreciably reduce those spillover effects over which people's reactions are divided, establishment of the $\bar{L}$ law, putting the burden ultimately on the manufacturers, provides the greater incentive to promote separate facilities solutions which as we have seen, can be productive of greater NB than optimal solutions constrained within single areas. The larger the proportion of the population in any given area that can be divided roughly into 'sensitive' and 'insensitive' types with respect to some given byproduct, the larger the potential NB to be found in a separate facilities solution compared with a constrained optimum solution.[30]

These three considerations merit some attention by economists, above all at a time like the present when the products of advancing technology in a growing economy tend swiftly to reduce environmental areas and city centres to a common and depressing pattern. So long as economists implicitly accepted the existing state of the law as being neutral in respect of allocation, the economic case against resisting the spread of subtopia could not be made with the necessary cogency. Recognition of the role played by the law, both in determining the pattern of the optimal output set and in determining the magnitude of the costs necessary to implement that pattern, plus the recognition also of the superiority of a separate facilities solution[31] to some externality problems, should enable economists to justify proposals for more radical social choices – the choice, for instance, of viable residential areas undisturbed by engine noises of any sort – than those which can be expected to emerge through the operation of the market under the existing laws. It follows, therefore, that legislation recognizing the citizen's rights to amenity – the right to such once-free goods as quiet, fresh air, natural beauty – and putting the burden of compensation squarely on the incidental destroyers of amenity without exception, would not only be equitable in itself, it would promote a wider range of choices than is offered under the present dispensation.

VII

(2) As a contribution to equity, the establishment of the L law would tend to produce a greater equality in the distribution of welfare insofar as the commodities and services that generate the outstanding diseconomies – air and water pollution, noise, visual disturbance, destruction of natural beauty – are purchased by and earn incomes for the wealthier groups in the community. More important than distributional considerations perhaps is the inequity *per se* of a law that countenances the inflicting of a wide range of damages on others without effective means of redress. In the absence of comprehensive sanctions against trespass on the citizen's amenity, existing institutions lend themselves inadvertently to a process of blackmail insofar as they place the burden of reaching agreement on the person or group ·whose interests have been damaged. Although the disabilities inflicted on innocent parties may be judged with less severity when they are generated as a byproduct of the pursuit of gain under the existing laws than when, instead, they are produced for the sole purpose of exacting payment, the Pareto principle is met in either case by the 'voluntary' agreement of the party whose rights, liberties, or interests are under threat. Indeed, the virtue of the Pareto principle resides in its alleged neutrality: if A habitually amuses himself by throwing smoke bombs through B's window, but agrees to desist on payment of $25 a week, both are made better off if B chooses to pay it rather than continue to suffer these depredations.[32] Though all existing law acts to prevent calculated blackmail and victimization, there is still this hiatus in the law that enables incidental damage – though frequently severe and lasting damage – to be inflicted on people unless they can find the means to bribe the perpetrators.

Such a depressing fact makes it all the more imperative to perceive a distinction within the notion of ethical neutrality, conceived, on the one hand, as a *disregard* of ethical implication – which is the sense in which the Pareto principle is, in fact, neutral – and, on the other hand, as *impartiality* between the alternative ways of giving effect to the principle, which is, albeit mistakenly, the sense usually attributed to it.[33] Thus the fact that whether A successfully compensates B, or whether B successfully compensates A, a Pareto improvement is effected, is all too frequently believed illustrative of the cardinal virtue of an economic principle that is above and independent of the law.[34] If the nonsmoker's enjoyment is reduced by the smoker's freedom to smoke, so it is argued, the smoker's enjoyment is reduced by abstaining for the sake of the nonsmoker. Each interferes with the enjoyment of the other. The conflict of interest, it is concluded, is symmetric in all relevant respects, and the determination of which of the parties ought, if possible, to compensate the other is either held to be of no interest to economists, or else may be settled by reference to the distributional implications (as, for instance in [9]). But this apparent ethical dilemma, at least, does not stand up to scrutiny. In accordance with the liberal maxim, the freedom of any man to smoke what he chooses and when he chooses would, indeed, be conceded – but with the crucial proviso that his smoking take place in circumstances which do not reduce the freedom of others. Insofar as it does, the freedom of the smoker is not symmetric with that desired by the nonsmoker who merely wishes to breathe unpolluted air and, in the pursuit thereof, and unlike the smoker, does not reduce the amenity of others. Similarly, the benefits enjoyed by any person as a result of the operation of noisy vehicles, lawnmowers, or aircraft, do incidentally damage the amenity of others; the person who lives quietly does not. The conflict of interest does not arise, therefore, from *reciprocal* effects and does not imply equal culpability. The conflict arises from the damage inflicted only by one of the parties on the other. It follows that unless the law is altered to provide comprehensive safeguards for the citizen's rights to certain fundamental amenities, the range of voluntary agreements cannot be vindicated, at least not on ethical grounds, by reference to invisible-hand arguments.[35]

In the current obsession with economic growth, little heed is paid to these critical features of the existing pricing system. Economists busy contriving yet more sophisticated growth models are already sufficiently occupied experimenting with a variety of production functions, with saving and investment coefficients and time responses. As for those engaged in empirical studies aimed at discovering the sources of economic growth, they are sure to invoke demarcation arguments: their concern with the growth of wealth, in some aggregative sense, as measured by indices of national output, being regarded as separable both from familiar distributional problems and from the ethical implications under the existing law that have been raised in this paper. However, whether or not they accept the arguments for a change in the existing legal framework, insofar as they justify their study of economic growth as evidence of concern with the real growth of wealth, they can hardly ignore the effects of those alterations in the legal framework that would promote Pareto improvements unattainable under the existing system. For the effect is surely to expand the range of society's choices in a significant way: not merely in the provision of more gadgetry, at least in affluent societies, but in ways that are vitally important to the individual's well-being and in the choice of environment.

Of course the growth economist may choose to ignore this implication also. But he cannot, with any pretence at consistency, claim to be concerned with ways of increasing real income, under any acceptable definition, and yet to be unconcerned with an existing legal framework that acts to inhibit socially significant choices from being brought into effect.

Appendix 1

Under the L law which, in section II, permits radio-playing, consider the 'perverse' case – each individual being faced with an *increasing* marginal utility of the good (the good being, in this example, the elimination of others' radio noise). Since the sum of payments offered by the remainder to bribe each additional person from playing his radio grows with the size of the population in consequence of the larger payment each is willing to offer to prevent the playing of the nth radio as compared with the payment of the $(n-1)$th, it should be clear that one can always choose a population large enough to ensure that the NB of the C outcome is positive. Thus, even if the order in which the radios were prohibited from playing were such as to yield negative figures for the first r column totals, a large enough population n will ensure that the remaining $(n-r)$ column totals add up to a positive sum that is larger, absolutely, than the sum of r negative column totals. The significant implication for the increasing marginal utility case is, therefore, that a population can always be chosen which yields a positive NB from exempting each member of the population from the L

law. As a corollary the C arrangement is, in effect, an alteration of the L law and produces the same positive NB as the B arrangement.

However, in such cases it is a sufficient condition for the D arrangement to yield a larger NB than the C or B arrangement, that not all the *row* totals are positive. For if all the $(n-h)$ persons having positive row totals are placed in a separate $\bar{L}$ area they become better off in not having to compensate the h individuals having negative row totals (as required in the C arrangement). And this is not all. The h individuals left in a separate L area may now enjoy their radios the more in the absence of the $(n-h)$ radios, the additional enjoyment being represented by the sum of the payments each was willing to pay to turn off the $(n-h)$ radios which have now been removed to the separate $\bar{L}$ area. And though it is possible that a different division of the population between the separate areas could be found to yield a still larger NB, the selection rule that allocates to the $\bar{L}$ area only those with positive row totals (those who, on balance, prefer a quiet area) will always produce a positive NB larger than that arising from the C or B outcomes, both of which result in total prohibition.

Although the result that a sufficient increase in population can always justify a change of law for the area as a whole makes the case of increasing marginal utility rather less interesting than the 'normal' case of diminishing marginal utility, the implications for the C outcome of populations below this crucial size may be briefly indicated.

If it is possible to arrange the order of individual prohibition as to begin with positive column totals, we should, as in the 'normal' case, begin with the highest positive totals. In that event it is possible, by prohibiting the radios of the first r persons having positive column totals, to secure a positive NB greater than that emerging from the B arrangement. As an instance, Matrix I(L) is reproduced here except that the row-wise direction of the positive figures is reversed in order to accord with the notion of increasing marginal utility.

Modified Matrix I(L)

	W	Z	X	Y	
W	-14	4	5	6	1
Z	8	-25	9	10	2
X	3	7	-33	9	-14
Y	10	15	16	-35	6
	7	1	-3	-10	-5

It is manifest that in this case also the C solution prohibits W and Z, although now yielding a positive NB of no more than 8. By the method discussed in the text, the D solution, placing W and Z in the $\bar{L}$ area produces an excess NB of 35. This instance serves also to introduce the possibility of column totals being initially positive, then negative, and eventually positive again. For if we continued to add population to this group of 4, the greater magnitude of the positive figures in each additional column would eventually produce positive column totals. If at some such population, the sum of *all* the column totals were positive but less than 8, the C outcome that would prohibit only W and Z is obviously to be preferred. If, on the other hand, this sum were greater than 8, the C outcome with the higher NB would require complete prohibition. The C outcome in such a case would then be the same as the B outcome both in respect of arrangement and NB.

Finally, there may be instances for which it is not possible so to arrange columns as to provide an initial positive column total. Nonetheless, if the population is large enough, the column totals eventually become positive and, as in the B outcome, we are faced with all-or-nothing decisions according as the sum of the column totals is positive or negative. In the example matrix, the NB of the C outcome is the same as that of the B outcome and equal to 2.

Example Matrix

	W	X	Y	Z	
W	−14	4	5	6	1
X	5	−14	8	10	9
Y	3	5	−14	7	1
Z	0	2	4	−15	−9
	−6	−3	3	8	2

If, according to our selection rule, we now allow W, X, and Y to move into a separate area under the $\bar{L}$ law they would be better off there than they were in the common area subject to the L law by 11 – the payments they would jointly make to be in a quiet area. Z, being placed in a separate L area, would be better off by 6. Thus $[NB(D)–NB(C)]$ is equal to 15.

The reader may satisfy himself that, for the zero welfare case, if the same population were subjected to the $\bar{L}$ law, the corresponding 'perverse' assumption of decreasing marginal disutility (of radio noise) produces symmetrical results.

Appendix 2

A general n-person model may be briefly outlined by identifying the $n \times n$ matrix V with the L law, and the $n \times n$ matrix $\bar{V}$ with the $\bar{L}$ law. The element v_{ij} $(\bar{v}_{ij})$ is individual i's compensation to exempt individual j from the existing $L(\bar{L})$ law. If the exemption of

individual j from the $L(\bar{L})$ law confers an advantage on individual i, v_{ij} $(\bar{v}_{ij})$ is positive and is interpreted as individual i's maximum payment to individual j for j's exemption. If, on the other hand, j's exemption from the $L(\bar{L})$ law inflicts some liability on individual i then v_{ij} $(\bar{v}_{ij})$ is negative, and is interpreted as the minimum sum acceptable to individual i as compensation for j's exemption. In particular v_{ii} $(\bar{v}_{ii})$ is the individual i's compensation for his own exemption from the $L(\bar{L})$ law, positive if it is an advantage to be exempt from the existing law, negative if it is a disadvantage. We need not in general impose any restrictions on the signs, but if all elements had all the same signs, whether positive or negative, the outcome of each of the decision rules would be the same. In order for the analysis to have any interest the matrix must have elements with positive and negative signs, and for an optimal or separate facilities outcome, at least one column total must have an opposite sign to the others.

From the relevant data Matrix V is arranged so that the sum of the first m column totals $(m < n)$ yields a maximum positive value. The small v in the bottom right-hand corner is the algebraic sum of the $m \times n$ elements of the V matrix.

Matrix V

v_{11}	v_{12}	.	.	v_{1m}	.	v_{1n}	$v_{1\cdot}$
v_{21}			.	v_{2m}	.	v_{2n}	$v_{2\cdot}$
.			.	.	.	.	.
.			.	.	.	.	.
v_{m1}	.	.	.	v_{mm}	.	v_{mn}	$v_{m\cdot}$
.			.	.	.	.	.
v_{n1}			.	.	.	v_{nn}	$v_{n\cdot}$
$v_{\cdot1}$	$v_{\cdot2}$	.	.	$v_{\cdot m}$	.	$v_{\cdot n}$	v

Each of our decision rules may result in some change from the initial (uncorrected) position in which all are subject to the L law. A change resulting from the A decision rule may, or may not, be a Pareto improvement as compared with the initial situation. Changes resulting from the B, C, or D decision rules are always Pareto improvements compared with the initial situation.

A. Single outcome voting. Designate the algebraic sum of any ith row as $v_{i\cdot}$, and attribute a value of +1 to each row having a positive total and −1 to each row having a negative total.[36] If so valued $\sum_{i=1}^{n} v_{i\cdot} > 0$, then the L law is changed to $\bar{L}$.

B. Pareto single outcome. We now require that each row total assume its actual algebraic value. Again, if $\sum v_{i\cdot} > 0$, the L law is reversed.

It is clear that, owing to the different systems of

weighting the row totals in A and B, the outcome from applying the B rule may differ from that of applying the A rule. If under the B rule, however, $\sum\limits^{n} v_{i\cdot} > 0$, and, accordingly, the law is changed from L to $\bar{L}$, there is a Pareto improvement compared with the initial situation, a net benefit of

$$NB(B) = \sum\limits^{n} v_{i\cdot}.$$

C. Pareto mixed outcome. Designate the algebraic sum of the elements in any jth column as $v_{\cdot j}$ and exempt all those individuals having positive column totals. As mentioned above, we have already arranged the matrix so that the first m columns have positive totals and together yield a positive value as great or greater than any other arrangement of the data. The remaining $(n-m)$ individuals will all have negative column totals and will remain subject to the L law. Compared with the initial situation, the net benefit of this outcome is

$$NB(C) = \sum\limits_{j=1}^{m} v_{\cdot j}$$

The superiority of the C outcome over the B outcome is easily demonstrated:

$$NB(B) = \sum\limits^{n} v_{i\cdot} = v$$

and where $v > 0$

$$NB(B) > 0$$

By arrangement of the matrix, however,

$$NB(C) = \sum\limits^{m} v_{\cdot j} \geqslant \sum\limits^{n} v_{\cdot j} = v = NB(B)$$

For the relevant case, $m < n$, however,

$$\sum\limits^{m} v_{\cdot j} > \sum\limits^{n} v_{\cdot j}$$

and therefore

$$NB(C) > NB(B)$$

D. Separate facilities outcome. We can partition the V matrix as shown, placing the first m individuals in a separate $\bar{L}$ area, the remaining $(n-m)$ individuals being placed in a separate L area. Partitioning results in the four submatrices, V^{11}, V^{12}, V^{21}, and V^{22}. First consider the case in which $V^{11} \leqslant 0$. The D outcome yields an excess NB over the C outcome equal to (a) the negative of the algebraic sum of the elements in V^{11}, plus (b) $\sum\limits^{m} v_{i\cdot}$.

This is explained as follows:

(a) If, in the C outcome, the algebraic sum of the V^{11} elements were negative, a net payment was required to compensate the first m individuals for their exemption from the L law. This net sum – equals $-(V^{11}I)$ – has to be met, in the C outcome, by the $(n-m)$ unexempted group from their net positive payments, equal to $V^{21}I$, to exempt the m group. Once the exempted m group is placed in a separate exempted area, the unexempted $(n-m)$ group is therefore able to dispose of a greater surplus, compared with the C outcome, to an amount exactly equal to $-(V^{11}I)$.

(b) The individuals of the exempted m group, however, are not in general indifferent as between (i) being exactly compensated for their exemption in an area in which the remaining $(n-m)$ individuals are unexempted, as under the C outcome,[37] and (ii) being exempted in a separate $\bar{L}$ area. If we continue to make the assumption that they are indifferent between being in a larger or smaller area in either of which there is total exemption, their net gain from changing from an L area (or its equivalence – complete compensation under a C outcome to an $\bar{L}$ area) can be calculated as the algebraic sum of their row totals. If this is positive, it represents the amount of money they would offer, on balance, to have the whole area under $\bar{L}$ law. The effect being the same when they are placed in a separate $\bar{L}$ area, this sum can be regarded as a positive surplus. If, on the other hand, the algebraic sum of the m row totals is negative, there is a negative surplus to be added to (a) above.

Thus

$$NB(D) - NB(C) = (b) + (a) = \sum\limits^{m} v_{i\cdot} - V^{11}I$$
$$= V^{11}I + V^{12}I - V^{11}I = V^{12}I$$

Or, more generally, for the case in which $V^{11}I \leqslant 0$,

$$NB(D) \gtreqless NB(C) \text{ according as } V^{12}I \gtreqless 0$$

In the case for which $V^{11}I > 0$, we set the (a) component equal to zero, as the unexempted group does not dispose of a greater surplus, compared with the C outcome when it remains in a separate L area. Thus,

$$NB(D) - NB(C) = (b) + (a) = \sum\limits^{m} v_{i\cdot} \text{ only}$$
$$= V^{11}I + V^{12}I$$

Or, more generally, in the special case,

$$NB(D) \gtreqless NB(C) \text{ according as } \overset{m}{\underset{}{\Sigma}} \, v_{i.} \gtreqless 0 \text{[38]}$$

The simplest plausible situation in which $NB(D) > NB(C)$ under the L law is that in which (i), for each individual the activity is advantageous to himself but disadvantageous to others, and (ii) each member of the m group attaches greater value to resisting his own exemption than he does to exempting the remaining members of the m group, conditions that were exemplified in Matrix I(L).

A change to the $\bar{L}$ law is to be associated with a $\bar{V}$ matrix having elements $\bar{v}_{ij}$. In the special case of zero welfare effects with respect to the activity in question, the $\bar{V}$-matrix is equal to a $-V$ matrix, with $\bar{v}_{ij}$ equal to $-v_{ij}$. With all signs reversed, the results are symmetrical and the outcomes the same.

A. If the voting under L was a majority for $\bar{L}$, under the $\bar{L}$ law the voting will be a minority for L. In both cases the voting outcome would be for $\bar{L}$. The converse is obviously true.

B. If, under L, $\overset{n}{\underset{}{\Sigma}} \, v_{i.} > 0$, under $\bar{L}$ it will be $\overset{n}{\underset{}{\Sigma}} \, \bar{v}_{i.} < 0$. The outcome in both cases is the adoption of the $\bar{L}$ law. Again, the converse is obviously true.

C. If the V matrix was so arranged as to have the first m column totals sum to a maximum, the remaining $(n-m)$ column totals must sum to a maximum (absolute) negative value. In the $\bar{V}$ matrix, with all signs reversed, the first m column totals now have the maximum (absolute) negative value, and the remaining $(n-m)$ columns the maximum positive value. These $(n-m)$ individuals, each having positive column totals will now be exempted from the $\bar{L}$ law while the m members remain subject to it. This is effectively the same result as that reached with the V matrix; $(n-m)$ members being there subject to the L law, and m being exempted. Thus if V is associated with the permissive law, the C outcome under both laws is that the $(n-m)$ group engages in the activity and the m group does not.

Though the optimal outcome is the same for both laws, the $NB(C)$ under the $\bar{L}$ law will not in general be equal to the $NB(C)$ under the L law. Under the $\bar{L}$ law $NB(C) =$

$$\overset{n}{\underset{j=m+1}{\Sigma}} \, \bar{v}_{.j} \gtreqless \overset{m}{\underset{j=1}{\Sigma}} \, v_{.j}$$

which is $NB(C)$ under the L law.

D. Again, under the $\bar{L}$ law we are guided by the C outcome in leaving the m group in a separate $\bar{L}$ area and the remaining $(n-m)$ members moving to a separate L area. The excess NB compared with the C outcome of this arrangement is equal to $-\bar{V}^{12}\mathrm{I}$. For if the algebraic sum

of the elements in $\bar{V}^{12}$ is negative, this represents, under the C outcome, a net compensatory requirement by the members of the m group for their agreement to exempt the $(n-m)$ members from the $\bar{L}$ law. Once the m group is placed in a separate $\bar{L}$ area then provided $\bar{V}^{12}\mathrm{I} \leqslant 0$,[39] it is no worse off than being in the initial situation under the $\bar{L}$ law (which situation is also exactly equivalent to being compensated for the $(n-m)$ exemptions in the C outcome). The $(n-m)$ group, however, no longer has to make this payment, equal to $-\bar{V}^{12}\mathrm{I}$. Hence,

$$NB(D) - NB(C) = -\bar{V}^{12}\mathrm{I} \text{[40]}$$

Or, in general,

$$NB(D) \gtreqless NB(C) \text{ according as } \bar{V}^{12}\mathrm{I} \gtreqless 0 \text{[41]}$$

The simplest plausible situation in which $NB(D) > NB(C)$ under the $\bar{L}$ law is that in which, again, the individual's activity though advantageous to himself is disadvantageous to others. Under the prohibitive law $\bar{L}$ each of the elements $\bar{V}^{12}$ is negative and therefore $[NB(D) - NB(C)]$, equals $-\bar{V}^{12}\mathrm{I}$, is positive.

If now, when L is reversed, we allow that welfare effects alter the absolute size of the compensatory payment – so that $\bar{v}_{ij} \gtreqless -v_{ij}$, and therefore $\bar{V} \neq -V$ – the outcomes of applying the decision rules *A*, *B*, *C*, and *D*, are no longer uniquely determined irrespective of the law. In particular, the optimal outcomes under the C rule will, in general, differ according as the law is L or $\bar{L}$.

Notes: Chapter 11

1 Provided the thing is a good. If, instead, it were a 'bad' there is a maximum sum he will pay to divest himself of it, and a minimum sum he will accept as compensation for bearing with it.

2 A discussion of this implication will be found in my paper [**10**, p. 603].

3 If, instead, we adopted the EV measure, the EV of each of the gainers from the change would involve a minimum sum to be paid to him (enough to compensate him to forgo the change). The EV of each loser, on the other hand, would involve a maximum payment from him (leaving him no better off than if he accepted the change). If the algebraic sum of the EVs were negative, an overall Pareto loss results from *not* introducing the change. This is awkward in respect both of sign and of interpretation – for this sum need not always be negative when the algebraic sum of the CVs is positive.

4 If the exemption is agreed upon for a particular individual, it is agreed, that is, to preclude his radio from the beach. If the law instead were prohibitive, an exempted individual plays his radio freely.

5 This 'independence' assumption, stating that the value to the individual of playing his own radio is determined

independently of the number of other radios that are playing, is not plausible. It is more reasonable to expect the value of his own radio-playing to be enhanced as other radios are switched off.

Taking 33 to be the minimum sum acceptable to individual X for not playing his radio when all others are permitted to play, if the first alteration in the initial situation, that in which all four were playing, was agreement to have one individual, say W, turn off his radio, the minimum sum acceptable to X might now rise to 36. The additional 3 that X's own radio-playing is now worth could be added to the amount he is willing to pay for the first other radio to be turned off, making it 12 instead of 9. If another radio turned off added a further 3 to the worth of his own radio-playing the next sum would be revised from 7 to 10, and so on. But this adjustment is possible only up to the point at which X himself is exempted, after which it becomes irrelevant. If, for example, X's radio-playing were excluded first, the positive figures would remain without revision. Without the independence assumption then, only when agreement has been reached on which individuals are to remain playing their radios, and which are not to play, are these negative numbers finally determined.

It is not, however, worth elaborating the problem to allow for this interdependence since, as we shall indicate in later notes, the qualitative results to be established do not depend on the independence assumption.

6 The independence assumption involves no sacrifice of plausibility when decision rules A and B are applied to the initial situation, since for each individual the value of his own radio-playing is to be estimated under the condition that all other radios are being played.

7 If r were equal to 4, NB would be the same as for the B outcome irrespective of the ordering.

8 If we remove the independence assumption, the negative numbers may be higher (absolutely) in the resulting matrix for the remaining radio-players X and Y than they are in the table. If so, the negative column totals for X and Y would be higher (absolutely) than they appear in Matrix I(L). If, for example, the figures -33, and -35, were revised respectively to -36, and -40, and the X and Y columns totals therefore to -12, and -25 respectively the NB from exempting W and Z would be increased by 8 to 32 altogether. To X and Y, the worth of their permission to play when W and Z are excluded is enhanced by 8. This should be clear whether we add this 8 to the sum of their minimum payments, as here, or whether instead we had revised upward their maximum payments to W and Z by a total of 8.

9 On the sufficient condition that, under a total-prohibition law, the individual is indifferent with respect to the size of the area.

10 These latter payments, however, equal to 47, or the sum of the elements in V^{21} (9, 16, 7, 15) exceed the required joint compensation of 23 by the amount 24, which, as already indicated, is the NB arising from the C outcome compared with the initial situation.

11 If we removed our rule on the separate facilities arrangements, W and Z could be made yet better off by changing, by common consent, their separate $\bar{L}$ area into a separate L area. Indeed, in the limiting case, the maximum net benefit accrues if each individual were placed in a separate L area. In order to highlight the practical alternatives we ignore these possibilities.

12 If the row totals for W and Z were negative, they would be added algebraically to the negative of the sum of the V^{11} elements, so reducing excess NB compared with C.

Again, if it so happened that the algebraic sum of the elements in V^{11} was positive, there would be no additional gain to X and Y from no longer having to make up a required compensation for exempting Z and W. For in such a case Z and W between them provide more than enough compensation for one another. However, in such a case the Z and W row totals are that much larger – by at least 23, that is. Separation of Z and W into an $\bar{L}$ area would then provide them with an excess benefit of more than the 3 in the text example (by at least 23).

13 If, for this case also, we remove the independence assumption, the negative elements for X and Y may again be revised upward (absolutely) owing once more to the exclusion of W and Z – in this arrangement, because of their being placed in an area separate from the L area for the X and Y group. If we assume the figures were revised upward (absolutely) by a total of 8, this revision holds both for the C outcome and the D outcome. Consequently the excess NB from moving from the C outcome to the D outcome remains unchanged at 26.

14 An alternative method of estimating this measure of excess NB is to sum the row-wise improvements for each individual in the D solution compared with the *initial* situation, and subtract this estimate of $NB(D)$ from the known $NB(C)$. (a') For X and Y, the improvement in being left in a separate L area consists in their no longer having to offer payments equal to V^{21}I to exempt Z and W, both of whom are now placed in the separate $\bar{L}$ area. As a result of this saving the joint minimum compensation necessary to move X and Y from a separate L area goes up by V^{21}I, or by 47 (compared with the original minimum joint compensation of 8 in the shared L area). (b') For W and Z, as indicated in the text, the improvement in being placed in a separate $\bar{L}$ area, indifferent to the shared $\bar{L}$ area, is equal to their row totals, 3, which equals (V^{11}I+V^{12}I). Thus

$$NB(D)=(a')=+(b')= V^{21}I + V^{11}I + V^{12}I=50$$

$NB(C)$, the W and Z column totals, is

$$NB(C)= V^{11}I + V^{21}I=24$$

$$\therefore NB(D)-NB(C)=(V^{21}I + V^{11}I + V^{12}I)-(V^{11}I + V^{21}I)= V^{12}I$$
$$=26 \text{ (as above)}$$

15 In general we should expect the NB yield by the C outcome to be different under the $\bar{L}$ law, as, in general, the optimal outcome will be further from the initial state under one law than under the other.

16 Again this result may be checked by comparing the row totals under the D outcome with those in the initial situation under the $\bar{L}$ law. (b'), W and Z are neither better off nor worse off. From being in a joint area where all are prohibited they are now in a separate area where all are prohibited. (a'), X and Y on the other hand, are better off. From being in a shared prohibited $\bar{L}$ area they are prepared to pay, for being placed in a separate L area, a sum, 55, equal to V^{22}I, the algebraic sum of their reduced rows. Since the D outcome would in fact place them in the separate L area, this sum is pure surplus:

$$NB(D) = (a') + (b') = V^{22}I = 55$$

$NB(C)$, equal to the X and Y column totals, is

$$NB(C) = V^{12}I + V^{22}I = 29$$

$$\therefore NB(D) - NB(C) = V^{22}I - (V^{12}I + V^{22}I) = -V^{12}I = 26 \text{ (as above)}$$

17 The reader will have noticed that under the $\bar{L}$ law, we calculated the excess NB for the D outcome without a contribution from the W and Z groups while under the L law we added their row totals to the surplus of X and Y to arrive at the excess NB. This apparent asymmetry arises from the fact that under the L law, W and Z are *not* (necessarily) indifferent as between being placed in a separate quiet $\bar{L}$ area and being exactly compensated under the C outcome as to be no worse off than they were under the initial L law (where all had permission). In contrast, under the $\bar{L}$ law, W and Z *are* indifferent as between being placed in a separate $\bar{L}$ area and being exactly compensated under the C outcome as to be no worse off there than they were under the initial $\bar{L}$ law (where all four were prohibited in a joint area).

18 The magnitude of the alterations made to the compensatory payments in Matrix $I'(\bar{L})$ are obviously exaggerated. This does not matter in a purely illustrative example. The significance of this asymmetry in important instances will be argued later.

19 Moreover, possible economies of scale in a joint area may have to be forgone if the area is divided. Any such loss is to be subtracted from $[NB(D) - NB(C)]$.

20 See in particular arguments of Buchanan and Tullock [3], and R. H. Coase [4].

21 One cannot be much impressed by the argument of noninterventionists that if some new arrangement, say a separate facilities solution, could in fact yield net benefits to the otherwise afflicted group, then it must be possible, if not for the group itself to come together and organize it, for some entrepreneur to make a profit by promoting the arrangement. And the fact that such an arrangement has not come into being is, therefore, held to be *prima facie* evidence that it does not yield net benefits. If this argument were taken seriously one would infer that no new form of enterprise could possibly be discovered in the future; that no further social or managerial innovation remains to be discovered. The ever-vigilant and omniscient entrepreneur has foreseen every possible opportunity for making profits; the only forms of innovation remaining are purely technological.

22 An example in which benefit is conferred by one individual upon the other is of small interest unless the individual who confers the benefit damages his interest in the process, in which case it is formally similar to the problem treated in the text.

23 A separate areas solution cannot be proposed in such a case since the effect enjoyed by Y depends upon his new house being located in the particular area that obstructs X's view.

24 This example is adapted from the one suggested by Buchanan and Stubblebine [2]. Their unique optimum is to be compared with the result above.

25 This sum is equal to its rent, or excess profit, in using that particular airfield compared with the next most suitable airfield available to the airline company, plus the costs of movement.

26 If represented on a diagram similar to the figure, with the company's compensation line as the Y line, there would be only one such Y line irrespective of the law, the difference in the optimal number of planes under the L law as compared with the $\bar{L}$ law arising only from differences in the X line.

The smoke nuisance case is treated in a similar manner. If the damaging effects from smoke can be completely offset by the purchase of soap, laundering services, and the like, the X line would be uniquely determined, and so also would be the optimal output – if we ignore all costs of implementation.

27 On issues that make a significant difference to the individual's welfare the difference between the maximum sum he would pay to avoid a certain fate (his view being permanently obscured, or his peace being shattered over a long period) and the minimum sum he would accept for submitting to that fate is likely to be far greater than is habitually suggested by our notions of differences in welfare effect, so frequently assumed negligible in order to reach elegant theoretical results. The current and prospective income and assets of a person form a limit to the maximum he can afford to pay and remain alive, while no such limit restricts the minimum sum he would consent to receive. A man dying of thirst in the middle of the Sahara could offer, for a bucket of water that would save his life, no more than his prospective earnings (above some subsistence level). And this sum would be infinitesimal compared with the sum of money needed to induce him to forgo the bucket of water and fatally reduce his chance of survival.

28 The determination of an optimal number of cars on a given stretch of road can, incidentally, be illuminated by this matrix scheme. In such problems, it is often supposed that only the individuals who actually use the road for driving suffer damages as a result of growing congestion. Provisionally accepting this assumption, we build up the matrix under an $\bar{L}$ law by introducing one car at a time in descending order of the values they set on driving over this stretch of road. As the number of cars increases from 1, 2, 3, to m, we represent the position by a 1×1, a 2×2, a 3×3, and eventually an $m \times m$ matrix. The mth car also has a positive v_{mm}. It inflicts damage on the $(m-1)$ other cars, hence the negative elements in the rest of the m column. However, it suffers damage from each of the $(m-1)$ other cars, hence the negative elements in the rest of the m row. In the conventional case, where it is assumed that the additional driver inflicts on each of the others the total congestion costs experienced by introducing his own car, each negative element in the rth column is equal to the sum of the negative elements in the $(r-1)$th row. In deciding whether to use the road, the individual driver consults only his row total; if positive he drives. The optimal solution, however, will admit all those cars having positive column totals.

29 If, on the other hand, the specific instance in mind was the disturbance caused within a residential area by motorized lawnmowers, an outcome with a higher NB than either the C or the D outcome may be reached by agreement on the pattern of activity within the period. The initial matrix, we could suppose, had reference to compensatory payments per week for exemptions under the L law from any lawnmowing during the week. Any optimal C solution would leave a certain number of individuals free to mow their lawns any time they wished, while prohibiting the

remainder from any motorized lawn-mowing at all. It is now entirely possible that a consensus on confining lawn-mowing activity to limited periods, say Wednesdays from 2 to 4 and/or Fridays from 4 to 6, would confer a larger NB than the C outcome.

30 If the world were otherwise than that described here, in particular, if on balance, (a) it were more costly to bring about optimal arrangements under an L law and (b) optimal arrangements under the $\bar{L}$ law resulted in a less satisfactory distribution of welfare, then clearly the case for a change from L to $\bar{L}$ would be weakened. The case for such a change would rest more heavily on the ethical considerations which considerations should in any case, I believe, predominate.

I do not find it easy, however, to think of instances in which the facts, in respect of G costs at least, are other than those assumed in the text. Widespread disamenity resulting from mass usage of the recent products of industry is no exception. Under an $\bar{L}$ law the initiative toward improved economic arrangements would come from the large firms or from trade associations which, being highly organized decision-taking bodies, could promote the new economic arrangements at much lower G costs than can the unorganized members of the affected public under the existing L law. Indeed, in many cases the cheapest method of correcting the externality, that of redesigning the product so as to remove the offending features, would involve practically no G costs under an $\bar{L}$ law while being almost impossible to bring about under the existing L law.

31 It is perhaps an unnecessary precaution to remark that there is no affinity whatever between my separate-facilities proposal and the doctrines of 'separate but equal facilities'. If anything, my proposal implies the reverse of that doctrine: facilities in the two (or more) areas are designed to be different, while the choice of area in which to reside is entirely up to each individual family.

32 Stigler in his 1943 note [14] protests that the compensating principle is repugnant to our moral code inasmuch as it would apparently sanction compensation of successful thieves for the amounts they would otherwise steal. I pointed out in a footnote in my survey paper [9, p. 219, f. 5] that this criticism did not apply to *hypothetical* compensation tests, which left the question of *actual* compensation to be determined on other grounds, generally by reference to the distributional implications – though, of course, one might bring in other ethical considerations.

Nonetheless, insofar as the working of the market is sanctioned ultimately by this Pareto principle and, indeed, the working of the market under the existing laws *does* place the burden of payment on the victims of the incidental damage caused by industry, the core of Stigler's criticism can be justified.

33 Paradoxically, perhaps, this interpretation is borne out by the familiar misgivings about the neglect of the distributional implications of applying hypothetical compensation tests. (For particular instances the reader is referred to the articles by Hotelling [6], Scitovsky [13], Radomysler [12], and Baumol [1]). A distributional proviso may be attached to the compensation tests, as has been suggested by Scitovsky [13], Little [7] and many others. What the distributional proviso should state, however, is not always clear, but it is generally conceded that the statement, to command general assent, must have reference to the ethics of society.

While this explicit concern with distribution rather than

the uncertain implications for distribution of the marginal utility approach may be seen as one of the redeeming features of the New Welfare Economics, the question of who, under the circumstances, ought to pay compensation, must also be referred to ethical considerations, distinct from and possibly in conflict with those invoked in discussing the distribution of welfare. If my neighbor's weeding machine is eccentric enough to blow his weeds into my garden, I should not like to think that the question of who compensates whom is to be decided by reference to our relative incomes.

34 Coase [4, p. 2] writes: 'The question is commonly thought of as one in which A inflicts harm on B and what has to be decided is: how should we restrain A? But this is wrong. We are dealing with a problem of a reciprocal nature. To avoid the harm to B would inflict harm on A. The real question that has to be decided is: should A be allowed to harm B or should B be allowed to harm A?' A conflict of interest does not *per se*, however, imply reciprocal damage. Thus, in one of the instances adduced, that of a confectioner, the vibration from whose machinery disturbed a doctor at his work, reciprocity would require that the doctor in his turn, damaged the production of confectionery, which was not alleged.

In the circumstances, the doctor (B) has an incentive to approach the confectioner (A) for the terms on which he, B, may obtain relief whereas A has no such incentive. Indeed the only incentive facing A is that of gratuitously adding to the noise in order to increase the amount of the bribe that B can be induced to offer.

35 Throughout the paper we have deliberately evaded the difficulties associated with checking the accuracy of subjective estimates of compensatory payments. It might reasonably be suspected that many people suffering from the existing disamenities, inflicted on them by industrial expansion, would make exaggerated claims. But, even if we assume that such difficulties are not likely to be satisfactorily resolved, exaggerated claims would tend to provide greater incentives for those generating external diseconomies to take the initiative in promoting a separate facilities solution. If, for instance, enthusiastic motorists were called upon to satisfy the claims of those sensitive to their disamenity-creating potential, the purchase of large motorized residential areas by the automobile interest is likely to prove a far more economical solution than a mixed Pareto outcome within each of the existing residential areas.

36 We ignore the rows whose algebraic totals are equal to zero. Such individuals are indifferent to being subjected, along with the others, either to the L law or to the $\bar{L}$ law.

37 The m group is, of course, indifferent to being exactly compensated for its exemption under the C outcome and remaining in the initial situation under the L law.

38 An alternative method of reaching the same result is to compare the row totals for each group under separate areas with their row totals in the initial situation. From the $NB(D)$ so calculated we can subtract $NB(C)$.

Compared with the initial situation the net benefit for the m exempted members when placed in a separate $\bar{L}$ area is, as explained in the text, equal to $\overset{m}{\Sigma} v_{i.}$.

As for the remaining $(n-m)$ group, remaining in a separate L area their net benefit in each row is increased by removal therefrom the algebraic sum of the first m elements, this sum being the net amount of all compensatory payments for exempting each member of the m group from the L law – no longer necessary when the m group is placed in a separate $\bar{L}$ area. The net benefit of this $(n-m)$ group, compared with the initial situation is, therefore, equal to $V^{21}I$.

Thus
$$NB(D) - NB(C) = (\overset{m}{\Sigma}\ v_{i\cdot} + V^{21}I) - \overset{m}{\Sigma}\ v_{\cdot j}$$

$$= \overset{m}{\Sigma}\ v_{i\cdot} + V^{21}I - V^{11}I - V^{21}I$$

$$= \overset{m}{\Sigma}\ v_{i\cdot} - V^{11}I$$

$$= V^{12}I$$

as above, for the first case in which $V^{11}I \leqslant 0$.

For the special case of $V^{11} > 0$, however, it is $\overset{m}{\Sigma}\ v_{i\cdot}$ alone.

39 If, on the other hand, $\bar{V}^{12}I > 0$, this indicates that, on balance, the m group derives net positive benefit from the $(n-m)$ group's exemption from the $\bar{L}$ law under the C outcome. Therefore placing this m group in a separate $\bar{L}$ area – without the presence of the exempted $(n-m)$ members – must make it worse off.

The $(n-m)$ group in the separate L area, on the other hand, is no worse off (unless, of course, we have it compensating the m group in the separate $\bar{L}$ area – in which case the m group is no worse off, having shifted the burden to the other group). However, if $V^{12}I > 0$ the n members as a whole are worse off by $-V^{12}I$ when placed in separate areas than they were under the C outcome.

40 This apparent asymmetry in calculating $[NB(D) - NB(C)]$ under the $\bar{L}$ law as compared with the L law springs from the two different ways in which the C outcome is reached. What we might call the prevailing group, $(n-m)$ in the C procedure are paying to exempt the others – the m group – under the L law, but paying to exempt themselves under the $\bar{L}$ law.

41 Again, an alternative method of reaching the same result is to compare the row totals for each group in the separate areas with their row totals in the initial situation. From the $NB(D)$ so calculated we subtract $NB(C)$.

Assuming the m group is no better or worse off in a separate $\bar{L}$ area than in the initial situation under a joint $\bar{L}$ area, we need consider only the $(n-m)$ group. Recall that the n row elements in the initial situation are the individual's compensatory payments to exempt each of the n members from the $\bar{L}$ law. Thus a negative algebraic sum of the first m elements in any of the $(n-m)$ rows entails a net compensatory sum required by that individual for consenting to exempt from the $\bar{L}$ law the m group as a whole. Once such an individual is placed in a separate area without the m group, _though without for the moment changing the existing $\bar{L}$ law,_ these m row elements are omitted for each of the $(n-m)$ individuals. The remaining

elements for this $(n-m)$ group comprise those in the sub-matrix $\bar{V}^{22}$. The sum of these elements is the net amount which the $(n-m)$ group is willing to pay to change this now separate $\bar{L}$ area into a separate L area. If, now, the area is put under the L law, these $(n-m)$ individuals do not in fact have to pay the sum $\bar{V}^{22}I$ which, consequently, measures $NB(D)$.

Since
$$NB(C) = \overset{n}{\underset{j=m+1}{\Sigma}}\ \bar{v}_{\cdot j}$$

$$NB(D) - NB(C) = \bar{V}^{22}I - \overset{n}{\underset{j=m+1}{\Sigma}}\ \bar{v}_{\cdot j}$$

$$= \bar{V}^{22}I - \bar{V}^{12}I - \bar{V}^{22}I$$

$$= -\bar{V}^{12}I \text{ (as above)}$$

References

1 Baumol, W. J., 'Community indifference', *Review of Economic Studies,* vol. 14(1), no. 35 (1948).
2 Buchanan. J. and Stubblebine, W. C., 'Externality', *Economica* (November 1962).
3 Buchanan, J. and Tullock, G., *The Calculus of Consent* (Michigan, 1962), esp. pp. 47–8 and 61–2 and ch. 7.
4 Coase, R. H., 'The problem of social cost', *Journal of Law and Economics* (October 1960).
5 Davis, O. A. and Whinston, A., 'Externalities, welfare and the theory of games', *Journal of Political Economy* (June 1962).
6 Hotelling, H., 'The general welfare in relation to the problems of taxation and of railway and utility rates', *Econometrica* (1938).
7 Little, I. M. D., *A Critique of Welfare Economics,* 2nd edn (London: Oxford University Press, 1957).
8 Meade, J. E., 'External economies and diseconomies in a competitive situation', *Economic Journal* (March 1952).
9 Mishan, E. J., 'A survey of welfare economics, 1939–1959', *Economic Journal* (June 1960).
10 Mishan, E. J., 'Welfare criteria for external effects', *American Economic Review* (September 1961).
11 Pigou, A. C., *The Economics of Welfare,* 4th edn (London, 1932).
12 Radomysler, A., 'Welfare economics and economic policy', *Economica* (1946).
13 Scitovsky, T., 'A note on welfare propositions in economics', *Review of Economic Studies,* vol. 9, no. 2 (1941).
14 Stigler, G. J., 'The New Welfare Economics: a communication', *American Economic Review* (1943).
15 Turvey, R., 'Side effects of resource use', in *Environmental Quality in a Growing Economy* (Baltimore: Johns Hopkins, for Resources for the Future Inc. 1966), ch. 3.

12

What Is the Optimal Level of Pollution?

On a theoretical plane, the question has not been properly answered. Its neglect may be partly explained by its seeming obviousness. And though the answer is indeed obvious once it is correctly stated, it is not the answer one gleans from a reading of the relevant literature.

Other factors have probably contributed to its neglect. One is the altogether commendable concern now growing among economic specialists, particularly in the United States, about practical methods for stemming rising levels of air and water pollution. Another reason is that, in theoretical discussions much attention is given to what I have called (1965) 'external diseconomies *internal* to the industry', or to the 'activity', the phenomenon associated chiefly with the names of Allen Young and Frank Knight (1924), whose contributions are summarized in the classic Ellis and Fellner paper (1943). The 'external diseconomy' here springs from nothing less familiar than the eventually diminishing returns to a variable factor arising from the fixity of other factors. Where – as in the case of agriculture – the scarce factor, land, is assumed properly priced – that is, by reference to the difference between the average and marginal product of labor – the resulting competitive supply curve is also the correct marginal cost curve of grain, and the perfectly competitive output is therefore the optimal output. Where, instead, the scarce factor is some common property such as a road or a fishing area, it is not priced at all. The competitive supply curve of the good produced on, or with, this common property factor is only an average curve, one that excludes rent to the scarce factor. Consequently, the competitive equilibrium (of traffic or output) exceeds optimality.

Restriction of one's attention to these external diseconomies that are internal to the industry, and therefore also to the theme of an unpriced scarce factor, suggests that the optimum external diseconomy to be borne by the industry (and by society) is that associated with the optimal output of the corrected supply curve – one that is an average curve that includes rent to the scarce factor. For all these 'internal-to-the-industry' cases the answer is satisfactory simply because it is assumed that the external diseconomy can be varied only by varying the industry's output. Such an assumption, however, is not justified for the class of external diseconomies that are external to the industry or activity, especially those which, under the umbrella term 'pollution', have engrossed the public's attention over the past decade. Though, again, an unpriced common property resource, such as air or water, is at the base of the problem, there are now ways of varying the amount of the externality other than by varying the output of the good itself. It is this fact – that a pollutant externality can be reduced in a number of ways – that calls for a more general statement about the optimum level of pollution.[1]

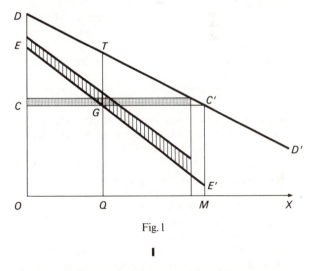

Fig. 1

I

Though not necessary to the conclusions, in the interests of simplicity the analysis which follows is strictly partial: in all other sectors outputs are already optimal, and our concern is then solely with reaching an optimal solution in this one industry or activity that produces an external diseconomy. To avoid obvious modifications, we shall assume that the welfare effects on the amounts demanded are zero; initially that there are no transactions costs broadly defined; and that the industry which produces an output X is perfectly competitive and has a constant long-period supply curve. If the reader can bear the tedium, we shall suppose that the external diseconomy produced in conjunction with X is, again, smoke, and that the value of the social damage associated with any increment of output is measured as the vertical distance between the demand curve DD' and the curve EE' in Figure 1.

The conventional analysis goes as follows. With the demand curve DD', the uncorrected long-period market equilibrium output of X is equal to OM. The 'optimal output' OQ occurs where the resultant marginal social valuation measured by curve EE' is equal to the marginal resource cost CC', an output that can be realized by imposing an 'optimal tax' TG on each unit of X.[2] The 'optimal pollution', which has to remain in the economy, and be suffered by the pollution victims, is that associated with output OQ, and valued, or rather, 'costed', by society at a sum equal to the area $EDTG$.

These conclusions would be satisfactory if there were no methods of dealing with the smoke other than by varying output of X, although the TG excise tax would be only one device through which this 'optimal' output OQ could be determined. For, in the last resort, quantitative controls alone could be used to ensure that no more than OQ of X is produced. Moreover, bargaining between the industry and the smoke victims would also result in OQ of X being produced, irrespective of which party under the law had to pay the other to take action.

But, as mentioned above, there can be a number of ways of curbing smoke pollution, and Coase's (1960) article has at least the merit of drawing our attention to this mundane fact. In section 9 of the article, for instance, he assumes a case in which the damage caused by the smoke is $100 per annum, but in which there is a smoke-preventing device costing $90 and also the option of moving all the smoke victims from the locality for the modest sum of $40 per annum.[3] For that matter, the relocation of the smoky factory to a more sparsely inhabited area may also be feasible. Clearly, there is no limit to the number of possible ways of reducing the pollution, but nothing is lost in generality of conclusions by confining ourselves to three forms of reducing it: A, the one most familiar to economics students, a reduction of the output of X; B, the employment of any particular smoke-preventive

technique; and C, the movement elsewhere of the smoky industry.

II

The impression conveyed by the literature on externalities that occasionally recognizes alternative methods of dealing with them – certainly in the Coase article but also in those of others[4] – is that where one method is not clearly more economic than the others, practical circumstances will suggest which is to be adopted. Thus, in the Coase example referred to, the most economical solution is that of moving the smoke-sufferers to a smokeless area, whereas, when it comes to practical considerations, the economic specialists have a marked predilection for an effluent tax, at least for water pollution.[5] In contrast, the theoretical solution to the problem of the optimal amount of pollution implies that if there are n methods of varying the pollution, then, in general, all n methods are to be simultaneously employed.[6]

In elaborating this conclusion, there are advantages in proceeding as follows. First, the 'optimal' B and C methods will each be summarized before being compared with the A solution. Following this, each method is compared with what we may call the 'composite' optimum solution inasmuch as this solution employs each of the three methods simultaneously, though using each method less intensively than if that method were used alone and to the exclusion of the other methods. Our results are then formalized, and some of their policy implications are briefly considered.

While the A method is the one which reduces the total increment of pollution that is generated by a unit of output of X by the expedient of reducing the production of that unit of X, the B method involves expenditure on resources in creating devices that act to reduce, in some degree, the existing level of pollution on all the X being currently produced. Thus, an initial increment of expenditure on some preventive technique will be worthwhile if it reduces an amount of pollution (generated by the existing output of X) that confers a social gain greater in value than the increment of expenditure. A marginal reduction in the value of social damage arising from a marginal reduction in the pollution generated by output OM – in effect the marginal social gain arising from a marginal decrease in overall pollution – can be represented in our Figure 1 by the area of the shaded strip lying on top of EE'. The (smaller) cost of effecting this social gain can be an overhead expense to each firm in the short period, but in the long period the industry supply curve is raised by the dotted strip lying on top of CC'. Since this adjustment raises the equilibrium price of X, the equilibrium output of X will be somewhat smaller than OM as indicated in the figure. Clearly, one may continue to improve matters, that is, to make net social gains, by incurring successive increments of pollution-abatement expenditure until the cost of doing so is no longer exceeded by the corresponding 'strip' of social gain.

The effect of the 'optimal' solution by method B could then be represented on the same diagram in Figure 2. Total expenditure on pollution abatement has raised long-period marginal cost to $C_1 C_1'$, thereby reducing equilibrium output of X to OM_1. The value of the pollution remaining – the 'optimal' pollution, since the marginal gain of pollution reduction by method B is equal to the marginal cost so incurred – is given by the area $DE_1 E_1' C_1'$, and this may be greater or less than $EDTG$, the 'optimal' pollution that remains when using the A method alone.

measured, and along the vertical axis is measured the marginal social value of the pollution damage and also the marginal opportunity cost of pollution abatement.[8] Thus, ON is the total pollution initially generated by the uncorrected OM market output of X, and $OV'V$ is the marginal social damage curve. Up to OV' units the pollution has no perceptible impact on people's welfare, after which successive increments of pollution entail increasing social loss – measured, say, by the maximum sum society is willing to pay to avoid that unit of pollution – the nth unit of pollution suffered being 'valued' at VN. If we look at the diagram instead from right to left, the $VV'O$ curve can be construed as the downward-sloping valuation or demand curve for pollution reduction, and CC' as the upward-sloping marginal cost curve of pollution reduction. The area VNV' in the figure is equal to area $DEE'C'$ in Figure 2, and both areas are equal to the total value of social damage when nothing at all is done about the pollution.

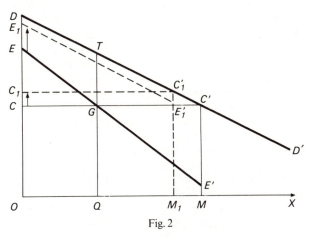

Fig. 2

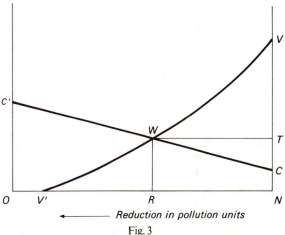

Fig. 3

Method B, involving preventive techniques, is implied by proposals for pollution or effluent charges, or by taxes designed to reduce pollution to some arbitrary 'tolerable' level.[7] Obviously, bargaining as between the industry and the victims of pollution – about the overall reduction of pollution to be aimed at by preventive techniques – will also result in a B-method 'optimal' level of pollution.

III

The diagram by which the 'optimal' pollution on the B method is commonly exhibited is that shown as Figure 3. Along the horizontal axis, units of pollution are

Figure 3 clearly suggests that net social gain from reducing pollution is maximized by a reduction of NR pollution units, at which point the (falling) marginal gain from pollution reduction is equal to the (rising) marginal cost of pollution reduction. A tax of TN per unit of pollution would therefore be 'optimal' since – without knowledge of, or reference to, the VV' curve – the levying of such a tax will impel the industry to reduce pollution by NR. For up to the first NR units of pollution, it is cheaper to reduce pollution than to pay the tax. After NR units, the reverse is true. The 'optimal' pollution remaining is, therefore, OR, and this is 'valued' at a sum that corresponds to the area of triangle $V'RW$ – the sum represented in Figure 2 as equal to the area $DE_1E_1'C_1'$.

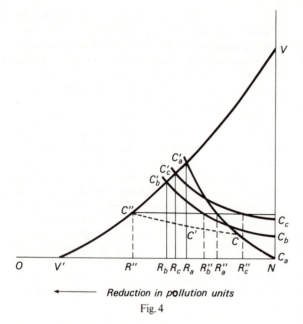

Reduction in pollution units

Fig. 4

Now, by measuring along *NO* the distance in miles that the polluting *X* industry can be moved from the boundary of the inhabited area,[9] we can interpret the *CC'* and *VV'* curves, respectively, as the marginal cost per mile of movement and the marginal social gain per mile of that movement arising from the associated reduction in pollution. We should then conclude that *NR* is the 'optimal' distance to move the industry. However, since it will be convenient to represent this method C on the same axes as method B, we assume the possibility of a unique transformation of distance into units of pollution reduction. Thus, in Figure 4, the horizontal axis measures units of pollution, and the marginal cost curve for method C with respect to these units appears as $C_c C_c'$, which curve can now be directly compared with the marginal cost curve $C_b C_b'$ for method B, which, like the marginal valuation curve *VV'*, is the same as that in Figure 3.

A similar marginal cost curve for method A can be shown on the same diagram as $C_a C_a'$. This is in effect a marginal opportunity curve derived primarily from the forgoing of excess benefit – demand price less marginal resource cost – as the output of *X* is reduced from *OM* toward zero.[10] Transforming reduced output of *X* into reduced pollution, simplified by assuming a fixed proportion between smoke and output, produces this required cost curve of reducing pollution by method A with respect to pollution units.

In general, the 'optimal' pollution levels when each one of the three methods is used alone will differ. In Figure 4 they are OR_a, OR_b, and OR_c, respectively, for

methods A, B, and C. Their corresponding 'optimal' pollution taxes also differ.[11] But if all three methods of reducing pollution are to be simultaneously employed, then economy requires that the amount reduced by each method is such that the marginal cost of each method is the same. This result follows from the idea of reducing the first, second, third, ... *n*th unit of pollution by whichever method is the cheapest for that unit, bearing in mind that eventually each of the methods is increasingly used. The succession of lowest incremental costs so derived forms the composite marginal cost curve, and the true optimal pollution reduction is determined where this curve cuts the *VV'* curve at *R''*.

For simplicity of construction, assume the marginal cost curve of each of our three methods is independent of the costs, if any, incurred by the other two methods.[12] We can then construct the composite marginal cost curve for pollution reduction, $C_a CC'C''$, by 'horizontally adding together' the three separate marginal cost curves. From C_a to *C* on this composite curve, method A only is used to reduce pollution. From *C* to *C'*, some reduction is effected by both A and B methods. From *C'* onward, further reductions receive a contribution from each of the three methods.

The reader will at once observe that the composite optimal pollution that remains, *V'R''*, is smaller than the 'optimal' pollution determined by the employment of any one method alone. Consequently, the composite pollution tax *C''R''* is also smaller than a pollution tax determined by reference to any single method of pollution reduction. Since the magnitude of the composite pollution tax is to be adopted by each of the three methods when they are used together, the pollution reduction contributed by each of the methods when they are used together is smaller than the 'optimal' pollution reduction effected by that method when it is used alone. Thus, of the total pollution reduced jointly, *NR''*, methods A, B, and C, are responsible, respectively, for amounts NR_a'', NR_b'', and NR_c''. Clearly, each of these amounts is smaller than NR_a, NR_b, and NR_c, these being, respectively, the 'optimal' pollution reductions of methods A, B, and C, when each method is used alone.

It may be revealing to depict the effects of this composite pollution optimum also on the original demand-and-supply diagram. The composite pollution tax implies an excise tax on the output of *X* that is smaller than *TG* in Figure 2.[13] It is equal, say, to *T'G'* in Figure 5 (derived by reference to *C''R''* in Figure 4). The optimal output of *X* resulting from applying the composite pollution tax to the A method is, therefore, OQ_1, which is larger than the output *OQ* corresponding to

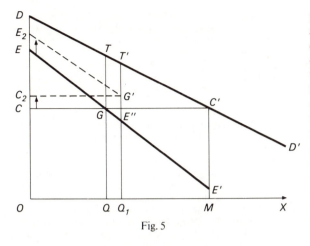

Fig. 5

the use of method A alone. The optimal employment of methods B and C has, between them, raised the unit cost of this output from OC to OC_2 and has reduced pollution damage by a value equal to the area $EE_2G'E''$. The value of the optimal pollution remaining, the area $DT'G'E_2$, is then also equal in area to triangle $V'R''C''$ in Figure 4.

These findings are easily formalized and extended. At any moment of time there will be a number of economically feasible technologies that can be used directly to reduce the level of pollution generated in the production of a given output of good X, including perhaps one or more methods of recycling the pollutant,[14] each having its own marginal cost curve of pollution reduction. Although under suitable conditions all these direct methods of pollution abatement will be simultaneously used, there can be indivisibilities of capital expenditure that demand an initial choice among the alternatives, one based on a comparison of estimates of the total costs to be incurred in reducing some expected amount of pollution. But for all these direct methods of pollution abatement that are simultaneously employed, the composite optimal solution requires that the marginal social gains from reducing pollution be equal to the marginal composite cost of reducing pollution, and equal also to the marginal cost of reducing pollution by each of the methods in use.[15]

IV

In a world in which transactions costs, broadly defined, are low in relation to net social gains from reducing pollution, an ideal institution, on grounds both of equity and allocation, would be a law that placed on all polluting manufacturers the obligation to compensate all pollution victims. Businesses would then have a direct incentive to seek new and more economical ways of reducing pollution damage in order to reduce their total costs, including residual compensatory payments. Since the conflict today is between polluting industry on the one hand and the public at large on the other,[16] the transactions costs associated with compensating the victims under such a law are likely to be heavy, including, as they must, the costs of information, of identifying claimants, of legal fees, of negotiating fees, and so on. Unless the available methods are so efficacious as to leave a negligible amount of pollution, such a law might cause a large number of polluting enterprises to close down altogether. And this 'polar' solution, though economically justifiable under such a law, may be economically worse, or better, than the opposite polar solution, that of no reduction at all of pollution, which comes about if the effect of existing laws is to place the burden of compensation wholly on the public at large.[17]

Better than either of these polar solutions are likely to be those that result when governments undertake some initiative and, therefore, come to bear a part of the consequently smaller magnitude of transactions costs (interpreted to include research, monitoring, and otherwise enforcing the law) that are involved in nothing more ambitious than maintaining 'tolerable' standards. As some economists have observed,[18] the costs associated with gathering the data necessary to estimate the $V'V$ curve in order to calculate the ideal tax could be disproportionately high compared with the anticipated value of the net social gains. It is then more practical to devise means of reaching agreement on standards – say the level of maximum 'tolerable' pollution – and calculating or discovering (by trial and error) taxes that give effect to them.

The foregoing analysis suggests that we bear in mind also that enterprising firms will, given the tax or other incentive, continue to seek ways of transforming the pollution tax into an output tax, into a zoning tax,[19] and so on, and that they will find it most economical to operate on all these 'antipollution fronts' simultaneously. We might then remind ourselves that for any required reduction in pollution, the tax set by reference to the simultaneous use of a variety of methods will be lower than that set by reference to any single method of pollution reduction.

Notes: Chapter 12

1 If ever an account of the development of this aspect of economic thought comes to be written, there is sure to be some speculation about the long neglect of a general statement about the optimum level of a pollutant externality. My guess is that one reason for it has been the intellectual energy absorbed by the reaction against the Pigovian doctrine, and especially against the classic tax-subsidy solution. In this connection one thinks immediately of the famous Coase article (1960), and also perhaps of the short piece by Buchanan and Stubblebine (1962), which together seemed to have started an iconoclastic movement to edge the master from his niche in the hall of fame. Although there have been earlier criticisms of parts of Coase's analysis (Mishan, 1965) and also of Buchanan and Stubblebine's paper (Shibata, 1972), the Pigovian doctrine and the tax-subsidy solution have been vindicated in an elegant and incisive article by Baumol (1972), which gently but firmly took these writers to task for discovering 'errors' in the Pigovian doctrine that were the result wholly of a lack of care in their own analyses. As for other critics of the classical doctrine who reached conclusions seemingly at variance with those of Pigou, the novelty of their findings has arisen simply from the novelty of their assumptions. To mention those that spring to mind, Plott (1966) concocts a counter-Pigovian (and counterintuitive) example of optimality, one requiring an expansion of the polluting activity, by assuming a production function that uses less of the factor directly responsible for the pollution as more output is produced. Dolbear (1967) uses a model in which changes in welfare affect the valuation of, and demand for, goods and bads, an assumption that – not surprisingly – undermines the uniqueness of an optimal solution (see also Mishan, 1967). Schall (1971) manages to produce an optimal increase in the market output of a good that generates an external diseconomy by assuming a simultaneous contravention of both factor efficiency and top-level efficiency conditions. For it is then conceivable that a correction of both conditions entails so large an improvement of productive efficiency that the resulting increase in output of the good in question swamps the movement that would otherwise reduce the output of this good originally having a marginal social cost greater than its price. In view of Mishan (1965) and Schall (1971), at least, the statement by Goetz and Buchanan (1971) – namely, that 'the impact of production externalities has heretofore been conceived of exclusively in terms of a suboptimal exchange equilibrium on the production possibility frontier' – is invalid. Not only do they fail to observe that the simultaneous infringement of productive and top-level efficiency conditions occurs when external diseconomies are internal to the industry, but they go to the unnecessary trouble of contriving a model in which – for some unexplained reason – the unit cost of the ith firm depends not on the output of all firms, but only on the output of the remaining firms. (This implies a cost advantage in producing a total output by a number of firms which is smaller than that in the uncorrected market equilibrium.)

2 It is yet more conventional, in the Anglo-Saxon literature, to add the value of the smoke damage to the cost curve so as to construct a marginal social cost curve rather than, as here, to subtract the value of smoke damage from the market valuation of the goods produced in association with it. But the analysis which follows is simpler to follow by adopting the latter construction.

3 As Baumol (1972) pertinently observes, however, if it costs the victims but $40 per annum to move elsewhere, they would of their own volition do so rather than put up with smoke damage that they reckon as equivalent to $100 per annum. Once they move away, no further smoke damage is suffered by people in the vicinity, and the question of a tax on the output of the smoky factory no longer arises.

4 This incidental impression is clearly conveyed by a splendid summing up of this aspect of the literature by Davis and Kamien (1969, 67–86), and also in Baumol's paper (1972, pp. 313–14), where, in his discussion of 'multiplicity of local optima', he suggests that we choose the maximum among them. The same impression arises in reading the otherwise excellent article by Baumol and Bradford (1972). Thus, toward the end of their section 4 on 'Spatial separation as a palliative', they state: 'These diagrams illustrate the proposition that sufficiently severe externalities make locational specialization economical.'

5 The reasons for this are nicely summarized in the article by Freeman and Haveman (1972).

6 I say 'in general' since the use of one method may, for technical or other reasons, preclude the use of one or more other methods. Also, some methods may be too costly to adopt for the particular levels of pollution in question. Thus, for all n methods to be simultaneously adopted, certain conditions would have to be met (which we can assume are met in our three-method model) in order for each to be economically feasible.

7 Though such a tax implies that firms coping with pollution with differing degrees of efficiency will undertake to reduce different amounts of pollution – so that their combined costs for reducing a given amount of pollution are minimal – this optimal aspect of such a tax does not emerge in our simple model in which all firms are assumed to be of equal efficiency.

8 These marginal curves are sometimes derived, respectively, from anterior curves of total damage value of pollution and total cost of reducing pollution, as, for instance, in Ridker (1967).

9 Alternatively, the horizontal distance from N can measure the number of factories to be moved some fixed distance away. It is part of our general conclusion that a combination of both methods can produce a better result than either alone. Although movement in some geographical directions will be more efficient than in others in reducing the effect of pollution on the inhabited area, there is nothing to be gained at this stage in making the analysis more 'real' in these respects.

10 In perfect competition, equilibrium output is M where long-run marginal cost is equal to price. At this output M, the marginal opportunity cost of reducing the output of X is therefore zero.

11 The 'optimal' pollution tax for the A method alone, equal to $C_a' R_a$ in Figure 4, can be transformed into an excise tax on good X, and the 'optimal' pollution tax for the C method alone, equal to $C_c' R_c$ in Figure 4, can also be transformed into a zoning tax based on mileage from the inhabited area.

12 The assumption facilitates the geometry, but, as we shall see later, the resulting marginal conditions remain unaffected when we assume, more realistically, that the marginal cost curve of any one method is affected – presumably shifted upward – by an increase in the use of the other methods (see note 15).

13 The *TG* can also be derived from pollution tax $C_a' R_a$ in Figure 4.

14 Recycling can be regarded as a combination of pollution reduction and goods production. The marginal social value of the goods that emerge in the recycling process is to be subtracted from the appropriate marginal cost of the particular recycling process to yield the relevant marginal cost of reducing pollution by this means.

15 Let Z be the total *reduction* of pollution units in the given area, and Z_1, Z_2, Z_3, be the amounts of pollution reduced by methods 1, 2, and 3 respectively. Write the social welfare as $V(Z)$, where $dV/dZ > 0$, and the cost of pollution reduction as

$$C(Z) = C(Z_1, Z_2, Z_3)$$

where $dC/dZ > 0$. By maximizing $[V(Z) - C(Z)]$ subject to

$$Z = Z_1 + Z_2 + Z_3,$$

we discover the first-order conditions

$$\frac{dV}{dZ} = \frac{dC}{dZ} = \frac{\partial C}{\partial Z_1} = \frac{\partial C}{\partial Z_2} = \frac{\partial C}{\partial Z_3}$$

We limit ourselves here to the necessary conditions only. Thus, we ignore the possibility that the overheads associated with any one method may exceed the net social gains from its employment; also, the possibility that the difference in overheads as between two methods may be so great that it may be economical to withdraw entirely the one with the larger overheads.

16 Since costs of pollution reduction will, in any case, be passed onto the purchasing public by the manufacturers, it is more accurate to talk of a conflict between people as consumers of the product and people as the inhabitants of the environment. Nonetheless, manufacturers can be regarded as representatives, in the first instance, of the interests of people as consumers.

17 See Mishan (1971, s. 10).

18 For a recent paper favoring the adoption of pollution standards, see Baumol and Oates (1971).

19 For the pollution tax effectively to become a zoning tax also, it is necessary that the tax on a particular pollutant be specified as that pollutant falling within a given inhabitable area.

References

Baumol, W. J., 'On taxation and the control of externalities', *American Economic Review,* vol. 62, no. 3 (June 1972), pp. 307–22.

Baumol, W. J. and Bradford, D. F., 'Detrimental externalities and non-convexity of the production set', *Economica* (May 1972), pp. 160–76.

Baumol, W. J. and Oates, W. E., 'The use of standards and prices for protection of the environment', *Swedish Journal of Economics* (March 1971), pp. 42–54.

Buchanan, J. M. and Stubblebine, W. C., 'Externality', *Economica,* vol. 29 (November 1962), pp. 371–84.

Coase, R. H., 'The problem of social cost', *Journal of Law and Economics,* vol. 3 (October 1960), pp. 1–44.

Davis, O. A. and Kamien, M. I., 'Externalities, information, and alternative collective actions', in *The Analysis of Public Expenditures: The PPB System* (Washington: Government Printing Office, 1969).

Dolbear, F. T., Jr, 'On the theory of optimal externality', *American Economic Review,* vol. 57, no. 1 (March 1967), pp. 90–103.

Ellis, H. S. and Fellner, W., 'External economies and diseconomies', *American Economic Review,* vol. 33 (September 1943), pp. 493–511.

Freeman, A. M. and Haveman, R. H., 'Clean rhetoric, dirty water', *Public Interest,* vol. 28 (Summer 1972), pp. 51–65.

Goetz, C. J. and Buchanan, J., 'External diseconomies in competitive supply', *American Economic Review,* vol. 61 (December 1971), pp. 883–90.

Knight, F. H., 'Some fallacies in the interpretation of social cost', *Quarterly Journal of Economics,* vol. 37 (August 1924), pp. 582–606.

Mishan, E. J., 'Reflections on recent developments in the concept of external effects', *Canadian Journal of Political Economy,* vol. 31 (February 1965), pp. 3–34.

Mishan, E. J., 'Pareto optimality and the law', *Oxford Economic Papers,* vol. 9, no. 3 (November 1967), pp. 255–87.

Mishan, E. J., 'The postwar literature on externalities: an interpretative essay', *Journal of Economic Literature,* vol. 9 (March 1971, pp. 1–28.

Pigou, A. C., *The Economics of Welfare,* 4th edn, London: Macmillan, 1946).

Plott, C. R., 'Externalities and corrective taxes', *Economica,* vol. 33, no. 129 (February 1966), pp. 84–7.

Ridker, R. G., *The Economic Costs of Air Pollution* (New York: Praeger, 1967).

Schall, L. D., 'Technological externalities and resource allocation', *Journal of Political Economy,* vol. 79, no. 5 (September 1971), pp. 983–1001.

Shibata, H., 'Pareto-optimality, trade, and the Pigovian tax', *Economica,* no. 154 (May 1972), pp. 190–202.

13

The Postwar Literature on Externalities: An Interpretative Essay

External effects on firms – or externalities, as they are now inelegantly referred to – make their appearance in Marshall's *Principles* as external economies; that is, economies external to the firm but internal to the industry. Little attention was given to this concept until Pigou's celebrated *Economics of Welfare,* where, developed and extended, it appears as one of the chief causes of divergencies between 'private net product' and 'social net product'. Expressed more generally, externalities today provide the standard exception to the equation of optimality with universal perfect competition. In addition to the increasingly overt recognition of this qualifying or limiting proviso, interest in the externality concept, as a phenomenon in the context of partial equilibrium analysis, has grown steadily and picked up momentum in the postwar period. Its current popularity warrants the demarcation of a new field of specialization within the broader terrain of welfare economics.

I

Other than R. F. Kahn's emendation of A. C. Pigou's general proposition in his classic paper on ideal output [**23**, Kahn, 1935, pp. 1–35] – to the effect that competitive industries having external economies (diseconomies) *above the average for the economy as a whole* should be expanded (contracted) – developments in the subject area during the interwar period appear to have consisted, in the main, in clearing up confusions about the nature of the long-period supply curve of competitive industry. Since the Second World War,

I wish to acknowledge with gratitude the helpful comments and suggestions of Abram Bergson, Otto Davis, Jack Ochs, and E. P. Seskin who read a first draft of this paper.

however, and especially during the last decade, contributions to the subject have been prolific – though not surprisingly in the opinion of those who discern a close association between the development of economic analysis and the economic problems of society. Nor is it altogether inexplicable that, although environmental spillovers have been prominent in the news over the last few years, the bulk of the recent literature has confined its investigations to inter-industry, interfirm, and interperson externalities. Economists respond to real world problems with a time lag, initially making use of more familiar, if less relevant, bits of apparatus.

Since one of the purposes of this interpretative survey is to acquaint the nonspecialist with the significance of the advances made on this front, and to leave him with a picture of works in progress, a chronological account would seem to be less suitable than one that divides the subject into a number of broad aspects. This treatment is, therefore, organized in the main around four topics: (1) the problems of definition, (2) the traditional doctrine in the light of later refinements, (3) the relation of external economies to public goods, and (4) the new concern with environmental spillovers.

II Concerning the Definition of Externalities

In popular expositions, an external effect is commonly defined in terms of the response of a firm's output, or a person's utility, to the activity of others. Insofar as the standard smoke and noise examples are cited, the correct impression is conveyed. This casual definition is unsatisfactory because the statement that a firm's output, or a person's utility, can be influenced by the activity of others, also holds true in the absence of external effects. Within the context of an interdependent system, for example, the Walrasian general equilibrium system, an exogenous change in the behavior of individuals can alter the equilibrium set of product and factor prices and thereby alter the utility levels of persons and the output levels of firms and industries. In the presence of universally perfect competition, however, such exogenous changes entail equilibrium solutions that are all Pareto optimal – and these solutions, therefore, cannot be ranked in the absence of a social welfare function.

In light of the above proposition, one is compelled to recognize the distinction between, on the one hand, instances where the influence upon the utility and outputs of others is exerted 'indirectly', that is, via relative prices only in a general interdependent system, and, on the other hand, those where such an influence is exerted on them 'directly', that is, via the arguments of their utility or production functions.

There is general agreement on the sort of mathematical notation required to indicate the presence of an external effect. Thus

$$F^1(x_1^1, x_2^1, \ldots, x_m^1; x_n^2)$$

will represent an external effect generated by entity 2 on entity 1. F^1 can stand for the utility level of person 1, in which case the x's are the amounts of some goods X_1, $X_2, \ldots, X_m$, utilized by him, x_n^2 being the amount of some good X_n (where X_n could, of course, be X_1, X_2, ..., or X_m) that is utilized by person 2, or produced by an industry 2. Again, F^1 can stand for the output of a firm or an industry, in which case the x's are the amounts of its inputs, while x_n^2 is the amount of the input or output of some other firm or industry. Alternatively, looking at the productive process from the standpoint of cost, F^1 can stand for the total cost of all the goods X_1 to X_m produced by firm 1, where cost depends not only on the amounts produced of these goods but, also, on x_n^2, the amount of good X_n produced by firm 2.

A consideration of this notation suggests that an external effect arises wherever the value of a production function, or a consumption function, depends directly upon the activity of others. What the notation alone does not succeed in conveying, however, is that the essential feature of the concept of an external effect is that the effect produced is not a deliberate creation but an *unintended* or *incidental* byproduct of some otherwise legitimate activity. This feature influences the

economist's and the public's attitude toward externalities and, consequently, also influences remedial policies.

In pointing up the allocative significance of an external effect, we shall find it convenient, for the present at least, to follow tradition in treating the subject within the context of partial equilibrium analysis: assuming, that is, that all optimal conditions are met in all sectors of the economy save in those under scrutiny.

The existence of an externality falling on entity 1 as a result of the marginal unit of entity 2's equilibrium output of X_n is indicated by the term $\partial F^1/\partial x_n^2 \neq 0$. Let p_n^2 and c_n^2 stand for price and marginal cost of any output of the good X_n chosen by entity 2. If the existing externality is ignored by entity 2 and a competitive equilibrium chosen so as to equate c_n^2 to p_n^2, then

$$p_n^2 - c_n^2 + \frac{F^1}{x_n^2} \neq 0$$

which can be abbreviated

$$p^2 - c^2 + F^{21} \neq 0$$

The externality then has allocative significance at the margin of the existing equilibrium, and corrective action is called for.

We may conclude that

$$p^2 - c^2 + F^{21} = 0$$

is a necessary condition for an optimal output of x_n^2. But it is not a sufficient one. If $F^{21} = 0$ at the competitive equilibrium $p^2 - c^2 = 0$, it may also be true that external diseconomies are generated only by intramarginal units of the x_n^2 output. If this is so, the equilibrium output of x_n^2 may not be optimal. For it is possible that although the external diseconomy is generated only by some initial units of x_n^2, or is invariant to output x_n^2, if it inflicts on third parties (such as entity 1) a total loss that is greater than the total benefit – conceived as the sum of factor and consumer surpluses – deriving from the production and direct use of the competitive equilibrium output x_n^2 then the optimal output of the externality-producing good is zero.[1]

Similarly, if $F^{21} \neq 0$, where $p^2 - c^2 = 0$, the optimal output of x_n^2 can be zero.

To summarize: (a) in order for an external diseconomy to have no allocative significance (in the sense that no output correction is called for), the condition $F^{21} = 0$ at the equilibrium output $p^2 - c^2 = 0$ is not sufficient. It is necessary also that in this equilibrium the total losses inflicted by external diseconomies do not exceed total surpluses; (b) in order for a certain marginal externality, $F^{21} \neq 0$ at output $p^2 - c^2 = 0$, to warrant a correction of the output so as to meet the condition $p^2 - c^2 + F^{21} = 0$, it is also necessary that at this latter output[2] the same total condition is met – total surplus exceeds total externality-imposed loss.[3]

Some further light is shed on the nature of an externality by the notion of 'internalizing' it. If the effluent of an upstream firm damages the product of a downstream firm, a merger of the two firms will internalize the spillover – for the upstream branch of the new firm has now to adjust its output in the light of the damage its effluent causes to the downstream firm. More generally, however, the externality can be internalized into the economy if a market for a product not previously sold comes into being. For example, straw might be simply one of the joint byproducts of the threshing of wheat which happens to have value for some of the poorer peasants who habitually gather it for fodder or for filling mattresses. It would, however, cease to be an external economy if commercial uses for it were discovered, and the demand for it grew so that a market for straw came into being. Both grain and straw would then become intentionally produced and jointly marketed, and the demand prices of both together would be equated to the marginal resource cost of wheat production. Again, if we can imagine a world in which the airspace were allocated as a form of mobile property rights among the inhabitants, a 'factor' market might be established for the services of smoke-absorbing space. Smoke-absorbing services would then appear as an item along with factor-payments as an integral part of the production costs of the goods in question.

Of course, the price placed by the market on the erstwhile spillover, regarded either as a good or a 'bad', may well be judged too high, or too low, by reference to optimality conditions – in which case one may be tempted to assert that the external effect is only 'partially internalized' into the economy.[4] But extending the definition of an externality to make it turn on an 'optimal' pricing of the products and factors in question would be too stringent a requirement – for then any item whose price might be altered to bring outputs closer to an optimum would be deemed to partake of the nature of externalities. Moreover, such a definition is unnecessary as irrespective of the resulting price, the market internalization of the externality implies that, once priced, it comes under the control of that person,

firm, or industry, which, hitherto, could only be a passive recipient. That is to say, beginning from a situation in which the function describing the response of person, firm, or industry 1 is written as

$$F^1(x_1^1, x_2^1, \ldots, x_m^1, x_n^2)$$

the internalizing of x_n^2 now brings the value of the function under the direct control of 1, so that this original function is now to be written as

$$F^1(x_1^1, x_2^1, \ldots, x_m^1; x_n^1)$$

For the price of X_n is now determined by the market along with the prices of all other goods and factors; to the extent that the levels of outputs and utility are dependent on X_n, they are, for everyone, now affected only 'indirectly' by price changes of X_n.

It follows, incidentally, that if every effect on social welfare arising in the production, and use, of all goods is entered into the price system, universal perfect competition would tend to a general equilibrium that would, indeed, be Pareto optimal. One could say more – provided only that relative prices remain unaltered in the presence of exogenous changes, the comprehension of all effects on social welfare by the price system implies that all admissible investment projects produce *actual* Pareto improvements.[5]

III   The Prewar Controversy

Before moving on to more recent developments, let us briefly re-examine the early controversy associated with the names of A. C. Pigou, F. H. Knight, J. Viner, and Mrs Joan Robinson. Not only is the outcome of the controversy of some interest in itself, it also provided us with the gratuitous term *pecuniary* external effects.

Recalling a useful division of externalities into two polar cases, those *internal* to an industry[6] (or activity), and those *external* to it, the controversy in question confined itself to the treatment of external diseconomies that are *internal* to the industry. Two related questions were at issue: (1) whether the upward-sloping supply curve of the competitive industry was an *average* curve, in which case the competitive equilibrium output would be too large, and (2) whether the traffic-congestion problem was an instance of external diseconomies within the industry or else of the misuse of a scarce resource – in particular, of the zero pricing of scarce land.

In summarizing the debate, H. Ellis and W. Fellner [**17**, 1943] made it clear that, contrary to an initial allegation by Pigou (but later corrected by him) the equilibrium output of a perfectly competitive industry is indeed optimal. Thinking in terms of a fixed factor, say land, and a variable factor, say labor, available in any amount at a fixed price, the rising supply curve of the product is average inasmuch as it includes, at each output, the rent of land. But these rents, which rise as output is expanded, are but transfer payments to the owners of higher quality intramarginal units of land –or, for that matter, to the owners of a fixed amount of land of uniform quality – and cannot be reckoned, therefore, in the *opportunity* cost of increasing output. *Excluding* rent-payments, therefore, the supply curve can be regarded as a true marginal cost curve of the product, comprising as it does, the cost only of the additional labor required to produce additional units of the product. The competitive equilibrium is, therefore, optimal. Yet, if the equilibrium output is one for which price is equal to marginal cost *excluding* rent, it is at the same time one for which price is equal to average cost *including* rent.

As for the other issue, congestion on the roads, the Pigou explanation [42, 1946], reduced to its elements, is that each of the owners of the vehicles operating on a stretch of highway would have regard to the costs incurred only as it affected his own vehicles; each owner, that is, would ignore the costs simultaneously imposed on all the other vehicles by the addition of his vehicles. In order, then, to take account of these external diseconomies suffered by the intra-marginal vehicles Pigou constructed a curve that is marginal to the per-vehicle average cost curve, optimal traffic being reached when this marginal cost curve is equal to price, or marginal benefit. This optimal traffic flow can be attained by levying a toll on all vehicles equal to the difference, at the optimal flow, between the average and the marginal cost.

Knight [25, 1924, pp. 582–606] took a different view. To him it was not so much an instance of the divergence between private and social net products but rather an instance of the wasteful exploitation of a scarce natural resource. If good land were free, farm produce would also be excessive. Put land under private ownership, however, and its price would be bid up as demand expanded. Rising rents, as output expands, would then be included in the average costs of the product; in equilibrium, each factor would then be paid its full marginal product. By strict analogy, if the road in question is placed under private ownership, a price will be imputed to it that is equal to the full earnings of the owner. In a competitive situation this price will be its true scarcity value.

Bearing in mind that under competitive conditions the private owner is deemed to maximize his earnings by 'exploiting' the supply curve – that is, by taking a curve marginal to the average cost curve – we perceive where the two explanations converge. Pigou's external diseconomy explanation elicits the marginal cost *excluding* rent concept. Knight's solution – the proper pricing of a scarce resource, road space – elicits the average cost *including* rent concept. And, as we have seen, the curves produced by each are coterminous, being but different ways of regarding the correct competitive supply curve.[7]

The above resolution of the controversy presents no difficulty *provided that* the upward-sloping supply curve is the result of adding increments of a variable factor that is infinitely elastic in supply to a factor that is fixed in supply. In that case the area above the industry supply curve (and below the resulting equilibrium price) can be imputed wholly to the fixed factor. If, however, the upward-sloping supply curve of an industry, composed of equally efficient firms, is the result of inelasticity in the supply of *both* factors, plus the familiar assumption that the factors are combined there in proportions different from the average of all industries, (i) the curve is still a *marginal* curve in the sense that – for production functions homogeneous of degree one – the long period marginal cost, in terms of either factor, is equal to the equilibrium price; (ii) it is also an *average* curve in the sense that the minimum average inclusive cost for each firm is equal to the equilibrium price. But the area above the supply curve can no longer be identified with a rent or a 'surplus' to either factor [36, Mishan, 1968, pp. 1269–82].

In his classic paper of 1931, 'Cost curves and supply curves', Viner [53, 1931, pp. 23–46] introduced some terminological innovations which have since become standard currency despite their being, in my view, superfluous and possibly confusing. The term external *pecuniary* diseconomies was proposed to cover the case of a rising supply price that is the result solely of changes in relative factor prices as output expands. But in the complete absence of external effects, rising supply price is an implication of any interdependent economic model having such familiar features as production functions homogeneous of degree one, imperfectly elastic factor supplies, and factor proportions differing from one product to another. Seen from this perspective there is nothing special about a rising supply curve, and no optimizing correction of equilibrium outputs need be sought under conditions of universal perfect competition. Therefore to invoke the term *pecuniary* external diseconomies to 'explain' supply curves that are in fact already explained by this familiar interdependent economic system simply in order to distinguish them from external diseconomies proper – which in the Viner article take on the appellation, external *technological* diseconomies – strikes one today as, perhaps, a verbal extravagance. Moreover, the use of *pecuniary* external *economy* to refer to a *reduction* in the average cost of industry *A* as it expands its purchases of materials or services from a falling cost industry *B*, will surely confuse most readers because this phenomenon is neither more nor less than the original Marshallian conception of external economies that are internal to the competitive industry *A*, and attributable to economies of scale in the *B* industry.[8] We shall, therefore, make no further reference in this paper to a distinction between *pecuniary* and *technological* external effects. We shall speak only of external effects proper.

However, as was pointed out in 1965 [**34,** Mishan, 1965, pp. 4–5], the original clarity of the externality concept has become blurred in consequence of the term being used over the years as a convenient peg on which to hang a variety of economic phenomena which might be used to justify intervention in the private enterprise sector of the economy. Thus, the growth in skill and technical expertise of an expanding industry, where economic advantages are generally assumed 'irreversible' (a consideration pertinent to the infant-industry argument) have occasionally been referred to as external economies. P. W. Rosenstein-Rodan [**45,** 1943, pp. 202–11] used the term to indicate an alleged reduction in risks, and therefore costs, arising from the central planning of industries producing complementary goods. Again, T. Scitovsky [**50,** 1954, pp. 70–82] classified as 'pecuniary external economies' such diverse phenomena as consumers' and producers' surpluses, unexploited investment opportunities to be found in complementary industries (arising, in the main, from inadequate information and co-operation), in decreasing cost industries (arising from indivisibilities), or in domestic import-competing industries (for reasons connected with optimal-tariff arguments).

In the remainder of this paper all such extensions of the original concept are ignored.

IV   The Renovated Traditional Doctrine

The received doctrine, largely associated with Pigou's monumental *Economics of Welfare,* expressed simply and without qualification, is that the equilibrium output of a competitive industry which generates an external *diseconomy* having allocative significance, is in excess of its optimal output. If positive, the optimal output is that at which the market price, less the social

value of the marginal external diseconomy, is equal to the marginal resource cost. Conversely, if the competitive industry generates an external economy that has allocative significance, its equilibrium output is below the optimal output obtained by equating to its marginal resource cost the market price *plus* the social value of the marginal external economy.

Moreover, assuming total conditions are met, the traditional remedy for external effects is the tax-subsidy one. For a good generating an external diseconomy, the required excise tax is equal to the value of the marginal external diseconomy at the optimal output. *Per contra,* for any good generating an external economy, an excise subsidy equal to the value of the marginal external economy at the optimal output should be offered to producers. Clearly, the effect of these measures is, in the former case, to reduce output below its competitive equilibrium and, in the latter case, to extend output beyond its competitive equilibrium.

To this oversimplified version there will now be appended a number of qualifications and modifications, some obvious, some less so.

(a) The cost of reducing the economic loss inflicted by external diseconomies is always to be minimized in the light of existing technological opportunities. In Pigou's example of the damage done to the crops by the sparks of a railway engine,[9] the unavoidable damage will not be the value of the crops destroyed if it transpires that the farmers can grow crops elsewhere, or can at least produce something with the movable factors and inputs used in growing the crops. For in moving his labor and capital to an otherwise less suitable location, the loss is ultimately carried by the owners of land adjacent to the railway. Given, then, that all factors other than land are mobile enough to be employed elsewhere at the market prices, the economic loss attributable to the railway service is equal to no more than the loss of rent suffered by the owners of the land. It goes without saying that the economic loss, total and/or marginal, will be still smaller if the switch to a strain of spark-resistant crops, or the installation of spark-preventive gadgets, costs less than the value of the loss of rent.

(b) If there are reciprocal externalities, competitive industry *x* imposing externalities on competitive industry *y*, and *y* also imposing them on *x*, the optimal outputs of *x* and *y* may both differ from their equilibrium outputs. However, at the optimal output for each industry, the marginal resource cost is equal to the market price plus the algebraic value of the marginal external effect. Thus, if there is a reciprocal external diseconomy that has allocative significance, optimal outputs in both industries are smaller than equilibrium outputs. If there are reciprocal external economies that have allocative significance, optimal outputs are larger than equilibrium outputs. For expository purposes, however, we shall assume henceforth that, unless otherwise stated, external effects are unidirectional only.

(c) The analysis of external effects has always been conducted within a partial equilibrium framework.[10] This condition means, as indicated earlier, that the outputs arising from the application of the *social* marginal cost pricing-rule to externality-generating sectors are correct only if all the optimum conditions are already met in the rest of the economy. If the conditions there are not fully met, then, as observed in 'The general theory of second best' [**26,** Lipsey and Lancaster, 1957, pp. 11–32], there is no certainty that the outputs satisfying optimal conditions in the sector(s) under examination will move the economy (as a whole) closer to the Pareto optimum.

Nevertheless, plausible conditions can be invoked to justify this partial procedure [**19,** Farrell, 1958; **21,** Green, 1961; **33,** Mishan, 1962; **13,** Davis and Whinston, 1967]. If, for instance, the initial price–marginal cost ratios at the nonoptimal equilibrium outputs of the externality-generating goods are sufficiently large – say they are outside a 'band' within whose limits are contained all, or nearly all, the social marginal cost–price ratios of the remaining goods – then 'correcting' the outputs of the externality-generating goods by the social marginal cost–price rule is likely to bring the economy closer to an overall optimum.

(d) Another qualification of the received doctrine arises from the possibility that, again within a more general framework, an uncorrected externality also entails the *inefficient* production of a batch of goods. The correcting of such an external diseconomy then involves a movement from an interior point toward a position on the production-possibility boundary. It is no longer certain in such cases that correcting the external diseconomy results in a smaller output.

Such factor efficiency conditions are not met in the case of those (uncorrected) external diseconomies that are *internal* to the industry inasmuch as scarce resources (such as land, or a road, in the Knight–Pigou controversy) are valued at zero. In the economy as a whole, therefore, factor rates of substitution are not everywhere equal, and the batch of goods chosen by society cannot be on the production-possibility boundary. Once the external diseconomy is corrected, however, the scarce factor in question is properly priced and both production and top-level optima are met – assuming optimum conditions obtain in all sectors other than that generating the external

diseconomy. This movement from an interior to a boundary point evidently does not preclude the possibility of an increase in the external-diseconomy good in the optimal position.

In contrast, an external diseconomy arising from product x that is *external* to the x industry does not violate the factor efficiency conditions. While it can be true that the greater the amount of x produced, the greater the scalar reduction of the production function of the other good y, this effect serves only to describe the locus of the production possibilities as between x and y. The uncorrected equilibrium amount of x in this case violates only the top level optimum, and the movement to an optimal position along the production boundary entails a reduction in the amount of x. If, however, this external diseconomy on y is attributable *not* to product x itself but only to one, or some but not all, of the *factors* used in x (or, more generally, if not all the factors used in x exert proportional external diseconomies on y), such factors are in effect overpriced. Thus, notwithstanding that factor rates of substitution are common to all goods, the uncorrected position is not on the production boundary.[11] The movement toward optimum in this case also entails a movement from an interior point to one on the production boundary, and it becomes possible that correcting for x's external diseconomy results in a larger output of x. The converse is true, in such a case, for external economies.[12]

Apart from such possibilities arising from the infringement of the factor efficiency conditions, there is always a temptation to concoct perverse cases by invoking unfamiliar postulates. An example [**43,** Plott, 1966, pp. 84–7] would be that of an external diseconomy on y generated by a firm's use of a factor A that varies inversely with the firm's output of x. Optimal output of x then entails an expansion. Clearly, it is this rather implausible assumption that the externality-producing factor A is 'inferior' which brings about this apparently perverse result – at least for a noncompetitive industry.[13] Provided only that the factors are 'normal' (that is, not 'inferior') the same correction is called for whether the externality arises directly from the use of any factor or directly in the process of producing or consuming the good in question.

V   External Economies and Public Goods (i)

Explication of such a relationship is primarily an exercise in taxonomy. No apology is offered for pursuing the matter however. The classification of concepts, and their relation to one another, are preconditions of effective economic analysis.

P. A. Samuelson's original conception [**47**, 1954, pp. 387–9] – to the effect that a public good is one that is enjoyed in common, or one where person 1's consumption does not interfere with person 2's consumption – is a beginning. It comes close to the heart of the matter without being entirely satisfactory. For one thing, there is no explicit reference to the amount of the public good consumed by each of the beneficiaries. For another, as Margolis pointed out at the time [**28**, 1955, pp. 347–9], the proffered definition does not seem to accord well with the more common examples of a public good, such as education, hospitals, highways, courts of law, and the police. It does not appear true that for the use of such goods one person involves no cost to others: there are capacity limitations, congestions, and rationing in all of them. Again, despite some hints [**6**, Buchanan and Kafoglis, 1963, pp. 403–14; **52**, Vincent, 1969, pp. 976–84] and notational distinctions [**37**, Mishan, 1969, pp. 329–48], the nature of the suspected relationship between public goods and external effects has remained elusive.

Finally, the necessary optimal conditions – for, let us say, a three-person community,

$$v_d^1 = v_d^2 = v_d^3 = c \ldots \qquad \text{(i)}$$

and

$$v_g^1 + v_g^2 + v_g^3 = c \ldots \qquad \text{(ii)}^{14}$$

where c is the marginal resource cost and v_d^1 and v_g^1 are the marginal valuations of the ith person for the private and public good respectively – proposed by Samuelson to distinguish private goods from public goods respectively are not unambiguous. Granted equation (i) applies to private goods, so also will the expression

$$v_d^1 + v_d^2 + v_d^3 = \delta c$$

(at least if the marginal cost is constant at the equilibrium output), where δc is the increment in the cost of producing the final three units of the good. On the other hand, though equation (ii) applies to public goods, if the short period marginal cost of the public good happens to be zero, it can also be true that

$$v_g^1 = v_g^2 = v_g^3 = c = 0$$

The difficulties of making a clear distinction between public goods and private goods, and of linking the former to external effects, appear to be attributable to a number of factors. (1) The use of such terms as 'public goods' (or 'collective goods'), on the one hand, and 'private goods' on the other, terms which have conventional associations, as a means of making a conceptual and functional distinction, is troublesome. Possible confusion can be avoided by provisional use of 'G goods' to indicate the functional category corresponding to something like public goods, and 'D goods' for the functional category corresponding to something like private goods. (2) Because of the conventional association of such terms, it was not recognized that what might be a G good in the long period could also be a D good in the short period. (3) There was a failure to abstract initially from congestion costs or, more generally, from external effects in determining which category a specific good falls into. (4) There was also failure to make a distinction between two types of G goods, optional and nonoptional, and (5) the attempt to link the definitions of D goods and G goods with distinct optimal equation forms when, as indicated above, either equation form might, under certain circumstances, be applied to one or the other type of good.

Be that as it may, the difficulties can be resolved, first, by making explicit the conditions necessary to transform an external economy into a G good – ignoring, for the time being, possible congestion costs.

Suppose person A buys an amount of X at a price p_x and, unintentionally, confers a benefit Y on person B. The amount of Y thus received by person B may be so great as to have a zero marginal valuation, in which case the marginal consumption of X by person A involves no marginal external economy on B, and the amount of X bought by A is optimal. Only if the spillover has a positive marginal value for B, will B's marginal valuation schedule for X (in consequence of the Y it generates for him), when added to A's schedule for X, result in the optimal amount of X being greater than A's initial purchase. If, however, the amount of Y absorbed by B is constrained by A's consumption of X, the marginal value of that amount of Y may be negative to person B – from being a good to person B, Y has become a 'bad' or a diseconomy. Addition of their marginal valuation schedules in this instance implies that the optimal amount of X is *below* the amount initially chosen by A.[15]

Needless to remark, the analysis is essentially unchanged if, instead of just one person B, there are a number of other persons, B_1, B_2, . . . , B_n, all of them benefiting at least from the first units of the spillover Y. The optimal amount of X, that is, may still be the same as the initial amount bought by person A, or more than, or less than, this.

If, instead of the externality produced by A being Y, it is X itself, the very thing that A consumes,[16] then although X is available to anyone at the market price, A's amount of X offers to others a larger, equal, or smaller amount of the beneficial spillover X than that which they otherwise would buy. Whatever X is thereby received gratis is, however, a perfect substitute for the X that can be bought. Each beneficiary from A's purchase of X will therefore reduce, wholly, or to some extent, the amount of X he would otherwise have bought. Once more, then, the optimal amount of A's purchase of X is found by adding, to A's schedule for X, those also of the beneficiaries. Under the condition mentioned, this optimal amount may be the same as, or greater, or smaller, than, A's initial amount of X.[17] What is to be noticed, however, is that there is now an optimal amount of a single kind of good X, shared by several, and for this optimal amount of X the algebraic sum of each intramarginal unit is positive, and greater, than its marginal resource cost.

If we now suppose that the amount of X bought by A suffices for a given number of beneficiaries, then, although we are still supposing A foots the bill, X may now be regarded as a 'shared' good – in the provisional sense that the benefits of this amount of X are simultaneously enjoyed by a number of persons.[18] A simple example would be that of a television aerial erected on A's roof to which B, living in the semi-detached house, could connect his television. Possibly others close by, or living in apartments below A, could do the same without inflicting any loss on A – the total numbers availing themselves of A's enterprise being limited by the costs of making the connection, their costs rising with the distance of their television sets from A's aerial.

The shared good X – which may be said to tend to a G good as the numbers sharing it increase – arises therefore as the special case of an external economy in which the spillover X is itself identical to the good X that generates it.

VI External Economies and Public Goods (ii)

(1) We may describe a G good as *optional* if the amount absorbed by any person can be reduced without incurring costs; otherwise the G good is *nonoptional*. The significance of this distinction is revealed by a consideration of the relevant optimal conditions.[19] Suppose the short-period marginal resource cost of the G good in question is zero. Whether it is optional or nonoptional the equation

$$v_g{}^1 + v_g{}^2 + v_g{}^3 = c = 0$$

is necessary. For an optional G good, however, each person chooses to absorb an amount that yields him a zero marginal valuation. Consequently the equation $v_g{}^1 = v_g{}^2 = v_g{}^3 = c$ is also realized by the optimal output of it.[20] For a nonoptional G good, on the other hand, although the amount each person is initially constrained to absorb may differ,[21] his resulting marginal valuation may be zero, positive, or negative, and the latter equation is not met.

Bearing in mind that the optimal equation of some D goods may be written as

$$v_d{}^1 + v_d{}^2 + v_d{}^3 = \delta c$$

and also, as indicated above, some G goods may meet the condition

$$v_g{}^1 = v_g{}^2 = v g^3 = c$$

it should be clear why neither G nor D goods can be associated in all circumstances, and for both short and long periods, with a particular form of an optimal equation even in the absence of congestion costs.

(2) Let us define D goods as those whose resource costs are attributable to each of the beneficiaries – G goods being defined as those whose resource costs are not attributable. The appropriate optimal equation of this definition of a D good is that

$$v^1 = v^2 = v^3 = c \, (c > 0)$$

notwithstanding that it may also be true that

$$v^1 + v^2 + v^3 = \delta c$$

If this optimal condition cannot be met, the resource costs cannot be attributable. The only optimal condition which applies is then $v^1 + v^2 + v^3 = c \, (c > 0)$, and the good is a G good.

A conventional public good, say a particular highway system, which has nonattributable costs in a short period, whether zero or positive, is a G good. If now, from variable costs being zero – or being positive but independent of the number of users – it is discovered that some small user cost can be attributed to the vehicles, the highway system (though still a public good in the conventional sense) is clearly no longer a G good. For variable costs are now attributable to users, and the optimal condition, $v^1 = v^2 = v^3 = c \, (c > 0)$ now applies.

(3) It follows also that although the discovery that user costs are attributable makes the highway a D good for allocative purposes, in the long period it again has to be regarded as a G good. True, the long period, where

all costs are variable, is to be associated with any sort of alteration – that affecting the size, shape, or quality, of the facility – in particular any alteration enabling it to cater to a larger number of persons. Indeed, this latter long-period alteration might be thought to afford a clear case of a cost-attributable good and, therefore, for allocative purposes, a *D* good. Such an interpretation is not warranted, for were we to extend the good to accommodate four persons instead of the former three,[22] if the new long-period optimal is written as

$$v^1 + v^2 + v^3 + v^4 = c'$$

then, as compared with the original optimal condition, we could indeed equate v^4 with $(c' - c)$. But if the contemplated extension in favor of this one additional person also has some effect on the benefits to the existing number of persons, the new optimal equation has to be written

$$\bar{v}^1 + \bar{v}^2 + \bar{v}^3 + \bar{v}^4 = \bar{c}'$$

where $\bar{c}' > c'$, and

$$\bar{v}^i >/=/< v^i \ (i = 1, 2, 3)$$

For example, in extending a highway system to pass by an additional number of residences, it is likely that the pre-existing number of highway-users also will derive some additional benefit. In that case the costs of producing the extra benefits are not attributable to the additional user, or users. For allocative purposes, then, the long-period adjustment requires the good be treated as a *G* good.

(4) Finally, congestion costs incurred in the use of the *G* goods have to be introduced. Though resource costs are not, by definition, attributable to persons in the case of *G* goods, congestion costs are attributable. As indicated earlier, extracting the maximum social valuation from the collective use of the existing facility requires that marginal congestion costs be used as a rationing device.[23]

It should now be manifest that if we restrict ourselves to long periods, at least, the definition of a *G* good – one having nonattributable resource costs – accords with a fair number of goods that are conventionally referred to as collective, or public, goods. External defense, police, street-lighting, broadcasting, a bridge, a park, a highway or railway system, are examples that spring to mind.

We may, therefore, if we wish, define collective goods as those having no attributable resource costs *in the long period*. Thus, highways, railways, and bridges,

which might in the short period have a small ratio of variable operating costs to inclusive costs, would still qualify as collective goods. Hospitals and schools, on the other hand, will not be collective goods in this definition insofar as an increase in long-period resource costs can be attributable wholly to an increase in the numbers admitted.

Originally we approached the concept of a collective good from the benefit side – as the limiting case of an external economy in which the spillover on others is identical to the good enjoyed by the generator himself. The alternative approach from the cost side can now be indicated. This also conceives the collective good as a limiting case – as a good for which the long-period ratio of attributable to total costs is zero.

(5) It remains to make explicit the close relationship between a collective good and an external economy. For the external benefits conferred on each of a number of people as a result of a person's consumption of a unit of a good also cannot be attributed to each beneficiary on any economic principle. Indeed, there is, in general, no formal difference; in either case the summation-over-persons form of the optimal equation is required. There is a difference only in motivation. The benefits generated by person 1's consumption of a private good are unintentional whereas the benefits generated by the public good are clearly intentional. An appropriate notation for the values created by the former is Σv^{1i}, and for the latter is Σv^i.

A second informal difference, more apparent than real, arises from the custom of considering an optimal amount of but a single public good in contrast to the habit of considering the optimal amounts of, say, *n* persons each conferring external benefits on a number of others. This apparent difference would, of course, disappear if we supposed instead a large number of identical types of public goods all produced by a competitive industry. In that event the optimal condition for public goods would be of the form

$$\sum_{}^{m} v_A{}^i = \sum_{}^{n} v_B{}^i = \sum_{}^{q} v_C{}^i = \ldots = c$$

where $A, B, C, \ldots$ are groups comprising $m, n, q, \ldots$ members, respectively, in different parts of the economy. If, instead, $A, B, C, \ldots$ were individuals, each conferring external benefits on *n* people (including himself), the optimal equation would be

$$\sum_{}^{n} v^{Ai} = \sum_{}^{n} v^{Bi} = \sum_{}^{n} v^{Ci} = \ldots = c$$

Finally, the capacity, size, or coverage, of a shared or collective good[24] – whether, that is, it serves a few people or many, or whether it serves a locality, a region, or the country at large – depends in the main on three features: (1) economies of scale, (2) costs of travel to, or in connection with,[25] the collective good, and (3) income *per capita* and population density. Thus, (1) the greater is the decline in the long period average cost of providing the public service, (2) the lower is the cost of connecting or moving to it, and (3) the greater are population density and *per capita* income – the larger will be the size and coverage of the public good.

Moreover, any growth of congestion costs, as a result of an increase in the number of users, or an increase in usage by the same number of people, provides an incentive to extend the long-period capacity of the public good. Any optimal extension of capacity in effect entails economies from the substitution of long-period resource costs for some, at least, of the short-period congestion costs.

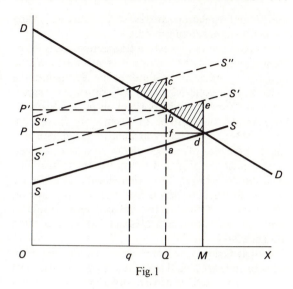

Fig. 1

VII Solutions to the Externality Problem

Let us now turn our attention to several of the more familiar methods proposed for correcting outputs for external diseconomies.[26]

(1) *Outright prohibition.* The economist is prone to think of this solution as naive. It would be prohibitively expensive, if not impossible, it is argued, to eliminate entirely all trace of some of the pollutants that inflict losses on others. Moreover, the argument continues, optimality does not require that external diseconomies be eliminated, simply that their amounts be consistent with the optimal amounts of the goods that create them.

This sort of argument is not conclusive for all pollutants. First of all, prohibition need not imply prohibition of every trace of a pollutant; it may be directed against producing 'discernible' or 'dangerous' amounts of the pollutant. Secondly, as we shall remark later, the cost of discovering and maintaining an optimal amount of the pollution may itself be prohibitive. The community may then be faced with the choice of zero or unchecked pollution.

(2) *The tax/subsidy solution.* This is the classic solution, and the one until recently most favored by theorists. The chief obstacle here is, of course, the costs of collecting the necessary information and the costs of supervision, costs which would be particularly heavy for industries in which demand and supply conditions are apt to vary frequently.[27] It is alleged, moreover, that this solution, even if feasible, overlooks a particular contingency that can result in 'overcorrection'.

See Figure 1 where *SS* is the 'private', or commercial marginal cost curve of the output of *X, DD* is the market demand curve, and the vertical distance between *SS*

and the *social* marginal cost curve, *S'S'*, is the unit cost of spillovers generated in the production of *X*.[28]

Optimal output, *OQ*, can be achieved by an excise tax equal, at *Q*, to the vertical distance between *SS* and *S'S'*. After the imposition of such a tax, however, the producers may regard *S'S'* as the new marginal cost curve.

At the new tax equilibrium, *OQ*, the marginal damage of the spillover effect is equal to *ab*. The victims of the spillover can then afford to pay producers as much as *cb*, equal to *ab*, to reduce output *OQ* by one unit, and so on for successive reductions. From such reasoning we construct a curve *S''S''* that is above *S'S'* by the same vertical distance at all points as *S'S'* is above *SS*. Clearly there can now be mutual agreement between producers and victims to reduce output to *Oq*, below the optimal output *OQ*.[29]

However, this possibility cannot be taken very seriously. If producers and their spillover victims can indeed reach voluntary agreement, they have more incentive to reach it before the excise tax is levied than afterward. The government, in any case, can always take measures to ensure that no further arrangements of this sort take place in order to prevent output being reduced below optimum.[30]

(3) *Regulation.* Insofar as regulation of the production of goods that generate externalities is intended, much the same sort of information is required, and much the same sort of costs are incurred, as in the tax/subsidy solution. If, however, regulation is to be applied to the extent, and manner, of the usage of spillover-generating products, there will be additional costs of enforcement – the more so if flexibility is

sought, and regulations are devised, to vary according to time, area, and circumstances.

(4) *Voluntary agreements.* If transactions costs in the broadest sense (to be defined presently) are *nil*, the initiative by either the producer or the recipient of the spillover in negotiating a mutually satisfactory agreement will bring about an optimal output. In Figure 1, for example, there will be an incentive to move from output OM to OQ since by so doing there will be a gain equal to the area of triangle *ebd* to be shared between the beneficiaries of X and the spillover victims. The maximum sum the spillover victims will pay to reduce the market output by MQ is given by the parallelogram area *abed,* while the loss to producers and consumers from reducing output by MQ is equal to the area of the triangle *abd.*

Such agreements, however, unless they are between firms or industries (and supported by legal sanctions) are likely to be so expensive to negotiate and maintain as to be impractical.

(5) *Preventive devices.* For obvious reasons the professional economist is more likely to interest himself in optimal-output solutions than in the opportunities for installing preventive devices. This latter form of remedy, however, cuts across those mentioned above inasmuch as either government regulation or voluntary agreements can bring them into being. Whether there are opportunities for few or for many such devices, and whether they are less costly to the industry concerned than the alternative course of reducing the spillover-generating outputs, are, of course, empirical questions and ones to which economists are now turning.

VIII The Abortive Consensus

Postwar developments seemed about to culminate in a broad consensus in the early 1960s when increased attention to environmental spillovers compelled economists to re-examine some of their basic simplifications as well as the conclusions based on them. The more crucial propositions of this emergent consensus are summarized below.

(1) On the assumption that the most economic way of dealing with an externality involves an output adjustment, the optimal output is uniquely determined. In this connection, it was also believed [**9,** Coase, 1960, pp. 1–44] that Pigou had failed to make explicit the duality of the tax/subsidy remedy. Whether the government offers an excise subsidy to the manufacturer to induce him to reduce the output of a good generating external diseconomies, or whether it imposes an excise tax on

such a good, was believed to be a matter of indifference so far as allocation is concerned. Similarly, in the absence of government intervention, and assuming transaction costs are low enough, it was believed to be a matter of indifference from the point of view of allocation whether a manufacturer is compelled to compensate the victims or whether the victims offer to bribe the manufacturer.

(2) Nor can the question of liability for the spillover properly be settled by a consideration of the equity involved. To use an example from Coase's 1960 paper [**9,** pp. 3–5], if the machinery of a confectioner disturbs the practice of a physician on the floor above, so also does the installation of vibration-reducing devices lower the profits of the confectioner. The interests of the two parties are mutually antagonistic, and with respect to equity the case is symmetric.[31]

(3) However the matter is actually resolved – whether an excise tax or an excise subsidy is used, or whether the one party or the other is compensated – optimality is not at issue, only the distribution of welfare. This statement does not, of course, imply approval of all measures that realize an optimum position, since in moving from a nonoptimal to an optimum position only a *potential* Pareto improvement, at best, is assured (gains exceed losses), and not an *actual* Pareto improvement. Thus a movement to an optimal position is quite consistent with one that makes the poor yet poorer.

(4) In the absence of government intervention, whatever the legal position, the unfavored party has a clear interest in trying to bribe the other party to modify the 'uncorrected' output. Successful mutual agreement between the parties, however, presupposes that the maximum possible amount of the shared gains, $G,$ in moving to an optimal position, exceeds their combined transaction costs, $T.$ Since the transactions costs, $T,$ are real enough, inasmuch as they are ultimately the valuation of scarce resources, successful mutual agreement produces a *net* Pareto improvement –

$$G - T > 0$$

Failure to reach mutual agreement, on the other hand, can be regarded as *prima facie* evidence that

$$G - T < 0$$

that is, a *net* potential Pareto improvement is not possible. Rationalizing the *status quo* in this way brings the economist perilously close to defending it.

Before subjecting the above propositions to scrutiny, it is as well to touch on an analytic difficulty of the partial analysis that seems to have been fudged.

The maximum social gain, G, from reducing the competitive output by MQ, in Figure 1, is generally calculated as follows: the gains to the spillover victims of reducing the output by MQ is equal to the area of the 'parallelogram' *abed*. From this gain, we subtract the loss from two other groups: consumers suffer a loss equal to the area of the 'triangle' *fdb*, and producers suffer a loss equal to the area of the 'triangle' *fda*. The residual gain – *abed* less $(fdb + fda)$ – is, of course, equal to the triangle, *dbe*.

However, if the supply curve is a long-period industry supply curve, one sloping upward in consequence of a relative price rise of the factor(s) used more intensively in this industry than in the economy as a whole, a zero Knightian profit is made by all firms in the industry in any long-period equilibrium. The area above the supply curve cannot then be identified with any surplus to the producers. Only if the upward slope of the long-period supply curve arises from the addition of increments of a constant-priced variable factor to the fixed amount of another factor – which may, however, include differences as between firms in the quality of the fixed factor – may the area between the supply curve and the price of the good be treated as a surplus. Moreover, it is not a surplus that accrues to the firms, but to the owners of the fixed factor whether of uniform quality or not.[32]

However, even if we suppose this long-period supply curve to slope upward as a result only of a fixed amount of the scarce factor, we may note that the conclusion that mutual agreement between producers and spillover victims, if feasible, produces an optimal output, commonly ignores the consumer interest. This neglect of the consumer interest is another consequence of the popular preference for the two-firm model, and of the occasional simplification of a horizontal sales curve facing each of the firms.

Ignoring transaction costs, the most favorable conditions for negotiation between producers and spillover victims would seem to exist when producers can be taken as a corporation, and the supply curve then treated as a long-period marginal cost curve (excluding rent). It will facilitate the analysis still further if we suppose the corporation to act as a discriminating monopolist, appropriating all the consumer surplus, thus equating its private marginal cost to the demand curve.

IX   Environmental Spillovers – Allocation (i)

The pertinent economic features of environmental spillovers, other than the observed fact that they appear to increase rapidly with economic growth, are (1) that their impact on the welfare of members of the public can be substantial, and (2) regarded as external diseconomies, they pose a problem not so much as between firms or industries, but as between, on the one hand, the producers and/or the users of spillover-creating goods and, on the other, the public at large. The implications of the latter feature are not diminished by the observation that, in important instances, the users of the spillover-creating goods and the affected public are all but indistinguishable – this being but a special case of external diseconomies internal to the activity in question.

A consequence of the first feature is that the so-called income-effects – or, more accurately, *welfare effects,* as we shall call them – can no longer be treated as negligible. A consequence flowing from the second feature is that the transaction costs are likely to be inordinately large. These two consequences assume particular relevance when we recognize that an alteration in the law, say from tolerating to the prohibiting of certain spillovers, or the reverse, has significant effects not only on the distribution of welfare, but on the outcome of the allocative criterion. In particular, the notion of a Pareto optimum, or, more accurately, since we are to restrict ourselves to partial economic analysis, a potential Pareto improvement, is no longer uniquely determined. Nor, for that matter, is a *net* potential Pareto improvement, $G - T > 0$, uniquely determined.

These propositions will now be demonstrated in connection with each of these two features in turn.

(1) If we assume that the welfare effects are positive, or 'normal', a man who is prepared to spend up to $60,000 for a particular house with a view will experience a rise in his welfare if, unexpectedly, he finds he can buy it, for, say, $40,000. In consequence of this 'surplus' of $20,000, the minimum price he will sell it for, after buying it for $40,000, will be more than $60,000, say $65,000. Invoking familiar Hicksian terminology, the difference of $5,000 in this case is equal to the difference between his *compensating variation* of $20,000 (the maximum sum he would pay – thus restoring his welfare to its original level W_0 – in order to be allowed to buy his house for a price of $40,000) and his *equivalent variation* of $25,000 (the minimum sum he would accept to forgo the opportunity of buying the house at $40,000, which sum raises his welfare to the level W_1 that he would have enjoyed had he indeed been permitted to buy the house at $40,000).

There is, however, another and possibly more potent factor in differentiating these magnitudes wherever the welfare involved is substantial. The maximum sum he will pay for something valuable is obviously related to, indeed limited by, a person's total resources, while the minimum sum he will accept for parting with it is subject to no such constraint. To take an extreme example, a man may be ready to sacrifice every penny he can spare in order to pay for an operation that will save his life. This may amount to a present value of $10,000 or $10 million, but it will be a finite sum. On the other hand, there may be no sum large enough to compensate him for going without the operation, and so parting from this life.

Let individual B, with disposable income of $12,000 per annum, be exposed to aircraft noise which can be escaped with certainty only by relocating hundreds of miles away in some deserted area. Given the choice, he would, if hypersensitive enough to aircraft noise, pay as much as $5,000 per annum to be entirely free of it. At the same time, if the law compelled the airlines concerned to compensate all injured parties, his true minimum claim could be, say, $15,000 per annum.

Now instead of regarding the maximum and minimum sums as compensating-variation and equivalent-variation measures of a change in welfare under the existing law, we can regard each respectively as the compensating variation corresponding to two opposing states of the law. Thus, if the existing law, L, is tolerant of environmental spillovers, in particular aircraft noise, the compensating variation of a contemplated change banning all aircraft noise is a payment by B of $5,000, this being the sum which, given up in exchange for the ban, maintains B's welfare at the level W_0 which prevails under the existing L law. If, on the other hand, the existing law is $\bar{L}$, one that effectively bans all aircraft noise, B's level of welfare is W_1, which is higher than the level W_0 that prevails under the L law. The compensating variation of a contemplated change introducing aircraft noise is then a receipt of $15,000 by B – this being the sum which, if the change occurs, will maintain his welfare at its original W_1 level.

Let A stand for the aircraft interests which extend, in this example, to all owning capital or employed in aircraft services as well as all the beneficiaries of air travel. The compensating variations of each of these persons will, in general, also vary according to which of the two kinds of law prevails. Let B stand for all those offended by aircraft noise. If the maximum sums that people are willing to pay to acquire a 'good' (or to avoid a 'bad') are prefixed by +ve signs, while the minimum sums they are prepared to accept to forgo a good (or to put up with a 'bad') are prefixed by –ve signs, the algebraic sum of all compensating variations indicates the social value of the change in question. In particular, if, under the existing law, the algebraic sum of a contemplated change is

+ve, a potential Pareto improvement is possible. If, however, the algebraic sum is –ve, the existing unchanged situation is optimal; the change in question would only result in a potential Pareto loss.

Imagine now that a costless and perfectly accurate method of obtaining all the relevant data has been invented. The end-product of much research into the aircraft noise problem might then be summarized in the figures of Table I.

Table I

Existing law	A	B	Total
L	– $55m.	+ $40m.	– $15m.
$\bar{L}$	+ $45m.	– $70m.	– $25m.

Reading along the first row we interpret as follows: given the existing law L, that is permissive of aircraft noise, the A group must be paid at least $55 million to secure agreement to change to $\bar{L}$ law, while the B group will offer up to $40 million to have the L law changed to $\bar{L}$. Since the changeover would incur a potential Pareto loss of $15 million, the existing situation under L law is deemed Pareto optimal. If, however, the existing law is $\bar{L}$ to start with, the second row indicates that the A group will pay up to $45 million to have the law changed to L. But this sum falls short by $25 million of the minimum compensation required by the B group to agree to the change. Again, therefore, the existing situation under the $\bar{L}$ law is Pareto optimal.

We are to conclude, therefore, that irrespective of the existing distribution it is possible, if not likely, that for significant environmental spillovers, the arrangement that is optimal under one state of the law is not optimal under the other state of law. In our example, if aircraft are already allowed to fly unchecked (L law), then that situation appears as optimal. If, on the other hand, aircraft were banned under $\bar{L}$ law, that situation, too, would be optimal.[33] Under such conditions, how do we decide how to act?

The above analysis, applicable to indivisible economic arrangements as appear, say, in cost–benefit calculations, can easily be extended to economic arrangements having perfectly divisible external effects. Suppose the number of aircraft permitted to fly over a residential area is to be determined by reference only to optimality considerations – the exercise being to locate the point at which the marginal benefit of the aircraft group A is equal to the marginal loss suffered by the residential group B. Prior to calculating the optimal number of flights, the existence of L law, which permits unchecked flying over the area, will result in a higher level of welfare for the A group that if, instead, the $\bar{L}$ law prevails and no planes are permitted to fly, the reverse being the case for the residents comprising the B group.

Suppose the L law to be in force; then, prior to any agreement between A and B, the number of planes flying over the area is given by OM in Figure 2. The

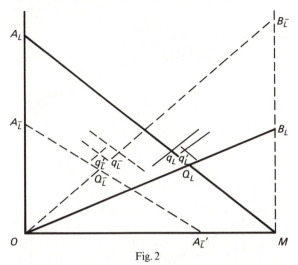

Fig. 2

minimum compensation acceptable to the A group for reducing successive flights is given by the marginal curve $A_L M$, while the maximum sums that the B group will pay for successive flight reductions is given by OB_L, the two curves intersecting at Q_L. If, however, $\bar{L}$ is in force to start with, then, prior to any mutual agreement between A and B, the number of flights over the area is zero, and the minimum sums acceptable to the B group for each successive flight are given by the marginal curve $OB_{\bar{L}}$, while the maximum sums that the A group is willing to pay for each additional flight are given by the marginal curve $A_{\bar{L}}A_{\bar{L}}'$. The intersection of these two $\bar{L}$ curves is $Q_{\bar{L}}$.

Now in reaching agreement, beginning from either initial position – OM flights with L law, or zero flights with $\bar{L}$ law – one, or both, groups are made better off and, therefore (assuming normal welfare effects), one or both marginal valuation curves shift upward, which implies that neither Q_L nor $Q_{\bar{L}}$ can be reached by bargaining alone. Nonetheless, if L law prevails, in which case flights are OM to begin with, and if we assume that in bargaining their way to an optimal position, all the gains go to the B group,[34] the increase in its welfare is still less than it would be, if instead $\bar{L}$ law initially prevailed and (without any payment from the B group) all flights were banned. Consequently the resulting maximum upward shift in B's marginal curve is still below the $OB_{\bar{L}}$ curve, the optimal point being

then q_L. However, if we suppose instead that A obtains some of the potential gains in the bargaining, B's marginal curve rises less and A's marginal curve rises somewhat, with the result that the revised optimal position, q_L' is to the right of q_L.

If, on the other hand, the $\bar{L}$ law prevails, and we assume first that all the gains in bargaining go to the A group, the increase in its welfare is less than it would be if the law were changed to L, and all flights were freely allowed. The resulting upward shift in A's original $A_{\bar{L}}A_{\bar{L}}'$ curve is therefore below the $A_L M$ curve, the optimal point being $q_{\bar{L}}$. However, according as the B group secures some of the gains in bargaining toward an optimal position, A's resulting marginal curve is somewhat lower while B's resulting marginal curve is above OB_L. The revised optimal position $q_{\bar{L}}'$ being to the left of $q_{\bar{L}}$.[35]

We may conclude, then, that however the bargaining goes, the resulting optimum output under the L law entails more flights than an optimum output under the $\bar{L}$ law[36].

X Environmental Spillovers – Allocation (ii)

(2) Assuming that, whichever law prevails, the state does not oppose agreements tending to a Pareto improvement, any movement by any method toward such improvements involves a variety of costs, for which the term *transactions costs* is in common use. In general, the more favorable the law is in promoting mutual agreements of this sort, the lower will such transactions costs be. If, at first, we restrict ourselves to the method of voluntary agreement between two opposing groups in their attempt to reach a solution, either by curbing the activity of the offending industry, by installing preventive devices, or by moving the industry (or, alternatively, members of the B group) elsewhere – whichever method is the cheapest – the transactions costs, T, may be divided into three sub-categories: T_1, the initial costs leading to negotiations between the two groups; T_2, the costs of maintaining and, if necessary, revising, the agreement; and T_3, the capital expenditure, if any, required to implement the agreement.

The more important of these, the T_1 costs, can be broken down, for each group, into a number of phases: (a) identifying the members of the group, (b) persuading them to make, or to accept, a joint offer, (c) reaching agreement within the group on all matters incidental to its negotiation with the other group, and (d) negotiating with the other group.

It cannot be assumed, without investigation, that

transactions costs would be any less under $\bar{L}$ law than they are under L law. What can be said, however, is that such costs, especially those subsumed under T_1, increase with the dispersion of the B group, and increase with the numbers involved, probably at an exponential rate. Whatever the magnitude of the T costs, however, relative to the maximum Pareto gains, G, three alternative cases exhaust the possibilities.

(1) A net potential Pareto improvement, $G - T > 0$, emerges for the industry under either type of law – though if $\bar{L}$ law prevails, the optimal output, both of goods and pollution, will be smaller.

(2) A net potential Pareto improvement for the industry emerges under neither type of law. By comparison with the (costless) potential optimum, therefore, we shall have 'too much' pollution with the equilibrium output under the L law, and 'too little' pollution under the zero output of the $\bar{L}$ law. Without further assumptions, however, it is not possible to say in general whether 'too much' (under the L law) or 'too little' (under the $\bar{L}$ law) is likely to be closer to the potential optimum, and, therefore, whether more is lost by adopting the L law rather than the $\bar{L}$ law.

(3) Where the potential optimum position is closer to the initial $\bar{L}$ position than to the initial L position, a net Pareto improvement may take place only if the L law prevails. If the reverse is true, a net Pareto improvement may take place only if the $\bar{L}$ law prevails.[37] The former possibility is illustrated in Figure 3(a); the latter in Figure 3(b) (welfare shifts being omitted so as not to encumber the diagrams).

Although it has been convenient to think of net potential Pareto improvements, through voluntary agreement between the A and B groups, in terms of output adjustments, if any, the above three possibilities are equally valid if other, and cheaper, methods of effecting net potential Pareto improvements are contemplated – such as moving factories, or processes (or members of the B group) to the other areas, installing any of a variety of preventive devices (or, in general, modifying the technology as to reduce spillovers), or government regulation of output either directly or through excise taxes.

In the absence of evidence indicating a clear connection between the magnitude of transactions costs and the type of law, there appear to be no firm allocative implications – save, perhaps, the advisability of thinking more closely of technical and institutional innovations that are likely to reduce transactions costs. Thus, with respect to the costs of government regulation of output, directly or through excise taxes, economists may like to remind themselves that the

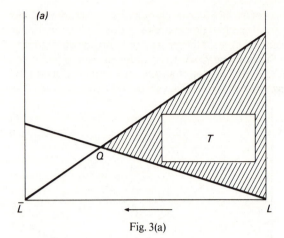

Fig. 3(a)

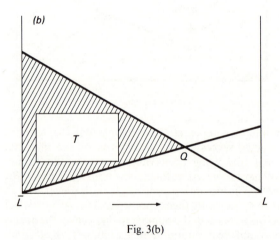

Fig. 3(b)

pursuit of the ideal is the enemy of the better. A roughly calculated excise tax imposed on a pollutant is likely to effect a distinct improvement, even if it were as much as 20 per cent or so higher, or lower, than the 'ideal' excise tax. As an immediate response to clear cases of excessive pollution, a roughly calculated tax is likely to be superior to not imposing a tax at all – or to procrastinating indefinitely while engaged in research to refine data and methods in the attempt to produce an ideal tax.

There are, nevertheless, a couple of considerations which appear to favor $\bar{L}$ law rather than L law. First, although the magnitude of transactions costs have been assumed independent of the type of law, the likelihood of a member of one group taking the initiative in approaching the other group is not independent of the law. If L law is in force, the possibility of some limited benefit for the person(s) taking the initiative on behalf of a large and widely dispersed B group has to be set against the certain loss of time and effort, and also against a large risk of incurring substantial and irrecoverable expenses in the attempt to complete phases (a) and (b). Under $\bar{L}$ law in contrast, the necessary initiative comes from industry. No personal risk is undertaken by one or more of the executives acting on behalf of shareholders – though, in any case, such an initiative would hardly stand out from the routine activities involving decision-taking by the managers of industry.[38] Indeed, under $\bar{L}$ law, firms are unlikely to invest in plant and machinery for the manufacture of pollution-prone products unless they are fairly confident that – after all economic 'preventive technology' has been employed – they can afford to meet claims for residual damage.

Secondly, under an L law, there is little incentive for industry to switch resources from promoting sales, or from research into product innovations or from cost-reducing technology, in favor of pollution-reducing technology. Assuming that firms allocate investable funds according to the equimarginal principle, they will then, under the existing L law, misallocate resources because they tend to ignore all opportunities for social gains made by directing research funds into preventive technology.[39] Under an $\bar{L}$ law, in contrast, full liability for pollution damage enters directly into production costs, along with expenditures on productive services, and the consequent incentive to engage in such research is inescapable.

Opportunities for private industry, under an $\bar{L}$ law, of reducing the social costs of pollution are not, however, restricted to curbing outputs and engaging in research on pollution-reducing technology. There will be incentives for the polluting industries to investigate many other possible ways of reducing their liabilities for damage to the public. They may find it cheaper to concentrate (parts of) their plant in remote areas, to redesign and reroute highways, to reroute air flights over less populous areas, in the pursuit of which they create conditions conducive to separate 'amenity areas' for the public.[40]

XI Environmental Spillovers – Equity

On the issue of the relative merits of L law and $\bar{L}$ law, there remain a number of considerations which may be subsumed under equity.

(1) *Distribution.* If it can be shown (a) that goods which generate spillovers also earn incomes for, and are purchased by, groups having above-average incomes, and (b) that the bulk of modern spillovers fall more heavily on families with below-average incomes, then it may be asserted that, compared with $\bar{L}$ law, L law is a force acting to increase the regressive distribution of welfare. In the absence of any systematic research into the question, however, one can say only that it is not implausible to believe that the introduction of significant disamenities into a large area is likely to reduce the welfare of the more mobile rich less than that of the poor.[41]

(2) *Malpractices.* If institutional innovations over time cause transactions costs to decline and initiative among the public to rise, there would be, under existing L law, a temptation for enterprising firms, and others in a position to do so, to produce unnecessary pollution in order to exact greater tribute from the public. This result can occur either prior to an initial agreement with the affected members of the public, or else subsequently – on the plea that market conditions have changed so radically that the existing agreement is irrelevant. Access to the detailed knowledge necessary to challenge businessmen's alleged expenditures on research and on consultations in attempting to meet public demands, or their subsequent allegations of changes in market conditions, is, if possible at all, likely to be costly and to lead to prolonged litigation.

(3) *Culpability.* A part of the recent consensus was the belief that the conflict of interest entailed by an external diseconomy was symmetric in all relevant respects. The freedom of either group to pursue its interests or enjoyments necessarily interfered with the freedom of the other group. Thus, if the nonsmokers' enjoyment is reduced by the smokers' freedom to smoke, so also, it is observed, is the smokers' enjoyment reduced by their abstaining for the greater comfort of the nonsmokers. The question of who should compensate whom, it was occasionally stated, can be settled only arbitrarily or by reference to distributional implications.

But although they are indeed Pareto symmetric, such conflicts may not be ethically symmetric. In accordance with the classical liberal maxim, the freedom of a man to pursue his interests is qualified insofar as it tends to reduce the freedom, or the welfare, of others. It may then be argued that the freedom of the smoker to smoke in shared quarters is not on all fours with the freedom of the nonsmoker to breathe fresh air, since the freedom to breathe fresh air does not, of itself, reduce the welfare of others. In contrast, the smokers' freedom to blow smoke into the air breathed by others does reduce their welfare. Similarly, it may be argued, the freedom to operate noisy vehicles, or pollutive plant, does incidentally damage the welfare of others, while the freedom desired by members of the public to live in clean and quiet surroundings does not, of itself, reduce the welfare of others. If such arguments can be sustained, there is a case in equity for the L law, and a case therefore for making polluters legally liable.[42]

(4) *Amenity.* If, over time, transactions costs, and perhaps the costs of regulation also do not decline, the choice of L law or $\bar{L}$ law may imply that for a large class of spillovers the effective choice for society lies between 'too much' spillover or 'too little'.[43] If the rate of growth of spillovers equals or exceeds[44] the growth of gross national product, and if one assumed diminishing marginal utility of man-made goods and increasing marginal disutility of man-made 'bads', the prevalence of L law will be a factor accelerating the rate at which *per capita* growth of real income approaches zero, and beyond.

(5) *Posterity.* Indeed, for a range of spillovers, government regulation, intervention, or prohibition may be justified notwithstanding an apparent consensus among the groups immediately affected. The possibility that the damage being wrought by particular spillover effects is virtually irreversible has to be taken seriously in the new vision of our tiny and unique planet. In terms of man's life span, the continuing destruction of our limited resources of natural beauty, the poisoning of lakes and rivers, may be regarded as irrevocable. Consequently the losses to be suffered by future generations[45] have to be added to those carried by existing populations.

(6) *Information.* If the pace of technological innovation extends the time lag between the immediate commercial exploitation of new products and processes, on the one hand, and, on the other, the knowledge of their long-term genetical and ecological effects, there is a presumption not only in favor of $\bar{L}$ law, but in favor also of direct prohibition of a number of hazardous polluting activities. There is a case, too, for public control over the adoption of new processes, and the marketing of new products, in particular, chemical products. The risks arising from insufficient knowledge of the long-term effects of any single innovation – or, indeed, the risks arising from insufficient knowledge of the long-term effects of any of a number of existing products and processes – may well be thought slight. But even allowing for this more favorable contingency, as the number of such products spread over the globe – and today they tend to spread with incredible rapidity – the chance of some uncontrollable epidemic, or ecological catastrophe occurring becomes increasingly probable.

XII Epilogue

Many of the considerations brought forward in the last section do not, I recognize, lend themselves easily to analytic elegance. But with respect to environmental spillover – the most urgent economic problem of our fragile civilization – they are more pertinent than those arising from traditional allocative analysis. It is not, of course, hard to understand the somewhat exaggerated weight attached by economists to the allocative aspects of an economic problem as distinct, say, from those connected with equity. For the former aspects lend themselves nicely to formal theorizing and, with patience and a little finesse, impressive measures of social losses and gains can be foisted on credulous civil servants and a gullible public.

Yet the priority given to allocative aspects in real economic problems cannot, I think, be justified; certainly not by recourse to welfare economics. The more 'affluent' a society becomes, the less important is allocative merit narrowly conceived. And in any society in the throes of accelerating technological change (one in which, of necessity, pertinent knowledge of the human, social, and ecological consequences of what we are doing is generally slight and partly erroneous) complacency on the part of any economist, guided in his professional decisions by considerations alone of allocative merit or economic growth potential, is both to be envied and deplored.

Notes: Chapter 13

1 Assuming that, under the existing technology, the least cost method of dealing with the external diseconomy is used.
2 Thus the optimal outputs remain positive though, in general, different from the equilibrium output x_n^2.
  It is commonly assumed that the equilibrium amount of the affected good, say X_m, is also altered by the external effect absorbed from the production of the good X_n. If however, the external effect on the production function of the X_m good is 'separable', the equilibrium amount of X_m is not altered; that is, there is an effect on X_m's total cost, but not on its marginal cost [11, Davis and Whinston, 1962].
3 This total condition may also be extended to cases where $\partial F_2^1/\partial x_n > 0$ – where, that is, external economies prevail at the margin –since it is at least conceptually possible that, although external economies are exerted at the margin, external diseconomies are generated by some of the intramarginal units of X_n.
4 An instance of this sort of reasoning is found in Mishan [34, 1965, pp. 6–8].
5 This is true whether or not perfect competition prevails. By assumption no one can be made worse off either through a change in relative prices or through external diseconomies, and some people will be made better off provided the new investment meets proper benefit–cost criteria.
6 The external diseconomy *internal* to an industry A might well be the result of an external economy absorbed by A from another industry B. J. Meade's example of apple-blossom providing food for bees [31, 1952, pp. 54–67] is

such a case. The scarce apple-blossom would cause the average cost of honey to rise as labor and capital were increased in the honey-producing industry (A). While the optimal amount of apples in the B industry has to take account of the value of the blossom as bee-food in honey production, the optimal amount of honey in A is below the competitive equilibrium, and is obtained by taking a curve marginal to the rising average cost of honey [34, Mishan, 1965].

7 A more detailed treatment of the controversy will be found in Mishan [34, 1965].

8 If, however, industry A were a monopoly, and used its size and buying-power to obtain more advantageous terms from its sellers, the gains it would make in this way are not those arising from the technological advantages of greater output, but only a transfer of revenue from weaker firms to itself.

9 Discussed by R. H. Coase in his 1960 paper [9] and again in Mishan [34, 1965].

10 An outstanding exception being the general equilibrium model produced by Ayres and Kneese [1, 1969]. In its present stage of development its heuristic advantages are more prominent.

11 If, in the uncorrected x output, the use of factor A alone exerts an external diseconomy on the output of y, then, although the factor rate of substitution in x and y is equal to the inverse of the common factor–price ratio, more of both x and y can be produced by switching some of A from x to y in exchange for some of factor B from y to x.

It should be evident, however, that this conclusion depends upon our assumption of external effects moving in one direction only – here from x to y. Assuming, instead, reciprocal effects in a two-good competitive economy, and also that, before correction, factor A used in y has an external effect on x that is proportional to the effect on y of factor A in x, the equilibrium amounts of the two goods will be on the production boundary. Indeed, in a two-good economy, a competitive equilibrium with proportional reciprocal externalities can be optimal.

12 Notwithstanding which, no striking new policy implications emerge. The tax/subsidy solution which realizes an optimal output simultaneously corrects both sorts of optimal infringement [34, Mishan, 1965].

13 If the x-industry were perfectly competitive, moreover, the standard result would obtain. The long-period social marginal cost of x would then be higher and the optimal output produced by fewer firms smaller than the uncorrected output.

14 Assuming, throughout, that there is always sufficient divisibility to warrant the equality signs.

15 If there is a reciprocal spillover arising from B's purchase of X conferring Y on person A, as well as A's purchase of X conferring Y on B, the optimal amount of X for B is determined in a manner symmetric to that for A. Thus it is determined by reference to B's marginal valuation schedule for X plus A's resulting marginal valuation for X (as derived from A's marginal valuation schedule for the Y generated by B's purchases of X).

16 An example would be the purchase by A of private protection of his home, which would benefit also the homes of his neighbors $B_1, B_2, \ldots, B_n$.

17 According to Buchanan and Kafoglis [6, 1963] the standard doctrine states that if private behavior exerts a 'Pareto relevant' external economy, the market-generated supply of resources used in this behavior falls short of the social

optimum. They then produce the example of the spillover from A's consumption of X being X also, and for B, the recipient of this spillover, a perfect substitute for the X he buys. However, since they did not discuss the possibility of B's having a negative marginal valuation of A's spillover of X (in virtue of B's being constrained to absorb the lot), their result, that an optimal amount of X could be *smaller* than the market amount, depended, in the nonreciprocal case, on the rather implausible assumption that the X received as spillover by B has a higher value to B than the identical X he buys on the market. In the reciprocal case, on the other hand, the smaller-optimal-output result is obtained by an implicit assumption of increasing returns to scale. Also see P. E. Vincent [52, 1969].

18 Buchanan [7, 1965] determines the optimal number of people sharing a good by explicit reference to external diseconomies. The reader is reminded that, at this stage, we are still abstracting from congestion costs.

19 These so-called optimal conditions are sometimes referred to as first-order, or necessary, or marginal, conditions, thereby distinguishing them from second-order, or stability, conditions and also from the all-important total conditions

$$\sum_i^n V^i \gtreqless K$$

where V_i is the (discounted) net value to the ith person of the total output produced, and K is the (discounted) cost of the total output.

20 This optimal condition, when valid for an optional G good, does not, however, entitle us to infer that the amounts of the good taken can be exchanged as between persons. Where the marginal resource cost is not zero, but positive, the equation

$$v^1 = v^2 = v^3 = c$$

applies only to D goods. In that case, the exchange optimum is also met, which implies that the total output of the D good is so distributed among the n persons as to maximize the valuation of that output.

21 For example, the seeding of clouds may cause some farms to catch more rain than others. In some cases the marginal valuation of the rain received by a farm may be negative. Alternatively, costs may be incurred in reducing the amount of rain absorbed.

22 We are concerned here with the long-period alteration in the capacity of some facility, the existing distribution of the population being accepted as a datum, and *not* with the possibility of people moving closer in order to avail themselves of the facility in question (in which case the additional resource costs required by the facility are nil). An example of the former would be increasing the power of an existing broadcasting station to reach a larger number of people. An example of the latter would be the movement of some families to be within range of an existing transmitter.

23 The optimal conditions determining the collective use of a G good in circumstances in which congestion occurs can be derived as a special instance of the more general formulation determining the output of a /D good where external economies and diseconomies are exerted by persons on other persons (either directly through their consumption activities, or indirectly through the effect of their consumption activities on the production of the good in question):

$$\sum_i^n V_k{}^{i1} + \sum_i^n V_k{}^{1i} \ (i \neq 1)$$
$$= \sum_i^n V_k{}^{i2} + \sum_i^n V_k{}^{2i} \ (i \neq 2) = \ldots = \sum_i^n V_k{}^{in} + \sum_i^n V_k{}^{ni} \ (i \neq n) = c_k$$

where

c_k is the marginal resource cost of the kth good;

v^{i1} is the algebraic effect of the ith person's goods on the value of person 1's marginal consumption of k (this is sometimes assumed to be zero for all i ($i \neq 1$), only the positive term v^{11} remaining); and

v^{1i} is the algebraic effect on person 1's marginal consumption of k on the ith person's valuation of his own (i's) goods.

Each person properly evaluates his first summation term but ignores the second summation term which the economist must take into account.

For external diseconomies *internal* to the kth activity, all the external diseconomies generated by each person (whose second summation term is therefore negative) are deemed to be exerted on persons engaged solely in the kth activity. Congestion costs are, of course, a common form of external diseconomies internal to the activity. Insofar as congestion costs are generated in the collective use of a G good, the above formulation still applies except that the marginal resource cost, c_k, is equal to zero.

Finally, in the special case in which each person is associated with only one unit of the kth good – as in the example of private automobiles using a highway – the optimal traffic flow is n, where for the nth person

$$\sum_i^n V_k{}^{in} + \sum_i^n V_k{}^{ni} \ (i \neq n) = c_k$$

24 The term collective (or public) good is used in two senses in the literature: sometimes to designate the phsyical asset itself, say a bridge, and sometimes to designate the services provided by that asset. The context usually makes clear the sense in which the term is used.

25 According as the potential beneficiaries have to travel to avail themselves of the collective service (as in the case, say, of a park of theatre), or to form a link with the generator of the service (as in the case, say, of a television transmitter).

26 A comparable though not entirely similar commentary on the more commonly proposed solutions to the externality problem can be found in a recent paper by Davis and Kamien [10, 1969, pp. 78–86].

27 It is, of course, possible that the industry producing the external diseconomy is a noncompetitive industry. A monopoly firm equating marginal cost to marginal revenue will in any case produce an output smaller than the marginal (private) cost–price output, which may then be closer to the optimal output. In this connection, see D. A. Worcester [56, 1969].

28 There is some slight geometric convenience in constructing $S'S'$ parallel to SS.

29 See J. M. Buchanan and W. C. Stubblebine [5, 1962] and Turvey [51, 1963].

30 A related objection to an effluent excise tax occurs in a paper by P. Bohm [4, 1970]. If the optimal excise tax increases with output, the firm (he argues) might become aware of the relationship. Subtracting the schedule of optimal taxes from the demand price of the product would result in a downward-sloping net average revenue curve from which the firm could derive a marginal revenue

curve. By equating marginal cost to this 'marginal revenue' curve, the firm reduces its output below optimal.

However, the government is not obliged to impose a *uniform* effluent tax. It could as well make it clear that it would impose a *discriminating* tax, one equal at each unit of output to the marginal effluent and, therefore, at any output raising a total tax equal to the total loss inflicted by the effluent. Such a tax, already marginal, effectively precludes the industry from 'exploiting' it by reducing its output. In addition, such a discriminating tax ensures that the total conditions are met. Thus, heavy effluent charges properly imposed on the initial units of the output could well prohibit production of the good.

31 This conclusion can be ascribed to the popularity in the literature of the two-firm or two-industry case.

32 The rents earned by lands of superior quality, or location, being one of the earlier examples in the history of economic thought.

33 The reader will observe that the above paradox (which depends on different compensating variations under different states of the law) has no affinity with that associated with the so-called 'Kaldor-Hicks' and 'Scitovsky' type welfare criteria. The latter paradox arises only from alterations in the set of relative prices (common to everyone) associated with the distributional changes whenever the community moves from producing one batch of goods to producing another.

34 That is, the B group pays for each successive flight reduction no more than the sums traced out by the $A_L M$ curve.

35 Another incidental implication of this sort of analysis, one making explicit allowance for welfare effects, is that an excise tax alone can no longer be counted on to realize an optimal position. In this connection see F. T. Dolbear Jr [15, 1967].

36 The reverse being true for the improbable case of negative welfare effects.

37 It is of incidental interest to note, however, that in the first case society would be better off if the $\bar{L}$ law prevailed (notwithstanding that it would not pay to move from the resulting zero output), since it would save the T costs incurred in moving to Q under the L law. As for the second case, society would be better off if the L law prevailed.

38 We have ignored welfare effects in order to avoid minor distractions from the shifting of the marginal valuation curves.

Under the $\bar{L}$ law envisaged, it is not necessary for a plaintiff to incur any expense in pursuing a claim against pollution in the courts of law, since pollution – in the absence of explicit permission to the contrary – is illegal. Punitive action which includes cessation of the pollution-creating activity is immediately taken by the public prosecutor unless the firm has a government permit issued periodically, which permit is never granted unless all claims to damages over the period in question are met. So severe a law will not prove costly to administer simply because businesses will almost certainly find it cheaper (a) to move away from populous centers and/or (b) to undertake further research into the technical changes necessary to reduce pollution as to be virtually undetectable.

39 Any hope that funds from the B group will be offered to industry to engage in research so as to reduce widespread pollutants can be ruled out both because of the heavy risks of initiative by individual victims and because of the costs of transactions referred to.

40 The conditions under which a separate areas' solution of group conflict is superior to the usual optimal solution that is constrained within a given area are discussed in Mishan [**35**, 1967].

41 The fact that in any given neighborhood the rich will respond to local forms of pollution by moving from the locality in larger proportion than the poor certainly bears on the question of whether disamenities tend to fall in the first instance more heavily on the neighborhoods of the poorer groups in the economy. But even if it were the case that disamenities were introduced into initially unpolluted neighborhoods, rich and poor, in an entirely random fashion – which is implausible – it does not follow that the growth in pollution does not have regressive welfare effects. Thus if a man earning $100,000 per annum is willing to give up a maximum sum of $30,000 per annum to be rid of some particularly noxious spillover, but discovers that he is able to move out of the polluted area for a loss of about $10,000 per annum, he becomes better off than he would be if he remained in the area (to the tune of $20,000 per annum). An equally sensitive man earning only $10,000 per annum may be willing to sacrifice a maximum of $1,500 per annum to be rid of the pollution. But if the movement out of the area would involve him in a loss (or in the risk of a loss) of more than $1,500 per annum, he has to stay put and bear the full loss in his welfare.

42 This argument, if coaxed a little, might be made to take a finer turn: thus, if a switch in my demand from x to y causes either the price of x or y to rise, it obviously affects the welfare of others also. Nevertheless, considerations of equity need not ignore differences of magnitude. If the world were indeed such that a simple increase in my demand for notepaper inflicted injury on innocent families, it is likely – though the question of equity was far from clear – that broad agreement could be secured on the need to develop countervailing government mechanisms. If, however, the effects of changing tastes on relative prices were slight and random, and the costs of continually tracing them back to those responsible were prohibitive, there would be an explicit agreement or tacit understanding to ignore them for the undeniable conveniences offered by a comprehensive price system.

43 As suggested, the adoption of $\bar{L}$ law will encourage the development of preventive technology more than will L law. The 'too little' will not, then, be likely to last as long as the 'too much'.

44 Which is more likely, since familiar growth industries (automobiles, motorboats, motorized garden implements, chemicals, nuclear power, tourism, and so on) also appear prolific of spillover.

45 Any discounting of the losses to be borne by *future* generations, moreover, cannot be justified on the usual arguments developed in the context of a single generation.

References

1 Ayres, R. V. and Kneese, A. V., 'Production, consumption, and externalities', *American Economic Review,* vol. 59, no. 3 (June 1969), pp. 282–97.

2 Baumol, W. J., 'External economies and second-order optimality conditions', *American Economic Review,* vol. 54, no. 3 (June 1964), pp. 358–72.

3 Bohm, P., *External Economies in Production* (Stockholm: Almquist & Wiksells, 1964).

4 Bohm, P., 'Pollution, purification and the theory of external effects' (mimeo., 1969); also in French in *Annales de l'Insee* (1970).

5 Buchanan, J. M. and Stubblebine, W. C., 'Externality', *Economica,* vol. 29 (November 1962), pp. 371–84.

6 Buchanan, J. M. and Kafoglis, M. Z., 'A note on public goods supply', *American Economic Review,* vol. 53, no. 3 (June 1963), pp. 403–14.

7 Buchanan, J. M., 'An economic theory of clubs', *Economica,* vol. 32, no. 125 (February 1965), pp. 1–14.

8 Burrows, P., 'On external cost and the visible arm of the law', *Oxford Economic Papers* vol. 22, no. 1 (March 1970), pp. 1–17.

9 Coase, R. H., 'The problem of social cost', *Journal of Law and Economics,* vol. 3 (October 1960), pp. 1–44.

10 Davis, O. A. and Kamien, M. I., 'Externalities, information and alternative collective action', in *The Analysis of Public Expenditures: The PPB System* (Washington: Government Printing Office, 1969), pp. 67–86.

11 Davis, O. A. and Whinston, A., 'Externalities, welfare and the theory of games', *Journal of Political Economy,* vol. 70, no. 3 (June 1962), pp. 241–62.

12 Davis, O. A. and Whinston, A., 'On externalities, information and the government-assisted invisible hand', *Economica,* vol. 33, no. 131 (August 1966), pp. 303–18.

13 Davis, O. A. and Whinston, A., 'Piecemeal policy in the theory of second best', *Review of Economic Studies,* vol. 34, no. 3 (July 1967), pp. 323–31.

14 Davis, O. A. and Whinston, A., 'On the distinction between public and private goods', *American Economic Review,* vol. 57, no. 2 (May 1967), pp. 360–73.

15 Dolbear, F. T., Jr, 'On the theory of optimal externality', *American Economic Review,* vol. 57, no. 1 (March 1967), pp. 90–103.

16 Duesenberry, J., *Income, Saving and the Theory of Consumer Behaviour* (Harvard: Harvard University Press, 1949).

17 Ellis, H. and Fellner, W., 'External economies and diseconomies', *American Economic Review,* vol. 23, no. 3 (September 1943), pp. 493–511; reprinted in *Readings in Price Theory* (Chicago: Irwin, 1952).

18 Evans, A. W., 'Private goods, externality, public good', *Scottish Journal of Political Economy,* vol. 17, no. 1 (February 1970), pp. 79–89.

19 Farrell, M. J., 'In defence of public utility pricing', *Oxford Economic Papers,* vol. 10 (February 1958), pp. 109–23.

20 Graaff, J. de V., *Theoretical Welfare Economics* (Cambridge: Cambridge University Press, 1957).

21 Green, H. A. J., 'The social optimum in the presence of monopoly and taxation', *Review of Economic Studies,* vol. 29, no. 1 (1961), pp. 66–78.

22 Hicks, J. R., 'The four consumer's surpluses', *Review of Economic Studies,* vol. 11, no. 1 (1943), pp. 31–41.

23 Kahn, R. F., 'Some notes on ideal output', *Economic Journal,* vol. 45, no. 177 (March 1935), pp. 1–35.

24 Kneese, A. V., *Approaches to Regional Water Quality Management* (Washington, DC: Resources for the Future Inc., 1967).

25 Knight, F. H., 'Some fallacies in the interpretation of social cost', *Quarterly Journal of Economics,* vol. 37 (August 1924), pp. 582–606.

26 Lipsey, R. G. and Lancaster, K., 'The general theory of

second best', *Review of Economic Studies,* vol. 24, no. 63 (1956–7), pp. 11–32.

27 Little, I. M. D., *A Critique of Welfare Economics* (London: Oxford University Press, 1957).

28 Margolis, J., 'A comment on the pure theory of public expenditure', *Review of Economics and Statistics,* vol. 37 (November 1955), pp. 347–9.

29 Marshall, A., *Principles of Economics,* 8th edn (London: Macmillan, 1925).

30 McGuire, M. C. and Aaron, H., 'Efficiency and equity in the optimal supply of a public good', *Review of Economics and Statistics,* vol. 51, no. 1 (February 1969), pp. 31–9.

31 Meade, J., 'External economies and diseconomies in a competitive situation', *Economic Journal,* vol. 62 (March 1952), pp. 54–67.

32 Mishan, E. J., 'Welfare criteria for external effects', *American Economic Review,* vol. 51, no. 4 (September 1961), pp. 594–613.

33 Mishan, E. J., 'Second thoughts on second best', *Oxford Economic Papers,* vol. 14 (October 1962), pp. 205–17.

34 Mishan, E. J., 'Reflections on recent developments in the concept of external effects', *Canadian Journal of Political Economy,* vol. 31 (February 1965), pp. 3–34.

35 Mishan, E. J., 'Pareto optimality and the law', *Oxford Economic Papers,* (November 1967), pp. 255–87.

36 Mishan, E. J., 'What is producers' surplus?', *American Economic Review,* vol. 58, no. 5 (December 1968), pp. 1269–82.

37 Mishan E. J., 'The relationship between joint products, collective goods, and external effects', *Journal of Political Economy,* vol. 72, no. 3 (May 1969), pp. 329–48.

38 Musgrave, R. A., 'Cost–benefit analysis and the theory of public finance', *Journal of Economic Literature,* vol. 7, no. 3 (September 1969), pp. 797–806.

39 Oakland, W. H., 'Joint goods', *Economica,* vol. 36, no. 143 (August 1969), pp. 253–68.

40 Olson, M., *The Logic of Collective Action* (Harvard: Harvard University Press, 1965).

41 Pauly, M. V., 'Clubs, commonality and the core: an integration of game theory and the theory of public goods', *Economica,* vol. 34, no. 135 (August 1967), pp. 314–24.

42 Pigou, A. C., *The Economics of Welfare,* 4th edn (London: Macmillan, 1946).

43 Plott, C. R., 'Externalities and corrective taxes', *Economica,* vol. 33, no. 129 (February 1966), pp. 84–7.

44 Ridker, R. G., *Economic Costs of Air Pollution* (New York: Praeger, 1967).

45 Rosenstein-Rodan, P. W., 'Problems of industrialization of east and south east Europe', *Economic Journal,* vol. 53 (June 1943), pp. 202–11.

46 Samuelson, P. A., 'Contrast between welfare conditions for joint supply and for public goods', *Review of Economics and Statistics,* vol. 51, no. 1 (February 1969), pp. 26–30.

47 Samuelson, P. A., 'The pure theory of public expenditure', *Review of Economics and Statistics,* vol. 36 (November 1954), pp. 387–9.

48 Samuelson, P. A., 'Aspects of public expenditure theories', *Review of Economics and Statistics,* vol. 40 (November 1958), pp. 332–8.

49 Schumacher, E. F., 'Clean air and future energy', *Des Voeux Memorial Lecture* (1967).

50 Scitovsky, T., 'Two concepts of external economies', *Journal of Political Economy,* vol. 62 (April 1954), pp. 70–82.

51 Turvey, R., 'On divergences between social cost and private cost', *Economica,* vol. 30 (August 1963), pp. 309–13.

52 Vincent, P. E., 'Reciprocal externalities and optimal input and output levels', *American Economic Review,* vol. 59, no. 5 (December 1969), pp. 976–84.

53 Viner, J., 'Cost curves and supply curves', *Zeit. Nationalokonomie,* vol. 3 (September 1931), pp. 23–46; reprinted in *Readings in Price Theory* (New York: Blakiston, 1953).

54 Williams, A., 'The optimal provision of public goods in a system of local government', *Journal of Political Economy,* vol. 74 (January 1966).

55 Wellisz, S., 'On external diseconomies and the government-assisted invisible hand', *Economica,* vol. 31 (November 1964), pp. 345–62.

56 Worcester, D. A., 'Pecuniary and technological externality, factor rents and social costs', *American Economic Review,* vol. 59, no. 5 (December 1969), pp. 873–85.

PART FOUR

Project Evaluation

Methodology

14

Flexibility and Consistency in Project Evaluation

The two questions of method that may be raised in connection with *Guidelines for Project Evaluation* (Dasgupta *et al.,* 1972) are not particular to that volume. They arise also in connection with other recent books on project evaluation, for instance, Dasgupta and Pearce (1972), and Little and Mirrlees (1969). But in view of the authoritative nature of this work, the weight it will carry among economic agencies in the Third World, and the respect in which each of the distinguished authors is justly held, it seems to me that these basic differences in method, possibly also in conception, of cost–benefit analysis should be made as explicit as possible. It should be noted that apart from the controversial methodological issues raised in this paper, *Guidelines* offers a more thorough treatment of cost–benefit techniques applied to poor countries than can be found today in any other volume or monograph. Though perhaps rather less accessible to the intelligent layman than the authors imagine, it is for the most part judiciously written and should be regarded as an essential work of reference for all students interested in project selection for economically backward countries.

The lesser question, discussed in section I, concerns the treatment of political and administrative *constraints* in the calculation of those 'national parameters' that are derived wholly from economic principles. The more important question, treated in section II, concerns the role, if any, in cost–benefit analysis of those 'national parameters' that do not derive from familiar economic principles but are in effect politically determined.

I Calculating Shadow Prices under Given Constraints

The decision by the authors of *Guidelines* to present specific and detailed formulae for calculating some purely economic parameters, in particular, 'shadow prices', rests on a belief that the political constraints adopted, whether implicit or explicit, are those most likely to prevail in the poor countries of the world. This, of course, is a judgment of fact. Whether it is always correct, and what difference it makes if it is not correct, the reader will judge for himself after reading this section. Nevertheless, there may, perhaps, be provisional agreement that it is useful to draw attention in such a treatise to the desirability and the possibility of occasionally persuading governments to adopt economically more rational constraints than those currently prevailing.

A. A shadow price in the context of project evaluation arises from the assumption of the certain yield to private investment, ρ, being greater than r, the social rate of time preference. Reckoning in terms of current consumption, this inequality implies that a dollar currently invested in the private sector is more valuable than a dollar currently consumed. For in the simplest case, in which the annual return ρ to the dollar so invested is wholly consumed, it has a present value (discounted at r) of ρ/r, whereas a dollar currently consumed has a present value of exactly a dollar. In general, the present value of a dollar of private investment is given by S, the shadow price of investment, this being equal to ρ/r only in the simple case just mentioned. In more complex cases in which some fraction θ' of the returns from investment is reinvested, S will exceed ρ/r. Provided that funds for a public project are raised from taxes, and provided $\theta' \rho < r$, equation (14:16) (*Guidelines*, p. 177) shows

$$S = (1 - \theta')\frac{\rho}{r} - \theta\rho'$$

This result follows the method propounded by Marglin (1963a, p. 282, equation 15). I follow the notation in that article as being less cumbersome than that in *Guidelines*, except that I use θ' for Marglin's θ_2, and later I shall use θ for his θ_1.

Incidentally, for the case in which $\theta' \rho > r$, the reader is referred to a more elaborate formula, (14:52) (*Guidelines*, p. 197) which, as it happens, does not work for θ' equal to unity – for the case, that is, in which all returns to private investment are continually and wholly reinvested. A moment's reflection on this case suggests that it can easily be managed by using ρ as the discount rate in the investment criterion.

Earlier on, however (*Guidelines*, pp. 161–3), the authors take exception to using ρ as a discount rate, apparently on the grounds that to do so implies that an initial outlay of K on a public project is financed through a reduction in private investment of the same amount, K. But this implication is not necessary. It is possible for the public agency to raise the amount K solely from current consumption and yet justify the use of ρ as the appropriate discount rate in the investment criterion for the public project in question. All that is required is a change of the political or administrative constraints that the authors assume to exist. Thus, the relevant constraints in *Guidelines* imply that the investment agency, faced with a decision whether to invest the sum K in a public project, asks itself simply what this amount K would fetch if left, instead, in the private sector of the economy. Unless the public project can produce a stream of benefits having a higher present value, it does not pass the investment criterion. This ignores the complications that may be introduced by distributional weights or 'merit parameters' without, however, affecting the gist of the argument.

However, the investment agency might well adopt another procedure. It could, for instance, ask itself how best it could use a sum K which is to be raised for a public project. Assuming that the best alternative use for such a sum K is that of wholly investing it in the private sector at yield ρ, and wholly reinvesting all returns at ρ, then the appropriate discount rate in the investment criterion for the public project is ρ. For, unless the present value of the benefits of the project, when discounted at ρ, exceeds K, there is nothing to be gained by introducing this project as compared with investing K wholly in the private sector.

One may, indeed, discuss the political feasibility of adopting this procedure and the likely economic effects over time. But it cannot be dismissed as something that is not worth arguing about.

B. The advisability of looking more closely at the political and administrative constraints in any treatise of this kind can be illustrated in another connection.

Let us suppose we accept the procedure that requires the public investment agency, in calculating the social opportunity cost of a public project, to consider only the loss of present value entailed by raising a sum for this purpose from the private sector. We can still reach conclusions that are quite different from those of the authors by adopting other rules about the sum to be raised.

If, for example, the public project requires an initial capital outlay of 100 then, for an S of 2·5 and a θ of 0·2 (where θ is that fraction of tax revenue that is made available by reducing private investment), the social opportunity cost of the project on their calculation would be

$$2 \cdot 5 (20) + 1 \cdot 0 (80) = 130$$

or $1·3 for each dollar of outlay on the project. If the present discounted value of the benefits of the project came to 120, or $1·2 of benefit per dollar of capital outlay, it would be rejected.

Now let us have the public agency raise, not 100, but 125 by taxation, and of this 125 let it invest 100 in the project and the remaining 25 in the private investment sector, all the time retaining the assumption that the return to this placing of 25 in the private investment sector is reinvested in exactly the same way as it would be by the private sector. The social opportunity cost per dollar from raising $125 by taxation is, of course, $1·3, as before. But the social *benefit* per dollar from the new use of this $125 is made up of 20 per cent at an S of 2·5 plus 80 per cent at 1·2, or $1·46. Using this procedure, the raising of 125 offers a social benefit per dollar of $1·46 as compared with a social cost of $1·3. Therefore what appears economically unfeasible under one constraint (a), raising exactly 100 to cover the capital outlay of the public project, now becomes economically feasible under the proposed constraint (b), raising a larger sum, 125, and investing 20 per cent of it in the private sector (so as to offset exactly the loss of private investment).

Certainly there is as much economic rationale in adopting the (b) procedure as the (a), since using the 125 in this way is Pareto-superior to the option of leaving it in the private sector.[1] The argument that it is possible to do better still by investing in the private investment sector more than 20 per cent of any sum raised by taxes – in the limiting case the whole of any sum raised by taxes – is not to be evaded. Indeed, in this limiting case we are back to the constraint examined in the preceding section; that in which the public investment agency always has the option of investing any sum raised for a public project wholly in the private investment sector, an option implied in the use of ρ as the appropriate discount rate for the project.

Whatever the outcome of a debate on any particular

proposal, it can hardly be denied that some increased flexibility in thinking about possible political and administrative constraints is worthwhile. Whatever the existing institutional constraints, there can always be alternatives which have economic advantages and which the conscientious economist may succeed in inducing governments to adopt.

C. The question to be raised about the shadow price of labour is an extension of the preceding argument, but is of particular interest in view of the important role which the concept has played in the literature on economically underdeveloped countries. Let us ignore the more exotic formulations that may be produced by a proliferation of saving propensities and distributional and other weights,[2] and adopt virtually the minimal assumptions needed to come to grips with the essential concept. It arises in connection with proposals to move homogeneous labour from low-pay sectors of the economy, say agriculture, to relatively high-pay public projects in which, however, the wage there is assumed to exceed the marginal product of labour. As a result of this latter assumption, the marginal product of labour in agriculture, m_a, which is forgone when the worker is transferred to the public project, is only one of the components[3] of the shadow wage – which concept refers to the *inclusive* social costs incurred in transferring the worker to the public project.

Since the employment of an additional worker in the public project requires a subsidy to bridge the amount by which w, the wage there, exceeds m_p, labour's marginal product there, a loss of private investment can arise from the necessary transfer of income in so far as the saving propensity of those financing the subsidy is higher than that of the workers receiving the subsidy. The present value of this accompanying loss of private investment is the· other component of the shadow wage.

In the simple case in which the workers save nothing and the private sector (which pays the subsidy) saves θ of its income, the latter component is calculated as θ times the subsidy per worker, $(w - m_p)$ multiplied by the *excess* shadow price of investment, $(S - 1)$. In these circumstances one can define the shadow wage, in any given situation, as

$$w^* = m_a + (S-1)(w - m_p)\theta \tag{1}$$

However, since a transfer of labour from agriculture to the public project entails a social benefit of m_p and a social loss of w^*, the transfer ought to continue as long as m_p exceeds w^*. Clearly, then, an optimal allocation

of labour as between these two sectors is reached when $m_p = w^*$. In this optimal situation we can substitute w^* for m_p in equation (1), which gives us

$$w^* = w - \frac{1}{S}(w - m_a)\theta \tag{2}$$

For the special case of θ equal to unity, equation (2) reduces to the formulation proposed by Little and Mirrlees (1969, p. 167).

Warr (1973) derives a general expression for the shadow wage for an optimal allocation of labour as between agriculture and the public project sector. From this general expression the shadow wage formulations of a number of writers are derived by using their special assumptions about the saving propensities of different groups.

But whatever the formulation used it clearly does make a difference whether we used the definition of a shadow wage as in equation (1) above, or an 'optimal' shadow wage as in equation (2), and as explicated by Warr. Thus in our simple formulation, if we begin with a situation in which $w = 10$, $m_a = 1$, $m_p = 8$, and $S = 3$, the existing shadow wage according to equation (1) is 5, and since $m_p = 8$, there would appear to be an allocative improvement in transferring workers from agriculture to the public project. The use of our equation (2), however, assumes that labour has been moved from agriculture to the project in such numbers that $w^* = m_p$, in which case both are equal to 7.

It would be useful to have more explicit statements from such writers about the considerations that require us to use as a shadow wage for labour that which would prevail if labour were already optimally allocated, in the way indicated, when it is altogether possible for a public project to be mooted in circumstances in which the shadow wage, as defined in equation (1), is below the marginal product of labour in the public project.

Now provided θ is less than unity, the loss-of-investment component arises (whichever formulation we use) only if government agencies are constrained to raise exactly one dollar for every dollar of subsidy required. If they can be persuaded to change their conventions so as to raise more than a dollar for each dollar of subsidy required, the value of the shadow wage can be altered. Once again, with a θ of 20 per cent, the government could raise $1·25 for every dollar of subsidy required, place 25 cents of each $1·25 raised (or 20 per cent of every dollar raised) in the private investment sector, and use the remainder for the wage subsidy. The loss-of-investment component would thus be exactly offset by this procedure, the resulting shadow wage being then equal only to the marginal product of labour in agriculture. Projects which would not be undertaken on any one of the conventional shadow-wage formulations might easily be admitted with a shadow wage equal to no more than labour's agricultural marginal product.

The economic rationale of adopting this procedure rather than the more conventional one is apparently quite valid, though it immediately raises questions, similar to those in the preceding section, about how far to move in that direction. For by placing in the private investment sector a greater proportion than θ of the funds raised, private investment can be increased rather than reduced, and the shadow wage therefore made to appear smaller than labour's marginal product in agriculture, and perhaps made equal to zero or to some negative magnitude. Fundamental questions are thus raised anew about the constraints to be aimed at, and also about the related choice of investment criteria.

If for example, a terminal-value investment criterion were adopted, rather than a present-value criterion, of any part of the benefits in the ith year that are in the form of factor rents – say wages in excess of the opportunity costs of labour to the project – the fraction consumed is compounded forward to the terminal period at r, the fraction reinvested in the private investment sector at ρ. The remaining benefits are also compounded forward at r or ρ (or possibly some other rate) according to their expected disposal which is determined by the nature of the project and the operative constraints.[4]

II Implications of the Use of Political Parameters

A word first on the general conception of project evaluation methods that would include politically determined parameters. To quote from *Guidelines* (p. 1):

> Projects should, therefore, be formulated and evaluated in such a way as to single out for implementation those that contribute most to the *ultimate objectives of the country.* It follows that the Government requires a methodology for comparing and evaluating alternative projects *in terms of their contribution to these objectives.* (my italics)

Later on, and more specifically, they write (p. 106): 'What precise values these national weights will take will, it is hoped, emerge from the policy makers' selection of projects. But their logic lies essentially in the policy makers' ethical values.'

These remarks, and similar ones found elsewhere

(Walsh and Williams, 1969, p. 19), relate the ultimate justification of politically determined parameters to the primacy of national objectives of which increasing aggregate consumption is only one. Recourse to such parameters, however, seems to have risen also from specific difficulties of economic measurement and from the recognition of the limitations of economic calculation in respect of particular goods: its inability, for example, to put a money figure on some of the less tangible consequences of an investment project, such as a better distribution of income within an area or the promotion of education or culture there.

The social rate of discount, for instance, is difficult to estimate not only because there is a large number of interest rates in any country, each reflecting different time periods and different degrees of risk, but for other reasons some of which are mentioned in *Guidelines* (pp. 158–60). Thus 'intertemporal rationality' is brought into question because it is unrealistic to assume that individuals learn from their experience in intertemporal contexts based on lifetime consumption and also because of individual uncertainty in estimating lifetime resources. Moreover, data from the United States suggest that, over their lifetimes, only the rich save from disposable income. All, however, may derive positive utility from society's aggregate saving whether or not they save individually.[5]

To these reasons one might add that, in consequence of progressive income taxation, the rates of return on investment income *net* of tax differ at the margin for different income groups. The amounts saved and invested by individuals differ, therefore, from those which would exist if the rates of return (net of tax) were the same for everyone in any given securities market (see Mishan, 1975, ch. 31).

After elaborating on some of these difficulties the authors of *Guidelines* conclude (p. 164), perhaps too hastily: 'There is thus no escape from the need for the Government to judge the relative weight to be accorded to aggregate-consumption benefits and costs at different times'.

Merit goods. It can be argued that cost–benefit analysis or, for that matter, the competitive price system ignores considerations of 'social merit'. The benefits of such goods as better health, better community relations, or the alleviation of poverty, though they might notionally be brought into relation with the economic calculus, are likely to elude attempts to translate them into money values. Socially desirable goods of this sort may also be roughly, and to some extent arbitrarily, measured by what have come to be known as *social indicators*. The interested reader is referred to the US Government's *Toward a Social*

Report (1969). For an application of a weighted index to a specific problem, see Mack and Myers (1965).

One way of making allowance for merit wants is, of course, to attach a weight or premium to the benefit associated with the social good in question. To quote from *Guidelines* (p. 149):

... one Government, preparing for a transition to collective agriculture may consider peasant ownership a demerit want and wish to penalize the subsistence variant accordingly. By contrast a second Government, holding private ownership to be a moral or political virtue, may attach a positive premium to the subsistence variant over and above its redistributional advantage. In either case the premium or penalty is to be ... discovered by ... [the economist].

Equity of distribution. The impact of large investment projects on the distribution of real income has attracted much attention. One form of response to this concern has been an attempt to incorporate distributional effects into a cost–benefit calculation by weighting gains and losses according to the income of the recipient. Such a procedure effectively transforms money estimates of compensating variations into *utils*. Thus a cost–benefit criterion that is not met in money terms might well be met when the calculation is translated into utility terms, and vice versa.

The particular weighting systems that have been proposed are of necessity arbitrary and all assume, not surprisingly, diminishing marginal utility of income. One method is that of adopting a particular form of the utility–income relation; for example, one that gives a constant elasticity of *minus* two with respect to income. Alternatively, the weighting system can be made dependent upon the political decisions taken in the past. A method of deriving such weights has been proposed by Weisbrod (1968) and rests on the assumption that all public projects which were adopted despite their failure to meet cost–benefit criteria over a period, were adopted because of an implicit set of utility weights attached by the political process to the earnings of different income or regional groups. Another method of deriving these political weights is by a more direct approach to policy-makers.[6] Yet another method is that of calculating them from the marginal rates of income tax on the premise that the object of the existing tax system is to share the real burden of any increment of tax equally among all income groups.[7]

A. Even if the principle of calculating politically determined national parameters were wholly accept-able, difficulties would arise in their implementation.

(i) There is always the risk of the numerical values of such parameters being determined by non-representative bodies. The 'policy-maker' so persistently invoked by the economist may, in plausible circumstances, turn out to be little more than a bureaucrat, even if a humane one. The figure he puts on a crucial price, say the social rate of time preference may have little social justification. In the poorer countries of Asia or Africa, for example, the bureaucrat is likely to be one among a politically powerful group that is imbued with 'Western' ideas or ideologies and with strong convictions about the desirability, or 'absolute necessity', of rapid economic growth. Such a person is prone to think of himself as custodian of generations yet unborn, entrusted with the sacred task of transforming a backward economy into a modern one in the face of the inertia, 'superstition', or resentment of the mass of the people. In the endeavour to achieve a faster rate of economic growth, the policy-maker will adopt a social rate of discount that is apt to be appreciably lower than any that would accord with existing patterns of behaviour or with any estimate of the subjective valuations of the citizens. In effect, he endeavours to impose sacrifices on existing generations that they themselves would not, given the choice, willingly accept.

Having acknowledged the difficulties of calculating some 'ideal' social rate of time preference from individual welfare functions, there is something to be said for the economist's confessing his current ignorance while persisting in his attempts to discover some useful proxy for this 'ideal' social rate of time preference. There is nothing to be said, as we shall see anon, for letting the policy-maker himself decide what it is to be.

(ii) Whether bureaucratically or democratically chosen, such parameters, purporting to represent 'ultimate national objectives', will vary not only from one country to another. Within any one country they may vary from year to year according to the particular regime in power, or according to the composition of the legislature or, again, according to political fashions and the exigencies of state. Moreover, since it will soon become recognised, in any representative democracy, that some projects which would be accepted on one set of weights, or national parameters, would be rejected on another set, one may anticipate continued lobbying and political infighting, both by regional and other group interests, over the weights to be adopted. The resulting vicissitudes and conflict would go far to discredit cost–benefit techniques and, possibly, economists also.

(iii) Even if it were possible to secure permanent agreement within any one country on the set of *distributional* weights to be attached to the benefits and losses of different income groups, it could not be counted on to prevent the introduction of a project having a markedly regressive distributional impact. Of the projects that meet a distributionally weighted cost–benefit criterion some might well make the rich richer and the poor poorer if the beneficiaries were rich and many and the losers were poor and few. Such distributionally undesirable outcomes can be avoided only by separate consideration of the distributional impact of any contemplated project.

B. The proposal to employ politically determined parameters in project evaluation appears, on the surface, to be one arising from the modesty of the economist who overtly recognises the limitations of his craft, and particularly, his inability to place a socially acceptable valuation on a variety of social phenomena that are influenced by an investment project and that alter people's welfare for better or worse. But it is a modest proposal which issues in more ambitious claims for the *resulting technique*, one that is then held to 'integrate project planning and national policy' (see *Guidelines*, p. 5). For it purports to reduce to a single critical magnitude a variety of considerations, tangible and intangible. And if the parameters have been successfully determined by reference to political processes, and therefore bear the mark of political authority, the findings of the experts will be the more difficult to challenge.

The traditional cost–benefit approach is actually more modest and more explicit. Within the limits of partial analysis, the basic criterion is that of Kaldor–Hicks; in other words, a potential Pareto improvement.[8] There are obviously difficulties of estimation, partly because of future uncertainty. But, purged of difficulties, the cost–benefit criterion is met if the algebraic sum of the aggregate of compensating variations is positive.[9] Although many investment projects will have perceptible effects on some of the broader constituents of social welfare – on defence, on democratic participation, on the distribution of incomes and so on – such intangibles are to be excluded from the economist's calculation, as also are those benefits or losses that are potentially measurable but, owing to lack of data, cannot be reasonably approximated. The duty of the economist in such circumstances is to make clear to the public just what these exclusions are and to claim no more for his resulting calculation than what it is – an estimate, in money terms, of the excess of the gains to be secured by some persons above the losses to be borne by others as a result of the introduction of the project in question.

In this traditional approach the calculation of these gains and losses is made on a purely economic principle; that is, by placing a value on them by reference only to the subjective valuation of the persons affected by the project. Thus, if the government calls upon the economist to undertake a cost–benefit study, it presumably expects him to employ economic principles and only economic principles. If for any reason the economist encounters difficulties in evaluating some particular social benefit or cost item, he has the option of leaving its calculation out of the analysis and making it clear that he has done so. If, instead, he attempts to derive a value for this social benefit or social loss by reference to values that are implicit in recent political decisions (assuming they are consistent) he is, in effect, presenting the government with a result that depends, *inter alia*, on the government's own preferences or valuations and *not* on those of the individual citizens whose welfare will be affected by the project. The government having referred the problem to the economist for a solution, the economist, by these means, surreptitiously hands it back to the government.

Even where these political parameters are derived explicitly, say by cross-questioning the so-called policy-maker, the effect is the same in that the resulting calculation is no longer determined by reference to economic principles alone.

The government, if democratically elected, may of course claim to represent the nation. But it is hardly necessary to remind the reader that the ballot box can produce results very different from those of the market or those reached by an application of the Pareto principle. A majority may well vote in favour of the use of weights or parameters that would justify the introduction of *uneconomical* projects to be financed by the wealthier minority. Thus, if the present value of the cost of building a funfair for the community were £4 million and the present value of the maximum sums the members of the community were prepared to pay were equal to £3 million, the funfair project would not meet a cost–benefit criterion. But if a majority wanted the funfair built, it would not be hard to pass it off as a 'merit good' so as to attach to each pound of a benefit a weight, say, of two. Alternatively, since the poor would visit the funfair more than the rich, while the rich, through taxes, would pay more than the poor, by judiciously weighting the expected losses and gains of rich and poor, a 'utility' cost–benefit criterion could be met and, therefore, the funfair project pronounced economical.

Now there may be some good reasons why the community should have a funfair built despite the fact that it cannot meet a purely economic criterion. These reasons could be brought out in public debate and the decision taken to build the funfair. But there is everything to be said for making it abundantly clear that the project does *not* meet an economic criterion. For by 'doctoring' the method of evaluation so as to accommodate current political predilections, the economic facts are concealed from the public which is then misled into the belief that the proposal has the sanction of pure economic calculation, a belief that is likely to influence the course and outcome of any debate on the subject.

C. Now those who have sanctioned the use in cost–benefit analysis of national parameters calculated by reference to political decisions, or by reference to some other non-economic principle, might choose to regard the issue being raised here as basically a semantic one. After all, they may argue, there is nothing to prevent governments from making use of, or social scientists themselves evolving, methods that employ some of the economist's expertise in order to compare alternative projects *quite explicitly* in the light of national objectives. If it is really thought improper to extend the term cost–benefit analysis to the resultant technique then surely some other term can be employed for that purpose!

It may be contended, however, that the issue is not one of semantics but one of substance inasmuch as there are advantages in adhering exclusively to a traditional economic cost–benefit criterion and apparent disadvantages in departing from it.

First, the traditional cost–benefit approach is based on an economic criterion which is of a piece with that used by economists in judging the allocative merit of the economic system as a whole, or any portion of it. Thus, the economist's statement that social value would be augmented if resources were shifted from one use to another rests also on an acceptance of the familiar concept of a potential Pareto improvement.

Secondly, in a fairly competitive economic system, or in one at least where price–marginal cost ratios fall within a tolerable range, a cost–benefit analysis raised on a purely economic criterion may be thought of as an extension of a reasonably efficient price system, one that tends to select those enterprises that are expected to produce the greatest excess of social value over resource cost. Thus a project admitted on a purely economic cost–benefit criterion is clearly less likely to be allocatively at variance with other parts of the economy than would be a criterion modified by political parameters. If, for example, a dollar gained or lost by the rich is to be valued, in the project evaluation, as some fraction of that gained or lost by the poor, then investment projects may be undertaken which, on an economic cost–benefit criterion, yield a negative rate of return.

There may, of course, be social justification for introducing some projects that do not meet a traditional cost–benefit criterion. But using an economic cost–benefit criterion we should at least know just when we were introducing such uneconomic projects and, presumably, the reasons for it.[10] Incorporating a system of politically determined weights into the cost–benefit analysis, we should know *neither* whether we were incurring allocative losses nor whether we were making the distribution of incomes worse.

I should add in passing that while arguing for the exclusion of politically determined prices or parameters in project evaluation, no inconsistency is committed in simultaneously acknowledging the existence of political constraints. These do not offer to the economist arbitrary or non-economic valuations of goods or bads. They act only to circumscribe the range of choices open to the economist. They can best be regarded as information on how the government is expected to act or react to a change in relevant economic circumstances. In accepting these constraints, the economist does not have to endorse the government's policy. Indeed, he may go on record as opposing it. In taking into account the expected actions and reactions of the government, the economist is seeking only to discover whether, in these circumstances, the introduction of the mooted project will yet realise a potential Pareto improvement. In the endeavour to discover this, however, the economist may not also accept politically determined parameters or prices. He must restrict himself to *economic* prices – those arising from the subjective valuations of the persons whose welfares are affected by the project.

Thirdly, once politically determined valuations are believed pertinent to some agenda, there is no obvious case for limiting the extent of political intervention for this purpose. If decision-makers can attach weights to merit or demerit goods, why not also to the more ordinary goods on the argument that, as among ordinary goods also, some will have smaller social merit than others? If political decision-makers may attach a valuation to accidents or loss of life, why may they not also attach their own valuations to a wide range of other spillover effects? And if so much can be justified, there seems to be no logical reasons against going further, and having political decisions over-ride all market prices and individual valuations. There would then seem to be no reason why each and every investment project should not be approved or rejected directly by the political process, democratic or otherwise.

In such a dispensation the economist could, of course, entertain the politicians and the public by finesse in explicating the implicit prices or weights necessary to justify any particular investment decision. In their turn, the politicians and the public might busy themselves comparing implicit prices or weights emerging from one investment decision with those emerging from other investment decisions. Some of them might even become worried at evidence of inconsistencies and attempt to resolve them by securing at least some provisional consensus. Whatever the outcome, however, the resulting role assumed by the economist – as the creature of bureaucracy, or the agent of political opinion entrusted with the task of translating its current prejudices into respectable-looking numerals – is far removed from his traditional role as an independent specialist drawing his inspiration wholly from economic principles of valuation.

Finally, there is the crucial question of interpretation. Methods of evaluation that can claim no virtues other than those of 'marshalling data systematically putting them in quantitative terms, and rendering them as commensurable as possible' (Walsh and Williams, 1969, p. 3), have little to commend them if, in the process, fundamentally different criteria are being employed to produce a single magnitude. The use both of economic valuations and political parameters in a single project evaluation implies the simultaneous use of two criteria – individual subjective valuations being used for some welfare changes, and arbitrary or politically inspired valuations for others.

In general, when two or more criteria are jointly used problems arise. Even if we may suppose that each criterion, taken on its own, has merit enough for it to be socially acceptable, the application of either alone to an evaluation problem as compared with the application alone of the other(s) can yield very different and, as we have seen, possibly contradictory results. One may employ, say, two criteria in project evaluation only (i) if there is general agreement on some higher principle to which both can be referred in case of conflict or which demarcates, in advance, the area of application for each of the two criteria, and (ii) if the single resulting figure emerging from the application of these two criteria has a clear interpretation and social rationale.

Those who have proposed varieties of weighting systems,[11] or the occasional use of political parameters, have not yet recognised, much less faced up to, these difficulties.

D. In conclusion, it cannot too often be stressed that the traditional cost–benefit analysis, based wholly on an economic criterion, is no more than one useful technique in the service of social decisions. Indeed, the acceptance of this traditional, and more rigorous and limited, concept of cost–benefit analysis clearly implies that the outcome of a cost–benefit analysis is not by itself socially decisive. It is certainly not to be thought of as a substitute for economic policy. After all, cost–benefit analysis not only neglects distributional effects, it neglects equity. It may also have to ignore intangible spillover effects – though the economist must always make this explicit. Of the occasional influence of a project on broad social goals, the cost–benefit study can only draw public attention to the fact. In sum, a well-conducted cost–benefit study can be only a part, though sometimes an important part, of the data necessary for informed collective decisions. To quote from the penultimate paragraph of Prest and Turvey (1965): 'The case for using cost–benefit analysis is strengthened, not weakened, if its limitations are openly recognized and indeed emphasized'.

For reasons given above, attempts to work more into the technique of cost–benefit analysis, to endow it with greater self-sufficiency for policy purposes by recourse to distributional weights or national parameters, formulated by reference to political decisions or, at any rate, to non-economic considerations, are to be resisted by economists. True, those economists who choose otherwise, who are prepared to accept the idea that society should be guided in its economic activity by prices that are set by or through the political process, can always plead that they are simply following the wishes of those elected to take social decisions. But if they do so, they should not overlook the fact that once they accept from the political process prices or weights that have no necessary correspondence with the relevant subjective valuations of the members of society, they not only cease to offer the public an independent *economic* appraisal of any plan or project (independent, that is, of the existing policies and preferences of the government of the day), they may be unable to provide a coherent interpretation of their resulting calculations and, therefore, unable to provide a clear vindication of any recommendation based on them.

Notes: Chapter 14

1 More generally, of any sum G the government raises in order to finance a public project requiring a capital outlay of K, the fraction θ_g is placed in the private investment sector. Since the remainder, $G(1 - \theta_g)$, is to equal K, in

choosing to provide an outlay K the government raises the sum

$$G = \frac{K}{1 - \theta_g}$$

The social opportunity cost (SOC) of this sum is

$$aG = [S(\theta - \theta_g) + (1 - \theta)] \, G$$

In the special case in which θ_g is chosen to equal θ,

$$SOC = (1 - \theta)G = K$$

and the appropriate investment criterion

$$PV_r(B) > aG$$

becomes

$$PV_r(B) > K$$

where $PV_r(B)$ stands for the present value of the public project's benefit stream discounted at r, the social rate of time preference.

Where θ_g is chosen to be greater than θ,

$$aG < (1 - \theta)G$$

and therefore

$$SOC < K$$

It is then possible that

$$SOC < PV_r(B) < K$$

In the limiting case in which θ_g is set equal to unity, nothing is left for K. The government simply transfers all the sum G raised by taxes to the private investment sector. (If this is *politically* feasible, there can be no purely economic objection – unless particular public projects can produce a yield greater than ρ.)

2 An impressive specimen of what may be accomplished in this regard with a little patience and determination is to be found as equation (2) in Sen (1972, p. 492).

3 For simplicity, we ignore non-pecuniary considerations and costs of movement, and so on.

4 For a statement of the advantages claimed for a particular terminal-value investment criterion see my 1967 *Economic Journal* paper, also my *Cost–Benefit Analysis* (2nd edn, 1975). In such a scheme the 'shadow wage' is no more than the opportunity cost of labour to this project (that is, without any private-investment-loss component).

5 See Marglin (1963b). In that paper Marglin assumes that saving more for posterity confers a positive externality on the existing generation. Others have argued that inasmuch as the presumption is that future generations will be richer, additional 'social' saving entails a redistribution of income from poorer to richer generations, and would probably be regarded as a negative externality.

6 According to the authors of *Guidelines* (p. 104): 'The additional weights to be attached to the consumption of these poorer classes or groups are also a set of national parameters reflecting the relative weights on the redistribution objective *vis-à-vis* the objective of pursuing aggregate consumption'. In various parts of the volume they propose cross-questioning policy-makers in the attempt to derive these national weights.

7 For an application of distributional weights based on marginal rates of income tax to the figures produced by the Roskill Commission, see Nwaneri (1970).

8 According to the Commission on the Third London Airport (1971, p. 39):

> The analysis has been guided by the principle of accepting the scale of values apparently held by the people concerned, as revealed by their choice and behaviour. For *potential* possessions or activities, they are valued at what people would be prepared to pay to acquire them. For *existing* possessions or activities, things are valued at the minimum which people would be prepared to accept as just compensation for their loss.

9 In recognition of Professor Meade's justified criticism (1972) of the first edition of my *Cost–Benefit Analysis* I am prepared to recognise – at least in the absence of radical legislation on amenity rights – that any project should be able to meet two tests; aggregate *compensating* variations positive and aggregate *equivalent* variations negative.

10 An example of a project that does not meet a purely economic criterion is a transfer in cash or in kind to members of an underprivileged group. Nevertheless, the economist may be able to propose the form of transfer – the proportion of cash and the types of goods and services – likely to maximise the benefits over time of the recipients. Such an exercise, is, of course, subsumed by the analysis of cost-effectiveness.

11 It has been put to me by colleagues that it may be appropriate in project evaluation to have recourse to a sort of sensitivity analysis. Thus, by systematically varying the weights to be put on the gains and losses of different groups of people we can discover the critical sets of weights above or below which the project would appear unacceptable. I do not take to this idea. If there is to be any consensus on the weights to be used in a cost–benefit analysis, it should be reached in advance of, and therefore independently of, the critical sets of weights yielded by any particular project. If, on the other hand, the more extreme view is taken that no set of weights can properly be regarded as more valid than any other set ('It all depends on your social welfare function!'), then no project can ever be wholly rejected: for there will always be a conceivable set of weights which, when applied to a given set of numbers, will render the algebraic sum positive.

References

Commission on the Third London Airport (1971), *Papers and Proceedings*, vol. VII (London: HMSO).

Dasgupta, A. K. and Pearce, D. W. (1972), *Cost–Benefit Analysis: Theory and Practice* (London: Macmillan).

Dasgupta, P., Marglin, S. and Sen, A. (1972), *Guidelines for Project Evaluation* (New York: United Nations).

Little, I. M. D. and Mirrlees, J. (1969), *Social Cost–Benefit Analysis* (Paris: Organisation for Economic Co-operation and Development).

Mack, R. and Myers, S. (1965), 'Outdoor recreation', in *Measuring Benefits of Government Investments,* R. Dorfman (ed.) (Washington, DC: Brookings Institution), pp. 71–100.

Marglin, S. (1963a), 'The opportunity cost of public investment', *Quarterly Journal of Economics,* vol. 77, pp. 274–89.

Marglin, S. (1963b), 'The social rate of discount and the optimal rate of investment', *Quarterly Journal of Economics,* vol. 77, pp. 95–111.

Meade, J. E. (1972), Review of *Cost–Benefit Analysis* by E. J. Mishan, *Economic Journal,* vol. 82, pp. 244–6.

Mishan, E. J. (1967), 'A proposed normalization procedure for public investment criteria', *Economic Journal,* vol. 77, pp. 777–96.

Mishan, E. J. (1975), *Cost–Benefit Analysis,* 2nd edn (London: Allen & Unwin).

Nwaneri, V. C. (1970), 'Equity in cost–benefit analysis – Third London Airport', *Journal of Transport Economics and Policy,* vol. 4, pp. 235–54.

Prest, A. R. and Turvey, R. (1965), 'Cost–benefit analysis: a survey', *Economic Journal,* vol. 75, pp. 683–735.

Sen, A. K. (1972), 'Control areas and accounting prices: an approach to economic evaluation', *Economic Journal,* vol. 82, pp. 486–501.

US Department of Health, Education and Welfare (1969), *Toward a Social Report* (Washington, DC).

Walsh, H. G. and Williams, A. (1969), *Current Issues in Cost–Benefit Analysis,* CAS Occasional Paper, No. 11 (London: HMSO).

Warr, P. G. (1973), 'Savings propensities and the shadow wage', *Economica,* vol. 40, pp. 410–15.

Weisbrod, B. (1968), 'Income redistributive effects and benefit–cost analysis', in *Problems in Public Expenditure Analysis,* S. B. Chase (ed.) (Washington, DC: Brookings Institution), pp. 177–208.

15

The Use of Compensating and Equivalent Variations in Cost–Benefit Analysis

In the first edition of my *Cost–Benefit Analysis* (1971), I argued that the basic concept by reference to which gains and losses are to be estimated is the compensating variation (*CV*). Aside from objections arising from the problems of measurement, in particular of the measurement of the more intangible gains and losses that result from the introduction of an investment project, a number of objections have been argued recently against the use, or against the exclusive use, of the *CV* concept in cost–benefit analysis. Among those objections that concern us here are three:

(a) that a cost–benefit analysis based on *CV* alone fails to take account of considerations of equity. In particular, it ignores the distributional effects of a project;
(b) that the *CV* concept is an unreliable indicator of gains and losses;
(c) that the equivalent variation (*EV*) concept is, no less than the *CV* concept, a valid basis for cost–benefit analysis.

The chief issues in the first objection, however, have already been the subject matter of a recent paper (Mishan, 1974) in which I discuss the problems involved in ambitious attempts to extend cost–benefit techniques beyond the economic arithmetic of money gains and losses. I concluded there that, in consequence of the difficulties of integrating into a cost–benefit calculation other aspects of a relevant (though incompletely charted) social welfare function, economists should continue to confine their efforts to obtaining estimates of monetary gains and losses – although with the strict proviso that the outcome of such a calculation be *not* regarded as decisive, but simply as one element in a social decision criterion.

However, since the proposal for the introduction of distributional weights, as a means of remedying an alleged deficiency of the *CV* basis of cost–benefit analysis, has arisen again in connection with the second objection listed above, I shall find occasion, later on, to summarise some of the problems that arise in any attempt to implement such a proposal.

The second and third objections have been put forward, respectively, in a paper by Boadway (1974) and in a review by Meade (1972) of the first edition of my *Cost–Benefit Analysis*. I have been persuaded by Professor Meade's arguments, and I amend my position accordingly in section V. On the other hand, I reject Boadway's analysis for reasons given below; notwithstanding which, I welcome his article as drawing attention to a possible misconception, and as affording the opportunity of developing my own views further with the object of sharpening our understanding of the seeming paradoxes that are latent in the economic concepts of gains and losses.

Boadway's reappraisal of the *CV* base of cost–benefit analysis is unsatisfactory for a number of reasons. First, it is marred throughout by an error that makes the use of *CV* in cost-benefit analysis appear paradoxical in conditions under which, in fact, it is quite unambiguous. Secondly, the seeming paradox that survives this correction is, as it happens, of ancient vintage and related to the Kaldor–Hicks–Scitovsky findings of over thirty years ago. The likelihood of its occurrence, moreover, had already been discussed in chapter 46 of my *Cost–Benefit Analysis* (1st edn), and the solution to that kind of paradox discussed at length in my 1973 paper. Thirdly, since no mention is made of these bits of analyses, and no mention is made either of another significant source of paradox arising from the use of the *CV* concept (Mishan, 1967), Boadway's analysis fails to place the issues in perspective. Fourthly, the solution proposed by Boadway of attaching distributional weights to money gains and losses is unacceptable in itself and, in any case, cannot resolve the apparent paradoxes.

Although each of the above criticisms are elaborated in that order, they also find a place as part of the structure of a more general analysis.

I   The Pure Redistribution Case

Let us first go over the analysis of Boadway's 'single batch – pure redistribution case' (p. 932). My Figure 1(a) reproduces the essentials of his figure 2, although I find it convenient to use different lettering, and to indicate the community's fixed collection of two goods, X and Y, by Q measured from the origin O. Person A's indifference curves are ordered from O, of which only two, a_3 and a_6, are shown. Likewise, person B's indifference curves are ordered from point Q, of which b_3 and b_6 are shown. Two efficient distributions, d_1 and d_2, are indicated on the resulting contract curve, the slope of the mutual tangencies at these points being given by the relative price lines p_1 and p_2 respectively.

A purely redistributive movement is one from d_1 to d_2. Clearly such a movement cannot achieve a Pareto improvement – nor, for that matter, a potential Pareto improvement. Yet, according to Boadway, the move to d_2 can meet the ΣCV test (the requirement that $\Sigma CV > 0$) since A's gain, measured in terms of Y, is equal to CE, a sum that exceeds B's loss of DE leaving a net gain of CD.

In calculating the ΣCV, A's gain and B's loss are measured, properly, at the p_2 prices. It is to be observed, however, that in order for A to show a CV gain equal to CE, his movement to d_2 along p_2 has to be *not* from the actual point d_1 on his a_3 curve, but from a point a' on his a_3 curve which is tangent to his p_2', the slope of the p_2 prices. At this point a', however, person A chooses Oy_a of Y and Ox_a of X. Similarly, in order to show a loss equal to ED for person B, the movement to d_2 that is envisaged is *not* from the actual point d_1 on his b_6 indifference curve, but from a point b' on that curve. At this point b', however, person B is choosing Qy_6 of Y and Qx_b of X.

It follows that, in order to obtain this result that $\Sigma CV = CD$, the amounts of X and Y that persons A and B are (together) assumed to hold prior to their movement to the chosen position d_2 at p_2 prices – amounts indicated by a' and b' respectively – are clearly *not* equal to those given by the Q collection. Indeed, the excess of X jointly required is measured by qa' and the shortfall of Y by $b'q$. In fact, the initial quantities of X and Y required jointly by persons A and B are given, instead, by the distribution d_1' on the contract curve of a quite different collection Q', shown in Figure 1(b).

By construction, QQ_0 in Figure 1(b) is equal to $b'q$ in Figures 1(a) and 1(b), and Q_0Q' in Figure 1(b) is equal to qa' in Figure 1(a) (and equal to qd' in Figure 1(b)). Again

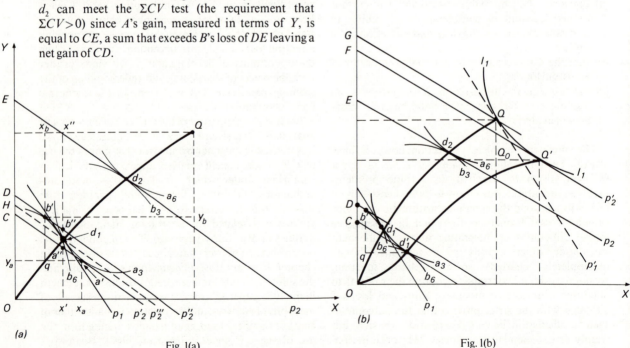

(a)

Fig. 1(a)

(b)

Fig. 1(b)

by construction, the points a' and b' in Figure 1(a) come together in Figure 1(b) in mutual tangency d_1' on the OQ' contract curve. Indeed, since points d_1 and d_1' on the Q and Q' contract curves, respectively, both represent welfare combinations a_3 and b_6, a community indifference curve I_1, comprehending all (efficient) welfare combinations a_3 and b_6, passes through Q with slope equal to p_1 and through Q' with slope equal to p_2. Therefore, what Boadway in effect ends up comparing is *not*, as he thought, points d_1 and d_2 on the contract curve of a single collection Q, but, instead, a point d_1', on the contract curve of another and quite different collection Q', with the point d_2 on the contract curve of the original collection Q. And in comparing two different collections, Q' and Q, with the p_2 prices, corresponding to the mutual tangency d_2, it is obviously possible for Q to be valued higher than Q'. Thus, by constructing price lines parallel to p_2 through Q' and Q, the Y axis in Figure 1(b) is intersected respectively at F and G. From this it follows that, at the p_2 prices, collection Q is valued higher than collection Q' by FG of Y in Figure 1(b) – where FG in Figure 1(b) is equal, by construction, to CD in Figures 1(a) and 1(b).

It may be noted, in passing, that since the *actual* distributions of Q and Q' are d_2 and d_1' respectively and, therefore, the *actual* prices at which the collections Q and Q' are marketed are equal to p_2 in both cases, Q will be valued higher than Q' both in the movement from Q to Q' and also in the reverse movement from Q' to Q. However, if the actual distribution of Q' were not d_1' (as required by the Boadway exercise), but were instead some other efficient distribution having a 'steeper' mutual tangency and, therefore, a 'steeper' price set, say p_1 – that is, X dearer in terms of Y – we should not be surprised to discover that, at this resulting p_1 price set, the collection Q' was valued higher than Q.

Let us now return for a moment to Boadway's 'single batch' construction in order to explore the implied quantity constraints in the CV measure of a pure redistribution of a fixed amount of goods as between persons A and B.

In determining the CV of persons A and B in moving from d_1 (chosen with the p_1 prices) to d_2 (chosen with the p_2 prices), it must be borne in mind that they will be unable to move from the d_1 division of the Q collection without, as indicated above, violating the quantitative restrictions of the model. If the implied quantity constraint in the movement from d_1 to d_2 is ignored, as it is by Boadway, then the *apparent* compensating variation, CV', for the gainer, person A, will in general be larger than the true compensating variation, CV. In contrast, the CV' for the loser, person B, which bears a negative sign, will in general be absolutely smaller than

the true CV. In general, therefore, the $\Sigma CV'$ will be larger than the true ΣCV – which true ΣCV is, not surprisingly, zero for any efficient redistribution of some fixed collection of goods. For the maximum sum person A will pay to move from a fixed d_1 to the new position d_2 with the p_2 price set is HE, whereas the smallest sum that will compensate person B for having to move from a fixed d_1 position to the new d_2 position at the p_2 prices is EH, the ΣCV being, then, exactly zero.

Let us be quite clear in our minds about the operation of this constraint since it is critical to the understanding of the two-batch case, which is pertinent to any cost–benefit calculation. Taking Y to be money (all other goods at fixed prices), suppose person A were asked to name the largest sum he would pay to have the opportunity of the budget line p_2, in Figure 1(a). If he ignores the quantity constraint, his true answer would be CE. By ignoring the quantity constraint also, person B's true answer to the question of the least sum he would accept to move to the budget line p_2 would be ED. The resulting $\Sigma CV'$ is CD, an apparent net gain. As a result, let us say, the change is made.

Person A now discovers that he offered too much for the benefit of the change to p_2. For he had counted on being able to move from d_1 to a' with the p_2 price set, involving an increase of X from Ox' to OX_a. If this could be done then, indeed, he would be no worse off than before when giving up as much as HE to move to d_2 on the p_2 budget line. But, of course, he cannot do this: he cannot, that is, increase his amount of X by $x'x_a$. Nor can B increase his amount of X by $x''x_b$. When A realises that he is stuck with Ox' of X, the sum CE he gave up leaves him at a'', on an indifference curve below his original a_3. He therefore suffers a loss equal to HC. Similarly, when B realises that he is stuck with Ox'' of X, the sum ED paid to him leaves him at b'' on an indifference curve below his original b_6. He therefore suffers a loss equal to DH. The sum of these unanticipated shortfalls equals DC, which exactly offsets the $\Sigma CV'$ equal to CD.

We may conclude that, in this gratuitous single-batch exercise, the fault lies not in the compensating variation concept, but in its misuse; in using the $\Sigma CV'$ measure, which, when the quantity constraint is operative, exceeds the true ΣCV measure.

II The Two-Batch Case

From the preceding analysis we may conclude that, for a given set of prices, say p_2, the value of a given batch of goods, say Q_1 in Figure 2, remains the same at OE (in terms of Y), irrespective of its efficient distribution. Since the other batch of goods, Q_2 in Figure 2, when valued at the same p_2 prices – the price set that happens here to coincide with the actual d_2 distribution of Q_2 – is equal to OF, again regardless of Q_2's efficient distribution, it is evident that $p_2Q_2 > p_2Q_1$ by the amount EF. This EF is, of course, the ΣCV (measured in terms of Y) of the movement from Q_1 to Q_2.

It is to be emphasised that, in calculating the ΣCV of the movement from collection Q_1 to collection Q_2, we attend to the actual (and not the hypothetical) changes in the amounts of X and Y affecting each person as a result of the movement from the d_1 division of Q_1 to the d_2 division of Q_2. From the construction of Figure 2, person A is seen to obtain more of both X and Y in the movement from d_1 to d_2, whereas person B is seen to lose some of both X and Y. In order to calculate the CV of each person, construct lines p_2''' and p_2'' parallel to p_2 and passing respectively through d_1 and d_2. The CV of the $d_1 - d_2$ change to person A is equal to CJ.

The geometric measure of person B's CV requires that his amounts of X and Y, given by d_2 with respect to point Q_2, be represented by d_2' with respect now to point Q_1. This point d_2' is determined, incidentally, by a downward movement from d_2 to q (a vertical distance equal to Q_2Q_0) followed by a rightward movement from q to d_2' (a horizontal distance equal to Q_0Q_1). Draw p_2'''' parallel to p_2 and passing through d_2'. On person B's indifference curves, as ordered now from Q_1, the movement is from his original d_1 quantities to the d_2' quantities chosen on the p_2'''' budget line. Measured along the Y-axis, B's CV of this loss of welfare is therefore equal to KC.

So calculated, the ΣCV is, therefore, CJ less KC, or a net gain of KJ. Since, by construction, d_2' is positioned with respect to d_2 as Q_1 is with respect to Q_2, this distance KJ is equal to EF – the alternative measure of ΣCV given above, as the value (in terms of Y) by which, at the p_2 prices, Q_2 exceeds Q_1. (Needless to say, if Boadway's CV' method of calculating compensating variations were adopted, person A's CV' gain would be gJ, person B's CV' loss would be Kh, the $\Sigma CV'$ being equal therefore to $(EF + gh)$; or gh more than the correct ΣCV sum. In fact, Boadway continues to calculate $\Sigma CV'$ to the end of his paper. Thus, in his final figure 5 (p. 937), the new price, say p_2, given by the slope of his bb line should pass through position I on the contract curve O_aO_b so as to correct for the quantity constraint in the CV measure of the movement from I to II with p_2 prices. Making this correction, it turns out that (by reference to the construction of his figure) the net loss from the movement – equal also to the vertical distance between two parallel p_2 lines drawn to pass respectively

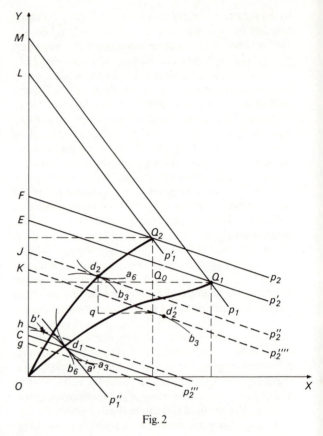

Fig. 2

through Ob and $O'b$ – is less than the $\Sigma CV'$, or bc; indeed, it is close to zero.)

It is, of course, just possible that the price set actually associated with d_1 distribution of Q_1 is also p_2, the actual price set of the Q_2 collection. In Figure 1(b), for instance, the collection Q' had to be constructed as to have just this property. But, in general, if the change from Q_1 to Q_2 involves large changes in aggregate quantities, one or more prices can be expected to change perceptibly. In this more general case, in which p_1 differs from p_2, the amounts of X and Y that persons A and B would each be willing to take at the p_2 prices *subject to the maintenance of their original welfares*, in the Q_1 position (indicated, respectively, by a' and b'), will differ from the amounts they are constrained to take at d_1. Consequently, as indicated, the constrained ΣCV must, in general, be less than the calculation of $\Sigma CV'$, based, as is the latter, on the false premise that, in contemplating the move to d_2, these former (hypothetical) quantities of X and Y are, indeed, available to A and B.

Although we do well to take note of the distinction between CV and CV', if only to guard against the exhilaration of discovering illusory paradoxes, the difference between a calculation of ΣCV and that of $\Sigma CV'$ is likely to be swamped by errors of measurement – bearing in mind, in particular, that the economist today is very satisfied if he can obtain good measures of the areas under the relevant demand curves as proxies for the true consumer surpluses.

III   Contradictory Possibilities in the Two- Batch Case

The larger the change in the quantities of goods involved in moving from batch Q_1 to Q_2, the greater the scope for differences in the price sets p_1 and p_2 associated, respectively, with their efficient distributions d_1 and d_2. Let us denote ΣCV from Q_1 and Q_2 as $\Sigma CV(12)$. The preceding section has shown $\Sigma CV(12)$ to be equal to the quantity difference between the two batches when calculated at the p_2 prices; equal, that is, to $(p_2Q_2 - p_2Q_1)$.

In the 'straightforward' case, a positive $\Sigma CV(12)$ is confirmed by a negative $\Sigma CV(21)$, and vice versa; that is to say, an apparent gain in moving from Q_1 to Q_2 (with p_2 prices) is confirmed by an apparent loss in moving back from Q_2 to Q_1 (with p_1 prices), and vice versa. Ignoring errors of measurement, the greater is the net benefit ratio of an investment project, the more likely is the case to be 'straightforward'. Put otherwise, the larger the positive value of $\Sigma CV(12)$, at least as a proportion of the investment, the more likely that $\Sigma CV(21)$ will take the opposite sign, even though the absolute figure will generally differ.

Yet it is, of course, entirely possible that the price changes accompanying the change in quantities are (as a result, perhaps, of the associated change in distribution) large enough to produce the awkward result that a positive $\Sigma CV(12)$ is accompanied also by a positive $\Sigma CV(21)$. In fact, Figure 2 has been constructed so that $\Sigma CV(21)$, measured as $p_1(Q_1 - Q_2)$ and, therefore, equal to LM, is also positive.

What may be inferred about the comparative merits of Q_1 and Q_2 in such a case? Before the answer emerges, we must make a distinction: for the outcome, $p_2Q_2 > p_2Q_1$ and $p_1Q_1 > p_1Q_2$ can be interpreted either as (a) precise measures of $\Sigma CV(12)$ and $\Sigma CV(21)$ respectively, or else (b), as sufficient conditions for two alternative tests of hypothetical compensation.

Consider the latter more closely. If we ask the question, whether everyone *could* (with costless distribution) be made worse off with the Q_1 batch than he is with the Q_2 batch, we are posing a test of hypothetical compensation. The answer to the question would emerge from comparing the community indifference curve based on the d_2 distribution, passing through Q_2, with a community indifference curve passing through Q_1, though based on a distribution of the Q_1 batch that is Pareto-comparable with the d_2 welfare combination. This sort of hypothetical test is, in effect, the crucial concept in the question asked by Samuelson (1939) and, later, by Kemp (1962): whether free trade, or some trade (the Q_2 position), is better than no trade (the Q_1 position). The information that $p_2Q_2 > p_2Q_1$ can, of course, always be interpreted more directly, as Samuelson and Kemp intended it should, as 'revealing' a social preference for the Q_2 batch. However, such information can also be interpreted as Hicks (1940) chose to: as a *sufficient* condition for the above test of hypothetical compensation to be satisfied. (The reader can easily assure himself that meeting this test is *not* necessary for the satisfaction of hypothetical compensation by drawing the p_2 line through Q_2 to pass, instead, just below Q_1, at the same time constructing the Q_2 community indifference curve to pass above Q_1.)

As we know from the literature, however, the information $p_2Q_2 > p_2Q_1$ is not only unnecessary for satisfying the hypothetical compensation test favouring Q_2. When that test is satisfied, it can be contradicted by a similar hypothetical compensation test favouring Q_1. Hence, the inference that $p_2Q_2 > p_2Q_1$ and $p_1Q_1 > p_1Q_2$ can be interpreted either as an apparent contradiction of the revealed preference tests or else as *sufficient* conditions for the apparent contradiction of tests of hypothetical compensation. (Again, the reader can convince himself that these 'contradictory' price–quantity data are not *necessary* for the apparent contradiction of the corresponding hypothetical compensation tests by constructing a figure in which the p_2 price line, passing through Q_2, and the p_1 price line, passing through Q_1, do *not* intersect between Q_1 and Q_2; yet at the same time the community indifference curve passing through Q_2, and based on the d_2 welfare combination, lies above Q_1, while the community indifference curve passing through Q_1, and based on the d_1 welfare combination, lies above Q_2. The sufficient condition for the related Kaldor–Hicks test to be met is, however, that $p_1Q_1 < p_1Q_2$. And the sufficient condition for it to be contradicted by the reversal test proposed by Scitovsky is $p_2Q_2 < p_2Q_1$.)

Now although the same techniques are used, and the same apparent contradictions generated, in (a) ΣCV tests, on the one hand, and (b) the tests both of hypothetical compensation and revealed preference just referred to on the other, the interpretation of these two sorts of test differ. In the hypothetical compensation (or revealed preference) test, the division of one of the batches of goods being compared, say the Q_1 batch, is purely *hypothetical*: for the question being posed is whether this Q_1 batch *could be* (costlessly) distributed among the individuals so as to make each one of them worse off (or, alternatively, each one of them better off) than he actually is with the Q_2 batch. In the ΣCV test, in contrast, we are algebraically summing the money gains and losses of all individuals in moving, say, from the Q_1 to the Q_2 quantities at a given set of prices, say p_2. We are, then, comparing the *actual* quantities held by each individual in the Q_1 position with the *actual* quantities held by each individual in the Q_2 position.

Notwithstanding this important difference in the question being asked by the two sorts of test, the underlying reality of both the questions being asked can be represented by a construction such as that in Figure 2, elaborated, if necessary, for our understanding by the inclusion of the relevant community indifference curves I_2 and I_1 (not shown in the figure) passing through Q_2 and Q_1 respectively. For this reason, if both $\Sigma CV(12) > 0$ and $\Sigma CV(21) > 0$; that is, if the data reveal that $p_2Q_2 > p_2Q_1$ and also $p_1Q_1 > p_1Q_2$, then we are sure that the I_2 and I_1 community indifference curves intersect between Q_2 and Q_1. And knowing this much, we can refer to a recently established theorem (Mishan, 1973) which says that, wherever such community indifference curves intersect, no allocative ranking of Q_1 and Q_2 is possible. Furthermore, since the welfare combinations associated with the d_1 and d_2 distributions of Q_1 and Q_2 respectively can be shown to be alternative distributions of a third hypothetical batch, say Q_3, the actual welfare combinations associated with Q_1 and Q_2 can be ranked, if at all, only by reference to a distributional ordering.

It follows, therefore, that if the economist discovers that $\Sigma CV(12)$ and $\Sigma CV(21)$ are both positive, he must perforce conclude – assuming, always, the accuracy and relevance of his calculations – that the ranking of Q_1 and Q_2 on an unambiguous allocative basis is not possible. This discovery does not, however, preclude a satisfactory ranking of Q_1 and Q_2 on some other social criterion. Smith and Stephen's note (1975) on Boadway is unacceptable simply because, in any cost–benefit approach, the ΣCV for their change from *I* to *II* (or *II* to *I*) would not be measured as *TU* in their figures 1–3, by reference to hypothetical batches. Moreover, the intersection of the two community indifference curves in all of their figures implies that allocative ranking of the change from *I* to *II* is in any case impossible (as indicated in my 1973 paper).

IV   An Alternative Source of the Apparent Paradox

By reference to the conventional definitions, the *CV* for a movement from situation 1 to situation 2 is exactly equal to the equivalent variation (*EV*) for the reverse movement, from 2 to 1. In Figure 2, for example, person *A*'s $CV(12)$ for a movement from his d_1 quantities of *X* and *Y* to the larger d_2 quantities chosen on the p_2 budget line is equal to a payment of *CJ* of *Y*. But his $EV(21)$, the sum of money to be transferred (here paid by him) in order to ensure the exact level of welfare corresponding to the new position, d_1, chosen with budget p_1, when in fact he has to remain at the original d_2 position, is also equal to *CJ*, and therefore also equal to $CV(12)$. Likewise, person *A*'s $CV(21)$, for a movement from his d_2 quantities to the d_1 quantities chosen with the p_1 budget line, is equal to his $EV(12)$.

The awkward cases, $\Sigma CV(12)$ and $\Sigma CV(21)$, both positive or both negative, can therefore be translated into the cases in which $\Sigma CV(12)$ and $\Sigma EV(12)$ both have the same sign; either both positive, as when $p_2Q_2 > p_2Q_1$ and also $p_1Q_1 > p_1Q_2$ (as in Figure 2) or else both negative (not shown in the figure).

So far, the explanation of the seemingly contradictory possibility, $\Sigma CV(12)$ and $\Sigma EV(12)$ of the same sign, has turned on a difference in the price sets p_1 and p_2, corresponding to Q_1 and Q_2, which are common to all the individuals. For convenience, this kind of explanation will be referred to as explanation (I). And a little more notation will be introduced in order to contrast this case more sharply with explanation (II), a different explanation of the seeming contradiction.

In general, where the number of goods and their corresponding prices exceeds two, we can write Σp_2 for the market prices of all goods in the Q_2 batch, and Σp_1 for the market prices of all goods in the Q_1 batch. For $(Q_2 - Q_1)$ we write ΔQ, and for the reverse movement $(Q_1 - Q_2)$, we write $(-\Delta Q)$. This sum of changes in the batch of goods, ΔQ, is of course equal to the algebraic aggregate of the changes in goods experienced by each person in the movement from Q_1 to Q_2, with $(-\Delta Q)$ being the algebraic aggregate of their changes for the reverse movement, from Q_2 to Q_1. We already know from the preceding analysis that, irrespective of the distributions of Q_2 and Q_1, the value of $\Sigma CV(12)$, say, measured by reference to the Σp_2 prices, remains unchanged. If *Y*, measured vertically, is taken to be the *numeraire*, or 'money', the *CV* of each person's welfare change is measured as the sum of money $\Sigma p_2 \Delta q$, where Δq represents the particular change in the amounts of goods he buys following the change from Q_1 to Q_2. By reference, instead, to a marginal indifference curve i_0

(where i_0 is the curve of the first derivative of his original indifference curve I_0 with respect to X), the individual's CV can be calculated as a line integral. The CV measure from this structure must obviously differ from that above, being approximated by the area Δp $(q + \frac{1}{2}\Delta q)$.

In Figure 2, the following relationships are represented:

$$\Sigma CV(12) = \Sigma p_2 \Delta Q = \Sigma p_2 (Q_2 - Q_1) = EF > 0$$
$$\Sigma EV(12) = \Sigma p_1 (-\Delta Q) = \Sigma p_1 (Q_1 - Q_2) = LM > 0$$

For this result, the (I) explanation applies. The prices, and therefore the price changes, are the same for all persons. The quantity changes, however, will in general be different as between persons. For an explanation in terms of the (II) case, on the other hand, the reverse is true. The change in the amount of the item in question – usually a collective good-cum-bad – is either the same for each person or, if different, is unalterable. More generally, the amounts of the accompanying bads, or external diseconomies, are alterable only if expenditures are incurred by the victims.

Inasmuch as each person cannot alter the amount of the collective bad affecting his welfare (nor, perhaps, the amount of the collective good), there being no market in these externalities, a uniform price for the relevant bad or good will not exist: in terms of the *numeraire*, the marginal valuation of the bad or good will differ from one person to another. What is more significant in this connection, however, is that whatever the valuation the individual puts on the increment of good or bad will also differ (in absolute terms) according as the change is included in Δq – the quantity changes affecting the individual in the movement from Q_1 to Q_2 – or in the reverse change $(-\Delta q)$. Thus, even if the prices of all market goods remain constant in the movement from Q_1 to Q_2 or from Q_2 to Q_1, there can be (absolute) differences in each individual's valuation of the *increments* of non-market goods or bads according as this change is included in his Δq or in his $(-\Delta q)$. And this difference in valuation arises specifically from the existence of welfare effects (or 'income effects'). A person who is ready to pay up to 100 for an increment of a good (or the removal of an increment of bad) will, if the welfare effect is positive, need to receive more than 100 if he is to be induced to part with the good (or put up with the bad).

It can be shown that the introduction of a project having no effect whatever on market prices but, in consequence of a collective item involved in it, raising the welfare of one group A while reducing the welfare of

the remaining group B can also produce a seeming contradiction. Given positive welfare effects, however, it is to be noted that if $\Sigma CV(12) > 0$, then the position is unambiguous. For it follows that $\Sigma CV(21)$, or $\Sigma EV(12)$, has to be negative. Indeed, in absolute terms, this $\Sigma EV(12)$ will be greater than $\Sigma CV(12)$. In other words, if for this case the project is accepted on the ΣCV test, it will *a fortiori* be accepted on the ΣEV test.

To illustrate, if the most that the A group will pay for the introduction of the project is 100 and the least sum the B group must receive in compensation is 80, the $\Sigma CV(12)$ is positive – an excess of payments over receipts of 20. In order to forgo the introduction of the project, however, the A group will want more than 100, say 120, whereas the B group will be willing to pay less than 80, say 70. The resulting $\Sigma EV(12)$ of –50, the shortfall of payments over receipts, confirms the net gain from introducing the project.

The logic of the above example also suggests that if $\Sigma EV(12) > 0$, then $CV(12) < 0$ by a greater (absolute) sum. Thus, for this case, if the project is rejected by the ΣEV test, it will *a fortiori* be rejected by the ΣCV test.

There are however two awkard possibilities: (a) if $\Sigma CV(12) < 0$, it is also possible for $EV(12) < 0$; and, of course (b) if $EV(12) < 0$, it is also possible for $\Sigma CV(12) < 0$. (For example, for the introduction of the project, A would pay 80 and B must receive 100, giving a $\Sigma CV(12)$ of –20. For the abandonment of the project, on the other hand, A must receive 100 and B would be willing to pay 90, giving an $\Sigma EV(12)$ of –10. Thus the project is rejected on the ΣCV test and accepted on the ΣEV test.) This means that, if a project is rejected on the ΣCV test, it may be accepted on the EV test; also, of course, if a project is accepted on the ΣEV test, it may be rejected on the ΣCV test.

V Relevance of Explanation (II) to Environmental Projects

This paradox arising from explanation (II) is of particular importance for appraising projects that have significant environmental impact, since there is no market for the collective good and certainly none for the accompanying collective bad, or external diseconomies, if there are any. Yet the effect on the community's welfare can be substantial. For this reason the difference in the (absolute) magnitudes of the ΣCV and the ΣEV tests can be large.

Now it was just because the introduction of a number of large projects having manifestly detrimental effects on the environment was being rationalised by cost–benefit techniques that sought to calculate the resulting disamenity by reference to the ΣEV test – which evaluates the disamenity by the maximum sums the victims would pay to avoid it – that I came down in my *Cost–Benefit Analysis* (1st edn) in favour of the ΣCV test. For such a test implies that the value of the amenity to be destroyed be calculated, instead, by reference to the minimum sums required to compensate the losers.

However, as Meade (1972) correctly remarks, not all public projects are, or need be, destructive of amenity. If, for example, we consider a project specifically designed to enhance environmental amenity, the value of the amenity to be created is to be valued on the ΣCV test as the maximum sum the beneficiaries are able and willing to pay for it. On the same test, the losses of those opposed to the proposed amenity is to be reckoned as the minimum sum that adequately compensates them. For such a project, the ΣEV test is clearly more favourable.

The pro-environmental economist would, of course, like to use the ΣCV test in order to deter projects that destroy amenity and to use the ΣEV test in order to encourage projects that create amenity. And it is interesting to reflect that he could, in effect, have it both ways in a society that recognised constitutional amenity rights for its citizens covering a specific range of environmental goods. For under such a dispensation, any project designed to create an amenity could legitimately be regarded as restoring to the citizen what is his by right, in which case the amenity in question is properly valued as the sum, compensating him for a presumed infringement of his right to it.

In the absence of such a law, however, the detached economist must agree that there is no morally binding reason why the ΣCV calculation should be the basic concept in cost–benefit analysis to the exclusion of the ΣEV calculation.

Let us remind ourselves, however, that the difference in the two tests matters only in the case of seeming contradiction. If this arises from the (I) explanation, which turns on changes in market prices, the economist recognises that an unambiguous allocative ranking is not possible anyway. If, on the other hand, the explanation of the seeming contradiction is of the (II) kind, the economist will, again, be unable to come down in favour or against the project on allocative grounds.

It may be mentioned in passing that where the seeming contradiction arises predominantly from the latter explanation – which implies that the project is one causing significant environmental effects but relatively insignificant changes in market prices – the economist does not necessarily have to undertake both calculations. He can begin with either. If, for example,

the ΣCV calculation were the easier, a positive sum would suffice to indicate an unequivocal gain since, as we have seen, it cannot be upset by the ΣEV test. If, instead, the ΣEV calculation were the easier, a positive sum would suffice to indicate an unequivocal loss since, again, it cannot be upset by the ΣCV test. Only if the ΣCV test rejects the project, or the ΣEV test approves it, can there be a seeming contradiction. The economist is then obliged to undertake both tests.

VI Summary and Conclusions

The use of compensation variation tests in cost–benefit analysis can, indeed, give rise to seeming contradictions. Among them, however, is not the one imagined by Boadway. Once such tests are amended to allow for the relevant quantity constraints implied by the model, no redistributions of a single batch of goods can generate a positive ΣCV.

A cost–benefit problem, however, can be represented only by a two-batch comparison involving a change in the total amount of goods. Seeming contradictions that arise from the use of ΣCV and ΣEV tests derive from two different explanations. In explanation (I), if the changes in market prices that accompany the changes in the quantities of the goods are large enough, a ΣCV test can give the opposite result to a ΣEV test. In such event, neither net benefit figure has economic significance, though the distributional effects may be important.

On the other hand, the explanation of the seeming contradiction may be of the (II) kind, the project in question generating goods and bads that have no market prices. 'For 'normal' (positive) welfare effects, it is possible for a project that is rejected on the ΣCV test to be accepted on the ΣEV test, and vice versa. If so, the net benefit figures given by the two tests are ignored, although, again, the project may be accepted or rejected on other than allocative criteria.

Even though the occurrence of seemingly contradictory tests may be unlikely in actual cost–benefit analyses, especially those arising from explanation (I), there is no satisfactory way of circumventing this possibility. True, a number of economists (recently, Weisbrod, 1968; Dasgupta and Pearce, 1972; Dasgupta *et al.*, 1972) have argued that considerations of equity or distribution can be promoted by applying explicit or implicit distributional (or other) weights to the calculated money gains and losses of different groups. Such proposals have impelled me to point out the difficulties that arise in determining and applying any system of weights (Mishan, 1974). Of particular relevance is the fact that, whatever the system of distributional weights employed, the resulting calculation might still approve projects that make the poor worse off and the rich better off – a contingency that can be guarded against, therefore, only by separate consideration of the distributional effects.

What is more to the purpose in our present concern, no system of distributional weights can prevent the possibility of a weighted ΣCV calculation being contradicted by a weighted ΣEV calculation. For particular projects, of course, the weights chosen could be such that the results of the weighted calculations would not seemingly contradict, whereas the unweighted calculations would do so. But for the same set of weights, there can be other projects for which the reverse is true, the weighted ΣCV and ΣEV calculations showing contradictory results in contrast to the unweighted calculations.

Only if we are ready to forgo the use of money, or any *numeraire* good, in the calculation of individual gains and losses and, instead, have recourse to measuring the change in each individual's welfare directly in terms of cardinal utility, can we ensure a unique 'util' measure of the change in social welfare caused by an investment project. Should this ever come to pass, however, we should be faced with the problem of bringing this 'util' criterion into relation with allocative criteria used in the economy at large. Perhaps we should be satisfied with the problems we already have.

References

Boadway, R. W. (1974), 'The welfare foundations of cost–benefit analysis', *Economic Journal*, vol. 84, pp. 926–39.

Dasgupta, A. K. and Pearce, D. W. (1972), *Cost-Benefit Analysis: Theory and Practice* (London: Macmillan).

Dasgupta, P., Marglin, S. and Sen, A. (1972), *Guidelines for Project Evaluation* (New York: United Nations).

Hicks, J. R. (1940), 'The valuation of the social income', *Economica*, vol. 7, pp. 105–24.

Kemp, M. S. (1962), 'The gains from international trade', *Economic Journal*, vol. 72, pp. 803–19.

Meade, J. E. (1972), 'Review of *Cost–Benefit Analysis* by E. J. Mishan, *Economic Journal*, vol. 82, pp. 244–6.

Mishan, E. J. (1967), 'Pareto optimality and the law', *Oxford Economic Papers*, vol. 19, pp. 255–87.

Mishan, E. J. (1971), *Cost–Benefit Analysis* (London: Allen & Unwin).

Mishan, E. J. (1973), 'Welfare criteria: resolution of a paradox', *Economic Journal*, vol. 83, pp. 747–67.

Mishan, E. J. (1974), 'Flexibility and consistency in cost–benefit analysis', *Economica*, vol. 41, pp. 81–96.

Samuelson, P. A. (1939), 'The gains from international trade', *Canadian Journal of Economics*, vol. 5, pp. 195–205.

Smith, B. and Stephen, F. H. (1975), 'Cost–benefit analysis and compensation criteria: a note', *Economic Journal*, vol. 85, pp. 902–5.

Weisbrod, B. (1968), 'Income redistributive effects and benefit–cost analysis', in *Problems in Public Expenditure Analysis*, S. B. Chase (ed.) (Washington, DC: Brookings Institution), pp. 177–208.

16

The Nature of Economic Expertise Reconsidered

Do we need another debate on the rationale of the economist's rules for resource allocation? Since the 1920s there has been a wide-ranging debate about the foundations of welfare economics. What seems to have been salvaged from that debate is that the economist's welfare propositions, and the allocative rules derived therefrom, are normative rather than positive: they *entail* ought statements that rest upon value judgments.[1] For the rest, the course of the debate after 1939 was shaped by two recurrent issues. (1) The first was the respective merits of building the edifice of welfare economics on the older neoclassical (diminishing marginal utility) foundations or, alternatively, on a Paretian foundation as proposed by the New Welfare Economics. Put otherwise, the issue was whether the welfare criterion of the economist should turn on 'cardinal' utility or on ordinal utility.[2] (2) In so far as the latter view prevailed, much of the ensuing debate was concerned with the apparent paradoxes of the various proposed criteria and with the means for guarding against intransitivity.

In consequence of the growing postwar interest in project appraisal – stimulated by the expansion both of the size of the public sector and of aid programmes to Third World countries – a new debate appears to be brewing. Unsurprisingly, it involves a reconsideration of the issues raised already by the debate on welfare criteria. But it also encompasses some new issues that have arisen in response to the pressing need to evolve operational procedures. For in the endeavour to meet this need, a number of manuals[3] directing their expertise to the problems of project appraisal in 'less developed countries', along with a number of textbooks on social cost–benefit techniques,[4] have taken up rather strong positions about the nature of the economic expertise in question. Yet, in the main, such positions are being adopted without careful attention to the methodological and ethical implications, without careful attention, either, to alternative positions. What is

more, the positions held by most of these authors are not free from ambiguity.

Therefore, while waiting patiently to be invited to a forthcoming conference on these fundamental issues – hopefully to be held somewhere in Hawaii or Bali Bali – I shall anticipate the debate to the extent, at least, of providing a framework within which the related issues can be aired. True, I have already taken up a strong position myself on the role of the economist in applying cost–benefit analysis and related techniques in the second edition of my *Cost–Benefit Analysis* (1975).[5] And although I shall indeed leave the impression that there is a balance of advantage in adopting that position, my academic detachment is to some extent assured by my basic disinterestedness in the outcome of such a debate.

This disinterestedness flows from a belief that the value of cost–benefit analysis, and other allocative techniques, is increasingly limited in a world that is being rapidly transformed by modern technology. For in such a world, people cannot reasonably be expected to foresee the range of significant consequences that follow in the train of innovations; much less are they able to place a sensible value on them. Bearing in mind that much of the consequent uncertainty borders on irremediable ignorance of the ensuing side effects of innovations and of new projects, or a succession of new projects, on an ignorance of the probability of their occurrence even if they could be foreseen, and bearing in mind also that such side effects can manifest themselves in irreversible changes in the physical and social environment, which may prove catastrophic, only an incurable and determined quantomaniac will continue to believe that a numerical estimate of the net social benefit, contrived from the data he assiduously dredges up, bears any relation to the actual social welfare.

Nonetheless, a personal disinterestedness in the outcome of this new debate is altogether compatible with an intellectual interest in its promotion. And so I proceed to outline the agenda of this debate, along with my own reflections.

I

Since this essay addresses itself to the operational techniques to be found in the literature on project appraisal, it is hardly necessary to remark that we are not to trouble ourselves with problems arising from a more general concept of the social welfare function. Working within this project appraisal literature, we shall, moreover, ignore the familiar paradoxes associated with valuation. Thus, we shall write the initial and basic data unambiguously as $\Sigma\Delta v$ – translated as the algebraic aggregate of the money values (positive, negative or zero) that each person in the defined community puts on the change of his welfare resulting from the project or programme in question. If this $\Sigma\Delta v$ is positive, economists may regard the change as 'economically efficient', and the magnitude of this positive sum as the measure of its 'social net benefit'.[6] The converse interpretation follows, of course, if $\Sigma\Delta v$ is negative.[7] Accepting this much provisionally, the art of the economist consists of ways of capturing the $\Sigma\Delta v$ data by both indirect and direct methods.

Let us first consider the position of those who take what Sugden and Williams (1978) call 'the decision-making approach' – in contrast, that is, to what they call 'the Paretian approach'.[8] Adopting this 'decision-making approach', the role of the economist is conceived as that of a technician or 'analyst' assisting the 'decision-maker' to make choices that are consistent with the values and objectives of the latter. Cost–benefit analysis, in consequence, is held to be no more than a technique, or way of organised thought, for comparing alternative projects or courses of action. As such, then, the virtue of the technique is to be judged by its consistency and explicitness – irrespective of the policy-maker's values or objectives. In any case, by providing the objectives, the policy-maker also provides implicitly the value judgments that the analyst has to accept. For 'it is no part of the analyst's job to judge whether the decision-maker's objectives are ethically right, nor whether they are acceptable to the community as a whole' (Sugden and Williams, 1978, p. 236).

On this view, therefore, the economist engaged on a cost–benefit analysis has no recourse to an accepted 'normative economics'. He is employed as a suitable analyst simply in the belief that his training ensures competence in the use of those quantitative techniques associated with the notions of value and trade-off.

It may be alleged that in this respect the economist is in no way different from, say, a medical officer, or engineer, or biologist, or any other expert who, *vis-à-vis* the political or decision-taking process, is expected to be 'on tap, but not on top'. But such an allegation could confuse the issue. The economist may, of course, restrict himself to positive economics – to an attempt, that is, to provide the policy-maker with forecasts about the range of economic consequences of the alternative projects or policies. But whenever he does more than this, as in fact he does in a cost–benefit analysis, and in addition seeks to rank alternative projects on the scale of better or worse, or else to talk of one alternative as being economically 'more efficient' than another, then an economic *criterion* is necessarily implied.

Now, it is acknowledged that the medical profession does use criteria both for determining the health of a patient and, more specifically, for determining the existence or extent of a disease in a patient. Yet, these criteria clearly have no connection whatever with the political will of the decision-maker. They are tests of health or disease *per se*. Likewise, the engineer has criteria for engineering efficiency and the biologist criteria for biological efficiency that are wholly independent of political decisions. The crucial question in this essay therefore is *not* whether the economist agrees to serve the policy-maker or the community in whatever capacity is thought proper. It is whether the economist, like the doctor, or engineer, or biologist, has an independent criterion for ranking phenomena within his field of competence – specifically, whether the economist can rank alternative economic situations or whether instead, and as distinct from these other professionals, the criterion or criteria he uses for ranking derive from, and are ultimately sanctioned by, the will of the policy-maker or political community.

To be sure, in the Sugden–Williams view the economist, as analyst, is not precluded from occasionally hazarding a private opinion that can perhaps modify the goals or values of the policy-maker. But it is clearly understood that ultimately the economist's criterion – the weights he uses and, therefore, also his findings – will conform with those of the decision-maker.

Thus, communication between the policy-maker and the economist, or analyst, is visualised as a dialogue by means of which they arrive at a set of weights, values or trade-offs that can be depended upon to be consistent with the objectives of the decision-maker or policy-maker. Such a dialogue may begin with the policy-maker's specifying some or all of the valuations to be attached to the range of effects flowing from the projects he may wish to implement, leaving it as a task for the analyst to discover whether, in fact, the specified set of valuations will indeed give priority to the desired number of projects and, if not, whether the implications of the changes in valuations necessary to do so will, at the same time, conform with the policy-maker's declared objectives. Alternatively, the dialogue may begin with the policy-maker's selection of a number of projects, leaving it to the analyst to work out the common set of valuation that, if acceptable to the policy-maker, is to be used thenceforth in the selection of further projects[9] – always provided the policy-maker retains his ultimate values and objectives.

One cannot be unaware of the difficulties that may arise in such a dialogue – the difficulties of discovering the more relevant implications of alternative courses of action, the difficulties of measurement, to say nothing of the sources of friction and frustration within the administrative and political systems. However, this particular debate is to be addressed primarily to the propriety of alternative *conceptions* of the rationale of a cost–benefit analysis under the far-fetched assumption that all procedures incidental to that conception are practical.

To continue now with the description of our decision-maker, he can be a single person, say an autocrat or bureaucrat, or else it can be a cohesive group of autocrats or bureaucrats, following its own objectives and guided only by its own ideas of right and wrong; at no level, that is, will such a group be answerable to the members of the community whose destinies they control. Alternatively, the decision-maker is but a shorthand term for the institutions by which collective decisions are debated and implemented – say, by the political systems that prevail in any of the liberal democracies. Let us consider these two alternatives respectively, under the headings of A and B.

A. A cost–benefit analysis so conceived could be made a sensible instrument for promoting the purposes of a personality such as Genghis Khan. The dialogue between him and his favourite analyst could begin with Genghis Khan's articulate and vehement desire to raze to the ground, this year, four Christian fortified cities, A, B, C and D, preferably in that order, from a score or so of tempting alternatives. Our analyst, after being permitted to confer at length with the generals about the relevant probabilities of death and destruction on both sides under a variety of conditions, ends up finally with the following system of weights which, he assures his sovereign, fits his desires exactly: the death of a Khan warrior –1, the death of a Khan general –10, the death of an adult male Christian +4·5, . . . , the destruction of a Christian church +85, and so on.

The four chosen enterprises of Genghis Khan, having been scientifically approved, and the relative weights made explicit and, indeed, toasted at each subsequent banquet, the cities A, B, C and D are razed to the ground in the order scheduled. Following these successes, however, recourse to the same set of weights reveals that the greatest social net benefit accrues if, in the new year, strongholds F, G and H are given the same treatment. But our belligerent policy-maker now proclaims his resolve to demolish, instead, strongholds H, J and K. (After all, there is nothing in the decision-making approach that precludes occasional revision of broad national objectives.) Our prudent analyst quietly goes to work and eventually comes up with a revised set of weights altogether fitting to the latest policy objectives as expressed by the policy-maker.

This A conception of a cost–benefit analysis, illustrated by the above, somewhat extreme example, has the undoubted advantage that no difficulties of principle arise with respect either to method or to sanction. The policy-maker can be as arbitrary as he wishes. And any conceivable benefit or cost can be ignored simply by attaching to it a weight of zero. The expertise of the analyst is directed entirely to quantification and, within the prevailing values and objectives of the policy-maker, to consistency.

Within a more contemporary context, we should be inclined to think of the A-type policy-maker as a bureaucrat, or a cabal of bureaucrats, that is not answerable in the last resort to the community at large. And the consistent set of weights that are to emerge from the analyst's researches may be referred to henceforth as *bureau-weights*. However, despite the emphasis placed by Sugden and Williams (1978) on the merit of 'explicitness' in addition to that of consistency in a cost–benefit approach to project appraisal, the calculation of a set of bureau-weights does not of itself imply explicitness in any sense other than the obvious one of the weights being made known to the bureaucrat. There is certainly no incentive arising simply from the calculation of such a set of weights to place them on public record in order to enable the community at large to monitor the projects and policies selected by the bureaucrat. Indeed, Little and Mirrlees have gone so far as actually to suggest concealing distributional weights from the public, since 'It may sometimes be politically expedient to do good by stealth' (1974, p. 55).[10]

II

B. Some obvious modifications to the above remarks are necessary when the policy-maker is a bureaucrat, but one who is, in principle and practice, subject to the will of political representatives, who are themselves responsible to an electorate based on, say, universal suffrage. True, the elaborate machinery of administration in a modern liberal democracy is clogged with intermediate procedures and personnel, is subject to corruption and intrigue, and is deflected by pressures from powerful minority lobbies and media. What is more, economic issues in particular are often more complex and far-reaching than is apprehended either by politicians or by the greater part of the public. Political outcomes therefore cannot be supposed invariably to reflect a political consensus or even a majority view on every issue. Yet, these facts of political life are not immediate agenda for our purpose. Such a tangle of imperfections in the operation of any particular form of Western liberal democracy becomes relevant to our investigation only according as we are persuaded that, ideally, the inspiration and ultimate sanction of a cost–benefit analysis should reside in the political will of the electorate.

Assuming for the present, then, that the political machinery operates smoothly, we have now to substitute what we may call *politico-weights* in this *B* conception for the bureau-weights of the preceding *A* conception. The economist is still, properly speaking, a technician or analyst only. But he is employed now to give quantitative expression to the political will of the electorate. Of course, he may never be consulted directly by the electorate. More commonly, he will be advised by its representatives or by the bureaucrats appointed by the representatives. Nonetheless, the basic sanction for the set of weights employed by the analyst derives from the political will of the electorate. More briefly, we may say that the required set of weights is derived from the 'political process'.

This *B* conception of a cost–benefit analysis again removes all the difficulties of principle from the path of the economist, who once more assumes the role of loyal analyst wholly absorbed in elaborating techniques that make use of, or issue in, a set of weights deemed to be consistent with the objectives revealed by the political process. The fruits of his labours will therefore take the form of a quantitative assessment, whose magnitude will depend upon the resultant set of weights – distributional, regional, merit, and so on – which reflect the priorities of the multiple objectives being pursued by the political process. And it goes without saying that no dimension of a proposed project or policy need lack

for an explicitly stated politico-weight, be it natural beauty, nostalgic sentiment, religious ferment, or possible tedium or perplexity.

Be this as it may, there are a number of implications of this *B* position which, on reflection, may reduce the composure of its advocates.

(1) It no longer becomes possible to make reference to an independent economic criterion in judging the 'economic' aspects of projects or policies under consideration. Thus, statements such as 'policy 2 is economically more efficient than policy 1' are no longer admissible. And the authors of manuals and textbooks adopting the *B* (or *A*) position can only mislead the public whenever they seek to justify their proposals for a revision of certain market prices by reference to such terms as 'price distortions', 'optimality' or 'sub-optimality' conditions, inasmuch as they encourage the impression that, in their own adopted approach, economics has a meaning and a sanction that is independent of the political will.

In fact, economics as such is swallowed whole by politics in the *B* approach. The quantitative assessment of a project, whether made in terms of dollars or of 'utils', is ultimately the byproduct of politico-weights, which are determined, in the last resort, by the political process alone. And it follows as a corollary that, although sectors of private industry may continue to be judged competitive and 'efficient' on some conventional standard, consistency of political purpose would require policy-makers, nevertheless, to seek to alter the outputs produced by the private sector of the economy, so that they too can be justified by reference to the chosen set of politico-weights.

(2) Assuming that a set of politico-weights is successfuly established, it is practically certain that it will be vulnerable to each major political change. The consistency sought may not in fact endure beyond a few years. Worse, the public itself will soon discover that the quantitative techniques employed in the assessment of alternative projects are pure 'window-dressing' – pure quantitative rationalisation for whatever policies are favoured by the political party or parties in office.

Such a discovery is not likely to predispose the public to take such quantitative assessments seriously. At best, the public may take some perverse pleasure in playing this numbers game – as a result of which the conventional political discussion about the merits of projects favoured by an existing majority is transformed into arguments about the appropriate system of politico-weights.[11]

(3) It will soon be realised also that the *distributional* politico-weights adopted cannot be counted on to exclude projects having unwanted distributional

effects. There is, of course, nothing to prevent a government from excluding such a project on distributional grounds. But if it chooses instead to favour the use of a cost–benefit technique that attributes a higher weight to the dollar gained or lost by the 'poor' than the dollar gained or lost by the 'rich', in order to impart a progressive bias to the calculation, it is still possible for a distributionally regressive project to yield a positive net social benefit if a large enough number of the 'rich' benefit at the expense of a very small number of poor people.

The expected and proper reaction to such a project would be to exclude it anyway on distributional grounds (always assuming that such distributional effects cannot be corrected through the tax system). But if such a reaction is accepted, distributional weights become superfluous. If we can assess the distributional implications of a project – and unless we can do so, obviously we cannot employ distributional weights – we can always exclude those projects having unwanted distributional effects without recourse to the charade of distributional weights.

To these three implications, two observations need to be appended. First, those who conceive of policy-makers, of either the A or the B type, as the final arbiters in all that passes for economic appraisal, disclose a fascinating ambivalence in their writings. For instance, the authors of manuals devoted to the appraisal of Third World country projects overtly defer to the broad national planning objectives of these sovereign policy-makers – whether of the 'bottoms-up' approach as favoured by the *Guidelines* (Dasgupta *et al.*, 1972) or of the 'tops-down' approach as favoured by the *Manual* (Little and Mirrlees, 1969) – when, for the most part, the formulae they offer their readers are directly deducible from the simple $\Sigma\Delta v$ concept of the Paretian approach. Thus, when it comes to the calculation of shadow prices of labour, or of capital,[12] or of imports, the formula proposed is of this $\Sigma\Delta v$ kind, elaborated so as to encapsulate the relevant money opportunity costs. At the same time these authors also suggest that politico-weights be attached to money valuations in order to give adequate expression to distributional, regional and merit considerations that are included in the national objectives, as conceived at least by the policy-makers. In particular, the social rate of discount, one of the more critical parameters, is clearly related to the policy-maker's own ideas of the 'optimal' volume of investment and, indirectly, to his own ideas of a desirable rate of economic growth.

Surely such authors cannot be instructing these policy-makers when they are to abide by the $\Sigma\Delta v$ formulation and when they are to choose their own

weights and parameters. For if so, the inquisitive reader of these manuals will also want to know just by reference to what master criterion this subdivision of authority is to be determined. After all, if the authority does indeed reside wholly with the policy-maker, these manuals' accounts of the appropriate techniques to use must be assuming that in fact the policy-maker himself will always choose to use estimating techniques based wholly, or largely, on the $\Sigma\Delta v$ data whenever the manuals use them, while in the estimating of other things this same policy-maker follows the manuals' proposals and has recourse to politico-weights.

All this is, of course, an assumption of fact for which no evidence is offered. A sceptic must therefore be forgiven for harbouring the suspicion that the authors of such manuals tend to favour the $\Sigma\Delta v$-based estimates whenever they believe that familiar economic principles enable them to cope with the calculations (although, even in such cases, they may propose that the $\Sigma\Delta v$ data be modified by attaching politico-weights to the money valuations), while invoking the authority of the policy-maker whenever there is some elusiveness about the appropriate allocative principles or some seemingly insuperable difficulty in measuring.

It is, of course, entirely possible that such authors would prefer to invoke an independent economic criterion. At all events, being economists by training, they must find it hard to wean themselves from the $\Sigma\Delta v$ fare on which they were reared. But if we suppose that they mean what they say – perhaps they do not – then, having officially handed the economic sceptre to the policy-maker, they cannot at the same time reserve for themselves any independent authority as economists.

Thus, although some of these authors continue to think that the term 'economic efficiency' can legitimately be used in so far as cost minimisation is at issue, this is erroneous whether in the context of a general or a partial equilibrium analysis. In a general equilibrium analysis, the minimum cost of any collection of goods is associated with a point upon the goods boundary. Such a point entails that factor prices be the same in all uses – where the range of relevant factor prices (or factor rates of substitution) is constrained by the given resource endowment.

But factor prices are the source of income to factor-owners. Once weights are to be attached to income groups, and factor returns expressed in, say, 'utils', the returns to labour (or some kinds, at least) may be revised upward and/or the returns to land or capital revised downward, so departing from an efficient set of factor prices as described above. The combinations of factors used in the production of each good in a collection that minimise its resulting 'util' cost can, then, be quite different from an efficient set of factor combinations – from which it follows that the util-determined collection of goods will *not* be a point along the production boundary.

Partial equilibrium analysis is, however, far more common in cost–benefit analysis. Within this context, opportunity cost is properly interpreted as the value forgone from shifting factors from their existing occupation to the project in question. It follows therefore, that the relevant opportunity costs will also differ in magnitude according as they are now weighted by reference to distributional, merit or other considerations. In general, then, and contrary to the impression conveyed by these authors, calculations of cost-efficiency or cost-effectiveness cannot stand on their own, invariant to the values and objectives of policy-makers in the *A* or *B* conception of a cost–benefit analysis. These costs too will vary with and reflect the objectives and values of the decision-maker.[13]

My second observation is in effect a footnote to the first. The national plan of the policy-maker is invariably envisaged by such authors as one comprehending some measure of economic growth – often an increase in the rate of economic growth.

To ardent proponents of economic growth, this component of a national plan must appear eminently reasonable, bearing in mind the extent of poverty in Third World countries. Presumably, they believe that, if a grand debate of the whole nation were to be held somehow on this subject, the economic growth objectives of the country's rulers would be approved.

Yet, if this were true in so far as economic growth is understood as involving no more than a rise in the living standards, it might *not* be true at all if the full social implications of the sort of modernisation entailed by economic growth are also made explicit. In some countries the implication would include checks to the power of religion, a weakening of traditional institutions, the disruption of a settled way of life and, in general, the transformation of a hierarchical society within which each person has a role to play, and within which the mass of people can be resigned to worldly hardship, into a more anonymous, mobile, secular and restless society.

The transitional phases in any modernisation programme for such countries, moreover, can hardly avoid the mass exodus from agricultural smallholdings to overcrowded cities unable to cope with the growing unemployment there – cities increasingly vulnerable to disease, crime, civic disorder and breakdown.

For authors who believe that decision-makers should defer ultimately, in their choice of multiple objectives, to the desires of society at large, the assumption by them that economic growth – regarded, as in fact it is, as a modernisation process involving Western technology –is sure to be a priority among these objectives, is something of a presumption.

III

C. A third conception of the role of economist in a cost–benefit analysis is that of a specialist who is licensed to provide only strictly 'economic' data in a particular format to the policy-maker, whether the latter is an autocrat or a democrat. These economic data are viewed as information only, much like chemical data on the heating or blending of gases, and carry with them no independent criterion whatever. In particular, since the economist claims no criterion by which such data enable him to rank a project *X* above an alternative project *Y*, the data he offers can be wholly ignored by the policy-maker. More generally, however, the policy-maker can attach whatever importance he wishes to the quantitative estimates provided, and can impress on any particular calculation his own set of weights – restrained, perhaps, only by a formal requirement that he be consistent in this respect.

Effectively, the status of the economist is no different in this third case from that in the preceding two cases, although his influence on the policy-maker is, if possible, even less. For in the two preceding cases the economist, as analyst, is at least envisaged as having a continuous dialogue with the policy-maker – a dialogue designed to explicate the trade-offs or weights that accord with the latter's broad national objectives. In the *C* conception of a cost–benefit analysis, in contrast, the economist simply presents his offering – the economic data in the usual $\Sigma \Delta v$ form – and retires from the scene, leaving the policy-maker and his advisors to decide whether, and if so how, these data should influence their appraisal of the alternative courses of action facing them.

The economist, incidentally, is now in the position proposed by a number of well-known writers (in particular, Tinbergen, 1966) who see no role in the decision process for a normative economics. To these economists the discipline of economics is regarded solely as a positive science and, as such, can only offer to policy-makers information that is the product of economic analysis and statistics. The economist in government service is, in their view, to confine himself to forecasts of the relevant economic implications of alternative projects or policies.

The actual role assigned to the economist in this *C*

conception may, of course, be more closely structured than indicated by the preceding paragraph. For example, he may be required to direct his expertise (a) to estimating the relevant $\Sigma\Delta v$, and no more, or (b) to estimating the relevant $\Sigma\Delta u$ (the aggregate of 'util' measurements) by reference to the politico-weights provided for his use, or else (c) to using, in addition to either $\Sigma\Delta v$ or $\Sigma\Delta u$, a particular formula in expressing the distributional implications, or indeed any other implications.

A few words about (a) and (b) before concluding this third possible conception of a cost–benefit analysis:

(a) This role would be congenial enough to many economists. True, such economists may find it useful, if only as a concession to force of habit, to continue to employ familiar terms like 'more efficient' whenever the change in question produces a larger $\Sigma\Delta v$, or to use the term 'optimal' whenever the relevant $\Sigma\Delta v$ cannot be made larger. But it is understood among them that such terms are a convenient jargon only and carry no commendatory undertones.

(b) Although the political process may prefer to have the economic data in the $\Sigma\Delta u$ form, as a measure of aggregate utility in some 'objective' sense, there is clearly no scientific way of determining the 'util' weights to be attached to the dollars gained or lost by different income groups. Inevitably, then, the economist has to be provided with politico-weights, and he may therefore be drawn into the so-called dialogue with the policy-maker for the purpose of giving consistent quantitative expression to the value judgments and broad objectives of the latter, as in the preceding A and B approaches. Alternatively, he may be excluded from this dialogue and simply handed the appropriate set of weights by courtesy of the policy-maker, and left to get on with the job.

Whether the (a) or (b) data are selected as the form more pertinent to the policy-maker's mode of appraisal, it follows in either case that $\Sigma\Delta v$ is required in the first instance. In both cases, however, the economist is once more entirely without any economic criterion, although – as distinct from the A and B conceptions – he may now be formally removed from participation in the decision-making process.

IV

D. The final conception of a cost–benefit analysis in this scheme of things is one that regards allocative techniques as embedded in normative foundations. Clearly, such a conception entails value judgments, which can be either the value judgments of the economist or else those of society as a whole. If they are of the former, they do not necessarily have any social sanction – although, it must be recognised, a good deal of modern 'political economy' has its origins in the writer's own (sometimes implicit) value judgments as well as his own (sometimes implicit) factual judgments. Yet, it is only when the economist's criterion, on which his prescriptive propositions are to turn, is at one with the ethical premises of the particular society to which such propositions are addressed, that they carry an independent sanction.

If this D conception of a cost–benefit analysis, or of allocative techniques generally, is conceded, then – ignoring for the present some issues that arise in the interpretation of this D conception – it follows that, whenever a situation II is ranked above a situation I on the economist's criterion, society also ranks II above I, *other things equal.* From this conclusion it also follows that normative economic judgments resulting therefrom are entirely independent of the judgments of policy-makers or, more generally, of political judgments. Hence, whatever the project or policy being debated or implemented by the political process, the economist is entitled, by reference to his criterion, to pronounce the project or policy to be economically efficient or inefficient as the case may be.

Nevertheless, this normative economic warrant is not to be construed as one that transcends any political decision on the issue, or one that has any claim to priority. A project may properly be declared economically inefficient; yet, other things not being equal in fact, it may legitimately be favoured by the political process. Indeed, even if all other things *are* equal, there is nothing to prevent the political process from adopting the economically inefficient course of action. And, as indicated below, there is nothing illegitimate or perverse about such an outcome. Nonetheless, in so far as political debate tends to oversimplify issues, and therefore to mislead public opinion on fairly complex economic proposals, a study that assesses the economic impact of a project, and attaches to it an efficiency-ranking based on an agreed criterion, serves a useful purpose in political debate.

In connection with this D conception, a number of issues have now to be faced.

(1) As indicated above, there can be differences in project-ranking as between the findings based on an economic criterion, on the one hand, and on the outcome of the political process, on the other. This fact, however, does not necessarily lead to conflict. True, the

economic criterion is held to build upon the ethical premises of society – in effect, to be part of a 'virtual constitution'. But then, the mechanism adopted (including voting rules) for reaching political decisions is also one that is sanctioned by a virtual or actual constitution.

In practice, of course, the political decision will always prevail, inasmuch as the political process is the ultimate source of power. The economist may reasonably hope that his independent assessment and economic ordering will be given serious consideration by the policy-makers, especially where his findings are clear and compelling, even though he has no power to ensure as much. Yet, it must be remembered that it is the political process itself that, from time to time, calls for the implementation of a cost–benefit analysis. Under the *D* interpretation at least, such a political demand implies recognition that an economic ranking is independent of a political ranking. Certainly, if economic expertise is viewed in this light, the public and the politician will come to regard economic assessment and ranking as a meaningful and independent contribution to the political decision-making process.[14]

(2) The second issue is that of the choice of $\Sigma\Delta v$ or $\Sigma\Delta u$ as the basic material for the economist's criterion. Before attending in the following section to some of the subtler implications of adopting the $\Sigma\Delta v$ basis, let us first list some of the apparent disadvantages of adopting instead $\Sigma\Delta u$ as the basis for the economist's criterion.

(a) As mentioned above, there can be no scientific means for comparing the utilities of different persons on a cardinal scale. The economist can, of course, decide to attribute util weights according to some simple but arbitrary function, or else he can attempt to deduce them, on certain assumptions, from the prevailing tax structure or from other politically influenced decisions – so inferring politico-weights. In either case he must be prepared to see these weights change with a change in economic personnel or a change in political alignments – a prospect that cannot but reduce the respect in which his criterion is held.[15]

(b) Again, as pointed out in our discussion of the *B* conception of a cost–benefit analysis, even an ideal set of distributional weights cannot prevent a cost–benefit study from favouring a project having marked regressive distributional effects. Such a choice can always be rationalised as reflecting the community's trade-off (embodied in its distributional politico-weights) as between more output and better distribution. But the political facts of life are such that, notwithstanding the implied trade-off, a project known to have a regressive distributional effect is likely to be rejected anyway. For the purpose designed, therefore, such distributional weights tend to be redundant.

(c) The initial set of politico-weights may well be distributional only, these being vindicated as the community's attempt, in its political capacity, to rank projects in terms of aggregate utility rather than money. But once the idea of a set of distributional weights is accepted, it will be difficult to prevent the political process from revising the set of weights to comprehend also considerations of 'social merit', of regional development, of growth potential, of ecological stability, and of other desirable social attributes or aspirations. The process can only come to an end when all possible dimensions of a project or policy have entered, albeit controversially, into the quantitative assessment, so that once more it reflects no more than the objectives of the political incumbents in office. Such an outcome effectively destroys the resulting $\Sigma\Delta u$-based economist's criterion as an independent economic criterion; it is transformed into the purely political criterion we encountered in our discussion of the *B* conception of a cost–benefit analysis. As suggested, a set of politico-weights can generally be found to rationalise all, or nearly all, the projects proposed by the political party in office in pursuit of its objectives.

(d) Even assuming that the politico-weights that emerge from the political process are relatively stable, it follows that the public sector, operating as it does on a $\Sigma\Delta u$ basis, is guided by a different criterion from the private sector of the economy, which is guided (ignoring externalities) by reference to $\Sigma\Delta v$ data. Such an anomaly cannot easily be overlooked, inasmuch as allocative efficiency, if it is thought to mean anything, means one thing to the private sector and quite another thing to the public sector. The resulting allocation of the economy as a whole is consequently difficult to rationalise.

In these circumstances, therefore, the political decision-making process will have pretext enough to extend its control of industry over the private sector – an extension of power having repercussions that go far beyond the merely economic. For the policy-maker could properly be accused of inconsistency in his vision of national objectives if he permitted such a transparent anomaly to go uncorrected.

V

It behoves us now to reconsider the advisability of adopting the familiar $\Sigma\Delta v$ calculations as the basis of our economic criterion. But what ethical judgments may be invoked in its favour, and what are the problems associated with its application?

Addressing ourselves for the present to the first question, its bearing on the concept of social welfare – a concept that appears repeatedly in the welfare economics literature – needs to be considered. Since the sanction for the economist's criterion has to derive from an ethical consensus, it follows that it is not (necessarily) the *fact* of an increase in society's welfare – allowing that it could be satisfactorily defined, detected and measured – that is to underwrite this criterion, but rather society's fundamental beliefs about what *ought* to count as a contribution to the social welfare. The welfare economist therefore should not seek to determine in some objective way the measure of actual change in society's welfare. In as much as the economist is to prescribe for a particular society, his criterion has to affirm a change as one conferring an increase in social welfare when, and only when, this society, in its *ethical* capacity, would also regard such change as conferring an increase in its welfare.

The basic ethical premises that have to be ascribed to any society for which $\Sigma\Delta v$ qualifies as the measuring rod of social welfare are simply stated – although it has to be borne in mind, also, that there can be a number of fundamental beliefs about what is right and proper, or wrong and improper, in each society, which can occasionally come into conflict with these basic ethical premises and which therefore may qualify the applicability of the economist's criterion.

The first ethical premise to which society has to subscribe in order to warrant the economist's use of $\Sigma\Delta v$ as a ranking device is that each person's welfare is to count and, what is more, to count according to his own valuation. If the economic change in question confers on him a net benefit that he values at $55, society has also to reckon this benefit as worth $55 to him.

Such a premise is likely to commend itself to a society that believes, as a matter of right, that each person should be treated as if he knows better than others what a thing is worth to him. It may generally be recognised that in fact each adult in the community does not always know what is best for himself, and that indeed the more complex the choice facing him the less able he is to appraise the full consequences of his decision and to place a money value on it – notwithstanding which, society as a whole would subscribe to the premise. Moreover, if the application of this premise is not, in practice, to be frequently suspended, it is essential that no exemption be made in virtue of the individual's imperfect state of knowledge. Thus, whatever the information in his possession at the time of his choice, or of the occurrence of effects that result from the community's choice, it is to be deemed sufficient to warrant society's accepting his own valuation of it as reflecting its worth to him better than any valuation determined by others.

The second broad premise to which society has to subscribe if the use of $\Sigma\Delta v$ as a ranking device is to be vindicated, is either of the following. (1) The valuation placed on a specific change by any person is *also* the valuation placed on the change by society itself. Thus, if person *A* perceives the change as a net gain and places on it a value of $55, whereas person *B* perceives the change as a net loss which he reckons at $25, then to society also there is a net gain of $55 and a net loss of $25, or an aggregate net gain of $30 (in so far as the welfares of persons *A* and *B* only enter into the calculus). Alternatively, (2) a change that meets a *potential* Pareto improvement confers, in aggregate, a net benefit on society.

The first possible premise (1) is not one that is likely to be embraced by a Western liberal society. It needs an unusual degree of complacency to count an additional gain of a dollar to a very rich man as equal in value to society as an additional dollar of gain to a very poor man. For to adopt such reckoning implies that society as a whole is, at the ethical level, wholly indifferent to adopting a project that inflicts on ten poor families losses they reckon as equal, in total, to $30,000 if, at the same time, it produces a benefit for a rich man that he values at $30,000.

The alternative (2) premise, that of a potential Pareto improvement, may not on first reflections appear much likelier to attract widespread support. It may be easy enough to secure general agreement that an economic change that actually does make every one in the community better off is a desirable social change. It is much less certain that there will be a consensus in favour of an economic change that, though it does not make every one better off, would be able to do so if a redistribution of the goods available in the new position were a costless operation, which it is not, so that the redistribution in question generally does not take place.

Nevertheless, an economic change that is a potential Pareto improvement may well qualify for society's seal of approval in virtue of any or all of the following beliefs about the working of the economy:

(a) that economic changes that are potential Pareto

improvements do not in fact have significant regressive distributional effects;

(b) that the existing progressive-tax structure provides adequate safeguards against the occurrence of such distributional effects;

(c) that over time a succession of economic changes countenanced by the potential Pareto-improvement criterion is, in any case, unlikely to produce regressive distributional effects of any importance; or

(d) that such a succession of economic changes has a better chance of raising society's living standards over time than a succession of economic changes sanctioned by any other economic criterion.

If, in the event, a potential Pareto improvement is adopted as the economic criterion, then by reference to it the term 'economic efficiency' has a clear meaning, and one that is entirely independent of political objectives and outcomes. Thus, if a correct calculation reveals that

$$\Sigma v(II) > \Sigma v(I)$$

– the algebraic sum of the valuations in the new situation II exceeds that of situation I – then II is held to be economically more efficient than I, even though, at the same time, the political system reveals that voters unanimously prefer I to II.

It follows that the economic assessment of situation II compared with situation I may properly be accepted as a distinct *economic* contribution to the decision-making process of society. When, therefore, the policy-maker, acting on behalf of the political process, proposes that a cost–benefit study be made by the economist in order to help him reach a decision, he is no longer requesting of the economist a quantitative rationalisation of his own (i.e. the policy-maker's) preferences and objectives. He is proposing that a distinct economic criterion be employed in producing quantitative estimates to which, presumably, he attaches some significance, even though such estimates explicitly ignore other dimensions of the policy or project that the policy-maker has to take into consideration.[16]

The $\Sigma \Delta v$ estimates could, of course, be supplemented by a distributional criterion – one that was also based on an ethical consensus, assuming it to exist. If so, such a distributional criterion would add some weight to an economic prescription based now on both criteria, even where the distributional implications were not politically fashionable. It is, of course, possible also that alternative II is ranked above alternative I on the

economist's Pareto criterion and below I on the economist's distributional criterion. In this case, as in others, the economist is not obliged to recommend a course of action or, for that matter, a course of no action. He simply passes on to the policy-maker, as a relevant contribution to the decision-making process, the findings based on his two criteria.

On the other hand, if an ethical consensus about distributional structures is not possible, the economist *qua* economist cannot offer a distributional ranking of the alternatives. He has then to content himself with offering only an allocative ranking based on the $\Sigma \Delta v$ estimates, leaving the distributional implications of the policy or project in question (about which, however, he may be able to provide information) to be considered along with other factors by the political process.

VI

Restricting ourselves in the remainder of this essay to the $\Sigma \Delta v$ measurements based on the Pareto criterion, there are still a number of questions to be raised.

(1) Inasmuch as his prescriptive propositions draw sanction from an ethical consensus, the economist is impelled to make a distribution within the set of those economic effects commonly designated as 'externalities' – a distinction that has been generally overlooked by economists immersed in the more technical aspects of this branch of the subject. The distinction is that between, on the one hand, those external diseconomies – such as undue concentrations of noise, smoke or other forms of pollution included in the term 'spillovers' – that are generally regarded as a legitimate form of grievance and, on the other, those external diseconomies that arise from resentment or envy of the possessions or the status of others. The latter are not atypical in modern societies. Yet, if they sometimes elicit sympathy or understanding, at least, they do not command moral approbation. Accordingly, the economist who derives his prescriptive propositions from an ethical consensus is bound to identify and evaluate the former and 'legitimate' external effects while, at the same time, categorically excluding the latter effects – those sometimes included in the category known as 'interdependent utility effects'. Such 'illegitimate' external effects are extended to offences taken by persons simply from their awareness of the private activities of others and to pleasure experienced at the misfortune suffered by others.[17]

It is to be especially noted that reference to an ethical consensus for guidance in these matters may preclude symmetrical reasoning. Thus, drawing on the notion of a consensus, the economist has to evaluate as being a legitimate externality any increase in satisfaction experienced by individuals from their discovery of the benefits conferred on other creatures by some project or policy. In its ethical capacity, for example, society may approve of the shame and resentment of citizens when they learn of the cruelty inflicted by man on animals or of the extinction of a species, animal or plant. Hence, for a project having as its primary purpose, or as one of its secondary effects, a reduction in the suffering of animals or a check to the destruction of flora and fauna, the assessment of the consequent increase in satisfaction felt by some members of society is properly an agendum for the economist. Any decrease in satisfaction felt by other members of society arising from the same phenomenon is not.

(2) The techniques devised by economists to deal with the problem of risk and uncertainty can be critical in any cost–benefit calculation and deserve further attention. So far, proposals for dealing with uncertainty have directed their appeal, in the main, to the attention of economists and other specialists in their technical capacity. It may well be the case that, if the more commonly used techniques for dealing with uncertainty were reduced to basic criteria comprehensible to the layman, they would indeed elicit approval. But unless there are good reasons for thinking so, economic estimates of projects having recourse to these techniques for dealing with uncertainty cannot be vindicated by the economist as deriving from an ethical consensus.

(3) Finally, allowing that the economist entrusted with a cost–benefit study has identified the relevant data and, in order to cope with uncertainty, has adopted a technique whose basic rationale meets with the required consensus, it is yet possible that he will meet with seemingly insurmountable difficulties in the attempt to evaluate one or more items. Of course, a sensitivity analysis may reveal their exact valuation to be of small consequence in the final reckoning. But it can be otherwise.

Since the acceptance of an independent economic criterion precludes appeal to the preferences of policy-makers themselves as a means of contriving any evaluation, the economist has no honest alternative to making explicit his omissions. Nonetheless, his incomplete appraisal of the project or projects would be more useful to the political decision-making process if he could describe the nature of the effects omitted, which descriptions would include estimates of their physical magnitudes where possible. He can, in addition, essay a range of 'contingency calculations' (Mishan, 1969, p.

80) with the aim of illustrating their potential economic significance for the choice to be made.

A concluding remark. There may be more in this essay to provoke a debate rather than to resolve it. Certainly, if this *D* conception of a cost–benefit analysis, which I currently favour, is accepted, there are questions additional to those above that press on our attention.[18] Not least is the question of whether there is in today's pluralistic and innovative societies a consensus on the first broad premise: that society accepts as the worth of a thing to each person his own valuation of it. And if so or not, there is still the question of whether there is a consensus on the second premise, interpreted as a potential Pareto improvement.[19]

Notes: Chapter 16

1 For a brief discussion of contrary views, see my 1969 monograph, especially chapter 1, 'On the current opposition to welfare economics' (pp. 13–22).
2 Following Kaldor's famous note of 1939, Hicks (1939a) proposed that the edifice of welfare economics as constructed by Pigou (1924) be re-erected on Paretian foundations rather than on neoclassical foundations. Again, Hicks's consumer surplus measure (1939b) eliminated any need for consideration of the marginal utility of money. It required no more of the individual than a continuum of ordered preferences.
3 Among the better known of these manuals are those of Little and Mirrlees (1969), often referred to as the *Manual*, of Dasgupta *et al.* (1972), often referred to as the *Guidelines*, and of Squire and Van der Tak (1975). For an appraisal and critical comparison of the first two, see Schwartz and Berney (1977), sometimes referred to as the IAD Symposium.
4 Among those I have read closely are McKean (1958), Tinbergen (1966), Dasgupta and Pearce (1972), Eckstein and Krutilla (1958), Maass *et al.* (1962), Pearce (1971), Chase (1968), Pearce (1978), Irvin (1978), and Sugden and Williams (1978).
5 In particular, see chapters 61 and 62.
6 Clearly, if a small change produces a positive $\Sigma \Delta v$, the positive social net benefit may be further augmented by extending this change, unit by unit, to the point at which (assuming sufficient divisibility) $\Sigma \Delta v = 0$. Allowing that the 'total conditions' are also met, the situation reached in this way may be referred to an 'optimal'.
7 Although almost all the postwar journal literature on resource allocation, particularly in connection with the treatment of externalities, accepts the relevant data in this form (and accepts also the implied criterion) in comparing alternative solutions, this is not true of the project appraisal literature, in which attaching weights to the money values of either different groups or different items is often recommended.
8 These authors correctly associate my work, of which my 1975 book is an example, with this 'Paretian approach' in contrast to the 'decision-making approach' that they favour. Since for pedagogic purposes I have thrown their

arguments into stark relief (although taking care not to misrepresent them), the conscientious reader is advised to glance through the last few pages of their book (especially pp. 238–41), where their position is carefully stated.

9 There may, of course, be a wide range of variation in the set of resultant weights, which range narrows as the number of desirable projects increases.

10 Such a remark raises doubts in the mind of the reader whether the 'Project Evaluation Office' of Little and Mirrlees is regarded by them as wholly responsible to a political authority that is itself responsible to the people.

In the IAD Symposium (Schwartz and Berney, 1977), Little talks of the need for 'a relatively powerful or influential Project Evaluation Office', and he says: 'What we have in mind is an integration of policy analysis and national planning at a high policy level, such as through a Planning Commission or a Treasury Department. In such a situation the representatives of the Project Evaluation Office could exert a considerable influence' (p. 60). However, in his criticism of the *Guidelines*'s 'bottoms-up' approach, Little takes a more autocratic view of this 'powerful or influential Project Evaluation Office'. As he puts it: 'There are thousands of decisions which have to be made and for which there is not time to refer to persons who have the political authority.'

11 One can imagine a stable society in which the relative weights and parameters become a part of the constitution itself and therefore are out of the power of governments to alter. Such a situation would provide strong sanctions for the resulting cost–benefit analyses. However, this sort of justification for a 'weighted' type cost–benefit analysis has not been advanced by any writer, and the possibility that a set of weights may be written into a country's constitution is a remote one.

12 However, the discount rate itself, which is required in order to calculate the shadow price of capital and possibly also of labour is – as indicated in the text – a parameter chosen by the policy–maker to correspond with what he believes to be the volume of investment proper to the realisation of the objectives of the national plan.

13 If there is a decision-maker in each of two separate areas, each decision-maker being guided in his economic policies by a set of weights that is different from the other, then (assuming negligible transport costs) profitable trade between the two areas is possible. This familiar proposition is set forth in Sugden and Williams (1978, pp. 188–90). In the simple case of two goods, x_1 and x_2, such trade can allow each area to have more of both goods, and certainly a greater value of both goods, in each area (when calculated at the initial set of values prevailing in each area).

Under familiar assumptions, moreover, trade between the two areas may expand to the point at which (neglecting transport costs) the relative valuations of x_1 and x_2 are the same for both areas. Trade can then be said to be 'efficient' in the same sense that free exchange of goods between two persons is said to be efficient: each is better off according to his own lights – an outcome described by an actual Pareto improvement. Only if the respective improvements of welfare of the two persons, or of the two areas, have to be aggregated into a single measure do the problems of weighting arise. But in a cost–benefit analysis this is, of course, the nub of the problem.

14 The notion of an independent contribution from the economist implies that other 'non-economic' factors are taken into account in the political decision-making process. Formally, it is possible to designate every 'non-economic' factor – such as considerations of distribution, merit or natural beauty – as an externality. With respect to distribution, the pertinent externality could be of the particular 'interdependent utilities' sort as proposed by Hochman and Rodgers (1969). Similarly, we could extend the $\Sigma \Delta v$ calculation to take account of merit goods, aesthetic appeal, religious conviction, or traditional values, simply by posing the question: what is the maximum sum each individual would pay for the particular effect on him in this respect (or what is the minimum sum he would accept to forgo it)?

However, such hyperformalisation, involving the attribution of money sums to intangible benefits and transcendental values, is foredoomed, if only because it is impossible either to persuade citizens consistently to extend the measuring rod of money to a range of factors charged with emotions along with the valuation of carrots, shoes and transistors, or to persuade the political community to waive its constitutional right to debate broad, complex and controversial questions and instead to resign itself to having all social issues settled by economic calculation alone.

15 Indeed, the existing $\Sigma \Delta u$ assessments are apt to be repudiated also by groups of economists, politicians and other bodies, whose political views in the relevant respects are at variance with those serving the government in office, so degrading further the authority associated with economic appraisal and making economic quantification yet more ridiculous in the eyes of the public.

16 This seems as good a place as any to remark that Harberger's 1978 paper, despite what its title may suggest, has little affinity with the broad argument of the present essay. Although his paper has intrinsic interest, it does not perceive the use of weights in project evaluation as a development which, if continued, must eventually emasculate the economist regarded as an expert offering an independent economic contribution to the decision-making process. Nor will his mildly deprecatory comments about distributional weights in cost–benefit analysis go far in dissuading the proponents of this art from continuing their practice. Indeed, his experimental calculations with a range of distributional weights, which form the bulk of his paper, can be taken to imply a belief that the radical use of distributional weights acts to prevent approval of projects that would otherwise generate regressive distributional effects (contrary to my observation in my 1974 paper).

Moreover, in his penultimate section IV, Harberger concedes – unwarrantably in my view –the treatment of distributional gains as commensurable with efficiency gains. He concludes with the brief observation that, if the distributional weights are small, their use will not make much difference to the results reached by the traditional (unweighted) cost–benefit methods, whereas, if they are large, 'considerations of distribution [could] swamp those of efficiency altogether' which would be 'unacceptable to the vast majority of economists'.

In his final section V, Harberger tentatively proposes (a) that policies should meet a criterion based on the use of both weighted and unweighted valuations, (b) that the unweighted procedure should be vindicated wherever the excess gains are large enough actually to effect transfers that would correct any regressive distributional change associated with the project, and (c) that in the traditional efficiency calculus we ought not perhaps to concern ourselves with distributional weights or with correcting undesirable distributional effects through cash transfers, in a society in which transfers in kind are an accepted means of meeting minimal standards of food, clothing, shelter, health care and education.

One response of all this by the proponents of distributional weights would surely be that Harberger is using the term 'efficiency' as being coterminous with the use of 'unweighted' valuations and is juxtaposing gains in efficiency so defined with possible distributional losses. In contrast, they, the proponents of distributional weights, require the use of weights in the endeavour to establish a concept of efficiency in 'real' or 'util' terms – a legacy of the neoclassical approach.

In the present essay on the other hand, I started with an awareness of their commendable ambitions to infuse more realism into the economist's criterion of efficiency, and have gone on to explore the consequences of such ambitions, if successful, for the survival of an independent criterion of economic efficiency and, therefore, for the status of the economist.

17 Under the dictum that 'all that is utility is not welfare', the distinction between 'legitimate' and 'illegitimate' external effects is drawn in my 1969 monograph (pp. 33–7).

18 One of them is the significance for the distributional structure of 'distributional' externalities – a question also raised in my 1969 monograph (p. 35). Another question is that of the Paretian justification for using a discount rate that is, say, common to all affected by a project when the project extends over a period during which some of the beneficiaries die and others are born.

19 I address myself to this question of consensus within today's 'pluralist' societies in a forthcoming paper in the *Journal of Economic Issues*.

References

Chase, S. B. (ed.) (1968), *Problems in Public Expenditure Analysis* (Washington, DC: Brookings Institution).

Dasgupta, A. K. and Pearce, D. W. (1972), *Cost–Benefit Analysis: Theory and Practice* (London: Macmillan).

Dasgupta, P., Marglin, S. and Sen, A. K. (1972), *Guidelines for Project Evaluation* (New York: UNIDO).

Eckstein, O. and Krutilla, J. (1958), *Water Resource Development* (Cambridge, Mass).

Harberger, A. C. (1978), 'On the use of distributional weights in social cost-benefit analysis', *Journal of Political Economy*, (May).

Hicks, J. R. (1939a), 'The foundations of welfare economics', *Economic Journal* (December).

Hicks, J. R. (1939b), *Value and Capital* (Oxford: Clarendon).

Hochman, H. and Rodgers, J. (1969), 'Pareto optimal redistribution', *American Economic Review*, vol. 59, pp. 542–57.

Irvin, G. (1978), *Modern Cost–Benefit Methods* (London: Macmillan).

Kaldor, N. (1939), 'Welfare propositions in economics and interpersonal comparisons of utility', *Economic Journal* (September).

Little, I. M. D. and Mirrlees, J. A. (1969), *Manual of Industrial Project Analysis in Developing Countries* (Paris: Organisation for Economic Co-operation and Development).

Little, I. M. D. and Mirrlees, J. A. (1974), *Project Appraisal and Planning for Developing Countries* (New York: Basic Books).

Maass, A. *et al.* (1962), *Design of Water Resource Systems* (Harvard: Harvard University Press).

McKean, R. N. (1958), *Efficiency of Government through Systems Analysis* (New York: Wiley).

Mishan, E. J. (1969), *Welfare Economics: An Assessment* (Amsterdam: North-Holland).

Mishan, E. J. (1975), *Cost–Benefit Analysis*, 2nd edn (London: Allen & Unwin).

Pearce, D. W. (1971), *Cost–Benefit Analysis* (London: Macmillan).

Pearce, D. W. (ed.) (1978), *The Valuation of Social Cost* (London: Allen & Unwin).

Pigou, A. C. (1924), *The Economics of Welfare* (London: Macmillan).

Schwartz, H. and Berney, R. (eds) (1977), *Social and Economic Dimensions of Project Evaluation* (Washington, DC: IAD Bank).

Squire, L. and Van der Tak, H. G. (1975), *Economic Analysis and Projects* (Baltimore: Johns Hopkins).

Sugden, R. and Williams, A. (1978), *The Principles of Practical Cost–Benefit Analysis* (Oxford: Oxford University Press).

Tinbergen, J. (1966), *Economic Policy, Principles, and Design* (Amsterdam: North-Holland).

Investment Criteria

17

The Use of DPV in Public Investment Criteria: A Critique

I Introduction

In an ideal Fisherian world in which the market rate of interest is equal both to society's rate of time preference and to the current rate of return on private investment, the ranking of alternative investment streams is accomplished simply by comparing their present values when discounted by the market rate of interest. Problems arise only when the rate of return on private investment, ρ, exceeds r, the common rate of time preference. There are many reasons why this should be so,[1] and we shall assume this to be the case from now on.

All the well-known criteria proposed for evaluating public investment streams embody a discounted present value (DPV) procedure.[2] However, a crucial distinction has to be made between:

(a) the older type criterion, which simply applies a discount rate to the given benefit stream, and within which category differences arise as to the appropriate rate to adopt; and

(b) a newer type of criterion, in which provision is made for the allocation of returns as between consumption and investment, and within which category there can be differences as between behavioural, institutional and political assumptions.

The differences within category (a) are brought out in a comparison below of formulations (1) through (4). Those within the (b) category are less controversial. They arise largely from differences in the degree of elaboration, which deserve no more than passing mention. The (b) type can therefore be represented by formulation (5) alone.

The plan of this paper is as follows. After some introductory remarks about the conventional framework of assumptions, the alleged rationale of each of the four type (a) criteria is briefly indicated in section II. In section III their crucial defect is revealed. Section IV shows the same defect to be inherent in criteria based on the internal rate of return (IRR). As observed in section V, this defect is recognised in the type (b) criterion represented here by formula (5), and provision is made to remedy it. Nonetheless, these criteria fall short of exploiting the full innovational potential implicit in the new perspective they provide. As argued in section VI, this potential is realised by a terminal value-ranking produced by simple rules rather than by formulae. In conclusion, section VII argues the advantages of the latter procedure in comparisons with those of the type (b) criteria.

II Public Investment Criteria of Type (a)

For methods of project evaluation that rest ultimately on a Pareto criterion, an unresolved difficulty arises if the lifetimes of the n people in the community do not overlap at some point over the period of expected benefits. Although there can be other factors, such as intolerable uncertainty about the magnitude of the benefits after a certain date, the former consideration is of itself enough to warrant the introduction of a finite time horizon in any actual procedure for ranking alternative public projects.

In order to economise on inessential elaboration of the analysis, the practice, common in the literature, of ignoring (initially at least) uncertainty in order to focus on a critical part of the logic of investment criteria is followed here. Again, the assumption of 'full employment' is maintained throughout the paper,[3] as is also the fiction that the market values of goods are equal to their social values, in particular that an outlay K on the public project is equal to its opportunity cost.

The convention that voluntary changes in current saving entail equal changes in private investment is also followed in the text.

Let r be the rate of time preference common to all n individuals affected by the public project, and let ρ be the yield on private investment. Although there can be many different rs and ρs (r_i for $i = 1, \ldots, n$, and ρ_j for $j = 1, \ldots, s$), and each r_i, ρ_j can also be dated ($t = 0, \ldots, T$), an analysis conducted in terms of such generality adds only elegant complexity, which may obscure the main lines of the argument. We shall therefore continue to regard r and ρ as single magnitudes, and not as vectors or matrices, except to comment on the proposals of others.

Writing $PV_a(B)$, then, as a shorthand for the present value of the stream of benefits (some of which can be net outlays, or negative benefits) when discounted at rate a, the four type (a) criteria to be reviewed are as follows:

(1) $PV_r(B) > K$;
(2) $PV_\rho(B) > K$;
(3) $PV_\rho(B) > K$;

where $\rho = \sum_{i=1}^{n} w_i r_i + \sum_{j=1}^{s} w_j \rho_j$

and $\sum_{i=1}^{n} w_i + \sum_{j=1}^{s} w_j = 1$; and

(4) $PV_q(B) > K$;

where $\rho > q > r$.

Criterion (1), the staple of textbook instruction, is superficially plausible enough. If r is the common rate of time preference, the community is indifferent as between receiving the stream of benefits $(B) = (B_0, \ldots, B_T)$ and receiving its present value, $PV_r(B)$. It is then convenient to rank the community's preference between any set of alternative investment streams, $B^1, B^2, \ldots, B^g$, each of which results from an initial outlay K, according to the relative magnitudes of $PV_r(B^1)$, $PV_r(B^2), \ldots, PV_r(B^g)$. In particular, any project having a benefit stream that meets (1) tells us that the present value of that stream of benefits exceeds the present value of its costs and therefore represents a potential Pareto improvement for the community.

The rationale for criterion (2), treated in Eckstein's paper of 1957 and also advocated in my 1967a paper and in Baumol's two papers (1968, 1969), is no less plausible. For it suggests that, if funds equal to K are to be spent on a public project, the average yield from the project should be no less than the ρ per annum that the sum K could fetch if it were placed instead in the private investment sector. If, over the period, the benefit stream yields on the average more than ρ, the $PV_\rho(B) > K$

criterion is met, and there is a net gain from adopting the investment project.

Clearly, criterion (3) is a generalisation of (1) and (2) extended to cover all the different rs and ρs in the economy. Since the weights, the ws, are the fractions of K contributed by the separable components of reduced consumption and of reduced private investment, the resultant weighted rate of return represents society's actual opportunity yield per dollar of investing a sum K in a public project. In general, then, ρ will vary according as whether K is raised by tax finance, by loan finance or as a mixture of both. Although (3) was originally proposed by Krutilla and Eckstein (1958), it was advanced again by Harberger (1968) in connection with a rise in interest rates in response to government borrowing[4] which is supposed to check both private investment and consumption.[5] With such a weighted discount rate Harberger claimed (erroneously, as we shall see), 'the so-called reinvestment problem disappears' (p. 308).[6]

The well-known Arrow–Lind paper of 1970 produced criterion (4) as a modification of the popular criterion (2), $PV_\rho(B) > K$, when for their analysis ρ can be taken as the highest actuarial rate of return corresponding, say, to the riskiest private investment. Accepting without criticism their argument that the risks associated with public projects, when divided among a large population of taxpayers, are felt by each taxpayer to be negligible – in contrast to the sense of risk apprehended by the private investor – a risk premium of $(\rho - q)$ can be attributed to the private investor. Inasmuch, then, as the investor is indifferent between the riskiest private investment at ρ and a virtual certain return of q on his money, a potential Pareto improvement is effected if funds are removed from this private investment, so forgoing ρ, and placed instead in public investment at a yield greater than q. Hence the proposed criterion $PV_q(B) > K$.

However, as Arrow and Lind acknowledge in their reply (1972) to critical comments, the crucial assumption on which their criterion rested – that the set of public investment projects excludes opportunities in the private investment sector – did not receive explicit emphasis. And if the assumption is lifted and the government, permitted to undertake private sector investment, can avail itself again of the yield ρ, the $PV_\rho(B) > K$ criterion comes into its own again.

Although criterion (4) is an interesting variation on the type (a) criterion, in other respects it is, as stands, subject to the fundamental criticism of this sort of criterion put forward in section III, which follows.

III   Critique of the Conventional (Type (a)) DPV Criterion

Since the demonstration that follows applies to any of the four criteria, we can use $PV_p(B) > K$ to represent the generic type.

Given the stream of benefits $B_0, B_1, \ldots, B_T$, the above criterion is explicated as

$$\sum_{t=0}^{T} \frac{B_t}{(1+p)^t} > K \qquad (1)$$

By multiplying through by a scalar $(1 + p)^T$, we obtain the equivalent inequality

$$\sum_{t=0}^{T} B_t (1+p)^{T-t} > K(1+p)^T \qquad (2)$$

which can be summarised as

$$TV_p(B) > (K)_p$$

where $TV_p(B)$ stands for the terminal value of the stream of benefits when compounded forward to T at the rate p, and $(K)_p$ stands for the terminal value of the outlay K when it is also compounded forward to T at rate p.

If, and only if, $PV_p(B) > (K)$ does $TV_p(B) > (K)_p$; one form of the criterion, that is, entails the other. But the latter form is more revealing. For it makes clear that, in order for the criterion to be met, the sum of each of the benefits $B_0, B_1, \ldots, B_t, \ldots$, *when wholly invested* and *reinvested to time T at rate p,* must exceed a sum equal to K when wholly and continually reinvested at p to time T. Such a criterion is clearly applicable when in fact both the benefits and the outlays are to be used in exactly this way. If, however, they are not to be used in this way –and it is unlikely that they will be – a criterion based on such a supposition can seriously mislead. Certainly, this $PV_p(B) > K$ criterion is misleading when it is applied to public investment projects without information in each case about the disposal of the returns to the project, and without information about the uses to which the sum K would have been put were it not used as initial outlay for the project.

To illustrate, suppose it to be the case that the outlay K required by a particular public investment is to be drawn entirely from the private investment sector, where it would otherwise have been reinvested at p to reach the value $(K)_p$ at a time T, whereas the project's benefits are to be entirely consumed as they emerge over time. The value of these benefits will grow over time only at r, the rate of time preference, reaching a

total value of $TV_r(B)$ at time T. Now, if the sum $TV_r(B)$ is smaller than $(K)_p$, the project is rejected on a Pareto criterion. Society, that is, will be better off leaving the sum K in the private sector than employing it on the public project. However, since $p > r$, the hypothetical sum $TV_p(B)$ exceeds $TV_r(B)$ and therefore $TV_p(B)$ can exceed $(K)_p$. If so, the project is approved on the $PV_p(B) > K$ criterion, even though it is rejected on a Pareto criterion.

Let us return now to the criterion $PV_r(B) > K$, regarded as a limiting case of the generic $PV_p(B) > K$ criterion. Its transformation into the $TV_r(B) > (K)_r$ form, however, enables us to appreciate immediately the sufficient conditions required for its valid application: namely, that all the returns from the project be wholly consumed as they occur and that the sum K be raised entirely from current consumption. Similarly, transforming the other limiting case, $PV_p(B) > K$ into the form $TV_p(B) > (K)_p$ enables us also to appreciate at once that its Pareto validity is assured if, in fact, it is applied to a case in which the benefits, as they occur, are wholly invested and reinvested in the private investment sector at prevailing yield p until the terminal date T, and if the sum K raised from the private sector would have been wholly invested and reinvested also at yield p until T.

Put otherwise, the correct terminal value of a project's benefit stream, and the correct terminal value of the opportunity cost of its outlay, are both functions, in the simplest possible case, of three variables, r, ρ and θ, where θ is the fraction of any income or investment return that is reinvested in the private sector. In contrast, a criterion $PV_p(B) > K$ makes the terminal value both of the benefit stream and of the outlay a function only of p, whether p is equal to r, or to ρ, or to a weighted sum of r and ρ.

To anticipate a little, the above stringent conditions for the Pareto validity of the type (a) criterion are sufficient. They are not strictly necessary, however.[7] For instance, where the consumption–investment ratio is the same for all the benefits and also for the outlay, a type (b) criterion can, as we shall see later, be reduced to the $PV_r(B) > K$ criterion.

Such simplifications are very agreeable. But one can go further. For on the procedure I propose, there is no need to discount at all. As will be seen in section VI, all that matters are the relevant rates at which returns are to be compounded forward to T. Indeed, once this is done, the terminal values can then be discounted at r or at ρ or at any conceivable rate without any alterations occurring in the ranking or in the criterion.

IV Critique of the Conventional IRR Criterion

In order to complete this part of the critique, we must also re-examine criteria based on the internal rate of return (IRR). There is a seeming advantage in being able to use the IRR for ranking projects without reference to the prevailing yields or interest rates in the economy. Nonetheless, it is not possible to accept or reject projects on the basis of the IRR alone. For this purpose the IRR has to be compared with whatever is believed to be the relevant opportunity rate.

In fact, letting λ stand for the IRR, the IRR criteria corresponding to the DPV criteria (1) through (4) are:

(1') $\lambda > r$,
(2') $\lambda > \rho$,
(3') $\lambda > p$, and
(4') $\lambda > q$.

As a ranking device the IRR has fallen into disfavour among economists, chiefly because there can, in general, be more than one IRR for a given investment stream.[8] However, this is the less important reason. The more important reason is that, even in the common case in which all benefits are positive, the unique IRR calculated for an investment stream does not accord with the true average rate of return over time of the value of that stream. In fact, as conventionally defined, the IRR when used as a criterion has the same defect as the DPV criterion: namely, that a reinvestment rate is entailed that has no necessary relation to the actual rates involved in the particular case.

This defect follows from the standard definition of the IRR as that λ for which

$$\sum_{t=0}^{T} \frac{B_t}{(1+\lambda)^t} = K$$

From multiplying through by $(1+\lambda)^T$ we obtain

$$\sum_{t=0}^{T} B_t(1+\lambda)^{T-t} = K(1+\lambda)^T \qquad (3)$$

So explicated, equation (3) reveals the IRR to be defined as the rate that, when used to compound the benefits forward to T, produces a terminal value equal to outlay K when this is also compounded forward at that rate. The resulting terminal value of the benefits is therefore calculated on the implicit assumption that they are wholly invested and reinvested to T at the rate λ –irrespective, that is, of whether this calculated λ is less than r or greater than ρ. Since, in any actual project, the disposal of the benefits depends upon behavioural and institutional factors, the actual terminal value of

the benefit stream is, again in the simplest case, a function of r, ρ and θ, and not, in general, of λ alone. In other words, before we can calculate λ as an average rate of growth of the initial investment K over the period to T, we must be able to calculate independently the actual terminal value of the benefit stream by reference to r, ρ and θ.

V The New Public Investment (Type (b)) Criteria

Recent recognition by a number of economists of the reinvestment problem had led to formulations of the type (b) criterion, which can be represented by:

(5) $PV_r(B) > AK$.

Marglin's treatment, in his classic article of 1963, assumes that the required sum K is raised from tax revenue and, that of every dollar so raised, a fraction θ_1, comes from an initial reduction in private investment having yield ρ, the remaining fraction $(1 - \theta_1)$ coming from a reduction in current consumption.[9] In addition, θ_2 is the fraction of each dollar of any return that is placed in the private investment sector. Under these conditions an amount K left in the private sector of the economy would generate a stream of consumption over the future, which, when discounted at r, would converge to $aK (a > 1)$.[10] This aK is the 'social opportunity cost' of a project requiring a nominal outlay of K.

However, the employment now of a criterion $PV_r(B) > aK$ can be justified only if the stream of benefits is entirely consumed as they occur. If, instead, the fraction $(1 - \theta_2)$ of each of the benefits is consumed as it occurs, the remainder being invested in the private sector at ρ, and the returns to these investment components treated in the same way, the consumption stream so generated can be discounted at r to a present value of $\alpha PV_r(B) (\alpha > 1)$. The corrected criterion

$$\alpha PV_r(B) > aK$$

can then be written as

$$PV_r(B) > AK \left(A = \tfrac{a}{\alpha}\right).[11]$$

Later contributions that explicitly recognised the reinvestment problem produced models that, although interesting in themselves, reproduced the same essential features of the Marglin model. Feldstein's two papers (1964, 1972), for instance, extend the formulation to cover other behavioural and institutional parameters. Bradford's 1975 paper is of the same family; and although he begins somewhat differently, his results conform to the same basic formula as Marglin's.[12] Since there is no fundamental novelty of conception in the later papers adopting this approach, remarks on the Marglin model are applicable also to their analyses.

Without doubt, the introduction of the type (b) criteria, which face up to the reinvestment problem, was an important step forward in the art of project evaluation and went far to remedy the defect inherent in the older DPV formulae. Yet, the insight that inspired the innovation was channelled into the conventional mould. In the light of the new perspective provided, however, it is possible to break out of the traditional mould – to adopt instead a *terminal value* procedure that depends upon the application of simple rules rather than on elaborate formulae. Since my criticism of the new type (b) criteria is made only by way of comparison with this proposed procedure, its broad outlines are etched in the following section.

VI The Terminal Value Procedure

The procedure I proposed in 1967 is one that transforms an investment stream $-K_0, B_0, B_1, \ldots, B_T$ into the stream $-K_0, 0, 0, \ldots, TV(B)$ (Mishan, 1967b). Of the initial return B_0, the amount consumed is compounded forward at the relevant rates of time preference, say r, to the terminal date T. The remaining amount of B_0 is divided among different investment opportunities actually anticipated, each component being compounded at its yield to the following year and producing in aggregate an amount ΔR_1. Thus, at time $t = 1$ we have returns $(B_1 + \Delta R_1)$ to allocate. Again, the proportion of this total $(B_1 + \Delta R_1)$ that is *consumed* at $t = 1$ is compounded to T at rate r, the remainder being allocated among the various investment opportunities anticipated in consequence of the existing political and/or administrative constraints. Continuing in this way until T, the original benefit stream is transformed into its terminal value $TV(B)$ at T.[13]

A valid ranking of, say, two mutually exclusive projects X and Y, both of which may be rejected, however, requires not only a common terminal date, T, but also a common initial outlay K_0. This requirement is not restrictive. If, say, Y's initial outlay is 20 less than that of X, the 20 left over from the Y investment can be treated as generating a stream of returns in the private sector of the economy, having a terminal value that is to be added to that of the Y stream of benefits.

As for the social opportunity cost of K_0 itself, this is allowed for simply by treating the stream of returns it would generate if left in the private sector, on a par with projects X and Y. For identification we refer to this alternative as the Z stream. Using the same rules, it compounds to terminal value $TV(Z)$.

In this way we end up with three values, $TV(X)$, $TV(Y)$ and $TV(Z)$, from which to choose, all generated by initial outlay K_0. No further operation is required for ranking purposes. If both $TV(X)$ and $TV(Y)$ are less than $TV(Z)$, neither public project is acceptable on a Pareto criterion. If, instead, say

$$TV(X) > TV(Y) > TV(Z)$$

then $TV(X)$ is chosen on the Pareto criterion. Any further operation that is acceptable – say reducing the terminal values to present social values, to present benefit–cost ratios or to IRRs – cannot alter this basic ranking.

Thus, corresponding present values for X, Y and Z are obtained simply by multiplying each of their terminal values by a scalar $(1 + r)^{-T}$. Corresponding benefit–cost ratios are obtained by multiplying them by a scalar $(1 + r)^{-T}/K_0$. As for the corresponding IRRs, when defined in accordance with the basic concept of an average rate of increase over time of the initial investment K_0, and therefore as that unique value of λ for which

$$\frac{TV(B)}{(1+\lambda)^T} = K_0$$

the resulting equations

$$\frac{TV(X)}{(1+\lambda_X)^T} = \frac{TV(Y)}{(1+\lambda_Y)^T} = \frac{TV(Z)}{(1+\lambda_Z)^T} = K_0$$

entails the ranking

$$\lambda_X > \lambda_Y > \lambda_Z$$

VII Rules versus Formulae

In a comparison with the terminal value procedure, the new investment type (b) criteria have a number of disadvantages. A minor objection to them is their employment of infinite time horizons. This assumption has obvious mathematical convenience. It makes possible an initial calculation of the shadow price of a dollar of private investment and, by putting bounds (not always plausible) on the magnitudes of the parameters, allows otherwise cumbersome equations to converge to a more manageable PDV form. Yet, there is a finite time horizon for the expected benefit stream of all actual projects. Indeed, as mentioned earlier, if the method of project evaluation is to have strict Pareto justification, the time limit cannot exceed a certain period. Certainly, if the particular time horizon adopted is short, the application of criteria based on an infinite time horizon can seriously mislead.

A more important consideration is that of economy of time and effort. There is at present unlimited scope for further elaboration of type (b) formulae. Differences between them can arise (1) because of differences in individual behaviour, especially with respect to saving and consumption; (2) because of differences in institutional postulates, especially those describing the collection and disposal of tax revenues and, possibly also, the balance-of-payments effects; and (3) because of differences in administrative and political constraints, especially with reference to the various methods of raising funds for public projects and to the directions for the sale and distribution of the benefits.[14] And since there is no limit to the degree of refinement involved in decomposing aggregates into smaller groups, or in distinguishing institutional factors, unless we break with old habits there is every reason to expect a proliferation of unwieldy public investment criteria over the future.

Given the clearer perception of the issues conferred by these new investment criteria, the need for increased flexibility in actual project evaluation suggests that we turn away from our habitual temptations to elaborate sophisticated formulae. Instead, we should avail ourselves of the facilities provided by high speed computers in producing a valid terminal-value-ranking guided only by simple rules appropriate to the occasion. For although the instructions to the computer for any particular project will vary according to the factors mentioned in (1), (2) and (3) above, and according to the degree of refinement sought, the simple rules in question follow the same basic principle: a dividing of the aggregate returns at each time t into consumption and investment opportunities, and then a compounding of each component forward either to T or to $(t + 1)$, respectively.

The proposed procedure also has the obvious advantage of conceiving the exercise in terms of a chronological movement forward through time, rather than the reverse. Thus, the instructions for the two-period sequence, t and $(t + 1)$, are explicit and easy to check. Moreover, the procedure is flexible enough to accommodate itself, if necessary, to political constraints that are expected to alter over time or are scheduled to take effect at later points in time, such as the provision of special investment opportunities in the public sector for the returns expected from the project in question.

Notes: Chapter 17

1 Among the reasons why, at any point of time, ρ can be supposed greater than r, the following are commonly mentioned. (a) The incidence of direct taxes (mainly income and corporation taxes) requires that yield ρ exceed r, since r is the net return the individual will have to receive if he is to continue to provide his current volume of saving. (b) Even in an economy having no direct taxes, the prevalence of subjective risk in investment undertaken by private firms and in the saving provided by individuals would raise yields on investments above r. (c) Again, in the absence both of direct taxes and risks, external economies in current investment would imply a social rate of return ρ on current investment greater than the market rate of return that is equal to r. (d) In the absence of direct taxes, risks and external economies from investment, the prevailing short-run market rate ρ can exceed the long-run equilibrium rate r. (e) In addition to these phenomena, there are always those imperishable 'market imperfections' which sometimes take the form of monopoly power among lenders.

I deliberately omit one possible explanation of the deviation between a social rate of time preference and market rates of interest: namely, one that has it that the social rate of time preference is to be decided by some political authority or decision-makers. For treatments that favour this notion of the social rate of time preference, see Dasgupta *et al.* (1972), Dasgupta and Pearce (1972) and Nath (1969). For arguments against this solution, see Mishan (1974).

2 My proposed normalisation procedure (1976b) is an exception, further reflection about which has resulted in the present critique.

3 The financial outlay necessary for a public project can be many times the project's opportunity cost if unemployment is so high that a large proportion of the labour used in the project would otherwise have remained unemployed. For empirical calculations of the opportunity cost of a dollar of outlay under a wide range of employment conditions, see Haveman and Krutilla (1968).

4 Not surprisingly, Chicago school economists favour loan finance of public investments. Others favour tax finance either on the grounds (see Musgrave, 1969) that it tends to reduce the volume of private investment less than does loan finance, or else on the grounds (see Nichols, 1969) that loan finance entails future tax levies in order to service the debt.

5 However, Drèze (1974, p. 60) asks if government borrowing does affect the rate of interest and, if so, whether a higher rate of interest increases current saving. His answer is simply that 'there undoubtedly exist cases where government borrowing does not affect the rate of interest, but is simply offset by rationing of private investment'.

Drèze compares his view with that of Arrow (1966), who argues that the divergence 'between the rate of interest implicit in consumption decisions and any market rate is so great that is must be accepted that savings are largely independent of the latter', and then goes on to say that the issue is 'to decide whether some consumers do react, at least, for some forms of consumption'.

6　The conclusion reached by Sandmo and Drèze (1971), that for a closed economy 'the public sector's discount rate should be a weighted average of the rates facing consumers and the tax-distorted rates used by firms', is similar to that of Ramsey (1969) and much the same as the proposal put forward by Harberger (1968).

7　See note 11 for conditions justifying the use of the $PV_r(B) > K$ criterion even when reinvestment effects are taken into account. As for the conditions justifying the use of the $PV_\rho(B) > K$ criterion, Feldstein (1972), associating its use with Hirshleifer *et al.* (1961) and Mishan (1967a) alleges that it is based on an ambiguity in the notion of opportunity cost. For the purpose of investment criteria, opportunity cost should relate not to the best alternative use to which the resource *could* be put, but to the alternative use to which it *would* be put.

I agree that it should be the latter, but there is more to be said. For Feldstein ignores the question of political constraint. To illustrate, if the public investment authority is invested with powers to make the best possible use of funds that are otherwise available for particular public projects, the use of ρ as discount rate is indeed justified, since in that case the best alternative opportunity open to such funds may well be that of investing and reinvesting them in the private investment sector at ρ.

8　A negative benefit (excluding the initial outlay) is a necessary condition for more than one value of the IRR, but is not sufficient. In general, if there are n periods of time, there can be as many as $(n-1)$ values for the IRR of the investment stream, although some may be complex numbers.

9　In fact, Marglin produces three models in this paper. His third model introduces alternative and less plausible behaviour assumptions, while his first model is little more than a stepping stone to the second model, which is treated above as *the* Marglin model.

10　In order for the infinite stream of consumption thus generated to converge, when discounted at r, to a finite sum, Marglin assumes that $\theta_2\rho < r$.

11　In a limiting case, where $\theta_1 = \theta_2$, $a = \alpha$ and $PV_r(B) > AK$ reduces to $PV_r(B) > K$. (In Bradford's 1975 model, θ_1 and θ_2 are denoted respectively as a_t and α_{t+1}; and when these are equal, his criterion also reduces to $PV_r(B) > K$.)

12　Bradford's 1975 paper, in some ways a development of his earlier paper of 1970, constructs a model that closely resembles that of Marglin. This resemblance is easier to appreciate by comparing Marglin's equation (8), condensed and cast in discrete form, with Bradford's equation (15), using a common notation. Marglin's criterion then appears as

$$\sum_{t=0}^{\infty} \alpha B_t \delta_t - aK_0 > 0$$

while Bradford's takes the form

$$\sum_{t=0}^{T} \alpha_t B_t \delta_t - \Sigma a_t K_t \delta > 0$$

where B_t is the tth benefit from the public project, K_t the tth net outlay, and α_t the shadow price of a dollar of the tth net outlay. The discount factor to be applied to B_t and K_t is δ_t.

Since Bradford's public-investment benefit stream is finite (and not infinite, as is Marglin's), his shadow prices α_t and a_t vary with t.

For the special case $\alpha_t = a_t$, both reduce to the general form

$$PV_r(B-K) > 0$$

which form includes the possibility also of a stream of net outlays.

13　If, instead, behaviour and political constraints are such that the annual *return* on the investment component of the preceding year is taken as the basis for consumption and reinvestment of the current year, the rules are different. In that case θB_0, the amount invested in the private sector out of the initial return B_0, is added immediately to the terminal value of the investment stream, while the annual return $q_1, = \rho(\theta B_0)$, on this θB_0, continues to appear annually at $t=1, 2, \ldots, T$. At $t=1$ this q_1 is added to B_1, the aggregate return now being $(B_1 + q_1)$, of which a proportion θ is placed in the private investment sector and the remainder consumed.

14　Thus, in addition to raising an initial outlay K_0 by any mixture of tax finance and loan finance, a part can also be raised by using the funds that otherwise go to replacing the capital of existing public enterprises – a possibility mentioned by Steiner (1959) and Mishan (1967b).

References

Arrow, K. J. (1966), 'Discounting and public investment criteria', in A. Kneese and Smith (eds), *Water Research* (Washington, DC: Resources for the Future).

Arrow, K. J. and Lind, R. C. (1970), 'Uncertainty and the evaluation of public investment decisions', *American Economic Review* (June).

Arrow, K. J. and Lind, R. C. (1972), 'Reply', *American Economic Review* (March).

Baumol, W. J. (1968), 'On the social discount rate', *American Economic Review* (September).

Baumol, W. J. (1969), 'On the social rate for public projects' in *The Analysis and Evaluation of Public Expenditures: The PBB System,* Vol. I (Washington, DC: Joint Economic Committee).

Bradford, D. F. (1970), 'Constraints on public action and rules for social decisions', *American Economic Review* (September).

Bradford, D. F. (1975), 'Constraints of government investment opportunities and the choice of discount rate', *American Economic Review* (December).

Dasgupta, A. K. and Pearce, D. W. (1972), *Cost–Benefit Analysis: Theory and Practice* (London: Macmillan).

Dasgupta, P., Marglin, S. A. and Sen, A. (1972), *Guidelines for Project Evaluation* (New York: United Nations).

Drèze, J. H. (1974), 'Discount rates and public investment: a postscript', *Economica* (February).

Eckstein, O. (1957), 'Investment criteria for economic development', *Quarterly Journal of Economics* (June).

Feldstein, M. S. (1964), 'Net social benefit calculation and the public investment decision', *Oxford Economic Papers.*

Feldstein, M. S. (1972), 'The inadequacy of weighted discount rates', in R. Layard (ed.), *Cost–Benefit Analysis* (London: Penguin).

Harberger, A. C. (1968), 'The opportunity costs of public investment financed by borrowing'; reprinted in R. Layard (ed.), *Cost–Benefit Analysis* (London: Penguin, 1972).

Harberger, A. C. (1978), 'On the use of distributional weights in social cost–benefit analysis', *Journal of Political Economy,* (May).

Haveman, R. H. and Krutilla, J. V. (1968), *Unemployment, Idle Capacity and the Evaluation of Public Expenditures* (Washington, DC).

Hertz, D. B. (1964), 'Risk analysis in capital investment', *Harvard Business Review* (January).

Hirshleifer J. (1966), 'Investment decisions under uncertainty: application of the state preference approach', *Quarterly Journal of Economics* (May).

Hirshleifer, J. *et al.* (1961), *Water Supply: Economics, Technology and Policy* (Princeton, NJ: Princeton University Press).

Krutilla, J. and Eckstein, O. (1958), *Multiple Purpose River Development* (Baltimore: Johns Hopkins).

Marglin, S. A. (1963), 'The opportunity cost of public investment', *Quarterly Journal of Economics* (May).

Mishan, E. J. (1967a), 'Criteria for public investment: some simplifying suggestions', *Journal of Political Economy* (September).

Mishan. E. J. (1967b), 'A proposed normalisation procedure for public investment criteria', *Economic Journal* (December).

Mishan, E. J. (1974a), 'Consistency and flexibility in cost–benefit analysis', *Economica* (February).

Mishan E. J. (1974b), 'Flexibility and consistency in project evaluation', *Economica* (December).

Musgrave, R. A. (1969), 'Cost–benefit analysis and the theory of public finance', *Journal of Economic Literature.*

Nath, S. K. (1969), *A Reappraisal of Welfare Economics* (London: Routledge & Kegan Paul).

Nichols, A. (1969), 'On the social rate of discount: a comment', *American Economic Review* (December).

Ramsey, D. D. (1969), 'On the social rate of discount: a comment', *American Economic Review* (December).

Sandmo, A. and Drèze, J. H. (1971), 'Discount rates for public investment in closed and open economies', *Economica* (May).

Steiner, P. O. (1959), 'Choosing among alternative public investments in the water resource field', *American Economic Review* (December).

18

The Difficulty in Evaluating Long-lived Projects

There are a number of problems in connection with public cost–benefit analysis – the pricing of 'intangibles', the treatment of uncertainty and alternative methods of discounting come to mind in this connection – that have not as yet been satisfactorily resolved. There is, in addition, a problem that, so far as I know, has not been explicitly recognised and satisfactorily treated: namely, the propriety of using a conventional discounting (or compounding) procedure when the stream of benefits is expected to cover a period over which beneficiaries expire and are born.

This paper is divided into five sections. Section I describes the nature of the problem. Sections II and III are developed under the assumption that *no* institutional mechanisms exist whereby benefits occurring at given times can be transferred to others or transformed into future benefits. Their object is to show that, although an individual's time stream of benefits and costs can be evaluated at any point of time (usually time zero) by reference simply to his time rate of preference, this procedure cannot automatically be extended to a community of individuals having the same time rate of preference. Section II makes clear that the conventional method of discounting to the present at a common rate of time preference is unwarrantable when applied to two non-overlapping generations. Section III shows that, in the absence of intervening mechanisms actually to transfer benefits as between generations – in effect transforming the original benefit system into one having particular properties – the Pareto criterion, as commonly understood (as a synonym for a potential Pareto improvement), cannot be applied to a succession of overlapping generations.

Sections IV and V introduce possible institutional mechanisms. Section IV considers the possibility of arranged transfers as between generations, while Section V considers the market mechanism, in particular investment opportunities whereby an original benefit stream can be transformed over generational time into one that apparently meets a Pareto criterion. The possible conclusion in each of these two latter cases, that a resulting positive net benefit is tantamount to a potential Pareto improvement, is shown to be invalid.

I

(1) Although economists have addressed themselves to intergenerational problems, they have done so only in connection with growth models, in particular with those featuring finite amounts of depletable natural resources.[1] For such models the focus of concern is on the distribution of *per capita* consumption over generational time. Despite complications introduced by alternative shapes of the production function, by alternative behaviour assumptions, by the existence of depletable natural resources and/or by technical progress, there is an observable tendency for more recent models to favour the original Ramsey (1928) solution of eventual constant *per capita* consumption over time.

A conventional cost–benefit analysis, on the other hand, in so far as it is raised on allocative criteria only, disregards distributional implications. For this analysis the relevant criterion proposed, the Pareto criterion, is met if the project in question meets a potential Pareto improvement – having special regard to the economist's basic axiom, that the value to be attributed to a good or bad at a point of time is the value placed on it by the person at that point of time. So restricted, the criterion proposed can be defined as purely economic. Its application requires, *inter alia,* that, if person X values $600 to be received in year 10 as equal to $60 today, the economist also has to accept this trade-off as part of the 'objective' data.

(2) The case of a single individual raises no problem in this connection. Where, however, a number of individuals have to be considered, an arbitrary element is unavoidable whenever the individual time rates of discount differ. To illustrate, suppose that the

introduction of the project affects the welfare of two persons only, X and Y, the result being that X gains 60 in the first year, while Y loses 200 in year 10. Person Y is indifferent as between a loss of 200 in year 10 and a loss of 100 in year 1. Person X, on the other hand, is indifferent between a gain of 60 today and 600 in ten years' time.

If we decide to discount values to the present, there is clearly a net loss of 40 from the project. If, instead, we compare equivalent values in year 10, there will be a net gain of 400. In this example the ratio of person X's benefit to person Y's loss varies with the reference year we choose to adopt in order to evaluate the net benefit of the project – as is brought out in Figure 1, in which the time-equivalent values (benefits and costs) of each person are measured vertically, on a logarithmic scale, for each point of time over the ten-year period.

In general, of course, there can be a matrix of rates of time preference, each element of such a matrix denoting the relevant rate for a particular person (or group) over a particular period of chronological time. This matrix conception of itself causes no theoretical difficulty. But from our example above we are impelled to conclude that, unless the (weighted) time rate of discount is the same for both gainers and losers from the project, the outcome of a cost–benefit calculation will depend, in general, upon the reference point of time to which all gains and losses are to be reduced. Since no purely economic consideration favours one point of time over another, the choice of any one point of time (including, of course, the present time, which is favoured by convention) is arbitrary.

However, we may reasonably disregard this possibility among others in the interests of facing up to the more crucial difficulty.

(3) Although not necessary to its demonstration, it will both simplify the exposition and discourage attempts (by invoking the notion of bequests or the investment of benefits received) to wriggle out of the quandary in which we shall find ourselves if, for the time being, we conceive of a public project the finance (and opportunity cost) of which is raised wholly by reducing current consumption and the benefits from which are entirely consumed as they occur. Moreover, in contrast to the above example, we shall henceforth assume the existence of a money market so accommodating as to produce a rate of discount, r, that is common to all persons affected by the project. From this assumption it follows that, *provided that all of them expect to remain alive during the investment period,* the ratio of benefits to losses – as distinct from the excess benefit magnitude – remains unaltered irrespective of the reference point of time adopted. The reader should

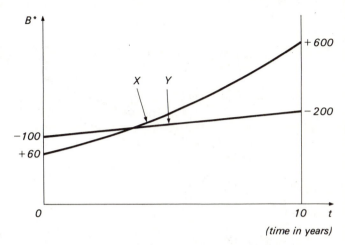

(log of benefit)

Fig. 1

bear in mind, however, that, inasmuch as a benefit–cost ratio greater than unity entails an excess of benefits over cost, it also meets the Pareto criterion whenever, in the valuation of benefits and costs, the basic economic axiom obtains.

The problem addressed in this paper is that which arises when the italicised proviso above is *not* met – when, that is, beneficiaries (which term includes 'maleficiaries') come into being at some point of time later than the initial year, and when some of those who are beneficiaries at the introduction of the project expire before the terminal date of the investment period.

To illustrate the problem, suppose that a benefit of 1,000 is to be received by person X in year 100 as a result of the introduction in year 0 of a public project. The common rate of discount, r, which (in accordance with our assumption) corresponds also to X's rate of time preference, is such, we shall suppose, as to discount this 1,000 in year 100 to 2 in year 0. But even though his rate of time preference over his own lifetime is equal to r, if X were born in year 80 he could not be said to be indifferent as between receiving 1,000 in year 100 and receiving 2 in year 0, this being eighty years prior to his birth.

Although the assumption of an investment period as long as 100 years helps to point up the problem, the same difficulty occurs in project evaluation generally – in fact, for any period over which some gainers and losers by the project expire while others come into being.

(4) This difficulty has been circumvented up to now

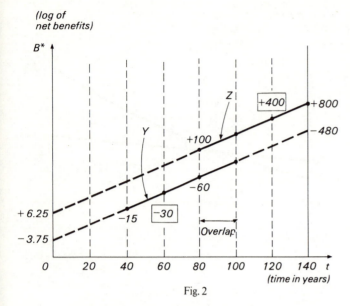

Fig. 2

by adopting either of two ruses. The first is simply that of assuming (implicitly) that the lifetime of each person affected by the project covers the whole period – although, as we shall see, this assumption is too strict. The second is that of adopting a 'social' rate of discount, regarded as a political datum that the economist alleges he has no right to question.

The latter device has been adopted as a matter of course by a number of writers,[2] and no one would deny that it simplifies matters wonderfully. Yet, the implications from introducing politically determined valuations into economic calculations are far from acceptable. All that need be said here, however, is that recourse to such devices entails the rejection of a purely economic criterion as defined above. And since it is just possible, in any case, that the political authority may require the economist to produce a purely economic calculation of the project in question – and since, in addition, some economists themselves may be interested in a purely economic evaluation – we have some excuse for thinking about it.

In doing so we shall follow the practice in cost–benefit analysis of evading the awkward question of the exact age at which a person is supposed to be sufficiently conscious of the benefits or losses associated with the project as to be able to assess them and to translate them into equivalent values over time by reference to r, his time preference rate.[3] Thus, in the examples that follow, the year in which a person is 'born' is interpreted as being the year in which he can first be trusted to evaluate consistently the benefits and costs accruing to him (or the first year to which the

values of benefits or losses received can confidently be attributed to him). It is therefore the earliest year to which subsequent benefits and losses can be discounted by him. This same person 'expires' when he is no longer able to make sensible and consistent assessments in these respects, even though he may be alive in the biological sense. The year of his expiration in this sense is the last year to which benefits and losses he experiences can be compounded by him.

II

(5) Chronological time is measured along the horizontal axis of Figure 2, and the logarithm of the value of net benefits or losses is measured along the vertical axis. The solid parts of the two lines marked Y and Z are to be regarded as the 'time indifference curves' of these two individuals, Y and Z, inasmuch as each of them is indifferent as between the different aggregate values of his actual stream of net benefits (or net losses) corresponding to any chosen points of time.

Given a common rate of time preference, r, for all persons, the time indifference curve for each person slopes upward from left to right at the same angle, equal to r. Thus, person Z (who lives from year 80 to year 140) is represented in Figure 2 as enjoying a net benefit stream worth 400 in year 120. Adopting an r such that \$1 compounds to \$2 in twenty years – an r of approximately 0·035 per annum – Z is then indifferent as between receiving the sum 400 in year 120 or the sum 800 in year 140. Person Y, on the other hand (who lives from year 40 to year 100), sustains a net loss over time equal to 30 in year 60 and, therefore, equal to 60 in year 80, and equal to a net loss of 120 in year 100. Since with this r the sum of 30 in year 60 discounts to 3·75 today, the sum of 400 in year 120 discounts to 6·25 today; a conventional DPV (discounted present value) method reduces this 'stream' of benefits to a benefit–cost ratio of 5/3.

In view of the fact that person Z appears on the scene much later than person Y, it is possible to demur at this result as being unfair to Z. It may then be suggested that a fair criterion would be one that compares the benefits to each person when his stream of benefits is discounted to his own year of birth. On this proposal Z's benefit of 400 in year 120 is discounted to 100 in year 80, the year of Z's birth, while Y's cost of 30 in year 60 is discounted to 15 in year 40, Y's year of birth. The comparison of these figures, 100 and 15, produces a benefit–cost ratio of 20/3, clearly more favourable than the conventional ratio of 5/3.

This proposal, however, contravenes the purely economic criterion. After all, the twenty-year period between (and including) years 80 and 100 is common to both persons. Taking year 80, arbitrarily, as the common reference point in time, person Z is indifferent at rate r as between 400 in year 120 and 100 in year 80, while person Y is indifferent as between −30 in year 60 and −60 in year 80. Thus, at year 80 both Z and Y are agreed on their respective equivalent valuations, 100 and −60. The benefit–cost ratio in the reference year 80 is then 100/60, or 5/3.

It should be obvious that the choice of any other reference year common to both lifetimes – the years 80 to 100 inclusive – will yield proportional values for each person that leave this benefit–cost ratio unchanged. For example, the equivalent values for, say, year 100 can be obtained simply by multiplying both the 100 for person Z and the −60 for person Y in year 80 by $(1+r)^{20}$, so leaving the benefit–cost ratio of 5/3 unaltered.

This ratio of 5/3, it will be noticed, is exactly the same as that resulting from the employment of the conventional DPV method, which is hardly surprising, since, starting from an agreed benefit–cost ratio of 5/3 in year 80, a discounting of both numerator and denominator by the common scalar $(1+r)^{80}$ does not alter the ratio. For the same reason, neither does the employment, instead, of a CTV (compounded terminal value) procedure alter the 5/3 ratio.

From this simple example we conclude as follows: accepting the benefit–cost ratio at any point of time as an index of the Pareto criterion, then, provided that there is a common rate of time preference, r, the existence of an 'overlap' in the lifetimes of such persons justifies the familiar calculation of a benefit–cost ratio. Moreover, the existence of this common r assures that the resulting ratio remains unchanged, whatever reference point of time is chosen. Consequently, the adoption of a DPV or of a CTV method under these conditions can also be vindicated.

(6) As a step toward our next construction we turn our attention now from the lifetime overlap of twenty years between persons Y and Z to a 'gap' of twenty years between the lifetimes of persons X and Z. The situation is that depicted in Figure 3. Person X is there represented as indifferent as between the actual stream of benefits he receives from the project and a net receipt of 60 in year 60. On the other hand, Z is indifferent between the actual stream of benefits accruing to him from the project and a net outlay of 100 in year 80. This net outlay figure of 100 appears as −100 at the beginning of Z's lifetime in year 80.

Using a conventional DPV procedure, the figures for persons X and Z are respectively 7·5 and −6·25, or a benefit–cost ratio of 6/5. For a conventional CTV procedure the figures are respectively 960 and −800,

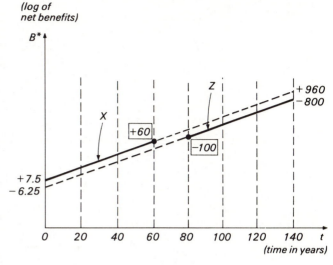

(log of net benefits)

Fig. 3

and again a benefit–cost ratio of 6/5. However, this ratio cannot be rationalised in the same way as that for the data in the preceding example, for the simple reason that there is no longer a common point of time at which each person can attach an equivalent value. We have already compounded X's benefit stream forward as far as we may to year 60, and discounted Z's benefit stream as far back as we may to year 80. And this is as far as we may go if we abide, as we intend in this exercise, by the basic axiom.

It is manifest, therefore, that the usual DPV method implies unwarrantably that this gap be bridged – that person Z's net outlay of 100 in year 80 be unwarrantably discounted to year 60, to become a net outlay of 50. Alternatively, the usual CTV method unwarrantably implies that person X's net benefit of 60 in year 60 be compounded to year 80, to become a net benefit of 120. Yet clearly, Z is *not* indifferent as between his agreed net outlay of 100 in year 80 and a net outlay of 50 in year 60, since he is not alive in year 60. *Mutatis mutandi*, X is *not* indifferent as between his agreed net benefit of 60 in year 60 and a net benefit of 120 in year 80, since he is not alive in year 80. In fact, the only comparison that may be warranted by the economist's basic axiom is a direct comparison of the equivalent values of both persons (−100 for Z and 60 for X) at any point of time within and including the two end points of the gap.

Bearing in mind that the so-called gap is the shortest distance in time separating persons X and Z from sharing a common point of time, a determination to adhere to the basic axiom would require that – with

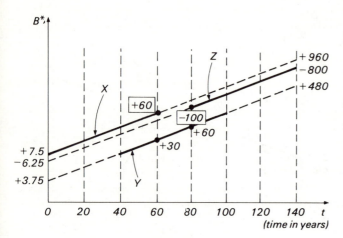

Fig. 4

respect to discounting or compounding – the time gap between the individuals be disregarded. The economist, that is, may *not* assume for *Z* an equivalent outlay value any smaller than the 100 equivalent outlay agreed to in year 80, nor for *X* an equivalent benefit value larger than the 60 units equivalent benefit agreed to in year 60. Separated by an unbridgeable time gap in the lives of these persons, the economist can either throw up his hands or else, by analogy with two persons separated by space, seek to justify a direct comparison between a net benefit of 60 for *X* and a net outlay of 100 for *Z*, and therefore a benefit–cost ratio of 60/100, or 3/5.

(7) Granted the warrant for the above comparison, the benefit–cost ratio of 6/5, resulting from the employment, instead, of a conventional DPV or CTV procedure, requires correction. The correction is obvious and, in the limiting case, can be looked at in either of two ways:

(a) Since the CTV of person *X*'s net benefit at year 60 is unwarrantably compounded forward on the conventional CTV procedure at rate *r* for twenty years, correction requires that the *numerator* of the conventional CTV benefit–cost ratio be multiplied by $(1 + r)^{-20}$.

(b) Alternatively, since, on a conventional DPV procedure, the DPV of person *Z*'s net outlay at year 80 is unwarrantably discounted for twenty years at rate *r*, correction requires that the *denominator* of the conventional DPV benefit-cost ratio be multiplied by $(1 + r)^{20}$.

It should be evident that these alternative corrections are equivalent and equal to a correction factor of $1/(1 + r)^{20}$. When this correction factor is applied to the conventional benefit–cost ratio of 6/5, the result is, of course, the ostensibly warranted ratio of 3/5.

This simple result can, if adopted, easily be generalised to comprehend more than two persons, *X* and *Z*, and therefore to comprehend more than two time gaps. But there is no point in doing so in view of the conclusion to be reached in the following section, where we introduce into the above example a third person, *Y*, whose lifetime overlaps with those of both *X* and *Z*, in this way producing an irreducible model of the intergenerational overlapping case.

III

(8) The addition now of a third person, *Y*, whose lifetime, from year 40 to year 100, overlaps with those of persons *X* and *Z* provides us with a critical example.

The hypothetical data are those depicted in Figure 4, which reproduces all the features of Figure 3 along with the solid-line indifference curve marked *Y* from year 40 to year 100. The actual net-benefit stream enjoyed by person *Y* from the project is such that it is equivalent to a net benefit of 60 at year 80 or else of 30 at year 60. Person *Y*, that is, is indifferent as between these two options and, of course, the stream itself. Thus, the figures +30 and +60, above the *Y* line at years 60 and 80, are equivalent options for *Y*.

By reference to the two sets of three figures at years 0 and 140 respectively, a conventional DPV or CTV procedure is seen to yield a benefit–cost ratio of 9/5, which, however, is economically unacceptable, inasmuch as it violates the basic axiom. By reference to it we must now determine the necessary corrections.

Let us recall for a moment the corrections to be effected in the case of persons *X* and *Z* only. Correction (a), applied to the conventional CTV method, in effect leaves us with +60 and –100 at year 80, whereas correction (b), applied to the conventional DPV method, in effect also leaves us with the same figures, +60 and –100, at year 60. Thus, a direct comparison of these two figures, either at year 60 or at year 80, can make no difference to the corrected benefit–cost ratio of 3/5.

Our third person, *Y*, is, as mentioned, indifferent as between a net benefit of 30 at year 60 and a net benefit of 60 at year 80. However, if we choose correction (b), with the year 60 as our reference point of time, then adherence to the basic axiom will sanction the figures +30, +60 and –100 respectively for persons *Y*, *X* and *Z*, and therefore a benefit–cost ratio of 9/10, which any

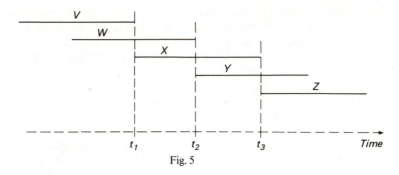

Fig. 5

further discounting or compounding at r will not alter. If, on the other hand, we choose correction (a), with year 80 as our reference point of time, we sanction the figures +60, +60 and –100 respectively for persons Y, X and Z, and therefore a benefit–cost ratio of 12/10, which discounting or compounding at r again cannot alter. Yet, it obviously makes a critical difference to the benefit–cost ratio which year we choose as reference year – year 60 or year 80. Conformity with the basic axiom, then, suggests that either of these years is a valid reference point. But economics has nothing to contribute to the choice.

We can check this result briefly by adopting in turn each of the two corrections proposed in the preceding section, where, however, it made no difference to the benefit–cost ratio for the two-person case, X and Z. Using a conventional CTV procedure, the required (a) correction, operating only on an unwarrantable compounding of person X's net benefit for twenty years, is that which multiplies X's CTV of 960 by $(1 + r)^{-20}$, so reducing it to 480. The corrected CTV benefit–cost ratio is therefore 12/10 – equal, then, to the warranted ratio when reference year 80 is chosen.

Using, instead, a conventional DPV procedure, the required (b) correction, now operating only on an unwarrantable discounting of person Z's net outlay for twenty years, is that which multiplies Z's DPV of $-6 \cdot 25$ by $(1 + r)^{20}$, so increasing its absolute value to $-12 \cdot 5$. The corrected DPV benefit–cost ratio is therefore 9/10 – equal again, then, to the warranted ratio when reference year 60 is chosen.

(9) In sum, adherence to the economist's basic axiom seems to justify either the type (a) correction of a conventional CTV procedure, or the type (b) correction of a conventional DPV procedure. The two different benefit–cost ratios resulting respectively from these two corrections are necessarily equal also to the two different 'warranted' benefit–cost ratios resulting from choosing respectively either year 80 or year 60 as the reference year. There is nothing in economics, however, that will enable us to justify the choice of one

reference year over the other, and therefore to justify also the choice of a corrected CTV method over a corrected DPV method, even though the choice can be critical, as indeed it is in our example.

There is, of course, scope for a more elegant and general presentation of these results. But nothing serves better than a crude example to rivet attention on the problem.

(10) To sum up, and abstracting from institutional mechanisms, Figure 4 reduces the problem to its simplest form in that there is an overlap between persons X and Y, so rendering them Pareto comparable, and an overlap between persons Y and Z, so rendering them Pareto comparable also. But clearly, there is no common point of overlap for the three persons X, Y and Z. As indicated, therefore, a comparison of X and Y alone, or else of Y and Z alone, can yield a benefit–cost ratio that is invariant to time. But since there is no common point of overlap between X, Y and Z adherence to the basic axiom forbids a Pareto comparison of all three, and a benefit – cost ratio that is the result of the conventional discounting procedure is invalid.

More generally, the number of overlapping persons may be increased from two to any number m, and the years of common overlap chosen arbitrarily without altering the above conclusion. Thus, if m were three instead of two, as in Figure 4, five persons, V, W, X, Y and Z, could conveniently be represented in Figure 5, which (as distinct from Figure 4) dispenses with a vertical axis by simply attaching a net benefit figure (positive or negative) – which increases at the common rate, r – to each of these overlapping horizontal lines.

The three successive persons V, W and X overlap at time t_1, and therefore a Pareto comparison in the form of a benefit–cost ratio is possible. Similar words apply to persons W, X and Y at time t_2, and to persons X, Y and Z at time t_3. But since there is no satisfactory way of bringing both V and Y into a Pareto comparison, a benefit–cost ratio for the four persons V, W, X and Y is not possible. Nor, for the same reason, is a benefit–cost ratio for W, X, Y and Z. Clearly, the spacing of successive persons closer so as to increase the number of overlapping persons at each point of time cannot alter the general conclusion once the chronological time is extended sufficiently.

We conclude that, in the absence of institutional mechanisms that will enable us to transform the project's original net–benefit stream into some new pattern, it is not possible in general to meet the standard Pareto criterion.

IV

(11) The next phase of the analysis should be apparent. First, it is necessary to show how the use of some institutional mechanism can transform the project's original stream of net benefits into one that meets or fails the standard Pareto criterion. Secondly, we are to examine the implications of this possible transformation in order to interpret the resulting criterion. Finally, we have to appraise the ethical appeal of such a criterion within an intergenerational context.

(12) Now, of course, it is possible to rearrange the receipts as between generations so as to appear to vindicate the DPV or CTV procedure. Returning to our example represented by Figure 4, instead of person X remaining in year 60 with the 60 conferred by the project and person Y remaining with 30 in year 60 (with person Z not yet born), the government could transfer the 60 received by X to Y at that point of time, leaving X with zero and Y with 90. This 90 in year 60 is equivalent to 180 in year 80 for Y, so that in year 80 it becomes possible to compare this benefit of 180 for Y with the loss of 100 for Z – a benefit–cost ratio of 9/5, which, of course, corresponds with the benefit–cost figure resulting from the conventional use of the rate of discount. Indeed, 100 of Y's gain of 180 could then be transferred to Z, in this way offsetting Z's loss of 100 in that year. The end result of such transfers would be that both X and Z are no worse off than they would be without the project, while Y is better off by 80 in year 80.

(13) If government could be depended upon to intervene in this way, it may seem to follow that such arrangements would in fact result in an *actual* Pareto improvement for the community comprising persons X, Y and Z. But this apparent actual Pareto improvement is simply the result of our treating X, Y and Z, up to now, as three *persons*, whereas we have now to recognise the need to treat them as three *generations*. Once we do so, the net gains of generation X can be divided into two sums: X_g, the gains of the

members of the X generation benefiting from the project; and X_1, the losses suffered from the project of other members of the X generation. Hence, letting X' stand for the net benefit of generation X,

$$X' = X_g - X_1 = +60 \text{ in year } 60$$

And since we assume a common rate of time preference, r, this net gain of 60 for generation X in year 60 is equal to a net gain of 30 in year 40, of 15 in year 20 and of 7·5 in year 0. Similarly, the net benefit of generation Y is denoted by

$$Y' = Y_g - Y_1 = +30 \text{ in year } 60$$

while the net benefit of generation Z is denoted by

$$Z' = Z_g - Z_1 = -100 \text{ in year } 80$$

It follows therefore that, *prior* to any government transfer, the original project effects a potential Pareto improvement for each of generations X and Y and a potential Pareto loss for generation Z. However, once the government intervenes in the way described above, each of generations X and Z ends up by realising a zero potential Pareto improvement (in each of these two generations, gains exactly offset losses), whereas generation Y enjoys a potential Pareto improvement (gains to some members of the Y generation exceed the losses suffered by other members of that generation by as much as 80 valued in year 80).

We conclude therefore that, if the government actually *does* intercede so as to transfer sums from generation X to generation Y and from generation Y to generation Z in such a way that, at least, no generations suffer a potential Pareto loss, then a potential Pareto improvement can be secured for at least one generation – in our example, generation Y – whenever the conventional discounting procedure produces a benefit–cost ratio greater than unity.

(14) However, the economist has not, as yet, made the application of his conventional discounting procedure explicitly contingent upon government intervention in the way exemplified above. He has always applied the discount rate directly to the original stream of returns generated by the original investment project, irrespective of the time span involved. It follows that, if this discounting procedure when applied directly to the stream of returns of the original project shows a benefit–cost ratio greater than unity (or an excess of benefits over costs), an assumption that appropriate transfers between generations have been made is implicit in the conclusion that a potential Pareto

improvement is thereby met. The requirement, then, of hypothetical (costless) transfers between generations, which are necessary to produce this resulting potential Pareto improvement, entails yet another 'potential' in the criterion.

Put otherwise, a potential Pareto improvement is realised if, within an existing community (or generation), a hypothetical (costless) redistribution of the net gains can be so arranged as to make 'everybody' better off. And it now transpires that this sought-for potential Pareto improvement can be realised only if, within an intergenerational context, there is in addition a hypothetical (costless) redistribution of each generation's net benefits arranged so as to make each generation enjoy a potential Pareto improvement or – in the limiting case (as in our simple example involving generations X, Y and Z) – so that no generation suffers a potential Pareto loss and one generation at least enjoys a potential Pareto improvement.

(15) It would not be inappropriate to call this dual hypothetical redistribution entailed by the discounting procedure a *potential* potential Pareto improvement, since, in order eventually to realise the familiar potential Pareto improvements at particular points in time, hypothetical transfers between generations have first to be assumed.[4] Irrespective of terminology, however, the dimensions of the hypothetical transfers now involved are manifestly more complex than those involved in the more familiar comparative-statics potential Pareto improvement. And, what is pertinent to the issue, the resulting criterion is less ethically acceptable than the ordinary Pareto criterion; that is to say, it is less likely to command an ethical consensus for the community for which it is intended: namely, the community composed of members of all successive generations covered by the period of investment. Certainly, the economist has never explicitly proposed that such a *potential* potential Pareto improvement be accepted as an economic criterion of social welfare.

To be more explicit, whereas the familiar potential Pareto improvement may commend itself to an existing community at a point of time, since members of the community are aware that there exist distributive mechanisms – the progressive tax structure along with a range of benefits available from the welfare state – that go some way to diffusing the net benefits of public projects among the members of society, no such distributive mechanisms can be counted upon to operate between generations. An intergenerational project that, using a conventional DPV or CTV method, happens to yield a benefit–cost ratio greater than unity – indicative, therefore, of meeting what we have called a *potential* potential Pareto improvement –

may well be one in which the bulk of the benefits accrues to existing or earlier generations, leaving heavy costs to be borne by later generations.

V

(16) The introduction of *investment opportunities* gives rise to much the same reasoning and reaches the same conclusion. Adopting the rate r as reflecting also the rate of return on current investment, the net gain of 60 received by generation X in year 60 can be invested at r for twenty years to compound to the sum 120. From the 120 so accumulated, generation Z can be paid 100. Thus, Z is left as well off as it would have been without the project (as is the case also with X, which expires twenty years earlier), while generation Y is left a net gain of 80 in year 80. And the result of these hypothetical operations apparently meets a Pareto criterion.

(17) The interpretation of the above simple example follows that of the preceding section. Yet, what is involved can be brought out more starkly by adopting the somewhat outlandish example used by Freeman (1977) in order to illustrate his assertion that, in project evaluation, it makes economic sense to discount to the present the value of damages expected to be suffered by generations who will live many thousands of years from now. Thus, a colossal amount of damage, equal in value to $D and expected to be experienced in 100,000 years' time, should, he alleges, be discounted to the present to equal, say, $80 today. If the immediate benefits of such a project are equal to $100, the benefit–cost ratio exceeds unity and, on an allocative test, the project should be admitted.

Freeman goes on to argue that justification for this conclusion resides in the fact that, if $80 were invested today and continually reinvested at the discount rate for 100,000 years (assuming always that we can know the relevant rates and that they will continue to be positive, which is questionable), the $80 would compound to this sum $D. The beneficiaries from this amount $D would then be able exactly to compensate those destined to suffer the $D amount of damages, leaving a net gain of $20 for today's generation. According to Freeman, a potential Pareto improvement would thereby be met, as required by the economist.

Now, with respect to the *hypothetical* time stream devised by Freeman, a potential Pareto improvement would indeed be met. But clearly, this time stream is *not* the original stream that would confer a gain on the present generation of $100 and inflict damages equal to $D on generations living 100,000 years from today. What his argument amounts to, therefore, is the sanctioning of an actual intergenerational project that, by recourse to investment opportunities, *could* be changed into a different intergenerational project, which different project could then meet the conventional hypothetical compensation test. Since both a hypothetical project and a hypothetical compensation test are involved in his exercise, he also is, in effect, ascribing allocative virtue to an economic change that meets a *potential* potential Pareto improvement.

The analysis is, of course, symmetric. For if, instead, a colossal benefit equal to B were to be conferred on some group that will be alive in 100,000 years' time by investing today the sum of $80, the project would also be approved on Freeman's logic if the discounted present value of B were equal to, say, $100. True, future generations cannot pass benefits backward in time to their predecessors. But it is always possible for current generations to consume $100 of existing capital, which, were it not so consumed, would have compounded to B in 100,000 years. Hence, if such action were taken, the generation alive in 100,000 years would, in addition, suffer a loss of potential value equal to B, which loss would exactly offset the benefit B conferred by the project. Future gains and losses would then cancel out, leaving to the present generation a loss of $80 (equal to the outlay on the project) and the gain of $100 from consuming that much of the existing capital which would otherwise have been passed on to the future. This contrived *hypothetical* stream would therefore also meet a potential Pareto improvement.

(18) In general, then, by appropriate intervention at points in time over the intergenerational period, an original investment project whose stream of benefits and outlays occurring over the distant future can be discounted to yield a positive net benefit today is one that may also be converted into any of a number of hypothetical projects, each of which would indeed meet a potential Pareto improvement.

In all such instances, therefore, two sorts of hypothetically costless transfers are involved, not just one. The first has reference to the sums that may be transferred from earlier generations and, possibly, invested for the time necessary to produce zero or positive net benefits for future generations. The second has reference to the distribution among the members of each of such generations now having the hypothetical zero or positive net benefits, so that no member of them is made worse off. Since the DPV method espoused by Freeman in this intergenerational context is *not* being regarded as contingent upon actual agreements being reached between the governments of all generations involved actually to invest the receipts of earlier generations, with the object of presenting later genera-

tions with sums calculated to offset the losses they are to suffer, this notional transfer between generations is clearly as hypothetical as the subsequent redistribution of net gains among members of the community at any point of time.

Again, of course, the terminology of the implicit criterion – a *potential* potential Pareto improvement – is itself of no consequence. The reader may indeed prefer simply to envisage instead a more complex form of hypothetical intervention over time, involving both transfers between generations (via investment opportunities) and between members of each generation. Yet, the same conclusion holds: namely, that, whereas a consensus on the acceptability of the familiar potential Pareto improvement as a criterion (involving, as it does, members of a given generation) may be presumed to exist, in contrast, a consensus between members of all generations involved in the long-lived investment project may not be presumed – inasmuch as there are no mechanisms that can be presumed to diffuse the net benefits among this intergenerational community.

If, meeting together behind 'the veil of ignorance', the members of all generations involved in the project cannot know when they are to be alive, they will all have a lively apprehension of the disadvantages of being born into one of the later generations to be affected by the project whenever positive rates of discount are used. Projects yielding immense benefits to later generations for very small net costs to the earliest generation can easily be rejected by this earliest generation, acting on the conventional criterion. Worse yet, projects inflicting immense damage on later generations in exchange for slight net gains to the earlier generations can easily be accepted by these earlier generations, acting on the conventional criterion.

At all events, it is certain that there has been no debate, much less agreement, among economists about the advisability of adopting this implied *potential* potential criterion in an intergenerational context. In the circumstances the economists are impelled to face directly the intergenerational distributional implications of such projects.[5]

Notes: Chapter 18

1 Among the better-known models are those of Strotz (1955), Solow (1974), Dasgupta and Heal (1974) and Page (1976).
2 See, for instance, Dasgupta *et al.* (1972).
3 If a river project designed to improve the water quality of an area is introduced, the benefits accrue also to unweaned infants. The subjective value to these infants of the benefits they receive would not be easy to assess even by the most

skilled psychologist. The economist might well seek to adopt figures that the infants, when grown, would not reject – an objective that would still introduce some arbitrariness into the calculation.

4   It is possibly useful to labour the point by analogy, within a static context. Suppose that we contemplate introducing a public good and discover that the data show that the algebraic sum of individual valuations is negative. We say it does *not* meet a Pareto criterion; we cannot, that is, reach a position from which, by costless redistribution, 'everyone' can be made better off.

But now some bright lad proves to us that there is some *other* distribution of income, d^*, that differs from the existing distribution d_0 and that, could it be costlessly brought about, would show the sum of individual valuations to be positive. Are we to conclude that the public project does, after all, meet a potential Pareto improvement?

No! What has been shown is that a potential Pareto improvement is hypothetically possible. Thus, only if the d^* distribution can be brought about costlessly (whether d^* is desirable or not is a separate question), and if, following that, the resulting positive algebraic sum can be costlessly redistributed, will an actual Pareto improvement have been achieved. In fact, neither of these operations can be brought about costlessly. Therefore, a proposal that the project be adopted because there is a d^* that would generate a positive algebraic sum of individual valuations is tantamount to adopting a *potential* potential Pareto improvement as a criterion.

5   It will occur to the reader that, even for a project having a relatively short time span, say twenty years, there may not be a common point of overlap; in other words, there may be a time gap between the deaths of some members of the community affected by the project and the birth of others affected by the project. In such cases a vindication of the discounting procedure also involves the acceptance of a *potential* potential Pareto improvement as a criterion.

However, within a shorter span of time, one not exceeding a generation of, say, thirty years or so, such a criterion may possibly command a consensus over the period in question, based on the beliefs that institutional mechanisms will continue to operate, so that no person affected by these relatively short-term projects is likely to suffer great loss, and that there is a better chance of capturing and diffusing opportunities of increased welfare by adopting this economic criterion than by adopting any other.

References

Dasgupta, P. and Heal, G. (1974), 'The optimal depletion of exhaustible resources', *Review of Economic Studies,* vol. 41, supplement, pp. 3–28.

Dasgupta, P., Marglin, S. and Sen, A. (1972), *Guidelines for Project Evaluation* (New York: United Nations).

Feldstein, M. (1964), 'Net social benefit calculation and the public investment decision', *Oxford Economic Papers.*

Freeman, M. (1977), 'A short argument in favor of discounting intergenerational effects', *Futures* (October).

Marglin, S. (1963), 'The opportunity cost of public investment', *Quarterly Journal of Economics.*

Mishan, E. J. (1976), *Cost–Benefit Analysis,* 2nd edn (New York: Praeger).

Page, T. (1976), 'Equitable use of the resource base', *Environment and Planning* (June).

Ramsey, F. (1928), 'A mathematical theory of saving', *Economic Journal,* vol. 38, pp. 543–59.

Solow, R. H. (1974), 'Intergenerational equity', *Review of Economic Studies,* vol. 41, supplement, pp. 29–45.

Strotz, R. H. (1955), 'Myopia and inconsistency in dynamic utility maximization', *Review of Economic Studies,* vol. 23, pp. 165–80.

PART FIVE

Reflections on Economic Efficiency and Social Welfare

19
What Is Wrong With Roskill?

The *Papers and Proceedings* of the Commission on the Third London Airport (the Roskill Commission) run to nine volumes, covering between them the first three stages of the commission's planned procedure. Under review here is the seventh volume, pertaining to Stage III.[1] It runs to over 500 pages, and embodies both the method of approach and the quantitative assessment of the commission's research team led by Mr F. P. Thompson, an economist formerly employed in the Ministry of Transport. I doubt whether an economist who, like myself, has had no hand in the writing of this volume could become familiar with all the aspects discussed in less than a couple of months of uninterrupted study. Nor would he be able to check all the calculations in less than about six months, and then with a goodly amount of research assistance. Since I can claim only to have perused a number of chapters – though I believe they are the more important chapters – the overall impressions left on me have to be regarded as provisional only. Some of my more critical judgments, however, in particular those in sections III and IV, are put forward with less reservation, since they were reached only after a close scrutiny of the text. And the more general reflections at the end of this review depend neither on my overall impressions of the Roskill Report nor on the more critical findings. They arise from a consideration of the relevance of such cost–benefit evaluations for the world we are living in.

I Cost or Cost–Benefit

It may be useful first to remind the reader of the limitations of cost–benefit techniques. As everyone knows, a cost–benefit analysis purports to measure in money terms all the benefits and all the costs to be expected over the future of some mooted project, and to admit the project if the sum of the benefits exceeds the sum of the costs by a sufficient margin. Under ideal conditions,

I am very much indebted to Mr A. Flowerdew for prior discussion and to Mr D. L. Munby for later comments on a first draft of this paper.

the adopted criterion of a cost–benefit analysis – requiring that benefits exceed costs – can be vindicated only by a social judgment, that an economic rearrangement which *could* make everyone better off is 'a good thing'.

There are two points to notice about such a judgment. First, nothing is said about existing institutions, economic, political or legal. But in order to be a valid judgment, the criterion adopted must be *independent* of existing institutions. This is far from being an esoteric refinement, as we shall see later on. Secondly, and more obvious perhaps, such a judgment does *not* require that everyone shall be made better off, or even that some people shall be made better off while no others are made worse off. The likelihood – a virtual certainty – that some people, possibly most, will be made worse off is tacitly acknowledged. The criterion is met simply if it can be established that, on the adoption of the project, hypothetically costless transfers of money *could* make everyone affected better off than he was before. A project admitted on a cost–benefit analysis is, therefore, quite consistent with an economic arrangement which makes the rich richer and the poor poorer. It is consistent also with transparent inequity: irrespective of the income groups involved, the opportunities for increased profit or pleasure provided by the new project may inflict direct and substantial injury on others.

In order, then, for a project to be socially acceptable, it is not enough to show that the outcome of a cost–benefit calculation is positive – allowing, always, that the evaluation of each of the component items has been thorough and consistent. It must also be established that the resulting distributional effects are not unduly regressive, and that no gross inequities are perpetrated.

In the light of an ideal cost–benefit procedure, what can be said of this report?

The first thing that ought to be said is that, for Britain at least,[2] the report has aimed at a level of sophistication that will not be easy to exceed. For the most part it is clearly written and well organised. The theoretical underpinning – much of it summarised in part I, *Proposed Research Methodology*, and in chapter I of part II – is respectable, and the tone is suggestive of a determination not to forsake principle for facility of calculation. The so-called intangibles are believed to be in principle quantifiable, and the research team has not yielded to the temptation to hand back part of its brief to the political process, which had offered it to the economists in the first place.[3] There are occasional manifestations of resourcefulness and ingenuity, as well as determination, in bringing disparate considerations 'into relationship with the measuring rod of money'. Nevertheless, paragraph 1.22 (on p. 43) makes it plain that the conditions mentioned above, relating to distribution and equity – though their relevance is acknowledged – are *not* to be taken into consideration in the assessment. For this reason, if for no other, the quantitative findings of the report cannot be used alone to decide the issue.

The second thing that ought to be said is that the urgency is apparently not so great as we have been led to believe. If their projections of future air traffic are accepted (and they are large enough in all conscience), the airlines could go on until about 1982 using the existing facilities at Heathrow and Gatwick. Although congestion costs at the existing airports are expected to increase year by year, it will not be until 1982 that they will exceed £22 million, which is the estimated annual worth of postponing construction of the third airport.

The third thing that ought to be said is that the assessment in this volume is *not*, properly speaking, a cost–benefit analysis. It consists only of a comparison of the costs of the four alternative airport sites on the short list: Cublington, Foulness, Nuthampstead, and Thurleigh. And in this connection it is important to notice that the full costs of each item are *not* always compared; sometimes only the differences in costs are entered, or a portion of the costs in which the differences are captured. We shall find it revealing to dwell a while on this peculiarity of the report.

This choice of a relative cost evaluation rather than a cost–benefit evaluation carries with it an implicit presumption that a third airport at any one of the four alternative sites can be justified on economic grounds. There are reasons to doubt this presumption, and we shall turn to them in section III.

In section II we concern ourselves only with the weight to be attached to the comparative figures produced by the commission in order to rank the four alternative sites on the scale of economic desirability.

II Costs to Passengers and Airlines

A comparison of the costs of the four sites discounted to 1975[4] is given by row 22 of table 29.1 (pp. 490–1). They are ranked below in order of increasing cost:

Cublington	£2,265 million	(0)
Thurleigh	£2,267 million	(£2 million)
Nuthampstead	£2,274 million	(£9 million)
Foulness	£2,385 million	(£120 million)

(The figures in the brackets indicate by how much the cost of that particular site exceeds the cost of the lowest site at Cublington.)

It is clear that the differences between the first three sites are too slight in proportion for likely errors to be taken seriously. Foulness – except for bird-lovers, the conservationists' favoured site – stands out clearly as the most costly of the four. One reason is that a loss of potential benefit amounting to about £44 million is chalked up against Foulness in consequence of the smaller air traffic it is expected to generate as compared with the three inland airports, all of which happen to be on the right side of London to attract traffic from the North and the Midlands. In the year 2000, for example, the total number of air passengers in the country is expected to be something between 6 and 10 million less if Foulness is chosen rather than one of the others.

How significant is this difference in cost for the Foulness site? The two largest items in table 29.1 are those for 'airspace movement' and 'passenger user cost'. They account for over 80 per cent of the total costs in the table, and they both depend heavily on the value placed on passengers' time. In particular, it is the additional time and cost of reaching the Foulness airport site that forces the figure for 'passenger user cost' there to £1,041 million, or £152 million more than the figure for the next most costly site in this respect, Thurleigh.

Value of Travel Time

It is at such points that one is tempted to challenge the figure of 46s per hour placed on business travel in 1968, rising to 72s per hour (all at 1968 prices) by the year 2000. The figure is derived from an estimate of business firms' average annual expenditure on their airborne representatives of £4,626 (in 1968), which sum includes an average business traveller's income of £3,200. For 'leisure passengers', in contrast, a mere 4s 7d an hour is deemed appropriate. Both figures are assumed to rise over time at 3 per cent per annum.

Since these estimates, made in consultation with the Ministry of Transport, are likely to be controversial, the report makes some additional calculations on the side, based on alternative evaluations of the worth of people's time. If, for instance, the value of business time is reduced by 25 per cent of the above figure, and leisure time is not valued at all, the total costs are so revised that the bracketed figures giving the *differences* in cost for the four airports become those shown below:

Thurleigh	(0)
Cublington	(£10 million)
Nuthampstead	(£28 million)
Foulness	(£42 million)

Clearly there is some margin to be got by playing around with such figures, and this makes any choice on economic grounds alone appear somewhat less satisfactory. The figures would appear less reliable still, and the differentials would narrow further,[5] if one could reasonably object to the notion of basing the value of time on a person's earnings. First of all, it is meaningful to say of a person that he values his leisure very little but that he dislikes his work a lot. Travel time for, say, a holiday-maker is simply one way of using his leisure. And it is not to be regarded as equivalent to work unless, at the margin, the person is indifferent as between, say, an hour spent on the train and an hour at work.

Secondly, the assumption of putting a positive value on the extra hour or so of businessmen's time if Foulness is chosen is also open to challenge. Dividing a firm's annual expenditure per travelling representative by the number of hours he is supposed to work produces an average hourly figure which, it can be argued, has no economic significance in this connection. The correct economic concept is the 'opportunity cost' to the firm, or rather to the country, of an hour or so's delay to its representative. Notwithstanding assertions to the contrary, indivisibilities of time are important here. If the delay were of a full day, it could matter to the individual firm – though, again, it might not matter that much for the country. If the difference in delay were of an hour's duration, one might think up circumstances in which it would matter. But such circumstances would not be relevant to the choice under consideration in the report. If Foulness is chosen, it is not to be supposed that many firms could make profitable use of the extra hour or so of representatives' time saved in travelling to the airport. To most firms, I should imagine, it would make no difference at all. The representative would simply have to get up a little earlier on the appointed day and travel a little longer. And if this is a disutility for him, it has to be taken out of the category of business time and put into the category of passengers' leisure time.

Airline Operation Costs

Let us suppose, however, that we accept the figures in table 29.1 as not seriously misleading. We may still wonder what importance we are to attach to them. Large though the absolute figure of £120 million is, it appears as only about 5 per cent of the total discounted costs of any of the sites. Actually, it is a very much smaller proportion of the total future resource costs of any of the airports; for, as mentioned, the table does not reveal all of the costs. The full airport construction costs are given. So also are all the 'passenger user costs' – the resource costs of travelling to each of the four sites, *plus* any difference in the 'disbenefits' of travelling to one airport site rather than another. But the cost of the largest item in the table, 'airspace movement', is only a fraction – presumably unknown – of the total airline operation costs over the future. For, on the assumption that, whichever site is chosen, all the aircraft will fly the same distances to their destinations from some common boundary containing the four sites, the authors of the report simplified their work by calculating only the costs of reaching this boundary from each of the four sites (allowance being made for the somewhat smaller air traffic expected if Foulness were chosen). If, instead, total airline operation costs were included, the discounted value of *total* resources could be more than double the figures given in row 22 of table 29.1. Accepting the report's valuation of time, the excess cost of Foulness would be more like $2\frac{1}{2}$ per cent of the value of the total resources involved. On the report's optional calculation of business and leisure time, the excess of £42 million for Foulness comes to less than 1 per cent of the value of total resources. On margins thus small, an economic case against the choice of Foulness cannot be seriously maintained.

Supersonic Flight

Finally, nothing is said about the particular sorts of damage currently associated with supersonic flight. I have been told that the omission was deliberate, and predicated on the recent White Paper of the previous government, in which it was stated that the Concorde would not fly at supersonic speeds over land. Such a statement of intent may reasonably be regarded with suspicion. If we suppose that there is a chance that, for any of a half-dozen reasons the aircraft industry or the airline companies can think up, supersonic speeds over land may some day become 'essential', the choice of any site other than Foulness would leave us in a sorry and angry state.[6]

III   Is a Third Airport Justified?

Let us now turn to what I regard as the major defect of the report: that the economic case for the construction of a third London airport was not a part of its terms of reference. In a brief chapter on 'The value to the nation of a third London airport', a number of considerations were put forward to convince the public that the benefits were almost self-evident: the popularity of the postwar package tour, it was pointed out, is sure to grow immensely. So also is business travel, conceived as a 'lubricant' of international trade through which the blessings of technology are spread throughout the world. Besides, airports are generators of high income in the surrounding areas, and the growth in traffic should benefit the aircraft construction industry and industry in general; and much more of the same sort of froth. I suspect that this industry sales talk got included in the report only on the insistence of interested parties. It contrasts with the more professional judgment shown elsewhere and is perhaps not expected to be taken seriously. There is, however, another argument in the earlier part of the chapter which, if it were accepted, would go some way toward establishing a presumption in favour of sufficient benefits to justify the undertaking. This takes the form of a belief that the expected revenues from passengers will be able to cover all the future resource costs involved in airline flights, and that, in addition, the estimated cost of all 'disbenefits' – noise, disamenity, demolition of historic buildings, and so on – could be more than covered by an increase in revenue from raising landing fees.

The Intangibles

Before this presumption is accepted, it is necessary to examine the estimates made of the value of the 'intangibles', more particularly of the value of the loss of amenity and recreation to the community, or rather to examine the methods used by the authors to estimate these values. For in a comparative cost analysis, whatever the magnitudes of the 'intangibles', one of the alternative projects has to be chosen. Under this constraint, the only relevant question is whether or not introduction of the 'intangibles' will alter the cost-ranking of the alternative projects. In a cost–benefit analysis, in contrast, one question to be answered is whether or not any one of the alternative projects is economically feasible. The magnitude of the 'intangibles' can, therefore, be decisive.

By and large, the conceptual underpinning of the report is, as indicated earlier, sound enough. It is in making the transition from the concepts to the measurement of the relevant effects that one begins to feel critical of the particular devices, ingenious though they sometimes are, which the authors make use of in order to place money values on the damages suffered by

others. Thus, in evaluating the potential disbenefits, the authors lay it down on page 39 that:

> The analysis has been guided by the principle of accepting the scale of values apparently held by the people concerned, as revealed by their choice and behaviour. For *potential* possessions or activities, they are valued at what people would be prepared to pay to acquire them. For *existing* possessions or activities, things are valued at the minimum which people would be prepared to accept as just compensation for their loss.

As a statement of intent, this reflects the doctrines of modern welfare economics, and is unexceptionable. But, in the event, what do they do?

Households Displaced

For those households moving out because of the airport, the loss suffered is reckoned as (a) estimated depreciation of their property, plus (b) removal expenses, plus (c) 'consumer surplus'. Thus, if the market value of a house before the airport is sited in the area is £10,000, but the family enjoys a consumer surplus of £2,000 on it (that is, the family would not sell it below £12,000) and would require £500 for removal expenses, a fall in the market price to £7,000 would involve the family in a total loss of £5,500 – equal to (a) £3,000, plus (b) £2,000, plus (c) £500. The estimate of (a), depreciation, was derived from consultations with estate agents and by reference to depreciation of properties in those areas around Gatwick and Heathrow that are subject to various degrees of aircraft disturbance. The estimates for (b) and (c) together, removal expenses plus consumer surplus, resulted from a sample survey in which householders were asked the following question: 'Suppose your house was wanted to form part of a large development scheme and the developer offered to buy it from you, what price would be just high enough to compensate you for leaving this house (flat) and moving to another area?' (p. 381). Subtraction from this subjective price of the existing market price provided an estimate for (b) and (c). A truthful answer to this question would be a satisfactory measure of the subjective value of the house only if the move contemplated by the householder were one that would take him completely out of the noise area (or, more precisely, if there already was some noise in the area, to another area suffering from no greater noise). Yet the question posed does not state how far the householder will have to move. Mention of a developer must surely give the householder the impression that a few acres, within which his house happens to be situated, are required. It would not occur to him that he would have to leave the neighbourhood. And it is, indeed, entirely a different affair if the household is to be displaced either because the site is needed for an airport or because the noise will be all but unbearable. This can be a real wrench for the family. A change of job location, a change of school location, to say nothing of a loss of friends and neighbours, have then to be anticipated. The figures used by the report in this connection are, therefore, certain to have understated the value of expected losses.

A more obvious reason why the figures derived from the sample answers to the above question understate the amount of compensation is that 8 per cent of those asked said they would not move at any price. The compensatory sum for such a householder was placed, arbitrarily, at £5,000. If those people mean what they said, the compensatory sum would be 'infinite' and this would obviously wreck any cost–benefit criterion. Yet, if the answers are believed, consistency of principle requires that an 'infinite sum' be entered. It may be that a good interviewer would have elicited a finite sum, though well in excess of £5,000 – perhaps £50,000? or £5 million? And, though unlikely, it is not altogether inconceivable that for some older, or unworldly, people all that money could buy for them would not suffice as compensation for having to live elsewhere. What is certain, however, is that by setting this arbitrary upper limit of £5,000 the authors' figure for 'consumer surplus' can be made much smaller than the 'consumer surplus' figure that would have emerged by an uncompromising application of their own adopted principles.

The disbenefits of an increase of the number of flights associated with the establishment of a third London airport is an underestimate for another reason, one which the report itself touches upon – though possibly without recognising its full significance (inasmuch as it applies to the evaluation of traffic noise in general). On page 368 (para. 20.12) it is observed that: 'People buying a house affected by aircraft noise would be very naive if they did not expect an increase in noise, at least for the next ten years or so.' Precisely! If noise is to increase over the next ten years – and, on present trends, who doubts it? – a family will have to search very much further afield if its members are to discover an equally congenial neighbourhood with the same degree of quiet. It is scarcely possible for them to discover an area which has reasonable amenities and facilities within commuting distance of work and at the same time is expected over the future to be as quiet as is their present habitation today. Anticipating the spread of noise

everywhere, the family, in effect, has only a limited choice: that of staying in the existing area or of moving to a new one, where *both* areas are expected to become much noisier. Indeed, as the level of noise in general increases, the perceived differences are likely to decrease, and so also, therefore, will the sum of money necessary to induce the family to move. But the disbenefit suffered from each contribution to a rising noise level is properly valued only by a sum of money large enough to compensate the members of a family for the loss of the original low-noise situation, this being the sum that will enable them to maintain their original level of welfare.

Households Remaining in Neighbourhood

The expectation of an increase over the future in the volume and spread of noise is yet more significant in evaluating the loss to the larger population who will continue to live within the noisier zones about the airport – those remaining within the 35 NNI contour line.[7] The statement quoted on page 39 of the report implies that the measure of the loss experienced by such people would emerge from a truthful answer to the question: 'What is the minimum sum you would accept to reconcile yourself to the increase in aircraft noise to which you are, and in the future will be, subjected?' Yet the loss for this larger group was measured, ultimately, by the expected depreciation of their property alone – that is, no more than the (a) component of the loss to the household that is moved from the airport site. A good deal of finesse was, of course, employed in working out the exact depreciation to be used for each sort of house in each sort of zone, allowance for sensitivity being made by using the figure for depreciation as the median point of a distribution of noise sensitivity. Again, however, if noise is expected to increase over time, such measures are sure to understate the loss. For as noise grows over time the absolute difference in noise between any two points on a map may be unchanged, and the difference in property values will also remain unchanged – yet people living in areas about these two points will be worse off. Indeed, as noise increases over time, it is far more likely that *differences* in noise will diminish within a given area, and the effect therefore on property values will be smaller – a prospect with which the estate agents consulted can be assumed to be familiar. In such circumstances, the use of differentials in property values does not only understate the loss; as an index of loss it is wholly perverse. In the limiting case in which there is no escape whatever from aircraft noise in all inhabited areas of the country, noise being everywhere uniformly unbearable, noise-induced differences in property values will vanish; the measure of loss for all of us, on this indicator, being zero.

In connection with noise, there is yet another weakness, which at first glance may seem a quibble but in fact is a critical weakness of the cost–benefit technique when extended to non-market disbenefits: its almost unavoidable asymmetry in the weighting of 'imponderables'. To illustrate in the present instance, the authors confine themselves to noise within the 35 NNI contour line, apparently on the grounds that the effects of aircraft disturbance below 35 NNI are difficult to determine. Now the population within the zones between, say, 20 NNI and 35 NNI is several times as large as that within the area enclosed by the 35 NNI contour. Despite the admirable statement of intent on page 39, no loss of welfare is imputed to this larger population. That decision can be justified only if it is known that all families are perfectly indifferent to the increase in noise up to 35 NNI. Yet there will surely be a proportion of such families who, at least, will come to resent the extra noise.

Illusory Benefits of Air Travel

Clearly the reaction of numbers of people in the larger population to noise levels below 35 NNI involves a judgment about significance. It is a purely subjective judgment, however, and it is in just such circumstances that the economist can be misled by a 'misplaced concreteness'. I am not suggesting that the economist is visibly stirred, as we imagine the technocrat to be, by a vision of a vast airport having all the familiar manifestations of highly organised bustle and breath-lessness. I am suggesting, however, that market-formed prices and quantities are regarded as somehow more solid than the values attributed to the 'intangibles'. If a person is willing to pay £50 for a flight from London to Palma, there is, indisputably, a figure of £50 of benefit to play with. If the resource cost of the flight were shown to be £40, the economist would have no hesitation in claiming an excess benefit of (at least) £10. Such a flight may well be, for the greater number of future passengers, a whimsical form of indulgence, a fashion good of which the deprivation would be resented in varying degrees – though probably much less as time passed and alternative opportunites were discovered.[8]

For business travellers, the case is simpler yet. For most of them the company pays air fares from business expenditures, so that, taking income and corporation taxes into account, the true cost to the firm is less than half the fare. Thus, the marginal value of the air trip to the business firm is, presumably, well below the marginal resource cost.

With the advent of air travel, the number of conferences, business, professional and academic, has been growing at an exponential rate. The same people who now rush about the world reading the same paper at a dozen conferences in as many months are those who, in quieter days, would have found time to read, write, and reflect. At any rate, the value of such trips cannot be measured by the air fare, simply because air travel is not, in such cases, one of the alternative goods a man can buy subject to a budget constraint. The conferees do not pay their own fares. And it is doubtful if the benefit they personally expect to derive from these occasions is such that many would attend the conference without additional inducements. Only the conveners of the conference can be said to benefit. Calling a conference is one among the alternative ways of disposing of funds provided by governments and businesses guided by the principle of self-promotion. Conference-creating activity is one of many growth industries produced by aircraft travel, and one of the many prestige uses of the massive funds accumulated by business foundations. The social benefit of all this hectic to-ing and fro-ing, however, is difficult to evaluate – which is no reason for not assuming that it is probably negative.

There is room for speculation here, but not for doubt, that much of the assumed benefit of air travel is illusory.

Asymmetry in Cost–Benefit Analysis

The purpose of carping at the nature of these assumed benefits is to draw attention to the asymmetry referred to, which arises, in the last resort, from institutional limitations. Whether he is motivated by strong desire, by the spirit of overindulgence, or by spurious business need, if a man pays £50 twice a year for an air trip a benefit of at least £100 will be entered against the cost of the resources used in the two flights. In contrast, the dis-benefit suffered by a person living within the 35 NNI – 20 NNI zone, whether it verges on fury for a hypersensitive minority[9] or whether it is the bearable annoyance of the majority, does not enter the grand computation at all. Yet it is, at least, a moot point whether the loss of welfare to any person subjected daily (and perhaps nightly also) to this *initially* lower level of noise-annoyance should properly be thought of as meriting no consideration as compared with the gain in welfare of any person who, at some time in the year, does the flight to Palma, or to Hong Kong for that matter.[10] If institutions happened to be the reverse of what they are for this particular case; if say, the universe were so designed that people could freely sell their quiet in a competitive market at the ruling price while, on the other hand, owing to some institutional factor (say, the cost of fare-collecting was fantastically high), a market in airline services were not possible, we should appreciate the asymmetrical treatment better. For then, *all* the disbenefits from noise would be priced on the market, and they would grow with the increasing noise of aircraft. They would be counted as part of the 'solid' price–quantity data, and would be added to the resource costs on the same economic principle – that payment has to be made to induce people to part with things they value, whether it be their property rights, their leisure, or their peace and quiet. And both in virtue of the change to a correct method of evaluating these disbenefits, and in virtue of the extension of the market to the population as a whole, the resulting loss figure would probably be many times that estimated in the report. On the other hand, in keeping with the current methods used in estimating the values of non-market items, the benefits of the trips would be calculated only for a fraction of the potential number of beneficiaries. This would be the fraction having greater claims according to some benefit-scale beyond which the economist would declare it difficult to believe that benefits were at all substantial. Moreover, if the methods used in estimating benefits were deficient in the same respects as those used by the report in estimating disbenefits, the total value of the benefits calculated even for this fraction of the beneficiaries would be an underestimate.

In sum, under such hypothetical institutions, the outcome of a cost–benefit calculation conducted on the lines of this report would be vastly different from that reached under the existing institutions, and could fail entirely to justify the building of a third London airport – from which we may conclude, at the very least, that the methods employed in the report do not meet the conditions of an ideal cost–benefit analysis as laid down at the beginning of this article.

IV   Social Costs and Equity

The conclusion of section II was that, on alternative – and, in my opinion, more plausible – estimates of the value of passengers' time over the future, the cost differences between the four sites as a proportion of total resource costs become so small as to be unreliable for the purpose of economic ranking.

In section III I gave some reasons for doubting whether, indeed, the construction of a third London airport could be justified by a respectable cost–benefit analysis. The chief reason I gave was that the methods used for the estimate of the benefits and the disbenefits are not independent of existing institutions: because the benefits are registered largely as market phenomena, and disbenefits largely as 'intangibles', the asymmetry of treatment tells heavily in favour of the benefits.

This reason is reinforced when it is discovered that a number of 'intangible' disbenefits have been omitted altogether from the commission's calculation. There may be some justification for these omissions in a study of cost comparisons; the evidence may suggest that they differ little as between one site and another. But in a cost–benefit study undertaken to establish economic feasibility such disbenefits must be counted. I mention two of these below, neither of which is negligible.

(a) *Loss of life.* Per million passenger-miles fatalities may be falling. But what matters in a cost–benefit calculation is the expected rise in absolute numbers attributable to the rise in numbers of passengers brought about by a third London airport. If choice of Foulness implies fewer passenger flights over the future, loss of life will be correspondingly smaller also – something the commission did not take into account.

(b) Most important of all, however, is the *destruction of natural beauty* at home and abroad. This disbenefit is sometimes rudely referred to as 'tourist blight' – a phenomenon of postwar affluence that has already caused irreparable destruction, all over the Mediterranean area and far beyond, to places of once rare scenic beauty, woodland, coastline, lakes and islands.[11]

The social costs inflicted as a result of air travel facilities may be ignored by governments, but a comprehensive cost–benefit analysis simply cannot ignore them. If they appear intractable to existing methods of computation, the economist must say so, in which case an otherwise favourable cost–benefit calculation must be deemed inconclusive.[12]

Finally, the economist is interested not only in the question whether a given project yields an excess of benefit over cost, but also in the *optimal* operation of an existing or future project.

From table 4.6, on page 86, one gathers that the number of air passengers taking off in the London area is expected to increase from 18 million per annum in 1969 to 294 million in thirty-seven years' time. Reference to such figures would seem to leave no room for doubt of the 'need' of a third London airport, and probably of a fourth and fifth also. After all, for every single air passenger today there will be, according to these predictions, as many as seventeen in thirty-seven years' time. And if fares continue to remain much the same relative to the prices of other services, and if there is no restriction on airports or air travel, some of us may live to witness the grand spectacle. But, inasmuch as air travel does impose disbenefits on the public, proper concern with allocation requires that fares be raised to take account of them. If this were done, the numbers would not rise nearly so rapidly. They might hardly rise at all, and the need for a third London airport might not then be in the least apparent. For the disbenefits do not consist only of the noise annoyance, fearful as this is going to be,[13] and increased air pollution – which disbenefits, be it noted, contribute to a spreading background of pollution and perpetual noise, by reference to which further aircraft and automobile projects are the more easily justified by cost–benefit techniques, since the perceptible contribution of each project to noise and air pollution that is already so bad is obviously limited.[14] As already indicated, the chief disbenefit, tourist blight, is the most difficult of all to measure. The popularity of package tourism need not be questioned. Let us accept airline receipts as a measure of benefit. We need attend only to the 'spillover effects' each additional person imposes on all others, present and future, but of which he himself takes no account. Indeed, not being 'very naive' either, the would-be traveller will expect tourist blight to rise over the future and will hasten to travel the sooner before the destruction is complete.

Measuring these adverse spillover effects would, as suggested, present some difficulties. In view of the commercial interests at stake, and in view of the commitment of governments to compete for a share in this growing market (for fear of losing on balance-of-payments account), research into methods for their quantification would also be a thankless task. As things stand, however, the process of destruction through mass tourism, instead of being slowed down by taxes high enough to cover the marginal spillover effects, is, on the contrary, accelerated by subsidies. In view of the magnitude of these spillovers, it is high time that governments began to think in terms of stiff taxes on air travel. Where the fare may cover only a small part of the social cost, a very roughly calculated tax is almost certainly better than no tax at all – even if it should eventually be found to reduce air travel below the optimum level.

Growth of Public Protest

Let me conclude with a more general reflection. There are the beginnings in this country and abroad,

particularly in the United States, of a strong antidisamenity movement among the public. At present, political parties are trying to absorb some of its force. My belief is that they under-rate the passion behind the protest, and its growing appeal, not least among the young. The movement shows every indication of growing rapidly in the next few years, and also every inclination to achieve its aims by large-scale political changes rather than by 'tinkering with the system'.

Cost–benefit techniques are, indeed, becoming more sophisticated. But they may be too late to exert much influence in the choice of projects which can be related to the 'quality of life' issue. A report such as the present one, excellent as it is, paying lip service to right principles and secure within its terms of reference, may have the unexpected effect of contributing only to the public's growing impatience with economic expertise, and perhaps with economics in general.

One reason for this impatience is that in such economic calculations *equity* is wholly ignored. If indeed, the business tycoons and the Mallorca holiday-makers are shown to benefit, after paying their fares, to such an extent that they *could* more than compensate their victims of aircraft spillover, the cost–benefit criterion is met. But compensation is *not* paid. The former continue to enjoy the profit and the pleasure; the latter continue to suffer the disamenities. Another reason for growing impatience is even more compelling. In an age of supposedly increasing prosperity, the choice of a more wholesome life than that we seem to be moving into should, it seems, be technically feasible. Yet, despite a succession of governments overtly obsessed with economic growth, we are being offered year by year continuously less choice in the one factor most crucial to our welfare – the physical environment in which we live, and in which we are fast being submerged.

Notes: Chapter 19

1 Commission on the Third London Airport, *Papers and Proceedings*. Vol. VII (Pts I and II): *Stage III Research and Investigation – Assessment of Short-Listed Sites* (London: HMSO, 1970).
2 Cost–benefit studies on the grand scale are more common in the United States, a large proportion being concerned with water resources and construction of dams.
3 Nevertheless, there are one or two blemishes in the proposed methodology which could be damaging in a cost–benefit analysis, though, if they were corrected in this cost-comparison report, they would not be likely to make much difference to the ranking of sites in table 29.1. (i) On page 38 (para. 1.7), for instance, it is asserted that goods and

services are to be valued at their resource costs on grounds that they 'most clearly represent the real cost to the community . . . in terms of resources embodied in their production. Indirect taxes and subsidies . . . are excluded'. This is a valid convention for estimating changes in national income aggregates, but it is an *incorrect* principle for cost–benefit evaluations. The cost to the economy of a resource to be used in the project is determined by the value it creates in the use from which it is to be moved. Consequently, if the resource is moved from the production of some good subject, say, to a 100 per cent tax, its cost to the project must be valued as equal to the price, which is not equal to, but twice, the resource cost. (ii) Again on pages 42–3 (para. 1.19) in the discussion on the costs of journeys to the airport, mention is made of the preference of some people for using their own cars, and the paragraph ends with the sentence: 'The measure of this benefit is found deductively by observing what the travelling public is prepared to pay, in time and money, for the convenience, at least in their own eyes . . . of using their own car.' Fair enough, but no allowance is made for the additional congestion costs that are imposed on all *other* vehicles, or for the additional spillover effects on the rest of the population of private transport as compared with public transport.

4 If the costs are discounted to a later date, 1982, the figures above are all roughly doubled, since a discount rate of 10 per cent per annum has been adopted.

5 In the limiting case, if no value at all were placed on the time required to reach the airports, the cost-ranking of the four airports (with the cost differences given in brackets) would be: 'Thurleigh (0), Foulness (6), Cublington (7), Nuthampstead (21).

6 There are deficiencies also in the measurement of other disbenefits. Their potential impact is probably less significant than that of aircraft noise, but they are worth touching on. For churches located off the airport site, the social losses entered are no more than the costs of strengthening the structures to withstand vibration. On the other hand, the social loss resulting from the demolition of churches and other buildings on the airport site is taken to be equal to the sum of their current market costs, as indicated by their insurance values. For architecturally undistinguished churches there need be no objection on secular grounds. But for irreplaceable churches of unique architectural value, this is obviously unacceptable. If Westminster Abbey is insured for £200,000 against destruction by fire, it does not follow that the nation at large is indifferent as between having Westminster Abbey or the £200,000. But this is the implied logic of accepting the fire insurance figure as the loss equivalence. The loss arising from damage to recreational activities is conventionally treated and arbitrarily quantified. Thus, on page 418 (para. 24.24) we read:

> Most of the recreational activities affected by aircraft noise, of which visiting historic houses, hunting, golf, fresh water fishing, predominate, are located within moderate noise levels. It was therefore assumed that visits would, on average, be reduced by 10 per cent, and that this would be directly reflected in lower admission revenues. It can be deduced from conventional demand analysis that this reduction in

participation could correspond to a reduction of about 20 per cent in the consumer surplus enjoyed by those continuing to visit.

The tone is tentative here: 40 per cent, perhaps 60 per cent, would be no less acceptable. But, frankly, the statement makes no sense as it stands. Admissions could change very little, and yet the loss be far in excess of '20 per cent in the consumer surplus enjoyed by those continuing to visit'. Indeed, the method is in conflict with the guiding principle laid down on page 39 and elsewhere: that the loss of an existing facility is to be measured by the sum necessary to restore the person's original welfare.

7 NNI is an abbreviation of Noise and Number Index. It was developed as an index of aircraft noise annoyance by the Committee on the Problem of Noise (Cmnd 2056).

8 I do not underestimate the extent of the potential protest, initiated by business interests with the support of mass media and inflated by the sheer joy of expressing protest. I speak only of the individual discomfort after the ban against this sort of travel has been generally accepted. Anger at being deprived, or the pleasure of expressing it, is no measure of the loss of utility of a thing.

9 On page 365 the authors refer to the survey conducted by the Committee on the Problem of Noise. In the *quietest* areas covered by the survey, 10 per cent of the population were classified as 'seriously annoyed'. In the noisiest areas, on the other hand, only 10 per cent denied that aircraft noise was a nuisance, and 10 per cent claimed a 'minimal degree of annoyance', leaving 80 per cent claiming more than a minimal degree of annoyance.

10 It might be objected that the person on the ground may, at some other time, be an air passenger on his way to Palma or Hong Kong. But this, as it happens, makes not the slightest difference to the calculation. His losses are no less real for his having benefits also, and vice versa. Nor does the fact that a person who resents aircraft noise also travels by air constitute evidence that, *on balance*, he prefers air travel along with the accompanying disbenefits to no air travel at all. Evidence of the latter proposition must await developments in which he is given the choice of being 'grounded' without any aircraft noise or of putting up with the noise along with the opportunity of flying. This sort of choice is not provided by the market, nor does the government at present look like presenting it to us.

11 I refer not only to the disfiguration of innumerable coastal resorts, once famed for their beauty, as a result of frantic 'development' in the attempt to accommodate increasing numbers: these are losses to be borne by future generations as well as ourselves. I refer also to the increasing discomforts endured in popular resorts in consequence of the greater numbers of people and the greater traffic. Indeed, in the expectation that in this respect matters can only get worse, there is every incentive to add to the crowds by visiting such places sooner rather than later. The reader will readily appreciate that the economic issue is not *who* should travel, but (thinking in terms of the spillovers borne by the intramarginal tourists today and other generations to come) *how many*.

12 The *otherwise* excess benefit over cost may be provided by the economist so allowing the public to judge whether such a figure compensates for the damage to be expected over the future.

13 Unless some effective aircraft-noise preventive device is

invented. This does not seem too likely just now, particularly as private and public airlines have no strong incentive to undertake such research – an incentive they would have if they were required to compensate the victims of noise pollution.

14 As has been pointed out frequently during the controversy on noise, the ground traffic is already so heavy in built-up areas that the addition of aircraft noise makes no great difference. So, too, once a third airport is built and the aircraft noise level rises over time and extends over the country, it will be that much easier to justify further noise-creating projects, including a fourth and fifth London airport.

20

The Folklore of the Market: An Inquiry into the Economic Doctrines of the Chicago School

According to a recent statement by Milton Friedman (1974, p.11):

> ... in discussions of economic policy, 'Chicago' stands for belief in the efficacy of the free market as a means of organizing resources, for scepticism about government intervention into economic affairs, and for emphasis on the quantity of money as a key factor in producing inflation ...
>
> In discussions of economic science, 'Chicago' stands for an approach that takes seriously the use of economic theory as a tool for analyzing a startlingly wide range of concrete problems, rather than as an abstract mathematical structure of great beauty but little power; for an approach that insists on the empirical testing of theoretical generalizations and that rejects alike facts without theory and theory without facts.

In this preliminary investigation into the validity and relevance of the economic presuppositions and the belief-system of the Chicago school, I shall concentrate chiefly on the arguments that bear on its belief in the efficacy of free markets in organizing resources, in extending individual choice, and in preserving political freedom.

I Introduction

Definition of a Market

In a press conference, an abridged version of which was reproduced along with the statement quoted above,

I wish to thank George Borts for his comments and to record my indebtedness to Milton Friedman for detailed and trenchant criticism of an earlier draft.

Friedman replied to the question of whether market forces were capable of redistributing wealth throughout the world as follows: 'Voluntary arrangements by people, voluntary giving of charity to other countries are market forces. Market forces means voluntary forces.'

The equation above of voluntary action with market forces implies a concept of the market broader than that usually entailed in the professional literature; and it is entirely possible that Friedman put it this way in order to emphasize the link between private munificence and nineteenth-century capitalist freedom. To most economists, however, the word *market* suggests a voluntary exchange of goods; a *quid pro quo* is involved. And in the more familiar economic contexts the word is indicative of an *organized* market, which adjective conveys the notion of a number of people offering to buy and sell at a money price various amounts of a particular good – a good being defined as something having value and including, therefore, products or services, final or intermediate, and, consequently, also productive services or factors.

However, when the term 'the free market' is used in a normative context, additional associations are invoked which purport to assess the social merits of the institution. As used by the Chicago school, at least, 'the free market' can be identified with, or can partake of, each of the following institutional features:

(1) the private ownership of capital, or productive (nonhuman) assets;
(2) the private management of economic enterprise;
(3) the decentralization of economic enterprise;
(4) competitive enterprise;
(5) a price system; and
(6) a market system.

These features, although distinct, are obviously not all mutually exclusive. But setting them out in this way has some heuristic value. It is possible to imagine the existence of (1), private ownership of capital, without (2), the private management of economic enterprises, or (2) without (1). It is no less possible to conceive an economy in which (3), enterprise is decentralized, without its being (1), privately owned, or (2), privately managed,[1] or (4), competitive. Again, (5), a pricing system, may be established in the absence of the remaining features, in particular without the existence of (6), a market system. On the other hand, it is hard to visualize a competitive enterprise system without a market system, and impossible to have a market system without prices.

An economy combining features (1), private ownership of capital, (2), private management of enterprise, and (6), a market system, can be expected to react to changes in the conditions of demand and supply. The more there is of (4), competition, the greater the sensitivity we should expect to changes in these conditions.

Since (4), competition, implies the existence of (5), a price system, and (6), a market system, and since (4) in the presence of (1) entails (3), we may conclude that the simultaneous existence of three features, (1), (2), and (4) – in which (1) and (2) have tended, historically, to grow together – forms the essentials of that economic system which is so attractive to the Chicago school. We may refer to this system as the 'competitive private enterprise economy'. Wherever the advantages to be considered are those flowing from private ownership or private management of enterprise the terminology may be abbreviated to 'the private enterprise economy' or 'the capitalist system'. Where, instead, the focus of our examination is upon the allocative merits associated with the competitive model, the term 'competitive market' or 'free market' will be used. But the reader must not expect rigor in this respect, and the terminology will vary not only according to context, but also according to any need to avoid monotony.

Terms of Reference

The existence of a 'competitive private enterprise economy' does not of itself, however, ensure smooth and rapid adjustment of the economy to changes in the underlying conditions of demand and supply. Whether market equilibria are stable, at least locally, is a question of fact in each case, one that depends on behavior and technological relationships. The productive efficiency of a competitive economy, and the speed of adjustment to changing patterns of demand, will vary from one type of good to another and will depend *inter alia* on the quality of management, the geography of the market, and the development of communications. Nonetheless, the clear belief of the Chicago school is that, in the absence of direct government intervention in the operation of free markets, the system will function at least as well as it would under any alternative economic arrangement. Moreover, when regard is paid not so much to the allocative properties of competitive equilibrium but to the dynamic consequences of the struggle for profits, the competitive economy, it is believed, can be vindicated by reasoning analogous to the Darwinian principle of natural selection: the inefficient do not survive long in a competitive economy.

Although this is legitimate conjecture, it does not suffice to establish a strong presumption in favor of the competitive market on these grounds. The inefficient go to the wall in a highly competitive economy, and they would go there more frequently if governments undertook fewer rescue operations. But how quickly would they go? And although, given enough time, the more efficient tend to survive, they are not necessarily as efficient as they might be. In a modern economy in which markets open up, close down, expand, and contract, from year to year, are there any forces at work to ensure that the most efficient firms are more than tolerably efficient? A more searching investigation would pursue such questions which (not because of limitations of space, but of competence) I can only raise here.

The tasks I set myself in this preliminary inquiry are the following: First, to examine the advantages commonly attributed to free markets; the extension of individual choice, the convenience offered to buyers and sellers of goods and factors, the tendency of resources to move in order to clear markets, and the resulting economic efficiency in the allocation of goods and factors. Secondly, to appraise the virtues attributed to a private enterprise economy, the encouragement it offers to managerial initiative, the continuing incentives it provides for service-, product-, and process-innovation, and its reinforcement of political freedom. Thirdly, to assess the social importance of other desiderata that are not claimed for the competitive economy, especially equity and the quality of life. Fourthly, to comment, in passing, on some of the better-known canons of economic policy associated with the Chicago school, such as:

(1) the removal of all legislation or government devices tending to strengthen monopoly among employers or employees;

(2) the removal of all impediments to the free movement of goods and factors, including the migration of peoples;

(3) the removal of government intervention in foreign exchange markets;

(4) the use of monetary policy rather than price controls in stabilizing prices; and

(5) the preference for transfers in cash rather than in kind.

Criteria

In appraising the virtues claimed for the competitive private-enterprise economy various yardsticks might be used.

First, it is possible to compare that economy with alternative economic systems, existing or seemingly feasible. Here, care must be exercised not to compare an existing imperfect private-enterprise system with an alternative ideal hypothetical system; nor to compare an existing and imperfect alternative economic system, say, that of some socialist country, with a hypothetical ideal private-enterprise system. Since this sort of comparison is a task better suited to those who specialize in comparative economic systems, I shall hardly do more than drop a stray remark here and there. It should be clear, however, that this sort of comparison is limited to answering the question: what sort of economic system, in a given social context, performs better in given respects?

Secondly, it is possible to engage in more immanent criticisms in the light of recent economic thought and to discuss how far from, or close to, realizing the virtues claimed for it is a competitive market economy. A supplementary question may then be posed: do these competitive market virtues, if indeed they are realized in existing societies, make a significant contribution to social welfare? A negative or uncertain answer to this question would cast doubt on the existing allocation of effort and ingenuity among economists to promote legislation and institutions tending to increase competition. Since, in the main, I shall be raising questions that are suggested by relevant theoretical developments in order, occasionally, to cast doubt on implied logical connections, the conclusions that emerge from this survey can only be tentative and impressionistic – an invitation to the profession to re-examine the validity of economic presumptions and the relevance of economic canons that have for so long exerted a dominating influence on the shape and content of economic literature, and to do so in the light of new knowledge and changing material circumstances.

As the reader will soon observe, I follow my exasperating habit of restricting social conjectures or factual judgments to the affluent countries of the world, although some of them may apply as well to the poor or – to use the popular inept euphemism – 'developing' countries of the 'Third World'.

An outline of the structure of this inquiry is easily conveyed by the section titles that follow:

II The Welfare Significance of Economic Efficiency

The Optimal Conditions Again

Since we are to examine briefly the welfare significance of the economic concept of allocative efficiency and, later, to make frequent reference to this concept, the first step must be to decompose a Pareto summit position arbitrarily into a convenient number of necessary conditions by reference to familiar simplifying assumptions.[2] The following four have been chosen:

(a) The '*exchange optimum*', which is met for any distribution of a collection of goods, wherever it is not possible to make 'everyone' better off.[3] When this necessary condition is met, the goods rate of substitution is (under the familiar behavior assumptions mentioned) the same for each person in the community. Since the condition can be met for an indefinite number of distributions among the community, a locus of optimal distributions can be generated which is represented geometrically as the 'contract curve'.

(b) The '*production optimum*', which is met for any collection of goods produced with a given factor endowment when it is not possible to produce any more of one good without producing less of another good. When this necessary condition is fulfilled the factor rate of substitution is the same in the production of each good. Again, the condition can be met for an indefinite variety of goods, the locus of which can be represented geometrically as a production frontier.

(c) The '*top-level optimum*', which is reached when it is no longer possible to make 'everyone' in the community better off with the given endowment of factors. When this necessary condition is met, the goods rate of substitution common to each person in the community is equal to the economy's goods rate of transformation. The geometric analogue is the tangency of the community's indifference curve with the production frontier, or product-transformation curve – a construct which also implies the fulfillment of the exchange optimum and the production optimum respectively.

(d) Finally, wherever the factors available to the economy are not fixed in supply, another condition has to be met; namely, the '*factor-use optimum*'. When this necessary condition is met, it is not possible to make 'everyone' better off by varying the supply of any factor. Its fulfillment implies that the subjective factor-product rate of substitution for each person is equal to the 'objective' factor-product rate of substitution with the existing technology. The corresponding geometric analogue is the tangency between the individual's factor-product indifference curve and the Knightian factor-product transformation curve.

Since a well-functioning market, whether competitive or not, tends to produce a common set of goods prices, the assumption of consumer maximization implies a tendency for the exchange optimal condition to be met. Inasmuch as it tends also to produce a common set of factor prices, the assumption that firms are cost-minimizers – although perhaps less plausible – implies a tendency for the production optimum condition to be met as well. However, in the presence of monopoly, the factor-use optimum is not met. Even in the presence of universal competition, it is not met unless, at ruling factor prices, factor-owners suffer no constraint on the amounts of factors they would choose to supply – which is unlikely to be the case in modern industry.

More interest is attached customarily to the top-level optimal condition, inasmuch as it is violated wherever goods outputs are such that one or more prices in the economy are not equal to their corresponding marginal costs.[4] Thus, although the general term *allocative efficiency* comprehends 'lower level' optima such as (a), (b), and (d) above, its use in the economic literature has reference in the main to the top-level optimum condition, as for instance in the treatment of taxes, tariffs, price controls, and monopolistic pricing.

The Chicago school's concern with the allocative advantages of increased competition would seem to imply a belief in two things; first, a belief in existence of some significant social gain from fulfilling top-level optimal conditions alone, since, however imperfect the market, these lower-level optimal conditions (a) and (b) could also be met. Nevertheless it could be argued that competition impels the economy closer to the production optimum. This belief in the social gains from increasing competition is obviously not easy to verify. There are difficulties enough in measuring such gains under the restrictive assumptions of partial analysis. As for the measurement of gains in a broader context, arising from a change to more competitive arrangements, the unlimited recourse to simplification and, often, to the fiction of a two- or three-sector economy, are such that nobody is inclined to regard the quantitative results as anything more than a bold guess, hopefully illustrative of the direction of gain.

The second implied belief is in the speed of adjustment in a competitive economy.

It is not enough to perceive a continuing *tendency* toward a better allocation of resources. The rapidity or otherwise of industrial adjustment to exogenous movements in demand and supply is also a determinant of allocative improvement over time. Factors other than the degree of competition – for instance, economic institutions, political and cultural features, the state and pace of technological development, and the extent of state intervention – will influence the speed at which industry adjusts to such exogenous changes. It is altogether possible that, however competitive the economy is, industrial equipment is such that the actual changes in the pattern of outputs take place slowly relative to exogenous changes in the pattern of consumption so that the welfare significance of the tendencies toward optimality is slight. To put it otherwise, if in fact, for whatever reason, the economy responds so slowly as to leave it uncertain whether, at any moment of time, we are moving closer to or further from optimality, the belief that 'distortions' can be eliminated by increasing competition is more tenuous, even though we ignore the problems of 'first-' and second-best' that are considered below. Casual judgments about the time factor may yet give way to methods for assessing the time-profile of 'economic' welfare by comparing the optimal price–quantity adjustment at each point of time with the actual price–quantity adjustment that takes place under given institutions and with given policies.

The opposition to the use of price controls as an aid in combating inflation on the grounds that, if effective, it creates allocative 'distortions' in the economy, is weakened by doctrinairism of this sort. Until some plausible estimates can be made of the actual welfare significance of the alleged distortions over the anticipated period of time, and until such estimates of social cost can be compared with that of the temporary increase in unemployment associated with the alternative monetarist solution, the allegation of 'distortions' raises an issue, but does not settle it.

Problems of Second Best

The traditional goal of promoting competition throughout the economy suffered a severe blow from the formal articulation by Lipsey and Lancaster in 1957 of 'The general theory of second best'. There it was demonstrated that the extension of marginal cost pricing in an economy in which some sectors were constrained to realize other pricing rules would not of itself increase social welfare and could, indeed, reduce it. Although it is not possible to infer from the theorem that, in the absence of a first-best solution for the economy, any allocation was as good or as bad as any other,[5] it certainly took the wind out of the sails of many a competitive model notwithstanding some limited counterblasts.[6] Technological unemployment among economists is unthinkable, however, and predictably the procession of allocative propositions continued undiminished with only a respectful salutation in the direction of second best, which theorem continues to this day to be more honored in the breach than the observance.

The upshot of the theorem is that recommendations of marginal cost pricing can be strictly justified only if it is believed that, as a result of such recommendations, marginal cost pricing will be universally adopted; an unlikely prospect. True, the predilection of the Chicago school for a more competitive economy receives support from consideration other than allocation. But it is the allocative significance of the Chicago doctrine that concerns us in this section.

Problems of First Best

Although economists are wont to distinguish with exaggerated care between allocation and equity – where equity includes distributional justice – we should recall that the original appeal of the Pareto principle, on which all allocation propositions are raised, was to a sense of ethical propriety: a change is deemed to be good if nobody is made worse off and at least one person is made better off. If the decentralized competitive economy could be depended upon to produce only these kinds of changes then – allowing for short periods of inconvenience – the esteem in which it is still held by many economists would be wholly vindicated. But the conditions for this outcome to obtain – a world of constant costs (in order to obviate the so-called 'pecuniary' external diseconomies) and a market that captures all goods and bads that are generated in society – will never be realized. Just because these conditions are never met, practically every significant change occurring in the market economy acts to make some people better off and others worse off. Needless to remark, a change from a nonoptimal position to an ideal, or top-level, optimal position will also produce these mixed effects. What is more, some of those who are made worse off could be among the very poor just as some of those who are made better off could be among the very rich. Unless the economist can discover the distributional facts associated with particular allocative improvements, or unless he has reason to believe that any resulting inequities will be overcome quickly with the passage of time, he should be cautious in their recommendation.

The above remarks also apply to potential Pareto improvements, of the Kaldor-Scitovsky variety – or tests of hypothetical compensation as they are sometimes called – for which, if costless distribution were possible, everyone could be made better off. Put otherwise, such tests are met simply if aggregate gains exceed aggregate losses, even though it is explicitly acknowledged that some, possibly the poor, will be made worse off.

Indeed, it cannot be too often emphasized that all purely allocative propositions, whether made within a partial or general economic context, turn on the concept of a *potential* Pareto improvement only. For this reason their ethical appeal is limited.

Recognizing this possibility, the outcome of a conventional cost–benefit study (organized as it is around the notion of the algebraic sum of the compensating variations of everyone affected by the project) is not to be regarded as a decision criterion. Indeed, the magnitude of the excess of gains over losses is to be regarded only as one of the essential bits of information, along with other information about distribution and equity.

Of course, in the limiting case of so progressive an income tax that everyone is left with the same disposable income, all potential improvements become translated into actual improvements for everyone – unless the costs of the transfer exceed the net gains. It is not, therefore, unreasonable to argue that in a market economy without significant externalities the pursuit of allocative efficiency – though perhaps difficult in view of the problems of first and second best – could at least lead to the bulk of the population being made better off over time *provided* the tax system was both highly progressive and efficient. Couched in such terms, however, the statement reveals only too clearly the extent of our ignorance about relevant magnitudes, in particular the order of magnitudes of the actual gains and actual losses arising from seemingly efficient reallocations, their distribution through the existing tax system, and, indeed, the long-run costs to society in maintaining existing tax systems which are neither highly progressive nor highly efficient. In sum, it reveals the extent to which current presuppositions in favor of economic efficiency depend no less upon faith than upon knowledge of the facts.

A final deficiency of allocative propositions in economics also arises from our acceptance of their formulation in terms of potential gains. As demonstrated initially by Scitovsky (1941), and on innumerable later occasions by other writers, if a collection of goods Q_2 is allocatively superior to a collection Q_1, in that everyone could be made better off by a movement from Q_1 to Q_2, the same may be said for the reverse movement, from Q_2 to Q_1. This apparent contradiction depends upon a correspondence between each efficient distribution of a given goods collection and a set of prices. Thus, thinking in terms of the related price-index criterion, it is hardly paradoxical to state that at one set of prices the goods collection Q_2 is valued higher than Q_1, whereas for another set of prices Q_1 is valued higher.

But there are further implications of this line of analysis that make one pause. First, it is no longer possible to show, in general, that a top-level optimal position is unambiguously superior – on a potential Pareto test, that is – to a nonoptimal position (Mishan, 1957). Indeed, it is not possible in general to regard as unambiguously superior, in this same sense, a collection of goods Q_2 that has more of all goods than Q_1 – even if, in addition, Q_2 is a top-level optimum and Q_1 is not only nonoptimal but is situated below the production boundary and, therefore, does not meet the production optimal conditions.[7]

The question of how important in the real world are these awkward possibilities is one which invites speculation. There may be important limiting conditions, but as yet they have not been discovered. I tend to think that it is less likely than it appears in the geometry of the two- or three-good case. Yet awareness of these possibilities does add something to the doubts about the welfare significance of allocative improve-

ments and, *a fortiori* therefore, to the presumption that an extension of the competitive economy enhances welfare.[8]

Interdependent Utilities

This phenomenon comes under the category of externalities inasmuch as a person's welfare depends upon variables – the utility, or the income, or the amounts of goods purchased, of other persons – that he cannot control. They are less amenable to correction, however, than the more tangible externalities inflicted by pollutants.

The implication of Duesenberry's 'relative income hypothesis' (1949) for social welfare in a growing economy, though of the utmost importance, is familiar enough today to warrant only brief mention before turning to the more recent exploration of other aspects of interdependent utilities. That people's satisfaction in life is not impervious to the wealth of their neighbors is an observation too banal to be worth the recording. Yet when nicely formalized and fed into the Pareto machinery, the resulting outcome gives economic respectability to current philosophical doubts about the value of sustained material growth. If it is true that the higher the level of 'real' *per capita* income the more does a person's well-being depend, not on his absolute income but on his income relative to those of others, the less the Pareto justification for further economic growth. People may continue, of course, to struggle to improve their position relative to others but clearly, in the limiting case in which individual welfare depends only on relative income, it would no longer be possible to make everyone better off: only redistribution possibilities would remain open to society. And, once real income were equally distributed, no rise in well-being would be experienced by anyone even though output *per capita* would continue to grow.

Although there is evidence from surveys of the increasing prevalence of this phenomenon,[9] much more needs to be known before any strong conclusion can be reached. The more prevalent it becomes, however, the more do the attractions of further economic growth diminish.[10] And although a disciple of the Chicago school may have no particular brief for economic growth *per se*, but only for that economic growth that is the collective result of individual decisions, the value of the growth of 'real' income resulting therefrom is also diminished.

In general, it may be said that the more the relative

income hypothesis operates the less value is to be placed on more goods satisfaction and on allocative improvements, even where free of all ambiguity.

In contrast to this negative relationship between a person's welfare and the income of others, in particular the income of those within his status group, recent writers have been paying more attention to the positive relation between a person's welfare and the incomes of those who are poorer than he. The first relationship can be referred to briefly as 'envy', the second 'benevolence'. Needless to remark, the two hypotheses are not mutually exclusive: person A's welfare may rise with an increase in B's income until it exceeds some critical proportion of A's income, after which A's welfare declines with increases in B's income.

However, by reference to the Pareto criterion, the 'benevolence' relationship has been employed to rationalize actual or possible patterns of distribution either in money or in kind.

Three kinds of argument bearing on distribution can be distinguished.

(1) One argument, associated with Hochman and Rodgers (1969), confines itself to money transfers that are actual Pareto improvements. Thus, if it is assumed that a dollar received by Mr Poor is valued by him at just one dollar, it is required of the donor, Mr Rich, that he obtain more than one dollar's worth of satisfaction from 'spending' the dollar on Mr Poor. Following this line of thought some distributions, at least, can be regarded simply as an extension of the Pareto principle.

(2) It is to be noted that a potential Pareto improvement criterion would imply a larger transfer of income than an actual Pareto improvement criterion. For on the former criterion we could justify transferring a dollar from Mr Rich even if the satisfaction he derives from its donation to Mr Poor were less than a dollar. It is enough that Mr Rich's satisfaction is not negative.

The distributional agreement associated with Thurow (1971) is, in fact, based on a potential Pareto improvement criterion. Classifying the structure of the income distribution as a collective good, each conceivable income structure (or tax structure) is assumed to affect the welfare of every member of the community. In consequence each person can place a value, or compensating variation, on each alternative structure. If it raises his welfare, this compensating variation is the sum he is willing to pay for the collective adoption of the structure in question. If it lowers his welfare, the compensating variation is the sum he must receive to restore his welfare. The largest potential Pareto improvement follows from implementing (costlessly) that distributional structure that commands the largest positive aggregate of compensating variations.

(3) A third argument linked with Daly and Giertz (1972) rests on a distinction between 'utility externalities' (the dependence of A's welfare on the levels of income of others) and 'goods externalities' (the dependence of A's welfare on amounts of specific goods consumed by others). In the former case, all the goods-exchange optimal conditions are met and, as indicated earlier, improvements can be effected only through transfers of purchasing power. In the latter case, however, since a person's welfare depends *inter alia* on the amounts of specific goods consumed by others, the existence of a common set of prices no longer ensures the existence of an exchange optimum: if negotiation were costless, person A, for example, might improve his position by bribing other persons to take more, or less, of those particular goods their possession of which affects his welfare.

From this implication, a case may be conceived for transfers in kind rather than in cash. The proponents of such a scheme agree what it costs to convert money into goods and to administer the distribution of the goods. They agree also that, as a rule, the recipients prefer cash to goods. Yet they conclude that to insist on cash transfers in all cases might imply a loss of possible gains in welfare. For if donors were not allowed to give transfers in kind, they might give away considerably less in cash than the value of the goods they would willingly have given. Not only would the donors be worse off if the cash-only doctrine were enforced, but the recipients also inasmuch as – though they prefer a dollar of cash to a dollar's worth of goods – the value of the total cash they receive is less than the value they attach to the goods they would have received. Thus, although transfers in kind may be stigmatized as 'paternalism', they can, it seems, be vindicated not only by the democratic process but also by the Pareto criterion which has some ethical appeal inasmuch as every one counts, donors as well as recipients.

I do not know whether adherents of the Chicago school were much impressed by any of these arguments.[11] But they do favor voluntary cash transfers which appear to be the policy implication of the first argument. However, Hochman and Rodgers also make use of their concept to rationalize the existing tax system, which is unacceptable to the Chicago school. Nor would the direct tax implication of Thurow's analysis appeal to it. The Daly and Giertz conclusions would go down no better. Although their analysis proceeds by reference to voluntary behavior, information and transactions costs are such that government action is necessary to implement the findings in favor of goods transfers. Indeed, not only are the required transfers to be compulsory, the sums raised are to be used for the purchase and distribution of specific goods, a policy which entails expansion of state bureaucracies.

Ethics versus Utility

The three distribution arguments summarized above are examples of analyses that omit a vital distinction in connection with the way distribution enters into each person's utility: the distinction between the 'Pareto efficient' distribution and the 'just' distribution. A movement toward the former can, as indicated, be justified beginning from an existing real world position. The 'just' or 'ethical' distribution, on the other hand, is one that is conceived to emerge from a constitution that is framed behind Rawls's veil of ignorance. In other words, it is an ideal distribution that men might hope to agree upon if the matter were debated in some hypothetical state prior to their entering into the real world – a state in which no man could foresee his genetic or material endowment in the real world or the circumstances that would befall him. Insofar as men succeed, in their actual deliberations, in projecting themselves into this imaginary state, they are addressing themselves to the 'just' distribution, not the Pareto-efficient one (Mishan, 1971).

The traditional separation between economic efficiency and distribution entails, in my interpretation, a concern with the 'just' distribution and not the Pareto-efficient one. It should be clear, moreover, that insofar as there is conflict between the two approaches to distribution, the 'just' distribution has the stronger ethical appeal.

Thus in the broader context of economy policy, the Pareto principle is not the only criterion acceptable to the liberal economist or, indeed, to the welfare economist. As I have indicated elsewhere (1969b), the choice of a utility base for welfare economics can be rejected in favor of an ethical base, the ethics being those of the society for which the prescriptive statements of welfare economics are intended to apply. As indicated above, these ethics, however, are sometimes those that would emerge only from deliberations taking place behind 'the veil of ignorance' and are, therefore, not always readily apparent from public expression. Nor then can they always be expected to be politically decisive. The most to be hoped for is that, in consequence of a continuing dialogue, they will ultimately prevail.

However, in some instances the ethics of an issue are more manifestly in conflict with the prescriptions flowing from a utility- or Pareto-based welfare economics. Excess benefits, for example, may arise from the expropriation by a majority of the property of a rich

minority. Again, a project that raises the material well-being of a given group of people sufficiently to warrant the real resources involved, may be vetoed on the Pareto criterion if it inflames the prejudices of neighboring groups. Yet the ethics of society might forbid that a policy be rejected simply because – although it improves the material well-being of one group without damaging the material interests of any other group – it could be resented by others.

What is more, there can be accord among economists against resort to the Pareto criterion on a wide range of policy issues simply because the public lacks both the relevant knowledge and the training to foresee the likely consequences of the alternative policies being mooted. On such issues the economist would prefer that decisions be reached through the political process, not necessarily because he is impressed by the wisdom of the multitude as expressed through the ballot box. After all, the democratic process has come out in support of many policies rejected not only by the Chicago school but also by a majority of economists – tariffs, trade restrictions, farm price supports, wage and price legislation, to mention just a few. The economist may prefer the political process because he is averse to extending a criterion appropriate for the choice of market goods – where its justification depends upon the notion of given tastes and on the belief, or fiction, that people know their own interests best – to broader or more complex issues in which given 'tastes' may be given prejudices, and which it is demonstrably untrue that people know their own interests best, much less those of the community at large. Employing the Pareto principle in such issues, assuming all measurement problems could be overcome, might well find in favor of existing and possibly higher tariffs, in favor of farm price supports, in favor of racial discrimination – and in favor of distribution in kind. In short, its wholesale employment, assuming its feasibility, would give the sanction of economic efficiency to policies that are today roundly condemned by liberal economists. Relegating such issues instead to the political arena, at least enables economists and others to participate in an ongoing dialogue in the endeavor to persuade an existing majority of people that it is not in their ultimate interests or desires to support policies they currently favor.

Thus, notwithstanding the recent analyses of Pareto-efficient distributions, the argument against proposed transfers in kind can draw upon ethical considerations touched upon in the paragraph preceding the above, as well as those of propriety mentioned in the preceding paragraph. The liberal economist may reasonably affirm that *in respect of market goods,* it is morally appropriate that all adults, even the poor and destitute, should be treated as if they knew their own interests best; they should be treated, that is, on a par with other members of society in this respect. Only exceptional circumstances warrant the implied indignity. And if it is true that donors prefer to give in kind because they believe that they know better what the recipients need than do the recipients themselves – or for whatever reason – then the liberal economist could well retort that it is quite improper for them to think in this way and would seek to convince them of the impropriety.

III Free Markets and the Environment

The proposition that the existence of perfectly competitive equilibria in all markets entails an optimal position for the economy always carries the standard proviso that there be no external effects. At the time Pigou was writing, the existence of such effects was thought to be more the exception than the rule. But with growing public concern over pollution after the Second World War and, in consequence, the vastly increased attention being given to environmental externalities in the professional literature over the last decade or so, the Chicago school could no longer avoid discussing some of the issues raised by their incidence.

The Chicago View

Not surprisingly, a more conservative approach was developed, in part inspired by Frank Knight's classic article (1924), and also perhaps by the no less celebrated paper by Jacob Viner (1931), which sought to weaken the popular arguments for government intervention, and to strengthen the presumption that unaided market forces would, or could be made to, bring about a proper allocation of resources, at least within the restrictive assumptions of a partial context. Caution against too ready a recourse to excise taxes or subsidies, or other controls, continues to be urged for a number of reasons.

First, and rather casually, members of the Chicago school maintain that the current preoccupation with pollution is out of proportion to the problems it poses[12] and they vent their resentment against 'environmentalists' by associating their articulate concern with elitist self-interest. 'The quality of the environment', it is repeatedly asserted, 'is predominantly a middle-class interest', which interest, were it to prevail, would tend to have regressive distributional effects – through the raising of the prices of a range of products that forms a significant proportion of the consumption of the 'poor', and through a possible slowing down of the rate of economic growth (as a result both of reducing resources otherwise available for new investment and of interfering with the decisions of private industry).

These allegations carry little conviction. It is not impossible that social marginal costs of a range of polluting goods exceed their prices and, if corrected, would reduce the 'real' incomes (measured in terms only of man-made goods) of the poor by a greater proportion than those of the rich. Yet conservative economists do not favor subsidizing particular goods for distributional reasons. They favor direct transfers of money. On the difficulties of estimating the distributional effects of combating a wide range of pollutants, see Kneese and Schultze (1975).

As for the concern with future economic growth, there is no apparent reason to suppose that allocative correction for environmental spillovers would act to reduce aggregate investment or innovation.

In the same spirit, caveats were uttered against state intervention in the attempt to improve the environment without careful thought of the consequences. If, for example, the measures taken by a government succeeded in improving the urban environment inhabited by the poor, the suburban rich might begin to move back to the urban area and, in the process, drive up rents so far as to displace the poor.

Secondly, a number of arguments found favor with these more conservative economists, many of whom disliked the tax solution associated with the writings of Pigou. There was a tendency, for example, to conclude that the calculation of an optimal tax was costly and its administration fraught with difficulties.[13] Another much favored maneuver was to discover circumstances in which an external diseconomy might warrant an expansion of output rather than a contraction.[14] These apparently perverse possibilities, however, do not rate as counterexamples to the broad Pigovian theme which, in the face of market failures, directed the state to bring about a 'reshuffling' of resources as between economic activities in the endeavor to realize an ideal allocation, one identified by the necessary condition that in the production of all goods prices should equal corresponding marginal *social* cost.

In the same category can be found the rather lame proposition (Buchanan and Stubblebine, 1962) that an optimal excise tax levied on a good producing an external diseconomy could result in a suboptimal contraction of output if further bargaining between the affected parties took place.[15] Also, another more plausible assertion; that the market left to itself raises the costs of pollutant-causing products by the required amount inasmuch as industries established in polluted areas have to offer a premium to attract workers from, and prevent workers migrating to, less polluted areas.[16]

Thirdly, a more convincing argument against state intervention can be made by relating the operation of the market to the distribution of property rights in scarce resources. Thus, in contrast to Pigou's optimal tax solution to the congested highway problem, Knight (1924) explained the congestion itself in terms of the overuse of a scarce resource, highway space, this being the result of its being treated as a common property. Regarded in this light, the appropriate remedy was to treat the highway as private property and so to price traffic as to maximize the return to the highway.[17]

In effect, Knight's proposed solution emerged as part of his analysis. It was a solution, however, that produced the same output as Pigou's optimal tax. The pragmatic question, then, turns on a comparison of the social costs of collecting the appropriate tolls or taxes either by the highway-owners or by the agencies of the state. Yet Knight's insight was impressive, and a *prima facie* argument against the necessity of state intervention was established – at least for those external diseconomies that result from treating as common property those scarce but appropriable resources associated with areas of land and water.

This seminal idea, however, was to lie in fallow soil until about 1960 when it began to produce much fruit after its kind. Coase's celebrated contribution of that year illustrated, among other things, the proposition that in the absence of income effects (or, more properly 'welfare effects') and in the absence of all transactions costs, the bargaining solution to an external diseconomy problem would be optimal and uniquely determined.[18] Coase also sought to dispose of the popular notion of one party's inflicting damage on another, a notion that lends itself to policies that favor compensation for the victim. What modest success he had in this endeavor arose from his choice of examples in which conflicts of business interest were mutual and therefore were such as to make the question of equity difficult to determine.

Fourthly, the explicit consideration of transactions costs could be made to tell against state intervention.

In the absence of all transactions costs, mutual bargaining would, as indicated by Coase (1960), tend to produce an optimal solution – even if there were scarce resources involved that were being treated as common property. In fact, it is the existence of transactions costs large enough to prevent bargaining that requires the consideration of other solutions among which, needless to remark, the one most favored by Chicago is that which would direct the scarce appropriable resource to be managed as private property. Thus, it came to pass that the concept of transactions costs, along with that of property rights, inspired a number of thoughtful contributions, many of which appeared during the 1960s in the *Journal of Law and Economics*,[19] designed to strengthen the presumption favoring the free market even in the presence of significant externalities. Indeed, arguments were pushed to the point of suggesting that the mere existence of an unchecked market output of a good x, one generating external diseconomies, could be accepted as evidence that transactions costs, more particularly bargaining costs, must be in excess of the net social gains that would otherwise result from optimal correction of the output. The existence of a *de facto* optimum could then be legitimately inferred. On the other hand, the nonexistence of a market for a good y could be interpreted as evidence that transactions costs, more particularly enforcement or policing costs, must be greater than the (otherwise) net gains to society. By extending the concept of transactions cost to encompass any inertia or lack of initiative in society, one comes uncomfortably close to the thesis that, in economics, whatever is, is best.

Fifthly, the conservative economist warns against premature action against pollution. Action must wait upon knowledge; and the eventual measures, if any, to be taken must be the fruit of prolonged and dispassionate research. Bearing in mind the costs of unearthing relevant information, the effect of such conservative advice is to put the burden of expense and proof on the antipollution faction.

Sixthly, although there is an absence of markets, in the conventional sense, for the more commonly recognized environmental goods, aesthetic amenity, quiet, fresh air, clean water, it may be contended that individuals retain some choice in the matter through the simple mechanism mentioned in the Tiebout hypothesis (1956). For environmental goods could be included in each of the packages of public goods offered by the different local authorities. In fact the extent of the choice in respect of environmental goods is limited by the size of the jurisdiction, by their number, by the pressure of business interests, and all too commonly, by the lack of initiative and imagination. Even if the differences in environmental goods as between locations were substantially greater than they happen to be, accessibility to them is limited by costs of movement, 'real' and 'psychic', which are likely to fall more heavily on the poor. There is, moreover, nothing in this mechanism to prevent a general erosion over time of environmental standards in all areas of a country, the direct result of the technologies and products associated with postwar economic growth.

Finally, by conceding the case, in principle, for the need of some form of property rights in environmental goods, it is seemingly possible to reconcile a concern over environmental disruption with a faith in the operation of free markets.

Assessment of the Chicago View

I should not want to under-rate either the ingenuity or the significance of the many contributions that served to strengthen the Chicago school's faith in the allocative virtue of the free market even in a society that is increasingly afflicted by external diseconomies. But there are a number of aspects of the problem, related to equity as well as to allocation, that the market cannot satisfactorily resolve. These appear more important as less attention is paid to interfirm or interindustry externalities and more attention to the overspill on the public at large from the processes or products of modern industry.

First, although the notion of some ideal distribution among the populace of property rights in environmental amenities – what I refer to more briefly as 'amenity rights' (1967b) – is suggestive in understanding the nature of the problem, there are insuperable difficulties in implementing it. A vision of a decentralized market in which, for example, each member of the public can sell or rent his allotted volume of air-space – to be regarded by buyers of the amounts of air-space needed by industry as a substitute for the air-space owned by any other member of the public – to be used as a repository for containing pollutants such as smoke, particles, fume, noise, and so forth, can be counted on to provoke the imagination to grasp the limitations of our universe. But just because, in those cases where the scarce resource is not appropriable, such schemes are impossible, we are constrained to compare an inefficient market solution with a solution requiring some form of state intervention. For there are, indeed, social costs in extending a bureaucracy over and above the usual list of transactions costs. And the latter will be high if economists insist on calculating the magnitude of the ideal excise or effluent tax. Without being optimal, however, rough and tentative tax calculations can effect a substantial improvement. Certainly the use of taxes to enforce tolerable standards may yield significant social gains over and above the costs of enforcement.[20]

Secondly, although the bargaining outcome will be optimal if there are no transactions costs, it will not be uniquely optimal if there are nonzero welfare effects. The incidence of these effects on the outcome can be assumed negligible only if the impact of the decision in question on people's well-being is small, which is not generally the case for environmental spillovers. Assuming normal (positive) welfare effects, what a person in a noisy environment is willing to pay for continuing quiet may be only a fraction of the minimum sum he is willing to accept to put up with the existing noise, or with the additional noise expected to be generated by a highway or airport to be built near his home. Whether the airport or highway is sanctioned on economic grounds can then depend on whether the law requires compensation for the residents in question or whether, in default of a legal ruling, the economic cost of the noise is estimated simply by what the residents can pay to prevent it. Thus, in the absence of marketable amenity rights, the disamenities inflicted on the public are ignored by the entrepreneur who will be induced to modify his scheme only if the sums they can offer him in return will more than compensate for his incidental loss of profit. Furthermore, even if the building of a proposed highway or airport is contingent upon a thoroughgoing cost–beneft criterion, one taking into account compensatory variations for all disamenities incurred, the question of equity is neglected.

Thirdly, as for the conservative principle that no action be taken unless and until relevant information is available, it could be a recipe for disaster in a world of rapid change. It is, of course, true that the ideal tax cannot be calculated in the absence of detailed knowledge about the environmental impact of the good or process in question. It is also true, as indicated above, that worthwhile improvements can be implemented without recourse to an ideal tax. What is more to the point, however, is that such a principle amounts to the methodological rule: when in doubt, continue to pollute.

For a community living on the margin of subsistence such a rule might be justified – at least insofar as it would countenance the introduction of polluting goods or processes that otherwise make a substantial contribution to the community's welfare. But in an already affluent society, the case for adopting such a rule is far from obvious. And if we include in the term *pollution,* the risk of grave and possibly irreversible genetic and ecological consequences – a subject we touch on in the following section – the reverse methodological rule would seem more prudent; namely, that all processes generating, or products containing, substances about whose effects we have limited experience, should be withheld until prolonged research has uncovered their range of consequences beyond reasonable doubt.

Fourthly, if the law were to prohibit any new developments having manifestly adverse environmenal effects without fully compensating all who were thereby injured, the outputs of some industries would tend to be smaller than they would in the absence of such restrictive environmental legislation. Indeed, if only because of the heavy costs also incurred in identifying and bargaining with potential victims, some industries would not be able to operate at all. Yet the equilibrium that the competitive market tends to, under this dispensation, would be no less of an optimal than the equilibrium it would tend to if, instead, the spillover victims had no rights whatsoever. The interesting question arises whether, in respect of net social gains and/or equity, the competitive equilibrium solution in the presence of this restrictive legislation is better or worse than the competitive equilibrium solution in the absence of any such restrictive legislation: or whether, perhaps, a mixture of the two, or else a system of effluent taxes that enforce environmental standards, is better than either – bearing in mind that the magnitude of transactions costs (which use up real resources) will vary from one solution to another. Without further reflection and some empirical study there is not much to be said that would command general assent. There are certainly no considerations that lead one to suspect that a pollutant-permissive competitive-market solution is likely to be best in respect either of net social gain or of equity.

Fifthly, and most important of all, among the great virtues claimed for the market, one apt to be overlooked in a professional literature that lends itself too easily to formal allocation propositions, is that of the freedom to choose. Notwithstanding Machlup's arguments (1969), there is no necessary restriction of consumer freedom if, without reducing disposable incomes, excise taxes and subsidies are used to make good x dearer and good y cheaper. So far as the consumer is affected, the resulting change of market prices could have as well been the outcome of changes in the conditions of supply. Indeed, the only difference between these two cases is allocative: the tax-subsidy alteration of goods prices is potentially Pareto inferior to a situation in which the relative prices reflect their corresponding social marginal costs.

The case is quite different for expenditure or quantitative constraints. As Milton Friedman has persuasively argued, the more the public sector takes over from the private market sector the less choice remains for the individual. His money is used, allegedly on his behalf, in the production of public goods that may not interest him and, insofar as these goods are nonoptional, he is compelled to consume them in amounts other than those he would prefer.[21] If this is true of public sector collective goods, it is no less true of nonoptional collective bads, or external diseconomies.

And it remains true whether or not allocative criteria are satisfied;[22] whether, that is, the optimal amounts of collective goods or collective bads are being produced.

Thus, if a person complains of smog or aircraft noise, it is not altogether to the purpose to remark the impressive growth of industry and its products, or the increase of travel opportunities. He may himself have little use for the smog-creating products or air travel services. And if he were observed to make use of them – if only because in the sort of environment developed in response to these products, and in particular to the growth in airplanes and automobiles, he is left with little choice in the matter – he still might not want to put up with the concomitant bads in the amounts he currently receives. Indeed, on balance, he may regard himself as worse off in consequence of the availability of such goods-cum-bads. In contrast, a tied sale (by which a person is compelled to pay for some items he may not want, or may dislike, in order to acquire the goods he wants) cannot make him worse off. For he can always refuse the tied sale offer if, on balance, it reduces his welfare. But where the package includes nonoptional collective bads, no matter how much or little he takes of the accompanying goods he cannot reduce the quantum of bads that fall on him – save, possibly, by incurring expenditures.

The point is not trivial. The virtue of extended choice claimed for the market resides in its ability, so to speak, to 'decompose' composite packages of goods, or bads, or both, for individual consumption – packages that could result, say, from a state decree or from a popular vote – into its constituent parts among which the individual may freely choose. Insofar as the market is to be successful in this vital respect, all the goods and all the bads of any welfare significance must enter the price system. Changes over time operating through this market will then tend to realize[23] actual Pareto improvements; those in which everyone is actually made better off.

The significance of the above passage may be brought out by imagining a market economy without a labor market. Allocative criteria in these circumstances would be met by taking proper account of the 'diswelfare', in terms of compensating variations, of all the labor forcibly directed into the production of amounts of goods being demanded; the costs of such labor being treated, quite properly in this economy, as an external diseconomy. In making the transition to an organized labor market in which, within the constraints of technology and custom, each worker can now choose for himself where among the alternative opportunities to place his labor, there will be a significant extension of individual choice which enhances social welfare. Its formal expression, however, is in terms of a movement from a potential to an actual Pareto improvement.

Now in the nature of things, one cannot literally set up a spillovers market, one in which each person can decide for himself how much of each spillover he will freely absorb at the going market price. The unavoidable treatment in economics of such spillovers as external diseconomies, or nonoptional collective bads, that is, entails the use of this more limited criterion – the potential Pareto improvement, and not the actual one. And the welfare significance of this limitation clearly depends upon the impact of the range of spillovers on individual wellbeing.

Considering the pace and scale of modern technology and the power of commercial interests,[24] it would be optimistic to anticipate much decline in the existing range of spillovers over the future. At best, we can expect new spillovers for old. Some pervasive spillovers, such as noise, visual distraction, urban litter and ugliness, are not likely to diminish much over the next decade. Bearing in mind the inertia of political processes, is it too pessimistic to conclude that, notwithstanding the operation of free markets, in all of that which is trivial the individual today has ample choice, but in much that is truly important to the state of his well-being – the environment in which he is enmeshed – he has very little choice? At any rate, if something like this conclusion is credible, the claims made for the virtue of the free market in purveying choice will, as a result of the technologies of economic growth, have to be considerably diminished. For the domain of its success in this respect, at least under existing laws, has come to exclude areas of great sensitivity.

The question then to be faced is whether any alternative economic organization can do better than the existing market system even when supplemented by effluent taxes. A fairly radical suggestion, one compatible with the operation of the market, has already been suggested: that in respect of a number of environmental spillovers suffered by the public at large legislation be enacted placing the burden of prevention or compensation wholly on the industries or persons responsible for them.[25] Enforcement costs may, of course, be so large that the optimum toward which the economy tends under this form of law, offers a smaller net social gain than the optimum toward which the economy tends under the existing laws. On the other hand, all adjustments involving environmental repercussions will, under the proposed law, tend to involve actual Pareto improvements: nobody will then suffer uncompensated damage. In effect, a trade-off between equity or justice, on the one hand, and (unweighted) real income on the other would be at issue, with society

requiring some idea of the magnitudes and some criterion by which to assess these incommensurables. In a materially prosperous society, however, it may be easier to secure assent to the maxim, that it is more important to prevent injustice and unnecessary suffering than it is to provide opportunities for further material aggrandizement.

IV Risk and the Market Economy

Some of the risks run by private businesses can be insured against. Some of the risks that cannot be insured against arise from the uncertainty of future prices and can be hedged against on futures or forward markets. Yet others can be, at least, partly unloaded onto willing speculators. Employees may also be able to insure against sickness, unemployment, or loss of earnings. Through such schemes, a variety of risks can be costed into the economic system and, since such schemes, like the production of any new good, offer social gains, there is warrant for some economic ingenuity being directed into innovations of this sort.

In this section, the risks that concern us are not those arising from the ordinary vicissitudes of trade – that is, from the uncertainty about future prices and availabilities – but those arising in the production and use of goods that bear on the health and survival of members of society. The treatment of this problem, then, involves an extension of the treatment of environmental externalities in the preceding section.

Although the line between risk and uncertainty, and between knowledge and ignorance of potential damage, is very blurred, some arbitrary classification will help us to come to grips with the problems.

Voluntary and Known Risk

The unchecked operation of the goods market will suffice wherever it can be supposed that each person knows from experience the probability of incurring particular disabilities from the consumption and use of the different goods, or else can acquire the relevant information at low cost and little inconvenience. As for those occupational risks that are correctly assessed, the operation of the market can be expected to produce factor prices that include the appropriate risk premia.

Voluntary and Unknown Risk

Exceptions always being allowed for the protection of minors, the position taken by John Stuart Mill continues to express the judgment of liberal economists today. In the absence of external effects,[26] the maxim, that no man should seek to improve the social welfare by interfering in any way in those individual choices directed to market goods, would also extend to any adult the freedom to imperil his life or health in any way he wished. Since knowledge of the kind of risks that are associated with the consumption of tobacco, liquor, or traditional drugs, such as opium, is fairly widely dispersed in society, the case in freedom for allowing a man to take what risks he will, provided they fall entirely on his person,[27] is buttressed by modern instances of the unhappier consequences of attempts by the state to control the traffic in liquor or drugs.

There is a case, indeed, for the freedom of any person to take drugs about which very little is currently known, either of the consequences or of their likelihood of occurrence, granted always that there is little chance of his hurting others. Suffice that he knows it to be a drug that could conceivably have dire consequences on his physical and mental health, there is a case in freedom for permitting him to experiment on his own person only if he so chooses.

Involuntary and Known Risk

If we accept this view, at least provisionally, we need concern ourselves in the remainder of this section only with instances in which risks fall on those who by their own activity do not incur them; in short with the externality aspects of risk-bearing. Where the external diseconomies that arise in the production or the consumption of the goods in question are those that increase the risk of damage to the health of others by a known probability, recourse to a system of excise taxes can, in principle, internalize the resulting social costs into the price system. No more need be said here about alternative solutions, however, since environmental damage, treated in the preceding section, includes any known health risks of intervention in the environment or biosphere.

Involuntary and Unknown Risk

In this category are those instances where the nature, magnitude, and, therefore, possibly the valuation of the damage that might occur are believed to be understood, but the probability of its occurrence is not; also included are those instances where we have no knowledge or very imperfect knowledge of the extent of the damage that could occur.

Game theory is one of the techniques favored by economists for dealing with such problems of uncertainty, especially those for which the magnitudes of alternative outcomes are known but not the

probabilities of their occurrence. For the case where the magnitudes themselves are unknown, our greater ignorance can also be formalized along game-theoretic lines by extending the spectrum of possible social costs from some negligible figure at one end to a figure at the other end that is large enough to shock anybody.

It is possible to make use of such techniques in social cost–benefit studies, although in fact they are seldom used in putting a value on the social hazards of large projects using complex technology. The greater the extent of our ignorance, the less satisfactory the outcome of a game theory exercise, bearing in mind also that it does not carry with it a rule for deciding which criterion to apply; whether, for instance, the more conservative *maximin* criterion or the more opportunistic *minimax* one. What can be said for sure, however, is that wherever such risks are borne involuntarily – wherever, that is, they are not confined to the individual, the firm, or the industry generating them – but instead fall upon the public at large, the free market cannot cope with them.

The popular examples of such hazards that spring to mind are, not surprisingly, the consequence of scientific and technological advance. Although in all cases it is possible (though not likely) that the full range of adverse consequences, and the probability distribution of each of them, will come to light with the passage of time, the social problem is that of somehow adjusting the economic system to the existence of our dangerous state of ignorance until we know more.[28] Recollecting the social consequences of the introduction of heroin at the turn of the century (advertised and prescribed for a while by the medical profession as a safe sedative), more recently those of Methadone, the genetic consequence of Thalidomide and, to a lesser extent, chemical food additives to say nothing of the far-reaching ecological effects of DDT and a growing range of chemical pesticides, it is obvious that no provision for them can be made by the mechanism of the market; nor, for that matter, by such traditional economic devices as a system of excise or other taxes.

The postwar cornucopia of drugs and synthetics about whose consequences, singly or in combination, we know next to nothing, now runs into many thousands. And although the probability of some genetic or ecological calamity in the production or use of any one of them might be very small indeed, as the number of such products continues to multiply, the resulting risk of some such calamity actually occurring increases to a point beyond which society is in grave peril. In these circumstances, measuring social gains against social costs with the aid of market prices is no longer that of a routine exercise in allocation economics. Indeed, any hope of translating these sorts of risk into money values that can somehow be internalized into the economic system is to be dismissed as chimerical.[29] The nature of many of the risks we are courting can be dealt with only at the highest political level and following considerable public debate.

In this connection one has only to think of the possible consequences currently associated with 'genetic engineering', with supersonic flights, with the operation of nuclear fission plants, to appreciate the magnitude of some of the problems that the technological society is running into. To continue much longer, therefore, to allow scientists to make their own decisions about fields of research, to allow research departments of corporations to decide themselves whether and when a new product should be marketed, to allow government agencies, guided by the advice of enthusiastic technocrats, to make critical decisions about vast projects and policies that could conceivably endanger the lives and health of thousands or millions of ordinary citizens, would amount to a victory of traditional *laissez-faire* doctrine, and of faith in elected governments, over society's instinct for self-preservation, a victory that could pave the way for social disaster. In this new and more dangerous world we are entering, adequate legislation would entail a wide range of democratic controls, not only over the activities of private enterprise, but also over the research activities of scientists.

Whatever the outcome, however, the variety of apprehensions that afflict a society in consequence of the perils, real or imagined, that flow directly from new research or technologies, or indirectly from the social consequences of technological growth, can reach levels that swamp any contribution to social welfare arising from the operation of free markets in a growing economy. In the present state of technological development this is not an idle fancy. As we shall see anon, technology has yet other consequences that run counter to the beneficient effects of free markets, in particular those extending individual choice and personal freedom; consequences, therefore, that relegate to that felicitous institution a diminishing role in the preservation of society's welfare.

V Intergenerational Equity and the Market

In an ideal Irving-Fisher type of capital market, the volume of current new investment is the collective outcome of individual decisions, each one the result of weighing the inconvenience of postponing consumption against the gains (from investment) of doing so. Insofar as economic growth stems only from the accumulation of capital in this manner, its path is determined by a market that reflects individual desires. The contribution to economic growth of technological progress need not, however, be regarded as an independent factor. For the advance and diffusion of technology may reach a stage at which the returns to investment in research itself will continually be compared with the returns to investment in known techniques of production.

It is unnecessary to remark that the operation of capital markets is unlikely to produce this ideal result and that, for a number of reasons, we should expect current social yields on new investment to exceed individual rates of time preference: they include income and corporation taxes, possible external economies of investment, uncertainty about the future felt by lender and borrower, and the borrowing advantages of large corporations. Yet even if capital markets were to operate perfectly and, at any point of time, the rate of time preference were equal to the current social yield on new investment, its merit would consist only in giving expression, through the accumulation of capital, to the saving and investment decisions of the existing generation. And in this connection, it is hardly necessary to remark that many people today still choose to save for and leave wealth to their children and grandchildren, and would continue to do so whether, through its collective actions, society's real income were expected to increase or decline. However, inasmuch as intergenerational equity is a desideratum that economists are having to think about in consequence of our concern with technological growth and the depletion of natural resources, the extent of the market's inability to promote it is worth exploring.

In the belief that people were naturally impatient to consume, Pigou favored the idea of the state's acting as guardian for future generations. But apart from a general directive that the state should act to increase the rate of capital accumulation above that resulting from the free play of the market, no explicit criterion was offered for the ideal rate of investment through time.

If the welfare of the existing generation alone were at issue, there would be little difficulty since – allowing, for argument's sake, that people's capacity to enjoy goods does not alter over their lives – this 'impatience' could be sensibly defined to exist if, at a zero rate of interest, people chose to consume more in their earlier years. Yet if such were the pattern of their behavior, the *laissez-faire* economist would perceive no justification for intervening in the market. Nevertheless, a case in justice or humanity for intervening in the market exists if there is reason to believe that the impatience or short-sightedness of present generations can imperil the survival of future generations.

Intergenerational Criteria

Touching on this question of the welfare of succeeding generations, three distinct criteria can be discovered in the economic literature.

(1) The simplest criterion is an egalitarian one; *per capita* income should, ideally, remain constant from one generation to another. If it is believed that, even without positive net investment *per capita* 'real' income will grow over time as a result, say, of incidental innovation, possible economies of scale, and improved managerial efficiency, the ideal can be attained only by net consumption of capital at some rate over time. Each generation would then pass on a smaller stock of more productive capital than it would inherit from the preceding generation, a policy that would require considerable state intervention.

(2) An alternative criterion is the neoclassical one of maximizing the utility that accrues over time. By assuming equal capacity for enjoyment within a given society along with diminishing marginal utility of 'real' income, aggregate utility *at any point of time* is maximized only when it is equally distributed among all members – each person (or family) having the same total utility as any other.

Once future generations are brought into the picture, however, the amount of goods to be consumed is not a fixed amount that can be distributed among a number of successive generations. Goods are produced continuously through time and their consumption, through the investment process, can be shifted in only one direction – forward into the future. Utility maximization which, under the above assumptions, requires that the *marginal* utility of consumption through time and, therefore, for each successive generation, be equal, is consistent with different patterns of aggregate and *per capita* consumption over time. Thus, if real output, *per capita* or in the aggregate, can be expected to increase over time, the utility maximization condition implies a rising level of *per capita* or of aggregate consumption respectively. Economic policy instrumental to this objective requires additional investment in any period for which the proportional expected (real) growth of a dollar invested exceeds the proportional expected decline in the marginal utility of a dollar of consumption. Thus, aggregate investment in any period t_0 has to be carried to the point at which the percentage yield on a dollar of marginal investment realized at t_1 is just equal to the percentage reduction in the marginal utility of a dollar consumed at t_1, compared with t_0.[30] Implementation of this policy, however, requires knowledge of the relation between aggregate consumption and utility, or – at any point of time – the elasticity of the marginal utility of money with respect to consumption.[31]

(3) For those economists who still eschew interpersonal and, therefore, intergenerational comparisons of utility there remains the Pareto criterion, the wellhead of all our allocative propositions. In any cost–benefit analysis, a potential Pareto improvement is the criterion, and it is met if the value of gains exceeds that of the losses. Yet those affected by the project in question are assumed to remain alive over the period so that the valuation they place on an item at any point of time is determined by reference to their own time preference. A person who anticipates a gain of $100 in twenty years' time with virtual certainty might value its worth today at $40, an equivalence that would be incorporated into the cost–benefit analysis.

If, now, the composition of the community alters over time, so that the $100 can be expected to accrue to someone else yet to be born, its present value is not $40. For the gainer is to be a person who does not have the option of receiving it today. Evaluating the future gains of long-term investment by reference to those who later come to enjoy them could realize potential Pareto improvements with projects that would be rejected by the standard discounting procedure. Thus, extending the potential Pareto criterion to long-term investments having yields that are wholly, or partly, enjoyed by members of a future generation would act to favor future generations as against earlier generations.

None of these criteria will be realized by the market, however, even under the most simplifying assumptions. By reference to the (1) criterion, the market makes too much provision for the future. By reference to the (3) criterion, it makes too little. As for the (2) criterion, since in fact judgments about the validity of interpersonal utility comparisons, *a fortiori* of intergenerational utility comparisons, are apt to differ markedly, any rationalization of existing market rates of return, in terms of some assumed value of the elasticity of marginal utility of consumption, carries little conviction.

The (1) criterion clearly has stronger ethical appeal than the others, and is the one most likely to command a consensus at some imaginary constitutional gathering made up of representatives of different generations (Page, 1976). Although, as suggested, under the once common assumption that economic growth (in some 'real' sense) will continue into the far future, the market makes too much provision for the future, there is today a countervailing consideration turning on the rapid depletion of natural resources for which no good substitutes may be available. It is then not impossible that, on balance, we are making too little provision for the future (Page, 1976).

Depletable Resources

Until very recently there was something akin to complacency among economists about current rates of exploitation of fixed natural deposits of minerals and fossil fuels, some of it arising from empirical studies of their relative prices over time (Barnett and Morse, 1963), perhaps more from general theoretical considerations of the sort advanced in Hotelling's classic (1931) paper. Defining an optimal rate of exploitation of a fixed resource as one that maximizes its present social value, the necessary condition follows that the discounted present value of the *net* price (marginal social valuation *less* marginal resource cost) for all years be the same. The question is then whether a competitive market can bring about this required optimal time path of exploitation. If so, the economist need concern himself only with possible externalities and those forms of government intervention (regulation, taxes, depletion allowances, and so forth) that imply a departure from the optimal path – at least in a first-best world.

Since the necessary condition is met if, through time, the percentage rise in the net price is equal to the rate of interest,[32] a competitive market, in which price is assumed equal to marginal social valuation, might seem on first thoughts to be an appropriate mechanism. For there would, indeed, be forces tending to bring the annual percentage net price increase into equality with the rate of interest. To illustrate with a 5 per cent interest rate and a current net price of 100, if the net price next year is expected to be 105, competitive mining firms are indifferent as between producing ore this year or next year. If, instead, next year's net price happens to be 108, competitive firms will defer production until next year.[33] But as the amount of ore marketed this year diminishes in consequence, its net price this year will rise until the 5 per cent differential is restored. *Per contra*, if next year's expected net price is 102, firms will switch to producing more ore this year.[34] The resulting decline in the current net price continues until, once again, the equilibrium 5 per cent differential is restored.

This seemingly providential mechanism, however,

ignores the formation of price expectations. If the elasticity of price expectations exceeds zero, so that a change in the current price of the mineral causes the market to revise its estimate of future prices – a not uncommon phenomenon – the rate of production will veer off the optimal path. Indeed, if the elasticity of expectations is equal to or greater than unity, the market response will be destabilizing:[35] any initial deviation from the optimal path, in either direction, gathers force – until, eventually, the elasticity falls below unity. There may, in addition, be autonomous revisions of future price expectations so that, even though the necessary condition through time is being met, the actual production path taken is above or below the optimal path. In fact, only if all future demand curves and all future costs happen to be known to the competing firms (or else to a perfectly competitive futures market) can there be assurance that prompt reaction by firms to profit opportunities will succeed in preventing the rate of production from straying too far from the optimal path. Thus no assumption about the intelligence of producers, or about their incentives, can avail, when the required knowledge is not available to them. Nor would any expenditure on better forecasts enable it to be made available. We conclude that one of the prime virtues claimed for a competitive market; namely that the decentralization involved tends to reduce relevant information costs – although it seems to be valid enough for the more commonly considered case of inexhaustible inputs – is not valid for the case of exhaustible inputs.

Finally, we are to remind ourselves that this ideal production path has Pareto justification only for a community consisting of an unchanged number of people. For some person of a later generation, say a person yet to be born who is destined to consume the mineral in question in year 50 from now, the value of consuming a marginal unit will be equal to its then current price, say 100; and not $100/(1 + r)^{50}$ or the discounted present value at the time the investment decision is made. This consideration might not seem to matter much for those cases in which cost–benefit analysis is applicable – at least, those for which the political constraints are such that all the net benefits of the project are wholly reinvested at existing market yields – since, as the mineral is depleted it is replaced by productive assets having greater social value. But where, as the practice is in mineral and fossil fuel exploitation, the bulk of the net benefits are, in effect, consumed contemporaneously by the public – through its direct consumption of the minerals or fuels, or through the consumption of products into which they enter[36] – the popular belief, that in using up finite natural resources no specific provision is being made for future generations, is far from being erroneous.

The complacent view of the matter has now to rest its case, not on any specific provision for the future inherent in the market mechanism, but rather in a faith that the future will be much like the recent past in two related respects: (1) in the discovery of substitute resources for those being depleted and (2) in the continuing secular rise of living standards[37] (at least in the industrialized countries of the world). Ultimately, it amounts to a faith in the capability of science in overcoming a multitude of social and environmental problems that have begun to absorb our attention.

In connection with natural resource substitutes, there is one more thing to be said. Technical substitution is not enough to secure a continued rise of social welfare; not enough even to maintain it. To touch on a trivial case first, the market has not prevented a decline in the quality of some foodstuffs over time: perhaps it cannot reasonably be expected to do this. If in thirty years' time, much of the food we shall be eating will taste more like plastic than it does today, the market may not be to blame. A lot of it may be chemical synthetics, time saving and much cheaper than more 'natural' foodstuffs. Again, we may rightly refrain from blaming the market if, in consequence of the absence of enforceable property rights, or of the absence of other devices or institutions that would internalize the externalities into the economic system, vast areas of natural beauty and wildlife continue to dwindle rapidly so that our grandchildren come to inherit a more desolate and monotonous world. But, then, neither can we repose any faith in the mere operation itself of competitive markets in maintaining a satisfactory allocation of resources over time in this crucial regard.

Over time, the terms of trade as between natural goods and man-made goods can be expected to alter in favor of the former. And although future generations may well have much more of the latter, it may not be enough to compensate them for the apparently inexorable disappearance of the variety of wild life and natural beauty. Perhaps no amounts of manufactured goods and recreational opportunities will suffice for the diminished accessibility to unspoiled coastline, to mountain, lake, and woodland, much less for escape for the sensitive into a world of solitude and grandeur.

VI The Consumer Bias of the Market

In the absence of all externalities, universal perfect competition, as described in the textbooks, is neither a necessary nor sufficient condition for optimal allocation. Since marginal cost pricing can be pursued by other forms of economic organization – for instance, by the state or by discriminating monopolists – it is not necessary. And since free entry of factors into each industry does not entail the fulfillment of the factor-use condition (the fulfillment of which, in the case of labor, would imply opportunities for workers to choose the amounts of time to work in each of the occupations that utilize their labor), perfect competition is not sufficient.

This proposition, however, is not of great interest. Much more important are the possible welfare losses that can be endured by workers subject to the 'discipline of the market'. Thus, if there were a shift of $10 million of consumption expenditure from good X to good Y which, in due course, was followed by a movement of, say, 1,000 workers from industry X to industry Y, the market would have done its job well, and, assuming marginal cost pricing were restored, allocation criteria would also be met.

But the welfare of the workers *qua* workers is apt to be overlooked: in particular, their rents, arising from occupational or locational preferences, and their costs of movement [38] and retraining[39] are often neglected. Of course, it can be argued that if workers are to be attracted into occupations they do not like, they will have to be compensated by higher wages or better conditions. And this net-advantages doctrine is useful as part of a long-run explanation of wage differentials. But if we are not surveying the opportunities facing new entrants into industry, but are instead concerned with the fortunes of the existing workforce in industry X, we cannot realistically suppose that workers always move out of X in response to attractions elsewhere. They may simply be discharged by industry X, and to that extent suffer a loss of welfare. Thus the gain to consumers from complete market adjustment to their shift in demand might well fall short of the losses in welfare suffered by the 1,000 workers.

Of course, a comparison of consumer welfare as between an equilibrium with the initial tastes and that with the new tastes is not possible. Once the new tastes are established, however, consumers become better off according as outputs adjust to the new demand pattern. But, as indicated, if workers who have to move from X to Y – not as a result of being attracted from X to Y so much as being laid off by industry X – they can be made substantially worse off.

In an imaginary world in which consumers' tastes remained constant, consumers also could be made worse off if workers moved voluntarily out of X into Y and, in consequence, output X were reduced leaving consumers perforce to spend more on Y; and they could be substantially worse off if X were important in their budgets. Yet the subsequent adjustment of consumer expenditure could be interpreted as consistent with marginal cost pricing in X and Y.

In sum, if the adjustment to an exogenous change in tastes (whether of consumers or workers) comes about wholly through price changes it does not reduce the welfare of the adjusters (whether they are workers or consumers). If, on the other hand, the adjustment comes about wholly through quantity changes (opportunities being withdrawn) it does entail a reduction in the welfare of the adjusters.

If the movements of labor necessary to implement the changing pattern of consumer demand lack proper allocative underpinning, once we turn from Pareto criteria to considerations of social equity, reservations about ideal market adjustments increase. For a dollar gained or lost by the consumer may have less welfare significance than a dollar lost or gained by the worker, and this without invoking differences in income. The average consumer in a wealthy economy is faced by a wide range of goods, substitution as between which causes him little inconvenience and no hardship. Indeed, a proportion of his purchases is aptly referred to as 'impulse buying'. Some may be the result of a recent advertising campaign, or seeing an item in a neighbor's home, or of being momentarily intrigued by some useless novelty, or of a bid to break the monotony of events. And though any frustration of his buying impulse at that point of time may elicit a protest,[40] the hardship he endures is negligible. On the other hand, the loss of welfare borne by workers who are displaced from the familiarity of their workplace and their neighborhood can reasonably be described as hardship.

Similar considerations apply to improved techniques of production. Even though labor's productivity and 'real' earnings rise in consequence, workers ultimately have little choice in the matter. They must perforce adopt the new methods and adjust accordingly. There can, therefore, be no presumption of net social advantage in any specific instance simply because consumers gain from lower unit costs.[41]

The conclusion of this argument is that the operation of the market is consumer oriented. Ideal market adjustments are compatible with net social loss on the Pareto criterion, a loss that can be magnified by weighting the welfare content of money gains and losses. How important this bias is depends upon the vicissitudes of consumer demand and the extent to which shifting patterns of consumer demand impose significant welfare losses on workers. Increasing affluence, which implies a growth of 'luxuries' and, consequently, of 'impulse buying', is likely to increase the threat to the security of workers unless there are countervailing forces at work, some associated with the welfare state.

In the circumstances, a doctrine that favors free markets specifically on allocation or equity grounds poses some difficulty. There is now more to it than the appealing notion of a continuing movement of scarce resources to uses in which their social value is highest, if only because of this built-in bias toward consumer valuation. In any assessment, however, the question of alternative economic organizations arises, including, of course, the feasibility of corrective institutions.

Again, although the liberal economist is disinclined to favor any innovation that extends power to the state, a simple-minded case could be argued for sustained advertising (as in Britain during the war and beyond) for being satisfied with what is, in the endeavor to maintain the pattern of currently produced outputs, and to alter it only to accommodate changes over time in occupational preferences. If successful, the scheme would entail no loss of welfare to consumers while conferring a gain in the workers' welfare arising from their increase in occupational security. It may, of course, seem to some an absurd objective for society to pursue, but that is largely because of the disproportionate importance attached to the notion of continuing change by postindustrial man and his relative unconcern with social welfare *per se*. At all events, once we free our minds from the simple equation between well-functioning competitive markets and allocative merit, we are likely to become less censorious than the Chicago school of such restrictive organizations as monopolies, cartels, labor unions, and of such restrictive practices as trade controls and immigration quotas.

Although it does not produce enthusiastic 'trust-busters', believing, as it does, that in the absence of active government intervention and legislation the extent and power of monopoly in the economic system would be limited, the Chicago school evidently looks on monopolies, cartels, price agreements, and government price supports with disrelish. Setting aside the question of the economic and political power wielded by large corporations, as discussed at length by Berle and Means (1933), we can recognize (in the light of the preceding remarks) that the allocative arguments against them are, on a general plane, inconclusive.

There is, moreover, another consideration. In a world of rapid change, in which the future is increasingly uncertain, the monopolistic propensities of employers and managers, their defensive advertising expenditures, their support for tariffs and price controls, can be understood as measures directed to stabilizing their markets in order to increase the security of their profits and personnel. Ostensibly, it is this same search for security in a highly uncertain world, as much as for higher real earnings, that inspires the formation of labor unions and of restrictive professional bodies. To the extent they reduce anxiety and increase security, such restrictive organizations and practices contribute to social welfare.

It may, of course, be possible to devise institutions that will afford to workers, professionals, business executives, and shareholders the sort of security that they seek in a world of increasing uncertainty, while at the same time encouraging them to alter their plans more readily to meet the requirements of changing technology and demand conditions. But until such institutions are operative, the belief in the paramountcy of consumer demand in calling the allocative tune, and the consequent opposition by conservative economists to any resistance of consumer expression by restrictive associations and practices, are open to challenge.[42]

VII Consumer Tastes and the Free Market

In the preceding section we have remarked on the consumer bias of the market and the bias, therefore, in the common interpretation of economic efficiency arising therefrom. Inquiry into this consumer bias can be carried further by broaching the question of consumers' tastes, which are generally treated in allocative contexts as an exogenous variable. More specifically, the question posed is whether the economist concerned with social welfare can be consistently indifferent to the changing pattern of consumers' tastes.

In order to distil the relevant issue from all extraneous matter, picture a competitive economy having an ideal distribution of income and free of all external effects. Everyone is buying and selling the amounts that he wishes, and at prices equal to unit costs that are as low as possible with the existing resource endowment and technology. In such an economic millenium, can the economist interested in welfare make any valid judgment about the effect of consumers' tastes or changes in tastes?

I have met distinguished economists who have declared emphatically, though seemingly without reflection, that their role as economists, insofar as it has any normative facet, consists only in making available to people what they (the people) want on the best terms possible. On this view, the task of the economist is discharged by facilitating the supply of goods for which

people – preferably through the market mechanism – express a desire.

It is debatable whether those – and they are not economists only – who assert that 'push-penny is as good as Pushkin', or words to that effect, personally believe this; whether they believe that others ought to believe it; or whether they simply think that people ought to act as if they believe it. What is certain, however, is that many people do not believe it; indeed, the idea of an educational establishment is raised on the contrary premise which, if accepted, is not without allocative significance, as we shall see.

Rather than argue about the proper role of the economist, it will be more useful, first, to assess the importance of the welfare contribution of the economist who, in respect of tastes, confines himself to the evidence of the market, and, secondly, to judge the adequacy of allocative criteria in the light of social welfare.

Allocative Assessment of Changes in Taste

To the economist concerned only with the working of the market, any exogenous shift in demand that calls for a shift of resources is as important as any other. But to the welfare economist, more significance is to be attached to exogenous shifts of demand that are 'price-inelastic' than to those that are 'price-elastic'; more significance to demand shifts as between broad categories of goods, say, as between housing, transport, food, clothing, and recreation, than to demand shifts as within these categories; and more significance to the movements in international trade as between countries whose economies are highly complementary than to movements as between countries trading goods that are close substitutes.

If the welfare economist is prepared, once in a while, to cross the Paretian Rubicon and to make the journey back north to the old neoclassical homelands, he can, on arrival, say more. He may still maintain that interpersonal measurements of utility are not 'scientific', or that fine judgments about the worth of a good, or a dollar's worth of goods, to different individuals or groups are unlikely to command universal support. But he will not be so far removed from reality as to persuade himself that the loss of $10 to a Rockefeller is no less important to him than the loss of $10 to a near destitute denizen of Calcutta, and that society ought to treat such losses as equally important. Such an economist will find no difficulty in believing that an additional $1 billion of consumption goods to a poor country yields more satisfaction than an additional $1 billion of consumption goods to a rich country. Following this reflection, he might surmise that a good allocation of resources is of greater importance in a poor society than in a rich one.

Indeed, without crossing the Paretian Rubicon, the economist can make sensible statements about the welfare significance of shifts in taste. If, as a result of the influence of fashion, or for any other reason, society is fickle in its tastes – consumer expenditure shifting from goods X to Y and, soon after, back to X again – the economist is inclined to accept this fickleness as a datum. In that case, it would seem to follow that social welfare is promoted by moving resources from X to Y and, soon after, back to X again. Nevertheless, the economist may also pertinently observe that, in the process, capital goods that are in good phsyical condition may thereby become obsolete. In comparison with a society in which tastes were less fickle, an effective loss of resources is incurred. More generally, in an economy in which goods are increasingly 'fashion goods', the period of capital amortization is shorter, and, therefore, unit inclusive costs of goods are higher than they are in a more stable-taste economy. Thus, rapid changes of taste, whether spontaneous, fashion created, or commercially induced, impose costs on the community inasmuch as in their absence – that is, if society had instead preferred to consume X continuously rather than X today, Y tomorrow, and X again the day after – it would have more goods at its disposal for the same resource endowment.

What follows? Were the economist truly indifferent as between a taste for X and a taste for Y, he would infer that welfare can be increased if the costs involved in persuading the public to stabilize their tastes (in favor, say, of their existing preference for X) are lower than the additional resource costs incurred in meeting the switch in demand from X to Y and, perhaps, back again to X. In an economy characterized by rapid changes of taste of this sort, substantial savings might be effected by the success of some organization in persuading the public to be less fickle in their tastes.

Of course, there can be trends in taste as well as oscillations. Insofar as demand shifts from X to Y, later from Y to Z, and then from Z to W, we cannot describe the change of tastes as wasteful in the preceding sense. Yet it is still meaningful to contend that some changes in the pattern of consumer expenditure have greater welfare significance than others, and that some changes in taste that are expressed through the market are more apt to reduce than to enhance social welfare – a judgment of fact, not of values. Thus, although Hayek (1961) is right to be skeptical of a distinction between 'natural' and 'artificial' wants, and right to associate the history of cultural advance with the invention of new wants, it

is *not* right to conclude that all product innovation, or even the greater part of it, at any moment in time constitutes a welfare advance much less a cultural advance – at least, not when the word *cultural* is used in the approved sense in which Hayek uses it.

Finally, by restricting ourselves, provisionally, to the conventional allocative context, it is possible to show that the market, regarded as an indicator of current tastes, new or old, is misleading by reference to what economists now call 'merit goods'. A merit good can be defined as one whose aggregate consumption enters positively into the utility functions of individuals. By symmetry, the aggregate consumption of a 'demerit good' enters negatively into individual utility functions. Clearly, merit and demerit goods fall into the category of external economies and diseconomies, respectively; in fact, they are a species of the 'interdependent utilities' family of externalities, the utility of one person depending in some way on the goods possessed or used by others.[43]

Opera, ballet, symphony orchestras, art galleries, libraries – including, possibly, a Pushkin reading room! – are among the common examples of a merit good.[44] People who seldom or never attend cultural events, who prefer cinema or television entertainment, may yet agree that high culture is a good thing and derive some satisfaction from its visible manifestation and in the knowledge that cultural activities are being promoted. Indeed, if a value judgment is permitted, some cultural activities are important enough in the civilization of the West to warrant a risk of overprovision rather than underprovision.

There are, to be sure, voluntary organizations for promoting good causes and cultural events. But inasmuch as a person's willing contribution to a merit good depends upon the amounts others are believed to contribute, and a person's declared willingness-to-pay is influenced by the 'free rider' opportunity open to him (especially where the number of beneficiaries is large), economists conclude that, whether such goods are provided through the political process or through voluntary action, their supply tends to fall below optimal (Olson, 1965).

On the other hand, pinball arcades, obscene literature, and pornographic theater are examples of a demerit good. People who willingly buy demerit goods, since they are available on the market anyway, may yet wish that there were less of them available to the public: they would think better of their fellow citizens if the demand for such things were to fall off.[45] Again, there will be voluntary organizations for combating the spread of some of these demerit goods. Yet, for the reasons given above, contributions toward their diminution tend to fall below those necessary to reduce them to optimal.

Thus allegations of a deterioration in the quality of life may have reference, among other things, to the manifest increase in demerit goods. In these circumstances, the economist who accepts the existing demand for demerit goods as expressed by the market as indicative of what society really wants deceives himself, and accepts a misallocation of resources in these respects.[46] And the fact that the information required to correct the existing situation appears, at present, difficult to obtain does not detract from the extent of the market's misrepresentation of what society wants and the consequent misallocation of resources.

Welfare Assessment of Ideal Allocation in a Growing Economy

A surprisingly common belief among students of economics is that in the absence of all externalities (including the absence of the aforementioned merit and demerit goods), a perfectly functioning competitive market will improve welfare in a growing economy – one in which productivity *per capita* increases over time.

The statement can be made to follow from restrictive assumptions that are useful enough in abstract models. Once the restrictive assumptions are discarded, and we turn to the real world, the preceding statement is not a tautology but a statement of fact and, therefore, open to dispute.[47] It may, of course, be very difficult or impossible to demonstrate conclusively whether such a statement is true or false, generally, or over any particular period of time. But it is always possible to adduce considerations that weaken the presumption that economic growth, even in a (competitive) externality-free economy, increases social welfare. I say *even* in an externality-free economy because there is no difficulty in weakening this presumption if account is taken of the variety of external diseconomies that, for technical or political reasons, are unlikely to be properly internalized into the economic system.

That a well-functioning market, under these postulated conditions, will enable choices to be made on 'nature's terms' is, of course, true. But there is nothing in the machinery of the market to ensure that free choice is wise choice. In a world of rapid technological change and continuing product innovation, relevant information about quality and performance of consumer goods is increasingly costly to obtain. It is still more difficult – for society as much as for the individual – to be *au courant* about such arcane matters as the cumulative toxic or genetic effects of drugs and food additives. And it is all but impossible to foresee the ultimate consequences on society's well-being of the adoption of outstanding innovations – though it is also far from certain that their adoption would be resisted even if the range of adverse consequences could be foreseen. For there is an apparent momentum about technology that sweeps all before it. As Jacques Ellul (1965) has remarked with understandable exaggeration, it is enough for a technology to be feasible to ensure its adoption.

The end result of improvements in all media and means of communication could be to accelerate the pace of life to a frantic degree. The longer-term effects on social well-being of a succession of labor-saving devices can be less impressive than the ingenuity that created them and the cost of resources used up in providing them. For instance, the trend in consumer innovation toward means of faster mobility, toward push-button gadgetry, toward physical self-sufficiency, may become subversive of welfare – at least, insofar as it is through our overt need of other persons that opportunities for human contact, kindness, and sacrifice arise in a community, as a result of which the seeds of mutual trust take root and friendships flourish.

VIII Advertising and the Competitive Economy

Our concern with the Chicago school's attitude toward commercial advertising focuses on two related aspects. First, whether commercial advertising is, as alleged by Henry Simons (1948), a 'major barrier' to competitive enterprise. Secondly, and more important, whether the institution can be justified on economic and social grounds. These questions are dealt with in that order.

Advertising and Competition

The sort of advertising expenditure that is the subject of our inquiry is other than that necessary to announce the existence of a firm, its premises, conditions of business, and so forth, or particulars of a sale – though even here, the size of the notice or repetition of particulars can influence taste beyond that warranted by the bare information itself. Clearly, it is not impossible for competition between firms to take place within an industry that is advertising the goods being sold by all the firms in that industry. It is also possible for the imaginative to conceive, as Telser (1964) does, of a large group of firms, each of which produces goods having identical characteristics, including identical kinds and amounts of advertising, and which are therefore in perfect competition with one another.

Now if one begins with a presumption against monopoly, a theoretic reconciliation of perfect competition with advertising, plus the finding that there is no marked relationship between advertising expenditure and industrial concentration, or between advertising expenditure and stability of sales (Telser, 1964), enables commercial advertising to evade discountenance. If, moreover, it is believed that continued 'consumer experimentation' is a good thing in itself, or that rapid entry and exit of firms into and out of an industry is 'a healthy sign,' then insofar as commercial advertising fosters taste-switching and so facilitates entry of new firms into an industry, something might be said in its favor. However, such beliefs are ancillary to those traditionally invoked in the economic concept of allocating scarce resources as to best satisfy human wants and, indeed, seem to conflict with them. This older and, perhaps, more static view, accepts wants as a datum with resources being distributed so as to satisfy them, whereas these other and more recent beliefs are compatible with an institution that uses scarce resources, also, to change wants; in effect, at least in the affluent society, perpetually to create dissatisfactions with existing goods in favor of rival goods or new goods.[48] Such a process could be vindicated by the belief that, over time, commercial advertising succeeds in inculcating tastes and living habits superior to those that would prevail in its absence, so making a contribution to civilized living. However, I do not suppose many economists would feel comfortable arguing the case for modern commercial advertising along these lines.

On traditional economic premises, a respectable case for commerical advertising does not look to be possible. Even a hypothetical advertising-cum-perfect-competition economy does not answer. For it is not enough that all the relevant marginal equalities be met: total conditions also have to be met in order to ensure that there is no 'waste' in the economy (in other words, that the optimal is not merely local but global). Thus, if resources were not used up in attempts to influence wants, they can always be used instead to produce additional goods which can be distributed as to make 'everyone' better off.

Some Popular Rationalizations of Commercial Advertising

Estimates of current advertising expenditures in the United States exceed $20 billion. Evidently there are people who believe that it is worth incurring such expenses, though from this belief alone one cannot infer social justification for the institution. The question to which much of the debate addresses itself is whether, and to what extent, commercial advertising influences consumers, a question that can be embarrassing to those who give it their blessing. For they have to steer their arguments carefully between Scylla and Charybdis. On the one hand, in order to justify advertising expenditures, they must not deny its efficacy – which is tantamount to an admission that consumers' tastes can be formed, unformed, and possibly deformed by business interests. If, on the other hand, they disclaim its effects, and insist that, on balance, it has little influence of consumers' choice,[49] it is hard to avoid the conclusion that commercial advertising is a colossal waste of resources.

Prior to a brief but more general statement in support of this latter conclusion, some of the more popular rationalizations for commercial advertising can be briefly disposed of.

There is, first, the oft-heard claim that advertisers help to pay for our newspapers and television programs. For instance, in addition to covering the real costs of an automobile advertisement, the manufacturers make a contribution to the costs of the newspaper which sum is to be recovered in the price of the automobile. In short, the buyers of the advertised car are made to subsidize newspaper-readers.[50] But unless there is good reason to believe that the newspaper (together with its advertisements) confers benefits on the community which, at the margin, exceed the value of resources in producing the newspaper, there is no economic warrant for the subsidy.

Secondly, there is the suggestion that the newspaper advertisement or television advertisement should be regarded as an essential part of a joint product, the other part being entertainment. But advertising and entertainment are clearly not inseparable products as are, say, wool and mutton. No good reason is offered why advertising, which piques itself on being a valuable service to the public, should not be sold at a price that covers its cost. Advertisers may, of course, suspect that if they tried to sell pure advertising 'by the yard' to the public at a price set to cover its cost, they would sell precious little of it; and that if they charged whatever addition was necessary to cover the costs of any 'entertaining' bits thrown in with the 'information', they would sell little more. Apparently they find it more profitable to provide advertising free, with or without entertainment, in the expectation of recouping these expenditures by selling enough of the advertised items at prices above their costs of production. The result is that the newspaper-reader, or the television-viewer, is subject to a 'tied sale': he receives advertising (and 'entertainment') along with his newspaper whether he wants them both together or not.[51]

A third rationalization is more cunning; it is to the effect that people actually prefer myth to truth. In connection with some aspects of life this is undeniable. Many people find solace and satisfaction in religious beliefs, in national myths, in a faith in the inherent goodness or ultimate wisdom of the people. Whether it is equally true for the mundane aspects of life, such as those that may involve a choice between one model of a television set and another, one brand of nylon tights and another, one can of peaches and another, is much more doubtful.

Finally, there is the justification in terms of information. Provided it is believed that the provision of information is desirable, in that it enables the public to make more satisfactory choices among the goods offered by industry, the critical distinction to bear in mind is not that between information and persuasion which can be very tenuous, but between *partial* information and *impartial* information.

The advertiser is not concerned with providing impartial information but with increasing the sale of the product. If the statements he makes happen to be accurate, this is incidental to his main task.[52]

If the buying public wants disinterested information about certain goods, then it is not reasonable for it to expect to obtain such information from those parties whose livelihood and success depend directly on the sales of such goods. Any advertising agency pledged to tell the whole truth and nothing but the truth about its clients' products would not be in business very long.

Consider, then, an alternative in the shape of one or more independent agencies, devoted to the task of providing impartial information, in the sense of providing 'complete' and 'relevant' information[53] from tests carried out under as objective conditions as possible. That the results of these tests, when published, can be very persuasive is nothing to the purpose. What is to the purpose is that the investigations be undertaken in a scientific spirit and free, therefore, from any conscious source of bias. It is not pertinent in arguing against such agencies that coverage of products is limited or that tests are not exhaustive. Such defects can be attributed to a lack of resources or to a lack of efficiency which, in the course of time, can be overcome. What matters is that such organizations operate on a principle entirely different from that of the advertising agency. The *aim* of the advertising agency is to promote the sales of his clients' goods: any information that is provided by the agency is selected to serve that end. The *aim* of the research agency, in contrast, is to provide impartial information to the consumer.[54]

Thus, if one accepts as a desirable social end, the provision of impartial and, increasingly, more accurate and complete information to the public, there does not seem much one can say in favor of continuing the present system of using substantial resources in providing the public with partial information at uneconomic prices and in tied-sale form that precludes choice. There is more to be said for the alternative of devoting the same resources to the provision of yet more and better consumer research services, the demand for which would be likely to expand if the existing tied-sale form of commercial advertising were to cease.

Is there a Political Case for Commercial Advertising?

Having raised doubts about the present system of commercial advertising on economic grounds, let us now examine the popular view that the doctrine of freedom to propagate opinions should be extended to cover the contending claims of private firms as embodied in commercial advertising. Why, it may be asked, should any disability be placed on organizations that choose to spend their own income or 'profits' in propagating a particular point of view?

First in respect of goods such as drugs or slow poisons that are believed to damage the mental or physical health, an ethical problem arises wherever vast sums are spent annually to promote their consumption, in particular among the young and impressionable, who are led to associate its consumption with initiation into adulthood or fashion. In the absence of tobacco advertisements, for instance, new addictions would decline and thousands of deaths from lung cancer could be prevented each year. If, to look at the matter otherwise, heroin promotion campaigns became legal, a rise in sicknesses and death, among other misfortunes, could be confidently predicted.[55]

For goods that are not widely believed to be dangerous to consumers or third parties, there are yet other considerations. Perhaps a difference in the degree of social significance between, on the one hand, political and philosophical issues and, on the other, judgments about the durability of doormats and the quality of breakfast cereals might be conceded. Certainly there are differences in conviction with which opinions are held about these two categories of phenomena. Yet there is no need for the case against a political right of freedom to advertise merchandise to turn wholly on these different degrees of significance or conviction.

John Milton's eloquent plea for freedom of speech is

raised on a utilitarian premise: that from the conflict of arguments, truth would surely emerge. If advertising supporters would conscript John Milton to their cause, they must embrace the belief that knowledge of the best kind of filter-tip cigarette or rubber sole will inevitably emerge from the counterclaims of competing advertisers.

More important, if we accept the utilitarian approach[56] – which conceives the public interest, in some sense, as the ultimate criterion of social policy – then, as with freedom of political expression itself, commercial advertising freedom has to be judged, not as an end in itself, but as a means of promoting the public interest. Thus, free political speech can be defended not only for the truths it uncovers, but also because it reduces the risk of violence in a context of continuing social change. For political ideas evolve over time and in the light of experience. At any moment of time, no political doctrine can be held as absolutely true, and if it were believed to be so, it is unlikely that the belief would remain unchallenged for long in the modern world. This being the case, it is a matter of political prudence to allow men openly to express their convictions on issues they believe to be of the highest moment; encouraging them always to try to persuade others rather than to coerce them.

Now such reasons cannot be invoked to justify the claims and counterclaims of competing manufacturers. The 'opinions' they propagate are not motivated by deep convictions about their truth, but solely by the search for profits. And the questions they raise – whether, in fact, one detergent really washes 'whiter than white', or whether one electric blanket is safer or warmer than another – are not those on which men are divided by deep conviction. In contrast to the conflicting claims of ideology, or to the conflicting opinions on social policy, there is very little about the competing claims of advertisers that cannot, in all relevant respects, be resolved simply by impartial testing – that is, by recourse to the facts.

IX Individual Freedom and the Competitive Economy

Let us turn, in this penultimate section, to that rooted belief in the social advantage of decentralized private enterprise, a belief that has exerted a lasting influence on the ideology and methodological presuppositions of Western economists. There is, first, the advantage of individual choice, itself a dimension of freedom, offered by the market sector of the economy. The smaller the public sector of the economy, the larger the area of choice remaining, at least for the consumer – a consideration which is decisive in the Chicago school's preference that any redistribution of income be effected through transfers in cash rather than in kind.[57] Secondly, there is the more general accession of freedom conferred on society by the competitive economy, not in virtue of its being a competitive market economy, but in virtue of its being a competitive *capitalist* economy. More specifically, a decentralized private-enterprise system entails a dispersal of economic power throughout society that acts as a counterweight to the economic power of the state. And since economic power is also a means of implementing political purposes, the larger the private sector of the economy, the greater the constraint on the ambition of bureaucrats and the power of the state.

It is in arguing the case for competitive capitalism on both these grounds that the Chicago school is most persuasive. Taking its stand there, it recognizes its advocacy to be in line with the great classical tradition that can be traced back to the economic thought of British and Continental writers of the eighteenth century, that came to fruition in the nineteenth century, and that was seemingly confirmed by the harsh experience of the twentieth.[58] Nothing I could say would so well remind the reader of the powerful appeal to utilitarian predilection and libertarian impulse than a quotation from Milton Friedman, the most distinguished exponent today of the Chicago school of thought:

The kind of economic organization that provides economic freedom directly, namely, competitive capitalism, also promotes political freedom because it separates economic power from political power and in this way enables the one to offset the other. (1962, p. 9)

Declaring that *economic* freedom (in the sense of individual freedom to choose man-made goods) is best realized through competitive markets, Friedman goes on to observe that:

... what the market does is to reduce greatly the range of issues that must be decided through political means, and thereby to minimize the extent to which government need participate directly in the game. The characteristic feature of action through political channels is that it tends to require or enforce substantial conformity. The great advantage of the market, on the other hand, is that it permits wide diversity. (1962, p. 15)

Yet this same competitive private-enterprise system that extends to economic freedom acts also to promote political freedom. For:

> . . . the fundamental threat to freedom is the power to coerce, be it in the hands of a monarch, a dictator, an oligarchy, or a momentary majority. The preservation of freedom requires the elimination of such concentration of power to the fullest possible extent and the dispersal and distribution of whatever power cannot be eliminated – a system of checks and balances. By removing the organization of economic power from the control of political authority, the market eliminates this source of coercive power. It enables economic strength to be a check to political power rather than a reinforcement. (1962, p. 15)

I confess that I am in sympathy with the broad sweep of this argument. Although, as indicated in the preceding section, the operation of a competitive private-enterprise economy cannot of itself prevent a deterioration of the quality of life or erosion of moral values, it is surely more congenial to the exercise of effective economic and political freedom than the concentration of economic power in the hands of giant corporations or, worse, in the hands of the state.

Nevertheless, in spite of the increasing resentment of ordinary citizens at the scale and frequency of government intervention, in spite of the articulate apprehension of liberals everywhere, in spite even of the occasional resolutions of government spokesmen, the size of the public sector has continued to grow in all major Western countries since the turn of the century. True, the US government does not yet directly control well over half the country's economic activity, as does the British government, but there can be little doubt that it is heading in this direction. As late as 1930, the upsurge in the total expenditure of the US government (federal, state, and local) following the First World War had subsided to about 9 per cent of net national expenditure, or what it had been in 1913. By 1940 the figure had risen to 25 per cent: by 1950 to 29 per cent, and by 1970 to 42 per cent. To some, this phenomenon may not be surprising in view of the growth of democratic or, rather, egalitarian sentiment over the last 100 years, and, accompanying it, a demand not only for greater opportunity to compete for the economic prizes, but also, and increasingly since the Second World War, for a share in whatever prizes are won – this latter demand being met partly through increased income transfers, but more through burgeoning public expenditures on health, education, and welfare services generally. Such an explanation of events – in terms, that

is, of misdirected humanitarianism and egalitarian aspirations – is not uncongenial to the liberal mind since it offers hope for the future. The good fight against persistent government encroachment could hardly be waged with conviction unless it were believed that this continuing trend could be checked, if not reversed; unless, that is, it were believed that the factors making for more government intervention in the economy are not decisive and, in the last resort, need not prevail against the expressed desires of that enlightened electorate which it is the task of the good liberal to bring into being.

From this liberal perspective, at any rate, the public sector in modern democracies grows in response to popular egalitarian sentiment which, as it happens, is linked to a strong preference for the government provision of specific services rather than for the straightforward money transfers favored by the Chicago school. What is more, this popular demand for more government services is directly facilitated by the operation of existing progressive-tax systems inasmuch as, in a growing economy (especially in an inflationary economy), it enables the government over time to collect an increasing proportion of the national product. From time to time, of course, nominal tax rates are lowered. But they are not lowered enough to counteract the aforementioned trend; a fact that makes it easier for governments to expand their economic activities. For this reason alone there is a strong case for proportional taxation, though one that will not be presented here.[59]

However, apart from popular egalitarian sentiment, reinforced perhaps by the empire-building propensities of bureaucrats, which are, incidentally, facilitated by a progressive tax structure, may there not be also a secular trend, arising from the shape of economic growth, that favors the continued expansion of government control over the economy? The fact that such a possibility did not occur to the libertarian economist must be attributed in some part to an ideological commitment to that material progress which he continues to regard, despite the accumulating evidence to the contrary, as a potent solvent of all social frictions and personal frustrations; though in some part also to the economist's habit of thinking about economic growth in terms of a rise in the flow of an abstract 'real' income.[60] As a result, they have paid too little attention to population growth and to the particular kinds of technology that, accompanying the process of economic growth, have come to increase the power and reach of the modern state. Thus the concomitant decline in personal freedom has to be regarded not only as a corollary of the reduction in the private sector of the economy, but also of a conscious surrender of personal rights and freedom, this being the unavoidable reaction of society to the consequences of population growth and of particular kinds of technology.

The Impact of Population and Technology on Freedom

In general terms it may be affirmed that the slower the changes taking place in any civilized society, and the greater the degree of moral consensus within it, the smaller the scope for legislation. *Per contra,* the more rapid the changes and the less the moral consensus, the greater the amount of legislation required. It is in this latter situation that we find ourselves today.

Concerning population growth in a technological society, its continuance, according to Ronald Ridker:

> ... forces upon us a slow but irreversible change in life style. Embedded in the folklore of what constitutes the American way of life is freedom from public regulation: freedom to hunt, fish, swim, and camp where and when we will; free use of water and access to uncongested, unregulated roadways; freedom to do as we please with what we own; and freedom from permits, licences, fees, red tape, and bureaucrats. Obviously we do not live this way now. Maybe we never did. But everything is relative. Americans of 2020 may look back with envy on what from their vantage point appears to be our relatively unfettered way of life, much as some today look back with nostalgia on the Wild West.
>
> Conservation of our water resources, preservation of wilderness areas, protection of animal life threatened by man, restrictions on pollutant emissions, and limitations on fertilizer and pesticide-use all require public regulation. Rules must be set and enforced, complaints heard and adjudicated. True enough, the more we can find means of relying on the price system, the easier will be the bureaucratic task. But even if effluent charges and user fees become universal, they would have to be set administratively, emissions and use metered, and fees collected. It appears inevitable that a larger proportion of our lives will be devoted to filling out forms, arguing with the computer or its representatives, appealing against decisions, waiting for our case to be handled, finding ways to evade or move ahead in the queue. In many small ways, everyday life will become more contrived. (1972, p.31)

Turning to technology proper, among those features whose development acts to diminish the area of individual freedom, the following deserve special mention.

(1) *The computer revolution.* The growing use of computers in controlling the operation of chemical plants, telephone exchanges, and public utilities such as gas, electricity, water supply, and sewage disposal, means that breakdowns are likely to be costly if not disastrous. In consequence, closer checks and tighter controls on personnel involved in the day-to-day management, maintenance, and repair of computers will be exercised, which requires detailed psychological knowledge of employees. Such knowledge will be provided by agencies and will be facilitated by the co-operation of citizens inasmuch as economic opportunities will come to depend increasingly upon its availability.

(2) *The internal combustion engine.* The postwar expansion of motorized pastimes, involving the use of such things as motorcycles, speedboats, snowmobiles, and so forth, has started a reaction among the more amenity-conscious citizenry which is manifestly on the increase and which is likely to result in substantial restrictions on the freedoms hitherto enjoyed by the motorized multitude. Again, the promotion of mass tourism, as a result of the popularity of air travel, has begun to run into the incipient resentment of populations in the host countries, or host regions within a country. Official attempts have already begun to limit the freedom of people to travel where and when they wish. Within countries, for instance, motorized travel to national parks and lake districts will soon have to be rationed, if not by price then by more direct measures.

(3) *The rise of toxic technology.* The mounting concern during the last decade with air, water, and soil pollution arising from new industrial processes – in particular, over the destruction of forests, wetlands, everglades, over the dumping of sewage in estuaries and oil on the high seas, over the wanton use of pesticides and chemical fertilizers – has been vociferous enough to precipitate a rash of restrictive legislation in the United States, both state and federal. The Environmental Protection Agency has recently been added to the several federal bureaucracies charged in effect with preventing businessmen from freely choosing their most profitable location and their most profitable type and scale of industrial plant.

(4) *Technology in the service of crime.* Whether or not the increase in the postwar incidence of crime and violence can be linked with economic growth, there can be no doubt of the increased power conferred on organized crime by technological innovation. It is by now abundantly clear that continued scientific research produces not only more expensive missile systems or

deadlier rays, gases, and bacteria. It also produces critical simplifications in the design of smaller thermo-nuclear or bacteriological bombs that place them not only within the capacity of the smaller and, generally, less politically stable nation-states, but also within the capacity of modern criminal organizations.

Furthermore, at a time when criminals and political fanatics – their effectiveness multiplied by air travel, radio communication, and other modern devices – are becoming active in intimidating the public by black-mail, kidnapping, and the torture or murder of hostages, the fear instilled into the ordinary citizen is the result also of the increased vulnerability of the large city or conurbation (itself a product of economic growth) owing to its dependence upon a single source of supply for its water, electricity, or sewage disposal. Once people come to recognize how vulnerable they have become in these respects, there will be less resistance to a closer monitoring of internal and inter-national travel and to a surrender to the police of more arbitrary powers of search and arrest.

(5) *The techno-military spiral.* In 1913 the US national defence expenditure was about 0·7 per cent of national income. In the 1970s it is over 10 per cent. The arms race among the 'superpowers' takes the form, not of expanding military personnel or the accumulation of military hardware, but of massive investment in developing more expensive and deadlier weapons. For every new weapon of offensive capability there will soon be designed a weapon of defensive capability, the response to which will be a yet more destructive offensive weapon, and so on.[61] The fears, real or imaginary, of ubiquitous enemy intelligence can sanction the use of special powers to be vested in government agencies, powers virtually to pry into the private affairs not only of government employees but also of every resident in the country. There is precious little a government, even a democratic government, cannot do today in the name of national defence or military necessity.

(6) *Atoms for peace.* Of the several sorts of risk associated with nuclear fission reactors, one will suffice to illustrate the theme of this section; the production of biological poisons, in particular that of plutonium, one of the deadliest elements ever handled by man. In a fully developed US nuclear economy some 200,000 pounds of plutonium will be generated annually. Bear-ing in mind that a mere half-pound of it, dispersed into the atmosphere as fine soluble particles, would be enough to inflict every living mortal with lung cancer, bearing in mind also that the half-life of plutonium is about 24,000 years, a containment level as high even as 99·99 per cent would hardly be acceptable. Yet inasmuch as plutonium is a necessary material for the fabrication of nuclear weapons, and is expected to be a lucrative item of illicit traffic, such a containment level is likely to prove unfeasible.[62]

The extent of the vigilance required by the planned expansion of a nuclear energy program will entail an unprecedented extension of the internal and inter-national energy program will entail an unprecedented extension of the internal and international security system.[63] Among other measures, this security system will involve armed protection of the transport network along which move the containers of atomic materials, a vast increase in internal surveillance and, inevitably, a surrender to special agents of extraordinary powers of entry, arrest, detention, and interrogation if, as they will surely claim, they are to move fast enough to prevent highly organized criminals, fanatics, and psychopaths from capturing positions from which they can effectively blackmail a nation or cause, in-advertently or deliberately, irreparable disaster.

It is, in sum, difficult to avoid the conclusion that competitive capitalism – even were it able to resist the growth of egalitarian sentiment and what Daniel Bell (1974) calls 'the revolution of rising entitlements' – will not suffice to shore up traditional freedoms against the continuing encroachment of the state. As we move into an increasingly dangerous world, the product of scientific and technical ingenuity, the instinctive desire for self-preservation, found in organized societies as well as in individuals, will prompt men, albeit reluctantly, to cede to governments far greater powers of surveillance, control, and repression, than are com-patible with contemporary notions of personal liberty.

X Summary and Conclusions

The progress of a science, especially a social science, can derive inestimable benefits from a widely recognized school of thought that produces a body of coherent doctrine. Such a school can be influential in imparting a distinctive method to the discipline and in demarcating its scope, as a result of which it can suggest promising areas of inquiry. The coherence itself of the doctrines held offers incentives to unify theoretical analyses, following which the original principles are extended to encompass a more diverse range of phenomena. In the last resort, it offers a framework for the discussion of new issues, and an edifice against which adversaries may try the strength of their un-orthodox idea. With these considerations in mind, my own judgment is that the influence of the Chicago school of economics has, on balance, exercised a sobering and salutary effect on the profession.

However, with the passage of time and, partly in consequence of continuing theoretical developments, occasions will arise when the disciples of any school of thought may be ready to disturb the dust of complacency that inevitably settles on doctrines long held against assault, and to examine anew their relevance, especially in a world that is changing rapidly. The adoption of new concepts and the discovery of new relationships act to reopen avenues of inquiry that once seemed to have been sealed off. Arguments that were once forceful and clear begin to look less certain in the light of new developments. And once the empirical judgments on which they rest are challenged, prescriptive policies and general presumptions may begin to lose their appeal.

This preliminary and somewhat incautious commentary on my understanding of the belief-system of the Chicago school of economists suggests that it is not too early to initiate a systematic reassessment of the validity and the relevance of the *political* economy, at least, that inspires its attitudes and activities. Such a reassessment may result in an increased sophistication of some of its views along with the qualification or discarding of others. Clearly, there is always a risk that, at some point in this process, the acceptance of one more major modification will begin to raise doubts about the affinity between the resulting edifice and the original.

My own opinion is that, on examination, some parts of the structure will appear weaker than its defenders suspect. The main findings of this paper, a summary of which follows, may not ruffle their equanimity unduly. But they are enough to raise important questions about the current relevance of some facts of the Chicago school's political economy in the minds of those who are less committed to its tenets.

Efficiency of the Competitive Economy

On these grounds the case for a competitive economy does not look so strong today as it did, say, before the Second World War. Although it may still be thought to have advantages over a strictly centralized economy, Western economists are today less complacent when comparing the merits of each. There is, of course, more scope in a competitive market economy for such dynamic intangibles as 'the spirit of enterprise'. But in highly industrial countries, this spirit of commercial enterprise may in fact confer little advantage in fundamental innovation, spending itself rather in the creation of consumer trivia. Moreover, a form of economic organization that nurtures the money-making instincts of a community, does not, for that reason alone, necessarily promote the social welfare.

Turning away from these less measurable consequences, however, the efficiency presumption favoring the competitive economy, at least when judged by standard criteria, looks weak today for a number of reasons.

First, the welfare significance of the concept of allocative efficiency, regarded properly as a normative criterion, is not compelling. The allocative 'first best' itself entails a *potential* improvement only, and, as such, may also issue in unresolvable ambiguities.

Secondly, the old allocative prescription that favored an extension of the competitive market so as to extend the dominion of the marginal cost rule, has been confounded by the 'second-best theorem'.[64]

Thirdly, the exceptions that suggest modification of the unchecked operation of competitive markets, in the shape of collective bads and goods, have begun to loom large with the spread of affluence and the progress of technology. In particular, the forms of industrial overspill that can be 'corrected' within the framework of the competitive market are issues in current controversy.

Fourthly, insofar as Duesenberry's relative income hypothesis becomes increasingly applicable in wealthier communities, the impress on social well-being of allocative improvements becomes increasingly faint.

Fifthly, judgments about the efficacy of the working of the market are apt to be consumer biased, the constraints on the choices of workers, and the psychic and pecuniary costs of their involuntary changes of job and location, in meeting voluntary changes of consumer demand being generally neglected by the market and often by economists also. The fears that beset workers and producers, subject as they are to the unforeseeable vicissitudes of trade, offer some explanation for the persistence of movements to erect tariffs, to establish monopolies, and to promote labor unions: they are protectionist, that is, not only in a power-seeking sense but also in a security-seeking sense.[65]

Reconsideration of Some Chicago School Prescriptions

These weaknesses in the concept and application of economic efficiency, reflected in the presumed merit of the competitive market, enter along with other factors into a brief reconsideration of the prescriptive policies of the Chicago school. To illustrate with three of the more familiar ones:

(1) Monetary restriction rather than price controls as

a means of controlling inflation. As I understand it, the opposition to price controls is based on an aversion to any extension of government powers, on the inefficacy of such controls, and on the allocative damage of restricting relative price movements. Yet much depends also on the length of time over which it is widely believed the controls are to be retained and on the willingness of the public to co-operate. If prices, or some key prices, become easier to control; if, in their control, allocative losses are not large,[66] or their welfare significance is not large; if the unemployment required to abate the existing pace of inflation is thought to be heavy; and if there is some risk of losing control for a time of an incipient recession resulting from the application alone of monetary controls, there might be a respectable case in political economy for supplementing monetary restrictions with price controls for a period of time. In short, although a presumption against price controls is in order, it ought not to be held with a tenacity that precludes the exercise of judgment fitting to specific economic and political circumstances.

(2) The support of Chicago economists for freely floating exchange rates as the appropriate equilibrating mechanism in international exchange rather than, say, the gold standard, arises from a recognition of the difficulties of operating a gold standard in the absence of universal wage flexibility. Their arguments against government-controlled exchange rates, which may or may not entail pegging the price of gold, turn on a general aversion to government intervention in free markets which, in the case of the foreign exchange market, causes inequities and distortions, prolongs a trade imbalance, and tempts governments into imposing trade restrictions.

Even if the aforementioned weaknesses in the concept of economic efficiency are conceded, therefore, the case for free exchanges appears to be strong on operational and political grounds. Thus, so long as free exchanges maintain current equilibrium in the balance of payments, each country is effectively insulated from variations in the aggregate employment and price levels of other countries: it neither 'imports' nor 'exports' unemployment or inflation.[67]

However, movements in the exchange rate will maintain balance-of-payments equilibrium only if foreign currencies bought and sold are chiefly for current transactions. The larger are speculative capital movements in a free market relative to current payments, the greater the influence they exert on the exchange rates. By analogy with price-stabilizing speculation on the domestic market for securities, which arises from a strong sense of a normal price (an alternative expression for a highly elastic liquidity preference), these speculative capital movements may tend to stabilize the rate of exchange in a free market, so putting a part of the burden of adjustment on changes of employment and price levels in the trading countries.

It follows that in order for complete freedom of international capital movements to be compatible with exchange rates that are flexible enough to prevent international transmissions of aggregate employment or inflation, the amount of speculative capital movements must be small relative to current international payments.

(3) A general presumption in favor of the removal of all political obstacles to international factor movements [68] includes a particular presumption in favor of removing all immigration quotas, which impede the free flow of international labor. In the absence of state welfare payments, this goal of policy would seem to fit easily into the political economy of the Chicago school: it extends personal freedom and improves the world allocation of resources.

The enlightened self-interest of the host country, however, does not point clearly in the same direction. Apart from the risks of short-term economic and social disruption form massive inflows of labor (which might be mitigated by government attempts to regulate the rate of immigration), the long-term implications for indigenous labor are not favorable. For a potential host country that is already worried about its population density, or about the growing congestion in urban areas, or about the erosion of environmental amenities, an awareness of the opportunities being offered to families in poor countries to better their material condition, or an awareness of the resultant expansion of world gross national product, may not suffice to allay its apprehensions. Bearing in mind the immense populations of the poorer countries of Asia, Africa and South America, and their current rate of increase, the prospect of an open-ended commitment to receive them in any numbers would strike Malthusian fears in many a liberal heart. To this one can add fears of a growing pressure on wages toward a subsistence level, and fears of social tensions that can arise at an apparent 'invasion' of new peoples differentiated from the local populations by race, language, and custom.[69] The American 'melting pot' splutters more than it melts, and western European countries have already experienced difficulties in their attempts to absorb relatively small numbers of immigrant labor since the war.[70]

If enlightened self-interest is translated into an interest in the welfare of one's countrymen, the net advantages of a wide-open door policy are far from evident.[71] If, on the other hand, one's vision is universalistic, a case might be made in support of such a policy, albeit an uneasy one resting on beliefs about the magnitudes involved and about the ability of the world to escape from the Malthusian nightmare.

Equity of the Competitive Economy

Few orthodox economists since J. B. Clark have argued that the market tends also to promote distributional justice. Recent attempts (Thurow, 1971; Hochman and Rodgers, 1969) to extend allocative criteria so as to embrace distributional problems only serve to confirm the inadequacy of the market in this respect. Yet, if the meaning of the term *equity* is extended to cover a person's freedom to select or reject, the operation of free markets, according to the Chicago school, promotes equity in this sense.

As indicated earlier, this exercise of choice is more evident for the consumer than the worker. Yet it is no more evident for the worker than for those citizens who suffer a decline in welfare as a result of external diseconomies generated by industrial processes or their products. Indeed, since there are free markets in labor, the worker has some choice in the matter; certainly he receives some compensation for the 'diswelfare' of his labor. However, inasmuch as environmental property rights are, in practice, difficult to distribute, and a competitive market for trading in such rights virtually impossible, the citizen is generally denied this choice. The sort of feasible solution that is common – either an unchecked competitive market or else a competitive market that is checked by excise or effluent taxes, or otherwise regulated – although it may meet allocative criteria is not such as to compensate the citizens for suffering collectively the residual bads. It entails a form of coercion no less onerous – and to many a sensitive citizen, far more onerous – than any arbitrary system of taxes. If, therefore, the incidence of these adverse spillovers tends to grow over time along with the conventional index of *per capita* growth, and if these spillovers come to be increasingly resented, the claims made for the market as an instrument for extending the area of individual choice will have to be seriously qualified.

Nevertheless, this defect is to some extent a consequence of the existing laws rather than wholly attributable to the market, which could operate well enough in a society pledged to pollution-repressive laws under which none of a range of pollutants could be incurred without paying adequate compensation. The case in justice for such laws is strong, but the enforcement and transactions costs could be heavy.

Touching on the question of intergenerational equity, we have already remarked, unnecessarily perhaps, that the market, even an ideal market, has no tendency to promote it. In respect of the amounts of man-made goods and their quality of efficacy, our descendents might well be wealthier than we. In respect of environmental goods, they will, if trends continue, be worse off. As for the depletion of natural resources, which is also related to man-made goods and environmental goods, the best outcome of a competitive market – which outcome, for reasons given, is not likely to occur – is the generation of an 'optimal' time-path of consumption which, however, makes no provision for our descendents. There is only the hope, or conventional expectation, that this manifest deficiency will be made good by continued technological progress and by the discovery of substitute materials over time.

The Competitive Economy and the Quality of Life

While it is true that the Chicago school does not consider the competitive economy to be a panacea for all social infirmities, it has, perhaps, been over-impressed by its economic and political virtues – by its potential for the creation and distribution of material wealth, for the extension of individual choice, and for the preservation of political freedom. Yet close attention to theoretical developments, to institutional constraints, and to the growing impact of modern technology, has served, as indicated, to uncover a number of weak connections that, taken together, must diminish one's faith in this sovereign institution.

Finally and moving a little away from these familiar haunts, the import of the phrase 'the neutrality of the market' can bear some comment. There is an obvious sense in which the competitive market is value free, or to put it otherwise, value blind. For it can serve a slave economy as faithfully as a free economy. So far as economic efficiency and consumer choice are concerned, it can work as well, or perhaps better, in an authoritarian regime than in a democratic one. Few markets can ever have been as competitive as those that flourished in Britain in the first half of the nineteenth century, when infants became deformed as they toiled their way to an early death in the pits and mills of the Black Country. And there is no lack of examples today to confirm the fact also that well-functioning markets have no innate tendency to promote excellence in any form. They offer no resistance to forces making for a descent into cultural barbarity or moral depravity.

Over the past two decades, rapid economic growth in the West has been accompanied by rapid growth also in the visible signs of social disintegration, as borne out by indexes of divorce, drug-taking, suicide, vandalism, delinquency, homicide, and crimes of violence, especially among the young. City streets are increasingly unsafe to walk in. Anxiety levels among parents have never been higher. Without implying a causal relationship between postwar economic expansion and these unhappier features of contemporary society, their effects on society's sense of well-being have to be weighed against those arising from the accumulation of material conveniences. It is a bold man who will declare that, over the postwar period, the contribution of economics to social welfare has been decisive.[72]

But however this contribution is assessed, those who are concerned primarily with society's well-being no longer look, today, to competitive markets for salvation. As, willy nilly, we are ushered into the postindustrial era, the focus of concern is shifting inevitably from traditional controversies about the economic conditions under which goods are produced towards a new controversy, one that turns about the sorts of goods themselves, both capital goods and consumer goods, that are now being produced – and their far-reaching effects on our environment, on our character, and on our chances of survival.

Notes: Chapter 20

1 As in Lerner's *Economics of Control* (1946), in which there is state ownership of the means of production, managed by public servants in a decentralized economic system that is designed to simulate a competitive economy under certain conditions.

2 Namely, that all consumption and production functions have nonzero second derivatives; that each person consumes some amount of each good; and that the production of each good requires some amount of each factor. Obvious amendments apply if these conditions are not met, but they do not modify our conclusions in significant respects.

3 I follow my own convention in using the phrase 'everyone' better off to include the case where one person or more are made better off and nobody is made worse off.

4 In the special case of fixed factor supplies, the optimal condition is violated if the price–marginal cost ratios are not the same for all goods. For further elaboration the interested reader is referred to Baumol and Bradford (1970) and Lerner (1970).

5 A first crude response to the theorem would be to include the price–marginal cost ratios of most sectors within a broad band, and to regard deviations from this range as being significant. See Green (1962) and Mishan (1962) for broad rules in the presence of second-best problems.

6 By, for instance, Davis and Whinston, McManus, Bohm and Negishi between 1965 and 1967.

7 I have shown in a previous paper (1973b) that wherever such apparently contradictory cases arise, it is not possible to attach superior allocative merit to either collection of goods inasmuch as the welfare combinations associated with each collection can be reduced to alternative distributions of a third hypothetical collection of goods.

8 A related criticism of economic practices that evade the problems of value or translate them into mechanistic allocative problems is elaborated in a recent paper by Klein (1974).

9 For a recent survey see the article by Mark Abrams in *Encounter* (1974).

10 This statement is valid provided all goods and bads are available on the market. To the extent that some goods are not available on the market exceptions can be made. Thus the provision of some collective goods, in particular when they are designed to reduce collective bads (external diseconomies) such as pollutants, that are a simultaneous form of annoyance to many people, can raise social welfare even in the limiting case of complete equality of distribution.

11 On an abstract level, the analysis of (1) and (2) cannot altogether solve the distribution problem since it begins, in each case, with the *status quo*. Allowing that, in principle, there is a different Pareto-efficient distributional solution corresponding to each initial distribution, society cannot escape having to make a choice among a wide range of alternative Pareto-efficient distributions. And for this ultimate choice, no criterion is offered.

12 Indeed, by focusing on some particular form of pollution – such as horse dung, sewage, or smoke – in some locations at some point in history, economists have argued that 'pollution-wise' we are better off today. For a recent example, see Beckerman (1972).

13 In this connection, see Coase (1960); see also Davis and Whinston (1962), who managed to compound the difficulty by using a model in which two firms of industries inflicted external diseconomies upon each other.

14 See, for example, Plott (1966) and Schall (1971). There are some brief comments on these models in my 1974 paper.

15 Clearly, if transactions costs were low enough to allow bargaining to take place in the first instance there would be no justification for an excise tax (in any case, the excise tax could be made conditional upon no further bargaining by the parties).

16 The assertion is unsatisfactory, however. It is not enough to show that the market can, in some circumstances, respond in the required direction. It has to be shown, also, that it will tend to respond by the *required magnitude*. For instance, congestion of itself tends to choke off traffic, but the resulting reduction of traffic falls short of that required by reference to the optimal condition.

The conditions necessary for the market solution to be optimal in a polluted industrial area are: (a) that the level of pollution in the industrial area be unrelated to the size of the working population, (b) that the workers' costs of movement are negligible, and (c) that pollution levels everywhere are not rising over time.

17 The analysis is on all fours with private property in farmland. Rent, the return to land, is to be maximized only through 'exploitation' of the upward-sloping supply curve of corn. 'Exploitation' of the demand curve, on the other hand, which is possible if land ownership is not diffused, produces monopoly rent and, therefore, a suboptimal output.

18 Useful insights into this proposition can be found in a short but valuable contribution by Calabresi (1968).

19 Particular attention should be given to the articles by Demsetz (1964, 1966) and more recently by Cheung (1970).

20 The advantages of this approach are discussed by Baumol and Oates (1975, ch. 10).

21 The distinction between optional collective goods (such as a public park or a public broadcast) and nonoptional collective goods (such as 'artificial rain' or internal security) is made in my 1969a paper.

22 For optional collective goods, exchange optimum is met inasmuch as (in the absence of congestion) the marginal cost to each person is zero. For nonoptional collective goods, however, exchange optimum is unlikely to be met since the amounts people are constrained to absorb are unalterable (except, perhaps, by incurring costs).

23 At least in the absence of 'pecuniary external diseconomies' or rising long-run unit costs.

24 In this connection see Freeman and Haveman (1972).

25 The suggestion does not, however, amount to the dictum that the pollution should be made to pay, which is ambiguous. Less ambiguous is the dictum that he who incurs the pollution should be made to bear the costs. Thus if a person chooses to move into a polluted zone, it is allocatively appropriate that he should be made to bear the environmental costs himself. Compensaiton in this circumstance is tantamount to a subsidy and can be shown to be allocatively unwarranted. If, however, he and others choose to move without pecuniary inducement, further social gains may be realized by curbing the activities of the polluting industries.

26 As a consequence of the spread of the welfare state into the field of medicine, the health risks that a person is ready to take can be partly spread among the taxpayers. But the 'external diseconomies' on them that appear to arise from this financial arrangement are what Viner would call 'pecuniary'; in effect, transfer payments only. Since the costs of any health damage fall in the first instance entirely on the risk-taker, there is no purely *allocative* justification for invoking the concept of 'social cost' in arguing a case for interfering with the individual's choice.

27 No man is an island unto himself, however, and there cannot be many persons whose health or survival is a matter of indifference to everyone else including the members of his family. Again, however, we are faced with a choice of grounding our welfare propositions in the Pareto criterion or in the ethics of society. The liberal welfare economist may consistently over-ride the Pareto criterion –which attitude, in this instance, implies a disregard of the reaction of others – in order to safeguard the freedom of the individual, and in doing so may be giving proper expression to the ethics of the community.

28 Our ignorance is dangerous whenever we produce, and market, complex chemical agents or new synthetic substances that are reasonably suspect of having genetic or ecological side effects yet to be discovered.

29 A sober account of the dangers accompanying the spread of breeder reactors is given by Kneese (1973).

30 Allowance being made for adjusting the base; so that, for example, a marginal dollar grown through investment to $1·25 is exactly offset by a 20 per cent decline in the utility of the resulting $1·25.

31 If this elasticity were equal to –4, and if average growth in *per capita* income were 2 per cent per annum, the use of 8 per cent as discount rate for calculating the present value of marginal gains and losses over time can be rationalized as a device for transforming dollar increments scattered through time into present dollars of equal utility weight. This sort of rationalization for the use of a discount rate is clearly distinct from that conventionally associated with its use in public investment criteria; namely, that it represents the yield of alternative uses.

32 In this context, the relevant rate of interest is that equal to the current social yield on new investment (before tax).

33 For if the firm produces a unit of ore this year at a net price of 100 and invests the proceeds at 5 per cent, it will realize 105 next year, whereas by postponing its extraction to next year a net price of 108 is realized.

34 For if the firm extracts a unit of ore today it fetches a net price of 100 which, when invested at 5 per cent, realizes 105 next year, whereas if the firm postpones its extraction to next year it realizes a net price of only 102.

35 For a fairly popular treatment of such possibilities, see Solow (1974).

36 In general, that is, only a small fraction of the stream of net proceeds (or net benefits) is saved and reinvested in productive assets. For a treatment of the usual assumptions made about the reinvestment of returns from public investment, see Mishan (1975, pt IV).

37 This second belief depends, to some extent, on the first being true.

38 Included are those intangible costs of separating himself from a neighborhood in which he has made close friends and from a pattern of life full of familiar associations.

39 Sometimes taxpayers are made to subsidize a proportion of the costs of movement or of retraining, a policy that also suffers from allocative deficiencies.

40 If the actions of all others were similarly circumscribed, he would feel less injured. And if, for political reasons – as in Britain between 1945 and 1954 – restrictions on consumer choice are accepted by society at large, his experience of welfare could, for a number of reasons, be as high or higher than it would be if such restrictions were removed.

41 There have, however, been recent reports in business journals of experiments that extend more choice to workers in respect of hours, or of work conditions, or of methods of production.

42 The suggestion that there can be considerations bearing on social welfare other than the seeming efficiency of markets that provide justification for some restrictive practices must not, however, be construed as blanket extenuation of extortionate pricing and dishonest dealings of many large corporations.

43 It is as well to remind readers at this stage that if transactions costs were zero, this interdependence would resolve itself through voluntary activity, which would produce the optimal amounts of these goods. But this ideal solution would require that merit good-producers have costless information about which persons benefit, and by how much, from the consumption by others of particular merit goods. Since such costs are likely to be prohibitive (involving, as they do, the free-rider problem), the effective choice society has is either to attempt to produce an optimal amount of some merit goods, or at least more of them than would be forthcoming on the free market, through subsidies financed by income (or other) taxes, or do nothing. A person strongly opposed to taxes, as being coercive, will choose to do nothing.

44 They also happen to be collective goods inasmuch as, in the absence of congestion, the costs of such services cannot be economically allocated among the beneficiaries. But this is not a necessary characteristic of merit goods which can also be private goods – for example, classical records or history books.

45   Even though people, on being directly questioned, declare in favor of freedom for the pornographic theater, it may well be simply because in their confusion they now believe they ought to feel ashamed of their (natural?) feelings of shame, and because they fear to be thought illiberal or in favor of censorship. Yet despite their intimidation by fashionable views, they might still feel better off if carnal displays disappeared from cinema and theater.

46   The reader will recall that I argued earlier (in section II), in connection with the transfers in kind and other issues, that the liberal economist is not obliged to raise his hat to Pareto on all occasions, and, indeed, where there is a conflict between Pareto-based allocative propositions and the ethical norms of the community, priority be given to the latter. However, insofar as the categorization of merit-demerit goods arises from the application of the more transcendental values of a society, this possible conflict between ethics and Pareto efficiency is circumvented.

47   Unless the meaning of *externalities* is extended beyond its conventional economic definition so as to exclude, in particular, all unforeseen and adverse consequences. But if so, it would clearly be impossible to know how to 'correct' externalities.

48   In private correspondence with me, Professor Friedman mentioned a Chicago study which found that the prices of identical optical goods were lower in the states that permitted advertising of opticians' services than in those states that did not. But this sort of advertising of services that the customer can judge for himself is more like simple announcements of place and terms of business. It is the sort of information that would or should be provided by consumer research agencies.

49   In support of such allegations, it is often remarked that a large proportion of competitive advertising is self-cancelling in its effects, and that the competitive firm's advertising mainly serves the purpose of maintaining its share of the market. However, it is not absurd to suppose that the market shares of the competitive firm would remain at least as stable in the absence of competitive advertising.

50   There is, in fact, both a distributional and an allocative effect. The distributional one involves no more than a shift of real income from car-buyers to newspaper-readers. The former pay more than the real costs incurred in the production of their cars, as a result of which the latter obtain the advertisement free and, in addition, pay less than the costs of the newspaper.

51   I do not think that Chicago economists would dissent from the above arguments. Some of them have long urged that television and radio channels be sold by auction, and that those who buy the rights to them should be free to distribute their programs by any means they wish, including pay television and pay radio.

52   I am not suggesting that advertising agencies are unscrupulous. They may well abide by what looks like a reasonable code of ethics. But the fact remains that, in virtue of his vocation, the advertising agent cannot be concerned primarily to disclose the whole truth (so far as he knows it) and nothing but the truth, but only those parts of it, along with some imagery, that would appear to him best able to promote the sale of the product.

53   By 'relevant', I mean information that enters into the consumer's decision. If he thinks that looking like, or acting like, other people is important, then information on the numbers of people using, or likely to be using, the article or service becomes relevant. By 'complete', I mean   *all* information that is relevant in the above sense. Clearly, completeness must be regarded as an aim; the more of it for a given outlay, the better. Yet the investigations have to be limited by the resources available to the agency, both financial and technical.

54   Of course, it could be argued that consumers prefer partial to impartial information. But if the law were amended to require manufacturers to sell their advertisements to the public at full cost, the public would be able to choose as between buying impartial and partial information, buying each at a price that covers its cost to the economy.

55   In his *Newsweek* column (16 June 1969) Milton Friedman attacked the then proposed prohibition of tobacco-advertising as constituting a form of censorship 'hostile to the maintenance of a free society', a view we shall examine in the text. To this general view, however, he appends a particular objection to arguments favoring prohibition of cigarette-advertising simply on the grounds of health risks. 'Every time we take an automobile ride, or cross the street', says Friedman, 'we knowingly risk our lives because we think that the gain from the ride or crossing the street justifies the risk.'

True, risk in varying degrees and in a variety of ways pervades our lives. The question at issue, however, is whether resources should be used in persuading people to take risks which otherwise they might not want to incur. Can there be no legitimate objection to advertising campaigns designed to persuade motorists of the joys of high-speed driving, or to persuade pedestrians of the exhilarations of running across city streets?

John Stuart Mill's argument for freedom of choice was reinforced by the consideration that the alleged ill effects on the consumers of drugs would themselves act as a deterrent to others once they became manifest to all. This deterrent effect, however, can be offset or overcome by sustained propaganda in its favor. It is hard to believe that tobacco and liquor addiction would be so widespread were it not for sustained propaganda by commercial interests.

Friedman's disapproval of the antismoking campaign of federal agencies on the grounds that 'government has no business using the taxpayer's money to propagandize' certain views is hard to understand. If a government, local, state, or federal, receives a mandate from the electorate for just that purpose, it cannot be accused of a misuse of the taxpayer's money, in particular since the views in question are not political in the ordinary sense. The government propaganda is better regarded as a collective good designed specifically to counter the propaganda of interested parties who are attempting to induce people to increase their exposure to health hazards.

56   It seems only fair to point out, however, that the Chicago school does not accept a utilitarian approach in which personal freedom is but one ingredient, though an important one, in the promotion of well-being. If I may quote from private correspondence with Friedman:

We regard the virtues and role of freedom as not simply instrumental ... for maximizing utilities, but far more fundamentally even in its instrumental role as a means for forming character and values and more basically as an ultimate end in itself derived from our lack of certainty about our own beliefs which seem to us to render it improper to try to impose these on somebody else.

However, even if this conception of the role of freedom is accepted it does not seem to me to upset the conclusion reached in the last two paragraphs of this section.

57 Although an ideal size of the public sector, judged on allocative grounds, may be related to the incidence and magnitude of the collective goods and bads emerging at some stage of technical progress, it is at least conceivable either (a) to have a public sector that embraces the entire economy even where all the goods produced are 'private' on the conventional definition, or (b) to have a private sector of the economy that contains nothing but collective goods. In arguments about the best size of the public sector, however, considerations arising from economic efficiency and from political expediency may point in opposite directions.

58 The chief lesson that was drawn by Hayek from the collectivist experiments on the Continent in the interwar period as described in his arresting monograph (1944), was the imperative of a large private sector of the economy as a means of preserving individual freedoms.

59 The case is cogently argued in Friedman (1962, pp. 172-6).

60 At best, liberal economists have been satisfied to think about economic growth in terms of more, or better, consumer goods which, it is said, 'expand the area of choice open to the individual'.

61 A fascinating account of the process of self-generating expenditures of the defence establishment by Charles Schultze appeared in 1970. Schultze concluded that 'continually advancing technology and the risk aversion of military planners, therefore, combine to produce ever more complex and expensive weapons systems and ever more contingencies to guard against' (p. 14).

62 According to the London *Observer* (9 March 1975), about 20 million Americans (on that date) were shown on their television screens how easy it was to steal plutonium and produce a home-made atomic bomb. If the report was accurate, the viewers were told that no nuclear plant in the United States – and probably in the world – is adequately protected against a well-planned attack by terrorists.

63 Writing in the *Bulletin of Atomic Scientists* (May 1972), Dr Hannes Alfven, Nobel Laureate in Physics, stated:

Fission energy is safe only if a number of critical devices work as they should, if a number of people in key positions follow all their instructions, if there is no sabotage, no hijacking of the transports, if no reactor fuel processing plant or reprocessing plant or repository anywhere in the world is situated in a region of riots or guerilla activity, and no revolution or war – even a 'conventional' one – takes place in these regions. The enormous quantities of extremely dangerous material must not get into the hands of ignorant people or desperados. No Acts of God can be permitted.

64 Nonetheless, the larger the discrepancy between the market price and the social marginal valuation of the product, the more certain is the standard correction to offer an improvement – a proposition that justifies treatment within a partial context of significant environmental diseconomies.

65 To be more obvious about it, losing one's market or losing one's job – even in 'the short run' – is an upsetting experience against which, in the scale of social welfare, additional consumer satisfaction may weigh very little.

66 This can be the case if adjustments to changing conditions of demand come about less through the movement of prices and more through the movement of factors in response to economic opportunities.

67 Under fixed exchange rates, in contrast, a full employment economy having a rate of inflation above those of the countries with which it trades, incurs an increasing balance-of-payments deficit. Attempts to eliminate this deficit by devaluing its currency *without* first improving the internal balance (reducing aggregate investment and government expenditures relative to saving and tax revenues) can only aggravate its inflation and restore the deficit.

68 The proposition that the international exchange of goods is a substitute for international factor movements, and tends to bring about international equality of factor prices, depends not only on the relevant number of traded goods being no fewer than the number of factors (which invites conjecture on the appropriate definitions of goods and factors) and on the absence of factor-ratio reversibility but also, and perhaps more important, on the assumption of identical linear homogeneous production functions in each country of the traded goods. The introduction of production functions having different degrees of technical progress (neutral or otherwise) is enough to vitiate the result that costless free trade equalizes factor prices.

69 An idea of the resentments felt by some people in Britain at the numbers of 'Commonwealth' immigrants is conveyed by Lord Elton (1965).

70 An account of these difficulties can be found in Power (1974).

71 Even though analytic considerations may suggest that economic gains to renters and capitalists exceed economic losses to workers.

72 Nordhaus and Tobin (1972) were too intelligent to be that bold. Whatever results were established by their figures were effectively disestablished by their explicit doubts and qualifications.

References

Abrams, M. (1974), 'Changing values', *Encounter,* vol. 43 (October), pp. 29–38.

Ayres, R. and Kneese, A. V. (1969), 'Production, consumption and externalities', *American Economic Review,* vol. 59 (June), pp. 282–97.

Barnett, H. and Morse, C. (1963), *Scarcity and Growth* (Baltimore: Johns Hopkins).

Bator, F. (1958), 'The anatomy of market failure', *Quarterly Journal of Economics,* vol. 72 (August), pp. 351–79.

Baumol, W. J. and Bradford, D. (1970), 'Optimal departures from marginal cost pricing', *American Economic Review,* vol. 60 (June), pp. 265–83.

Baumol, W. and Oates, W. E. (1975), *The Theory of Environmental Policy* (Englewood Cliffs, NJ: Prentice-Hall).

Beckerman, W. (1972), 'Economists, scientists and environmental catastrophe', *Oxford Economic Papers,* vol. 24 (November), pp. 327–44.

Bell, D. (1974), 'The public household', *Public Interest,* vol. 37 (Fall), pp. 29–68.

Berle, A. A. and Means, G. C. (1933), *The Modern Corporation and Private Property* (New York: Macmillan).

Breton, A. A. (1966), 'A theory of the demand for public goods', *Canadian Journal of Public Economics,* vol. 32 (November), pp. 455–67.

Buchanan, J. and Stubblebine, W. M. C. (1962), 'Externality', *Economica,* vol. 29 (November), pp. 371–84.

Calabresi, G. (1968), 'Transaction costs, resource allocation, and liability rules: a comment', *Journal of Law and Economics.*

Cheung, S. (1970), 'The structure of a contract', *Journal of Law and Economics,* vol. 13 (April), pp. 49–70.

Coase, R. H. (1960), 'The problems of social cost', *Journal of Law and Economics,* vol. 3 (October), pp. 1–4.

Daly, G. and Giertz, F. (1972), 'Welfare economics and welfare reform', *American Economic Review,* vol. 62 (March), pp. 131–8.

Davis, O. and Whinston, A. (1962), 'Externalities, welfare and the theory of games', *Journal of Political Economy,* vol. 70 (June), pp. 241–62.

Demsetz, H. (1964), 'The exchange and enforcement of property rights', *Journal of Law and Economics,* vol. 7 (October), pp. 11–26.

Demsetz, H. (1966), 'Some aspects of property rights', *Journal of Law and Economics,* vol. 9 (October), pp. 61–70.

Duesenberry, J. (1949), *Income, Saving and the Theory of Consumer Behavior* (Cambridge, Mass.: Harvard University Press).

Ellul, J. (1965), *The Technical Society* (London: Jonathan Cape).

Elton, Lord (1965), *The Unarmed Invasion* (London: Geoffrey Bles).

Epstein, E. J. (1974), 'Methadone: the forlorn hope', *Public Interest,* vol. 36 (Summer), pp. 3–24.

Freeman, A. M. and Haveman, R. (1972), 'Clean rhetoric, dirty water', *Public Interest,* vol. 28 (Summer), pp. 51–65.

Friedman, M. (1962), *Capitalism and Freedom* (Chicago: University of Chicago Press).

Friedman, M. (1974), 'Schools at Chicago', *University of Chicago Magazine* (Autumn), pp. 11–16.

Gaffney, M. (ed.) (1967), *Extractive Resources and Taxation* (Madison, Wis.: University of Wisconsin Press).

Georgescu-Roegen, N. (1975), 'Energy and economic myths', *Southern Economic Journal,* vol. 41 (January), pp. 347–81.

Gofman, J. (1972), 'Time for a moratorium', *Environmental Action,* vol. 4 (November), pp. 11–15.

Graff, J. V. (1957), *Theoretical Welfare Economics* (Cambridge: Cambridge University Press).

Green, H. A. J. (1962), 'The social optimum in the presence of monopoly and taxation', *Review of Economic Studies,* vol. 29 (February), pp. 66–78.

Hayek, F. A. (1944), *The Road to Serfdom* (London: Routledge & Sons).

Hayek, F. A. (1961), 'The *non sequitur* of the "dependence effect",' *Southern Economic Journal,* vol. 27 (April), pp. 346–8.

Hicks, J. R. (1939), *Value and Capital* (Oxford: Clarendon).

Hochman, H. and Rodgers, J. (1969), 'Pareto optimal redistribution', *American Economic Review,* vol. 59 (September), pp. 542–57.

Hotelling, H. (1931), 'The economics of exhaustible resources', *Journal of Political Economy,* vol. 39 (April), pp. 137–75.

Johnson, H. (1973), *Man and His Environment* (British North American Committee).

Kaldor, N. (1939), 'Welfare propositions in economics and interpersonal comparisons of utility', *Economic Journal,* vol. 51 (September), pp. 549-52.

Klein, P. (1974), 'Economics: allocation or valuation', *Journal of Economic Issues,* vol. 8 (December), pp. 785–811.

Kneese, A. (1973), *The Faustian Bargain* (Washington, DC: Resources for the Future).

Kneese, A. and Schultze, C. (1975), *Pollution, Prices and Public Policy* (Washington, DC: Brookings Institution).

Knight, F. H. (1924), 'Some fallacies in the interpretation of social cost', *Quarterly Journal of Economics,* vol. 38 (August), pp. 582–606.

Krutilla, J. A. and Fisher, A. (1975), *The Economics of Natural Resources* (Washington, DC: Resources for the Future).

Lerner, A. P. (1946), *The Economics of Control* (New York: Macmillan).

Lerner, A. P. (1970), 'On optimal taxes with an untaxable sector', *American Economic Review,* vol. 60 (June), pp. 284–94.

Lipsey, R. G. and Lancaster, K. (1957), 'The general theory of second best', *Review of Economic Studies,* vol. 24 (November), pp. 11–32.

Machlup, F. (1969), 'Liberalism and the choice of freedom', in *Roads to Freedom,* edited by E. Streissler (London: Routledge & Kegan Paul).

Maddox, J. (1972), 'Raw materials and the price mechanism', *Nature,* vol. 236 (14 April), pp. 331–4.

Mishan, E. J. (1957), 'A reappraisal of the principles of resource allocation', *Economica.*

Mishan, E. J. (1962), 'Second thoughts on second best', *Oxford Economic Papers,* vol. 14 (October), pp. 205–17.

Mishan, E. J. (1965), 'Reflection on recent developments in the concept of external effects', *Canadian Journal of Political Economy,* vol. 31 (February), pp. 3–34.

Mishan, E. J. (1967a), *The Costs of Economic Growth* (New York: Praeger).

Mishan, E. J. (1967b), 'Pareto optimality and the law', *Oxford Economic Papers,* vol. 19 (November), pp. 255–87.

Mishan, E. J. (1969a), 'The relationship between joint products, collective goods, and external effects', *Journal of Political Economy,* vol. 72, no. 3 (May), pp. 329–48.

Mishan, E. J. (1969b), *Welfare Economics: An Assessment* (Amsterdam: North-Holland).

Mishan, E. J. (1971), 'The postwar literature on externalities: an interpretive essay', *Journal of Economic Literature,* vol. 9 (May), pp. 1–28.

Mishan, E. J. (1972), 'The futility of Pareto efficient distribution', *American Economic Review,* vol. 62 (December), pp. 974–6.

Mishan, E. J. (1973a), *Making the World Safe for Pornography* (London: Alcove Press), ch. 6.

Mishan, E. J. (1973b), 'Welfare criteria: resolution of a paradox', *Economic Journal,* vol. 83 (September), pp. 747–67.

Mishan, E. J. (1974), 'What is the optimal level of pollution?' *Journal of Political Economy,* vol. 82 (November), pp. 1287–99.

Mishan, E. J. (1975), *Cost–Benefit Analysis,* 2nd edn (London: Allen & Unwin).

Nordhaus, W. and Tobin, J. (1972), 'Is growth obsolete?', in National Bureau of Economic Research, *Economic Growth* (New York: Columbia University Press).

Olson, M. (1965), *The Logic of Collective Action* (Cambridge, Mass.: Harvard University Press).

Packard, V. (1972), *A Nation of Strangers* (New York: David McKay).

Page, T. (1973), *The Economics of Involuntary Transfers* (New York: Springer-Verlag).

Page, T. (1976), *Conservation and Economic Efficiency* (Washington, DC: Resources for the Future).

Pigou, A. C. (1946), *The Economics of Welfare,* 4th edn (London: Macmillan).

Plott, C. (1966), 'Externalities and corrective taxes', *Economica,* vol. 33 (February), pp. 84–7.

Power, J. (1974), 'The new proletariat', *Encounter,* vol. 43 (September), pp. 8–13.

Ridker, R. (ed.) (1972), *Population, Resources and the Environment* (Washington, DC: US Government Printing Office).

Schall, L. (1971), 'Technological externalities and resource allocation', *Journal of Political Economy,* vol. 79 (September), pp. 983–1001.

Schultze, C. (1970), 'Re-examining the military budget', *Public Interest,* vol. 18 (Winter), pp. 3–24.

Scitovsky, T. (1941), 'A note on welfare propositions in economics', *Review of Economic Studies,* vol. 9 (November), pp. 77–88.

Simons, H. (1948), *Economic Policy for a Free Society* (Chicago: University of Chicago Press).

Solow, R. (1974), 'The economics of resources or the resources of economics', *American Economic Review,* vol. 64 (May), pp. 1–14.

Telser, L. (1964), 'Advertising and competition', *Journal of Political Economy,* vol. 72 (December), pp. 537–62.

Thurow, L. (1971), 'The income distribution as a pure public good', *Quarterly Journal of Economics,* vol. 85 (May), pp. 327–36.

Tiebout, C. (1956), 'A pure theory of local expenditure', *Journal of Political Economy,* vol. 64 (October), pp. 416–24.

Turvey, R. (1963), 'On divergencies between social and private cost', *Economica,* vol. 30 (August), pp. 309–13.

Viner, J. (1931), 'Cost curves and supply curves'; reprinted in *Readings in Price Theory* (New York: Blakiston, 1953).

21

Do Economic Evaluations of Allocative Changes Have Any Validity in the West Today?

It has often been suggested that economists, when advising governments, should restrict their activities to describing the range of consequences expected to arise as a result of any proposed economic measure, leaving it to the political process to decide whether or not the proposed measure ought to be undertaken. Nevertheless, practising economists continue to tender prescriptive economic advice to governments, which advice – if we exclude, as we must, the concept of a specified social welfare function for society as having any practical value in guiding the formulation of economic policies – generally falls into one of two categories: one that can be conveniently labelled political economy, and the other which goes by the name of allocation economics.[1] A brief word about each.

Political economy, in addition to making use of positive or analytic economics, and possibly also allocation economics, draws upon the particular economic adviser's own judgments – his judgments of the facts, political and social, and his judgments of value. These personal judgments play a large part in his appraisal of economic events and in enabling him to strike a balance between apparently conflicting objectives, such as those of equity and incentive, high employment and price stability, free trade and domestic tranquillity – also between conflicting social evils, such as misallocation of resources or inequities, on the one hand, and increased government intervention, on the other. The economic adviser will also have opinions about the nature and the limits of government intervention in the economy.

The authority, then, for statements about political economy derives in large part from the experience and prestige of the advocate, from the acceptance of his political ideology and from his standing in the community. It goes without saying that his assessment of the economic situation and his recommendations carry weight according as his political philosophy accords with that of the party, or parties, currently in office.

Allocation economics, in contrast, does not draw upon the value judgments of the individual economist. It derives from the premises of welfare economics and is restricted in the main to prescriptive propositions, often at the microeconomic level. Its theory and application address themselves to the reallocation of resources between different sectors of the economy, and its application finds expression in a number of techniques, among which the most popular are mathematical programming and cost–benefit analysis, both designed to yield numerical calculations of alternative social values or of net social gain.

I The Basic Maxims of Normative Allocation Economics

We are concerned in this essay chiefly with the status of allocation economics and, by extension therefore, with welfare economics, which may be said to encompass propositions concerning allocation, distribution and equity.

Economists are by training most fit to pronounce on the allocative aspects of an economic change. Although they may undertake also to make prescriptive statements about the distributional aspects of the change, as a rule they seem to prefer to assess the distributional changes, where perceptible, in terms of more or less progressive (or more or less regressive) distributions, in the belief that greater equality is the existing goal of policy. The question of equity, as distinct from that of distribution, has never formed part of a formal welfare criterion, even though in a world of proliferating and far-reaching externalities the question of culpability is of increasing relevance. However, we do not touch on this latter aspect here.[2]

A definition of welfare economics, at once serviceable and widely accepted, is that branch of the subject which seeks to formulate and justify propositions by which economists may rank, on the scale of better or worse, alternative economic situations. It follows that the conclusions of an analysis raised on the premises of welfare economics, as defined, may reasonably be interpreted as having prescriptive content.[3]

The task I set myself here is to make explicit and reassess the prescriptive content of welfare propositions, concentrating for the most part, and initially, on the allocative aspects. The resulting inquiry discloses something of an impasse, in consequence of which the import of allocation economics may have to sustain a drastic reinterpretation.

Restricting ourselves for the time being to the more widely accepted ordinalist development of the subject, generally associated with development of the New Welfare Economics, allocative propositions in economics may be said to rest on two basic maxims:

A. *The individualist maxim,* that the 'objective' data of the economist are the choices or subjective valuations of the individual members of society and nothing more. These data, incidentally, are assumed to remain constant over the period in question – a somewhat frail assumption, which, however, we need not challenge here.

B. *The Pareto maxim,* sometimes referred to as the Pareto criterion, which has it that an economic situation *II* is ranked above situation *I* if, in a costless movement from *I* to *II,* the aggregate value of the individual gains exceeds the aggregate value of the individual losses.

If the above condition is met, situation *II* may be regarded as a 'potential Pareto improvement' as compared with situation *I,* inasmuch as (assuming sufficient divisibility) everyone can be made better off in *II* following a costless movement from *I.* Needless to observe, this potential Pareto improvement is identical with that more commonly designated as an 'allocative improvement' or an 'economically more efficient' use of resources, such a criterion being the basis for the standard recommendation that resources be shifted from one use to another if, in consequence, their net social value can be increased.[4]

The individualist maxim, A, is usually defended by economists by invoking the proposition that each man knows his own interest best. This proposition, as enunciated by Adam Smith and others, is open to criticism when regarded as a factual statement. Its popularity in the West resides rather in its political expedience in a libertarian society that seeks to act on the principle that each man knows his own economic interests better than others.

As for the Pareto maxim, B, which purports to assess the social value of the mooted economic change simply by comparing the aggregate of the individual valuations in each of the alternative situations – even where, as is generally the case, the change makes some persons worse off – it has been widely accepted by economists in spite of some initial protests that followed in the wake of the Kaldor–Hicks criterion – a criterion that, seen in retrospect, only made explicit the import of those allocative recommendations which Pigou and other neoclassical economists had regarded for decades as self-evident.

The acceptance, however, by the economist of allocative propositions as prescriptive ones entails a belief that in the last resort there is an ethical consensus in favour of both maxims. And it should be manifest that this consensus cannot be derived from individual welfare functions, no matter how elaborated. On the contrary, the acceptance of individual welfare functions as relevant data in any prescriptive statement is conditional upon this ethical consensus.

II The Neoclassical and the New Welfare Economics Compared

Accepting the A maxim for the present as common ground to all economists, let us express the B maxim in the strong form,

$$II \, \mathrm{p} \, I \text{ wherever } \Sigma v_{II} > \Sigma v_I$$

which is to be read as stating that economic situation *II* is deemed socially preferred to situation *I* wherever the aggregate of individual valuations in *II* exceeds the aggregate of individual valuations in *I,* it being tacitly understood that it costs no more to realise *II* than it does to realise *I.*

It is of passing interest at this stage to introduce an alternative 'utility maxim', B', to represent the neoclassical position, expressed again in the strong form,

$$II \, \mathrm{p} \, I \text{ wherever } \Sigma u_{II} > \Sigma u_I$$

which is to be read as stating that situation *II* is deemed socially preferred to situation *I* wherever the aggregate of individual utilities in *II* exceeds the aggregate of individual utilities in *I*. Since in this latter case the exercise is to be carried through in terms of 'utils' rather than in terms of money valuations, it becomes necessary to multiply each individual valuation by a util weight. If we employ the two neoclassical postulates rejected by the ordinalists – (1) that individual utility increases with real income but at a diminishing rate and (2) that (allowing, perhaps, some time for adjustment) the utility functions of all members of society are much the same, say identical – the util weight to be attached to each dollar of gain or loss of the individual varies inversely with his income.

Now, if we are concerned as neoclassical economists only with distributional problems, a transfer of income from rich to poor *ceteris paribus* always raises aggregate utility, irrespective of the actual weights used. Indeed, a necessary condition for maximising society's aggregate utility is that its aggregate income be equally divided among the members of that society. If, instead, however, we wish to compare alternative economic situations *I* and *II*, the question of the exact weights to be used is of the utmost importance. For almost any project could be admitted on a net aggregate utility criterion, $\Sigma \Delta u > 0$, if there were no limits on the pattern of util weights. The actual methods proposed for determining these income weights have been either arbitrary (such as the adoption of a utility–income function having an elasticity of marginal utility with respect to income of unity, or some other number) or political. If the latter, the util weights are to be derived directly from past political decisions (following, say, the method proposed by Weisbrod, 1968) or else indirectly, on a particular interpretation of the rationale of the existing marginal-tax rates.

The weakness of the neoclassical welfare position is evident. For one thing, it is at least as questionable whether the B′ maxim represents a social consensus as whether the B maxim does. But what is more important in this connection is that the application of the B′ maxim, in comparing alternative situations *I* and *II*, would require exact util weights, which, when they are not arbitrary, are explicitly political. They are therefore also subject to political controversy and will tend to alter with political office – as a result of which, it may be argued, the role of the economist (at least in respect of comparisons of non-optimal situations) is reduced to that of a technician in the service of the existing government.

In contrast, if the B maxim is taken to rest on an ethical consensus, its application to alternative situations is non-political. Indeed, Kaldor (1939) distinguished between the 'economic efficiency' aspect of the change being considered, which he identified with the B maxim, and the distributional aspect, which he declared to be a political issue – one upon which the economist *qua* economist has no authority to pronounce.

Since the weight of the argument turns on this notion of economic efficiency, I shall spell out carefully my understanding of its prescriptive implications. The term 'economic efficiency', when it is not being used by economists simply as a shorthand for $\Sigma \Delta v > 0$, entails a norm by which alternative economic situations may be ranked. And since alternative economic organisations are agenda that affect the welfare of the members of society, the norm has to be one that is acceptable to the members of that society.

One way of expressing society's will with respect also to alternative economic organisations is through the political process – in a democratic state, through the voting mechanism. Yet, the outcome of a political decision, democratic or otherwise, about a set of economic alternatives is not regarded as necessarily efficient by the economist. Indeed, he often is highly critical of democratic legislation. It follows that the norm of economic efficiency is distinct from an expression of the political will and therefore that, it may properly be criticised by reference to the adopted norm of economic efficiency.

Now, if there has to be a sanction for the norm of economic efficiency that is adopted, inasmuch as it has to be acceptable by the society for which it is intended, it cannot be grounded in any single individual's value judgments. And since, as indicated, it cannot be grounded either in the political will of that society, since it is regarded as independent of its continuing expression, the norm perforce has to rest on an ethical consensus, or on what I have called elsewhere (1969) a 'virtual constitution' – a consensus that is deemed to be impervious to political fashions and to the vicissitudes of political office. It is, of course, right for economists to debate the nature and the relevant components of the prevailing ethical consensus in their assessment of alternative criteria or norms of economic efficiency. For this debate is a way of reaching agreement on the facts of the matter. On the other hand, any debate about the appeal of their own individual value judgments, no matter how fascinating, has no immediate bearing on the question of the existing ethical consensus.

Assuming, then, that there does exist a consensus on which a norm of economic efficiency can be raised, it also follows not only that it is independent of current expressions of the political will – in Western democracies, independent of the expressed will of a majority of voters – but also that is transcends the political will.

As indicated earlier, there can be little doubt that the adoption of an *actual* Pareto improvement – one that makes 'everyone' actually better off than he was before – as the norm of economic efficiency would be ethically acceptable to society. But if no less restrictive a norm were acceptable, the economist would have very little allocative advice to offer society. Can we then assume that the B maxim, on which all allocative propositions and recommendations are in fact raised, is also ethically acceptable? Although at first glance it is far from compelling, a belief that society as a whole would agree to abide by it may draw upon a number of arguments arising from beliefs about the actual operation of the economy, namely: (1) that such changes that are in fact potential Pareto improvements do not generally have marked regressive distributional effects; (2) that a progressive tax system in any case provides safeguards against pronounced distributional consequences resulting from any economic change; (3) that over time a succession of economic changes that are countenanced by this Pareto criterion will not have significant regressive distributional effects and will therefore tend to bring about an actual Pareto improvement; and (4) that a succession of economic changes that meets the Pareto criterion has a better chance of raising the general level of welfare over time than a succession of economic changes that meets any other criterion.

An acceptance of Kaldor's distinction has at least the merit of assigning a role to the economist that is wholly independent of the political process. Yet, if economists do in fact give primacy to 'economic efficiency' over considerations of distribution, it is not necessarily because they accept the Kaldor distinction, nor necessarily because they believe that economic efficiency takes precedence over questions of distribution or equity. It is simply because, provided that they abide by the B maxim, their craft enables them, from time to time, to come up with unambiguous results or with specific numbers. Concern with distributional changes, on the other hand, enables them to come up only with very general statements or abstract theorems.

Nonetheless, the Kaldor distinction was rejected by Little (1950), who proposed a dual criterion raised on two premises: (i) that, *ceteris paribus,* an actual Pareto improvement is a good thing; and (ii) that, *ceteris paribus,* a 'better' distribution is a good thing. The dual criterion he proposed, that the economic change be sanctioned if it meets either form of a potential Pareto improvement without making the distribution of income worse off, purports to be one that accords with one or both of his premises.

Without implicating Little in the suggestion, it is possible to regard his premises (i) and (ii) as an interpretation of society's ethical consensus. If the interpretation were correct, and assuming that there was an accord on the meaning of a 'better' distribution, any properly drawn conclusions deriving from the premises – whether purely allocative, purely distributional or, as would be more common, partaking of both – would be entirely independent of any politically determined outcome or proposal. The economist would therefore be in a position to criticise legislation or executive action on both allocative and on distributional grounds. For his criticisms and recommendations would have ethical sanctions that transcend the ephemeral decisions of the political process.[5]

However, as it has been shown impossible to decompose this dual welfare criterion into the apparently acceptable ethical premises (i) and (ii),[6] the Pareto B maxim has once more to stand on its own as the basic premise on which all allocative propositions and calculations are raised.

III   The Possibility of a Positive Allocation Economics

The preceding summary interpretation of developments in welfare economics is by way of a ground-clearing operation to enable us to perceive more clearly the nature of the impasse that allocation economics seems to have reached as a result of continued economic growth and social change in the West.

We have expressed the B maxim above as $II \text{ p } I$ wherever $\Sigma v_{II} > \Sigma v_I$. Such a maxim is indicative of a normative allocation economics, which is how the subject is generally understood. It is, however, possible to conceive allocation economics as a positive subject. Exactly the same data may be presented to society or its representatives by the economist, although without his attaching to the results any prescriptive content. That is to say, from the calculation $\Sigma v^{II} > \Sigma v_I$, the economist does not infer that $II \text{ p } I$. The economist can restrict himself simply to the gathering of data in the form of expected valuations, which, when aggregated, show that $\Sigma v_{II} > \Sigma v_I$ or that $\Sigma \Delta v > 0$. He can explain his methods and the meaning of the data when cast in this form, and offer the resulting figure as an input to the decision-making process in society.

If the economist elects to follow this positive approach, the mere fact that for some mooted project $\Sigma \Delta v > 0$ does not, of itself, warrant the recommendation that the project be adopted. Indeed, there is now no ground on which the economist, *qua* economist, may challenge the allocative decisions reached by the political process. He may, of course, always draw attention to the economic consequences of the course of action to be adopted and give his opinion that, on balance, they are favourable or unfavourable. What he cannot do, however, is to pronounce the politically determined allocation to be good or bad by reference to an independent economic criterion. Put otherwise, he may no longer judge the allocation to be 'economically efficient' or 'economically inefficient' by reference to a criterion that transcends current expressions of political opinion.

Clearly, then, if allocation economics is to be treated as a normative branch of the subject, the economist has to believe that the B maxim is indeed sanctioned by society. In particular, in order for the B maxim to be independent of any political expression about allocative matters, and for all the propositions raised upon the B maxim to be relevant for that society such maxim has to be grounded in an ethical consensus.[7]

IV A Consensus also on Exceptions to the Basic Maxims

However, if the economist opts for a normative allocation economics, consistency demands that it be raised entirely on an 'ethical base' as distinct from what we may call a 'utilitarian base'.[8] And it is from the implications of this consistency that problems arise. For although we may continue to suppose that society, in its ethical capacity, accepts the B maxim in ordinary circumstances, there can be circumstances in which society would unanimously reject it. The economist who ignores all exceptional circumstances of this sort, and continues to base his allocative recommendations entirely on the criterion $\Sigma\Delta v > 0$, is said here to be building his allocative propositions upon a 'utilitarian base', which is to say that he restricts himself to the utilities, or welfares, of the individuals affected as expressed in their own valuations (whether declared or inferred), without exception. If he does so, however, his recommendations may no longer claim to be grounded in the ethics of society, and therefore they may no longer be applicable or relevant to that society. For example, a person B may be willing to sell himself into servitude for the rest of his life to person A for a sum that is smaller than the most A is willing to pay him. Alternatively, a poor man B may agree to his being flagellated by a rich man A for a sum that ensures mutual gains. Ignoring externalities, the bargain that could be struck in either case would, of course, meet the B maxim;[9] indeed, such bargains would effect actual

Pareto improvements. Yet, the economist who in consequence recommended that the transaction take place would be prescribing a course of action that runs counter to the prevailing ethical consensus in the West.

Clearly, if a normative allocation economics is to be a valid instrument, as it can be only if it accords with the prevailing ethics of society, it cannot be raised in all circumstances on a utilitarian base. Ultimately, it has to be raised on an ethical base. Thus, in addition to the difficult problems of measurement that the economist faces in deducing allocative propositions or in calculating net social benefits, he has now also to vet his results in the light of his understanding of society's ethics. Adherence at all times to the B maxim is therefore not enough.

But this is not all. The B maxim subsumes the ethical validity also of the A maxim. Yet there can also be occasions on which society would not regard adherence to the A maxim as ethical either; it would refuse, that is, to be bound by the individual valuations that comprise the data of $\Sigma\Delta v$. The calculation of externalities in a cost–benefit analysis provides a useful example. Thus, a distinction can be made between 'tangible' external diseconomies, on the one hand, which cover the range of familiar pollutants that are commonly quoted for illustrative purposes in the economic literature, and, on the other hand, 'intangible' external diseconomies, which comprehend people's responses to a change even where no physical discomforts are anticipated therefrom. A well-known example of the latter is the 'interdependent utilities' hypothesis, in which each person's welfare is a function also, positive or negative, of the level of welfare (or, by extension, of the income or possessions) of others.

If a person B is expected to suffer as a direct result of the noise or fumes emitted by the automobiles of group A, the cost of the damage he sustains – as measured, say, by his expenditures directed to reducing the damage plus a minimal compensation for the residual inconveniences suffered – should indeed be entered into the $\Sigma\Delta v$ calculation of net social benefit. For it is reasonable to believe that such a cost will be endorsed as a legitimate item in measuring the social value of the project in question. In contrast, if the automobiles of group A have no effect whatever on person B's health and cause him no inconvenience, his welfare may yet decline in consequence only of his envy of group A. If this be the case, it is reasonable to suppose that the considered opinion of society will be wholly unsympathetic to his claim for compensation. Thus, if our allocation economics is erected upon an ethical base, as it should be, this distinction between 'tangible' and 'intangible' externalities – ignored in an allocation economics erected upon a utilitarian base – can be crucial in the economic calculation of net social benefit.

Clearly, this sort of distinction between 'tangible' and 'intangible' effects is operative also in the field of public works and economic policy generally. If, for example, a project were to raise the incomes of a group of people, the additional income would be included among the positive benefits of the project. The fact that awareness of this group's material improvement will also cause resentment among members of another group may in some circumstances enter strongly into a political decision. But in its ethical capacity society may well repudiate the idea of counting as costs the envy claims of the latter group on a par with the claims, say, of the financial losses or physical discomforts of some other group. It is possibly true that modern society is one in which the Commandment, 'Thou shalt not covet thy neighbour's property' is honoured by individuals more in the breach than in the observance. But if, as yet, society accepts the tenth Commandment as part of its ethical code, the inclusion of envy claims in a calculation of net social benefit violates the ethical consensus.

On reflection, however, it is manifest that we cannot stop here. If, in its ethical capacity, society is deemed to discountenance the envy or resentment experienced by people at the good fortune of others, to the extent of repudiating any claims arising from these 'intangible' externalities in an economic calculation of net social benefit, consistency also requires that society's ethical position be extended to cover the individuals' valuations of market and collective goods also. For society may well have strong ethical reservations about the motives that impel people to buy certain goods – motives such as resentment, spite, hatred, exhibitionism or merely a desire to keep up with the Joneses. Even where the motives are not deserving of censure, society may regard them with contempt enough, as being too petty or trivial, and rule that their reckoning be dismissed in any calculation designed to determine a reallocation of resources.

V Erosion of the Consensus Necessary for a Normative Allocation Economics

Allowing that a normative allocation economics is faced with the problem not simply of describing or calculating the money equivalence of the effects on the welfare of individuals arising from different economic changes, but also with the problem of prescribing economic changes for a particular society, we reach the following conclusion. The economist, having to base his normative allocative propositions on an ethical consensus is also saddled with the task of determining the ethical judgments of society with respect to a wide range of possible transactions. Unless he is successful in his endeavours, society will (or ought to) ignore his economic recommendations or calculations. As a corollary, then, the economist will have no criterion of economic efficiency to juxtapose against a politically determined allocation.

Clearly, such a task is easier to discharge the lower the level of consumption in a society and the slower its pace of change. A society in which goods are scarce in a more literal sense, and in which the patterns of consumption and production are largely determined by tradition, is one for which the economist may prescribe with confidence, in the belief that allocative propositions or calculations derived directly from a utilitarian base will be little different from those derived from an ethical base. Within a modern growth economy, on the other hand, in which it may be alleged, and is indeed frequently alleged, that a 'Jones effect' is increasingly important, or that personal attire is increasingly exhibitionist or that the norms of taste are declining, or that much of the economy's output appears to be increasingly trivial, if not regrettable, the task of the normative allocation economist is not enviable. In such circumstances it can reasonably be contended that the ethical consensus, to which the normative economist has to defer, is itself breaking down. Worse yet, if the consumption of some goods or some activities is believed by some proportion of the population to be unworthy or degrading, and at the same time is believed by the remainder to be innocuous, if not liberating, the task of the welfare economist becomes impossible.

Therefore, *if,* as is commonly asserted, the so-called permissive society, the child of Western affluence, is 'pluralistic' in the sense that a traditional or a dominant belief system no longer exists, and there is a tendency toward approval of the idea that each person go his own way or 'do his own thing' – in effect judging his own actions and those of others by the light of his own privately-constructed conscience – the economist is no longer able to justify his prescriptive statements. Fragmentation, of course, does not have to go that far. Suffice it that two or more main groupings in society differ noticeably in their attitudes about the merits of the products, services and processes of modern technology. For instance, it may be impossible to secure a consensus that more of society's resources should be diverted from their existing employment in order to make available increased outputs of pornographic literature or of 'You're Welcome' flash signs for automobiles, or in order to extend the range of tobacco products regardless of expected consumer expenditure on these items.

Reflection on recent developments may well reinforce the suspicion that the consensus necessary for a normative allocation economics is dissolving. First, there appears to be a greater reluctance today among segments of the public – made explicit in debates between economists, lawyers and sociologists – to accept without reservation the judgment of the market in the face of substantial expenditures on commercial advertising designed to influence the valuations placed on goods by the buying public. Secondly, there is now the question of rates of depletion of a large number of fuels and materials. Although prior to the Second World War the question was one of limited concern to society at large, and of limited importance in economics, the current scale of resource consumption has made it a topic of growing concern to the public, at the same time as it has become one of controversy within the ranks of economists themselves.

There can be little room for doubt that there is currently a deep division of opinion among informed members of the public, including economists, about the wisdom of current and proposed economic policies in these respects, which amounts also to a division of opinion about whether the valuations currently attributed to 'finite' resources (either under existing economic arrangements or under 'ideal' competitive arrangements) have any normative significance. Certainly, a number of reputable economists have argued that the existing valuations of fuels and minerals, and their current rates of consumption, cannot be justified by reference to any criterion that excludes the opinions of future generations.[10]

Finally, there is a growing agreement that, inasmuch as the untoward consequences of consumer innovations – one thinks in this connection of food additives, chemical drugs and pesticides, synthetic materials and a variety of new gadgets – tend to unfold slowly over time, their valuations at any point of time by the buying public (as determined by the market prices to which individual purchases adjust) may bear no relation whatever to the net utilities conferred over time. Indeed, the very pace of change today with respect to new models and new goods, it can be cogently argued, is such that it is no longer possible for the buying public to learn from its own experience to assess the relative merits of a large proportion of the goods coming on to the market. In consequence, society can have no confidence that the valuations of such goods have any *ex post* correspondence with people's subjective wants (whether socially approved or not) as to justify them, on the standard argument, as indicators of claims on society's resources.

Assuming that this latter belief becomes so widely accepted as virtually to become unanimous, it follows that, for a growing proportion of goods, the subjective valuations, upon which the normative allocation economist has to depend, will no longer be indicative even of the overall subjective utilities of the buyers. On the other hand, the continuance, instead, of a division of belief about the extent and importance of this development must also act to prevent the would-be normative economist from invoking an ethical sanction for his use of these valuations.

The reader will have noticed that, despite my opinion that there does not at present appear to be a relevant consensus, I have posed the question in tentative terms. The question is open to debate. And it has to be debated if the economist has any interest in vindicating his claim to be able to pronounce on the economic efficiency or otherwise of projects and policies.

We may, of course, have to conclude that there never has been a consensus in Western countries for fifty, or a hundred, or more years, and that only in a tradition-bound society, connected perhaps with a low-level of technology, can such a consensus exist. Whatever the conclusions reached, however, it is high time that the economist took stock of the validity today of his allocative prescriptions and his statements, numerical or otherwise, bearing on the economic efficiency of alternative projects and policies.

Of course, on particular issues the would-be normative economist may be able to speak with greater confidence than on others. He may have no hesitation in employing Dupuit's arguments in calculating the net benefits of a bridge, or in calculating the net benefits of a better system of food production or distribution in one of the poorer countries in the world – at least, if he is willing to disregard the possible long-run effects associated with the growth of population. But for many of the public projects in an affluent society, even where they are designed to provide the population with lower cost inputs of different forms of energy or basic materials, the conscientious normative economist can no longer speak with authority. For he is amply aware that the values to be placed on such basic inputs are part of a highly controversial topic and, moreover, that such inputs are used in a wide range of items and gadgets about whose social justification the community may be deeply divided.

VI   Summary and Conclusions

First, I argued: (1) that in order for economic allocative propositions to be regarded as normative, and by implication independent of politically determined allocative decisions, the maxims on which an allocation economics are raised must conform with the ethical consensus of the society for which it is intended; (2) that the basic maxims in use today are two in number, being the Pareto criterion (maxim B), which subsumes acceptance also of maxim A, that individual valuations alone should count; (3) that if these maxims do *not* accord with the ethical consensus of the society in question, an economic allegation to the effect that any particular politically-determined allocative decision is 'inefficient' cannot be vindicated; and (4) that in that event the role of the allocative economist is reduced to one of gathering information for the use of political decision-makers, whose authority for resolving and pronouncing upon allocative issues is final.

Granted that the above arguments are accepted, I then went on to make the following observations about the actual society or nation that is today often referred to as Western, liberal and democratic: (i) that a number of arrangements that accord with the Pareto criterion, or even an actual Pareto improvement, are likely to be rejected by the ethics of any civilised society; (ii) that the individual valuations of external diseconomies sustained by a group, as the result of some economic change, do appear to be rejected by the ethics of a libertarian society, and indeed by those of contemporary society, wherever such externalities are regarded as the result only of unworthy responses to the good fortune of others; (iii) that by extension the specific individual valuations that are placed on a range of market or collective goods may also be rejected or discounted by an ethical consensus either by reference to the inferred motives of the consumers (whether 'sadistic', 'narcissistic', 'prurient', or simply 'keeping up with the Joneses') or, more directly, by reference to the nature and purposes of the goods themselves (for example, when such 'goods' are held by common consent to be pernicious to the health or character of the user, or damaging to the social or physical environment or to the amenity of others); and finally (iv) that if the ethical consensus has broken down in these relevant respects, there is no 'virtual constitution' by reference to which the allocative economist can vindicate his normative propositions.

From these arguments and observations I then drew the following two conclusions. (1) Whereas the normative allocation economist should be able without much difficulty to take cognisance of (i), and possibly (ii) also, it would impose on him a considerable strain to have to adjust his allocative propositions and calculations to take account of a social situation (iii) in which an existing consensus had, at some historical stage, become intricately discriminating in its assessment of the worth of individual valuations. (2) However, of more immediate concern is the possibility that the affluent countries of the West, where growth is powered by continuing technological innovations, are moving closer to the breakdown of an ethical consensus, as mentioned in (iv) above. *If* such a society is divided in its ethical judgments about issues involving taste, propriety, decency and morality (as in fact is commonly observed), or in its convictions about the reliability or significance of individual valuations in the presence of commercial advertising, resource depletion and rapid change (as appears to be the case), then there can be no consensus, either, about what sort of individual valuations are to count. Indeed, on a yet more general level, at which judgments about particular sorts of goods are not explicitly in issue, the problem is compounded by doubts, increasingly expressed during the last two decades, as to whether – as implied by employment of $\Sigma \Delta v > 0$ as a normative economic criterion – more is always better than less both at the individual and at the community level. Under these conditions it is obvious that the task of the normative allocation economist is impossible to discharge. For his prescriptive propositions no longer have the ultimate sanction of an ethical consensus.[11]

It follows that, *if* the circumstances described in (iv) prevail, the more restricted conception of the role of the economist, as one whose task is simply to describe the economic consequences expected to follow from the introduction of alternative projects or policies, becomes the appropriate one. And the calculations of Σv or of Δv, currently used in allocation and cost–benefit analysis, then become no more than a convenient and popular method of presenting the economic effects expected from a proposed policy or project. Such net benefit aggregates, of course, no longer carry any independent economic recommendation. They are of value only in so far as they are made use of by the political authority as an input into the decision-making process – an input to which any weight (including a zero weight) can be attached.

VII   Epilogue

Assuming that the tentative observations (iii) and/or (iv) are reinforced by sociological research, continued use of the term 'economic efficiency' would be misleading, inasmuch as it conveys the notion of an independent criterion by which such efficiency can be determined; whereas if the condition mentioned in observation (iv) were to prevail, there could be no appeal to an ethical consensus that transcends the current will of society as expressed in its political mechanisms. This conclusion, incidentally, holds for all levels of economic efficiency. For once the ethical consensus by which individual valuations are to be judged has eroded, there can be no virtue either in a movement toward an *exchange optimum* (realised in respect of market 'goods' by an equilibrium in which members of society consume all they wish at the prevailing set of prices) or in a movement toward a *production optimum* (realised in an equilibrium in which, with given factor supplies, it is impossible to produce more of all 'goods').

Terms such as (a) 'increased economic efficiency' or (b) 'optimal position', whether used within a partial or general equilibrium context, may, of course, continue to be used by economists, although only as a sort of professional shorthand respectively for (a) an economic change for which $\Sigma \Delta v > 0$ or (b) an economic situation for which $\Sigma \Delta v \leq 0$, where the vs refer either to the individual valuation of all of the goods and bads experienced by members of society or else to any specified category of them.

After all, there is no good reason why the economist should allow the elaborate structure of allocation economics to go to rust merely because, just at present in the West, there are no foundations in which to embed it. There may well be other and more traditional societies in which the required consensus exists. What is more, even if there are no existing ethical consensuses, one may yet emerge from the ethically fragmented or, to use the common euphemism, 'pluralistic' societies of the West. In the meantime, however, so far as the West is concerned, prescriptive economics will have to go into cold storage.

Notes: Chapter 21

1 As with other phenomena, drawing a firm dividing line between one category and another is a difficult task. But the categories are worth distinguishing whenever a large number of instances fall easily into one or the other.
2 Some brief remarks on the subject of equity, suggestive of its importance in an allocative context, can be found toward the close of my 1971 paper.
3 To deny this interpretation it is necessary to deny also that a conclusion that 'on economic grounds' a situation *II* is ranked above a situation *I* implies that 'on economic

grounds' *II ought* to be adopted whenever the costs of the changeover from *I* to *II* are zero.
4 The possibilities for apparent contradiction – the movements from situation *I* to situation *II* and from *II* to *I* both meeting the Pareto criterion – do not affect the validity of the argument, which would hold even if conditions were such that contradictions of this sort could never arise. The reader interested in distinguishing two sources of possible contradiction, and in appraising their significance, is referred to my 1976 paper.
5 It is doubtful whether the writings about the concept of a social welfare function (SWF) for society is a part of the literature of welfare economics on this definition. Abstracting from the influence upon them of continued political debate, the individual SWFs, like individual valuations, may be accepted by the economist, or political scientist, as basic data. Yet, assuming that acceptable rules can be agreed upon for constructing a SWF for society from all the individual SWFs, the resulting SWF for society can hardly be said to be part of an ethical consensus. True, one of the rules proposed for passing from individual SWFs to a SWF for society is the Pareto rule (expressible as dominance). Other rules are such as to reject arbitrary decisions and inconsistencies. However, each individual is, so to speak, invited to go beyond revealing his pattern of choice for his own goods and factors and, *inter alia,* to rank alternative amounts of goods and factors for all individuals in society.

In effect, then, each economic man ranks alternative distributions according to his personal preferences. If from these individual rankings a social ranking of distributions can be derived, this resulting ranking is of a *political* nature, not an ethical one. In fact, the distributional aspects of the individual SWFs, although (more realistically) in terms of structure, were isolated by Thurow (1971) in order to construct therefrom the distributional structure of a SWF for society. By allowing each member of society to place a compensating variation (positive or negative in value) on each of the alternative distributional structures to be considered, he presented the distributional structure that commands the largest aggregate value of compensating variations as that which is preferred by society – again, however, a political solution, not an ethical one.
6 The fact that Little's attempt was unsuccessful, as explained in my 1965 paper, is not important for the purpose of this essay. We may, if we wish, continue to ignore all the apparent paradoxes that inhere in welfare criteria based on hypothetical compensation. The paradoxes have, in any event, been resolved in my 1973 paper.
7 It is perhaps unnecessary to point out at this juncture that the distinction being made here between 'normative' and 'positive' propositions differs from that proposed in connection with welfare economics by Archibald (1959) and has graver consequences. In his paper Archibald argued that controversies about appropriate welfare criteria are futile, since it is open to any economist to construct or define a welfare criterion that interests him; that such a definition may well take a simple form, as involving, say, an overall expansion of the production possibility surface; and that since in principle the fulfilment of such adopted criteria can be the subject of empirical tests, welfare economics should be regarded as a branch of positive economics.

As I remarked in my 1960 survey article, however, if welfare economics is not to be conceived as a private game for connoisseurs but rather as a study seeking to elaborate propositions that have general validity for the welfare of the society for which they are intended, its fundamental premises have to accord with the ethics of that society. It is not surprising, then, that much of the controversy about welfare economics should address itself to the question of criteria that will indeed be sanctioned by the ethics of society.

The choice I am concerned with in this essay is that between, on the one hand, the possibility of a normative welfare economics, or at least a normative allocation economics, from which prescriptive propositions for society are derived, and, on the other hand, a purely descriptive study of allocative problems, from which (no matter how the data are organised) no prescriptive propositions for society follow at all.

(Whether or not the fulfilment of an adopted criterion for social welfare can be directly tested has no bearing whatever on the normative nature of the criterion.)

8 A distinction introduced in my 1971 paper.

9 I have excluded externalities in these examples lest the reader be tempted to switch inadvertently to a 'utilitarian' base – to conclude that, once all relevant externalities are taken into account, it must appear that $\Sigma\Delta v > 0$, in which case the proposed economic arrangements cannot meet the Pareto criterion. Whether aggregate valuations are positive or negative, however, these arrangements violate the ethical consensus from which the economist derives justification for his criterion.

10 For a review and bibliography of this literature, consult Page (1977).

11 Allowing that existing Western democracies correspond with the description of social situation (iv), there is nothing to prevent liberalist economists from asserting sturdily that society has no right whatever to sit in judgment on the declared preferences of any individual (provided that he is adult and not insane). And they may reinforce such assertions by argument, and by illustrations, current and historical, of the folly of society's acting on any presumption other than that each man knows best his own interests. But until such time as their arguments prevail, and the liberalist doctrine is absorbed into the ethics of contemporary society, allocative prescriptions of economists raised on a utilitarian base remain without constitutional sanction.

References

Archibald, G. C. (1959), 'Welfare economics, ethics and essentialism', *Economica,* new series, vol. 26 (November).

Arrow, K. J. (1951), *Social Choice and Individual Values* (New York: Wiley).

Kaldor, N. (1939), 'Welfare propositions in economics', *Economic Journal.*

Little, I. M. D. (1950), *A Critique of Welfare Economics* (London: *Oxford University Press*).

Mishan, E. J. (1960), 'A survey of economics, 1939–1959', *Economic Journal* (June).

Mishan, E. J. (1965), 'The current debate on welfare criteria', *Oxford Economic Papers* (June).

Mishan, E. J. (1969), *Welfare Economics: An Assessment* (Amsterdam: North-Holland).

Mishan, E. J., (1971), 'The postwar literature on externalities', *Journal of Economic Literature* (March).

Mishan, E. J. (1973), 'Welfare criteria: resolution of a paradox', *Economic Journal* (September).

Mishan. E. J. (1976), 'The use of compensating and equivalent variations in cost–benefit analysis', *Economica* (May).

Page, T. (1977), *Conservation and Economic Efficiency* (Baltimore: Johns Hopkins).

Thurow, L. (1971), 'The income distribution as a pure public good', *Quarterly Journal of Economics* (May).

Weisbrod, B. A. (1968), 'Income redistribution effects and benefit–cost analysis', in S. B. Chase Jr (ed.), *Problems in Public Expenditure Analysis* (Washington, DC: Brookings Institution).

22

Whatever Happened to Progress?

I Introduction

The idea of Enlightenment can be traced back through the centuries, but for the West the idea is rather more specific and has its origins in what used to be known as the 'European Renaissance', which, beginning in Italy in the fifteenth century, soon spread to the rest of Europe. The quickening interest in the secular world, the world of art and nature, later took in the 'scientism' of Francis Bacon and Galileo and moved on into the eighteenth century, by which time it appeared to have reached its high point. Influenced by the French philosophers and the encyclopaedists, by Comte and Condorcet, the movement began to associate itself with agnosticism and empiricism, on the one hand, and, on the other, with a boundless optimism about the future and a growing concern for social justice. Not surprisingly, it was during this period, and particularly during the second half of the eighteenth century, that this broadly humanistic and humanitarian movement allied itself with the notion of progress as we understand it today: at first, intellectual and moral progress, which fused into a belief in the perfectibility of man; but later, under the impact of the writings of economists – Cantillon in France and, in the first half of the nineteenth century, the philosophical radicals in Britain, and others too numerous to mention – material progress also. The faith in progress, and especially material progress, reached its apogee in mid-Victorian England, and that faith, although less powerful today, has never lost its hold over the minds of the intellectual guardians of Western civilisation.

The result of these developments has been a continuing climate of 'respectable' intellectual opinion, reaching back at least 200 years – a climate of opinion that (for lack of a better word) we may refer to as the *Established Enlightenment*. Although it has never been so strong as to determine the course of events in opposition to strong vested interests or political repression, the Established Enlightenment could never be wholly ignored by the state. I do not argue that this intellectual climate of opinion could always produce a single view on any contemporary issue, but only that it was the source of inspiration from which flowed an enlightened dialogue – one that continues today between members of the middle class 'intelligentsia', the professional classes, the scientific and academic community, and the 'higher journalism'. And it is one of the sadder facts of political life that – far from there being a liberal tolerance extended to any arguable point of view at variance with those currently held by the Established Enlightenment – anyone so bold as publicly to challenge any of its cherished preconceptions (as I know to my cost) cannot hope to escape ridicule, abuse and unconscionable misrepresentation.

The thesis I wish to propound here is that, if we are concerned chiefly with social welfare, or with what is loosely spoken of as 'the quality of life', the benefits espoused by the Established Enlightenment – beliefs that have lighted our way for the past two centuries – are inadequate and inexpedient. They are just beginning to be challenged, perhaps to be challenged too late.

The idea of progress – which, broadly interpreted, encompasses the growing and interacting forces of knowledge and wealth – today holds the key position among the ideas of the Established Enlightenment. The growth of knowledge is pursued almost as an end in itself. (I say *almost,* because the pursuit of knowledge is occasionally justified, albeit briefly, by reference to seemingly accepted but vaguely defined ends, such as 'emancipation' or 'the realisation of human potential', or as a heroic destiny, a challenge man must not shirk, and so on.) As for the growth of material wealth, its desirability is hardly questioned; it receives occasional benediction in the economic literature from such phrases that depict economic growth as 'widening the area of choices open to men'.

The growth of wealth and knowledge together has made possible the continued advance in universal education – again regarded in the main as a self-evident good, although strengthening its appeal by phrases about 'freeing men from ignorance and superstition', or about 'promoting increased understanding and tolerance between men', and justifying its finance by the state as promoting equality of opportunity and encouraging the growth of skills required by modern societies that depend increasingly on sophisticated techniques.

According to the faithful, moreover, with the increased tolerance anticipated from the spread of wealth and knowledge, women will be emancipated from disabilities long and (until recently) patiently endured, social bigotry will disappear, and men and women of diverse races and creeds will live together in harmony.

Closely connected with the presumption by economists in favour of free international trade is that in favour of free migration of peoples – a presumption that, by reference to social justice, extends itself easily enough to the notion of increased mobility, geographical and, of course, also social and occupational. A yet further extension, allied with the presumption that favours the spread of knowledge, or at least of information, reinforces the case for increased media of communication.

A final example is the belief – still widely held, although at one time amounting to an article of faith among the Established Enlightenment – that continued progress will eventually overcome all the chronic social evils; poverty, corruption, crime, war. For sustained material progress not only implies the elimination of poverty, an end that is good in itself, but also the removal of conditions under which delinquency and criminal activity flourish.

These and other 'enlightened' beliefs have been, and to a large extent still are, held by men of otherwise different political ideologies. They are held by socialists, by liberals and by communists. For what separates the liberal (at least the old type liberal) from the socialist or communist lies simply in the deep-seated differences of opinion, amounting to ideological conviction, about the efficiency of the means whereby such believed goods are realised. The old liberal firmly believed in the efficacy of private enterprise and decentralised markets, and in limiting the compass of state activity, as the surest means of promoting economic growth and meeting the wants of citizens and consumers. In contrast, the socialist or communist holds that these ends are more surely realised by centralised planning and state custody. In particular, the communist holds that social justice and the good life require strengthening the state against the 'enemies of the people', in appropriating the means of

communication in order to spread 'the truth' among the masses, and in monopolising education so as to provide equal opportunity and so as to undertake massive scientific research.

Although my own commitment in this imperfect world of disintegrating societies is to a liberal democracy, to a decentralised and institutionally pluralistic order – an order that is increasingly difficult to maintain in the face of rapid technological advance and manifest economies of scale – it is so only on broad political grounds, chiefly as a safeguard against mounting encroachment by the state. Other than that I do not care to choose between the rival ideologies. In particular, it is becoming harder to decide the respective merits of centralised and decentralised planning in terms of economic efficiency, narrowly conceived. Not that it matters much to me anyway, as I am far from enamoured of the economist's idea of economic efficiency or of economic progress as commonly understood.

II Photo Album of Progress

Rather than couch my arguments in abstract and general terms, I shall present the reader with a succession of tableaux. First, I shall depict, sparingly, the social scene today compared with the prewar period, and then invoke examples to illustrate how these 'enlightened' beliefs – some of the chief ones and some of the auxiliary ones – are coming to conflict with the basic wants of common aspirations of ordinary men and women. It will be both convenient and instructive, although not necessary, to take our bearings by reference to a Western-type society – one boasting liberal–democratic institutions of a sort, and one in which, although a mixed economic system prevails, there are still the remnants of a presumption in favour of private enterprise and in favour of economic growth. (As a footnote comment I ought to add, however, that the general thrust of my conclusions would not be deflected if I developed my thesis by reference instead to some hypothetical, ideally decentralised, perfectly functioning, market system, as envisaged perhaps by Milton Friedman – one that has the economic textbook virtue of providing the consumer with whatever goods the world market produces at the lowest prices.)

Only if measured by technological achievement and commercial aggrandisement does our civilisation, the civilisation of the West in the 1970s, rate high. Apart from these undeniable technical and commercial achievements, the sort of progress impelled by economic growth, and to some extent influenced by the

Established Enlightenment, looks impressive enough only if one does not look at it too closely.

Thus, a quick glance down the credit side of the ledger would reveal the following items: maintenance, until recently, of something close to full employment since the war; a continued rise in 'real' income *per capita;* a phenomenal expansion of higher education, accompanied by a rise in the school-leaving age; a vast proliferation of social welfare services provided by the state; an extension of the suffrage (to younger people in Britain and the United States and, effectively, to many blacks in the southern states of the United States); a reduction of class distinctions and a reduction in regional and racial discrimination; an increased recognition of the rights of self-determination of once subject peoples; a growing awareness by women, and also by some men, that the fair sex was being unfairly treated and, in response, some incipient remedial legislation; the appearance in almost every household of the affluent West of new labour-saving gadgets and television sets; an unprecedented increase of mobility and, over the last two decades especially, increased foreign travel for the multitude. In addition, some possibly controversial, but nonetheless authentic, 'enlightened' measures have been introduced into a number of countries: for instance, the abolition of corporal punishment and of the death penalty, the abolition of theatre censorship, plus a number of smaller legal adjustments making for a more lenient attitude toward sexual deviance, toward juvenile violence, and toward overtly aphrodisiac literature and entertainment.

The traditional liberal, and indeed the non-revolutionary socialist also, may well be excused for feeling satisfied with the bounty of progress as he surveys these features of national life and compares them with the social scene some fifty or even twenty-five years ago. The fashionable intellectual, he is pleased to observe, is today quite properly a little touchy on the treatment of non-whites in the community. This same trendy spirit, he will also observe, is by and large 'anti-Victorian', 'anti-imperialist' and condescending of patriotic sentiment and has a marked predilection for debunking past heroes, national myths and anything that savours of 'the glorious days of old'. Withal, it exhibits an impatience of reverence, privilege and ceremony.

Nonetheless, if the advance of a civilisation is associated in our minds with order, with propriety, with a refinement of sensibilities, with the acceptance of norms and procedures, with a sense of things being in place, with ideals of harmony and proportion, then the kind of progress we have experienced over the last few decades can hardly fail to arouse also a great deal of cynicism, if not alarm.

A society has come into being whose members are daily encouraged to make invidious comparisons, and habitually to feel disgruntled at not having more – tendencies that are sometimes euphemistically referred to as 'motivated'. For the momentum of economic growth in the wealthier countries, it is believed, can be sustained only by the unremitting efforts of industry to create dissatisfaction with existing possessions and to promote unbridled covetousness. The resulting restlessness and discontent are accompanied and aggravated by a degenerating environment, and by the movement from the villages and smaller towns to the increasingly congested and polluted metropolises and their suburbs.

Each year sees more massive office blocks erected in our large cities, cheap, nasty and, for the most part, depressing. With the passage of time, once distinguished streets and squares have become tawdry with amusement arcades and sleazy bazaars. The litter of the 'throw-away' society is everywhere in evidence, with the means of sex titillation displayed at every corner news-stand and offered in various doses by the greater number of modern films. With each new summer millions more surge like lemmings toward places that rapidly become like the places they want to get away from. The determination of so many of the young today to look different has come to defy space and time; it has reached proportions where virtually 'anything goes', and where campuses and sometimes railway stations appear to have been taken over for a marathon tramps' carnival. As trends go, the number of cars on the roads, noise levels in the cities and the number of air passengers are expected to continue to grow year by year. The figures for crime and juvenile violence over the past two decades continue their inexorable climb upward. 'White collar' crime – business theft, embezzlement, bribery, tax frauds – appears to be rampant in the United States. As the young today see it, 'everyone is on the make'.

Some of these unprepossessing features of modern societies – greed, corruption, degenerative activity, public spectacles of sadistic violence – it may be remarked, can be found in one form or another during certain periods of other civilisations, although admittedly on an incomparably smaller scale, since the means of communication were limited, cities fewer and smaller, and populations and their resources then but a fraction of a fraction of those available today. What is today deeply disquieting, however, is not only their unprecedented scale, but also the growing suspicion that all these unhappier features of Western civilisation that have come into prominence since the Second World War are the products, perhaps the inevitable products, of 200 years of sustained economic growth in the West.

Such an outcome was never suspected by the brave reformers and humanists of the eighteenth-century Enlightenment. Nor did such disturbing possibilities ever cloud the splendid visions of those nineteenth-century apostles of progress, who – observing everywhere the spread of industry and knowledge, the establishment of institutions of learning and the introduction of labour-saving contrivances – foretold of a future of universal plenitude. harmony, leisure and culture. To expect that some great good will yet emerge from these unpromising developments – if only we press on with economic growth, with technical innovation, and with more liberal measures of aid and assistance – is to cling more tenaciously to doctrine as the facts become grimmer.

III Are We Approaching Human Fulfilment?

Concerning human needs, I think there is a fair consensus about them among thoughtful men. Like any other mammal, man has a need for physical activity and exertion. He also needs a sense of security, which depends upon the continuity and stability of institutions, upon a framework of law and custom, and upon his familiarity with places, people and things. Obviously, he also has a strong need of love and trust – a need to love and to be loved, to trust and to be trusted. In all of us too, there is a need for self-respect, allied to the need for love and trust but also deriving from the need for communal esteem; a man wants to feel that he matters to other people. And he craves too a distinct origin – an identity, a destiny, from which arises the desire to belong to a group, a folk, having a common history and a common pride. Irrational though it sounds in these wonderfully scientific times, he also wants to believe in a benevolent deity – in a source of infinite wisdom and compassion.

Finally, although stemming not directly from the same instinctual roots, but from a slow refinement of character and taste brought about by the civilising process, he aspires toward the good life – one offering him more leisure, more space, more margin to his life; one placing him closer to the pulse of nature, yet offering him access to magnificent cities, where each building adds beauty and proportion to the whole and in which concourse and gaiety thrive.

Now, as a result of chance events or in the inherent nature of things, progress in its various manifestations, far from meeting these basic needs or realising our aspirations, has begun to run counter to them. For instance, the pursuit of knowledge for its own sake cannot always be vindicated by reference to human well-being. Unless the search for knowledge is itself motivated by humane ends, it can be destructive of people's contentment. The Copernican theory started a revolution in astronomy that was to displace man from his unique position at the centre of the universe, the chosen and beloved creature of the Lord, and to relegate him to some inconsequential speck of matter whirling about the rim of but one of an uncountable number of star systems in an infinite and inhospitable universe. Three centuries later another dedicated scientist, Charles Darwin, revealed his findings to the world, and in doing so drove another deadly shaft into the heart of men's cherished beliefs. Far from having descended from the angels, our ancestors could be traced through an evolving species back to primeval slime. And all the wonder and variety of nature that once affirmed the infinite wisdom of God was from thence to be understood as the outcome of the mindless forces of natural selection.

Thus, the disinterested pursuit of knowledge saps the spiritual sustenance of men. It destroys also the myths that shore up their morale, the bonds that hold them together, their ideas of kith and kin, their pride in their history and in their folk heroes – beliefs that one by one are doomed to be shattered by troops of eager young historians in search of professional recognition. There is, in short, much knowledge that we should be happier to live without.

As for increase in understanding, tolerance and humanity – the products, supposedly, of universal education – the allegation is blatantly at odds with the facts. Few periods of history reveal such rooted antagonisms based on differences in race and nationality. This is not altogether surprising. Higher education is today overwhelmingly vocational and highly specialised. Its over-riding purpose is to produce the manifold skills required by a complex technical society. It teaches men more and more about less and less. It narrows their horizons, weakens their imaginations, perverts their judgments and cramps their spirits.

Finally, the process by which, necessarily, knowledge advances bodes no good for men. The extent and depth of modern knowledge, scholarly and scientific, is beyond the imagination to grasp. Its further progress, on a myriad of fronts, depends above all on a continued splintering of already highly specialised fragments of knowledge. There are signs already of incipient breakdown in communication at various points along the extending frontiers of modern knowledge, although this is not to my purpose just now. What is to the purpose here, however, is that, as specialism grows, wisdom recedes. Not only does the specialist see no more than some of the technical aspects of what is basically a social problem; he also acquires an interest in bringing to bear on it as much of his own technique as possible, so making the world more complex and thus more vulnerable. And his success in doing so brings him his reward, since the greater the number of accidents and breakdowns in any complex technological system, whether foreseeable or unforeseeable, the more scope there is for his expertise and the stronger the case for devoting yet more funds to scientific research.

But to what avail? As one urban expert, Harland Cleveland, said: 'There isn't anything we do not know about the modern city; its demography, its water table, its engineering design, its slums, its economics, its politics. We just don't seem to know how to make it beautiful, accessible, safe, and clean.'

IV Emergent Consequences of the Transport and other Revolutions

Let us turn now to those technological innovations which have provided us, among other things, with the means of swift travel both within our own countries and to the furthest part of the earth. We are a generation privileged to enjoy the variety and treasure of the whole world, or at least we thought so in the immediate postwar period. We did not reckon then with the sheer pressure of numbers making itself felt through the automobile and the airliner. As I asserted on a previous occasion, the invention of the automobile is the greatest disaster to have befallen mankind. For sheer irresistible destructive power nothing, save perhaps the airliner, can compete with it. In our towns and cities every principle of architectural harmony has been perverted in the vain struggle to keep the mounting volume of motorised traffic from coming to a standstill. Clamour, dust, fume, congestion and visual distraction are the predominant features in all built-up areas.

Even where styles of architecture differ between cities – and they differ less from one year to the next – these traffic features impinge so blatantly and persistently on the senses as to submerge all other impressions. Whether we are in Paris, Chicago, Tokyo, Milan or Stockholm, or any of 10,000 other towns and cities, it is the choking din, the dust and endless swirl of motorised traffic, that dominate the scene. Yet, such is the

hypnotic power of this satanic contrivance that we continue frenziedly to create a physical environment that makes us increasingly dependent upon private motorised transport. Worse, we continue to follow with bated breath the fortunes of the automobile industry, regarded as the prime indicator of economic health and progress.

The social costs of this hapless choice of means of travel include not only the rapid erosion of traditional amenities. They also include such mundane facts that robbery, crime and violence today all depend heavily on the fast getaway car. Motorists kill off other people at the rate of about 140,000 each year (55,000 in the United States alone), and they maim for life well over a million people annually. Through the emission each year of millions of tonnes of foul gases, the automobile's contribution to sickness and death from cancer and from bronchial and other disorders is just beginning to be understood. We are just beginning to understand that perhaps the most impressive example of postwar growth is the increase in the number of places that everyone wants to get away from. What, in contrast, is already fully understood – but about which, for commercial reasons, nothing at all is being done – is the connection between air and motor travel and the greatest holocaust of natural beauty since the dawn of creation. The postwar tourist blight has ravaged the once famed beauty of practically every resort along the coastline of the Mediterranean, and much of the hinterland besides. As I wrote in 1967:

We have already, and within a few short postwar years, all but destroyed a heritage of tranquil unmarred natural beauty that had else endured the passage of centuries and millenia. With a hubris unmatched since the heyday of Victorian capitalism, and with a blindness peculiar to our own time, we have abandoned ourselves to ransacking the most precious and irreplaceable good the earth provides without thought to the desolation of the future and the deprivation of posterity.

Of course, it is not only the economist who knows that, relative to the social damage they inflict, motor car and air travel are vastly underpriced, and a variety of remedies continue to be mooted by the public. But the power wielded by automobile interests is awesome to behold, and the rationalisations invented for maintaining the existing bedlam by otherwise respectable politicians and writers would be amusing if their implications were less tragic.

What may yet be more subversive of social welfare are the kinds of goods that come to be produced by a commercial or consumer-oriented economy and the kinds of innovation favoured by a growth-oriented economy. These are aspects of economic life about which economists do not wish to pass judgment, but such aspects are, of course, critical to my thesis. A word, therefore, about each.

The kinds of goods produced by industry, in order to keep growing at all costs, are no more neutral in their effects on the character and taste of the citizen than are art, literature and entertainment. A society that creates institutions devoted to frenziedly gutting the earth's resources in order to meet that evergreen figment of the business world, 'the needs of industry', an industry that disposes annually of masses of trivia, can escape a sense of its own abasement only by surreptitiously perverting human instincts and civilised values. And I cannot see the existing economic momentum in the West being maintained over the future except by increasing the outputs of just such trivia – by the production of yet more of those 'luxuries' that are a form of 'neogarbage', or of goods that are positively inimical to health and sanity.

As for the trend in innovation, both process innovation and product innovation, it is perhaps inevitably of a labour-saving kind. This may seem no more than an economic platitude, yet it is fraught with fearsome consequences for human relationships. For this type of technological innovation, favoured by the growth-oriented economy, is undoubtedly such as to reduce over time the need for direct communication and direct dependence between men. Human contact has declined since the war with the growth of supermarkets, automatic lifts, turnstiles and vending machines, with increased ownership of motor cars, transistors and television sets, and it will continue to decline with the growth of computerisation in offices and patient-monitoring systems in hospitals, with closed circuit television instruction and teaching machines. We are in effect about to enter an era of incredible artifice in the purveying of services and entertainment – a veritable push-button world in which our whims are instantly to be gratified, although at the expense of our deeper human needs. The thought of such a world may elate the businessman and inspire the technocrat. But the inescapable consequence is that the direct flow of communication and sympathy between people becomes even thinner, and to that extent the quality of their lives becomes the poorer.

As a final instance, consider the broad social consequences of economic progress, irrespective of the goods it brings into being. Based as it is on rapid technological change, it is profoundly unsettling to ordinary men. The call by technologists is not merely for yet more change, but for the adoption of a state of continuous rapid change as a way of life in its own right. The emergence of something like this state of affairs was attested to by Alvin Toffler in his recent book, *Future Shock,* also in Gordon Taylor's new book, *Rethink: A Paraprimitive Solution.* These authors quoted evidence to show that all significant changes of situation or environment, whether regarded as good or bad, adversely affect a man's health. For the truth is that the psyche of man seeks a settled pattern of life, craves the reassurance of familiar landmarks, the solace of familiar sounds, scenes, faces and accents, a community of shared experiences and shared affection.

Alas for man! In response to the pressures for economic growth, all things about him are in a perpetual state of dissolution. Even if he does not move house or job every few years, the environment around him is continuously and visibly changing. Where there were once open fields or a small copse, there are now rows of new houses. Where once there was a woodland path, there is now a concrete highway. And amid the din of endless drilling, old or historic buildings are being reduced to rubble and their places taken by towering plate-glass office blocks. The sorts of goods a man buys also change year by year – the models, the designs, the packaging, even the flavour of the more common foods. There is no time to form tastes, to learn to discriminate, to come to anticipate the satisfaction of things that are tried and trusted.

In a society that cultivates obsolescence as a prime virtue, nothing lasts long enough to gather affection or evoke memories. And men themselves too live on the brink of obsolescence, apprehensive that the skills and the specialised knowledge they have acquired through diligence and effort over the years will, with some new innovation, become superfluous. Legions of academics and professionals struggle to keep abreast of the relentless advance of knowledge in their specialised fields. There is no respite for fear of being left behind to sink under the waves of anonymity. Thus is the new leisure transmuted into preoccupation and eternal study.

With all their shortcomings, then, as they would appear to a chrome-plated affluent consumer society, we may well envy the small-scale preindustrial communities of the past, steeped in nostalgia and tradition. In those unhurried days familiarity was unfeigned. There was time for the idiosyncracies of life to unfold, time for lasting attachments to form, time to idle and sit around and gossip and take no heed of the morrow.

V   Can the Young Save Us?

Let me pause to anticipate the reader's remonstrances: that I take too sentimental a view of the past and too gloomy a view of the present. Space does not suffice to defend myself against both charges. I have indicated elsewhere how – by counting centennial disasters, evoking 'black' plagues, quoting 'real' income figures, citing mortality statistics, describing primitive toilet facilities, and so on – a modern historian can easily misjudge the robust sense of well-being common among ordinary people in earlier civilisations. I shall therefore restrict myself briefly to answering the latter charge: that I pay no heed to the more hopeful signs about us.

Thus, notwithstanding the postwar growth in the wealthier countries of the incidence of violence and corruption, the decay of city centres, and the manifest collapse of standards of taste and propriety, optimistic voices can be heard on both sides of the Atlantic. They talk of a new awakening among the young, especially among the middle class young in America, who have become increasingly cynical of the Protestant ethic of their fathers, and who largely reject their materialism and their striving for respectability and status.

As the young themselves see it, they are breaking the fetters of traditional values and seeking a freedom from the pressure of society – a freedom to experiment in life styles, a freedom to 'do their own thing'. 'Hippy' colonies, less popular today than they were in 1970, account only for a small proportion of the growing army of seemingly easygoing footloose youngsters, ready to talk to anyone and to try anything.

If anyone is pinning his hopes for a brighter future on this development, let me urge him to think again. For if the colour of the garment that the young choose to wear differs from that of their parents, the shape is much the same. This becomes clearer once it is understood that the motto I once associated with the spirit of economic growth, 'enough does not suffice', has relevance not only to the acquisition of material goods, but also to any object or objective that compels the attention of the citizens of the new affluence, old or young. For the essence of the growth ethos is not materialism; it is insatiability. Although there has been a perceptible shift of emphasis from absorption in material accumulation to absorption in 'lifestyles', there has been no diminution of appetite. The young may preen themselves on being in a different league from their fathers, playing for different prizes. But whatever the prizes, the more of them the better. From head to foot, from crown to toe, they too are maximisers.

Their apparently unlimited tolerance is chiefly a product of the moral vacuum in which they are reared; in the main it reflects their growing insensibility and promiscuity. Their inordinate fondness for 'mixing' with the world takes them by land, sea and air, in every kind of vehicle and in every kind of company, to every city and resort over the globe – there, like disoriented termite colonies, to swarm into parks and squares; to pour through castles, palaces and galleries; to squat and sprawl, smoke and munch, over the once-hallowed steps of spired cathedrals. Travelling in groups, large or small, they extend their experience from the best hotels to the worst, seeking consciously to be equally at home everywhere; to 'slum' with the rich and 'slum' with the poor; to ape the clothes both of other countries and of other periods of history; to eat the food, borrow the accents, play the instruments and adopt the customs of other cultures; to enter the tabernacles and revel in the rituals, alike of primitive tribes and of ancient civilisations – in short, to be excluded from nothing that may pass for experience, bright or dull, good or evil, sublime or seamy.

Thus, the young of the affluent countries are today among the most ruthless and persistent plunderers of the earth's vanishing variety. Their unchecked gluttony, intensified by commercial interests, is today one of the most active forces at work combining to produce an admass civilisation and to promote a cultural entropy – one that is in the process of dissolving all hierarchies, flattening all barriers, blurring all distinctions, erasing the mosaic pattern of centuries, transforming the once rich diversity of our universe into an inextricably blended monotony.

The effect on the character of the young may seem to be of less consequence, but it is no less pernicious. For this craving for endless experimentation, for savouring new 'lifestyles', for tasting new experiences, is of the nature of a compulsion among them – a determination to wriggle like mad in every newly detected current of experience in the avid pursuit of hedonic satiation; a determination perhaps partially hindered by the few years' cramming necessary to acquire professional credentials, and later diluted only by economic constraint.

On reflection, I find these new postures, and the attitude that informs them, both less promising and less laudable than the stodgy 'bourgeois' values that are allegedly being rejected. Not only do they entail activities that are, conservatively speaking, no less profligate of natural resources; they also are a good deal further out on the scale of human folly. For after sitting through some bubble-gum courses on 'personality development', 'self-assertion', 'relationship enhancement', 'stereotype avoidance', 'creative awakening', 'cognitive amplification' and the like, being offered today by the extracurricular departments of American campuses, the fashion among these newly emancipated spirits is in effect to select their maxims and arrange their thoughts and feelings so as, above all, to be able to 'travel light', unhampered by affective ties. Indeed, as observed by H. Hendin in his *Age of Sensation* (1975), all too many of the young at American colleges are unabashedly resolved to avoid falling in love and, generally, to resist surrender to feelings of love and trust, since these feelings are perceived to retard pace and 'turnover', so encumbering the search for pleasure.

However, these fashionable excesses of the young are, on my interpretation of events, only the tip of the iceberg. Their prodigality is symptomatic of a spiritual malaise that pervades our civilisation. One has only to reflect on the growing range of expendable products, of 'luxuries', of exhibitionist attire, of extravagant inanities, currently absorbed (despite pockets of destitution) by the consumer society to recognise that today it is less than a half-truth to assert that industry serves the needs of people. For the continuing expansion of modern industry depends directly on its continuing success in enlarging the appetite of the consuming public, so as to enable it to engorge a burgeoning variety and volume of goods. Traditional restraints on self-indulgence must perforce give way. The unrooted society, the permissive society in fact, is one of the preconditions of sustained economic growth.

As I observed in my *Costs of Economic Growth* (1967), the secularisation of society, consequent upon the rising prestige of science and the collapse of ecumenical faith, has also contributed to this transformation. The emerging generation (in spite of its commendable concern with environmental and other causes) lives in a society without religion, without patriotism, without civic pride and apparently without transcendental purpose. Not surprisingly, it is impatient of authority and of any institution believed to impede its claims to immediate gratification. Increasingly, it espouses an 'own ethic' designed to rationalise its conduct, no matter how wayward or deviant, resting its case merely on the depth of its convictions.

Economic determinism is a frightening doctrine. But is it too far-fetched to trace both the animus and the success of women's liberation to those familiar labour-saving innovations that, over the century, have rendered their domestic services increasingly expendable? And what of the permissive society, which, beginning with the joyous rejection of 'Victorian' guilt, progresses to an abandonment of the vestigial sense of shame, moves on to a clamorous rejection of any

restraint on appetite and culminates in adopting the experience of pleasure as an infallible guide to the good life? It is surely a providential development by means of which the modern innovative economy, continuously under institutional compulsion to expand, can be kept going.

Yet this seemingly inevitable outcome produces a 'contradiction'. As Fred Hirsch perceived in his *Social Limits to Growth* (1976), the ethos of the permissive society, in so far as it erodes the traditional sense of personal responsibility and obligation, acts also to undermine the efficient working of the economic system itself, whether privately owned, state directed or mixed.

To where does this tend? I have argued elsewhere that economic growth in the West is producing innovations that create unprecedented social conflicts and ecological hazards, both of which demand increasing government control. This consequent trend toward more government is aggravated by the perils of the permissive society. For as the moral restraints on which any civilisation is founded are scrapped in the name of individual emancipation, so, in the name of public safety, must the state expand its powers. Internal repressive mechanisms are replaced by external ones.

The permissive society, it transpires, is the precursor of the totalitarian society.

VI   Can Society Move off the Growth Path?

If the reader accepts my interpretation of recent developments (although not perhaps without some reservations), and concurs in the broad conclusion that nothing very promising can be detected along the horizon toward which we are moving, he will surely be wondering whether the radical changes required to move us from the growth path are in fact politically feasible. Assuming always that popular opinion becomes increasingly sceptical of the ultimate beneficence of economic growth, will Western civilisation, which has for centuries been guided by the idea of progress – expressed in material plenty, in the advance of knowledge and in free institutions – be able to wrest itself gradually from the responses ingrained in its way of life? Will it be able to place science and technology under permanent constraint and otherwise reshape its institutions, in order to realise a saner society and a more viable economic system?

Attention to three features of the modern world tempt me to doubt it: (1) the conventional rationalisation, (2) entrenched interests, and (3) international distrust. We take them up in that order.

(1) *Conventional rationalisation* can be described as dogged persistence in the belief that, irrespective of the past record of science and technology, it is to science and technology that we must continue to turn for salvation. Certainly, if the application of some new technology results in distress or disaster, the remedy is invariably sought in more technology, never in less. This uncompromising spirit is epitomised in a sentence of Sir Peter Medawar's address to the British Association in 1969: 'The deterioration of the environment produced by technology is a technological problem for which technology has found, is finding, and will continue to find solutions.' While admitting the difficulties that technology will have to overcome, Sir Peter ended, inevitably perhaps, with an affirmation of faith in science. He scornfully dismissed the faint-hearted with the words: 'To deride the hope of progress is the ultimate fatuity, the last word in poverty of spirit and meanness of mind.'

I should have thought that the charge of 'the ultimate fatuity' ought, instead, to be reserved for that hubris which blinds a scientist to the enormity of the risks to which his continued research is subjecting the human race. Nonetheless, the sad fact is that many thoughtful people today would echo his sentiments. For to many scientists the new sorts of risks being incurred do not suggest the existence of limits to empirical research, beyond which we trespass at our peril. Rather they suggest, at worst, the existence of unsuspected mines, strewn along a zone through which we must pick our way carefully before entering the promised land.

As for members of the larger public in the affluent society, many of them are still high with hopes that sooner or later science will unearth some breath-taking discovery – some new pill or potion that prolongs youth, maintains sexual potency or cleaves the kernels of sensation. Perhaps it will effect some genetic breakthrough that will enable us all to have brilliant children. Perhaps it will learn to decode signals received by radiotelescopes, telling of a superior form of life, which, we naturally hope, will be benignly disposed to us.

The newspapers, of course, keep these hopes simmering by occasional headlines announcing some miraculous scientific achievement or other. And although our apprehensions also are aroused by popular reports of things to come, there are so many of us today who suffer from a sense of vacuity, an absence of purpose in life (for which 'motivation' is no substitute), that we cannot but hope that the future will have something exhilarating to offer. In fact, much of the popular support of science can be attributed to that

restlessness and discontent which are the product and the precondition of sustained economic growth. Indeed, with the spread since the war of populist sentiment, personal disadvantages and ordinary frustrations have come to be regarded by large numbers of people as intolerable forms of discrimination – as evidence of an urgent need for state provision and for the enactment of new rights.

And although there is a growing awareness among intellectuals that institutional changes alone may not suffice to usher in the millennium, that much of the inequality among people is basic and the tedium of life seemingly ineradicable, their hopes also turn toward a science for which, it is claimed, nothing is impossible. From today's massive research, it is hoped, ways and means will eventually be discovered for removing all the pain and frustration from people's lives and for making them whole and beautiful again. There is, then, rationalisation enough in this discontented world of ours for public support of scientific and technological research.

(2) *Entrenched interests* is a term that brings to mind the organised power of wealthy stockholders, business magnates, landlords, bankers, industrial executives and state bureaucrats – supporters of the 'Establishment' all, and fearless growthmen at that. Their vocational purpose, as they see it, is to foster the growth of something, whether private profit, or sales, or revenues, or exports, or numbers of employees, or branches, or customers. This great exhilarating numbers game absorbs them thoroughly, from day to day and from year to year, the social life they lead being ancillary and subservient to the game; indeed, that social life is an extension of it, through which connections are made and maintained and power is exercised and exhibited. The very spirit of the individual caught up in this game becomes expansionist, thrusting, restless, rejoicing in the rise of the relevant indices and impatient of 'setbacks'. He may pay lip service at public meetings and conferences to emerging social ideals, but the full implications of the economics of the steady state are anathema to him.

In sum, the seemingly most powerful economic group in the modern nation-state is unwaveringly committed to continued economic growth. It may be 'purified' growth, 'humanised' growth, 'harmonious' growth or any other variety; it may be given a new title, a new set of credentials and 'a new direction'. But growth it has to be.

Although their day-to-day occupation is not so charged with expansionist impulse as their executives, the bulk of the working class – using the term to cover both blue- and white-collar workers, skilled and unskilled – have as yet hardly begun to question the growth gospel. What is more, with price and wage indices sprouting from every research centre, the members of every pay group have come to take the liveliest interest in their material prospects from one week to another. After three decades of gorging themselves from a cornucopia bulging with 'the good things of life' (enabling them, incidentally, to wreak havoc upon the environment in which they are immersed) and of quaffing periodically at the fount of unlimited expectations, workers in the affluent West are all but convinced that they are entitled by natural law, if not by common law, to a yearly rise in their real incomes.

Indeed, however difficult the economic circumstances, an interruption of this customary postwar process, even for a year or so, is apparently not to be brooked without every manifestation of impatience and displeasure. Some of the more thoughtful workers may have begun to appreciate the possibility of an eventual change to the economics of a steady state. But the Western world will have to suffer some pretty terrifying experiences before the labour unions will be ready to give their official blessing to the idea of a steady state economy.

Now, strong though these economic interests are, they are not the most powerful. They would not, I think, prevail against sustained resistance by today's 'third estate', the scientific community in the West, whose influence in society is undoubtedly on the ascendant. Despite the emergence of dissident voices over the last ten years, it is within the scientific establishment that the support for economic growth is most deeply entrenched. This support is not expressed directly, of course, not as a crude support for faster rates of gross national product. More fundamentally, it is expressed as a demand for 'freedom of inquiry', which can be translated today into a demand for continued support and expansion of the immense facilities needed for research and development – facilities that are provided currently by industry, by governments and by the universities. Add to this sacred principle of 'freedom of inquiry' the spur of 'social need', the problems galore that in many instances arise from the applications of science itself, and the case for sustaining the expansion of research and development – which, of course, support the scientific community and provide its members with social privilege and influence – becomes irresistible.

But, of course, one of my conclusions is that the continued expansion of research and innovation is ultimately incompatible with the good life. I would not go so far as to argue that, only if *all* scientific and technological progress were to be halted, could there be

any hope of creating a good life. To do so would be to claim both too little and too much: too little, because there is already in existence enough of the products of technology to make the good life impossible; too much, because one cannot exclude the possibility of stumbling upon innovations that are wholly beneficial on any reasonable criterion, even though we cannot foresee them. What, instead, I would argue, on the basis of observation and reflection, is that the sum of enduring happiness cannot be much augmented by further scientific discoveries, even under the most favourable circumstances.

If this much were conceded, an essential part of a social policy for the good life would be the enforcement of a general ban on all scientific research, on all new technology and on all new products – exception being made, on appeal, only for research closely directed toward discoveries serving clear humanitarian purposes. If, for example, there were the strongest grounds for believing that specific kinds of research would eventually discover remedies for a particular malignant affliction, permission to undertake or continue it might be granted, provided always that safeguards against possible accidents and side effects were regarded as paramount considerations.

The implied controls on scientific freedom of such a policy would, however, be so drastic as to amount to a virtual ban on empirical research and technological innovation. For all practical purposes economic growth would come to an end.

But imagine the plight of scientists in a steady state economy. Scores of thousands of them would have to move from their prestigious niches in industry or in a university to far humbler tasks. Hundreds of thousands of academics would have to abandon their wistful hopes of status and recognition. The ambitions of an army of technocrats would be permanently thwarted. Design departments in every industry, in every country, would close down. Research laboratories of every size and description would go to rust. Complex and ponderous computers would cease to hum. Sackfuls of learned journals would no longer appear. It would seem to many as if the vital core of society's machinery were being dismantled and that collapse must surely follow. One has but to contemplate the prospect, and the consternation it would produce, to dismiss it almost out of hand – to conclude, then, that scientific research and its translation into technological progress will indeed continue to impel us forward into the future of increasing hazard and anxiety that I have elsewhere described.

(3) *International distrust.* Finally, even if wisdom were somehow to prevail – as a providential result, we

could suppose, of a succession of well-publicised near-catastrophes arising from new synthetics or technologies, none of which, mercifully, was fatal to mankind – a policy evolved to establish a steady state economy would run into another formidable obstacle: namely, the universal apprehension that any steady state control of technology would cause the country adopting it to slip behind in 'the arms race'.

I myself doubt whether these apprehensions are warranted. Technological innovation is no longer what it was in earlier times – a product of the spread of enterprise and the growth of markets. Today, it is increasingly the outcome of highly organised research and development, controlled and directed toward specific objectives. Western governments, disposing annually of scores of billions of dollars on military defence, could in principle maintain an up-to-date war technology in virtual independence of the rest of the economy. They could organise research on any required scale and build large scale plants for all specific weapons.

Whether this view of the matter is substantially true or not, we shall probably never find out. For the experiment of not likely to be undertaken. The notion of 'spin-off', the notion that innovations in one branch of industry become an important source of progress in others, is a very persistent one. And in the last resort, so long as the defences of the West are the primary considerations, the military can convincingly argue that serious attempts to swerve from traditional pro-growth policies cannot but introduce some element of risk.

It is not possible, then, to end on a note of even qualified optimism. Nor would it be responsible of me to contrive to do so. But if the outlook is grim indeed, it does not follow that we should feel depressed and impotent. The growth in our understanding of what has happened, and what is happening, to our civilisation, does of itself afford some satisfaction. At least, we are not as sheep lost in the wilderness. Each of us can cling to his individual sanity even amid the collective insanity.

What is more, our forebodings need not encourage an attitude of quietism. And although one possible reaction would be to 'eat, drink and be merry', for tomorrow comes the holocaust, it is not a reaction that I should expect. For one cannot bring oneself entirely to rule out hope, if only because human beings are incurably obstinate and because they still believe in miracles. Although slender in all conscience, what filament of hope there is depends upon the creation of a growing public awareness of the forces at work in society – awareness of the traditional rationalisations of science and technology, and awareness too of the power of the entrenched material and intellectual interests that support them. Without a growing public awareness, without a growing disbelief in the still prevailing attitude that, by and large, economic growth serves us well – or, with some institutional rearrangements, can be made to serve us well – the little hope that there is for mankind would dwindle to nothing. The best that we could then hope for would be rescue by 'the man on the while horse' and thereafter a social order controlled by a benevolent but repressive bureaucracy.

References

Hendin, H. (1975), *Age of Sensation* (Boston, Mass.).

Hirsch, F. (1976), *The Social Limits to Growth* (Cambridge, Mass.).

Mishan, E. J. (1967), *The Costs of Economic Growth* (London: Staples Press).

Acknowledgements

1 Reprinted from *Economica* (November 1957), pp. 324–42, by permission.

2 Reprinted from *Oxford Economic Papers,* NS, vol. 14 (October 1962), pp. 205–17, by permission. © Oxford University Press.

3 Reprinted from *Oxford Economic Papers,* NS, vol. 17 (July 1965), pp. 219–36, by permission. © Oxford University Press.

4 Reprinted from the *Economic Journal* (September 1973), by permission.

5 Reprinted from *Zeitschrift für Nationalökonomie,* vol. 37 (1977), pp. 281–306, by permission.

6 Reprinted from *Zeitschrift für Nationalökonomie,* vol. 37 (1977), pp. 1–24, by permission.

7 Reprinted from the *American Economic Review* (1959), pp. 386–94, by permission.

8 Reprinted from the *American Economic Review* (1968), pp. 1269–82, by permission.

9 Reprinted from the *Journal of Political Economy* (1971), pp. 687–705, by permission.

10 Reprinted from the *Journal of Transport Economics and Policy* (May 1967), pp. 184–9, by permission.

11 Reprinted from the *American Economic Review,* vol. 57, no. 3 (June 1967), pp. 255–87, by permission.

12 Reprinted from the *Journal of Political Economy,* vol. 82, no. 6 (1974), pp. 1287–99, by permission.

13 Reprinted from the *Journal of Economic Literature* (1971), pp. 1–28, by permission.

14 Reprinted from *Economica* (February 1974), pp. 81–96, by permission.

15 Reprinted from *Economica* (May 1976), pp. 185–97, by permission.

16 A shortened version of this paper, entitled 'A difficulty in the economic evaluation of long-lived investment projects', has been published in *Zeitschrift für Nationalökonomie,* vol. 39 (1979), pp. 365–76.

19 Reprinted from the *Journal of Transport Economics and Policy* (September 1970), pp. 221–34, by permission.

20 Reprinted from the *Journal of Economic Issues* (December 1975), by special permission of the copyright-holder, the Association for Evolutionary Economics.

Index